ADVANCE PRAISE FOR

THE CONSPIRACY OF THE GOOD

"We are forever misremembering history, either through outright distortion or, more commonly, through simple neglect. Michael E. James adds a brilliant new dimension to our understanding of race, power, and schooling across the so-called American century."
Jonathan Zimmerman, Professor of Education and History,
Steinhardt School of Education, New York University

"Michael E. James writes with the knowledge of a scholar but in the style of more accessible writers. James has found a literate voice with which to tell the important story of race and civil rights in the United States."
John Beineke, Dean and Professor of Educational Leadership/Curriculum,
Arkansas State University, Jonesboro, Arkansas

"Michael E. James has provided a powerful lens by which to rethink my myths, motivations, and actions and their unintended outcomes. In short, James has helped me understand my Southern roots. This book is America's history—and mine as well."
Mollie Quinn, Professor of Educational Philosophy,
Adelphi University, Garden City, New York

THE CONSPIRACY OF THE GOOD

HISTORY OF SCHOOLS & SCHOOLING

Alan R. Sadovnik and Susan F. Semel
General Editors

Vol. 30

PETER LANG
New York • Washington, D.C./Baltimore • Bern
Frankfurt am Main • Berlin • Brussels • Vienna • Oxford

MICHAEL E. JAMES

THE CONSPIRACY OF THE GOOD

Civil Rights and the Struggle for Community in Two American Cities, 1875–2000

PETER LANG

New York • Washington, D.C./Baltimore • Bern
Frankfurt am Main • Berlin • Brussels • Vienna • Oxford

Library of Congress Cataloging-in-Publication Data

James, Michael E.
The conspiracy of the good: civil rights and the struggle for community
in two American cities, 1875–2000 / Michael E. James.
p. cm. — (History of schools and schooling; vol. 30)
Includes bibliographical references and index.
1. Charlottesville (Va.)—Race relations. 2. Pasadena (Calif.)—Race relations.
3. Charlottesville (Va.)—Social conditions. 4. Pasadena (Calif.)—Social conditions.
5. African Americans—Civil rights—Virginia—Charlottesville—History.
6. Minorities—Civil rights—California—Pasadena—History. 7. African Americans—Education—
Virginia—Charlottesville—History. 8. Minorities—Education—California—Pasadena—History.
9. School integration—Virginia—Charlottesville—History. 10. School integration—California—
Pasadena—History. I. Title. II. Series.
F234.C47 J36   305.8'009755'482—dc21   2002075710
ISBN 0-8204-5779-5
ISSN 1089-0678

Bibliographic information published by **Die Deutsche Bibliothek**.
Die Deutsche Bibliothek lists this publication in the "Deutsche
Nationalbibliografie"; detailed bibliographic data is available
on the Internet at http://dnb.ddb.de/.

Cover design by Lisa Barfield

The paper in this book meets the guidelines for permanence and durability
of the Committee on Production Guidelines for Book Longevity
of the Council of Library Resources.

© 2005 Peter Lang Publishing, Inc., New York
275 Seventh Avenue, 28th Floor, New York, NY 10001
www.peterlangusa.com

Printed in the United States of America

TABLE OF CONTENTS

ACKNOWLEDGMENTS

A multiyear project like *The Conspiracy of the Good* can ring up debts of immense grati-
tude. I would have never completed this manuscript were it not for the numerous individuals who selflessly gave of their time and expertise. Although their help was certainly
appreciated, any mistakes in fact or interpretation are mine and mine alone.

First, my family. To Anna, Marissa, David and Cristina, none of this would have
been possible without your continual support (and occasional chiding), love and respect.
There were many days when I doubted I would ever finish, but all of you in your own
ways, refused to let me quit. My love to you all.

Kudos to the many librarians and archivists around the country: at Connecticut
College, especially the reference librarians and the staff at the interlibrary loan office
(thanks Bridget); the Pasadena Museum of History, my "home" on my many trips West
(thanks Tanya, Lian, Sid and Mary); the Pasadena Central Library; the archives at the
California Institute of Technology; the Huntington Memorial Library; University of
California at Los Angeles; University of Southern California; the Bancroft Library at the
University of California; the Special Collections at Vassar College; the Special Collections
at the Jean and Alexander Heard Library, Vanderbilt University; the Virginia State
Library; the Virginia Historical Society; the Special Collections at Virginia State
University; the Southern California Library for Social Studies and Research; George
Washington University; the University of Virginia, especially the Alderman Library
Special Collections; Hampton University; Virginia Commonwealth University; and the
Albemarle County Historical Society; the California State University at Los Angeles and
the Los Angeles Public Library.

My deep appreciation to my colleagues and friends who read parts or all of the
manuscript (or patiently listened to me try to work through some problem): Bud Church,
Theresa Ammarati, Helen Regan, Sandy Grande, Lisa Wilson, Jon Zimmerman, Jim
Wallace, John Beineke, Wayne Urban, Alan Sadovnik, Susan Semel, Mike Apple,
Bernardo Gallegos, Tom O'Brien, Molly Quinn, Barbara Beatty, Kathryn Weiner, Ron
Cohen, Jennings Wagoner, O.L. Davis, Ann Scheid, Peter Carbone, Jim Giarelli, Ed
Ayres, Peter Wallenstein, Joe Newman, George Van Alstine, Bill Trimble, Irv Hendrick,
David Gamson, Kathleen Weiler, John Kneebone, Sandy Treadway, Brent Tarter, Ken
Teitlebaum, Sunil Bhatia, Lynn Burlbaw, Marlene Smith-Baranzini, Janet Fireman and
the many unnamed readers and respondents at professional meetings. I also want to men-
tion four scholars who have passed on but whose support is not forgotten: Malcolm
Douglass, Ken Benne, C. Vann Woodward and Armstead Robinson.

The book is, in part, a collection of interviews. To those who gave of their time to
talk with me about Pasadena, the West, Charlottesville and the South, my thanks: Walter
Shatford, Sara Shatford, Marge Wyatt, Ruby McKnight Williams, Elbie Hickambottom,

Maurice Morse, Sylvia and Vernon Jones, Jim and Bobbi Spangler, Skipper Rostker, Albert Lowe, Lynne Vernon, Sid Gally, Louise Egan Steele, Lydia Fernandez, Walter Rogers, Howard Schorr, Roland Walker, Betty Purcell, Connie Foster, Dr. Edna Griffin, LuVerne LaMotte, Lee Hines, Don Wheeldon, John (Russ) Holmes, Fred Ruynon, Ken Rhodes, Rev. Marvin Robinson, Morgan Padelford, Jessie Moses, Caroline Kidd, Karen Wilkes, Donald O'Dell, Katie Nack, Sam Madden, Ethel Guldersleeve, Thomas Downing, Mary Alexander Craig, Jack Allen, Ella Goslin Howell, Jane Goslin, Marguerite Duncan-Abrams, Shelton Beatty, Charlie Padelford, Kay Hallberg, Charles Johnson, Booker Reeves, Florence Bryant, Jacky Taylor and Liz Sargent.

There were special people who opened their homes, became document hunters, fed me and put up with my incessant questions: Roberta Martinez, Tony Gonzalez (gracias grandpa) Tanya Rizzo, Sid Gally, Sara Shatford, Ray Walker, Walter Nelson, Rolando and Karen Santos, Bill Trimble and Mary Borgerding.

I want to give special thanks to one friend who, because of his steadfast support and criticism, this project has seen the light of day: Chris Cory has read (and reread again and again) every word I've written. His cogent questions and yeoman's editorial advice served me well. Chris, you're my genius.

I should also mention my students, particularly those at Connecticut College that sat through my lectures and discussions in "School and Society." Their patience needs to be commended as I struggled to better understand the dynamics of race, class and schooling. Three deserve special mention: Sarah Grogan, Rob Hanover and Sarah Miller. As undergraduate research assistants, they responded to the project as if they were graduate students. I was lucky to have them around.

I want to acknowledge those who helped with transcriptions, proofreading, and technical assistance. Thanks to Sheila Susen, Mary Howard, Felicia Brown and Sarjit Rattan.

Finally, many thanks to Alan Sadovnik and Susan Semel, my two fine series editors, who labored with me as this book came to a conclusion.

Grateful acknowledgment is hereby made to copyright holders for permission to use the following copyrighted materials:

Permission credits:

An earlier draft of Chapter One was published as "The City on the Hill: Temperance, Race and Class in Turn-of-the-Century Pasadena," in *California History,* Winter 2001/2002, p. 186–203.

An earlier draft of Chapter Six was published as "Southern Progressivism and the Great Depression: Virginia and African-American Social Reconstruction," in *Social Reconstruction Through Education: The Philosophy, History and Curricula of a Radical Ideal,* edited by Michael James. Greenwood Press, 1995, p. 109–138.

Cover photographs:

top: Lane High School *(Courtesy of the Albert and Shirley Small Special Collections Library, University of Virginia)*

bottom: John C. Fremont School *(Courtesy of Pasadena Unified School District)*

Every effort has been made to secure permission for usage from copyright holders. If any rights holder feels that material was used incorrectly, please contact the publisher.

INTRODUCTION
Bridges and Drive-Bys

Let me begin with two "snapshots" from Pasadena, the California city best known for the Rose Parade:

> On Halloween night 1993, six young African-American boys, all in their early teens, were gunned down on a quiet residential street in a working-class Pasadena neighborhood. Three died. It was a senseless act of violence that few could understand. They were not members of any gang. They were walking home from a friend's Halloween party. No alcohol, no drugs, no guns, no attitude; just a crazed act with a semi-automatic. One eyewitness said the gunmen opened fire without provocation. Two of the boys were dead before their bodies hit the ground. The third died at the hospital. The eyewitness reported laughter as the gunmen sped away. There was much public grieving. The city council offered a reward for the killers. City leaders created a "Coalition Against Violence." Mayor Rick Cole pushed for a citywide ban on the sale of ammunition.
>
> *****
>
> On June 11, 1994, in celebration of Pasadena's $27-million restoration of its famous century-old bridge across the Arroyo Seco—known since the Depression as "suicide bridge"—hundreds of people, nearly all white and well-off, many from Pasadena's oldest and most respected families, mingled and danced on the bridge under a moonlit sky. They nibbled nouvelle cuisine, sipped self-congratulatory toasts of California sparkling wine, and marveled at how fortunate they were to live in a city that would go to such lengths to value the past. There was no mention of the murders in the official remarks.

My guess is that no one on the bridge that evening knew any of the boys, even though the murders happened in an area not far from the celebration. But given the social distance between those who get to dance on bridges while they drink bubbly and young, dark-skinned boys who walk at night in neighborhoods that are stalked by gun-toting killers, the boys might as well have come from another planet. The evening's celebration was organized by Pasadena Heritage, an upper-crust preservation and civic group made up of mostly white and prosperous women. In speaking with some of the people involved with the celebration, I learned that no one saw any reason to have the bridge reopening honor or even recognize the memory of the boys. I asked one organizer, more than a year after the celebration, if in retrospect the bridge rededication might have been used to somehow help unite the community. I was told, in a rather defensive tone, "What's the bridge got to do with them?"[1]

Similarly, some six months before the Heritage event and just weeks after the killings, the bridge was "officially" reopened to auto traffic after having been closed for nearly three years. Just before the reopening, the head of Pasadena's Public Works said in a gush of civic pride, "We are terribly excited. I think everyone in Pasadena ought to be celebrating." At first, the rededication ceremony was planned as an invitation-only affair, but Mayor Cole changed that and turned the opening into a spontaneous public affair. He rode his Appaloosa horse across the bridge at the head of a carnival-like procession of vintage cars, bicycles, baby buggies and a dog dressed in a tuxedo. Quoting from the first bridge dedication in 1913, Cole said future generations would praise the "wisdom, liberality and farsighted good judgment" of the community in building the bridge. Cole made no mention of the murders then, either. The bridge rededication was one more lost opportunity to reach across the chasm that divides the two Pasadenas.

Fig. 1. Erected in 1913 over the then treacherous Arroyo Seco canyon, the Colorado Street Bridge has become an icon for Pasadena tourism. Unfortunately, for many city boosters, the bridge is still referred to by too many by its Depression-era name, "Suicide Bridge." *(Photo courtesy of the Security Pacific Collection, Los Angeles Public Library)*

The murdered boys had lived in a multiethnic, working-class neighborhood of the city, not far from the neighborhood where baseball great Jackie Robinson grew up. The boys, in fact, played ball in a park named in Robinson's honor. In many ways, the city Jackie Robinson knew has changed drastically since he and his brother Mack learned to play games in front of their home on Pepper Street during the 1930s. The population has more than quadrupled, and the city has been intersected twice by billion-dollar freeways that have decimated entire neighborhoods. Since an early 1970 court order to desegregate Pasadena schools, students have been transported from school to school in the hope that the racial, ethnic and class heterogeneity that eluded Robinson's Pasadena could be accomplished using yellow buses. The courts have relented; the city is no longer legally bound to bus children, and Pasadena still is clearly divided. Tragically, Pasadena's poorer neighborhoods, including the one where the Robinson family lived, have become battlegrounds for the gang wars that have bloodied Southern California. Since the 1993 Halloween murders, at last count more than 50 young men and women of color have died in gang-related deaths in and around the city.[2]

Not long ago, I walked Robinson's old neighborhood. In addition to the games kids still play on Pepper Street, one thing remains unchanged. The northwest section of the city is where nearly two generations of poorer Pasadenans have lived while they drove the cars and cleaned the houses of wealthier Pasadenans. Some who were dancing on the bridge that evening may have recalled, as youngsters, having black domestics around the estates that flank the arroyo the bridge spans. Today, well-off white folks in Pasadena have their houses cleaned, their gardens tended and their meals prepared by largely immigrant "help" from Mexico and beyond.

The murders and the bridge celebration reflect a community that has never come to understand its common past. The obligation to understand falls most heavily on Pasadena's elite—those who have marshaled the region's resources over the generations to project and then protect the image of progressive grandeur that matched the once brilliant vistas of a city that still calls itself "The Crown of the Valley." Today, smog and the blight that comes from a region that can no longer support its massive numbers of people make Southern California's air (and traffic) some of the worst in the world. A cynical friend tells me the only thing that flourishes in Los Angeles these days are cars.

Pasadena has not always been this way. I could argue that the community and its varied neighborhoods once deserved its laurels and crown, if not for its natural beauty then maybe, briefly, for the healthy tension produced by its progressive politics. Lamentably, much of that history has been ignored. One way to look at how racial and class segmentation occurred and persists in Pasadena is to closely examine the history of the community before *de facto* segregation, when the numbers of black, Mexican and dark-skinned people were small and the city lacked restrictive real estate covenants. Long before Pasadena became the first city west of the Rockies to fall under a mandatory federal school desegregation order, even before the city began planning its first "Mexican School" in 1912, Pasadena had developed "progressive" structures of city building that relied on separating citizens by class and color. Often, these policies were born of genuinely good intentions. But those impulses were no match for the resiliency of an entrenched political economy that reformers then and now often woefully underestimate. The multimillion-dollar rebuilding of the Colorado Street Bridge was more than simply restoring a fading tourist attraction. It symbolized a reaffirmation that in America, wealth often speaks louder than justice. In the tragedy that was the senseless death of three young boys, a community failed to see itself. On re-dedication day, a newspaper reporter wrote that "the bridge connects Pasadena to a time that no longer exists." He could (or should) have said that the bridge remains a symbol of a community that refuses to recognize how the past still defines the present.[3]

What has occurred in a city like Pasadena allows us to focus intently on how Southern California and the West built their institutions at the same time they marketed themselves as the Promised Land. A place as near physically perfect as the mind can imagine, Pasadena, as well as all of Southern California during the latter decades of the 19th century, was to many the Christian "City on the Hill," the mythic Utopia. Pasadena has been a beacon for wealthy and working class alike throughout its history. During the first half of the 20th century, its schools were touted as some of the most progressive in the country. Its air was clean. Its streets were safe. Its natural beauty was superlative. Yet beneath this marketed vista of "Paradise Found" was a community in conflict with the very forces it publicly disavowed: race and racism, social class segmentation, and the inequalities of housing and education.

The tension that is produced when the rhetoric of Paradise collides with preservation of power is the central theme of *The Conspiracy of the Good*. By examining how the struggle for an inclusive community was contested during the expansion of Pasadena's institutions, especially its schools, we get a clearer picture of the larger issues that define the history of power, race and class struggle in this country.

The Conspiracy of the Good, however, is not confined to Pasadena. Although I initially set out to write a book on the history of civil rights and community building in a single Western city, the book became (as 10-year projects can) much more. I wanted to better understand the struggle that ensued as various groups— defined by class, color and politics—clashed over how best to characterize "the community." I began the book with an unproven assumption (more like a hunch) that the civil rights movement was somehow "different" in the West. Growing up in Southern California, in a working-class community 20 miles from Pasadena, I was convinced that the Western states somehow were unlike the rest of the country. That idea was nurtured by countless references to Western distinctiveness, both contemporary and historical. In fact, there is an academic cottage industry that bottles that feel-good elixir. It is called Western "exceptionalism," but as historian Patricia Limerick, the past president of the Western History Association, confesses, too much has been made of Western differences. Herbert Gutman, the venerable labor and working-class historian, went further. He argued that regionalism is a gimmick that has been passed along to ward off attempts to create a more progressive synthesis of the American experience. The West remains different, but it is because of topography and climate, not culture, economics or politics—despite the popular fiction of California's so-called flamboyant culture.[4]

As I began my research on Pasadena and the West, however, I decided that my work needed a larger context. Therefore, I added an additional location, a second city that I believed would provide another perspective to my analysis. I wanted a community similar in size and "character" to Pasadena, and since the book was focused on civil rights, it was logical that the other city would be in the South. After spending the summer of 1992 as a fellow at the Virginia Foundation for the Humanities, I chose Charlottesville, Virginia. The history of Charlottesville a city, like Pasadena with a rich and problematic past, has helped me understand more about the shifting meaning of other staples of our national self-perception, like "community," "neighborhood," "race" and "civil rights." Throughout the history of both cities, I found those concepts constantly undergoing redefinition. Today, the "neighborhood school," the defining slogan during the school desegregation wars in the 1960s and 1970s, no longer arouses the same passions it once did. Now, in both cities, the "neighborhood school" has come to mean something very different.

What I learned from Charlottesville and Pasadena convinces me that the historiography of civil rights can no longer be isolated to a single region—the South. Nor can it be viewed as the single message of black versus white. By seeing the struggle primarily as "race relations," we miss the many structural developments that help us better understand why, as the new millennium begins, the gap between those who hold most of the nation's wealth and the rest of us is greater than at any time since the second half of the 19th century. America has become, in Andrew Hacker's words, "Two Nations." Hacker's division is color, but if we continue to see our segregated society as divided only between black and white, we fail to get at the crucial nexus of race and social class. I want to make it very clear that I am not dismissing race and racism from my story. Nor, to paraphrase sociologist Jack Bloom, am I suggesting the primacy of class over race. Whites, rich and poor, labor and the business elite, have profited from racism. However, as Bloom wrote, racial practices are embedded within class and economic and political systems. By the study of those systems, over time we can come to better understand how race and racism have been used to justify inequalities.[5]

The book follows a chronological format, beginning with Pasadena's founding in the 1870s, covered in Chapter One, and the creation of Charlottesville's public schools during the same period, discussed in Chapter Two. The book then alternates chapters between cities, concluding with an epilogue that brings the reader to the year 2000 and the new millennium. I have used a broad set of categories to analyze what I believe is, at the bottom, a struggle for community. I have, for instance, included the labor movement, especially the more radical worker's movements in the early 20th century. In Chapter One, the laboring class that flooded to Pasadena in the 1880s was confronted with a gentry that professed Christian goodwill. The city's founders, all originally from the Midwest, white and Protestant, went about restricting the movement of labor so extensively and with such zeal that the first act in the history of the city of Pasadena—its incorporation—was designed to legally exclude itinerant workers from the city after dark. Simply put, the gentry wanted labor around during the day but did not want to live among them.

I have emphasized gendered politics in both communities (wealthy and working-class whites and poor women of color) to better understand how various ideologies of power flourished and then diminished. In Chapter Three, the emphasis is on the role that radical white women, known as the Women's Socialist Union, played in Pasadena's turn-of-the-century political movements. The failure of these women to secure any cross-class alliance with working women, especially working women of color, despite their professed statements of "sisterhood" and "solidarity," worked against a more democratic polity. Likewise, Virginia's women's movement, discussed in Chapter Four, was too class-bound to recognize that self-interest ruled the day, even as the women were applauding the selflessness of their community action.

The volume emphasizes issues of social class that seem to continually get pushed aside in the discussion about race and power in America. For too long, the majority white opinion of black and Latino communities has been of single entities, all alike, bound alone by color and culture. Yet Charlottesville's black community has always been as vexed with class conflicts as the city's white community. As discussed in Chapter Eight, during World War II in Charlottesville the black community was caught up in a controversy over the role of the high-school principal, a man who many, including a contingent of the city's black elite, argued was unfit to lead the school. Interestingly, some of his support came from other prominent black families who disliked the fact that students were cutting classes and frequenting the local pool halls and shoe shine parlors. Today Charlottesville struggles to decide if the old Jefferson Colored School building should be torn down to make way for the promised renaissance of "urban renewal." Some African Americans in the city like that idea; others—mostly old timers and those interested in historic preservation—object.

Although I have used many themes to tell the story of the two cities, *The Conspiracy of the Good* is principally about the educational policy and practice that has marked the phenomenal expansion of the American school since the Civil War. I do not see public schooling as an isolated institution—although, too often, too many parents, reformers, observers and analysts isolate public education from the larger context of American politics. I can only understand the history of schooling when it is rooted in larger themes of class conflict, racial unrest, industrial development and political economy. Schools have always been sites of community building, places where an assortment of groups, often with disparate intentions and means of expression, have battled for ideological elbowroom. I have emphasized "race" and "race relations" only when and if the ideas focus attention on the actions that constitute racism. In addition, I use no category called "difference." I have tried to illuminate supposed "differences" with an analysis that substantiates similarities. As with race and class, however, I have not reduced "difference" to "commonality." America's "melting pot" does not exist. It never has. Instead, I have treated multiple communities—African Americans, Latinos, organized labor, the white and male working class, wealthy and poor women and the business elite—as players, but certainly not equal players, in a larger story about power and its ramifications.[6]

I see Pasadena and Charlottesville as two sides of the same coin. I do not see a one-to-one correspondence between the two cities and it is not my intention to compare and contrast their histories, although I suspect that comparisons are inevitable. Rather, the history of each city is reflective of larger, common social, political and economic themes. The themes are often confusing and contradictory. The role of politics in shaping class concerns is an example. In the 1960s, as I discuss in Chapter Seven, mainly prosperous white members of the westside Pasadena community around the Arroyo Seco, that canyon-like draw where the Rose Bowl sits, came to realize that their status was rapidly being eroded by demographic shifts that placed increasing numbers of poor black students in the local high school. They argued that resources were being diverted to the now more prestigious eastside Pasadena High School, which remained nearly all white. They spoke about the "quality" of education, about "growing segregation" and about "fairness." The coalition that was formed as a response to the city's repeated stonewalling—a multiethnic alliance that squabbled some over who was to lead, whites or blacks—led to the federal court order that mandated the landmark desegregation of Pasadena's schools. The irony of Pasadena was that the political struggle to desegregate schools was led by well-off whites, not, as it was in the South, by black political organizations like the National Association for the Advancement of Colored People (NAACP).

To those who take issue with the "legitimacy" of my questions (I was once asked, "*why* did you write this?"), let me answer by pointing out something Michael Katz wrote a few years ago. "All written history," he said, "is part autobiography." For social historians like Katz (and me) "objectivity" and "advocacy" means that more often than not we find ourselves caught between our passion and the "requirements" of the profession. Throughout *The Conspiracy of the Good,* my passion and advocacy for "the others" is testimony to my belief that, although we may strive to remain "objective" in our storytelling, our own stories relentlessly guide our hand.[7] I have little interest in grand homes, Rose Parades or the aristocracy of the Old South—traditional icons in race and class history. Instead, I am trying to understand how exclusion is justified in the name of "necessity" and "goodness." Those are emotional terms for me. Too many times I have heard them used as justification for acts of power that perpetuate systems of inequality. Growing up in southeast Los Angeles after World War II, in a small working-class town called Maywood, I know firsthand how deception works to favor those who use it. Maywood was founded after World War I as a bedroom community for the white working class, complete with restrictive covenants to exclude blacks and Mexicans. But over the years, along the edges of town, near the borders of industrial Vernon and Los Angeles, near where the Bethlehem steel plant was located, grew patches of Mexican neighborhoods. Poor whites (*really* poor whites) lived there, too. There were no African Americans. These were Maywood's "slums"—or at least that is what we called them. Social practice among the kids I grew up with was "whites rule," and too many teachers and administrators reinforced that misbegotten notion at school. I remember more than one high-school teacher—especially our sports coaches—encouraging racist behavior. Looking back, I know my mates and I had much in common with those who lived along the edges of town.

I intend *The Conspiracy of the Good* not only for a scholarly audience but even more for general readers, including public officials, educators, parents and citizens. I want to address the nagging question that is part of the public debate over schooling. Why have our public schools, especially those in poor and working-class communities of color, failed to live up to the promises contained in the American Dream? Reforms appear to come as often as political elections, yet meaningful change seldom gets the traction promised by its proponents. I suspect this is because "progressive," well-meaning, good-hearted men and women, who often espouse "good intentions" in the name of "helping those in need," have ended up doing more harm than good. Why is that? I am not speaking only of church and independent charity work, although in both cities studied here the history of charity outreach plays a significant role in the history of good intentions gone bad. No, I am speaking more to those institutionalized, mainly governmental efforts that preach about addressing the community's "needs" but end up creating structures that attempt to "fix" the so-called "morally depraved," correct the antisocial behavior of the "riffraff," and remake "the others" into model citizens who hopefully know their place, and more important, stay there without complaint.

The Conspiracy of the Good is about how these plans go awry. If the volume has a thematic undercarriage, it is that the core value of the American experience is conflict, not consensus, no matter what mainstream historians have tried to sell us over the decades. In places like Charlottesville and Pasadena, the past has been twisted time and again to meet the needs of an elite that uses the politics of self-ishness, cloaked as "communal goodness."

In writing this book, what was perhaps most surprising was the dearth of documentable voices speaking out in both communities against the prevailing order. Those oppositional voices were, no doubt, there at one time, but largely have been lost. A central question, then, is how historians can interpret social change and what occurs when less powerful groups come into contact with a more dominant culture. In the last half of the book, Chapters Five through Eight, I have attempted to place at the center of my analysis the role of resistance to "conventional wisdom." For instance, conventional wisdom in Pasadena during the 1920s suggested that after a period of "adjustment" (conflict), the Mexican immigrant "blended" (assimilated) into the "American" culture. Indeed, the public transcript suggests there was little, if any, resistance to policies that attempted to "Americanize the foreigner." Resistance, however, has a history in many forms. Behind the public transcript lies a world of resistance to oppression that is the terrain of undeclared ideological warfare. To understand it, as political anthropologist James Scott argues, requires us to enter the world of everything from rumor, gossip and disguises to linguistic tricks, metaphors, folktales and euphemisms. Written by the powerful, the public transcript (the source for much of our conventional wisdom) most often gives legitimacy to the dominant worldview, and, in fact, is what Scott calls "a self-portrait of how they would have themselves seen." Recent scholarship, much of it by Scott but also others like public historian Robin D.G. Kelley, reveals another, different reality behind "our" history. In Pasadena and Charlottesville, the less powerful have always resisted change that was packaged "for their own good."[8]

It has been pointed out to me (more than once, especially by conservative historians) that the crimes of the past cannot be judged by present standards. I agree, but it is my contention that the past helps us understand what we confront today. Yes, the persistent "fixing" of the "others" at the turn of the 20th century must be judged by the lens of history, not by the colorations of contemporary hindsight. But what if the mechanics of "goodness" persist even as the evidence mounts that "fixing" people is not the solution? I now teach in the small city of New London, Connecticut, its former glory as a whaling port long gone, a section of its waterfront now home to tenements that were built in the late 1960s amid grand pronouncements that public housing would somehow rescue the poor. Nothing of the sort occurred, and now the city leaders are clamoring to tear down the buildings amidst speculation that there is more to be made off the land than the rescue of what are mostly Puerto Ricans and African Americans. In the first decade of the new millennium, educational policy coming out of Washington, D.C., and most state capitals preaches that a cultural and economic renaissance is at hand if only educators and children will work harder. Simple solutions abound. More and more testing, "uniform" standards and competition have supplanted calls for justice and equality. Political slogans have always been around to rally communities to this or that cause, but I am increasingly doubtful that state coercion cloaked as "higher standards" can keep children from being left behind.

Let me conclude this introduction with a story Ruby McKnight Williams told me a few years ago. McKnight Williams, who died recently at the age of 104, was the longtime president of the Pasadena branch of the NAACP. She was originally a schoolteacher. In the late 1920s, she came to Pasadena to visit her aunt. Intrigued by letters from her mother's sister, stories of the sweep and splendor of the West, McKnight Williams, like many would-be immigrants, wanted to see for herself. She had been educated at the Topeka Colored Normal School and thought Southern California might be her home. She had heard stories of a softer stance on race in the West and believed she should explore her future profession in Southern California. Once there, she was convinced she had made the right decision. Pasadena appeared to be everything the travel brochures advertised. She was puzzled though, one day as she walked along Colorado Boulevard, at why so many white faces seemed to stop and stare and why no one like her was shopping at Nash's department store. In fact, somewhat to her amazement, there were no other black people out that day. What McKnight came to find was that African Americans in Pasadena shopped mainly on Tuesday—the designated "day-off" for colored help. McKnight was there on Thursday. She also came to learn that Pasadena did not hire "colored teachers" or, for that matter, any professionals who did not adhere to the principles established by the founders. To gain access to public Pasadena, one had to be white, Protestant and at least middle class—certainly not black and certainly not Mexican.

McKnight's story of her stroll along Colorado Boulevard indicates that by the late 1920s, the life of the laborer of color was, at least to the majority white populace, thought to be so ordered and efficient that whites could stop and stare at a young black woman they believed was so out of place. It mattered not that they were staring at a young professional woman. What mattered was that this black woman was not where whites believed she was supposed to be. There are similar stories from Charlottesville in the chapters ahead. *The Conspiracy of the Good* asks how these social practices become the norm.[9]

NOTES

1. Marina Milligan and Roberto Ceniceros, "Trick-or-treaters gunned down; ambush kills three teens on Pasadena street," *Pasadena Star-News,* 1 November 1993, p. A1; "Shot Down," editorial, *Pasadena Star-News,* 3 November 1993, p. A4; "Violence and Hope," editorial, *Pasadena Star-News,* 12 December 1993, p. A4. For a description of the bridge party, see Pasadena Heritage press release and poster in Pasadena Central Library, Centennial Room, "Colorado Street Bridge" folder. The bridge party committee was made up of women with names like Kitty, Bunny, Hope, Corky and Tonie. The quote from the volunteer is anonymous. I am indebted to Charles Johnson, longtime NAACP attorney and Pasadena activist for his insights on the shootings and the bridge rededication. It was Mr. Johnson who first made it clear to me that the rededication was one more instance in which the city's majority wealthy white leadership failed to address the chasm between the two Pasadenas.

2. Susan MacLean, director of the Coalition for Zero Violence, Pasadena, telephone interview with author, 24 July 2003.

3. See Jennette Williams, "The Reopening of a Landmark," *Pasadena Star-News,* 13 December 1993, for a description of the rededication ceremony, including the dog in the tuxedo. See Keith Sharon, "Bridge is born again," *Pasadena Star-News,* 12 December 1993, p. A1 for the comment on civic pride.

4. William Cronon, George Miles and Jay Gitlin, eds., *Under an Open Sky: Rethinking America's Western Past* (New York: W.W. Norton, 1999), p. 62 and Ira Berlin, ed., *Power and Culture: Essays on the American Working Class* (New York: Pantheon Books, 1987), p. 5–6.

5. Andrew Hacker, *Two Nations: Black and White, Separate, Hostile, Unequal* (New York: Charles Scribner's Sons, 1992); Jack Bloom, *Class, Race, and the Civil Rights Movement* (Bloomington: Indiana University Press, 1987), p. 1, 3–5.

6. My categories have evolved since I began the book. Many thanks to Barbara Jean Fields, "Origins of the New South and the Negro Question," *The Journal of Southern History* 67:4 (November 2001), p. 811–812, 814, for illuminating the particulars of race, racism and "race relations."

7. James C. Scott, *Domination and the Arts of Resistance: Hidden Transcripts* (New Haven: Yale University Press, 1990), p. 18, 100. Also see Robin D.G. Kelley, "'We Are Not What We Seem': Rethinking Black Working-Class Opposition in the Jim Crow South," *The Journal of American History* 80:1 (June 1993), p. 78–112.

8. Michael B. Katz, *Improving Poor People* (Princeton: Princeton University Press, 1995), p. 10.

9. Ruby McKnight Williams, longtime Pasadena NAACP activist, interview with author, Pasadena, 16 March 1994.

CHAPTER 1

THE CITY ON THE HILL

It was clear and cold the morning of December 9, 1886, as Amy Bridges, a young, precocious college girl from a wealthy New England family, rushed off to the station to board the westbound train to Chicago. Nearly two dozen sorority sisters came to see Amy off as she boarded the train with her mama, papa, sister and more than 125 other tourists. Amy had in her possession a small, brown-covered journal from the Harvard Co-operative Society, reserved, she wrote, to describe her adventures. As the train pulled out of Boston's station that early morning, Amy made her first entry:

> Many friends came to see us off. Such a party of the college girls ... How I did hate to say good-bye to them for so long, as they crowded about our window. We had some lovely hyacinths given us—They shall be the first flowers I press here ... a sweet memory of the girls—also they gave us a pretty little paper book of selections of Browning which will give us so many happy thoughts while we are gone ... It is very hard to leave our dear home and friends.[1]

This was the family's second trip West in as many years, each member eager to revisit the soft, tranquil Mediterranean winter of Southern California that had become such a draw for those in America who could afford such extended periods of leisure. The Bridges were part of a throng of Easterners assembled by Walter Raymond of Raymond and Whitcomb Tours, the forerunner of what we might today call the all-inclusive travel package.[2] Their destination was a string of elegant hotels running from San Diego to San Francisco. Amy's favorite, though, would be Walter Raymond's flagship hotel and namesake, The Raymond of Pasadena.

We know very little about Amy and her family other than her travels out West. Earlier, in 1882, she had kept a rather pedestrian journal as she and her family traveled to Los Angeles and Yosemite Valley.[3] We know during the winter of 1885–86 she and her family traveled with Raymond Tours to Southern California but we have no written record of that trip. Knowing what we do, we can be assured that Amy was a young woman of status and wealth. Quite possibly

Amy was related to the prominent Daniel Thurber Bridges, of the D.T. Bridges and Co. Boot Manufactory in Hopkinton, Massachusetts.[4] Amy's descriptions of her trips West are packed with wonderful detail yet, oddly, she did not tell us where she attended school. Although the Bridges' name does not appear within the network of New England women's colleges, we do know that "those college girls" that came to see her off were the Alpha Gammas, a sorority in many of the East's most elite schools. We also know that she was an exceptional writer, with an eye for detail, occasionally bent to late Victorian sentimentality but nonetheless a writer of obvious talent. Other than that, her life is conjecture.

East through Chicago, then southbound along the great rivers of the Midwest, Amy gazed out the window of her Palace Car and recorded the sting of winter's harshness as it whistled by. "We have crossed these little streams with wooden sides before," she reminded her diary. It was during the previous spring when the rivers and streams "were so muddy and swiftly flowing, the banks were so green with flowers growing and the trees fresh with their leaves." She told her diary, "They seemed so pretty to me then—now all is bare and cold ..." As she moved west, she was anxious to put behind her the gray melancholy of the Eastern winter.

As her tour moved out of the rangelands of the Midwest and into the highlands of Santa Fe, New Mexico, Amy's privileged, Eastern urbanity ran headlong into life in the preindustrial Hispanic Southwest. To Amy, Santa Fe and all of the great western territory violated her New England sense of place and order. Santa Fe was most assuredly not Hopkinton. It was "mysterious and dangerous." She was less assured, less familiar in the West because her cultural boundaries were missing. She called Santa Fe a "strange town, of queer, low adobe houses with narrow streets full of strange things." Those streets and sidewalks fascinated Amy. Instead of flat Hopkinton, they "were up and down" and most improperly, they broke with the rigidity of the East as they passed directly through the "broad piazzas of the houses" and then out the other side.

But it was what was on those "narrow streets full of strange things" that intrigued her most. "Burros," she wrote, "loaded heavy with amoli or other wood driven by foreign looking men with swarthy faces" with "broad, soft, light felt hats ... and women, often with deeply wrinkled and very dark skin ... crouching by the dim rays or gliding along with their black shawls pressed over their heads." Amy was fascinated by the mystery of Mexican Santa Fe. There were dogs and pigs everywhere because everywhere, she lamented, it was "nothing like New England." Everything appeared "strange ... and incomprehensible." The poor girl was in culture shock. Like the proverbial fish out of water, Amy Bridges was ill prepared to define what she observed by what she had experienced in her familiar, conventional Hopkinton. A day later, expressing regret that a delay with her luggage resulted in her not having time to see the Romona Indian School, Amy left, but not before she criticized the Mexicans as "slow ... and unable to understand English so poorly that [the] trunks almost missed the train." There were "moments of despair, but alas," she told her diary, "everything was settled quite satisfactorily."[5]

Indeed, Santa Fe and the entire southwest was nothing like Amy Bridges' New England. What Amy could not see was a central contradiction of late 19th-century America. The men that Bridges saw as so "foreign looking" were part of a centuries-old Indigenous Mexican society unchanged culturally and linguistically for them, but transformed virtually overnight into a place Anglo Americans called "New" Mexico. Amy's consciousness—shaped by the culture of class-bound New England—did not prepare her for the fact that the transformation from ancient Indian-Mexico to "New" Mexico occurred only in the minds of privileged tourists like Amy.[6]

A few weeks later, after a brief stop at the Coronado Hotel in San Diego, Amy and her family stepped off the train at the base of what the locals now called "Raymond Hill." A mere bump compared to the majesty of what Amy had seen on her tour through the mountainous West, "Raymond Hill" was nonetheless a defining piece of real estate that marked the southern boundary of the village of Pasadena. For the next few months while her college sisters shivered in the Eastern deep freeze, Amy and her family would stroll through fields ablaze with red-orange poppies so brilliant they could be seen 50 miles away on the channel island of Santa Catalina. Her walks took her under huge sheltering oaks she came to call cathedrals and through lush rose gardens that by mid-February would be fragrant with bloom. The climate of Southern California, thanks to prolific science writers such as the imminent Charles Frederick Holder, was becoming world-famous and would soon draw tens of thousands of visitors.[7] In a few years, over-wintering tourists in Southern California would watch a parade of flower-adorned carriages and thrilling chariot races advertising the contradiction of rose blooms in January. By the middle of the 20th century when television took the Rose Parade and Rose Bowl football game into millions of homes nationwide, the standing joke in Pasadena would be: "What sound is that?" The New Year's Day reply: "the packing of a million suit cases."

Raymond and Whitcomb's just-opened hotel was the brainchild of Walter Raymond, son of Emmons Raymond, one of the 40 original stockholders in the Santa Fe Railroad. The hilltop project needed father's capital when construction ran into more rock than the engineers predicted. After 250 pounds of blasting power convinced Walter that his hill was, indeed, "bastard granite," as the 250 workmen came to call the obdurate material, Emmons Raymond opened his purse and the hotel became everything the Raymonds and the recently incorporated city of Pasadena wanted it to be. The Raymond Hotel was one of those synergistic, back-scratching opportunities so common to the history of capitalism. A deal was cut between the Raymonds and the city fathers. The Raymonds would stop the railroad at the base of the hill and build a hotel if the city would furnish gratis the needed water and power.[8]

The Raymond Hotel opened the fall before Amy arrived and was unlike anything the West had ever seen. This was arguably one of the finest hotels in the country. The building's foundation was laid on top of Emmons now flat hilltop; it took 1.3 million brick, all cast and fired on site. The wooden structure that rose atop those brick took 2.5 million board feet of lumber and a half million roof shingles. When finished, The Raymond, with 43 bathrooms and an equal number of water closets, soared seven stories into the valley sky. Much like the monster hotels that have sprung up a century later along Mexico's Caribbean coast, The Raymond was not intended for locals or for that matter any Californian. The Raymond was built for the Eastern establishment, a sanctuary from the cold of New York and Boston, a retreat from the social ills of industrial America.

The Raymond, commanding both a view of the valley to the south and the majestic peaks of the San Gabriel mountains to the north, was magnificent. Advertised as a place for "particular people with means—people who seek the same care in their own homes," guests at The Raymond were catered to at every turn.[9] Visitors could ride fine horses, play croquet and shuffleboard, paint, sit, walk, eat, read, nap and play tennis. By the turn of the century, they could take automobile driving lessons, play golf and drink schnapps as they rode the electric car up Mt. Lowe to a snow-covered alpine lodge. They could even cross the channel 26 miles away to semitropical Santa Catalina island to look back on the flaming flowered hillsides of the San Gabriels. Children—for this was an establishment that catered to wealthy families—could play games under the watchful eye of a staff of trained nurses, or "bareheaded and happy" they might "ride the hotel's patient burros." It was Amy's train that brought the first of those 25 "patient burros" from Santa Fe to The Raymond.[10]

Walter Raymond made sure his guests were pampered: lavish dinners, evening concerts, guided tours up the rugged mountain canyons to paint or hunt or down into the clang and clamor of pueblo Los Angeles—a place Amy called the "dirtiest town I ever saw." (Seventy years later, Christopher Isherwood would call his adopted Los Angeles, "... perhaps the ugliest city on earth.") Dining was in a grand hall where the very whim of every guest was met. Meals were served, as Amy said, by "table girls." Jenny, a dark-eyed, tall and slender girl from Vermont, out West "to get a chance to teach" served the Bridges' table. She was a recent graduate of the nation's first teacher-training college, Vermont's Normal School. For Jenny, her chance may have come in any one of a dozen rapidly expanding Southern California communities but it was not to be in Pasadena. There is no record of Jenny landing a job in any of the city's four schools, includ-

Fig. 2. The Raymond Hotel, c. 1890, for decades dominated the hilltop that separates Pasadena from Los Angeles. Arguably one of the finest hotels in the country, the original Raymond burned to the ground in 1895 only to be rebuilt a few years later with a different look but just as grand as the original. The second Raymond, long neglected due to stiff competition from other, newer super-hotels in the city, was razed during the 1930s. *(Photo courtesy of the Pasadena Museum of History)*

ing the recently opened elementary, California School, that Amy could see from her room atop the hill.[11]

After dinner, guests could stroll around the huge veranda—as wide as a broad city street—or sit "gathered about some Chinaman who had brought up his odorous wares in two great baskets suspended from a pole across his shoulders. He spread them out in tempting piles—dainty boxes, delicately carved woods, soft pale colors in crepe and silk and paper." Coquettish Amy remembered "the ladies and I having a lively time bargaining with him."

Steeped in a culture of wealth that expected its iconic women to do little more than serve as moral props, Amy and her tour friends would often "talk in little groups" or "sit idly in a big chair gazing dreamingly off to where the low hills parted and a gleaming line marked the Pacific, enjoying the clear air and lovely flowers and all the days beauty reading or doing fancy work." The Raymond was all a wealthy tourist could possibly imagine. Walter and his father had thought of everything.

Walter Raymond never expected guests to leave the hotel unescorted. More to the point, most guests never expected to leave the hotel. Most, that is, except

Amy. Beneath that chic veneer of Victorian sensibility beat the heart of an adventurous young woman. She may have been culturally naive and thoroughly WASP-ish but Amy certainly did not lack nerve. She would take the horse-drawn jitney at the base of the hill and wander off into what was fast becoming "boom town" Pasadena.

Quickly Amy came to realize that the village of Pasadena had in one short year been transformed. With an air of Eastern condescension, she described a community,

> like a beehive. It is a bustle [of] business and building ... such an enterprising, thriving place it is, one can see it grow daily. It seems bound to be a city and even now to assume the dignity of a city as children love to play grown up. That is what amuses me most.[12]

The Bridges had arrived that tourist season of 1886–87 to find their quaint Pasadena, along with the enormity of Southern California, in the euphoric rush of a great land boom.[13] What was once a village that marked the center of a quiet collection of mid-Western gentry farms was now fully involved in the "bustle and business" of urbanization. If Amy had cared to record what she surely saw at the base of that topographic bump called "Raymond Hill," we would have more than her romantic descriptions of warm, winter blue skies, lush green-hued, tree-lined streets and tales of bargaining with Ah Wong, the silk-stockinged Chinese peddler. We would also have a picture of the squalor of the city's South Raymond slum of some 500 tents and assorted shacks, home to a mix of working-class blacks, southern Europeans, men from China, and Mexican *traqueros,* laboring as section hands for the newly arrived Southern Pacific and Santa Fe railroads. Pasadena was in the midst of capital accumulation. A village once, now by the end of the 1880s, a city of nearly 10,000 who had begun to craft their own vision of city building in the progressive West, a vision that would somehow attempt to reconcile the needs of rapidly accumulating capital with the needs of a rapidly growing, ethnically diverse laboring class. In spite of the altruistic intentions of a generation of progressive reformers, the unfortunate consequence was the systematic segregation of workers and their families into slums that the California Conference on City Planning would describe nearly 40 years after Amy's visit as "the worst housing conditions in the state of California."[14]

THE EARLY YEARS

Ten years before Amy's winter visit, Pasadena was a mere wide place in the ancient road from Mission San Diego to Los Angeles. With the coming of the railroad and the tremendous flexing of postwar Eastern capital, urban Southern California was born. Local historians have retold the founding of Pasadena so often that the myth of the early settlers has found a purpose beyond its original form. According to the story, a group of winter-cold Indianapolis citizens, sitting around Dr. Thomas Elliott's dining room table, decided to pull up stakes and move to a warmer climate. Mrs. Elliott told the group she was going because she was sick of the winter—a particularly harsh one even by Indiana standards—and the group, not wanting to be left behind by the good doctor's wife, pooled their funds, appointed a search party and waited until Paradise was found. It was not long after that the partners moved West to their Indiana Colony, a cooperative venture where members bought shares or plots of land. Every colonist was Protestant, everyone middle class and white everyone from the midlands of the nation. Later, as the city lost its utopian predilections, access to power remained firmly defined by those criteria. The founders squabbled some over water rights; like much of the arid West the struggle over water would come to help make Pasadena what it is today.[15]

So goes the story, grounded like all oft-told stories in some truth but over time retold again and again to meet needs that are more contemporary. To the early colonists, no matter the heat, bugs, lack of water or choking dust, Pasadena and all of Southern California was their Promised Land. Yet, regardless of how local boosters have used the legend of the founding for their own purposes, the early Pasadena gentry, mainly small capitalists like the Elliott family or, a few years later, Hiram Reid from Iowa, came to this valley in Southern California with the intent to profit. The Elliotts, Reids and scores of other early settlers were fleeing not only the sting of winter's cold but also the shock waves of a rapidly industrializing culture. What took place in Southern California as the 19th century drew to a close reflects what was occurring in many cities and towns across the nation. The tensions that existed between a dominant and exceedingly ethnocentric Protestant middle class and the profiteering inherent in large-scale capital investment were played out in Southern California no less visibly than in the great cities of the East. The reality of capital accumulation would come to contradict the myth of the West-as-Paradise.[16]

The late 19th-century historian Frederick Jackson Turner's thesis of the ever-moving frontier as an incubator of democratic values and rugged individualism fed the psychology of Western mythmaking. Supposedly beyond the Great Divide, the settlers of early Pasadena would find a place fundamentally different from anywhere on earth, a land free of the deceit and immorality that for centuries conditioned life in Europe and now had infected the expanding industrial centers of the Eastern seaboard. At the core of the myth was the notion that community building in the West was somehow going to be very different from what had transpired before. The development of uniquely different "Western" institutions, in politics, science, industry and education were to mark this New Paradise.[17]

The age-old myth of the West-as-Paradise was in full flower as Amy Bridges settled into her routine that warm December in 1886. And why not? To Amy and the hundreds who flocked to The Raymond from the icy East, this surely was Paradise: waterfalls of crimson roses cascading down old adobe walls, brilliant blue skies laced with "fleecy clouds," warm breezes and the sweet smell of orange blossoms, all on a winter's day. Amy's cloistered, very privileged experience was, though, to the many who served her, little more than artifice. Paradise in Pasadena and the rest of Southern California had a seedy, malevolent underside. To a degree, community building in the West was no different from what had occurred elsewhere in the country as the economy shifted from agriculture to the factory. But only to a degree. City building in this western Paradise was invariably idiosyncratic as the mythmakers of Southern California built their empire from the late 19th-century progressive ideology of freedom and precision, a contradiction if there ever was one. When played out in the day-to-day lives of its citizens, Pasadena's grand but contradictory aspirations became for the wealthy precisely what the mythmakers promised—a material Paradise free from the constraints of urban life in the hide-bound East. For the laboring class—especially African Americans and Mexicans—Pasadena's progressive aspirations became little more than deceit and empty promises.

Examining how Pasadena and the territory west of the Rockies responded to the pressures of urbanization—to the increasing numbers of Anglo-European and nonwhite immigrant laborers who would continually contest the prevailing ethnocentric middle-class ideology—exposes how a community rich in its own mythology of Paradise compromised a set of progressive ideals into social distance and then segregation. The history of civil rights in the West is marked by an ideological terrain shaped by the conflict over race, gender, labor and, ultimately, schooling. This, then, is the politics of the margin: how the disenfranchised—women, both working and wealthy; people of color; and the working class in general—organized to resist the demands industrialization made on them.

During the 1870s, Southern California was idealized as biblically idyllic. This climatically gentle, Mediterranean-like coastal zone, once the domain of the Mexican Dons, was ironically now being "colonized" by Midwesterners bent on securing a vision of collective, Christian utopia. Described as "this *Italia* of America," Southern California was a refuge from what immigrants like John Bingham called the "4 yoke of oxen and sled, breaking out roads ... through ... drifts 8 to 10 feet, 30 degrees below zero and the ground froze 4 feet in depth." Instead, Bingham sat in shirtsleeves on a January day in Anaheim:

> with doors open and in sight of the rose, calla lily, and other flowers in bloom ... the banana plant, the date palm, and all about ... large lemmon [sic] and orange groves loaded with their golden hued fruit, beautifully contrasting with their glossy evergreen foliage, enough enchanting sights to make one think of Eden, the forbidden fruit tree left

out ... the most lucious [sic] fruits that will grow any where on God's green earth flourish in great profusion here.[18]

Edens like Anaheim, Redlands, Orange and Pasadena were settled with the
intent not only to escape the cold of "ground froze four feet" deep but also the
creeping blight of industrialism and urbanization. Settlers like the Elliotts and
John Bingham, who wrote about his heavenly Anaheim, were not the dispossessed dirt farmers of the mid-West and South. Jeanne Carr, a writer, feminist,
educator, and during the 1880s, proprietress of a garden spot in Pasadena she
called "Carmelita," wrote that not one of the village founders was experienced at
farming or horticulture.[19] Hardly, then, can we attribute the Elliott's migration
as simply a desire for shirtsleeve winters, although warm climate certainly has an
appeal to the psyche of any half-frozen citizen—that certainly was the case for the
Bridges family. If climate had been the single trump in their move, then
Pasadena's founders might very well have been off to some other warm weather
site. We know the Elliotts and their shareholders certainly discussed alternatives,
among them Florida and Louisiana, but no matter, it was to be Pasadena. To the
flood of migrating mid-Westerners, big city dwellers from the East, and overnight
entrepreneurs from everywhere, Southern California in the late 19th century more
than any other location, was the mythic "Frontier," now pacified and angelic
compared to a few decades before when Mexicans, Indians and cattle shared the
land and eked out a living despite the hardships of drought, war and famine
which constantly lurked. To this new breed of genteel pioneers, the lands tum-
bling down from the San Gabriel mountains were colored with renewal and cer-
tainty. Southern California was the land of opportunity that absolved—or at least
obscured—the uncertainty inherent in older, industrial communities. Pasadena's
founders saw in the lands that spread out before them the potential for Heaven-
on-Earth, and the city's boosters have romanticized that notion ever since.
    As alluring as the vision of a western Paradise may have been, profit is what
drives colonization and it was no different in Southern California. Throughout
the Civil War and the years that followed, unrelenting economic pressure exerted
by surplus American capital collapsed the old Mexican ranchero system. By 1875,
the holdings that made up the great Spanish land grants of the southwest had all
but been absorbed by Eastern capital.[20] During the decade after the war, hundreds of thousands of immigrants, a significant portion dislocated from Eastern
factories after the Panic of 1873, flowed into the state. By the early 1880s, the
ranchero cattle economy of California had been replaced by large-scale agriculture using plentiful, cheap labor and a rapidly growing manufacturing base,
fueled by expanding railroads engaged in a cutthroat fare war that saw migrants
from as far away as Kansas City arriving with tickets paid for by the change in
their pockets.[21]

By the winter of 1887, the seasonally rhythmic lifestyle that characterized pastoral Pasadena just six years earlier was gone. On more than one occasion, young Amy Bridges would leave behind her needlework and ride the horse-drawn jitney through either the mud or chaparral dust that passed for Pasadena's streets, to the hustle and bustle of downtown. After a sudden heavy downpour in February, Amy tiptoed her way across a narrow muddy plank "to the muddy side-walk thick with damp looking men and children." She observed men coming out from their stores bearing boards "of all sorts and descriptions which they threw down into the mud" and "after a careful balancing and choosing of footsteps" Amy was amused to see that "the mud was so slippery that men floundered around on these boards in a very funny manner and sometimes had to lay their crossings two boards deep to do any good." Her excursions from The Raymond revealed a chaotic and dirty city center, a place for Amy not as repulsive as pueblo Los Angeles but equally mysterious.

Amos Fletcher Jr., one of the founders, had laid out the original city plat map.[22] Fletcher's original Pasadena was intersected at right angles by streets and boulevards. The main east/west boulevard, Colorado Street, where New Year's Day millions watch the Rose Parade, crosses Fair Oaks and, here, Amy wrote,

> is the very center of town. At these corners is the greatest confusion. The narrow dirty wooden sidewalks are crowded with all sorts of foreign looking men and children ... Near here the Mexicans have driven up their teams full of roots and split wood for sale and stand in little clusters—foreign and dirty in appearance—foreign and incomprehensible to me in their talk—several dogs are with them. Horses stand harnessed to carriages for somebody to hire.[23]

Amy saw Chinese peddlers "in their blue cloaks and green shoes, shinny white stockings and white soles glide quickly along the street." She described a town center with "low dirty white [buildings] with narrow [doorways]" with signs that read "Lodging—25 cents" and what she called "shanties ... only a little more respectable ..." that served the booming town's transient population. Colorado and Fair Oaks had plenty of "little stores ... full of goods of all sorts, variety, and quality and seem to do a thriving business." Amy could not help but laugh that compared to her commercial Boston, these were "such queer little stores." Nonetheless, Amy was impressed with the rapidly expanding commercial center and the "two or three—even more than that—five business blocks with nice fronts and gilded signs especially one bank and the new Hotel Carleton." To a sophisticated New England girl out West, the Carleton was "small scale."

Everywhere she saw evidence of the boom. As Amy walked along Colorado Street—or dodged, depending on the circumstances—she peered up and down the north/south cross streets. Here she saw "building everywhere, so the sides of the streets are filled with piles of brick and blocks of stone." Swirling about her

Fig. 3. The Raymond horse-drawn jitney along Columbia Avenue c. 1890, taking passengers to the "hustle and bustle" of boomtown Pasadena. *(Photo courtesy of the Pasadena Museum of History)*

like some as yet unfinished kaleidoscope, Pasadena was "so very dirty the first weeks and the horse and carriages and foot passengers seemed to get all mixed up with the bricks, stores and lumber with the dust and with each other in a very confusing way to a stranger."

What Amy experienced on those adventures down from The Raymond to the civic center was the material representation of a clash between the values of a now very real Protestant middle-class culture—but once an idealized utopia— and the means secured by capital as it accumulated and consolidated more and more wealth. On those crowded, dirty sidewalks, Amy saw all sorts of "foreign-looking" strangers. To her they were the odd assortment of day laborers, transients, hucksters, Mexican section hands and wood peddlers, Chinese laundry-men and vegetable peddlers, capitalists, evangelists, merchants, all bent on finding their fortune, whatever it might be. Over the next decades, Pasadena's wealthy would measure the quality of culture through the conflict that was erupt-ing between labor and capital. The tranquility of preboom Southern California was gone forever.

Just across the municipal border in Los Angeles, labor would become engaged in an epic battle with Harrison Gray Otis, publisher of *The Los Angeles Times,* and the conflict would spill over into Paradise. Pasadena's working men and women would begin to organize in the years after Amy visited The Raymond. By the first decade of the new century, coupled with an incipient but vigorous socialist movement, the city's laboring class would proudly pronounce Pasadena a "union town." But it was temperance, or rather the intemperate laboring men and women of the city in the late years of the 19th century, that first defined the clash between the values of the gentry and the needs of capital.

Temperance

During the industrial expansion that followed the Civil War, temperance emerged at the cutting edge of national social reform. Prohibitionists and anti-saloon zealots saw moral decay in the big cities and, in their mind, the cause was drink and its effects on the character of the laboring class. The founders of Pasadena, believing their new community would benefit from a "dry" ordinance, wrote into their charter an antiliquor provision that forbade the production or sale of alcoholic drinks within the colony's borders. Theirs was a Christian utopia and devil drink had no place within the homes or shops of the village. Certainly they would never condone something as blasphemous as a saloon.

The founders' motivation to remove alcohol from the public place, typical of antidrink crusaders around the country, was framed by their zealous religious orthodoxy.[24] They firmly believed that liquor would undo all their hard work and they made sure that those who joined them in the West were of like mind and spirit. As their utopian vision of Pasadena collapsed around them in the boom of the late 1880s, enforcing their antidrink ordinance took on all the melodrama of a crusade. In Pasadena, as in nearly every Protestant community around the country, temperance workers were nurtured in the belief that industry, sobriety and thrift were more than a set of behaviors. They defined a character that the middle class sought to develop not only in themselves but in others as well. In places like Pasadena and Long Beach, Monrovia and Alhambra, Southern California's Protestant middle class idealized themselves as disciplined, orderly, hard-working, frugal, responsible, morally correct, and self-controlled, apt projections for an early settler from Iowa, Hiram Reid, a physician, antidrink zealot, and self-appointed first historian of the city. Reid later would hook up with another more famous evangelical prohibitionist, Amos Throop, founder of the Throop Polytechnic Institute, who like so many "antis" of his day, hated slavery nearly as much as alcohol. Throop Polytechnic would later become the California Institute of Technology-Caltech. Testament to his abolitionist sentiments,

Throop proudly stated, was the charred remains of a tree where his burning effigy once hung while he was Alderman of Chicago.

Throop's public life—for we have no record of his private one—was a model of self-control, frugality, piety and hard work. Well into his senior years, Throop could still pinpoint with exactitude when he decided on his life of moral probity. As a young boy of 12, he told how he worked a logging "bee" in upstate New York. As the loggers toiled and the logs piled up, his job was to keep the men well supplied in whiskey. By nightfall they were mauling each other more than the logs, and, he wrote, "the blood was flowing as freely as the liquor ..." As if plucking a scene from a late-century dime novel, Throop captured the moment of his redemption when, "Frightened, I ran to my mother. When she took me in her arms and said: "My son, my son, will you ever be a drunkard?" I promised I would not and have kept that promise."25 To men like Throop and Reid, intemperance was much more than an inability to abstain from drink. By lacking self-control, one would be unable to marshal the necessary will to forestall the evils of modernity. For Pasadena's antidrink leadership in the progressive milieu of the late century, having the worker acquire more self-control—or if that failed then controlling the worker—were the tools of redemption. If the worker could be taught some of those idealized notions of Throop's Victorian character—discipline, order, hard work, frugality, responsibility, probity, and especially punctuality—then the aberrant culture of the working class could be controlled and the needs of capital would continue to be met. For Throop, Reid and many others, including the ladies of Pasadena's Women's Christian Temperance Union (WCTU), reconciling how middle-class, Protestant culture could coexist with a lesser, often Catholic worker culture was defined on the daily level by their crusade to rid the community of the devil drink.

What Amy Bridges saw on those dirty sidewalks was the labor building Pasadena. With it came the inevitable market for drink and working-class leisure. During the boom, even with wages at four to six dollars a ten-hour day for skilled carpenters and masons, developers had to scramble to find sufficient labor. J.W. Wood was such a builder and, during the winter Amy Bridges walked Colorado Street, it was his bricks she surely saw being put up. Wood, who would later open the city's first pharmacy, found his barely sufficient labor force living in those 500 tents spread out in the only area of the city where they could be accommodated. Labor lived on the city's southern edge, along what would become South Raymond Avenue and Fair Oaks Boulevard, south of Colorado Street and within sight of Amy's hotel. Wood tells us the tent city was colorful: canvas in red, blue, and green, some with multicolored flaps and awnings, pitched in and among the orchards, feed pens, and garbage dumps.26

Here was a lucrative market for any entrepreneur and, in the winter of 1884, Jerome "Jerry" Beebe, a "well-liked and well-known" self-described capitalist opened a billiard hall on Colorado Street about a mile from where Amy would board the Hotel's jitney for her trips to the civic center. With a touch of vaude-ville, Beebe hired the recently formed Pasadena Brass Band, ironically made up of some of the town's most ardent antidrinkers, to open his game room. Initially dry, Beebe's Billiard Hall soon became Beebe's Billiard Hall and Saloon. The civic-minded, led by Reid, asked Beebe to remove the alcohol but he refused. Besides, he said with a smile when presented with the antis' resolution, he had a lawful license and his patrons would not play their games without drink. Business became so profitable that Beebe's Billiard Hall and Saloon quickly became known . simply as "the Saloon." Undeterred, the prohibitionists by the first week of November were calling for an antiliquor town hall meeting. Sensing that not only his livelihood but potentially his life was in danger, Beebe armed himself with a pair of loaded revolvers, and, backed up by a Los Angeles sheriff, warned the zealots that he would shoot anyone on sight if they attempted to interfere with his lawful saloon.27

Fig. 4. A Raymond Hotel work crew, living in their tent city, during construction of the hotel in 1883. No doubt these and other workers consumed buckets of beer carried up to the site from Beebe's saloon. *(Photo courtesy of the Pasadena Museum of History)*

The town meeting was held at Central School, directly across the street from Beebe's wood frame, two-story establishment. Within a year of Beebe's opening, the school property would be sold at auction, the proceeds being used to expand the public system to create new school buildings away from the "stir and confusion" of the business center.28 At Central School the crusaders drafted what would be the first of many antidrink resolutions over the next quarter century. With resolution in hand, a small delegation of clergy and Women's Temperance Christian Union ladies was sent off to confront the lion in his den. They were armed with God's Word—their "moral suasion"—but Beebe would hear none of it.

Beebe had hung an American flag over his doorway to show his patriotism— or to flaunt his God-given right to earn a buck. How Beebe responded to their demands underscores what was at the heart of the crusade: he offered to sell them the property and not engage in the saloon business again if he was paid $7,000. Apparently not wishing to go into the business of purchasing saloons, the crusaders refused his offer, although one suspects that Jerry Beebe knew all along that temperance money would not supplant temperance zeal. No, simply buying out Beebe would not eliminate the saloon business. Hiram Reid and the others believed that with the big money liquor business just across the municipal border in Los Angeles, someone would merely replace Beebe. What was needed was to control consumption by controlling the patrons who were consuming the drink. The prohibitionists were after more than the mere elimination of liquor. Their ultimate mission was the salvation of the working class.29

EXCLUSION: THE LABORER AS "OTHER"

The temperance campaign provides an insight into the politics of class formation in late-century Southern California. Pasadena's temperate middle class came to perceive the laborer as the "other." However, if the crusade is seen as simply an effort by a small group of religious zealots to keep liquor from a handful of workers at the end of a ten-hour day, then we fail to understand the campaign for what it was: an extremely complex negotiation that bartered power and compromise to reduce conflict. More important than the elimination of alcohol, the antidrink campaign reveals how the city's leadership, both the religious zealots as well as the less temperate business community, went about systematically controlling the movement of the poor and working class within the city's borders. During this first saloon campaign—there were to be many more in the years to come— Pasadena's elite did not publicly differentiate labor by ethnicity or race. However, what the city's leadership learned about the mechanics of exclusion during their many "Whiskey Wars" would have direct bearing 80 years later when Judge Manuel Real handed down his decision to desegregate Pasadena's schools.

This is not to say that the subsequent further marginalization of the working class by the city's business and cultural elite was a conscious, back-room plot to subordinate a disreputable lot of working-class stiffs. Certainly labor's response to the various efforts to manipulate and deceive working men and women should never be considered as passive acceptance. To understand Pasadena's "Whiskey

Wars" as the initial segmentation in community building requires more than the convenient application of a "religious benevolence as social control" thesis.[30] Ideology is too complex a phenomenon to be reduced to a simplistic dynamic of the powerful beating up on the less powerful. As political anthropologist James Scott argues, ideology is deception—sometimes self-deception—but seldom the conscious use of fraud and deceit. Reid's efforts were not disingenuous acts intended to dupe or trick.[31] To the contrary, the efforts to reduce the working class to marginal status in this new western community can be thought of as the by-product of what we now understand as a failed social reform model. Indeed, if we allow ourselves to criticize Reid and his zealous cohort and Wood and his business elites, then the real deception was their own. The turn-of-the-century middle-class ideology espoused by the city's leadership required a reform model—progressivism—that reinforced the perception that their worldview represented, and more importantly preserved, the public good. It can be argued that it was in the interest of the city's leadership to systematically differentiate the community because they believed it would help stabilize what they felt was a precarious social order.

Throughout Pasadena's progressive era, first the drinking laborer, then the Chinese, Mexican and black migrants would be channeled into specific neighborhoods delineated by race, ethnicity and social class, all, as more than one reformer claimed, "for their own good."[32] Over the next few decades, the anti-drink crusade was but one banner under which the reform campaign would march. Intending to remake the character of the working class, "Temperance for Christ!" over the years blended with "The New Education" and its manual training and "Opportunity School," which in turn were mediated by the ideals of progressive women and their "Mother's Aid Society." These were only a few of the organizational impulses found in nearly every urbanizing community experiencing the effects of a rapidly changing work force with its different cultural and religious orientations. Good-hearted, intelligent women and men hoped to create the kind of virtuous, orderly and efficient community where everyone was Godly, healthy, and clean—and knew their place and accepted it. Pasadena's reformers did what they knew how to do: taking their cue from missionaries working in big cities and foreign lands, they tried to remake the worker into their vision of what constituted a good, Christian American. They exerted such energy, so many resources and such unbridled passion that Pasadena's reformers became national models in the Americanization movement, that early 20th-century effort to transform dark-skinned immigrants into "Americans." These reconstituted New Americans were to be a mirror image of their patrons, minus their middle-class standing in the community. In the penchant to save the immigrant worker from himself, Pasadena's progressives tried to squeeze the "foreignness" out of them.

That meant ridding the worker not only of their drinking, but their native language and folkways.[33]

In a multiplicity of ways, immigrant workers and their families resisted assimilation into the dominant worldview. Like most that reside on top, a young girl like Amy Bridges was ill equipped to discern all but the most openly hostile forms of resistance. From her diary, it is obvious that Amy viewed those below her station as different, rather odd creatures, most there to serve her and her class. Her anger over the lack of prompt, English-speaking Mexicans in Santa Fe was quite logical.

The foot dragging Amy so deplored was to her little more than cultural lethargy. But, more importantly, the Mexican worker behavior that so exasperated Amy helps define the "infrapolitics of resistance," the unofficial, unorganized, every-day actions by ordinary people as they construct a separate sphere, a life in opposition.[34] What Amy experienced in Mexican Santa Fe was neither new nor bound by nationality. At least as far back as the preindustrial era, workers' communities in the commercial centers of the East were rife with suspicion and apprehension. Workers' mistrust of capital became on the shop floor a callous indifference toward the planned profit that comes from increasing precise efficiency.[35] In the urban workers' schools of the East, in places like New Bedford, Norwich and New York, a father's resistance to the exploitive conditions of the factory might have been acted out by his children as rampant truancy.[36] As industrialization moved West, urban centers like Chicago and St. Louis, and then San Francisco and Southern California would experience the cultural dissolution associated with industrialization. As capital centralized and labor organized, resistance to the dehumanizing effect of industrialization was played out all over the country. As the century turned, the conflict in Pasadena was over how to reconcile the wealth produced by industrialization just as urbanization tore away at the bonds of an idealized pastoral community. Pasadena's powerful had the same choice that urban leaders in the East employed, namely, abandon the city center as idealized visions of a better city were created in the suburbs. But Pasadena was already a suburb, no matter how the city's boosters have historically rejected that label. Looming just over their western border was a rapidly industrializing Los Angeles that over the next decades would see strikes, labor violence, and an increasing population of poor ethnic, African-American and Mexican families. Furthermore, Pasadena's civic center was indeed just that, a civic place without belching smokestacks and crumbling tenements housing the dispossessed. Pasadena's leaders were carefully crafting an image of "the City on the Hill." For the devout like Reid it meant an absence of immorality; for others, less zealous in their religious approbation, it meant a retreat away from the squalor, violence, and confusion of lesser places. The city was a refuge, an escape to Paradise. The question for Pasadena's elite was how to continue to acquire material wealth and yet keep the city as Paradise.

Many thought that segregating workers and their families was a logical extension of progressive ideology. Yet, paradoxically, the progressive impulse to rid the
immigrant of his folkways was at the same time a humane and beneficent effort
to rescue a generation from what industrialization and the factory had wrought—
the disease, filth, class violence, and cultural dissolution of the urban slum.
Throughout the middle years of the 20th century, in every urban center in the
country, from Los Angeles to New York and Chicago to Houston and Detroit,
the poor have been cordoned off into "projects" that, when built and for decades
after, were celebrated as livable places. Today, not far from the corner of Colorado
and Fair Oaks where Amy once dodged Wood's bricklayers, poor, mostly black
and Latino Pasadenans live in the "projects," cut off from the rest of the community by the very benevolence that created the Martin Luther King Village
housing project. The late 20th-century policymakers relied on an ideology that
was firmly rooted in the late 19th-century idea that the poor needed to be "fixed"
and that by restricting the movement of the poor the social service systems could
be brought to bear on these "problems."

THE WHISKEY WARS

Pasadena's "Whiskey Wars," as it came to be known, was a fragile compromise
negotiated between investors who respected and believed in the temperance ideals
but feared that the overzealousness of the crusade would drive away labor needed
to build Paradise or, worse yet, discourage the wealthy from enjoying the fruits of
that labor. Conversely, most prohibitionists, knowing their zeal was the hand of
God, eventually came to understand that they had to find common ground with
capital. Nothing of substance could be accomplished until both sides developed
a plan that would end the indiscriminate sale of alcohol, keep the laborer working and allow the wealthy tourist wine with dinner. The linchpin of the campaign
would be the phrase "indiscriminate sale of liquor."

Reid's crusade was not universally accepted in the community. We would
expect labor to resist being driven from their only public watering hole.
Increasingly, however, the major opposition to Reid came not from the working
class but from prominent businessmen heavily invested in projects along
Colorado and Fair Oaks. The opposition came when Reid and his group
demanded that *all* alcohol be banned from the city. Opposition surfaced from
five newspapers, three in Pasadena and two across the border in Los Angeles.
Initially, business supported the campaign, but as Reid and his cohort ratcheted
the cause into a crusade, investors like Ed Webster and A.K. McQuilling who
were heavily engaged in speculative ventures in and around the civic center worried that Reid's radical prohibition might restrict the flow of cheap, plentiful
labor into Pasadena. Moreover, business cringed when Reid's crusade painted the

city as a community in conflict over its morals. That was bad for business. After years of struggle—and before prohibition became federal law in the early 1920s—an unwritten yet tenuous compromise was reached between Pasadena's more centrist prohibitionists and the business community. The accord came when both moderate temperance and business understood the antidrink campaign was counterproductive if wealth determined that the city was uninhabitable. As is always the case, the business community abhorred conflict—it was not good for profit. The temperance campaign hated liquor and its effects on the working class. Together they developed responses to the liquor question that over time became institutionalized. The truce that ended the "Whiskey Wars" was the result of strategies that grew out of an exclusionary ideology firmly rooted in the principles of capital and profit. The strategies were tested and perfected again and again when conflict threatened the stability of capital investment. The tactics the city used in excluding the working-class laborer developed over time into *de facto* "agreements" that became fundamental to the workings of Pasadena's schools, health care, housing, law enforcement and civic government. For a community like Pasadena that was nurtured in the belief of an attainable Paradise, public conflict was to be avoided at all costs. Pharmacist Wood summed it up best when he said that business grew tired of the agitation. He chastised Reid because his efforts to rid the city of the saloon only "advertised [Pasadena] as having a saloon, which brought working men there to drink."[37]

In 1912, the "dry" element led by a newly arrived Methodist attorney named S.W. Odell proposed an amendment to the city charter that would prohibit "anybody from having liquor in their homes."[38] Opposed by the more liberal element, including Adolphus Busch, the beer king, who wintered in Pasadena, the moderates countered Odell with their own charter amendment. The liberals proposed banning "now and for ever" any saloon in the city but would allow liquor in private homes as well as liberalizing the hours alcohol could be served in the most-favored hotels and restaurants. *The Daily News* sided with the liberals, adding, with an ever-present eye toward profit, that

> Scores of persons who are strictly temperate and unalterably opposed to saloons have stated to *The Daily News* their belief that our visitors should be entitled to the same privileges in their temporary homes they are accustomed to back east. If we continue to deny them it is a reasonable assumption that they will go elsewhere. This is the question the people have the right to decide.[39]

They did. Pasadena continued to prohibit working-class saloons but welcomed liquor into private residences and the "select hotels and restaurants" of the city. Just after the vote, Odell's wife, Clara, who was the first woman elected president of the Board of Education, would begin a campaign to segregate all Mexican children into one school on South Raymond Avenue. One of Odell's

Board colleagues (or it may have been Odell) said the school was "for the indus-trial needs of the city."[40]

It took nearly ten years for the city to resolve the first of what would be many prohibition battles and, in doing so, the middle and upper classes more often than not put property—and profit—ahead of religious conviction. Modeling their program on the national antiliquor campaign, temperance workers formed The Mutual Protection Association (MPA). With an executive council that Hiram Reid claimed was comprised of 30 of the most influential business inter-ests in the city, the MPA initiated a coercive campaign. The antis came to see the enemy as anyone who had not publicly joined the MPA. Reid created his own temperance newspaper, *The Standard,* and the inaugural issue trumpeted, "NO SALOON IN THE VALLEY," a poem Reid wrote with an opening stanza wor-thy of the Cause:

> Rise, Pasadena! march and drill
> to this your bugle's rally—
> A church or School
> on every hill but
> NO SALOON IN THE VALLEY[41]

A mass psychology was developing that saw drink and its working-class abusers as something odd and very separate from the culture of the Protestant middle class. The majority white, middle-class Protestants saw the world divided in a life-and-death struggle between the forces of darkness and light. If the poor and the working class were not in the business of reforming themselves, which they surely were not, then Reid and his brothers and sisters would do it for them. Increasingly the apostolic and reform-minded saw the laborer as strangely "for-eign." The ideology of the temperance movement defined the world in terms of "otherness." The temperance crusaders used language that reduced the immigrant and working class into caricatures thought so evil and threatening that efforts to remake the laborer would erupt into fits of rage and violence against those deemed too foreign to be compatible. In the mind of an evangelical like Hiram Reid, this was, indeed, a holy war:

> [Be it resolved that] ... every place in Pasadena, where intoxicating liquors are dispensed contrary to the law, is an infamous invasion of our territory by a foreign foe; as a nesting place of anarchy and outlawry; as in flagrant defiance of the very ground principles of Republican government. And against any and all such we declare unremitting war.

> ... aiders, abettors, and supporters of such places, whether openly or secretly, are allies of the common enemy, and are helping to destroy the peace and safety of our homes, the value of our property, the good name of our city, the rights of local government.[42]

By March of 1885, Reid and the MPA were convinced Beebe would not budge. They drafted a resolution supported, Reid said, by 63 businesses and 272 voters. The resolution, distributed as a handbill, demanded an end to the indiscriminate sale of liquor in the city. Openly boycotting businesses not supporting the crusade, Reid and his followers aimed the resolution at the profit side of temperance:

> We the undersigned, citizens of Pasadena, realiz[e] that the indiscriminate sale of intoxicating liquors in our midst depreciates the value of our homes, retards immigration, injures our business interests, endangers our lives and property, leads our young men and boys into habits of vice and crime, and lowers the moral tone of our society.

Here is evidence that the temperance leadership had altered its original position. No longer was this a single-issue campaign. The antis understood all too well the declining moral tone brought about by the saloon. Arrests had skyrocketed in their once peaceful village and most, according to Reid's history, were alcohol related. The leadership knew that intoxicating liquors devalued and depreciated their community but only when the sale of liquor was, as they put it, "indiscriminate." In a friendly newspaper editorial, one of Reid's allies told the community that for 10 years there had been no "saloon, no criminal record, and no paupers." The message was clear. With Beebe's saloon, Pasadena would experience what other, less Christian cities found commonplace: the criminal ways of the poor and the working class. Therefore, the

> practical business object of this anti-saloon agreement is to keep out of our midst that class of men who would spend their earnings at the saloon thus sustaining the nuisance here, with all the crimes and other evils that naturally occur at such a place or by reason of it.[43]

The MPA resolution was aimed not only at ridding the city of the indiscriminate sale of alcohol, but also more effectively eliminating the need for "that class of men" to remain after they had done the day's labor. The trick was how to keep labor plentiful, complacent, but out of the city by end of workday. The goal was the elimination of the saloon.

The MPA boycott did little. Liquor still flowed at Beebe's saloon and under California law, the crusaders were legally powerless to do anything about it. Reid believed that no more than a handful of Pasadena men refused to support the boycott, yet Beebe's business still thrived. Reid was wrong. There may have been a majority of signatures but the majority did not support his campaign. Wood claims many were intimidated by the crusade. Granted no upstanding member of the community wished to see drunks sleeping off the night's pleasure in some public place, but Wood and his business allies were more concerned with Reid's overzealous campaign than about inebriated laborers. Wood and the others could agree to restrict the drinking laborer but they could not agree to indiscriminately restrict drinking.

The antialcohol forces were convinced that it was the liquor business in Los Angeles that continued to support Beebe, further proof to the temperance forces that the problem was outside Pasadena's borders.[44] Control those borders, they argued, and control "the problem." And Reid's "problem" was becoming more and more acute. The number of laborers streaming into the city looking for work and remaining after hours to drink was "changing and increasing so rapidly,"[45] wrote Reid, that something drastic had to be done.

The response was an attempt to close the borders; in effect, to wall off the community through incorporation. Under California law, in a fourth- or fifth-class city, citizens could petition to declare the sale of alcohol illegal, thereby removing the saloon, and with it, the reformers reasoned, the appeal for workers to remain in the city after work. To incorporate, Pasadena would have to go to the polls and in June of 1886, nearly a year after the petition was sent to the County Board of Supervisors, Pasadena became an official city under California law.[46] It is ironic that Pasadena's incorporation, which was in and of itself a legit-imate public effort to create a community, grew out of an effort to exclude a community of working-class men and women.

All the while Beebe's saloon "had been gaining a stronger foothold by the great influx of a drinking class of mechanics and laboring men who flocked to Pasadena in swarms—drawn by the high wages paid, and the great demand for labor in the booming rush of new buildings ..."[47] When the issue of alcohol in public places was finally joined in legislation it turned out that what really mat-tered in Pasadena was where those public places were located. When the temper-ance workers brought to the city attorney's office enough signatures to create an ordinance that would restrict the sale of drink, a quiet deal was cut between the city and the owners of the Carleton, the new hotel Amy Bridges so admired.[48] Advised that no law preventing beer and wine from being served with meals in a hotel would ever be upheld in the courts, the antidrink forces winked at the Carleton, and took what some lamented as a tainted victory.[49] The antidrink Ordinance 45 was read into the books not mentioning the hotels, yet all knew that no arrests would be made.

The compromise allowing the tourist hotels in the city to serve liquor was not a contradiction. The reformers still believed Ordinance 45 to be a victory over the forces of evil. Ignoring the alcohol being served at the Carleton, Reid boasted that they had "cornered the California Whiskey Lion in his Den."[50] More to the point, the antidrink forces accomplished what they had set out to do: corner the working class by closing the saloon. Within months, Beebe sold to a man named Campbell, and Campbell, unable to prevent the ordinance from closing his saloon, left town much to the delight of the crusaders and the business-men along Colorado. Still, alcohol continued to be served at the Carleton, The Raymond, and a scattering of other smaller hotels and restaurants in and around the civic center, including one owned by the fire chief, Pete Steil.[51] These, however, were not places that catered to the working class. What Pasadena got in return was an underground liquor business. Open defiance of the Ordinance, as well as thriving illegal liquor distilleries—the "private porcines of obscure vision," or "blind pigs" as Wood called them—began to pop up. The city was now confronted with having to enforce an unenforceable ordinance.

Reid's crusaders did not wait for the municipal government to respond. Within the week they created an Enforcement Committee, headed by 12 men representing the Protestant churches, civic organizations such as the YMCA and three banks. The WCTU, apparently believing Reid could better represent their interests than they could, threw their support behind the good doctor, for as they told him, "The Philistines are upon us ... and after fervent prayer ..." they appointed Reid to act "for God, home, and native land."

This was serious business. The Ordinance was worthless if the liquor interests could continue to manufacture and sell their trade. There was the additional fear that the Philistines were planning to test Ordinance 45 by opening two wholesale businesses in the city. As chairman of the committee, Reid vowed to "whip these sly and scaly law brakers [sic]" and within the week, hired two well-known Los Angeles temperance lawyers, a detective agency to canvass the city for the scaly lawbreakers and a chemistry professor to check for any "falsely named liquors." Reid's detectives went about town making life so hot that laborers apparently retaliated and the detectives were "beaten, gouged, [and] severely injured" along with one of Pasadena's policemen. The temperance effort had gotten out of hand. Reid's vigilantes found themselves in repeated brawls; one had a near fatal gunfight before the disgruntled townsfolk ran the detectives out of town.

Reid and his committee had gone too far. The streets had become a battleground and business interests would not abide such a contentious atmosphere—there was entirely too much money at stake, now and in the future. A new law, Ordinance 125, with the infamous hotel liquor clause intact, was put forward to be decided in the municipal election of 1890. The city had been a Republican stronghold since its founding and would remain so throughout the 20th century. Yet the politics of temperance had become so volatile during this first Whiskey War that traditional party lines became amorphous. Men who once supported a less divisive antisaloon campaign—men intimately involved in the bustle and business of the boom—became candidates for trustee seats by forming the Citizens party, with a platform that was nearly identical to the Democratically controlled antisumptuary Progressive League. Yet none of these men were Democrats. Reid's temperance crusaders and their party, "The People's Ticket," protecting the "moral prestige of Pasadena," opposed the hotel loophole and demanded that the city be teetotalling dry. Just before the vote, the Citizen's candidates published a disclaimer that under no circumstances would they support a saloon, bar or tipping house, and further, they "unalterably opposed ... encouraging the promiscuous sale or use of intoxicating liquors."[52] Everyone saw the election as a referendum on who could drink and where that transaction could take place.

Ultimately, it was an election that would legalize the eradication of a working-class saloon at the same time sanctioning alcohol in particular places. The Citizen's ticket of real estate broker T.P Lukens, his business partners A.K. McQuilling and C.M. Simpson along with one of the founder's nephews, Deputy Sheriff Thomas Banbury, and James Clarke won a narrow election.

The election turned out to be a disaster for the temperance forces. All of their candidates lost trustee seats. The saloon may have been eliminated but alcohol was not. After years of engaging in a haranguing, finger-pointing, fist-throwing campaign to rid the city of rum-holes, the prodrink forces celebrated by taunting Reid and the crusaders. Let Reid describe the scene:

> That night after the result was announced, a drunken mob went around yelling and howling as if pandemonium had broke [sic] loose. Old tin pans and empty oil cans were pounded on, fishhorns blown, and every other device used to make a hideous racket. A mob of men and boys thus equipped, and variously estimated at 40 to 70 in numbers, went to the residence of Rev. Dr. Breese, pastor of the M.E. church; went into the archway between the church and the parsonage and go [sic] close up to doors and windows, yelling like savages bent on a cannibal feast; hooting, howling, groaning; making mock prayers; banging their pans and hooting their fishhorns.[53]

Merely closing a saloon did not make for a dry city. Not long after the election, and contrary to what Lukens and the others professed, alcohol continued being openly sold. Reid claimed that beer was being served to carriage passengers coming to and from Los Angeles. Someone mocked Reid by declaring at a public hearing that they could get liquor in the city "And we don't have to go behind a screen to drink it, either!"[54] The city marshall would on occasion haul in someone for illegally serving or distilling liquor. In 1890, Thomas Twaits, a colored man known as "Cheap John" was arrested and arraigned for violating the ordinance. No matter the crusader's efforts, the working class refused to be remade into teetotalers.[55]

By legalizing liquor in only a few hotels and restaurants, Ordinance 125 would buckle under its blatant illegality. The city was recovering from the collapse of the speculative boom and there was renewed vigor in the business community. Eastern wealth had discovered that Pasadena could be home year-round and the very wealthy began to build magnificent homes—mainly overwintering mansions—along south Orange Grove Boulevard, so many, in fact that by the turn of the century the street was called "Millionaires Row." Restaurants and hotels were springing up in and around the city. In March of 1892, the trustees enacted a new prohibitory law, "Ordinance 195," with the hotel clause embellished allowing beer and wine with meals in "any hotel, restaurant, or boarding house." The trustees did not sanction a saloon but allowed liquor with meals anywhere in the city. Fourteen months later, the same trustees apparently realizing that they had erred in not specifying which hotels and restaurants could serve alcohol, amended the ordinance to read: "that prohibition shall not apply to sale of vinous or malt liquors when sold with and as part of a regular *meal costing not less than twenty five cents* ..." The italics were put there by the trustees who, once again, demonstrated to the working stiff that his labor was welcome but not his off-work dining and drinking.

Passing ordinances, which proclaimed the city free of the dreaded saloon, was apparently sufficient. The national Anti-Saloon League yearbooks, printed and distributed free to libraries, schools and organizations around the country, listed Pasadena in 1913 as having been "dry for twenty-four years." Saloons were forbidden by charter, said yearbook editor Cherryton, and during those 24 years, the assessed valuation of property "has increased from one million to nearly forty-five million dollars." Cherryton went on to say that Pasadena's businessmen "are a unit in declaring that being a "no-saloon city" has greatly helped business."56 Slightly exaggerating the length of dryness—24 years would put it two years before Beebe's saloon—the city's boosters continued to promote a persona that was at best contradictory. Pasadena's elite was crafting a vision of a privileged class of residents and guests residing in grand homes and magnificent hotels—built by labor that no one was supposed to see. It was a vision that promoters, politicians, realtors and others would continue to advance throughout the 20th century.

THE CHINESE RIOT: EXCLUSION PERFECTED

The city's effort to exclude the working class involved more than the expressed tension between labor and the business elite. Unlike Europe where social class dynamics was the engine that drove social provision, the development of social policy in the United States was determined "by the clash between racial diversity and an idealized American citizenry."57 As the 19th century turned, social class "otherness" so prevalent in urban, Eastern communities became indivisible from ethnic/religious/racial "otherness."58 As wealth and workers moved West after the end of Civil War hostilities, and the pace of foreign immigration quickened, class politics increasingly became the politics of race. It can be argued that in the volatile expanse of the Western territories, race has always been the progenitor of social policy. It is not coincidental, then, that Pasadena's exclusion of the working class occurred simultaneously with the forced expulsion of Pasadena's entire Chinese population. The racial/class dynamic that was defining politics Pasadena-style developed out of the contested ideological terrain where an idealized democracy met the principal of profit. In Pasadena, the virtuous demanded an end to public displays of immorality caused by the indiscriminate use of liquor by an expanding workforce. Compounding this, Pasadena was now subject to a darkening labor force. Amy Bridges' "foreign-looking men and boys" were threatening the stability of the sanctuary on the hill. Urbanization had destroyed the homogeneity of the population.[59]

The racial and ethnic heterogeneity that was becoming common on the streets of the city nurtured a fear of racial "otherness" in white Pasadena. White Pasadenans witnessed the arrival of darker-skinned workers—Chinese, Mexicans and a burgeoning number of southern and central Europeans. These foreigners provided the founders of Pasadena with the tangible evidence that these "others" would permeate their close-knit homogeneous community and destroy the foundation of Paradise. In defense of "God, Home, and Native Land," white Pasadenans joined together in "America for Americans," otherwise known as the American Protective Association, a national nativist organization that was anti-Catholic, racist and prone to fits of violence against dark immigrants from the south and the east. Their emblems were the American flag and the little red schoolhouse. They campaigned for laws in the city that would restrict land ownership to "Americans" and require literacy tests in English as a perquisite to suffrage. In 1895, 450 red-blooded Pasadenans—easily 10 percent of the adult population—had joined the local chapter.[60]

The Chinese, with their "strange and incomprehensible ways," were especially vulnerable to a community that felt threatened by the sudden and seemingly uncontrollable demographic changes. Since the Depression of 1873, the mood of the country had been growing steadily antilabor, and now as the century was drawing to a close, economic instability had become in the minds of many an expectation rather than an aberration. As the country was involved in an intense period of economic and social stratification, the monied classes saw strikes and labor violence as the unfortunate consequence of industrialization. What would result was the emergence of a racially and hierarchically segmented labor market with a surplus of workers.[61]

Pasadena felt the effects of these changes as the boom of the 1880s intensified. Around the state, the Chinese, the least powerful and most visible "outsiders" in an increasingly stratified cultural hierarchy, were subject to acts of violence as workers were pitted against one another for jobs. Throughout the 1880s, Chinese communities across the western United States were attacked, often by members of nascent labor unions as many of the existing jobs were subject to sudden shifts in capital investment and seasonal vagaries. The Chinese had become the scapegoat for California's economic ills.[62]

Used as laborers in the orchards and as cooks and servants at home, some two dozen Chinese were employed by the 200 or so gentry farmers of Pasadena throughout the 1870s and early 1880s.[63] With railroad connections to Los Angeles and the East completed, the number of laborers, not only Chinese, but also white, black and Mexican increased tremendously. Amy Bridges saw it—on those dirty and narrow wooden sidewalks were swarms of "foreign looking men and children." These were the laborers coming to build the West.

The Chinese were part of the influx into Pasadena. Denied all but the most menial of occupations, they found in urban life one occupation that could give them the stability of proprietorship—the laundry.[64] By the 1880s, three fourths of all the laundries in California were run by Chinese. Usually the laundry was small, occupied by anywhere from three to five men, often related by kin or province. Using what little capital they could save or borrow from their kinship cooperatives, washhouses served the needs of both the white and Chinese community, exchanging Chinese labor for cash. The first Chinese washhouse in the village might very well have been on South Orange Grove. The Chinese had occupied the building after a German grocer named Rosenbaum was routed by temperance folks when he tried to sell liquor along with his millinery and canned goods. Another Chinese business venture was started in the early 1880s, this one a much larger concern. It was located in a cluster of buildings on south Fair Oaks, just below Colorado—which placed it directly in the path of the rapidly developing financial center. The enterprise included not only a washhouse but also a store, an employment office, and lodging rooms. The washhouse occupied a rough-board building owned by Jacob Hisey. The store, boarding house and employment office were located in two buildings owned by another investor, Alexander F. Mills. That many businesses, occupying that many buildings indicate Pasadena had a fairly prosperous Chinese community. In addition, an employment office and boarding rooms suggest Pasadena's Chinese community was growing. *The Los Angeles Times* put the number of Chinese living in the "Celestial village" between 60 and 100. During the boom, when property values were rising at astronomical rates, land in the city center of Pasadena had become some of the most valuable property in the West. There were fortunes to be made and with the increasing anti-Chinese sentiment in the region, Pasadena's "Celestial village" was about to be moved.[65]

The Chinese business community occupied buildings owned by some of the earliest land speculators in Pasadena. In 1877 Alexander F. Mills bought 15 acres at the southwest corner of Fair Oaks and Colorado. He then sold a parcel to Jacob Hisey in 1882. In between the two transactions, he and scores of other investors bought and sold land so often that by the middle of the 1880s some of the property had changed hands dozens of times. During the height of boom madness, a single parcel of land was often sold and resold 20 times in one week. The transactions were very nearly always on the margin, meaning little hard currency was exchanged with the deed. This was the pattern of capital accumulation, where commodities are traded in an atmosphere of constant speculation. In Pasadena, speculation was the very heart and soul of the community's economic vitality. The city was founded by land speculators who, not surprisingly, wished to protect their investment by isolating their community from the ravages of urbanization.

The creative entrepreneurial spirit crystallized in what Reid called "one of the most notable historic events in our city's career." In 1886 the city fathers partitioned the 5-acre Central School property—where Reid and the others began their temperance wars—into 35 business lots and auctioned them off to the highest bidders. Many concede it was the single most influential land sale in the city's history and it ignited the boom of the eighties all over Southern California. Those were 35 prime lots that ran along Colorado and Fair Oaks and they were snapped up at unheard of prices ranging as high as $150 a front foot. In comparison, Mills' initial purchase seven years earlier of 15 acres in the same area cost $1,500.

Throughout the early 1880s, property in the civic center was rapidly being consolidated by a handful of investors, among them real estate broker Lukens, his partners McQuilling and Simpson, and speculators like Ed Webster and his business partners, the Ward Brothers. By October of 1885, Webster and his syndicate owned enough property contiguous to Colorado and Fair Oaks to begin building a three-story, block-long brick building that would eventually house much of the city's financial empire. The Ward Building was a stone's throw away from the Chinese washhouse.

On the evening of November 6, 1885, just a few weeks after the Rock Springs Mine massacre in Wyoming where white miners killed 28 Chinese, a group of white "transient laborers, local men and boys," sitting across the street from the Chinese washhouse "worked themselves up into a collective rage." Reid says they were talking "Chinaman" and they began throwing rocks at the men ironing clothes inside the washhouse.[66] Over went a kerosene lamp, and the building was ablaze. One of the laundrymen tried to smother the flames with a blanket but it was too late. The Chinese had to flee for their lives abandoning all their belongings to the now rapidly spreading fire. The laundrymen barricaded themselves in Mills' adjacent building but not before the mob looted the burning washhouse. The mob followed and with "vile imprecations"—including lynching—they stormed the Mills' building trying to force the "Mongols" out into the open. Wisely the laundrymen refused but the crazed mob then began to tear away at the door trying to get inside. Luckily, Deputy Sheriff Thomas Banbury and three or four other quickly deputized businessmen in the down-

Fig. 5. The only surviving photograph taken the day after the "Chinese Riot." To the right of the burned-out building, a "Chinaman" hangs in effigy, testament to the creation—and intended demise—of Pasadena's "other." *(Photo courtesy of the Pasadena Museum of History)*

town area persuaded the mob to disperse, but only after they had ordered the Chinese to be out of downtown within 24 hours.[67]

What has been dismissed as an unfortunate but isolated incident in Pasadena history very nearly became the carnage Los Angeles had already experienced. Ten years before, near what is now the cultural and historic center of Los Angeles, a crazed mob dragged Chinese men and women out of their homes along "Nigger Alley" and hung them from propped-up wagon hitches.[19] Chinese were lynched. No one was convicted of the crime. Pasadena's washhouse incident, known in local lore as the "Chinese Riot"—as if the Chinese had been the ones doing the rioting, was a violent manifestation of a larger, regional pattern of segregating the Chinese into areas away from urban investment zones.[68]

Even in the atmosphere of anti-Chinese hysteria that was rampant in the West during this period, the spontaneity of the violence seemed contrived. *The Valley Union* reported the next day that two weeks before the violence Deputy Sheriff Banbury had made "arrangements" for the Chinese to leave downtown by the first of December. The newspaper said he "leased premises" for the Chinese to relocate their washhouse "... away outside the town center." Indicative of the prevailing mood of the time, *The Valley Union* added the new Chinese laundry would be "... out of the way of annoying anyone." In addition to the Deputy Sheriff, a Mr. Clark, "the carpenter ... made arrangements with the other two

Chinese tenants to erect places for them immediately in the same neighborhood; thus removing the entire lot of Chinamen from the center of town."[69] The Chinese lost everything they owned. The next day "persons hunting in the burned out buildings raked out" nearly $100 in coins. *The Valley Union* makes no mention of a lease between the laundrymen and Mills and Hisey, but *The Los Angeles Times* mentioned that although Mills returned some rent money to the evicted laundrymen, the matter of the lease was still to be resolved.[70]

All the maneuvering, including an agreement with a city official weeks before the Chinese were burned out, points to the very real possibility that the laundry-men were either resisting the move or at the very least had begun to smell a rat. Given the speculative fever in town, the wealth to be acquired coupled with the low status the Chinese had in the West, the riot may very well have been little more than a vigilante effort to forcibly remove the Chinese.

Whatever the genesis of the eviction, within a matter of hours the Chinese relocation was institutionalized. The following day, 35 businessmen from the downtown area crowded into Lukens' real estate office to sign a resolution restricting the Chinese to an area outside the civic center. The signatories of the restrictive covenant reads like a who's who in the business community. Besides Lukens, there was pharmacist Wood, McQuilling, Webster, James Clark, Mills, Hisey, carpenter Byron Clark, Arthur Cruickshank, and the president of the First National bank, P.M. Green, plus nearly every other important landowner along the Colorado/Fair Oaks axis.

Taking their cue from the temperance crusade and putting distance between themselves and any complicity with the vigilantes, the resolution blamed the working class for the violence and then warned that business interests in the city would tolerate no "mob law." They cordoned off the Chinese from the civic body of the community. The resolution said it was "the sentiment of this community that no Chinese quarters be allowed within" what was the financial heart of Pasadena. The anti-Chinese resolution went on to insist "that everything [must] be done decently and in order [because] ... the good name of our community depends on its law-abiding character, and that we will use all necessary means to preserve such character." Just as the temperance crusade worked to restrict labor from occupying the city center after hours, "all necessary means" in the Chinese resolution meant the relocation of an entire "other" community away from the city center and its prime real estate. In other words, Pasadena did not want the Chinese too close but they did not want them too far either. *The Times* reported that the "respectable portion" of the community says the Chinese "may stay indefinitely ... [because] ... their labor is needed" but only if they remain outside the civic center.[71] Below the names of the 35 businessmen who had signed the resolution, *The Valley Union* concluded, "the Chinamen are gone and order reigns."[72]

Indeed, as the century turned, Pasadena had firmly established its policies of order. The city was consumed by the pursuit of profit as the city's fathers (and as we shall soon see, its mothers) continued to negotiate municipal strategies that attempted to manage growth through racial and class exclusion. By World War I, the City on the Hill could very well have shown itself to the outside world as "The White City" as racial practices, religious orthodoxy, class and racial violence, were all cloaked behind a carefully planned gentility that rejected, at least publicly, any suggestion of social discord. The city planners created a fictitious domestic ideal, as historian Kevin Starr notes; by the first decade of this century, Pasadena was "a liberal, Protestant upper-middle class daydream."[73] Men like Hiram Reid, T.P. Lukens and J.W. Wood laid a foundation of civic culture that, by policy and social "custom," marginalized working men and women. Wealth required immigrant labor but the city's leadership refused to recognize the civic right of labor to live and play in the city. In short, Pasadena was, in the early years of its beginning, a city fantasy unlike any in the country. By the early 1920s, Pasadena had the wealthiest per capita population in the country as the rich and superrich continued to make the Crown of the Valley their home. Given this wealth, it is not hard to imagine a community so wrapped up in itself as to exclude any group or any idea that might bring the risk of social conflict. Even Hollywood's movie stars, by the 1920s America's alter ego, were given a cold shoulder by Pasadena's elite. Over the next decades as the city struggled with growth, depression, and the consequences of institutionalizing racial and class exclusion, Pasadena's hierarchy came to believe that its destiny was to be a new world Shangra La, where wealth, racial superiority and a quietly conservative Protestantism would thrive amidst the chaos of the 20th century.

Notes

1. Amy T. Bridges, *Journal kept on a Raymond Excursion from Massachusetts to California and return, including a 3 month stay at The Raymond Hotel in South Pasadena, the Del Monte Hotel, and in San Francisco. 1886–1887,* Huntington Memorial Library, HML 48978, not paginated. Hereafter cited as Bridges' Diary. Her diary still shows the faint imprint of the hyacinths and other pressed flowers.
2. W. Raymond and I.A. Whitcomb, "Grand Tour Through the Sunny South, Mexico, and California," pamphlet (Boston, 1887) cited in Richard A. Van Orman, *A Room for the Night: Hotels of the Old West* (Bloomington: Indiana University Press, 1966), p. 78–80. Also see Thomas D. Carpenter, *Pasadena: Resort Hotels and Paradise,* (Pasadena: Castle Green Times, 1984).
3. The two other Bridges' diaries are also located at the Huntington Memorial Library.

4.   The only information Amy Bridges left in her diaries was her hometown, Hopkinton, Massachusetts. The records at the Hopkinton Historical Society indicate Daniel Thurber was married with a granddaughter named Eliza. Could that have been Amy? Possibly. The other diaries at the Huntington Library in San Marino, California, are of no help.

5.   Bridges' Diary.

6.   Sarah Deutsch, *No Separate Refuge: Culture, Class, and Conflict on an Anglo-Hispanic Frontier in the American Southwest, 1880–1940* (New York: Oxford University Press, 1987), p. 3–10, 13–39.

7.   Charles Frederick Holder, *Southern California: Its Climate, Trails, Mountains, Canyons, Watering Places, Fruits, Flowers and Game. A Guide Book* (Los Angeles: Los Angeles Times-Mirror Company, 1888). Also see Holder's *All About Pasadena and Its Vicinity*, (Boston, 1889). The single most authoritative book on migrating to Southern California in the post-war years was Charles Nordoff's *California for Health, Wealth and Residence* (New York: Harper and Bros., 1873).

8.   Hiram Reid, *The History of Pasadena* (Pasadena: The Pasadena History Company, 1895), p. 390, 467–471.

9.   "The Raymond Hotel, Pasadena, California: A Place for Particular People," pamphlet (San Francisco: Norman Pierce Company, 1904), not paginated.

10. Ibid.; Bridges' Diary.

11. Bridges' Diary; the Christopher Usherwood quote in Mike Davis's *City of Quartz* (New York: Verso Press, 1990).

12. Bridges' Diary.

13. The boom was an extraordinary event in real estate speculation. Parcels were bought and sold, almost exclusively on the margin (without hard currency), dozens of times each week. See J.W. Wood, *Pasadena, California, Historical and Personal* (Pasadena?: printed by author, 1917), *The Concise History of Pasadena (Los Angeles, 1923)*; Henry Markham Page, *Pasadena, It's Early Years* (Los Angeles: Lorrin L. Morrison, 1964); and Reid for succinct observations on the impact of the boom on the life of Pasadena. Also see Glen Dumke, *The Boom of Southern California* (San Marino: The Henry Huntington Library, 1944); and Carey McWilliams, *Southern California Country* (New York: Meredith Press, 1946), p. 144–145.

14. "Takes Whack at Slums of City," *Pasadena Daily News,* 7 June 1915, p.1. The "business and bustle" quote is from Bridges' Diary.

15. Reid, p. 106–108.

16. Thomas Elliott and Daniel Berry, the two principal partners in the speculative venture, called the "Indiana Colony," that became Pasadena, were nearly bankrupt just before the colony was founded in 1873. Although of "good character," neither was considered much of a credit risk. See James Madison, "Taking the Country Barefooted: The Indiana Colony in Southern California History," *California History* LXIX: 3 (February 1990), p. 238–239.

17. For an overview of the "New Western History," see William Robbins' historiographical essay, "The 'Plundered Province' Thesis and the Recent Historiography of the American West" *Pacific Historical Review* (winter 1986), p. 577–597. Also see Earl S. Pomeroy's *In Search of the Golden West: The Tourist in Western America* (Lincoln: University of Nebraska Press, 1957) for a discussion of the great expectations of the West as salvation. Also see the introductory essay, "Becoming the West," by editors William Cronin, George Miles and Jay Gitlin, *Under an Open Sky: Rethinking America's Western Past* (New York: W.W. Norton, 1992), p. 3–21.

18. "John Burham to Mrs. Vaughan," 7 February 1894, Amos Gager Throop Collection, Folder 3.13, Box 1.5, "Letters," California Institute of Technology Archives, Pasadena, Calif.

19. "Jeanne Caroline Carr Papers, 1842–1903," J. Carr to George Hall, 30 August 1892, Box 4, Huntington Memorial Library.

20. On the destruction of the California economy and culture, see Leonard Pitt, *The Decline of the Californios: A Social History of the Spanish-Speaking Californians, 1846–1890* (Berkeley: University of California Press, 1966) and Douglas Monroy, *Thrown Among Strangers: The Making of Mexican Culture in Frontier California* (Berkeley: University of California Press, 1990).

21. Dumke, p. 221.

22. Reid, p. 108.

23. Bridges' Diary.

24. John S. Blocker, *"Give to the Winds Thy Fears:" The Women's Temperance Crusade, 1873–1874* (Westport: Greenwood Press, 1985), p. 85–161, is an analysis of why women were so heavily involved in the national crusade. The Pasadena temperance movement, however, is a study in contradictions as women, especially the Women's Christian Temperance Union (WCTU), played a secondary role to men in this late-century confrontation. Also see Barbara Leslie Epstein, *The Politics of Domesticity: Women, Evangelism, and Temperance in 19th Century America* (Middletown: Wesleyan University Press, 1981); Elliott West, *The Saloon on the Rocky Mountain Mining Frontier* (Lincoln: University of Nebraska Press, 1979); and John J. Rumbarger, *Profits, Power, and Prohibition* (Albany: SUNY Press, 1989), p. 3–20, 123–183.

25. See Amos Throop's autobiographical sketch: "Memorandum of a few of the Incidents of my Past Life," (not paginated) in the Historical Files, Box 1.5, California Institute of Technology Archives, Pasadena, Calif., 1875.

26. Henry Markham Page, *Pasadena, Its Early Years* (Los Angeles: Lorrin L. Morrison, 1964), p. 78.

27. Hiram Reid, *The History of Pasadena,* p. 240–243. The reference to Beebe's smile comes from Wood, p. 217. For the reference to the Brass Band and Beebe's "well-liked" status, see *The Valley Union,* 24 February 1884, p. 77. The newspaper was edited by Wood and J.E. Clarke, both ardent antis who ended up playing prominent roles in the ensuing "Whiskey Wars."

28. Reid, p. 174 and Page, p. 78–79.

29. Reid, p. 242–243; for reference to the flag-draped door, see Page, p. 59. One of the WCTU delegates was Reid's wife, Dr. Rachel Reid, Pasadena's first woman physician.

30. Lois Banner, "Religious Benevolence as Social Control: A Critique of an Interpretation," *Journal of American History* 60:1 (June 1973), p. 23–41; and William A Muraskin, "The Social-Control Theory in American History: A Critique," *Journal of Social History* 9:4 (Summer 1976), p. 559–569.

31. James C. Scott, *Domination and the Arts of Resistance: Hidden Transcripts* (New Haven: Yale University Press, 1990), p. 1–16.

32. There are repeated references to the "goodness" of their actions in the temperance literature. See Ruth Bordin, *Women and Temperance* (Philadelphia: Temple University Press, 1981), p. 3–33; Rumbarger, p. 69–151; and Epstein. The idea of "saving" the working class has an extensive literature. See Paul Boyer, *Urban Masses and Moral Order in America* (Cambridge: Harvard University Press, 1978), p. 191, 221–232; Ivan Greenberg "The Half-Day Mill School Movement of the 1870s," *Education in Massachusetts: Selected Essays,* eds. Konig and Kauffman (Westfield: Institute for Massachusetts Studies, 1992), p. 65–77.

33. There were numerous Pasadenans involved with the Americanization movement. Most notable was Dr. J.H. McBride, a Pasadena psychiatrist and founder of the Encitas Hospital, who served as a member of the founding board of directors of the California Commission

on Immigration and Housing, the most influential governmental arm of the national Americanization movement. See "Americanization: The California Answer," *Commission of Immigration and Housing of California* (June 1920), California Printing Office, Sacramento, Calif. For a more complete discussion of the movement in the West, see Gayle Gullett, "Women Progressives and the Politics of Americanization in California, 1915–1920," *Pacific Historical Review* LXIV:1 (February 1996), p. 71–94; and David George Herman, "Neighbors on the Golden Mountain: The Americanization of Immigrants in California—Public Instruction as an Agency of Ethnic Assimilation, 1850–1933" (Ph.D. diss., University of California, Berkeley, 1981). For recent studies of Americanization nationally, see Laurie Olsen, *Made in America: Immigrant Students in Our Public Schools* (New York: Norton, 1997); and Paula S. Fass, *Outside In: Minorities and the Transformation of American Education* (New York: Oxford, 1989). See Chapter 5 for a lengthy discussion of Americanization in Pasadena.

34.   Scott, p. 183–184, 199–201. Also see Robin D.G. Kelley, "'We Are Not What We Seem': Rethinking Black Working-Class Opposition in the Jim Crow South," *Journal of American History* 80:1 (June 1993), p. 78–112.

35.   Herbert Gutman, "Work, Culture, and Society in Industrializing America, 1815–1919," *Journal of American History* 63 (Fall 1973), p. 531–587.

36.   Greenberg, p. 65–77.

37.   J.W. Wood, *The Concise History of Pasadena* (Los Angeles: 1923), p. 228.

38.   *The Anti-Saloon League Yearbook of 1913,* ed. E. H. Cherrington (Westervale, Ohio: Anti-Saloon League Association, 1913), p. 44. Also see Cherrington's *The Evolution of Prohibition in the United States of America* (New Jersey: Patterson Smith Publishing Company, 1920; reprint, 1969).

39.   *The Daily News,* 27 February 1912, p. 4.

40.   *Minutes,* Pasadena Board of Education, 9 September 1912.

41.   Reid, p. 243.

42.   See *The Whiskey War in Pasadena* (Pasadena: 1888), a pamphlet probably written by Reid, Huntington Library, MSS Collection. Although there is no specific mention of temperance and the working class, Sarah Deutsch's discussion of ethnic/racial "otherness" is useful in *No Separate Refuge: Culture, Class, and Gender on an Anglo-Hispanic Frontier in the American Southwest, 1880–1940* (New York: Oxford, 1987), p. 3–12, 13–40, and her essay "Landscape of Enclaves: Race Relations in the West, 1865–1990," *Under an Open Sky: Rethinking America's Western Past,* eds. W. Cronin, G. Miles, and J. Gitlin (New York: W.W. Norton, 1992), p. 110–131.

43.   Reid, p. 244 and *The Valley Union,* 2 June 1885.

44.   Reid, p. 244; also see John Blocker, *American Temperance Movements: Cycles of Reform* (New York: Twayne Publishers, 1989), for data on liquor investments, drinking patterns, and profit.

45.   Reid, p. 244.

46.   Reid, p. 245, also his chapter on "Incorporation." Page makes little reference to incorporation as a method to control drinking, although he does suggest that the zealots were motivated by the state's incorporation laws, p. 76.

47.   Reid, p. 245.

48.   Reid, p. 245 and Carpenter, p. 14.

49.   Reid, p. 245–246. Reid and his Los Angeles–based attorneys were opposed to the loophole.

50.   Reid, p. 250.

51. Reid, p. 251. Carpenter, in *Pasadena: Resort Hotels and Paradise*, p. 14, believes Steil was forced from office for his position on drink, yet there appears to be little to support this idea.
52. Ibid., p. 273.
53. Ibid., p. 273–274.
54. Ibid., p. 275.
55. Ibid., p. 276.
56. Cherrington, p. 46.
57. Gwendolyn Mink, "The Lady and the Tramp: Gender, Race, and the Origins of the American Welfare State," *Women, the State, and Welfare*, ed. L. Gordon (Madison: University of Wisconsin Press, 1990), p. 92–93.
58. Gordon, p. 25–26.
59. Mink, p. 92–98.
60. Reid, p. 505.
61. Boyer, p. 125–126, and 128; Paul Ong, "An Ethnic Trade: The Chinese Laundries in Early California," *Journal of Ethnic Studies* 8, (Winter 1978), p. 95–99; Paul Sui, "The Chinese Laundryman; A Study of Social Isolation" (Ph.D. Diss., University of Chicago, 1953), and "The Chinese Laundry on Second Street: Papers on Archeology at the Woodland Opera House Site," *California Archeology Reports* No. 24 (State of California, Department of Parks and Recreation, September 1984).
62. Ong, p. 100.
63. *U.S. Bureau of the Census, 1880: Population Schedules, California—City and County of Los Angeles, "Pasadena Village."*
64. Ong, p. 95.
65. In 1875, according to Reid, a German named Rosenbaum opened a small store on South Orange Grove Avenue, where, among his pharmaceuticals, millinery and pickle barrel, he sold liquor. There was such a public outcry that he was forced to abandon his store. Reid did not tell us if he sold or rented the building. He did tell us the building became a Chinese laundry. The "Celestial village" comment is found in "Fire and Fury: Angry Flames and Angry Citizens in Pasadena," *The Los Angeles Daily Times,* 7 November 1885, p. 1.
66. See Henry Tsai Shi-Shin, *The Chinese Experience in America* (Bloomington: Indiana University Press, 1986), for references to the 38 anti-Chinese riots in the Western states.
67. "Chinese Laundry Fire," *The Valley Union,* 7 November 1885, p. 1 and "Fire and Fury: Angry Flames and Angry Citizens in Pasadena," *The Los Angeles Daily Times,* 7 November 1885, p. 1. The *Times* reported over 100 men marched against the Chinese community, which the newspaper estimated to be between 60 and 100 individuals. Four buildings and a barn were destroyed.
68. Ong, p. 106–107; "The Chinese Laundry on Second Street: Papers on Archeology at the Woodland Opera House Site," cites a Woodland newspaper demanding that the Chinese in that community be banned to an area on the outskirts of town and "a fifty foot wall be built" to keep them confined.
69. *The Valley Union,* 8 November 1885, p. 1.
70. "It Was Not 'John,'" *The Los Angeles Daily Times,* 8 November 1885, p. 1, and "The Pasadena Trouble," *The Los Angeles Daily Times,* 8 November 1885, p. 2.
71. "It Was Not 'John,'" *The Los Angeles Daily Times,* 8 November 1885, p. 1.
72. *The Valley Union,* 8 November 1885, p. 1.
73. Kevin Starr, *Inventing the Dream: California Through the Progressive Era* (New York: Oxford University Press, 1985), p. 107.

CHAPTER 2

FEAR ITSELF
White Over Black and the Creation of
Public Education in the New South

When the Civil War began, Albert Sidney Johnston, like many future Confederate officers stationed throughout the territories and states of the Union, found himself on the wrong side of the conflict. Johnston was brigadier general and commander of the United States Pacific Department, encompassing California and Oregon, as well as all of the territories of Nevada, Arizona and New Mexico. His headquarters were at the Presidio (Spanish for fort) in San Francisco, California.[1]

When Johnston took command of the Western department in early 1861, he was at the zenith of his career as an U.S. Army officer. He led the military occupation of the Utah territory when President Buchanan believed that the Mormons were threatening rebellion.[2] Before the Utah occupation, he fought in successive campaigns against the Black Hawk and Cherokee and then against the Mexicans as a Texan patriot with Sam Houston. Johnston, a West Point graduate, was a seasoned, highly respected officer. Friends and colleagues thought he might occupy an important political office, but he never let on, at least publicly, that he wanted to do anything other than lead his men in "a great and noble cause."[3]

Johnston was a Kentuckian by birth, though he was from a long line of New England Presbyterians.[4] He was raised a fervent, patriotic Southerner, with firm opinions about states' rights and his country's manifest destiny. As a young man, he adopted Texas, on the western edge of the old South, as his home. In a life colored by irony, Albert Sidney Johnston, general of the Confederacy and tragic hero of the battle of Shiloh, would live much of his life in the West. He died leading his troops at Shiloh, defending the South's western territory in a battle that firmly established Ulysses S. Grant as President Lincoln's premier field marshal. There was speculation that Johnston's early death severely limited the South's military prowess. Only Lee and his tactical brilliance matched his skills as a leader.[5] It was only later that his star shone less brightly when both Grant and Confederate general Beauregard tarnished his image as a strategist at Shiloh. Still, the Confederacy lost a great leader.[6]

When Johnston took command of the Pacific Department, he brought his wife, Eliza Griffin, and their three children to San Francisco. California enchanted Mrs. Johnston; the temperate climate in the bay area was not at all like the hot, heavy air of her native South. Both she and the general praised San Francisco schools and wished their children would remain to cast their lot in the Golden State.[7] Mrs. Johnston relished that this Western jewel by the bay had few colored citizens, "one hardly sees one here in the streets," she wrote.[8] She could tolerate the few free coloreds she passed on Market Street, but when Eliza Griffin Johnston encountered an African population of any size, as in her native Virginia, then her racial proclivities were blunt: "the darky ... in any number should be slaves." [9] When the Johnstons departed for California, a free state under the provisions of the Compromise of 1850, they were compelled to dispose of their slave servants. Their "girl," Mary Washington, was sold to a family member but General Johnston's personal attendant, Randolph Hughes, protested being sold. Johnston set him free, but so he might not fall sway to the possibilities California presented to a freed slave, the general bound him to a five-year labor contract.[10]

Like many Southerners in service to the federal government, Johnston was torn by conflicting loyalties brought on by the politics of slavery and abolition. His record on slavery is sketchy though he firmly believed in the white man's right to human ownership. Eliza Griffin Johnston, on the other hand, was much more explicit in her racialized beliefs. She would beat a slave when she thought necessary and she held a deep and abiding hatred of the abolitionists with their "meddlesome interference" in Southern ways. Her brother, Dr. John Griffin, a physician who had come West with Fremont and Kearny in 1848—but remained to practice medicine and speculate in Southern California land—was such an ardent Southern nationalist that when he heard of Lincoln's assassination, he had to be restrained from running triumphant into the streets of Los Angeles "hurrahing for the Confederacy."[11] Johnston believed, as did his wife, that if only the abolitionists would cease their incessant clamor, all could be resolved: "If our Northern brethren will give up their fanatical, idolatrous Negro worshipping we can go on harmoniously, happy and prosperously and also gloriously as a nation."[12]

But it was not to be, "the Republican Party," he wrote a month before Fort Sumter, "is just too persistent[ly] obstinate."[13] When all else was said, Johnston would find it impossible to go to battle against friends and former neighbors. When word came that the Union was breaking apart and Texas had joined with other Southern states in succession, Johnston resigned his commission. A week later, after Lincoln's appointee, General E.V. Sumner had arrived to assume command, he took his family to Eliza's brother's home in Los Angeles. The now ex-general told friends that he and Eliza would abstain from any participation in the conflict; he wished to purchase a rancho in Southern California and retire from public service.[14]

Johnston's Southern California experience was short lived. His thoughts were with his comrades in the Southern campaigns, and he meant to leave California as quickly as possible. He asked to join a group of Southerners in Los Angeles planning to march overland to the Confederacy. This was to be no leisurely gallop east; once Johnston declared his allegiance to the Confederacy, Sumner would send troops to arrest him. His departure had to be quick and without public notice. He also knew Eliza, late in pregnancy, and the children would be unable to make the trek with him. They agreed to join one another as soon as she was able to travel east. He rode out of Griffin's rancho on June 16, 1861. He would never see his family again.[15]

Johnston's ride to the Confederacy took him along a route not dissimilar to the one taken by Amy Bridges on her train ride some 25 years later. Johnston and the men, armed with rifles stolen from federal armories, meant to ride by night to avoid the blistering desert heat and great clouds of soda dust kicked up as they crossed the Mojave Desert. This was a difficult ride as they dodged Union patrols from waterhole to waterhole.[16] At Fort Yuma, they crossed the Colorado River and then angled east along the Gila River into New Mexico territory. When he and his men reached Mesilla just above El Paso in west Texas, they joined the Texas Confederates. Johnston then left the men and departed to New Orleans; he then went by rail to Virginia. He arrived at Richmond early in September 1861 and immediately reported to his old friend Jefferson Davis, who said later that the "South could not have received a better gift than the service of Albert Sidney Johnston."[17] President Davis appointed Johnston commander of Confederate Department Number Two—the entire area west of the Appalachians to the Mississippi River, which included the states of Missouri, Tennessee, Arkansas and portions of Alabama, Mississippi and Louisiana. He left at once to assemble and train his army. In a few months, he would lead his men in that "great and noble cause." He died at the battle of Shiloh, wounded in the leg by an errant rifle ball. The general bled to death on a Tennessee hillside less than seven months after he rode out of his brother-in-law's rancho in Los Angeles.[18]

For reasons unknown, Eliza Griffin never left Los Angeles to join her husband. Instead, she decided to remain close to her brother.[19] From his vast land holdings in Southern California, she purchased a few hundred acres of land east of the San Gabriel mission. Apparently, it was her hope, once the war concluded, to carry out the family plan of retiring from public service as a California rancher. Eliza built a simple white frame house on the property nestled close to a seasonal wash that would come to be known as Eaton Canyon, named after a judge who purchased the property from Dr. Griffin. Eliza's brother had repurchased the land from her—for a profit—after her husband's death.[20] Eliza Griffin had named the rancho "Fair Oaks" after her childhood family plantation in Virginia. The name stuck, for the principal north-south axis of the city of Pasadena would later be known as Fair Oaks Boulevard. During the middle decades of the next century, as the city was buffeted by conflicts over class and race, the street represented, in the minds of many Pasadenans, a color line. Whites lived on one side, blacks lived on the other. Ironically, Griffin's Fair Oaks property in Virginia was destroyed by troops under the command of Albert Sidney Johnston's successor at the Presidio, General E.V. Sumner.[21]

THE RECONSTRUCTION OF THE SOUTH

In the end, the Confederacy lay in ruins. After four years of war, nearly all waged in the South, the Confederate states were decimated. In the years to follow, the South's reliance on the old social order prevented the region from capitalizing on its abundant natural resources, namely its people, both black and white. Postwar tensions surrounding social equality and economic uplift began as two sides of the same coin, but in less than 30 years from the close of the war, the region had devolved into a violent, biracial state that defined equality in terms of advantages for the few at the expense of the many.

Reconstruction began in earnest when Andrew Johnson, now occupying the presidency after Lincoln's death, issued an amnesty proclamation in May of 1865. By the end of the year, every Southern state had organized governments, elected senators and representatives and accepted the Thirteenth Amendment abolishing slavery. Johnson now recommended these new state governments to Congress.

But full acceptance remained elusive; if the Republicans agreed to readmit the former Confederate states, the balance of power would shift to the rival Democrats. To exacerbate the problem of reconciliation, the Southern white electorate initially turned to the region's elite, many of whom had served in the Confederate Congress or were officers of the rebel army. The North was willing to allow the Southern states to refill the borders of the original Union—but was unwilling to accept the Southerners' notion of racial equality. To whit, the Southern states enacted a series of "Black Codes" that severely limited the freedmen's citizenship, including his right to exchange his labor for cash. In most Southern states, legislators created harsh vagrancy codes aimed at keeping blacks confined to the land, always on terms dictated by white landowners. Anyone deemed "without work" was a "vagrant" and subject to arrest, then hired out to landowners in lieu of the fine.[22]

These and other statutes outraged the North. Simply readmitting the former Confederate states was impossible. President Johnson, a Tennessee Democrat, complicated Reconstruction efforts when he refused to endorse two important pieces of legislation—an expanded Freedmen's Bureau, the federal office that was set up in 1865 to care for refugees; and a Civil Rights Act that declared ex-slaves as citizens and protected their right to hold property and testify in court. In April of 1866, Congress rejected Johnson's veto and overwhelmingly passed the Civil Rights Act by a two-thirds majority, the first time in American history that a major piece of legislation became law over the veto of a president. This was a watershed event in postwar Reconstruction politics; Congress, not the president, now held the upper hand. For the next 10 years, the former rebellious states would be under the heel of Northern military occupation.[23]

One of the most important contributions of the Reconstruction period was the work of the Freedmen's Bureau.[24] Before emancipation, it was illegal for slaves to read or write. Formal literacy instruction, if it happened at all, was clandestine, often taking place in remote outbuildings away from suspicious whites. As the Confederate states fell to Union troops, Northern missionary societies sent teachers, mostly women, many with formal ties to abolitionist organizations, to set up schools for the ex-slave. From 1865 to the end of Reconstruction in 1877, thousands of Northern teachers came south to work in freedmen schools, many already established by ex-slave communities too impatient to wait for Northern philanthropy.[25] Given that there was little if any public education in the South before the war, it is paradoxical that out of the effort to educate the masses of illiterate ex-slaves came the foundation for public schools in the South. Through a close examination of the region's initial efforts to educate the new postbellum black citizen, we can unmask the systematic effort by the Southern white elite—the old aristocratic planters together with the newly enriched bourgeoisie—to perpetuate a racial state that relied on hierarchy by color and caste. Looking carefully at how one Southern community responded to the necessity of universal education, with its complex hidden meanings embedded within the rhetoric of state's rights and individual freedoms, we can better understand how public schooling and its most fervent, progressive patrons conspired to nurture the South's resistance to democracy.

THE RECONSTRUCTION OF VIRGINIA

Much of Virginia was destroyed during the war; when Lincoln visited Richmond, the capitol of the Confederacy, in 1865, the city was a rubble of broken, burned-out buildings. At war's end, state government was bankrupt; its ability to draw needed revenue from taxes was severely curtailed by the devastation brought on by the relentless military campaigns of the preceding four years. James Johnson, one of the first black historians of the 20th century, believed that Virginia had been ravaged more by the war than any other Southern state.[26]

Most of the carnage was in the seaboard counties where some of the war's great battles were fought from Petersburg north through Richmond to Fredericksburg and Chancellorsville. Toward the end of the war, Grant ordered Virginia's western Shenandoah Valley, a region essentially untouched by the conflict, to be laid bare in an attempt to prevent the breadbasket of the South from continuing to supply Lee's army.[27] Sherman's invading army overran Griffin's Fair Oaks plantation, not far from present-day Fincastle. Just to the north, less than 50 miles from Fincastle, Sherman's troops, under the command of Brigadier General George Armstrong Custer, swept through Albemarle, county seat to Jefferson's Monticello and occupied the only principal community, Charlottesville, home to the University of Virginia. Then a town of 2,500, Charlottesville was spared the Union's wrath when Custer was convinced by city and university elders that the town was of no military importance. Its only real strategic value had been as a military hospital, caring for 22,000 wounded and sick during the war. He apparently agreed and kept his troops in check, although they did manage to round up all the livestock and as many ex-slaves as were willing to join the Union troops. Custer's occupation would be Charlottesville's only direct contact with Union forces until surrender next spring.[28]

Still, even with Custer's passive occupation, at war's end commerce in Charlottesville had come to a standstill. Food supplies were dangerously low. Surrounding communities like Scotsville had not faired as well and had been all but destroyed. Rail travel was essentially nonexistent, restricted to short stretches between burned-out bridges, and the fields and orchards were in a state of neglect.[29] Because the state had few populous cities (by the turn of the century Virginia had only eight cities over 10,000), farming held the only chance for economic recovery.[30] But the fields and orchards of Albemarle required extensive labor. At war's end, Charlottesville's citizens faced a most vexing question—a question all Southerners would confront in the coming months of peace—how could the ex-slave be convinced to remain and work land he did not own? If former slaves rejected the appeals of their former masters, then how would communities like Charlottesville, no longer able to rely on chattel labor, respond? The answer came in the form of an unmarried teacher from New England, hell-bent on fixing the South.

FREEDMEN SCHOOLS AND THE DEVELOPMENT OF PUBLIC EDUCATION

She arrived in the fall of 1865, and, to the horror of Charlottesville's white citizens, Anna Gardner was a zealot. A seventh-generation Quaker from Nantucket, Massachusetts, she was a leader in the Northern abolitionist movement. Gardner brought to Charlottesville a rage against slavery—and slaveholders—that white Southerners found impossible to comprehend.[31] As a young teenager, she cared little about "fashions and follies" but instead had set her "heart on human welfare and social reforms." At the age of 18, a free black living on the island introduced her to firebrand William Lloyd Garrison's abolitionist newspaper, *The Liberator*. Gardner, an enthusiastic Republican before she was an abolitionist, honed her radical politics on Garrison's paper.[32]

Gardner's politics of race, though, came more from her family's activism than from Garrison's *Liberator*. When she was six, the family harbored a runaway slave family for weeks. It seems a slave hunter had come to Nantucket from Alexandria, Virginia to recapture Arthur Cooper and his family. As the slave hunter, with warrant in hand, approached the house, Gardner's family—grandfather, father, aunts and uncles—surrounded the house and prevented the agent from entering,

> While the altercation was proceeding, and the warrant was being read at the front of the house, my father and my uncle slipped around to the back window and adroitly assisted the trembling fugitives to make their escape from it. Disguised in father's coat and uncle Thomas' broad-brimmed Quaker hat. Arthur Cooper had nearly reached our backdoor before the wrangle was so far over for the officers to dare enter the house, when behold! The house was empty! The fugitives had flown![33]

When Cooper was hustled to the back door of the Gardner home, there stood young Anna. Her memory of seeing the runaway at the back stairs of the house—"black as midnight, with lips so paled with fright that they were as white as snow ..." so shocked the youngster, she could recall the details nearly 60 years later. It would be weeks before the family could spirit the Cooper family to safety. Gardner's experiences cemented her commitment to end slavery. At the age of 25, she organized the island's first Anti-Slavery Convention, which included Garrison as well as the debut of a new speaker for the cause, none other than Frederick Douglass.

She was no ordinary abolitionist, coming south to rescue the freedman from his own ignorance. Her commitment spoke of a deep and profound belief in the evils of slavery, nurtured over three decades of social action. But to the white land-owners of Albemarle County, she was nothing more than one of those "... slab-sided old maids ... [with] palpitating bosoms ... coming south to teach the Negroes to lie and steal."[34] If Gardner had any palpitations they came because of her enormous devotion to republican ideals and to the education of freedmen. But white Southerners, even a century later, would countenance none of her radical, racialized beliefs. To Charlottesville's whites, she was a "meddling fanatic," who failed to understand the peculiarities of "Southern institutions," and, most damning, "she aroused the Negro to unattainable dreams ..." which would later cause such racial animosity to call into question Gardner's "extrem-ist" teachings.[35]

Gardner arrived a few months after Appomattox, having already spent nearly two years in North Carolina creating "freedmen schools behind every cannon."[36]

Fig. 6. Anna Gardner in her September years, from an undated photograph in the Nantucket Historical Society. *(Photo courtesy of the Nantucket Historical Association)*

When she left Charlottesville in 1870, she had in five years as "Principal of Freed Schools" been a close observer as Virginians debated the possibilities of a more egalitarian society including racially mixed schools. In the end she must have been bitterly disappointed when conservatives pushed through a segregated, biracial social structure. Separate schools would quickly spread to separate accommodations, separate conveyances and even separate churches. In little more than a decade, Virginia, like the rest of the South, devolved into separate worlds for whites and blacks. By the turn of the century, the "peculiar institution" of slavery had metamorphosed into a perverse form of racial exclusion so rigid that Southerners would change their state constitutions and prevent Afro Southerners from voting.[37] Moreover, by demonizing the former slave, white Southerners created a class of "others" that, by the beginning of the 20th century, was thought to be so barbarous and alien that a black man's word or glance in the wrong direction could mean death by lynching.[38]

Freedmen schools established in Charlottesville just after the war were only supported by whites because they understood the education provided by teachers like Gardner would continue to underscore white superiority. When freedmen teachers, both white and black, challenged that assumption, whites rejected outright the ex-slave schools and moved to establish a public system that taught not only the rudiments of literacy and numbers in separate schools but, more important, socialized both communities to accept a culture of white dominance and black deference. The creation of community schools for poor whites as well as the emerging middleclass, something that did not exist in the South prior to the Civil War, was done so out of fear that universal black education would create a literate black citizenry that would call into question the very notion of the myth of white superiority. It was black education that created the impetus for white education. The real compromise—as significant as the Compromise of 1877, which led to the removal of federal troops from Southern soil—was the union of Southern elite and the rising commercial class championing universal white education as a countermeasure to the gains made by blacks in the years immediately following the war's end.[39]

Gardner established her first school in what was left of the old Delvan building, used during the war as a hospital and now housing federal troops and destitute freedmen. It was also initially Gardner's place of residence, for she had searched in vain for three days upon her arrival for housing.[40] The old hospital was in such a state of filth that Gardner "gathered up my garments out of the confluent streams of tobacco juice" and set about to turn the wreck of a building into a useful school. Her "tobacco juice" comment was not without malice. She never seemed to pass up an opportunity to remark just how base these Southerners were—an attitude that would fail to endear her to Charlottesville's white population. Two years later in an appeal for donated school supplies, she told a local newspaper editor that she "did not know any Southerners personally," a statement that irked at least two 20th-century historians. How could a white woman, even a Northerner, living in the community for two years, not come to know *any* white folks? They failed to understand the degree by which white Southerners refused to accept Northern presence in schools for the ex-slave.[41]

For effect, Gardner may have exaggerated her isolation from Southern society. Like many of her sisters in freedmen schools in the South, her aloofness arose from her own feelings of superiority to a defeated enemy. Many, including Gardner, were indisposed to treat Southerners as anything more than rank traitors who had openly rebelled against the Union. Gardner thought the Southerner "haughty and self-asserting ... primitive in appearance and habits." But more telling, Gardner never came to trust in Southern hospitality. "The seductive blandness, the peculiar suavity," she wrote, was a distinctive feature of Southern society. "There are among them many who may be metaphorically characterized as: the mildest mannered men ... that ever scuttled a ship or cut a throat."[42]

Although she believed open threats of violence by university students was a real possibility, what was never far from her thoughts was the fear that somehow through legal chicanery "those subtle and slippery Virginians" would find a way to close her schools.[43] Gardner's estrangement, though, was also a matter of protection against the violence aimed at Northern teachers. Although she makes no mention of Klu Klux Klan activity in the area, the threat of violence was always there, if not from university students, then in reports from every state in the South.

A state of terror reigned in parts of the Southland and it was aimed at driving Northerners out of the business of black education.[44] Virginians never came to see Northern teachers as anything other than emissaries of a new social order bent on destroying the old ways of caste. The prevailing attitude was if these "fantactical intruders" from the North are allowed, unencumbered, to poison the minds of the gullible freedmen, it would be nothing more than "social suicide."[45] Many Southerners believed that if Northern whites came south to help the ex-slave then surely these freedmen teachers were race traitors. One Virginia Baptist minister summed up the prevailing opinion as, "If you teach niggers, you're no better than a nigger yourself."[46] To Southerners, these apostles of change were hell-bent to remake the community, to disrupt the long established social system so completely they would "put the bottom rail on top."[47] Moreover, they were fearful that the "comic characters ... and dangerous fools," would spread the gospel of racial equality and make the freedmen "discontented with their lot."[48] Gardner was no comic nor was she a fool, but she was dangerous. She set out to do exactly what whites feared most—make the freedman discontented with his lot.

When the school opened in November of 1865, 90 "scholars," as ex-slave students were called, appeared at her door. With the assistance of a local white man by the name of Musgrave, who had opened a tuition school for ex-slaves, she split the students into two groups, taking most of the females and leaving Musgrave with the males. Surprisingly, nearly all the scholars were over 16 years of age. She wrote that "these repressed, down-trodden victims ... rushed in like water into an open lock."[49] Between the two classes, daily attendance was well over 80 percent.

Gardner's plan was to build a multitiered system of schools, beginning with primary levels and ending with a teacher-training academy. By April of 1866, a year after Appomattox, the primary school had nearly 250 students and four teachers, all on the payroll of the Freedmen Bureau. Two of the teachers were white—Gardner and Philena Carkin, recently arrived from Boston, and two black men, Robert Morris and Paul Lewis. Each was paid $25 a month, except Gardner, who was, for some unknown reason, paid $3 less. In 1869, the county Freedmen Bureau agent, William Tidball, reported that there were four Charlottesville schools, including two primaries, "The Savage School" named after the radical Republican mayor of Charlottesville, who was said to have been the only voter for Lincoln, and the "John Brown School." The intermediate school, headed by Miss Carkin, took the name "Abraham Lincoln." Finally, Anna Gardner directed the normal school, named in honor of Thomas Jefferson. Her Jefferson school, at least in name, has remained part of Charlottesville's educational landscape since its founding more than a century ago. Today, not far from where the Delvan building once stood, is Jefferson High School, built in the 1920s but now empty. For generations Jefferson was the city's only school for African Americans. Tragically, it is being threatened with demolition as developers eye the potential profit of urban renewal.

Gardner's approach to black education was classical New England liberal arts. Heavily influenced by Quaker beliefs, her schools were more egalitarian than the regressive and narrow conception of schooling promoted by advocates of manual education. In the first years of peace, black schools in Charlottesville and the county, whether they were Gardner's schools or those founded by ex-slaves, did not stress the reproduction of caste, but rather the training of black leadership.[50] The freedmen knew the fundamental importance of schooling was more than an apolitical approach to literacy. Reading and writing were important but only as the "silent instrumentality," as Gardner put it, of self-determination. Gardner saw education for the ex-slave as a means to acquire a semblance of economic independence. [51]

She held no preconceptions about the ability of the freedman to learn, in fact, she gives us numerous citations in her memoirs of how quickly the ex-slaves took to formal education. Although we have no definitive data on what curriculum was used, Gardner's devotion to her church probably led her to use materials published by the Quakers. This is significant, in that the Friends' curriculum was markedly different from curriculum prepared by the more conservative evangelical American Tract Society, with its books and pamphlets preaching racial subordination.[52]

Gardner tells of an incident that may indicate the source of her curriculum. In a conversation between a young ex-slave who worked at a white estate and the landowner's son, Gardner tells us that the young African American, a student in one of Charlottesville's schools, had told the owner's son that "the first clock in America was made by a colored astronomer, Benjamin Banneker, and that Euclid, whose works were studied at the university, was a colored man."[53] Where would an ex-slave have learned about Euclid and Banneker? Friends materials specifically aimed at black independence had been written by Lydia Maria Child, a Garrisonian abolitionist and acquaintance of Gardner. Child's intent was to create what today would be called "critical studies" of leaders from Banneker to Frederick Douglass and Toussant L'Ouverture. Child's materials might very well have been in use in Gardner's schools. Whether Gardner would have agreed with historian Ron Butchart, who considered the Quaker biographies strong affirmations of the equality of blacks and whites, remains open for debate. Still, her work with Southern black communities in both Virginia and North Carolina focused on more than simple schoolhouse instruction in the 3Rs.[54]

In the spring of 1867, as tensions escalated over Northern efforts to radically reconstruct Southern society, Gardner's schools came under severe criticism from Charlottesville's white leadership. She made her comment about "not knowing any Southerners ..." in a letter she sent to J.C. Southall, the conservative editor of the town's newspaper.[55] Gardner asked Southall for a donation to help in purchasing diplomas for the normal school graduates. Southall published her letter—with or without her consent, we do not know—and took the opportunity to admonish her.

> The impression among the white residents of Charlottesville is, that your instruction of colored people who attend your school contemplates something more than the communication of ordinary knowledge implied in teaching them to read, write, cypher, etc. The idea prevails that you instruct them in politics and sociology; that you come among us not merely as an ordinary school teacher, but as a political missionary; you communicate to the colored people ideas of social equality of the whites [sic]. With your first object we sympathize; the second we regard as mischievous, and as only tending to disturb the good feeling between the two races.

Within 48 hours, Gardner let Southall and the rest of the community know exactly her educational mission:

> Mr. J.C. Southall, I teach <u>IN SCHOOL</u> and <u>OUT</u>, so far as my political influence extends, the fundamental principles of 'politics' and 'sociology' apply, viz. 'Whatever you would that men should do to you, do ye even so unto them.'
> Yours in behalf of truth and justice,
> Anna Gardner

Southall's claim that Gardner's politics only tended to "disturb the good feelings between the races" presupposes that after the war the white community, if left undisturbed by Northern meddling, would advance the cause of black education. Everything points to the opposite. Ex-slaves understood that their former masters were working against black autonomy and so argued that black schooling must be about black self-determination. Even the more liberal schools supported by the bureau, intending to intellectually arm ex-slaves in their fight against Southern racism, were viewed with skepticism by the black community.

Early on, African Americans in both the North and South began to voice their suspicions about the intent of the Northern missionary schools. Less than a month after Appomattox, Frederick Douglass wrote that he had his "doubts about these Freedmen's Societies ..." fearful that the aid societies would "furnish an apology for excluding us ... [and] serve to keep up the very prejudices, which it is so desirable to banish from the country." Douglass ended up supporting the mission schools but only under protest.[56] He was not alone; his skepticism of the Northern schools was mirrored by freedmen in every Southern state. "Believe not in these School teachers," wrote Martin Delany, black abolitionist and Freedmen Bureau agent in North Carolina, "because they do not tell the truth ..."[57] Education was important but only as the means to gain full independence, a fact Northern aid teachers and the Freedmen Bureau failed to advance.

In Charlottesville, regardless of the apparent advantages of Gardner's four schools, local black leadership founded the Freedmen's Mutual Aid Society. Although we have no record of the black community rejecting Gardner's schools, there are instances in other Southern communities in which Afro-Southern self-determination found voice. Bureau agents from Maryland to Alabama were baffled that ex-slaves would refuse the better facilities and teachers of the Northern aid societies in favor of their own schools, much poorer in material quality but nonetheless autonomous institutions of the Afro-American community.

Well before Northern aid societies arrived, ex-slaves were in the business of education. Northern agents found schools operating in abandoned buildings, in churches, log cabins, virtually anywhere the former bondsmen created communities. The demand for schooling was urgent and for every bureau agent, overwhelming. In mid-summer of 1866, William Tidball, the Freedmen Bureau agent for Albemarle county, asked the Richmond office for funds to establish 19 additional schools in the county. Tidball understood the serious impediments to such an enterprise. Freedmen had no funds to buy land and build the schools, and there were certainly not enough suitable teachers, but, he reported, "Negroes stood ready to maintain the buildings and to furnish the wood for heating." The Richmond bureau did not respond, so local blacks agreed to build at least three of the schools without bureau assistance. In fact, Tidball reported in the spring of 1867, that there were several autonomous black schools in the county, supported by freedmen alone. As for the schools in Charlottesville, the existing facilities were unsuitable. Tidball recommended, with the support of the black community, that the bureau schools be moved out of the Delvan building and onto land owned by freedmen that would be donated rent free. Clearly, as it was in every Southern state, ex-slaves actively campaigned for community control.

But it was not to be. Gardner's bureau schools and the other black community schools in Albemarle County never survived. During the spring of 1867, Virginians recoiled at radical reconstruction brought south by the Republican party. Southern states would accept, as a condition of their defeat, the 13th Amendment ending slavery, but the 14th Amendment, which guaranteed suffrage to Afro-American males, was being forced on the former Confederate states as a condition of readmission to the Union. J.C. Southall's *Chronicle* claimed that Virginians would never support the black franchise and vowed that

Charlottesville would rather accept military rule than give the colored man the vote.[58] Southall and every white citizen in Albemarle County knew that the vote in the hands of the ex-slaves, who outnumbered whites in the county by 2,500, would forever alter the balance of power. Further, black citizens with their radical, Republican white allies were campaigning for universal public education. There was even wild talk of racially mixed schools. The conservatives rallied. Virginia's old regime would not die so easily.

In the spring of 1867, the Virginia Senate called for a constitutional convention to end the confusion of the postwar period and begin the process of readmitting Virginia to the Union. Before the lower house could endorse the Senate's call for a convention, Congress passed the Military Reconstruction Acts that gave the ex-slave an equal voice in state constitutional matters. Suddenly, the balance of power had shifted. Voter registration in succeeding weeks affirmed the worse fears of conservative whites: nearly 2,500 blacks in the county had registered against less than 2,200 whites.[59]

Late in April 1867, Charlottesville's black community called for a large assembly in the Delvan school building.[60] Blacks and whites crowded together to discuss the sea of changes afflicting the nation. A few weeks earlier, conservative whites tired to convince the ex-slave that his former master was his only true friend and the economic recovery of the county depended upon their mutual cooperation. That message fell on deaf ears. Southall told his readers, "We have perhaps the most intelligent colored population." But it was abundantly clear that white leadership was engaged in what Gardner referred to as their "peculiar suavity" and was trying to convince the black community to reject the tenants of reconstruction and remain wed to the old order. It was an argument that had no merit in the black community.[61]

The meeting at Delvan was a raucous affair. The landowners appealed to the ex-slaves to once again reject Republican ideas and "submit to white leadership."[62] Southall's *Chronicle* reported that three black speakers then stood to express a range of ideological positions within the community. In all actuality, there was only one position with which the great majority of black citizens would subscribe: total freedom and independence; economic and political rights equal to whites; admission to the University of Virginia; and free, universal public education. Fairfax Taylor, who had attended Gardner's school, told the audience that the black man had few friends in the South, including the Northern carpetbaggers, "who might turn and rob you." Apparently a Union soldier had relieved Taylor of his watch. To a thundering ovation, Taylor called upon the black community to establish their political independence, especially the right to serve on juries and attend the university.[63]

Two additional speakers tried to convince the audience that cooperation with whites was the only wise and prudent course of action. The first was ignored, but the second speaker, Reverend Nicholas Richmond, a Baptist minister, advised the audience not to oppose the white community directly, that their social status depended on how hard the ex-slave was willing to work himself out of poverty and ignorance. Two weeks later, when the good reverend rose to lead his church in a hymn, the entire congregation got up and walked out.[64]

The black community and their radical white allies drew up their platform based on Taylor's call for political independence and free schools. Conservative Republicans were stunned. They refused to support the platform and instead called for a party convention in August. Meanwhile, Charlottesville area planters met to conspire against the black Republicans and their allies. They organized the "co-operation" movement, a euphemism for white control of the Republican party. Led by ex-Confederates including Southall's brother, William, the planters played the race card and worked to undermine black influence. Charlottesville's black leadership and the radical whites met in July and blocked the conservative attempt to dismantle the party. They elected two delegates to the August convention, including Paul Lewis, one of the freedmen teachers in Gardner's school.[65] It appeared that the momentum of the radicals, coupled with the newly enfranchised black voter, would carry the day. If the alliance of black and white Republicans held, the state would have a constitution that would remake Virginia culture.

During the late summer and fall of 1867, Virginia's white conservatives worked to oppose the upcoming Constitutional Convention. With a clear majority, blacks and radical white Republicans would dominate the convention. White conservative leadership knew the radical Republicans would demand—and probably get—a constitution with universal suffrage and free-school amendments. Southall and other influential whites feared that mixed schools would so violate their notion of status and power that Virginia, as they knew it, would be finished. Southall told his readers: "Mr. James C. Southall is opposed to a convention, is opposed to universal Negro suffrage, and in favor of the supremacy of the White Race." His paper told white voters to ignore their differences with individual candidates and vote the race card, "You have no right to break the ranks."[66]

Southall's appeal failed. With the October election of delegates to the convention, black and radical white Republicans held a clear majority. Only 300 black men in the county did not cast their ballot as opposed to nearly 1,000 absent white voters. The Constitutional Convention would take place in December, and free, mixed schools were high on the agenda.[67]

When the convention opened, radical Republicans outnumbered conservatives more than two to one, but whites outnumbered blacks nearly four to one. Earlier Reconstruction-era historians have tried to cast the Republican delegates as a motley assortment of vagabonds and freebooters. Politically they were "dangerous demagogues" with little connection to Virginia except through their pocketbook. The 24 black delegates were worse, often described as semiliterate plantation bumpkins nominated by equally moronic former slaves with little understanding of republican government. White historians have generally failed to separate racist depictions from fact, too often quoting uncritically from newspaper accounts that reduced black speech to a grammarian's nightmare. The black voice was a comic rendition of what whites thought of as plantation-speak. In one of the less offensive quotes (illustrated here by Horace Mann Bond, the eminent black historian and educator), a black delegate to the convention was supposed to have said he "didn't want to see no such claws in the Constitution, and the fust thing we know, dere would be similar claws regards waship. Ez fer dis, dere was worser company of white children dan he wished his children to be wid; and dese was secesh children."68

Bond points out that the supposed use of "claws" for "clause," yet spelling "children" and "similar" correctly, more than suggests that the reporter manufactured the alteration in an attempt to reduce the arguments for mixed schools to the level of absurdity. Dr. Thomas Bayne, a delegate from Norfolk, went further. He told the white convention delegates and the newspaper reporter that "t-h-a-t didn't spell dat." And if any reporters wanted to "argue the principles of education he had only to lay down the glove."69 *The Richmond Dispatch* then mocked Bayne's concerns with a comment about not enough "dat-a ... in the convention for the reporters to go upon."70 Wealthy whites were advancing an argument, based on their own misdeeds and ignorance, that blacks were morally and intellectually deficient enough to prevent their equal participation in the affairs of the community. Weeks earlier, as the delegates departed for Richmond, editor Southall vowed to work to "keep the government out of the hands of a misguided and ignorant race."71

The debate over mixed schools began in early January and would occupy the delegates until April 1868. Conservative delegates immediately offered a separate schools amendment, but black delegates rose to argue that such a provision would be unmanageable. The state could barely afford one system let alone the efficient maintenance of two. The amendment was tabled but when whites again moved to segregate schools, Thomas Bayne, the black delegate from Norfolk then stood to introduce a motion that public schools accept all children with no pupil excluded on account of race. By the time Bayne's motion was read to the Education Committee, black delegates sensed that their alliance with radical Republicans was about to fracture over mixed schools. Blacks reminded the white delegates that the radical Republicans would collapse without black support, but to no avail. There were attempts by a few white radicals to advance motions that would have permitted integrated schools by parental choice, but these and other mixed school motions repeatedly died in committee.

Finally, in late April, weary over four months of debate, the Education Committee sent the Bayne amendment to the convention floor. Without white support, the motion failed 67 to 21. Mixed schools had split the radical Republicans along the racial fault line. The measure to ensure equal schooling had been defeated because white delegates, no matter their professed adherence to social equality, abandoned their black colleagues. The constitution contained no direct reference to mixed or segregated schools, but the intention of the convention was clear. Virginia would have no integrated schools.[72] On July 1, 1870, Virginians overwhelmingly endorsed the new constitution that called for schools to be free and open to all students between the ages of five and 21 whose fathers had paid the head tax. Blacks and radical whites capitulated; the community's children were to be educated in separate school buildings.

THE DISENFRANCHISEMENT OF AFRICAN AMERICANS

Southern white historians have championed the creation of state-supported universal schooling as a compromise that rescued the South from the chaos of Reconstruction. Yet after little more than three decades of segregated schooling, black education was worse off than it was in the years immediately following the Civil War.[73] The conservative elite feared that school integration would so alter the cultural landscape of Virginia, that they were willing, in 1870, to exchange black suffrage for an end to any discussion of mixed schools. By the Constitutional Convention of 1901, however, there was no real black or radical white opposition to disenfranchisement, and conservatives moved without hesitation to eliminate the last vestige of Radical Reconstruction in Virginia.

Since the ratification of the Constitution of 1869, whites had enacted a number of duplicitous restrictions that reduced black political participation to a trickle.[74] Every type of extralegal gimmick imaginable was used to restrict the black franchise, including head taxes, literacy tests and segregated voting booths that closed before blacks could cast their ballot. With the new constitution in 1902, the vast majority of black males in the state were legally prevented from voting. The means remained the same—mainly the poll tax and bogus literacy tests—only now they were made legal by the new constitution. *The Richmond Times* congratulated the delegates, "It is more courageous and honorable and better for public morals and good government to come out and boldly disenfranchise the Negro than to make a pretense of letting him vote and then cheating him at the polls."[75]

The insidious nature of Virginia's biracial society had skewed human reason. White Virginians had come to believe that at one level the black man lacked the intellectual and social maturity to participate effectively in a democratic government. The new constitution, then, did what everyone understood was necessary to preserve the white state. At a much deeper level, now evidenced by the increasing number of violent acts against the black community, white Virginians had become so isolated by their separation from black society that they were convinced that the black male was an alien beast. In one of the most revealing statements ever made about the insanity bred by racial doublethink, convention delegates took the position "that the unlawful, but necessary, expedients employed to preserve us from the evil effects of the thing (Negro enfranchisement) were debauching the morals and warping the intellect of our race ..."[76]

White Virginians removed the black man's legal right to full political participation not only for his own good, but, more importantly, the new constitution put Virginia's racial house in order. Free now of debauching the morals and warping the intellect of the white race, Virginians would no longer have to surreptitiously block the ballot box from the black man. When, 30 years before, black Republicans and their white allies appeared poised to redraw the racial boundaries of Virginia, editor Southall wailed in the *Charlottesville Chronicle,* "This is reconstruction. This is the 'Union as it is'. How long, O Lord, How Long!"[77] To answer Southall's question, less than a lifetime.

CONCLUSION

The freedmen's efforts at education were an attempt, as historian Ronald Butchart has written, to put distance between themselves and slavery.[78] To a degree, it parallels efforts by poor and working-class families everywhere to create community. The ex-slave of Albemarle County and the working-class laborer in Pasadena saw the ends of social equality and education in much the same way. Black families in Charlottesville and working-class families in Pasadena wanted schooling, as much for the obvious economic advantages as for their own sense of self-worth. When, in 1865, Frederick Douglass dedicated the Douglass Institute, an entirely black-owned and -controlled school in Maryland, he said, "The mission of the school and that of the colored race are identical ... It is to teach [blacks] the true idea of manly independence and self-respect."[79] As we will see, substitute "working-class" for "blacks," and the tradesmen in Southern California at the turn of the century could have made the same mission statement about public schools in Pasadena.

It has been argued that freedmen were permitted a publicly funded education only when the ruling, planter class understood that education could be useful to socialize the former slave into his role in the new, free labor economy. This argument makes sense when one sees schools as important places for the transmission of cultural values. Symbolically, Virginia's separate schools taught values that communicated to both communities that "whiteness" was significantly more important to the larger culture. Virginia's schools, as an instrument of state-enforced segregation, socialized whites and blacks to accept the stratification of the community as the natural order of things. All one had to do was look at the material representation of segregation: black schools were nearly always lesser places, a message that spoke volumes to both communities. The separateness of Southern society enforced the legitimacy of segregation.

Ironically, Northern freedmen teachers helped enforce that separateness. By not recognizing the ex-slaves' call for self-determination, but instead, treating the freedmen as objects in their assumption that slavery had left the African illequipped to realize full citizenship, Northern teachers gave legitimacy to a hier-archical racial ideology. Even Anna Gardner, like many of her colleagues in other schools, aided in the cleavage of Southern society.

Gardner was first an educator intent on bringing to her students all she believed to be good and wise. She was not, as were many of her associates, opposed to black suffrage or to Afro Southerners holding office. But her support may have been less her belief in black self-determination than her bitterness toward the slave owner and Southerners in general. Still, this does not diminish her role as an educator in Charlottesville. She openly endorsed black schools and probably used a curriculum that advanced black independence. There is no evi-dence that she supported a more restrictive manual education. In fact, there is evidence to the contrary, as she held no trade classes in the Delvan building.

If she believed the new black citizen was her equal, then she first understood that the freedman needed "uplift." Many Northern teachers saw the future in terms of black advancement, but that advancement did not entail blacks and whites living together once the Northern military presence was withdrawn. Freedmen teachers, including Gardner, wanted the ex-slaves to achieve beyond their modest beginnings, but it is doubtful many wanted blacks to achieve status equal to whites.[80]

As we shall see, Gardner was not unlike later, progressive white women in urban centers in the West. She believed social uplift was a necessary condition of evolution. Blacks simply had not progressed as far but were fully capable of "catching up" to Northern, white society. Gardner was described by a contempo-rary as "toiling for coming generations, and sowing seed for a glorious harvest,"[81] a description similar to that of the feminist and evolutionary socialist, Charlotte Perkins Gilman who lived and worked in Southern California at the turn of the century. Gardner was eager to use education as a social uplift, but she was well aware that education took many forms. Her comment that her teaching was both in school and out suggests she used her craft to advance social change.[82]

By the turn of the century, black education had been essentially abandoned by Southern state legislatures. The appropriation of public funds was so skewed in favor of white communities that the dollar-to-dollar ratio was as high as 20 to one. After public funds, the main source of money to support black schools came in the form of Northern philanthropic assistance. Over many years, the Slater, Peabody and Rockefeller General Education Board funds contributed millions to the education of African-American children. But this Northern philanthropy came with strings attached. Funds were restricted to manual education, that is, schools were not only segregated and criminally underfunded, but the liberal arts curriculum used by black communities after the war was replaced with schooling designed to restrict the ex-slave to manual labor. Education for leadership in the segregated New South was limited to the middle- and upper-class white community.

As the 19th century turned, "usefulness," a watchword of school progressives, would come to mean different things to different communities. For the white middle class, "manual training" was seen as having the potential to transform education from a static system of arcane ideas into schooling for social reconstruction. "Doing education" would become symbolic of the "New Education" of John Dewey and other progressive educators. For African Americans in the South, manual training meant menial labor.

Paradoxically, for the turn-of-the-century white, working class in Pasadena, "usefulness" would come to mean the acquisition of job skills that could translate into increased wages and enhanced status and self-respect within the larger community. In a complex story of race and the construction of class and community, the white, working class in Pasadena would reject the classical, liberal-arts model of education. As community organizational patterns solidified around the structural expectations of industrial capitalism, the working class would come to see traditional schooling as less useful because it failed to teach their children the skills of the new, free labor market. Ironically, the classical, New England education that the Southern ex-slaves demanded to honor the new African-American citizen, was rejected by the white laboring class because it failed to honor the values and aspirations of their working community.

NOTES

1. The following material on the life of Albert Sidney Johnston is taken from Charles P. Roland's excellent biography, *Albert Sidney Johnston, Soldier of Three Republics* (Austin: University of Texas Press, 1964).
2. Ibid., p. 188.
3. Ibid., p. 238–240.
4. Ibid., p. 6–7.
5. Ibid., p. 261.
6. Ibid., p. 345–351.
7. Ibid., p. 242.
8. Ibid., p. 242.
9. Ibid., p. 242.
10. Ibid., p. 241–242.

11. Harris Newmark, *Sixty Years in Southern California, 1853–1916,* 3rd ed. (New York: Houghton Mifflin Company, 1930), p. 337.

12. Roland, p. 182.

13. Ibid., p. 242.

14. Ibid., p. 248, 251.

15. Ibid., p. 251–252.

16. Ibid., p. 253.

17. Ibid., p. 260.

18. Ibid., p. 260, 336–339, and Newmark, p. 316.

19. Alberta Johnston Denis, "Mrs. Albert Sidney Johnston," *Texas Magazine* 11:13, May 1897, p. 429–431, and Newmark, p. 320. One possible reason she never left for the South was the death of their eldest son, Albert Sidney Johnston Jr., who died in the steamer explosion of the *Ada Hancock* in the harbor at Los Angeles in April 1862.

20. Newmark, p. 316; Harold D. Carew, *The History of Pasadena and the San Gabriel Valley* (Los Angeles: S.J. Clarke Publishing Co., 1930), p. 275; and Henry Markham Page, *Pasadena, Its Early Years* (Los Angeles: Lorrin L. Morrison, 1964), p. 10–15. Apparently, the early historians of Pasadena were confused as to whom Eliza Johnston sold the land. Was it sold back to her brother or to Judge Eaton? Newmark says Eaton; Carew and Page say Griffin.

21. Newmark, p. 294, 316; Carew, p. 275; Page, p. 10–15. There is some discrepancy as to the exact location of Fair Oaks in Virginia. Eliza Griffin's obituary in the *Texas Magazine* of 1897 has her place of birth in Western Virginia, in the Shenandoah Valley near present-day Fincastle. Yet the only reference to an antebellum property with the name of Fair Oaks is found in Henrico County, near Richmond. Also, Sumner led his command in the Seven Day Campaign against the Confederate capital in 1862, but as far as the author can determine, Sumner was never in the Shenandoah Valley campaign.

22. James McPherson, *Ordeal By Fire: The Civil War and Reconstruction* (New York: Alfred Knopf, 1982), p. 511–512.

23. Ibid., p. 513–524.

24. James Anderson, *The Education of Blacks in the South, 1860–1935* (Chapel Hill: University of North Carolina Press, 1988), p. 4–32.

25. Sandra Small, "The Yankee Schoolmarm in Freedmen Schools: An Analysis of Attitudes," *Journal of Southern History* XLV, August 1979, p. 381 and Anderson on exslave schools.

26. James Johnson, "The Participation of Negroes in the Government of Virginia From 1877 to 1888," *Journal of Negro History* 14:3, July 1929, p. 251.

27. Bruce Caton, *A Stillness at Appomattox* (New York: Doubleday and Company, 1953), p. 267–276.

28. John Hammond Moore, *Albemarle County: Jefferson's County, 1727–1976* (Charlottesville: University of Virginia Press, 1976), p. 208–213. Also see Chalmers L. Gemmill, "The Charlottesville General Hospital, 1861–1865," *Magazine of Albemarle County History* 22 (1964), p. 91–160 and "John B. Minor's Civil War Diary," ed. A. Freudenberg and J. Casteen, *Magazine of Albemarle County History* 22 (1964), p. 45–55.

29. Joseph Carroll Vance, "The Negro in the Reconstruction of Albemarle County, Virginia" (Master's thesis, University of Virginia, 1953), p. 9; William Edward Webb, "Charlottesville and Albemarle County, 1865–1900," (Ph.D. dissertation, University of Virginia, 1965).

30. *Report of the Commissioner of Education,* 1904, Volume 2 (Washington, DC: U.S. Government Printing Office, 1906), p. 1341.

31. Gardner recorded her memories and her rage at Southerners in *Harvest Gleanings in Prose and Verse* (New York: Fowler and Wells, 1881).

32. Ibid., p. 16–17.

33. Ibid., p. 14–15.

34. *Tuscaloosa Observer,* July 1866, cited in Sandra Small, "The Yankee Schoolmarm in Freedmen Schools: An Analysis of Attitudes," p. 389.

35. Vance, p. 50–51.

36. Gardner, p. 24.

37. Ralph Clipman McDaniel, "The Virginia Constitutional Convention of 1901–1902," in *Johns Hopkins University Studies in Historical and Political Science* 46 (Baltimore: The Johns Hopkins University Press, 1928), p. 243–408.

38. Robert Zangrando, *The NAACP Crusade Against Lynching, 1909–1950* (Philadelphia: Temple University Press, 1980); *Under Sentence of Death; Lynching in the South,* ed. W. F. Brundage (Chapel Hill: University of North Carolina Press, 1997).

39. Anderson, for comments on planters and education, p. 17–25; also see Louis Harlan, *Separate and Unequal: Public School Campaigns and Racism in the Southern Seaboard States, 1901–1915* (New York: Athenaeum Press, 1968), p. 8–9.

40. Gardner, p. 40. Lodging and food were constant concerns for the Northern teachers. See Small, p. 386; and William Preston Vaughn, *Schools for All: The Blacks and Public Education in the South, 1865–1877* (Lexington: University of Kentucky Press, 1974), p. 34–35.

41. In Vance's Master's thesis from the University of Virginia, he parenthetically references Gardner's two years (p. 81), then John Hammond Moore (p. 232) in his *Albermarle County: Jefferson's County, 1727–1976* picks up on Vance's editorializing and references the two years. Both were mistaken as freedmen teachers from the North were ostracized throughout the South. See William Preston Vaughn, *Schools for All,* for an excellent discussion of the treatment received by these teachers, p. 33–38.

42. Vance, p. 78; Gardner, p. 27–28.

43. Vance, p. 79.

44. Vaughn, p. 36, and Richard Morton, "Life in Virginia by a 'Yankee Teacher,' Margaret Newbold Thorpe" *Virginia Magazine of History and Biography* 64 (1956), p. 201.

45. Harrison W. Daniel, "Virginia Baptists and the Negro, 1865–1902," *Virginia Magazine of History and Biography* 87 (1968), p. 344.

46. Daniel, p. 361.

47. Small, p. 392.

48. Wilbur Cash, *The Mind of the South* (New York: Knopf, 1941), cited in Small, "Yankee Schoolmarm," p. 382.

49. Gardner, p. 26.

50. Anderson, p. 28–30.

51. Gardner, p. 84.

52. Anderson, p. 30; Ronald Butchart, *Northern Schools, Southern Blacks and Reconstruction* (Westport, Conn.: Greenwood Press, 1980), p. 135–168.

53. Gardner, p. 43–44.

54. Butchart, p. 151–152.

55. Vance, p. 81–82.

56. Butchart, p. 169.

57. Ibid., p. 177.

58. Vance, p. 15.

59. Ibid., p. 15–16; Moore, p. 226; Anderson, p. 19–20.

60. Richard L. Morton, "The Negro in Virginia Politics, 1865–1902" (Phelps-Stokes Fellowship papers No. 4, University of Virginia, 1918), p. 32.

61. See the *Charlottesville Chronicle,* 23 April 1867, p. 1, cited in Vance, p. 17.
62. Vance, p. 17.
63. Ibid., p. 19.
64. Ibid., p. 20–21.
65. Ibid., p. 23; Morton, p. 33; Moore, p. 228–229.
66. Vance, p. 29.
67. Vance, p. 30; Moore, p. 229.
68. Edgar W. Knight, *Public Education in the South* (New York: Ginn and Co., 1922), p. 321, as quoted in Horace Mann Bond, *The Education of the Negro in the American Social Order* (New York: Prentice Hall, Inc., 1934), p. 52.
69. *The Negro in Virginia,* Writers' Program of the Work Projects Administration (Richmond: Hastings House, New York), p. 228.
70. Ibid., p. 228.
71. Vance, p. 31.
72. William Preston Vaughn, *Schools for All: The Blacks and Public Education in the South, 1865–1877* (Lexington: University of Kentucky Press, 1974), p. 72–73.
73. Anderson, p. 31.
74. Ralph Clipman McDaniel, "The Virginia Constitutional Convention of 1901–1902," in *Johns Hopkins University Studies in Historical and Political Science* 46 (Baltimore: The Johns Hopkins University Press, 1928), p. 26–29.
75. Ibid., p. 33.
76. Ibid., p. 33.
77. Vance, p. 31.
78. Butchart, p. 169–179.
79. Ibid., p. 176.
80. Small, p. 392.
81. Gardner, p. 10.
82. Ibid., p. 84.

CHAPTER 3

"IN THIS ARISTOCRATIC TOWN?"
Labor, Women and the Gospel of Discontent

She arrived in the fall of 1888, just as the real-estate boom collapsed. Suffering from severe depression and physically exhausted—"that ghastly, below-zero weariness"—Charlotte Perkins Stetson, like so many late-century arrivals, had come to Pasadena to escape. Stetson's flight, though, was not from some real or imagined urban chaos but from a failed marriage. With the help of family friends wintering in Pasadena, she found a "little paper and wood four-room house" on Orange Grove Avenue. In the rapidly declining local economy, which Stetson described as "this land of low cost," her rent was $10 a month. There, nestled in a forgotten orange grove, "with roses running over the roof … and a tall olean-der pink against the sky," she lived a pauperish, bohemian existence. Charlotte purchased her fruits and vegetables for pennies from a roving "vegetable Chinaman," and she "scraped by" (if one so connected to bluestocking wealth ever really "scrapes"), writing story and verse (seldom sold), overseeing the inte-rior decoration of the new Opera House, and teaching art to middle-class chil-dren, who, she complained, had their instinct for drawing wrung out of them by the public-school teachers. She wrote, at times voraciously, between bouts of depression so severe they would drive her to her garden hammock for hours, too feeble to do much but contemplate her "weakness, [and] the dark, feeble mind." She wrote short stories, plays (one with her closest friend, Grace Channing), essays and poetry and sent them off to new "progressive" magazines. Most were rejected. She and Grace joined a local theater, Charlotte often being cast as the fool. When the city intelligentsia campaigned for a library to match their cultural appetites, Stetson set up a one-woman booth at the outdoor library fair, adver-tising on-the-spot poetry, created "while you wait." No one did. Verse from an unknown writer would not sell even in the city's small but active literary circle. Instead, Stetson relied on friends and family (but not her estranged husband, the painter Charles Walter Stetson) to help make ends meet.[1]

Charlotte Perkins Gilman (she dropped Stetson with her divorce from Walter, taking the name Gilman when she remarried 10 years later) would go on to become the most famous feminist of her Victorian generation; although today she is remembered mainly by academics specializing in Gilded Age feminist literature. With the birth of her child, Kate, in the mid-1880s, she fell into fits of deep depression she described as the "constant dragging weariness miles below zero." She cried incessantly, was so weak she could not hold a knife and fork, and, though she nursed her baby for five months, found no joy in maternity. She blamed no one but herself. "You had health and strength and hope and glorious work before you—and you threw it all away," she told her diary. Gilman saw herself as a champion for humanity, but she felt useless, no good as a mother, a writer or a wife. So, two years before she moved to her "little paper and wood four-room house," she took her doctor's advice and fled alone to spend the winter with the Channings out West. She spent a few weeks with her brother in Ogden, Utah, and a few days with her father in San Francisco. He was a man she hardly knew, having left the family when Charlotte was two years old. After a few reserved days with her father, she left "down the great inland plain of California, over the Mojave Desert, and to heaven."[2]

Heaven was Pasadena. She recovered quickly, her passion for beauty finally "satisfied ... [as] this place did not seem like earth, it was paradise." Amongst kind friends, her "amusements, out door sports," and "the blessed mountains, the long unbroken sweep of the valley, with snow-peaks at the far eastern end," Stetson found hope again. She paid close attention to her finances, and, although it would take her back East earlier than she wished, she took advantage of the railroad fare war, paying $5 for a private berth to Chicago. She knew that if she waited any longer she might have to either share her berth or, worse yet, sit with the regular passengers the entire return trip. A few days later, the few berths remaining were filled with two and three travelers, and what seats were left sold for $1.[3]

She returned to a dreary East in late March and was once again met with severe depression. Apparently, Stetson was suffering from what Freud described in the late century as "hysteria." Her doctor, the eminent S. Weir Mitchell of Philadelphia, told his patient to become "domestic," be with her child always, rest one hour after meals, be "intellectual" two hours a day, and never touch a pen, pencil or brush for the rest of her life. She followed his absurd prescription for months and "came perilously close to losing [her] mind." Finally, in the fall of 1887, she solved the riddle of her manic depression and separated from her husband. Although she harbored no ill feelings toward Walter Stetson, domesticity was a prison to Charlotte.[4]

A year later in 1888, she decided to return to Paradise. With her daughter in tow, she left for Pasadena to find a new life as an independent writer. She had never worked before, had no formal training except as an illustrator—a career that she never intended to follow—and was deeply depressed over her failed marriage and state of affairs. She had sold her family home and possessions to pay for the trip, everything, that is, except some 4000 pounds of furniture and belongings that she shipped to Pasadena. When she boarded the train in Providence for the West, she had little Kate in one hand and $10 in the other. Carrying her bags was an older Irish woman, a dressmaker by trade, who Charlotte had retained promising room and board and a return ticket East. Since Gilman despised the life of a domestic, it was logical that she brought one with her. The problem was that she disliked this "mother's helper" as much as the work she wanted her to perform. Charlotte described her variously as an "incubus," "dull," "useless," "dense," "uncompromising" and a "moron ... She could not cook, she would not sweep nor dust nor wash dishes—said it coarsened her hands!" Eventually, and somewhat gleefully, Charlotte sent the teary-eyed Irish woman packing. She now had to clean her own house, even the hated dirty dishes.[5]

Gilman had hoped to find in the West a "natural world" to her liking, a culture of gentility where a woman of her intellect might grow to her fullest capabilities, not a place where she would be forced by the economics of domesticity to perform the kind of work unsuited to a woman of her cultural station. In Gilman's autobiography, her tongue-lashing of this "under-witted" Irish servant woman underscores her allegiance to the prevalent Darwinian convention that society was "naturally" stratified. She believed, as many of her contemporaries did, that the stratification was not fixed but malleable, and, as Darwin hypothesized, continually evolving to a higher, more "perfect order." She knew too, that her social philosophy—what she called "this organic unity of the group"—would eventually wash away the pain of a lonely, single woman, burdened with an unwanted child and saddled with an incompetent house-woman.[6]

During these early years in Pasadena, which Gilman described as the foundation of her literary career, she developed a worldview that assumed progress without strife.[7] She wrote often that culture, through natural selection but without the brutish competition and violence associated with the more conservative evolutionary theory of Edward Spencer, would progress naturally without struggle toward its more perfect end. She believed that removing the social and economic impediments to growth would lead to a future of "better people." Gilman and her contemporaries were ardent evolutionists, who saw their social philosophy translate as nonviolent natural selection. Her unnamed Irish servant woman was simply on a lower evolutionary plane. Charlotte Perkins Gilman and the upper crust of society were at a higher, more refined evolutionary stage, better equipped, they believed, to carry out the intellectual work needed to bring about a new social order. By changing the social relations, those occupying the lower strata of society would be "fixed."[8]

Gilman's professional life began with her arrival in Pasadena during the autumn of 1888. She earned a few dollars with various literary endeavors—she was prolific despite her depression, completing 33 short articles, 23 poems and 10 children's verses. All that effort brought her little revenue. It was not until 1890, when she published "Similar Cases," a poetic tongue-in-cheek undressing of the conservative Spencerian evolutionists, that she had something to call important. William Dean Howells, the prominent editor of the *Atlantic Monthly*, and Lester Frank Ward, the father of modern sociology, publicly applauded Gilman's contribution to the growing body of late-century criticism that challenged the conventional notions of social organization as deterministic, excessively competitive and violent.[9]

Gilman's "Similar Cases" was published in the *Nationalist*, the official organ of an avant-garde socialist movement associated with author Edward Bellamy's *Looking Backward*. In Bellamy's novel, published in the late 1880s, he prophesied the evolution of culture, examining 100 years of "natural evolution." Bellamy believed that the end result would be a form of centralized, state socialism. Bellamy's novel was an instant success and sparked a near-miraculous, cultish, middle-class following. In the violent, stratified world of late-century industrial capitalism, Gilman and other middle-class intellectuals discovered in Bellamy's book a nonviolent solution—a form of socialism they called Nationalism—which gave meaning to their nascent thoughts of progress. Gilman, along with thousands around the country, rushed to join Bellamy reading circles, called Nationalist Clubs. Beginning first in the West and then spreading throughout the country, Nationalist Clubs provided middle-class reformers, many of them women, the opportunity to read, discuss, debate and promote a nonviolent socialism that was highly centralized, authoritarian and, ironically, exceedingly militaristic.[10]

Gilman joined the Pasadena Nationalist Club, founded early in 1890. In her first-ever public speech, titled "Human Nature," Charlotte told a standing-room-only audience that the brutish nature of capitalism would come to an end and be replaced by a humanitarian socialism. In Bellamy's Nationalism, she told her audience, "Everybody would share and nobody would suffer."[11] What mattered to Gilman were the social conditions. "Change the conditions," she argued, "and the organism changes." In an effort to bolster her notions of a malleable culture, she repeatedly used a litany of homegrown analogies as proof. She told her Pasadena audience,

> *Instinct*, mind you, is the result of habit—not habit of instinct. It is the transmitted effect of repeated actions and can be changed like every other form of life. Look at the instinct of the wild dog and the instinct of the tame dog. Who gave the dog what we now call his *"nature"*—faithful, obedient, self-sacrificing? Why we did. The wild dog is not faithful, obedient, self-sacrificing. We have developed those instincts by making the creature perform the action whose repetition formed the instinct."[12]

Gilman, like many late-century Darwinians, equated evolution with material and social progress. She advocated changing culture through "moral suasion," not unlike what the Women's Christian Temperance Union (WCTU) attempted when they met Jerry Beebe in his saloon. Changing the social relations would therefore change the modes of production. This was a radically different view of the coming revolution than that of Marx.13 For Gilman and those advocating an end to the greed of capital, Nationalism had "struck a great taproot in striking at our business system." But for Gilman, nationalism meant much more: "There is another root as deep—possibly deeper," she said. "The struggle," she wrote, was "between man and woman."14 Gilman saw class submerged by gender. She considered herself an intellectual, and although she spoke the language of cross-class solidarity, she did not live it. The great taproot may have struck at business, but for Charlotte Perkins Gilman and thousands of reforming middle- and upper-class women, Bellamy's socialism promised more egalitarian gender relations.

Gilman's socialism was the "early humanitarian kind ... not the narrow and rigid economic determinism of Marx," with its class-consciousness and struggle.15 She found in Pasadena a paradise she had never experienced, a place that nurtured for the "first time her boundless appetite for beauty." Paradise-Pasadena was tainted only by the struggle that comes from competition and greed, biological characteristics that were decidedly male to Gilman. Her socialist vision dismissed the Marxian precondition of struggle, because contained in struggle were the male determinants of avarice, competition and brutality. Gilman's middle-class Bellamyite socialism was anticlass struggle because working-class activism, especially labor unions and the more radical, male-dominated Socialist Labor party, was rooted in a male ideology that was antiwoman and therefore unscientific, unnatural and dangerous.16

To Gilman and her middle-class sisters, evolution and a passive form of natural selection helped define the woman's movement during the late Victorian era. Change was created, not through competition and struggle, as Spencer advocated, but "by superior process[es] supplanting inferior process[es]." Women were, by nature, patient, tireless workers. They were the "mothers" of society. Men were the opposite—they were individualistic, egoistic and competitive. If egoism was a masculine trait, then altruism, in terms of love, service, care, teaching and improvement of conditions for the sake of the young, was decidedly female. The prevailing views of society that reflected male attributes of greed and violence were wrong. Freeing women from the constraints of a male-imposed domesticity would free society to evolve to a higher state.17

Looking back, we can see that Gilman's feminist politics were flawed. Believing society was unequal was one thing; sanctioning equal status within society was quite another. In 1907, Gilman wrote that society was unequal and diverse, with particular members inferior but "essential to the life of the whole."

She believed it was her duty and the duty of her middle-class intellectual sisters to teach the lesser folk the same attributes one would teach a wild dog, namely obedience, faithfulness and self-sacrifice. Her notions of a just society were not based on equality. On the contrary, to many reforming middle-class women and men, "society was not composed of constituents all alike and equally developed, but most diverse and unequal." When Gilman wrote about blacks in her essay "A Suggestion on the Negro Problem," in 1908, her humane socialism becomes something less than egalitarian:

> A man would rather lose all ten toes than two eyes; and both feet than his eyes and ears. Our special senses are far superior to our meat and bones; yet it is quite essential to the body's life that even its least important parts be healthy.[18]

It was important that the "least important parts" of the body politic—and here she is referring to African Americans—be healthy lest the entire body become diseased. In the opening of her essay, Gilman wrote that if we had "left them [the Africans] alone in their own country … their dissimilarity and inferiority would have been none of our business …" She argues, then, that in their "own culture" they would have "not evolved," but since [they are] "here it was our responsibility."[19] Gilman's idea of socialism meant improving the quality of life, so eventually there would come a less class-bound society. She believed in the "mutability of the race," but her scientific nascence was clearly aligned with the pseudo-scientific racism of the era. She had no desire for a color-blind, more democratic culture.[20] Science would help, but menial labor would always be accomplished by lesser folk. Intellectuals (like her) would lead by creating ideas. Until that new age arrived (she thought in two or three generations), she worked to organize a more autonomous female culture.[21]

The larger, turn-of-the-century woman's reform movement (of which Bellamy's socialist movement was but a single branch) would justify women's autonomy from male culture on the grounds that science supported a separate woman's sphere. The woman's socialist movement that would develop in the Western states would have its own agenda and would be decidedly different from that of their husbands' and socialist brothers.[22] Socialist women would, along with their male counterparts, issue calls for an end to the greed and violent nature of capitalism. However, they would depart from the male socialist and labor union agenda by calling for an end to the servile status of women of all classes. They would often call for sisterly cross-class solidarity in the name of feminism, suffrage and socialism and then seemingly, without equivocation, marginalize working-class women, as Gilman did to her unnamed servant, as underwitted morons.

The failure of the late-century middle-class women's movement to connect to working women, especially ethnic women who were organizing as unionized labor, would have far-reaching consequences in cities like Pasadena. The turn of the century came to be extraordinarily important for the U.S. woman's movement. During the period in which Gilman emerged as a popular leader amongst many feminists, the movement rejected the opportunity for women to organize across class and ethnic lines in favor of a woman's movement more influenced by class standing than by cross-class solidarity. The impact of a woman's movement that was divided by class and ethnic biases altered forever how cities such as Pasadena and Charlottesville were to determine social policy. Increasingly, wealthy women came to influence social and moral policy in the name of cultural equality. The results for working women and especially for their children would be profound. By 1930, the city of Pasadena was rigidly divided along class and ethnic lines. Ironically, the community's schools were touted as the benchmark of progressivism, schools that were designed "to meet the needs of all children." The many ways in which those needs were determined exposed the strict social class biases cloaked as social policy.

LABOR AND SOCIALISM

In 1902 Gilman left Pasadena for San Francisco, believing her career and personal life would fare better in the Bay Area. She would end up splitting her time between San Francisco and Oakland, "preaching," writing, teaching "little classes" and doing club work.23 Before she left Pasadena, Gilman found that many women who had accompanied their tuberculosis-infected men had been stranded in Southern California when the disease became deadly. She tried to promote what she called a "residence shop," her idea of a hiring hall for out-of-work women. Gilman's plan was for the women to sew and mend for the city's winter visitors, a sort of for-profit spin on the Salvation Army—with the profit going to Gilman. This was "good business and a double benefit," but she found no sympathetic takers in the city, suggesting the idea was too much for "the residents to visualize." This was neither the first nor last time Gilman would criticize Californians for what she believed was their provincial nature. She finally washed her hands of the state late in the decade, giving the newspapers a field day criticizing her decision to permanently leave her daughter, Kate, with Walter Stetson and his new wife, her close friend, Grace Channing.24

Early in the 1930s, stricken with terminal cancer, Gilman returned to Pasadena to live with her daughter, Kate. In her autobiography, published just before she committed suicide by chloroform in 1935, Gilman remained committed to the ideas she formed in her youth and lamented "the rapidly descending extinction of our nation ... [by the] conglomerate races."25 It is ironic that the house where she ended her life was recently rescued from demolition and moved to the "Lincoln Triangle," a neighborhood Pasadena now recognizes as the city's first working-class enclave.26

The San Francisco Gilman came to know at the turn of the century was the vortex of the Western states' labor/capital struggle. During the 1890s, the economy of the country limped along, suffering from a haphazard fiscal policy that fluctuated from gold to silver and back again. By 1895, the nation appeared on the brink of bankruptcy. Compounding a stagnant economy was a severe breach in the public trust as strikes turned violent at the Homestead Steel plant near Pittsburgh, and at George Pullman's Palace Car factory. In its quest to limit the power of the working man and woman, big business found the federal army, the courts and the office of the presidency to be quick allies.

As the century turned, the financial and trade union superiority San Francisco held over the rest of the state began to wane. As California's economy emerged from the long slumber of the 1890s, Los Angeles and the surrounding communities were poised to enjoy a prodigious expansion. Increased exploitation of Southern California's oil fields and renewed interest in bringing water to this perennially dry region sparked an economic boom not seen since the mid-1880s. With the economic expansion came a great organizing flourish by labor, as union field organizers pursued both craft and semiskilled workers in nearly every trade. For the first time, the American Federation of Labor (AFL) gave Southern California more than token recognition. Never before in the history of organized labor had there been a period of such untrammeled opportunity. Dozens of trades and crafts were absorbed into the AFL. In the December 1903 issue of the AFL *Union Labor News,* the Los Angeles Council of Labor reported more than 60 affiliated unions represented at the Labor Hall on Spring Street. In addition, the Union Hall sponsored some 22 unaffiliated unions, including the Electrical Helpers, Blacksmiths and their helpers, Switchmen and various organizing councils, including the Pasadena Building Laborers No. 8998.[27]

The first two years of the century saw the number of unions rise an astonishing 75 percent with overall membership jumping some 125 percent.[28] With union strength came strikes, boycotts and assorted job action as labor flexed its new-found muscle. Throughout California, organized trades either threatened job action or walked out, often with the same results. Labor became increasingly centralized and efficient as trades and crafts adapted organizing tactics used by business. Public relations became instrumental as unions built a constituency of support throughout the community. There were sympathy walkouts by affiliated locals in support of their striking brothers. Plumbers walked to support the carpenters, and the electricians went out in support of the bricklayers. Some years were more volatile than others, but even in periods of apparent calm, the tension between capital and labor was acute.

The goal of organized labor was to expand its membership so trade unions would be an effective counterweight to the expanding influence of capitalists. Labor saw the widening gulf between the monied class and working people as the most threatening, antidemocratic influence in the country. Unions campaigned for an effective, democratic, honest government that honored the work that men and women performed every day. Writing in the "Pasadena Department" of the *Union Labor News* in 1905, city editor G.C. Keyes (an architectural draftsman by trade, who moonlighted as an editorial writer) advised union men to reject any political candidate who was self-nominated. "Ten to one," Keyes wrote, "the man who asks for office will 'graft' at the first and every opportunity." Capitalists bought politicians and "positions of public trust are, by right, places of honor, to which those whom the people of a district wish to honor are invited." Union men should never "vote for a man who asks for office," only for a candidate "nominated by his neighbors." Clearly, Keyes was reminding his nearly all-male readership that their franchise was reserved only for candidates endorsed by the "neighborhood," in other words, the union brotherhood.29 Ironically, three years later Keyes would be fired from his editorial post amidst charges of embezzlement.30

Keyes' admonishment had a larger purpose. Across the border in Los Angeles, powerful men opposed the rising preeminence of trade unionism. Driving through the streets of Los Angeles in his armor-plated touring car (complete with a small-bore cannon mounted to the hood) was labor's Public Enemy Number One: "General" Harrison Gray Otis, owner and publisher of *The Los Angeles Times*.31 No single individual in the history of the labor/capital conflict did as much to destroy the labor movement as Otis. Together with allies like Henry E. Huntington, owner of the Pacific Electric Railroad and their associates in the Merchants and Manufacturers Association, Otis vowed that Los Angeles would never become another San Francisco.

From 1900 until the Times building was bombed under mysterious circumstances in October 1910, labor's single-minded focus was the defeat of Otis. Los Angeles—"Otistown" to the unions—was subjected to daily antilabor attacks in the *Times,* as Otis used his newspaper as a bully pulpit to beat, batter and discredit working men and women and their unions in an orchestrated effort to destabilize the labor movement. Although he concentrated his energies on metropolitan Los Angeles, Otis's influence and his public tirades against unions tended to rally conservative interests everywhere. By the time his newspaper building was destroyed in October 1910, no community in Southern California was immune to his efforts. Affiliates of his Citizen's Alliance and the Merchants and Manufacturers Association would spring up in nearly every Southern California community, including Pasadena.32

By the fall of 1910, the tension in Los Angeles and much of the southland was electric. City editor Keyes reported "monster" rallies in Los Angeles, attended by hundreds from Pasadena in a show of solidarity with their laboring brothers and sisters across the river. Keyes and the other *Citizen* writers (the *Union Labor News* had been renamed *The Citizen* in 1905) told of boycotts, strikes and repeated false alarms, including L.A. police—which many working men and women believed were in Otis's pocket—"discovering" bombs ostensibly planted by prolabor forces. The situation compounded when the labor movement took a rapid turn to the political left.[33]

In the first decade of the new century, trade unions and the Socialist Party began to court one another, intending to forge a powerful new party that would effectively represent the political interests of the working class. This was the "fusion" between labor and the radical left that many thought would push the Socialist message mainstream. It was, at best, an uneasy, suspicious alliance. The working-class unionists did not trust the middle-class Socialists, believing them bound too tightly to notions (like Gilman's) of an intellectual elite. The Socialists, no matter their pronouncements of working-class solidarity, could not dispel labor's mistrust of a class-bound intelligentsia. What made the fusion work, at least initially, was the charismatic Job Harriman, a Los Angeles attorney and long-time Socialist activist. In 1910, Harriman announced his candidacy for mayor of Los Angeles. His labor/Socialist platform called for community ownership of the means of production, worker control of the local schools, improved job safety and an assortment of other progressive ideals that Otis and the business community immediately branded as dangerous. Harriman's campaign reflected his ideological commitment to the fusion as he surrounded himself with Socialists and trade unionists alike. His ticket included an African American, women and numerous labor union officials.[34]

In this increasingly tense atmosphere, the catastrophic happened. Late in the night of October 1, 1910, a bomb leveled *The Los Angeles Times* building, killing 21 and injuring nearly a dozen others. When two labor organizers, the brothers John and James McNamara, were arrested (they were actually kidnapped by Otis's private detective and brought to Los Angeles to stand trial), working men and women were outraged at the apparent frame-up.[35] A correspondent for the Socialist press proclaimed the brothers "innocent as new-born babes."[36] A year later—just days before Los Angeles was to go to the polls and elect, in a predicted landslide, Job Harriman as its first Socialist mayor—the McNamaras stunned the nation by changing their story. They admitted their guilt in a plea bargain brokered by their attorneys, saying they single-handedly planned the destruction of the *Times* building but never intended harm to anyone. Organized labor was stunned and immediately blamed the Socialists for a betrayal—it was reported that the streets turned blue as Harriman's supporters tossed their blue-colored campaign buttons into the gutters. Thorny questions persisted, including questionable behavior on the part of the McNamara team of attorneys, headed by Clarence Darrow. But the end result was never in question. The labor/Socialist alliance collapsed, never recovering its momentum. Job Harriman, discredited as complicit in the *Times* bombing, was crushed in his bid to become mayor as was his entire labor/Socialist ticket. The worker campaign to move labor to the center of social and political life in America collapsed in the rubble of the *Times* building. From that moment forward, the mainstream American labor movement would keep any alliance with politics of the radical left at arm's length.37

Fig. 7. What was left of *The Los Angeles Times* building, the day after the bombing in October, 1910. A year later, and just days before the general election in Los Angeles, the Socialist-leaning McNamara brothers confessed they were the bombers. That breach of public trust effectively ended any alliance between the radical left and organized labor in Southern California. *(Photo courtesy of the Security Pacific Collection, Los Angeles Public Library)*

The end of the first decade of the new century was the watershed years in the history of the labor/Socialist movement in the Western states. By the early 1920s, there was little to recognize of the old labor/Socialist movement in America. Events on an international scale had conspired to deal a deathblow to any fusion between the Socialists and organized labor in the United States. World War I and the political repression that followed, coupled with the internal dysfunction of the Socialist party, ruptured the party so badly that any hope of a unified Socialist front disappeared. Organized labor, already reeling from attacks by capital before and after the war, distanced itself further from the Socialists. The *Times* bombing and the subsequent trial signaled a change in the political landscape of the far West. However, two years before the *Times* bombing, Pasadena experienced its own flash point that would come to define the ideological landscape of the city for the next half century.

THE LABOR MOVEMENT AT THE TURN OF THE CENTURY

Although Pasadena's historians have never given the labor movement any notice and made only mocking mention of the city's legacy of Socialist "gadflies," during the first 20 years of the century, the trade unions, the Socialists and Pasadena's elite were locked in a pitched battle that would determine who was to rule the richest city in America. As it was in Los Angeles, Pasadena's cultural and economic space was contested terrain throughout the first decade of the 20th century. The long-standing myth of Pasadena as a community of grand homes, great wealth, tranquil politics (or no politics at all) and Anglo-Saxon cultural hegemony was established in the first decades of the 20th century. Before World War I, however, Pasadena was anything but tranquil. The labor movement and a small but energetic Socialist movement were contesting the prevailing definition of what Pasadena's elite called "civic values."[38]

In 1909, the Pasadena working man (if he was white, skilled and unionized) would not have hesitated in declaring that Pasadena was "his city" and a solid union town. Given every measure of labor's influence—in the cultural affairs of the community, in politics, the economy, even the society pages of the city's newspapers—Pasadena was clearly moved by the rhythms of organized labor. The unions had permeated much of the fiber of city life. A succession of mayors during the first decade were sympathetic and supportive of labor's agenda. By mid-decade, two union men served on the city council, one by election and the other by appointment. Numerous laboring men were appointed to the city's most important commissions and committees, helping guide policy on everything from water rights to electrical power. Union muscle had firmly planted the idea that municipal ownership of the public utilities was a good idea, and, through union backing, both would become reality before the end of World War I. By 1910, most of the construction sites in the city were unionized. The typographical union boasted a closed shop, and the other skilled trades were not far behind. The union influence in the city was so pervasive that Pasadena merchants purchased enough advertising in the West Coast AFL *Citizen* to carry the newspaper through the hard times of the decade. Possibly the best illustration of union ascendancy was the fact that the *Citizen's* "Pasadena Department" was the largest regional coverage outside of central Los Angeles.[39]

By 1910, Pasadena's unions and their annual Labor Day festivities, held the first Monday of September, would rival the more prestigious Tournament of Roses. Alternating annually between parades and picnics, Pasadena's unions during the first years of the century put on a Labor Day festival that "promoted a closer feeling of fraternity among the laboring classes and their friends."[40] When the Labor Day Organizing Committee decided to picnic in 1909, 4,000 workers, together with family and friends, made their way to Tournament Park for games, speeches, a basket lunch and, mindful of the city's aversion to alcohol consumption, "all the coffee you could drink, compliments of the Labor Day Association." The day began early when nearly a thousand union men marched with their families to the First Methodist Church to listen to a prolabor sermon by the "reverend gentleman" Matt S. Hughes, who avoided (thankfully, wrote *Citizen* editor G.C. Keyes) any "harping" on the "tendency of the laboring people [to] stay away from the churches."[41]

Labor Day was intended to be fun and games and, at the century's turn, the country's newest sport, baseball, moved center stage. The Electrical Union nine lost a slugfest to a mixed team of trade union bombers (dubbed the "Miscellaneous"), 16 to 15. Presumably, given the family crowd, "cussing" (and presumably fisticuffs), which the union ball players admitted had gotten so out of hand at their other games that they needed a police officer to keep order, was held in check. Once the ball game was over, the crowd was entertained by relay races and games, including a "Ladies Nail Driving Contest," a "Fifty Yard Dash for Young Ladies," and a "Ladies Baseball Throwing Contest." All three, incidentally, won by a young woman named Venice Hess, who could wield a carpenter's hammer so deftly she drove tenpenny nails into a two-by-four in half a minute. The popular image of the turn-of-the-century labor movement as a singularly—and bawdy—male enterprise is not supported by what occurred in Pasadena. Women served on the Labor Day Organizing Committee, walked alongside the trade union parade floats, and participated in the games with their men.[42]

It is important to note that the organized working class marching in those parades and playing in those games represented white, skilled tradesmen. Mexicans, blacks, Japanese and the Chinese were relegated to the most menial occupations and were not, except for isolated examples, unionized. Only in the case of the Japanese, who had some clout as artists, restaurateurs, pool hall proprietors, and merchants, could it be said that Pasadena's "minority" population was "well treated" during the first decade of the century.[43] There are examples of African Americans being admitted to union locals, but their numbers were few.[44]

Moreover, wage-earning white women continued to remain on the margin, relegated to occupations that seldom carried the union label. Only in a few instances, such as the large non-Chinese laundries, did the AFL extend its organizational muscle. As with many community histories, the life of working women

Fig. 8. A rare photograph of a "Labor Union" entry, found in the archives of the Pasadena Museum of History. The photo was filed as a Tournament of Roses parade entry, but given the antipathy toward labor expressed by the Tournament sponsors, this float might have been in a Labor Day parade. *(Photo courtesy of the Pasadena Museum of History)*

in Pasadena remains obscure. Women were employed as clerks, typists, teachers, seamstresses, waitresses and, in a processing plant on South Raymond Avenue, fruit and vegetable handlers. In addition, the city had two large laundries, together employing nearly 250 launderers and drivers. By 1910, both were at least partly unionized. In a rare glimpse into gendered politics in the labor movement, some women were elected to the laundry union leadership, an extraordinary event in the worker movement at the turn of the century.[45]

LABOR, SOCIALISM AND THE PUBLIC SCHOOLS

Throughout the first decade of the new century, organized labor made a significant impact on the politics of managing Pasadena's schools. The working men and women of the city felt they had some measure of influence in their children's education. There were repeated references in the *Citizen* to the condition of school buildings, but one would expect wage earners to be concerned with new construction and repair; it meant work and steady pay. In fact, the labor movement also was actively involved in more communal issues. It pursued textbook changes that recognized labor's influence on world affairs, stumped for school board candidates, advocated for particular teachers who were being marked for job reductions and coordinated with the mayor and the school board to push building code improvements. By 1906, every school construction contract except one was awarded to Pasadena contractors, something the *Citizen* reported as "near to being the right thing."[46] A few years later, the refurbishing of Roosevelt School was done entirely with union labor. City editor Keyes reported that as far away as New Jersey, organized labor had taken notice of how influential Pasadena unions had become in its efforts to improve school construction. Union men and women were exceedingly proud of their efforts to make schools in Pasadena clean, safe, modern and friendly to the prounion message.[47]

That union message was often carried by Pasadena plumber and Socialist J.J. Hicks, owner of a small shop on west Colorado Street. Hicks, and his wife, Mattie (herself influential in the Socialist movement), were vocal advocates of the union/Socialist agenda. Plumber Hicks (also the Socialist party candidate for mayor in 1907) led a delegation of union men when they met with the board of education over the unsanitary conditions at two schools. Complaining that the urinals were outdated and unsanitary, these working-class men knew it was within their power to argue for better conditions for their boys and, by implication, everyone. The city's plumbing inspector, J.C. Sheff, concurred and convinced Mayor Thumm, one of the few mayors during the decade who was not openly friendly to labor, to allocate funds for new sanitary facilities.[48]

Throughout the decade the Hicks family were no strangers to the maelstrom that passed for Pasadena politics. Whether it was campaigning for school urinals, Socialist reform, curriculum reform or an end to corporal punishment, the family was a force few could ignore. J.J. and Mattie Hicks were forever in the thick of things and, not surprisingly, so were their two boys, Lester and Eugene. Lester, or "Leslie" as he was known, the older of the two boys, was certainly no shrinking violet. During the summer of 1907, at the age of 12, he had been injured riding his bicycle through the streets of Pasadena. The *Citizen* reported young Hicks had ran into a horse and wagon.[49] Maybe the boys took after their father, for the senior Hicks always seemed to lead with his mouth—or his fist.

One morning in early February 1909, a Pasadena newspaper headline blazed: "SOCIALIST AND TEACHER IN PASADENA IN FISTIC AFFRAY." The *Pasadena Daily News* reported that "J.J. Hicks Attempts to Horsewhip Principal Thompson." Hicks and his eldest son, Leslie, were waiting in their wagon for the arrival of E.A. Thompson, the principal of Washington Street school. Leslie had told his father that Thompson had beaten him because he defended his nine-year-old brother, Eugene, who had been accused of throwing rocks at Thompson's young son. Hicks later said the man had beat Leslie once before "with a cat-o-nine tails." When Hicks saw Thompson arrive, he jumped off his wagon menacingly cracking the air with his horsewhip. As if on cue, Thompson took off his overcoat. The two adversaries circled each other once, then, before anyone knew what was happening, both were rolling in the dirt. Leslie flew from the wagon and tried to trip Thompson. Later, Mother Hicks told the newspaper that she believed her husband had gone to the school hoping to find a peaceful solution. She was wrong. The elder Hicks wanted nothing of the sort. "I wanted satisfaction …" he said. "I went up with the intention of licking the principal or being licked." Eyewitnesses said Hicks got licked. The plumber, though, claimed the fight was unfair. "Whenever I would get on top, they pulled me off, but whenever he got on top, they only said, "Now professor, you've hit him enough, you've hit him enough." Superintendent Hamilton, fed up with Hicks' and his boys' antiestablishment behavior, raked the family by telling the newspaper that the entire clan were "troublemakers."[50]

Even if the plumber's school stories were a bit blind to his children's reported behavior (to Hicks' credit, he never once wavered in his boys' defense; to Thompson's discredit, he never once denied beating the boys), the severity of punishment at Washington and Lincoln, two working-class schools attended by the Hicks boys, was, even by turn-of-the-century standards, exceedingly harsh. Mother Hicks told the *Citizen* that Leslie was once beaten so badly with a piece of garden hose that the bruises and welts stayed with him for weeks. When Mrs. Hicks complained that Eugene should not be hit without her permission ("he was a sensitive boy …"), the principal told her, "I've been teaching school for 25 years … without [your] assistance and [I will] whip Eugene whenever and for whatever [I] please …"[51] Hicks felt his side of the story was not reported fairly by the local newspaper, so the *Citizen* ran a pro-Hicks follow-up. Still, this was not the kind of press—in any newspaper—that Pasadena's boosters wished. During this first decade of the new century, the Board of Trade, the predecessor to the Chamber of Commerce, had settled on an advertising theme they hoped would market the virtues of Pasadena nationwide. "The Ideal Home City" appeared alongside newspaper mastheads and throughout the Tournament of Roses brochures. Obviously, stories about school beatings and fistfights with whip-wielding Socialists did little to enhance the city's "ideal" and "aristocratic" image.

Hicks' Socialist politics were just as provocative as his heavy-handed school work. To feminists like Charlotte Perkins Gilman, the writer and former Pasadena resident, men like Hicks and their street-fighting ways exposed the violence and male avarice women should disdain. J.J. Hicks belonged to a growing number of Pasadena men who had joined the Socialist party, a prolabor union, anticapital—and in the Western states nearly all white and all male—political party that would cast Eugene V. Debs as its presidential candidate more than once. Founded in 1902, the Pasadena local registered 83 new members within a few years. During the 1906 state convention, Pasadena sent more delegates than any city except Los Angeles. By the end of the first decade, the Pasadena local numbered in the hundreds. Pasadena Socialists held huge rallies under a sprawling tent-like contraption they called the "Socialist wigwam." The rallies would attract 1,500 to 2,000 people who came to listen to left-leaning speakers from around the Western states. "Wild Bill" Haywood came to talk of the miners' fight in Idaho. Presidential candidate Debs and his African-American running mate, the Rev. George Woodbey, came to preach socialism and worker's rights. So did the Socialist mayoral candidate from Los Angeles, Job Harriman. Yet the city's Socialists and labor unions never went so far as to welcome the "Wobblies," the radical International Workers of the World tried more than once to recruit in Pasadena but failed to establish any toehold.[52]

Just before the school election of 1909, it was estimated that there were more than 400 Socialists registered in Pasadena. To the chant of

> "Rah! Rah! Rah!
> From the town of the millionaire
> We're from Pasadena!
> Rah! for the Proletaire!"[53]

The Socialists had become a presence to be reckoned with. During the last school election of the decade, the Socialists had a critical mass that could force its agenda into mainstream party politics. Their success would depend upon party unity and a supportive labor movement. The election became the talk of the town from early May 1909, when the Socialists announced their campaign to elect three from their party to the school board—including the first woman to that office. The day after the early June election it was apparent that, as would occur two years later in Los Angeles, the fusion between labor and socialism had collapsed. Furthermore, it was the Women's Socialist Union (WSU) that failed to support the campaign, a campaign that ironically centered on many women's issues including the employment of married women as teachers.

THE WOMEN'S SOCIALIST UNION AND THE POLITICS OF CLASS

As the male-dominated Socialist party gathered steam early in the decade, many white, middle- and upper-middle-class women in the Western states believed the party was just the opposite of what politics ought to be. The Socialist party, to women like Charlotte Perkins Gilman, was antiwoman. So Gilman and others helped organize a group of like-minded women. It included Ethel Whitehead, a Pasadena seamstress and the daughter of a longtime Socialist. They created a Western states alternative to the male-dominated Socialist party, something they called the Women's Socialist Union.[54]

However, the formation of the WSU split the woman's Socialist movement. The urban, Socialist locals in the East were mixed (men and women), and their mainly ethnic, working-class women tended to be concerned with joining men in proletarian fights. But in California and the West, the WSU locals were distinctly separate from their Socialist brothers (and husbands). Socialist Western women were determined to create a feminine version of socialism organically tied to the women's movement rather than intermingled with the quest for working-class liberation. It was no mistake that the organization's title would begin with "Women" rather than "Socialist."[55]

These Western Socialists were more apt to be native-born white women of some wealth, like Gilman and Whitehead. Their sisters in the East were likely to be foreign-born, often tied to organized labor through their husbands' or their own wage-labor status. These Eastern, ethnic Socialists saw the world differently from their Western sisters. They were more class conscious, and they distrusted the motives of the Western, "bourgeois" women, who were calling for an autonomous Socialist movement for women. For women like Gilman and Whitehead, the Western Women's Socialist Union would ameliorate the constraints the male-oriented culture had created. Whereas Eastern, immigrant women saw class emancipation as a precursor to the overall liberation of women, the WSU rejected that position. "The labor question is also a woman's question," said Gilman, "and the emancipation of women must precede that of the worker."[56] It was an argument, not coincidentally, used by the Socialist male leaders, when they debated the question of race in the American labor movement—Socialist emancipation of the worker first, then the question of "the Negro."[57]

Regardless of the rhetoric of class solidarity used by Gilman and many of her Socialist colleagues, most were too far removed from the means of capitalist production to feel they could affect labor issues. Most of the WSU locals in California and the West were made up of middle-class women, many of whom had never worked as wage laborers. They had a far different agenda for themselves.

The WSU argued that within the male-dominated Socialist party locals, women were never given positions of power and authority. Too many women in charge of refreshments and entertainment meant too few women's concerns being expressed within the socialist platform. A separate political sphere meant that women could practice the skills of organization and leadership denied to them by men. Their goal was, "Women of various classes working together for women's self-determination."[58] They were, at least initially, even reluctant to join the suffrage movement for fear they would lose their autonomy. As historian Mari Jo Buhle has argued, "[T]he preference for separate organizations ... was politically salient." These Western Socialists believed that they could serve their "special interests" only in a separate group. It is ironic that their definition of a separate sphere was at least partially responsible for their undoing. Their reluctance to reach out in a more forceful way kept them from matching action to rhetoric. Then again, it may have been the reluctance of the male Socialist party to accept earlier overtures that helped convince the women that an autonomous organization would best serve the Socialist movement and women's emancipation. Ultimately, though, as historian Buhle and others have argued, women like Gilman knew too little about how "the others" lived to make any meaningful cross-class organizational effort. So they concentrated on a class-bound definition of feminist socialism.[59]

The Pasadena WSU may be the best example of the contradictions inherent in the women's turn-of-the-century Socialist movement. Throughout the Western states and especially in California, the WSU assimilated into local class politics. In other words, in cities like Los Angeles and San Francisco, where the membership was essentially middle class, the WSU seldom came into meaningful contact with working-class women, especially women of color. However, in communities like Oakland, with its largely working-class population, the WSU was more successful in forging a cross-class membership. It would be expected, then, that in a community such as Pasadena, with its penchant for antiworking-class politics and upper-crust women's clubs, the WSU local would be decidedly less inclusive.

The Pasadena local, one of the most active in the state, appears at first glance as a radical union of Socialist sisters engaged in organizing the city's working class, especially Pasadena's working women. These Socialist women participated in fund drives to enable labor to have a meeting hall, organized families into a Socialist Sunday school called "The School of the Red Flag," joined mass Socialist assemblies, and expressed their outrage at the failure of capitalist doctrine to address the needs of the poor and working class.[60] They campaigned for the Mexican trackmen during the 1903 strike and, along with the Central Labor Council in Pasadena, condemned the incarceration of Mexican revolutionaries being illegally detained in Arizona. They called on all working women to join them in the fight. "[The] latch-string of this Union is always out," they told the readers of Common Sense in 1908, "and all women, without regard to race, color, previous condition of servitude, politics or religion, are cordially invited to drop in upon us at any time." Then, undermining their call for cross-class solidarity, the Pasadena WSU organizational meetings were held during the day when working women worked.[61]

Just as their "latch-string" may have been well meaning but contradictory, these Socialist women defy any easy characterization. If they had a leader, it was Ethel Whitehead, a dressmaker. Her father, a widower, was a tailor and one of the founding members of the Pasadena Socialist party. Her brother, John, was a musician and a member of the party but both were not affiliated with any trade or musician's union.[62] From 1905 until the end of 1906, Ethel Whitehead was the principal writer for the Pasadena local in Common Sense. Her articles were lengthy, at times biting, never doctrinaire, and often focused on women's issues. When the Pasadena WSU began to have its own newspaper coverage in 1905, Whitehead wrote both columns. In the winter of 1907, she spoke at the monthly Socialist party meeting about the advantages of a woman's "Worker's Exchange ... where, different articles, such as staples of dairy products and women's productions could be sold or exchanged." She also called for a woman's employment office and a Socialist reading room in the same location. She then handed over a five-dollar bill "as a nucleus of a building fund."[63]

A year later, in March of 1908, 19 of the 20 members mentioned in the newspaper, pledged to protest the Los Angeles city ordinance prohibiting public gatherings without a permit. This "anti-free-speech ordinance" was clearly the doings of the *Times* publisher Otis and his Citizen's Alliance. The lone dissenting WSU vote offered a substitute motion to "tender sympathy" to the L.A. free-speech movement but the majority wanted "more than sympathy." Whether the women actually put themselves on the street corners to test the constitutionality of the ordinance is unknown. What we do know is that the data suggest the women were activists. Were they, though, like other more middle-class locals, focused exclusively on women's issues, or were they engaged in a broader, labor/Socialist agenda? Mattie Hicks, the Socialist plumber's wife, may help answer that question.[64]

On the same day as the free-speech vote, Mattie Hicks, who had seceded Whitehead as president of the local, urged the women to "greater activity in the organized Socialist movement ..." Mattie Hicks, who was one of the first members of the Pasadena WSU, went on to say that the supreme importance of the propaganda for socialism, dominated "all other interests of collective womanhood ..." She called on the membership to devote their "best energies ... to establish the cooperative commonwealth ... under the Socialist party discipline."[65] Hicks' talk is important in that she called for her sisters to put the party before women's concerns—in effect advocating that women's emancipation be subsumed by party doctrine, something Whitehead, who may have been in the audience, would have refused to support. Under Hicks' leadership, could the Pasadena WSU have fractured over the woman's issue? Given Whitehead's prior commitment to "parlor politics" associated with the earlier woman's movement, a split over organizational tactics might very well have spelled the end for the local.[66] Moreover, under Hicks' presidency, the local began to meet in the evening.

The same winter as her "worker's exchange" speech, Ethel Whitehead held an organizing "social" in her family home. The social was reported by *Common Sense*:

> The sock social was given by the Woman's Socialist Union and proved a most enjoyable affair. Each one as they entered received a small red or blue sock that was pinned on the

coat or dress. In this they were requested to place the number of cents corresponding to the sock size. A large stocking was hung by the door into which the small socks were dropped. The rooms were decorated with green ivy and ferns among which was [sic] nestled dainty red socks cut from pasteboard. Socks were of all sizes and shapes and were disposed about the draperies and on the walls bearing mottoes such as "A Socking Socialist Social" "What a Socking Sight" and "Sock It To 'Em."

The evening was made up of poetry readings, a piano solo and a vocal solo. The main speaker discussed Rose Pastor Stokes's poem "Dream of Things." Refreshments were served, and the evening concluded with everyone singing "Auld Lang Syne."[67]

This was not an unusual organizing effort. Under Whitehead's leadership, the Pasadena WSU engaged in "parlor politics," a form of organizing drawn from the earlier club and WCTU movements. Later Socialists like Whitehead solicited new members by creating a more "feminine" setting. Whitehead might have explained, as did one of her contemporaries, that "the social intimacy of women was necessary for carrying out the important work" of the Socialist cause. Once comfortable in their own homes, the women could then move more confidently into the male world. The parlor rather than the saloon better matched the sensibilities of middle-class women.[68]

THE SCHOOL BOARD ELECTION

The 1909 school board campaign began like all prior board elections—quietly, without fanfare. Interested men (nearly always businessmen), some better heeled than others, submitted their names as candidates. James W. Morin, a young attorney who had been educated in Pasadena, was the first to announce his candidacy, on May 6. A few days later, another name appeared, J.D. Macpherson, representing rapidly growing Altadena, an area just north of the city. There were three seats up for election. A current member of the board, J.E. Chamberlain, stated he would stand for re-election; two others would step down. It seemed to school patrons that the list of candidates was always too thin to adequately represent what should be the centerpiece of Pasadena's culture, the city schools. If this election were to be like prior campaigns, a mere 10 percent of the electorate— approximately 600 voters—would cast ballots on election day. Six hundred voters would elect the next school board.[69]

On May 14, the Socialists announced three of their own as board candidates—two men and a woman. Helen Firmin, a Socialist and labor leader, has the distinction of being the first woman in the history of Pasadena to run for any office. Firmin, a thin, wiry-faced, middle-aged woman, was the daughter of an Illinois judge (who, the Socialists claimed, was an "intimate associate of Douglass and Lincoln") and a "successful school teacher." She was president of Pasadena's

Women's Union Label League (WULL), a quasi support group that grew out of the men's Carpenter Union just before the turn of the century. Since then, the Pasadena WULL had taken on a more serious, activist position. Firmin was involved outside the city in labor and Socialist politics, but she apparently had little to do with the WSU. A year before the election, in a national, Socialist *cause celebre,* she was reportedly the first American visitor allowed to confer with three imprisoned Mexican revolutionaries. The three had been arrested—unjustly believed the Socialists—by U.S. federal authorities after they had crossed the border claiming political asylum. The two other Socialist candidates were O.T. Nichols, a Methodist minister, who was active organizing Methodists to the Socialist way, and J.E. Collier, of whom we know little. All three were obviously well-known Socialists, but none were openly endorsed by any trade union. Nichols sometimes took the lead and spoke for the three. Because the city's influential had ignored prior Socialist campaigns, the local paper buried the announcement on page five with the title, "Socialists Want Woman on Board." The reporter said nothing about Firmin or the Socialists' advocacy of women's issues. There was no mention by the Socialists of a campaign platform—just the promise from Hicks that they would be working hard in the next few weeks to get out the vote. Within a week, Firmin and the others were the talk of the town.[70]

On the same day the Socialists announced their intentions, the school board announced they would enforce a one-year moratorium dismissing women teachers whose husbands, the board claimed, were "fully capable" of supporting them. Of the eight targeted for removal, three were wives of school principals or department heads. The local paper, the *Pasadena Daily News*—whose publisher, Lon Chapin, had moved to Pasadena from Los Angeles in 1900—speculated that the board's decision would have consequences for the upcoming election. Chapin's wife was active in the women's club movement in Southern California and had been a prominent figure in earlier efforts to keep the color line intact within the women's clubs in the state. She was also a vitriolic opponent of socialism. *The Daily News* seemed to entertain the idea that this election might turn controversial. Indeed, for the next few weeks until the Socialists made their campaign platform public, married women as teachers was the only school issue that occupied Chapin's paper.[71]

A few days after the Socialists announced their three, a "mass meeting" brought out a dozen or so men to debate who should or should not join the board candidates. Chapin's paper asserted that the board's planned removal of the women had "raised a storm," although *The Daily News* claimed that "most of the women accepted the ruling." We do not know if Chapin meant all women in the city or just the eight targeted for dismissal. Whatever, acceptance does not always convey agreement. Prominent women in the city, which by 1900 had become a leading center of the state's Women's Club movement, had an ideological stake in the outcome of the board's action. Would the socially active women of, for instance, the Shakespeare Club or the Friday Morning Club enter the debate over the question of who is most fit to teach? How would the separate sphere in this aristocratic town be played out? Would the "woman's question" become a school question or would socially prominent women marginalize teachers as little more than "working women"?[72]

If the dearth of candidates concerned anyone, there was little in the newspaper to indicate that any effort was under way to recruit additional candidates. That was until a few weeks before the election when Chapin's paper reported a flurry of activity. Names were "flying in all directions" as candidates "cropped up ... galore." A week before the election, there were nine candidates including the Socialists. If this election were to replicate prior elections, then 600 votes spread between nine candidates—three of which were Socialists—would ensure at least one Socialist the election. It looked as if Pasadena would have its first elected Socialist and, if Hicks' gleeful speculation was accurate, maybe a school board with three Socialists—one of whom was a woman. Then, with just a week before the election, Hicks' party announced its campaign platform, and all hell broke lose.[73]

The Socialist campaign advanced eight principles, and it was apparent that they had drafted a platform that, at least to Chapin, "appealed to a considerable number of people." To Chapin and his friends, this broad Socialist appeal to the city's working class was "especially dangerous." The first two principles or planks of the platform were familiar Socialist campaign promises free textbooks and free medical care. Hicks and the three candidates did not specify if the medical care was for students, teachers or both.[74]

At the national level, earlier Socialist efforts at school reform were, according to historian Kenneth Teitlebaum, too often narrowly conceived notions of equal educational opportunity that paid attention to a "rather mechanistic view of the relationship between capital relations and school practice."[75] The Socialist argument for a more equitable education for working-class children was focused on matters like improved school buildings (or urinals), smaller class size and free books and medical care. Little critical exploration into what really occurred *inside* the schoolhouse framed Socialist discourse.[76] Yet what happened in Pasadena in the 1909 school election can be seen as a harbinger of future Socialist doctrine. Equally important, the election was a tale of what was to come for the city's working-class children.

Apparently Pasadena's Socialists had developed a more complex response to capitalist relations than their comrades elsewhere, because the platform illustrates a rather sophisticated understanding of the relationship between what is today called "the market" and educational practice. The labor/Socialist platform was drafted not only to address the more immediate needs of Pasadena's working class but to erode further the impact industrial capitalism had on educational policy-making. Pasadena's Socialists were responding to a school system that was structurally unresponsive to the needs of the poor and working class. Although Chapin's newspaper tried to turn the election into a referendum on patriotism and the "absurdity of socialist politics," this election had little to do with the emotions evoked by flag-waving or Hicks' eccentricities. This election was about the threat Socialists made for fundamental change in the definition of community and power.[77]

The core of the Socialist platform spoke to the needs of the city's working class. Two of the planks can be seen as expedient. There was to be no discrimination against married teachers and there was to be a significant increase in the grade-school teachers' salary, to $100 a month. The Socialists knew that every elementary school teacher was a woman. They also knew that even if these women could not vote, they had the potential to influence the men in their lives. The Socialists understood that teachers were wage earners and that the promise of $100 a month to a working-class family meant something. Clearly, the Socialists situated women teachers as members of the working class, and, by doing so, advocated a significant shift in the political economy of the city's schools. How would Pasadena's middle class and very wealthy women respond?

The remaining campaign promises struck at the heart of what provoked working-class families about school practice—the impact public education had on the formation of class relations and, by implication, the impact those relations had on their pocketbooks. The platform called for a reduction in the number of hours of after-school study "in order to eliminate a large portion of night work." To the working class, Pasadena's schools failed to take into account that many of the students needed to work for wages after school. Laboring over hours of "night work" or homework had potentially serious consequences for the family's budget. Moreover, having to work after school and then come home to hours of study placed working students at a distinct disadvantage with their more affluent classmates.

In addition to important issues of teacher salaries and study time, the Socialists argued for a modification in the city's classical, liberal arts curriculum. The platform urged the city schools to reflect a curriculum that would "better prepare the pupil more thoroughly for the practical duties of life." The Socialists believed the schools were promoting a two-tiered curriculum. They saw public education advancing a narrow, elite conception of learning that further advantaged wealthy students at the expense of the working class. In Pasadena, the Socialists and organized labor understood the need for schooling as utilitarian *and* intellectual. Aware of the progressive critiques of education by Socialists such as William English Walling, both the trade unionists and Socialists believed that

Pasadena's schools ought to provide the means to a better way of life for every-one. Therefore, they thought public education should focus more on the "practi-cal" than the esoteric.

Since the city's 1884 incorporation, working-class families had come to understand that the system was structured to undercut their children's ability to compete. In an era when social promotion did not exist, working parents knew that too many of their children were being held back after they failed end-of-year examinations. As historian David Tyack has argued, the system was geared to pro-duce failure. The superintendent's annual reports for the years 1900 to 1910 indi-cate that more than 30 percent of all elementary students were retained, mostly in schools with significant working-class populations. Superintendent Arthur Hamilton's system was increasingly focused on a particular set of progressive beliefs that highlighted "saving" the "out of school" child—the "incorrigible boy," as Hamilton put it. Too many children were failing to attend school, so Hamilton and his administrative staff devised plans to bring those children into the fam-ily of public schooling. The irony is that many of the children Hamilton brought into the system had left school because the system had classified them as failures.[78]

The Socialists proposed that the end-of-year test, which resulted in far too many students being retained, be done away with. They proposed that grade-level promotions be "determined by the class work of the pupil not by the final exam-ination." The poor and working-class parent has always known their children to be as inherently capable as their more privileged classmates. By eliminating the single test that favored the more affluent student (who in many instances has access to extra help and was already advantaged by the standard curriculum) and instead relying on the much larger body of work gathered over the entire school year, the Socialists hoped to alter the structural mechanisms that had so badly tilted the schoolhouse playing field.

Finally, Hicks' party endorsed a revision in the state law that required what the working class believed were an excessive number of changes in school text-books. This appears as a contradiction given the campaign promise of free text-books. However, working families knew all too well what costs were encumbered because of these frequent changes. Books that changed year after year could not be passed down from child to child. Someone had to pay for the new books. In keeping with their campaign that the city's schools were not meeting the real edu-cational needs of the working family, the Socialist platform urged changes.

The Socialist platform became public on May 29, six days before the elec-tion. Three days later, on June 2, Chapin's paper called for a mass meeting the next day to name a slate of candidates that could defeat the Socialists. The head-line was telling: "MASS MEETING IS CALLED TO NAME SCHOOL DIRECTORS," as if somehow the city's elite could circumvent the election and name three of their own. Through it all, plumber Hicks remained confident. Possibly sensing the panic around him, he told *The Daily News* that he expected all three Socialists to be elected.[79]

Chapin's strategy to defeat the labor/Socialist ticket was simple yet risky. A "mass meeting," chaired by a respected retired judge, attended by as many "prominent men" as could be found, would be called. They would try to convince the less prominent candidates to withdraw in favor of a slate of "better-known" men. Too many candidates cluttered the ballot and would end up splitting the vote, playing directly into the hands of the labor/Socialist block. Men such as Chapin, Wood and Hahn would be appointed as the "interview committee." Nominations would then be made, a vote taken and the field narrowed.[80] Still, given the seriousness of the election, it was a risky plan because the city's attention was now focused on the Socialists and their prolabor platform. Then a socialite, Mrs. Calvin Hartwell, dropped her bombshell.

On the same day Chapin and the others met to find more suitable candidates, his paper headlined charges by Mrs. Calvin Hartwell (her given name, Mary, was used only once in the press) that Pasadena's schools were a "HOTBED OF SOCIALISM." Hartwell, wife of the Los Angeles county coroner and chairman of the Shakespeare Club's civics committee, said, "There are a dozen Socialists ... among the teachers ..." who are openly "boast[ing] converts to Socialism." Hartwell told *The Daily News,* "People do not realize what is taking place in the schools ..."

> When you simmer it all down, socialism means treachery and traitorism to the country and these are being instilled in the minds of some of our pupils in some of our schools ... I think it is time that we awoke to the situation before a generation is raised up that does not know what socialism really is, but has been led to believe in some fanciful conception of vague and impractical men and women who ... most perversely blind their eyes to the consequences of the doctrines they are instilling in the minds of the young.[81]

What most shocked the community was Hartwell's flagrant charge that these "treacherous" Socialists were teaching Pasadena's children to dishonor the flag. She claimed, "Socialism is opposed to the American government," saying that Socialist party candidate Eugene Debs said "no Socialist can carry the United States flag." Debs said, "They [the Socialists] belong to an international organization, [therefore] they carry the Red Flag." Hartwell had actually twisted Debs' comments to suit her "righteous civics" agenda. Hartwell believed that "mischievous sins both of omission and commission are creeping in ... [and] the pupils are not being grounded in love of country or even respect for its authority." Nearly 40 years before the notorious Red Scare tactics of the McCarthy era, Pasadenans were told by the press that their way of life was threatened from within. Hartwell, through her strident position ("treason in our schools!"), was able to alter the community discourse and divert attention away from the politics of Socialist possibility.

The day after Hartwell's charges appeared—one day before the election—*The Daily News* headlined a series of wire reports, some days old, on the bloody strikes in Pennsylvania's rail yards and at the Northern California lumber mill town of McCloud, where state militia were ordered to shoot any striker who stood in their way. The Philadelphia strike, called by unionized rail workers, was being broken by hundreds of Southern African-American "police" hired by the railroad. In McCloud, lumbermen had struck a company town over pay, working conditions and the right to organize. The majority of the mill men were Italian immigrants, who, *The Daily News* reported, were being provoked by "outside agitators." Chapin's paper had not covered the strikes before this June 3 edition. After the election, the paper was again silent.[82]

The powerful in Pasadena were responding to the threat against a politically "neutral" school system. Politics had "no business in the schools and anyone, Protestant, Catholic, Socialist or otherwise …" *The Daily News* editorialized, had no right to force their beliefs on the children of the community. The day after the election, Chapin's paper argued that the Socialists, by the very nature of their "politico-religious … cult" were "required [to be] propagandists." Teachers "were not supposed to impart any 'ism' or sectarian belief." Yet the Socialists are "radically at variance with the existing order" and, therefore, committed to its destruction. Socialism, *The Daily News* concluded, "teaches irreverence for our institutions and disrespect for the flag that symbolizes them."[83]

Hicks's labor/Socialist alliance never had a chance to respond to Hartwell's charges. Within 24 hours, the polls would open and there was no time to counter the charges of anti-Americanism. The mass meeting Chapin had called was a resounding success. Enough candidates dropped out of the race to narrow the field. The fear that the Socialists were about to seize the city's educational system had been firmly planted by the business class through Chapin's paper and the electorate was convinced that this election was too crucial to ignore. Foreshadowing what would come, automobiles were enlisted for the first time to help get out the vote. Wagon after wagon and automobile after automobile brought voters to the polling place; enough, poll watchers contended, to assure that this school election would be different.[84]

As past practice had allowed, the school board published an official ballot, but Chapin's associates, now referring to themselves as the "Citizen's Ticket," printed their ballot as well. So did the Socialists. One of the independent candidates, Dr. W.A. Cundy, handed out his ballot printed with only his name and then two blank lines. As voters approached the polling place at Wilson School, they would walk through a gauntlet of election workers for every party and candidate. There was no official voter register and no checking of names and addresses. Voters walked to the official table, signed their name and handed over their marked ballot. The secret ballot in this election did not exist, and "... nothing besides the memory of the election officials and that man's sense of decency [kept] him from voting twice." *The Daily News* tabbed the election "queer and amusing." When the ballots were counted late that night, Pasadena was to look to the heavens for the results. If the electric lights were turned off, it signaled that the Citizen's Ticket was the winner. If the Socialists were elected, the lights were to go off twice.[85]

Late that night, Pasadena knew that the Citizen's Ticket had won. The next morning, when the final tally was announced, the community found out that the labor/Socialist alliance had been overwhelmed nearly four to one. Regardless of the impropriety of the election procedure, more than 1,600 ballots had been cast on June 4, more than in any previous school election. The three Socialists received fewer than 250 votes apiece. In an editorial Chapin wrote a few days later, he predicted that the Socialist light would never again shine in the community.[86]

THE POLITICS OF POSSIBILITY

In retrospect, the 1909 schoolboard election offers an insight into the politics of community formation in Southern California. The school election evidenced the struggle between the aspirations of Pasadena's wealth and those of "outsiders"— in this instance, the working class. In a larger sense, the period was one of conflict, when the wealthy's aims for the working class and poor increasingly diverged from the notions of self held by the laboring class and poor. The city's business elite used its numerous community resources, especially their privileged access to the media and political officials, to respond to a threat to what was arguably a nascent social order. Although Pasadena was in its infancy as a community—its institutions, neighborhoods and commercial districts were still evolving—the campaign illustrates how the structural components of capitalist-social relations, put in place by the middle class and wealthy, operated against the working class. Chapin and his "Citizen's Ticket" claimed to defend Pasadena's schools against party politics. In other words, as he editorialized days after the election, the "Citizen's Ticket" was a campaign to "take the schools out of politics."[87] Chapin and his friends did nothing of the sort. What they did was change the political process, as historians David Tyack and Larry Cuban have written, so to "set the agenda of reform, to diagnose problems, to prescribe solutions, and often to influence what should *not* be on the agenda of reform." As Tyack and Cuban remind us, the template of the elite set the dominant pattern of school reform for the next 50 years.[88]

The fusion of labor and Socialists was too weak to support a slate of even moderately progressive candidates. In hindsight, we now know that the labor

Fig. 9. Three views of a rapidly urbanizing Pasadena, all taken from the intersection of Colorado and Fair Oaks. The top left photo was taken in 1887, less than 2 years after the Chinese expulsion. The impressive buildings to the left of the simple storefront (center) replaced the structures burned in the washhouse fire. The top right photo, c. 1890, is looking east from Fair Oaks. The bottom photo, a mere 25 years from the Chinese washhouse fire, was taken in 1910. *(Top left photo courtesy of the Security Pacific Collection, Los Angeles Public Library. Top right photo courtesy of the Pasadena Museum of History and bottom photo courtesy Security Pacific Collection, Los Angeles Public Library.)*

alliance failed to understand the lengths to which the opposition would go to discredit the politics of progressive change. Maybe it was not so ironic that there were trade unionists at Chapin's mass meeting working against the Socialist ticket.[89] The *Citizen* reported that the election was a "laughable affair," but "in all such cases one good results—the placing of the best men before the public for their choice."[90] Certainly not a rousing endorsement from organized labor. The rift that had for years defined labor/Socialist infighting could not be overcome during the campaign of 1909. This, even with the professed similarities between labor's goals and Socialist doctrine. The campaign and the subsequent *Los Angeles Times* bombing ended any real participation by labor's left wing in the politics of Progressive-era Southern California. Some historians contend that the bombing and the subsequent trial of the McNamara brothers effectively ended any real worker movement in the country.[91]

What is perhaps most confusing is the absence of the WSU in the campaign. Where were Ethel Whitehead and her Socialist sisters throughout the election? After Mattie Hicks's call for party unity in 1908, the Pasadena WSU appears less and less in local politics. Sometime around the election, Whitehead stopped writing her Pasadena column for the Socialist newspaper *Common Sense*. During the school board election, there was nary a WSU word in the local press, the *Common Sense,* or the trade union *Citizen.* This remains a mystery, although, given the concerns generally expressed by the WSU, the election of working-class Socialists and even a Socialist working woman was not in its perceived best interest. The WSU typically shunned political office and was more than once critical of the labor/Socialist Party fusion as decidedly male and self-serving. To a majority of the WSU membership, the slate of labor/Socialist candidates may very well have been more a cadre of labor than a Socialist cadre. More than likely, under Hicks' leadership, the WSU may have become an auxiliary of the Socialist party, therefore losing much of its autonomy.

Clearly the WSU voice was missing from the campaign. By not initially allying with working women, they lost their opportunity under Whitehead to forge a true cross-class coalition. By not working closely with working men and women, the WSU failed to help organize enough of a broad-based constituency to effectively counter Hartwell and her accusations and Chapin with his Citizen's Ticket. Under Hicks' presidency, they may very well have been subsumed by the male-dominated labor/Socialist party fusion. Whatever the reason, by not reaching out to form a multiethnic, multiclass perspective on women's concerns, Pasadena's more radical women would ultimately end up leaving social policy, the very heart of the woman's movement, to Pasadena's wealthy and conservative women and men. Although the WSU and other women's organizations pushed for even greater benefits for women and children before World War I, "child saving" in Pasadena was essentially the work of moderate to conservative women, who believed in a more minimalist approach. In the Western states, too often the more radical women would speak for the working class but choose not to include the working class in their organizations.[92] Beginning with the election of 1909, the intent of public education in Pasadena would be cloaked in pronouncements of equity and democracy for the masses yet, as we shall soon see, in practice the schools would increasingly serve as an agency for social stratification.

At its most sanguine, the city's hierarchy hoped to create a community that met the needs of all its children. It was in creating the definition of those needs, however, that wealth and the middle class separated from the laboring class and poor. By the 1920s, the city had become a national model for the scientific use of intelligence testing. Every child was tested, interviewed and then guided into his or her "scientifically determined" course of study. The city adopted the progressive but unconventional 6-4-4 Plan of school organization, beginning with six years of elementary, then four years of junior high school, followed by four years of high school. In reality, students did not spend eight years in junior/senior high school, but rather the 6-4-4 Plan added a voluntary first two years of college to the end of high school. The junior high/high school plan ended up meaning that the more wealthy clientele had choices beyond the conventional. By the time the plan was in place, Pasadena had created a vocational or manual arts high school to meet the needs of the "others." By the 1920s, the debate over the usefulness of manual arts in the middle-class community no longer existed. Manual arts were now vocational arts. Black and Mexican students attended schools where IQ tests told them that vocational skills were best suited to their talents. More affluent, white students learned that the IQ tests underscored their talents as professionals, teachers, engineers and businessmen. The vocational, manual arts high school was where the great majority of black, Mexican and Japanese students went to school. In the 1930s, as the population of students of color continued to increase, Pasadena High School admitted fewer and fewer black students. Ironically, the manual arts high school that ended up meeting the needs of black, Mexican and Japanese students was named after the naturalist John Muir, a man who had spent his adult life championing nature's dispossessed.

NOTES

1. Unless otherwise noted, all quotes are from Charlotte Perkins Gilman's autobiography, *The Living of Charlotte Perkins Gilman,* (New York: D. Appleton-Century Company, 1935).
2. Ibid., p. 91, 93–95.
3. Ibid., p. 93–94
4. Ibid., p. 95–96
5. Ibid., p. 108
6. Ibid., p. 107–108; Mark Pittenger, *American Socialists and Evolutionary Thought, 1870–1920* (Madison: University of Wisconsin Press, 1993) p. 72–86.
7. Gilman, p. 131–132; Ann J. Lane, *Her Land and Beyond: The Life and Work of Charlotte Perkins Gilman* (New York: Pantheon Press, 1990) p. 230–232.
8. Pittenger, p. 74.

9. Gilman, p. 111: Pittenger, p. 72–73.
10. Pittenger, p. 70. Also see the introduction in Larry Ceplair's edited volume of Gilman essays, *Charlotte Perkins Gilman: A Nonfiction Reader* (New York: Columbia University Press, 1991) p. 29–31; Mary Hill, *Charlotte Perkins Gilman: The Making of a Radical Feminist, 1860–1896* (Philadelphia: Temple University Press, 1980) p. 170–173.
11. Gilman, "Human Nature," cited in Ceplair, p. 50.
12. Ibid., p. 46.
13. Lane, p. 230–232.
14. Gilman, "Human Nature," as cited in Ceplair, p. 50.
15. Gilman, p. 129–131; Pittenger, p. 73–74.
16. Gilman, "Human Nature," cited in Ceplair, p. 53; Pittenger, p. 75, and George Cotkin, "Working-Class Intellectuals and Evolutionary Thought in America, 1870–1915" (Ph.D. diss., Ohio State University, 1978) p. 3, 124–145.
17. Lane, p. 124–125; Pittenger, p. 72–88.
18. Gilman, "The Negro Problem ..." cited in Lane, p. 176.
19. Ibid., p. 178.
20. Pittenger, p. 186.
21. Lane, p. 157.
22. For a full examination of the women's movement and Socialism, see Mary Jo Buhle, *Women and American Socialism, 1870–1920* (Champaign: University of Illinois Press, 1981) and Sherry Katz, "Dual Commitments: Feminism, Socialism and Women's Political Activism in California, 1890–1920" (Ph.D. diss., University of California, Los Angeles, 1991).
23. Gilman, p. 131–134.
24. "Charlotte Gilman: the 1880s Gloria Steinem," *Pasadena Star-News*, 3 November 1988, p. 4.
25. Gilman, p. 129; Pittenger, p. 86–87; "Immigration Scored in Lecture," *Pasadena Star-News*, 10 March 1926; "Death Takes Noted Poet," *Pasadena Star-News*, 20 August 1935, p. 8.
26. "Pasadena's Lincoln Triangle," *The Los Angeles Times*, 6 August 1987, San Gabriel Valley section, IX-p. 1; "City Keeps Local Landmark on the Map Renovation: Former home of feminist Charlotte Perkins Gilman is relocated, where it will be refurbished and sold as low-income housing." *The Los Angeles Times*, 16 May 1993.
27. "Council of Labor," *Union Labor News*, 18 December 1903, p. 4; Stimson, p. 274–277.
28. Ibid.
29. "Political Economy," *Union Labor News*, 10 November 1905, p. 5.
30. "To the Patrons of *Citizen*," *The Citizen*, 7 August 1908, p. 1 (hereafter cited as *Citizen*).
31. Carey McWilliams, *Southern California Country* (Freeport: Books for Libraries Press, 1946, reprint, 1970). See especially the chapter, "The Politics of Utopia," p. 273–313.
32. Stimson, p. 258; "Citizens Alliance," mentioned in Pasadena in "Pasadena Department," *Citizen*, 26 July 1907, p. 3; "Here and There," *Citizen*, 2 August 1907, p. 4; see Stimson, p. 36, for "Otistown" quote.
33. See Keyes's many reports in *The Citizen*. Also see Paul Greenstein, *Bread and Hyacinths: The Rise and Fall of Utopian Los Angeles* (Los Angeles: California Classic Books, 1992).
34. Stimson, p. 324; Greenstein, p. 23–24, 35; "The Los Angeles Election," *Citizen*, 10 May 1910, p. 1.
35. Stimson, p. 366–406.
36. J. Anthony Lukas, *Big Trouble* (New York: Simon and Schuster, 1997) p. 751.
37. Stimson, p. 407–430; Greenstein, p. 68.

38. In 1915, Socialist Upton Sinclair moved to Pasadena to play tennis, enjoy the heat and dry air, and partake in his vegetarian diet of dried fruits and nuts. When asked why he moved to the richest city in America, he wrote, "But wherever there are millionaires there are also Socialists—they are cause and effect." Soon thereafter he became acculturated into the community's Socialist circle, which included the eccentric Kate Crane-Gartz, widow of the multimillionaire plumber from Chicago, Charles Crane who had helped finance Jane Addams's Hull House. Upton Sinclair, *The Autobiography of Upton Sinclair* (New York: Harcourt, Brace, and World, Inc., 1962) p. 213–214. On Pasadena's "gadfly" Socialists, see Kevin Starr, *Inventing the Dream: California Through the Progressive Era* (New York: Oxford University Press, 1985) p. 211–214.

39. There is no working-class history of Pasadena. This book serves as a starting point. See the many issues of the American Federation of Labor–affiliated newspaper, *The Citizen,* published by the Los Angeles Central Labor Council. For references to sympathetic mayors, see "Labor Day Association," 23 August 1907, p. 2. For references on city council elections and appointments, see "Pasadena Department," 10 August 1908, p. 3; "Pasadena Department," 12 March 1909, p. 2 and "The Pasadena Department," 9 April 1909, p. 4. For references on municipal ownership of water and power, see "Town Topics," 11 December 1908, p. 2, "Here and There," 26 July 1907, p. 6, "Pasadena Department," 30 August 1907, p. 4, "Here and There," 11 October 1907, p. 5, "Here and There," 20 December 1907, p. 6 and "The Reason Why," 22 March 1907, p. 3. For references on construction sites, "Pasadena Department," 29 April 1910, p. 3. For references on school construction and repairs, "Pasadena Department," 23 May 1907, p. 4, "Here and There," 14 June 1907, p. 5, "Pasadena Department," 12 February 1909, p. 2. For references on Pasadena merchants buying advertising in *The Citizen,* see Stimson, p. 236.

40. "Labor Day Association," *Citizen,* 30 August 1907, p. 4. Also see, Michael Kazin and Steven Ross, "America's Labor Day: The Dilemma of a Workers' Celebration," *Journal of American History* 78:4 (March 1992) p. 1294–1323.

41. In 1907, the Pasadena Central Labor Council, one of only three Central Labor Councils in Southern California—the others being Los Angeles and San Pedro—called for a parade through the streets of Pasadena. The parade included floats, bands and workhorses under the care of the Humane Society. Pasadena's unions were often critical of the Tournament of Roses officials who were accused of occasionally abusing animals in the New Year's parade. The Labor Day parade stretched for more than a mile and took well over an hour to view. Sitting alongside the union leadership in the procession's second car was the mayor and the city council. The first car was filled with members of the Women's Union Labor League. See "Labor Day Association," *Citizen,* 16 August 1907, p. 4; "Labor Day Association," 23 August 1907, p. 6; "Pasadena to Honor Men Who Toil," 30 August 1907; *Pasadena Daily News,* p. 2. For a description of the 1909 festivities, see the "Labor Day Program," *Citizen,* 3 September 1909, p. 4.

42. "Labor Day Program," *Citizen,* 3 September 1909, p. 4–5.

43. For references to the Japanese, see "Town Politics," *Citizen,* 7 May 1909, p. 2; "Pasadena Department," 23 May 1907. One of the earliest restaurants in the city was the Mikado, owned and operated for years by a Japanese family. The "well treated" comment comes from a remark made by producers of the 1984 centennial video, "The Changing Rose" a history of the African American community in Pasadena.

44. The *Citizen* reported the admission of a black carpenter to the union in "Carpenters 769," 10 May 1907; see the editorials of the *Citizen,* 14 November 1911, p. 1, and 27 September 1907, p. 2, which urged better relations with black workers in Los Angeles and makes

reference to "many colored workers" as members of trade unions. However supportive, The
Citizen editorial called for wariness on the part of labor as the antiunion forces in Los
Angeles were attempting to flood the market with cheap (black and Chinese) labor.

45.   On AFL organizing of women in laundries, see Simpson, p. 244–246; see the *Citizen,*
"Laundry Workers No. 79," 25 August 1911, p. 4 on women elected as union leaders.

46.   "Here and There," *Citizen,* 20 July 1906, p. 3.

47.   "Contracts Awarded," *Citizen,* 24 July 1908, p. 3; "Town Topics," 1 January 1909, p. 2;
"Pasadena Department," 29 January 1909, p. 3.

48.   "Pasadena Department," *Citizen,* 4 June 1907, p. 3; Pasadena Board of Education, Minutes,
23 April 1907.

49.   "Notes and Personals," *Citizen,* 19 July 1907, p. 3.

50.   "Socialist and Teacher in Pasadena in Fistic Affray," *Pasadena Daily News,* 5 February 1909,
p. 1. Hicks wrote *The Citizen* editorial. See "Hicks vs. Thompson," 12 February 1909, p. 3.
In addition to Hicks's objections to Thompson, *The Citizen* quoted the plumber as saying
his children had been singled out because they had defended "two little white girls" who
were being accosted by older "colored children" outside the Roosevelt School grounds.

51.   "Hicks vs. Thompson," *Citizen,* 12 February 1909, p. 3.

52.   The Pasadena local was organized by John Murray, who was editor of the *Los Angeles
Socialist,* and one of the most influential labor/Socialist leaders in the country; see Stimson,
p. 226; "Pasadena," 1 February 1902, *Los Angeles Socialist,* p. 2; "Pasadena Active," 19 April
1902, p. 4, "Murray Speaks at Pasadena," 12 April 1902, p. 5; on the "wigwam," see
Common Sense, "The Pasadena Wigwam," 22 October 1904, p. 1; Heywood coming to
Pasadena, "Haywood to Speak," Citizen 19 February 1909, p. 8. For comments on
Woodbey, see Phillip S. Foner, *American Socialism and Black Americans* (Westport:
Greenwood Press, 1977) p. 153–173. For comments on the rejection of the IWW, "Want
No Union Busters," *Union Labor News,* 23 March 1906, p. 6.

53.   "Pasadena Wigwam," *Common Sense,* 22 October 1904, p. 1.

54.   The authority on the Women's Socialist Union is Sherry Katz, "Dual Commitments:
Feminism, Socialism, and Women's Political Activism in California, 1890–1920" (Ph.D.
diss., University of California, Los Angeles, 1991). Also see Mari Jo Buhle, *Women and
American Socialism, 1870–1920,* cited above. Buhle refers to the W.S.U. as "socialist
women's clubs ..." p. 106.

55.   Buhle p. 107, 138; Katz, p. 103–104.

56.   The "bourgeois" quote is found in Buhle, p. 107; Katz, p. 112–134.

57.   Foner, p. 110–115. Debs wrote in 1903 "The Negro in the Class Struggle," in the
International Socialist Review (4 November 1903) p. 258–260, that "blacks were not one
whit worse off" than whites and that there was no Negro problem "apart from the general
labor problem ... we have nothing special to offer the Negro ... The Socialist Party is the
Party of the whole working class regardless of color." Cited in Foner, p. 114. Also see Katz,
p. 175.

58.   Katz, p. 133.

59.   Katz, p. 157; Buhle, p. 107, 118–140.

60.   The Pasadena Socialist Sunday School was given the title of "The School of the Red Flag"
by Ethel Whitehead, the principal founder and later the president of the WSU. See Katz, p.
170–173. Also see Kenneth Teitlebaum, *Schooling for "Good Rebels" Socialism, American
Education, and the Search for Radical Curriculum* (New York: Teachers College Press, 1995)
p. 48, 169. In *The Citizen,* "Sunday School Bazaar," 4 December 1908, p. 2, "Santa Claus
on a Donkey," 1 January 1909, p. 2; in *Common Sense,* "Socialist Sunday School in Pasa-

dena," 25 May 1907, p. 6. On the WSU speaking out on capitalist doctrine, see the many articles by Ethel Whitehead in *Common Sense*, all "Pasadena Department," 13, 21, 28 October 1906 and 2 February 1907. On the Mexican trackmen, see *Common Sense*, "Huntington's Receipt for Skinning Car Men," 3 May 1902. On the arrest of the Mexican revolutionaries, see *The Citizen*, "Resolution of the Pasadena Central Labor Council," 1 February 1908, p. 8.

61. "Pasadena Women Socialist," *Common Sense*, 10 January 1908, p. 6.
62. *Thurston's Directory of Pasadena* ((Pasadena: The Thurston Company) 1906–07; 1908–09; 1911.
63. "Pasadena Department," *Common Sense*, 2 February 1907, p. 7.
64. "Pasadena Women Ready: Will Support Free Speech Campaign," *Common Speech*, 21 March 1908, p. 4.
65. Ibid.
66. Katz, p. 158. For the tag, "aristocratic," we can thank John Murray, who announced in the *Los Angeles Socialist* on 12 April 1902, "The aristocratic town of Pasadena is not without its revolutionists. The Socialist party at that place has secured a hall at the corner of Fair Oaks and Colorado streets where the gospel of discontent will be preached every Sunday evening."
67. "Pasadena Department," *Common Sense*, 9 February 1907, p. 6.
68. Buhle, p. 112–113. For an early treatment on the "centrality of social events and personal relations in building political structures," see Catherine Allegor, *Parlor Politics: In Which the Ladies of Washington Help Build a City and a Government* (Charlottesville: University of Virginia Press, 2000).
69. "Candidates for School Board," *Daily News*, 6 May 1909, p. 1.
70. "Socialists Want Woman on Board," *Daily News*, 14 May 1909, p. 5.
71. "Married Women Teach No More," *Daily News*, 14 May 1909, p. 7; Gayle Gullett, *Becoming Citizens: The Emergence and Development of the California Women's Movement, 1880–1911*, (Champaign: University of Illinois Press, 2000) p. 112–114.
72. "School Board to Hear Woes," *Daily News*, 17 May 1909, p. 2.
73. "School Trustees By the Dozen," *Daily News*, 17 May 1909, p. 7.
74. "More Money to Teachers of Grades," *Daily News*, 29 May 1909, p. 7. Chapin's comments came in the editorial of the same edition, p. 4.
75. Teitlebaum, p. 23.
76. Ibid.
77. "Editorial," *Daily News*, 29 May, 1909, p. 4.
78. *Annual Report of the Pasadena City Schools*, 1912, Jeremiah M. Rhodes, Superintendent, Pasadena, California, "Comparative Statistics of Promotions and Non-Promotions" 1907–1912, p. 63. Superintendent Hamilton's comments on "saving" children are found in his *Annual Report*, 1908–1909, p. 18–20. David Tyack and Larry Cuban, *Tinkering Toward Utopia* (Cambridge: Harvard University Press, 1995) p. 90–91.
79. "Fear Result of School Election," *Daily News*, 1 June 1909, p. 1; "Mass Meeting Called To Name School Directors," *Daily News*, 2 June 1909, p. 1.
80. "School Board Election Will Determine Fate of Candidates," *Daily News*, 1 June 1909, p. 3. More than 150 men attended the "mass meeting." There was no mention of Firmin in the audience, although the other two Socialist candidates were present. O.T. Nichols told the gathering that the Socialists would not participate in the discussion, apparently concerned that any outcome from the "town meeting" might jeopardize the Socialist campaign.
81. "Are Schools Hotbed Socialism [sic]" *Daily News*, 2 June 1909, p. 2.

82. "Martial Law Declared," and "Strikers in Philadelphia Increasing," D*aily News,* 3 June 1909, p. 1.
83. "What is Socialism?" *Daily News,* 4 June 1909, p. 10.
84. "Citizen Ticket is Declared Winner," *Daily News,* 5 June 1909, p. 2, 9.
85. Ibid.
86. "Have Met the Issue," *Daily News,* 7 June 1909, p. 4.
87. Ibid.
88. Tyack and Cuban, p. 8–9.
89. "School Board Election Will Determine Fate of Candidates," *Daily News,* 1 June 1909, p. 1. J.W. Chick, a trade union official, was active at the meeting.
90. "School Board Election," *Citizen,* 11 June 1909, p. 2.
91. Stimpson, p. 366–430; George Mowry, *The California Progressives* (Berkeley: The University of California Press, 1951) p. 46–56.
92. Sherry Katz, "Socialist Women and Progressive Reform," *California Progressivism Revisited,* eds. William Deverell and Tom Sitton (Berkeley: University of California Press, 1994) p. 117–143.

CHAPTER 4

COMING OF AGE IN THE NEW SOUTH
Urbanity and Schooling in the Old Dominion, 1900–1940

During the early summer of 1905, in between reading about the weather and its effects on the apple crop, thoughtful readers of Charlottesville's two dailies may have taken note of events on the other side of the world. It appeared Czarist Russia was about to collapse. With violent worker strikes and Cossack atrocities against them, troops repeatedly clashed with rioters in Moscow and other major cities. Czar Nicholas was rejecting any demands for change; the old Russia of Catherine the Great and Peter was in chaos. In June, headlines reported that sailors aboard the Russian battleship *Potemkin*, outraged when a fellow sailor was shot for protesting his maggot-infested meat rations, mutinied, shooting their captain and several officers and unceremoniously throwing the others overboard. Newspaper wire reports lacked detail, but Charlottesville's readers knew the battleship, now under the mutineers' command, had steamed to Odessa harbor in support of thousands of striking workers in that city. Just days before the *Potemkin* mutiny, Cossacks had gunned down Odessa demonstrators who were afire over the Czar's iron-fisted rule. When the *Potemkin* sailed into Odessa harbor, the city was in open rebellion. Surely the old empire was about to come undone.[1]

During that long, hot summer of 1905, Charlottesville also read of other revolutions much closer to home. Since the conclusion of the Constitutional Convention of 1903, Virginia had been abuzz with talk of fundamental changes to the structure of the Old Dominion. Now that the new Constitution had "redeemed" Virginia from the destruction wrought by the evils of Reconstruction and the black franchise, Charlottesville read about the "school campaigns" that were energizing the region, all in the name of the "New Education." Indeed, the entire South was being awakened to the ideas of Progressive-era America. Throughout the region, huge rallies, purposely reminiscent of evangelical tent revivals, criticized the shopworn ways of the Old South. Prominent speakers promised that new methods in commerce, industry, government and education would lead to increased profits, both material and cultural.

In July 1905, James Alderman (the distinguished North Carolinian educator recently appointed president of the University of Virginia) was in New Haven, Connecticut, speaking to a gathering of notable Yale alumni. He told the audience of mainly Northern business and government leaders that it was time for the North and South to "march all one way to the music of national progress and righteousness."[2] Alderman went on to propose a student exchange between Northern and Southern colleges and universities. "I suggest that Northern boys come down South, preferably to Virginia, of course. There ..." he went on to say,

> among the people and in the land, they could teach and learn many valuable things, teaching us power and patience and orderly achievement, and learning—I won't say what, but I believe there is something good to learn of a people who have suffered for ideals and clung to loyalties, who are homogeneous in blood and who exalt personality and conduct.

Alderman's speech—the *Charlottesville Daily Progress* called it a "brilliant effort" and headlined his talk "Idealism Has Ruled America"—is important, for it mirrors what Southern reformers believed was fundamental to the South's advance into the 20th century as equals with the progressive North. Throughout the states of the old confederacy, from Virginia and North Carolina to the black belt of Alabama and Mississippi, the reformist leaders—all well-off, young, white males—campaigned for a "New South" that would ironically spring from the rejection of the Jeffersonian ideal of "democracy of the masses."

As in Russia, Southerners sensed the eminent collapse of the old order and, just as in far-off Pasadena, Charlottesville would clamor to adopt the much ballyhooed practices of industrial America: workplace efficiency through order, regulation and standardization, all tightly managed within a highly centralized bureaucracy. Southerners would apply these progressive methods to everything from markets to schools. To those bent on changing the future, embracing the tenets of Northern capitalism would usher their backward region out of its fettered allegiance to the gods of localism and parochialism. As one Virginia historian wrote, "It was urgent that ... Virginians move forward out of a world of inertia, poverty and parochialism and into an environment of energy, growth and cosmopolitanism."[3] Ironically, reformers came to understand that for the South to embrace the idealism that Alderman believed had ruled America, they would need to convince their fellow Southerners that it was in their best interests to abandon what they may have loved most about the South, the "democracy" of their small towns and villages.[4]

In the early years of the new century, Virginia reformers had begun to argue that the traditional notions of democracy, through local control, had masked contempt for needed social change. To one Virginia reformer, the villages and hamlets of the state were at a "stupid standstill" controlled by "poor and ignorant" citizens who were only "semi-civilized."[5] These were harsh words for communities that were exalted as the Jeffersonian ideal of a nation of small farmers a generation before. Alderman and his fellow reformers were relentless; the South would be remade for the "good of the country," a theme that was fast becoming common talk during the early decades of the 20th century. The South could only join the family of modern states if they collectively rejected the old ways. Northerners had embraced what early 20th-century reformers called "cooperative" democracy; cultural "betterment" could not rely on the old ways of "rugged individualism" and "democracy by the masses." The reform effort, however, was not to democratize the New South. Quite the opposite, progress, at least to Alderman and the elite cadre of reformers, was dependent upon the distribution of power (and ultimately profit) from the top down.[6]

As Alderman stressed in his 1905 Yale speech, the movement to "democratize" Southern society would, by unquestioned necessity, begin in the schools. The "New Education" of the New South was to expand and solidify a hybrid industrial/commercial culture that was to be highly stratified and bureaucratic. Schools were the training ground for the New South, and teachers would be, in the words of another North Carolinian reformist Walter Hines Page, "the servants of democracy ..."[7] There, in the "progressive" classroom, the new Southern citizen would come to embrace cooperation and organization instead of individualism and isolation. The expected changes would imbue the South with a "new sense of nationality."[8] Interestingly, a generation later, during the Depression of the 1930s, many of these same "servants of democracy" were espousing a radical progressivism called "social reconstruction," as they called for "cooperative planning" and an end to America's century-old love affair with "rugged individualism." They were attacked as "communists" because they favored the redistribution of wealth, ideological territory that turn-of-the-century Southern reformers like Alderman distained.

Early on, Alderman and his fellow reformers understood that to successfully reconstruct Southern society would require huge sums of money, funds the nearly bankrupt state governments did not possess. Further, any idea that the federal government could—or would—subsidize Southern social reform on such a magnitude was clearly out of the question. Southerners, fresh from the meddlesome doings of Northerners such as Anna Gardner, and their Radical Reconstruction feared that the federal government would tamper with Southern racial proclivities. So, Alderman and others turned to private interests. In what came to be known as the Southern School Campaigns, giant, Northern philanthropic resources, like the Rockefeller and Slater fortunes, were enlisted to finance the education of the New South. Under the auspices of the Southern Education Board (SEB), of which Alderman was a founding member, and later the General Education Board (GEB), Rockefeller and others fed nearly $150 million to

Southern states for school and health reforms by 1930. This was money reform-minded Southerners desperately needed if the Old South was to be reinvented in the image of the progressive North.

The irony of the New Education in the New South was found in the strati-fied, hierarchical nature of the schools. School reformers advocated a more cen-tralized, cooperative, efficient "democratic" system by limiting the democratic nature of local control. In his Yale speech, Alderman called for Northern students to come south and "teach us power, patience, and orderly achievement," traits he thought were in short supply. One might argue that Alderman contradicted his calls for an end to Southern traditionalism when he suggested Northerners might learn something from a people who had suffered for their traditions for so long. More important, though, was Alderman's reminder to his audience of the South's racial homogeneity, for this reform impulse was to be built on the bedrock of white power.

SCHOOLING AND THE BIRACIAL STATE

Many believed that a progressive-minded South would reap benefits for the entire nation, so it was in the national interest that the South's racial views should be left unexamined by Northern philanthropists. With Robert Ogden, the New York department store magnate presiding over the GEB, funds flowed south without entangling racial strings. The state constitutional conventions during the first decade of the 20th century effectively disenfranchised black voters. Increasingly strict segregation laws further divided the region into two cultural zones, one white with potential upward mobility for most (but not all), the other black and severely constricted for all. Yet these influential philanthropic agencies lent their support to the biracial state in the name of national reconciliation and the public good.

To better understand the North's complicity with Southern segregation, one needs to situate the racial doublethink in national turn-of-the-century social rela-tions and political economy. Middle-class Southern reformers, along with their ideological brethren in the North, had come to see regional regeneration as dependent on a pacified, complacent labor force. The previous 40 years had seen Southern society ripped by a brutal war; Reconstruction; white, working-class populism; and racial violence. Any hope for a rebuilt Southern economy would require a stability the South had not experienced since before the Civil War. When Alderman wrote that "to educate one untaught white man is worth more to the black man himself than the education of ten Negroes," he was placating white resistance to black education as much as he was reinforcing the emerging racial order of the New South.[9] Reformists believed that it was imperative for the descendants of ex-slaves to understand that denying them access to an equal public education would, in the long term, benefit everyone. In a now all too familiar trickle-down narrative, white social reformers called on blacks to be patient. "The less the Negro talks about his civic rights under the Constitution," wrote a Presbyterian minister in New York in 1916, "particularly his right of suffrage, the sooner he will attain all the rights that justly belong to him."[10] White Southerners feared Northern interference in education reform and made it clear that the money was welcome but not at the expense of "our customs."[11]

Even though Ogden and the other Northerners involved with the GEB were reportedly put off by the South's racial politics, they still chose a reform agenda that put white education ahead of any aid for black schooling. The internal workings of the two boards reflected the strictly racialized lines of Southern society. All meetings of the GEB and the SEB were segregated: no public displays of any kind suggested that racial equality was tolerated. Contacts with black leadership were beyond the public eye, often through intermediaries. It should be understood that the racialized funding was not without its critics. Booker T. Washington, who most whites believed was the embodiment of the "good Negro," was more than a little skeptical. Though Washington once promised Northern business that his accomodational approach to black uplift would deliver a "Negro labor force that would avoid unions and radicalism," he strongly criticized the white education campaigns as meaning "almost nothing so far as the Negro schools are concerned." Washington's complaint meant little to Alderman and his Virginia reform group.[12]

The decision by the GEB and SEB to concentrate first on white school reform was justified as politically pragmatic.[13] Historians such as Louis Harlan and James McPherson have argued that philanthropists had but one choice— support the existing social order or see the reform movement collapse and the South retreat further from modernity. Given the severity of Southern racial antipathies, coupled with fears of Northern interference that had lingered since Reconstruction, any reform movement directed at Southern society would, by necessity, need to avoid direct criticism of Southern racial mores. According to historians Harlan and McPherson, to ignore the fact that Southern society rested on a foundation of white over black—or worse, to entertain ideas of racial justice—was political folly.

Northern and Southern white school reformers in both regions had accepted the severity of Southern racism as a legitimate response to the post Reconstruction "New Negro." Well before the first trickle of Rockefeller money, Southerners had begun to rally around a tale of redemption and moral reconciliation that helped ease the postwar feelings of inadequacy and loss. After the Civil War, Southern whites, longing for an imagined past of the "good darkie" like those found in the tales of Uncle Remus, began to construct a narrative of Southern society that rationalized the impact slavery had on Africans. By the second decade of the 20th century, the myth that the antebellum plantation had begun to "civilize" a "barbaric people" was firmly planted in Southern thought. The slave trade had actually "rescued" Africans from "savagery." This "seepage of the imagined past," as historian Grace Elizabeth Hale has written, infected the minds of Southern whites as "the truths of Southern history."[14]

This narrative of redemption has spread well beyond the borders of the South. Northerners, too, read of slave owners who had "Christianized" the Africans, bringing them out of their "fetishes," civilizing them away from their "tribes" and "cannibalism." This redemption narrative spun the historical record on its head: Reconstruction, not the war to end slavery, was the evil that ruined the South. D.W. Griffith's *The Birth of a Nation,* the 1915 film that depicted a reconstructed South gone mad, succinctly captured the main themes of the narrative, showing how Northern "carpetbaggers" and Southern "scalawags" conspired with the former slaves to rape the Old South of its virtue. The "true history" of the slaveholding South conveniently inverted this apologist myth to show that it was now the white slave holder who wore the shackles, not the African slave. By the turn of the century, Southerners and many Northerners had come to believe that Reconstruction had twisted the largely imagined "good slave" of the plantation into a beast. The now benevolent New South was positioned to rescue the nation from the deranged black man.[15] Indeed, the redeemers had romanticized the plantation Old South into a pathological New South.

Southern whites invented black inferiority. After Reconstruction, they went about creating the apparatus to fit the model. The rationalizing myth of black subordination went something like this:

- African Americans were inferior because they were uneducated;
- they were uneducated because they attended schools that were inferior to white schools;
- they were a child-like race and, therefore, could not vote because they were unworthy of the franchise;
- they overbred because they were primitive and, like all children, were prone to give in to their urges;
- the most primitive black men deserved lynching because they were beasts bent on violating the wives and daughters of white men.

The segregated South—and a complicit North—created the biracial state for the common good of the nation.[16] This redemption motif has been so tightly wound that a century later nearly all analyses of the plight of the African American remain strangely disconnected from slavery.

THE NEW SOUTH AND UNIVERSAL EDUCATION

During the first decade of the 20th century, reformers began to articulate a new vision of universal education that included, in different spheres, both white and black. The new vision that Alderman, Robert Ogden and others advanced relied on the belief that any hope of a reunited nation lay with a pacified Afro Southerner. The smooth flow of commerce through an industrialized and urbanized South depended on a compliant black population. A coalition of Northern businessmen associated with the GEB, and Southern reformers, like Alderman and Hines, pointed to the booming Northern and Western states that had adopted a particular form of universal education that schooled workers in the new economy. The mission of the "New Education" was to teach more than the mechanical skills needed in the factory. Its apostles were advocating an educational enterprise that better socialized the working class to the aims of the new industrial capitalism. Reform advocates made no pretensions that the new education would lead workers to believe they could cross class lines.[17]

The Southern school campaigns were not without detractors. Initially (and especially in the black belt region of the lower South), school reformers ran headlong into the old, entrenched planter class. These elite, aristocratic landholders, had for generations derived their wealth through the exploitation of their field labor. Before the war, African slaves worked the land; after the war, it was poor whites and ex-slaves who were bound to the land as tenant farmers. To the planter class, education demeaned laborers by giving them the "unnatural" aspirations of status and mobility. It made the field hand "uppity." Southern landlords were fearful that literate field hands would abandon the land in favor of the promise of more lucrative employment in cities, especially northern cities.

During the first two decades of the education campaign, the debates within school reform circles, both North and South, were aimed at alleviating planter resistance to universal public education. At first the state crusades focused on white-only reforms. In Virginia, for example, reformers made no mention of black education for the first three years of the campaign. Like good progressives everywhere, Virginia school reformers believed that universal schooling would create a healthier, more efficient, productive and stable culture. Schools would socialize children into useful worker/management relations and "acceptable" standards of communal behavior. Slowly reformers began to include black education in their definition of universal schooling.

What was central to the Southern progressive ideology was that whites and blacks would be educated to accept their place in a biracial society as if segregation was the natural order of the universe. Hence Alderman could claim, without fear of recrimination, that the education of one white man was worth more to black education than the schooling of 10 black Southerners. This was not about democratizing the New South; it was about quite the opposite.

PROGRESSIVE EDUCATION AND BLACK LABOR

Booker T. Washington's promise of a black workforce that eschewed labor unions and radical politics did not fall on deaf ears. William H. Baldwin Jr., the Northern railroad executive and member of the GEB inner circle, believed that black workers, not only in the South but in the more industrialized North, could be used to break the power of advancing white labor unions. In fact, in 1909, Philadelphia railroads "hired" black Southerners as "police" to help break the unionized rail strikes, the same strikes that were reported in Pasadena's newspapers. Baldwin wrote that he believed "the strength of the South [lies] in the labor of the ... Negro." Therefore, according to Baldwin, the struggle would be to keep blacks in the South but as agricultural laborers. To do so, Baldwin argued that public schooling would need to educate Afro Southerners "for their [Southern] environment and not out of it."[18] What Baldwin meant by "their environment" was the solution to the vexing problem of black education that the planters and reformers had sought.

Baldwin's solution was black agricultural education. His vision points to the changes within the white reform organizations, both North and South. Increasingly, after the turn of the century, school reformers began to see the necessity of some form of black educational "uplift." But the incorporation of black schooling into the definition of universal education occurred only when reformers became convinced that the appropriate model of black schooling was industrial and agricultural education. The change of mind was advanced by Northerners smitten by an approach to black education being advanced at the Hampton Normal and Agricultural Institute in Hampton, Virginia.

Samuel Chapman Armstrong, son of a New England missionary, who spent 40 years in the Hawaiian Islands, founded the school after the Civil War. At the age of 21, Armstrong was sent to Williams College in Massachusetts, where upon graduation in 1862, he was commissioned in the U.S. Army as a colonel in command of a black regiment. Serving with distinction as an officer with the Eighth Regiment, U.S. Colored Troops, Armstrong was given a field promotion to brigadier general. Being in charge of black foot soldiers, his wife would write, allowed Armstrong to become "thoroughly familiar with the civil needs of the newly-made citizens."[19] It was that combination of missionary work among the Pacific island "natives" and military training during the war that Armstrong's wife believed so eminently qualified her husband:

> [Armstrong] brought from Hawaii to Virginia an idea, worked out by American brains in the heart of the Pacific, adequate to meet the demands of a race similar in its dawn of civilization to the people among whom this idea had first been successfully tested.[20]

Mrs. Armstrong thought it important to mention that her husband's father, the Rev. Richard Armstrong, was an "intimate friend" of the Rev. Dr. Junkin, president of Carlisle College. Carlisle was the infamous "Indian school" in the East, and it was at Carlisle that the ideology of deculturalization as assimilation was worked out as the school put into practice its proudly marketed cultural reconstruction of "kill the Indian and save the man."

Under Armstrong's direction, Hampton Institute became the antithesis of the social and educational ideologies of the freedmen. Despite Mrs. Armstrong's illusions of "meeting the needs" of the freedmen, "General" Armstrong (as he was called) intended his school to serve the needs of "wealth and power," not by advancing an educational ideal that challenged the fundamental economic and social dislocation of black Southerners, but by rescuing the ex-slaves from themselves.[21]

Baldwin, a member of the Hampton Board of Directors, told Southern reformers and Northern philanthropists in 1899 that the benefits of a "properly educated" black workforce were "incalculable." At Hampton (where Booker T. Washington had been educated), Baldwin, Ogden and other influential Northern business leaders found the perfect model of black "self help." Baldwin told the reformers that "[in] the Negro is the opportunity of the South .... [because] time has proven that he is best fitted to perform the heavy labor in the Southern States." What Baldwin called for was black industrial education that would school,

... him as a suitable citizen... [therefore,] willingly fill the more menial positions, do the heavy work, at less wages, [thereby] permitting the white laborer to perform the more expert labor, and to leave the fields, the mines, and the simpler trades to the Negro.[22]

The Hampton Institute and later the Tuskegee Normal and Industrial Institute founded by Booker T. Washington, developed a model of black education that marketed the illusion of black "self help" through model farms and manual skills training. In reality, the two schools were teacher-training institutes that promoted "the dignity of labor," coded language, historian James Anderson convincingly argues, that devalued academic training and black political participation. The Hampton-Tuskegee model favored education for menial labor that would promote the removal of black citizens from any effective role not only in Southern politics but wherever African Americans gathered as a community. Washington had explicitly called for an end to black political participation in 1895 and African Americans hotly debated Washington's proposal in Southern towns like Charlottesville and in Afro American League meetings in places like Pasadena. Looming over Washington's proposal was Samuel Chapman Armstrong's theme that ex-slaves were, as he wrote, "weak and blind," with leadership that was, at least to Chapman, more often than not "morally bankrupt."[23] In Charlottesville and Pasadena, black leadership was neither.

Baldwin's call for a particular form of black education reinforced the post-Reconstruction cultural hierarchies of white over black. Northern philanthropists defined the Hampton-Tuskegee model as the *only* legitimate approach to black education. For the next 30 years, during the apogee of Northern monetary influence on Southern schooling for blacks, the only schools to receive GEB funds were those that mirrored the Hampton-Tuskegee approach. The white reformers were so sure that black education should follow industrial lines—and so fearful that it would not—they sent inspectors to verify that black school officials were not masking academic education as industrial education.[24]

The GEB leadership had good reason for their suspicions. The black community rejected the white reformers' definition of the *intent* of industrial education. While industrial, agricultural and vocational education for whites (such as that offered at the Miller School for Boys in Charlottesville) promoted skills that were intended to correct environmental problems associated with postwar poverty, black industrial education focused on correcting the perceived deficiencies of the black Southerner.[25] In some ways, the Southern ex-slave community at the turn of the century found itself arguing, as did the white working class in Pasadena, for a similar new model of schooling. Both rejected the forms of education that they believed would further segregate their communities. In Pasadena, the labor union/Socialist alliance opposed a traditional form of schooling that further reinforced the perception that the working class was culturally "deficient," thereby justifying the continued subordination of working-class families. In schools like Hampton, Southern white educational leaders, fully backed by Northern business and philanthropic concerns, put in place an industrial education for former slaves and their descendants that would provide, as Episcopalian minister Charles Murphy wrote, "those elements of skill, those conditions of industrial peace, which our fathers supplied under the conditions of slavery."[26]

MARY JOHNSTON, "MISS LUCY," AND THE CONTRADICTIONS OF THE SOUTHERN WOMAN'S MOVEMENT

By the end of the first decade of the 20th century, the campaign for a New South, with its inherent contradictions of race and power, was in full bloom. As it was in many communities around the country, school reform had increasingly fallen under the banner of the woman's movement. Certainly in cities like Pasadena, progressive women saw school betterment as the natural extension of women's work. Moreover, an expansive woman's movement in many communities came to define social reform during the Progressive era. Up until the turn of the century, what had been missing from the reform effort, at least in Virginia, was the concentrated energy of the progressive woman. The Southern crusade for better schools—followed quickly by the campaign for the franchise—brought for the first time large numbers of Southern women to the edge of national politics where they joined moderates and radicals alike in an effort to redefine national politics as feminist politics. Nearly all the leadership of the woman's movement in Virginia, as it was in Pasadena, was drawn from the elite—the wealthy and middle class—both white and black. It is within this cadre of reforming women that the contradictions of the New Virginia, with its complex themes of race, power, status and democracy, can be most clearly understood.[27] Further, within the larger progressive movement to reform Virginia and the nation is located the contradictory impulses of "progress" and "race betterment."

Two distant cousins, Mary Johnston and Lucy Randolph Mason, epitomize the state of women's politics in Virginia during the first 30 years of the 20th century. Johnston, one of the South's most revered novelists and author of *To Have and to Hold* and numerous other works of romantic historical fiction, was drawn to the suffrage movement in 1909 as part of the inner circle of the Richmond Woman's Club. She went on to national prominence as a speaker, first for suffrage and then for causes associated with the larger woman's movement, including child labor, women's health, and, during the First World War, pacifism. As Johnston's national reputation grew during the early years of the suffrage campaign in Virginia, she concerned herself mainly with "the vote," always managing to navigate clear of controversy that might have a negative impact on the movement or her reputation as a "Southern lady." Early in her suffrage work she courted organized labor and the Virginia Socialist party. Yet in these more radical causes, Johnston chose to be a part-time player. At about the same time as the passage of the 19th Amendment that gave women the vote, she retreated to her beloved estate, Three Hills, in Warm Springs, Virginia, and retired from public view. She spent the remaining years of her life trying out various self-help psychologies, including psychic phenomena, the "Fourth Dimension," and mysticism.[28] As we will see, it is within her rather idiosyncratic world, her "Oneness" with the universe as she liked to call it, that we locate her most perplexing contradictions.[29] She referred to herself as a "progressive," and, by the war years, she was wed to "race betterment" as the solution to the ills of industrial America. Mary Johnston, unlike her cousin, saw progress as the manipulation of science. Mary Johnston became a devotee of eugenics.

Lucy Randolph Mason, like Johnston an early entrant into the suffrage wars in Virginia, carried in her ancestry "the blood of a constellation of Virginia heroes," including George Mason, author of the Virginia Bill of Rights, Supreme Court Justice John Marshall, and General Robert E. Lee.[30] Her father, Landon Mason, an Episcopal minister, had fought with Mosby's Raiders in and around Charlottesville during the Civil War.[31] However, Lucy Mason's parents were far from wealthy aristocrats. "Miss Lucy," as she was fondly called later in life as a labor organizer, railed at the assumption that her blue-blooded heritage carried monetary privileges. She told the story that her father's salary of $500 a year was "mostly paid in black-eyed peas and bacon."[32] Unlike Johnston, after the passage of the 19th Amendment, Mason did not retreat into private life. She went on to become one of the most powerful and respected labor union organizers in the country. Her memoir, *To Win These Rights,* was published in 1952. In the foreword, Eleanor Roosevelt called Mason's union organizing during the 1930s "a really remarkable piece of work for the achievement of democracy." Given the radical labor union environment that Mason worked in during her career as an organizer—or maybe *just because* of that radical environment—Mason never identified herself as a socialist nor did she sympathize with the Communist party. She remained a "Southern lady," liberal but never "Red."[33] Unlike her more conservative cousin, Mason believed the ills of industrial America might be ameliorated by racial and cross-class alliances. Clearly, these Virginia cousins took different paths.

"MISS LUCY AND THE CIO"

In 1911, two years after Johnston joined the Equal Suffrage League (ESL), Lucy Randolph Mason decided she could no longer remain on the fringe. Mason had been cautious, fearful that her stance on suffrage might embarrass her prominent father. But, as she told Lila Valentine, the president of the ESL, "[it is my] moral conviction ... to join the Equal Suffrage League." Still, the fear of public ridicule and family shame kept her under wraps. She initially insisted on publishing her suffrage writings under the pseudonym, "Lucy Cary." Within the year, Mason had discarded the pseudonym and published her coming-out essay, "The Divine Discontent." It was her vision of women—middle- and upper-class white women—using their newfound power of the vote to minister to the less fortunate. Mason argued that it was the "higher duty" of women to use their "unique" gifts to bring about a more divine social order.

By 1919, Mason had moved beyond the hesitant, passive activist space her cousin Mary Johnston occupied. She told *The Richmond News Leader* that her famous ancestor, George Mason, had believed that all men had the right of suffrage and that all men were created equal. Lucy Mason argued that if her great-great-great grandfather had been alive in 1919, he would have been a strong advocate for women's suffrage, just as he had been a strong advocate in the opposition to slavery. Her *News Leader* interview marked an important turning point in her life. She had publicly connected suffrage with abolition. In a few years, she would become one of the few white women in Virginia to openly work for interracial cooperation between black and white suffrage leagues.

Over the next 10 years, Mason worked mainly for the Richmond YWCA, chairing the Richmond branch of the League of Women Voters, including the league's Women in Industry Committee. She accepted an appointment from Samuel Gompers, president of the American Federation of Labor, to become Virginia's chairman of the Committee on Women in Industry of the National Advisory Committee on Labor. By 1923, Lucy Randolph Mason was a public figure, known outside of Virginia for her activism and commitment. Florence Kelley, one of the country's most famous feminists, asked her to assume the presidency of the national Consumer's League. Always her own person, Mason stunned Kelley and turned down the offer to remain in the South as the general secretary of the Richmond YWCA.

By the end of the decade, Mason was taking repeated public stands against segregation. She chaired the influential Council of Social Agencies committee that studied the economic conditions of Richmond's black community and was the only white woman to stand before the Richmond City Council to oppose the city's attempt to expand the limits of segregation within the black community.

By the early 1930s, during the depths of the Depression, Mason finally decided to accept Kelley's offer and moved to New York City to lead the Consumer's League. One of her biographers believes she doubted herself then, not sure what she could contribute to the "new social order." What Mason may have lacked in confidence, she made up for in action. The director of the Virginia Commission on Interracial Cooperation told her "no one can accuse you of being a coward or a hypocrite."34 As Mary Johnston became ever more insulated in her Warm Springs estate, Mason moved outward, toward her most difficult, yet rewarding endeavor—the massive Southern unionizing effort by the Congress on Industrial Organization (CIO) . Her career as the CIO "Operation Dixie" organizer would forever mark Lucy Randolph Mason as anything but a passive activist.

In June of 1937, John L. Lewis, head of the newly formed Congress of Industrial Organizations, met Lucy Mason and convinced her to become one of the CIO's "roving ambassadors" in the South. The CIO was committed to being an interracial labor union, and it was Mason's job to define the "new social order" within the existing racial politics of the South. In 1938, not long after she moved to Atlanta, she wrote President Franklin Roosevelt that her South "was leaning on the Fascist system as I have never seen it before." She spent the next 19 years as the CIO public relations director in the South, negotiating for strikers, interceding on behalf of both white and black laborers and working tirelessly to convince white and black working-class communities that an interracial labor union was stronger and better and would help ensure that the South would be a member in good standing with the rest of the nation.

Lucy Randolph Mason died in 1959, just as the modern civil rights movement was gathering steam. Although she may have been exceedingly optimistic, perhaps even a bit naive about the role of labor organizing, she nevertheless was committed to a progressive and democratic new social order. Mason saw progressivism less on personal terms than as cultural reconstruction. Progressive change and the benefits of social and economic transformation would come to the individual rather than coming from the individual. In contrast, Mary Johnston's definition of progressivism was self-actualization; it grew from her need to understand herself. Social change came from "fixing" the "others."

MARY JOHNSTON AND HER "SUPER RACE"

Both Johnston and Mason left the relative safety of their social position to venture into the highly visible world of the woman's suffrage movement. More to the point, both used, with varying degrees of success, their status as "respectable" Southern ladies against the status quo. Mary Johnston joined the Virginia suffrage movement because it appeared to be the logical extension of her Richmond Woman's Club circle of activities. She later wrote that the room where those first meetings took place held all the trappings of the "respectable families" of Richmond and Southern society.[35] After the Equal Suffrage League was formed in 1909, Johnston was hesitant to connect publicly to such a highly controversial organization. She told the press she was merely considering membership. Johnston seemed to be on the edge of the movement, more cautious than committed.

Throughout her career as a social activist, this would be her *modus operandi*. She seldom put her position as a "respectable Southern lady" at risk. When she disagreed with the direction of the Southern States' Woman's Suffrage Conference, with its overtly racist leadership, she quietly resigned but chose not to take any public stand.[36] When Lila Meade Valentine, the conservative president of the ESL, called her to task for her flirtations with the Socialist party (which she never joined) and organized labor (with which she was never affiliated), she avoided any further public displays of support. She did so even though she professed, at the time, that both organized labor and socialism could greatly empower the woman's movement. With the passage of the 19th Amendment in 1920, she shocked and angered many when she refused to join the newly established League of Women Voters. By then, she had come to believe that the universe was a seamless "One" and to countenance divisions around issues such as gender—like the League of Women's Voters—would be counterproductive to the "Oneness."[37]

These contradictions in Johnston's social activism should be seen as symptoms in her search for personal identity in a rapidly changing world. Whether she joined with the socialists, affiliated with the trade union movement, or led the newly formed Virginia League of Women Voters, it mattered little. Johnston's social activism was situated within the acceptable spaces most aristocratic, Southern white women were allowed to explore. Moreover, though she pushed at the edges of conventional wisdom—especially during the years just after the founding of the ESL, it appears she was driven more by a personal mission to better understand her evolving consciousness than a compelling desire to right political and social wrongs. That evolving consciousness would lead her to a more reactionary form of progressivism, a belief that the science of "human betterment" would bring about a more perfect union. Mary Johnston would embrace eugenics, the "science" of extreme social engineering that eventually would be embraced as the ideological framework for Hitler's Third Reich.

Johnston saw the women's movement as the means by which society might evolve toward a higher order. In an argument that was heard early and often during the Progressive era, Johnston believed women were "mothers of the race," and it was their "natural" calling to minister "goodness" to the needs of the nation. Yet Mary Johnston would rarely take a resolute, politically charged position. As her evolving consciousness would dictate, she would leave her "causes" and move on, from suffrage and trade unions to child labor, then to pacifism and finally to mysticism and transcendentalism. Toward the end of her life she tried to rebuild her family's land holdings in an effort to return to the lost days of the Old South.

Mary Johnston was uncomfortable as a public critic. She would criticize the social milieu, as she did when she addressed the Virginia legislature during the early suffrage campaign, but her arguments were embedded in a larger concern framed by her compelling desire to see a "better race." She saw suffrage as "but a part" of the larger "human movement." She would say, "While I am a suffragist, I am not simply a suffragist; I am a feminist rather than a suffragist. And while I am a feminist, I am not simply a feminist; I am a humanist rather than a feminist."[38]

In her search for moral order, Mary Johnston's belief in humanism became a belief in the power of race purification. It was Johnston's deep and profound commitment to the "science of human betterment" that would "strengthen the human race through the improvement of the human condition." Johnston believed, as did many of her generation—including Charlotte Perkins Gilman, that the woman's vote was but one step in the inevitable progress of the human race. The suffrage question, she wrote, was proof of "the evolution of the human species." She saw no distinction between women getting the franchise and the "evolution of the race."[39] From the "science" of eugenics—with its forced sterilization and segregation—would emerge the "science" of mental measurement and the IQ test, the Progressive Era effort to make legitimate the artificial ranking by ability.

EUGENICS AND A "BETTER WORLD THROUGH STERILIZATION"

In her belief in the possibilities for a scientifically formulated "better race," Johnston was not alone. Many white, progressive social activists joined her in the decades before the rise of Hitler and the discrediting of hereditarian studies. In a speech in Pittsburgh in 1911, this shy Southern woman told her audience a new age was upon the world, "a fresh blowing wind, the spirit of ardor, the spirit of mysticism..."

> We are on the eve of a very great age in the world's growth, of a spiritual century, of a rise in the level of the mind of the men. Everywhere we feel it ... Very great ideas are abroad today ...

And in Johnston's new age "... the greatest, the widest and deepest and most hopeful" idea was the "eugenic idea ... not in its narrower and more technical meaning and application," but eugenics in the "widest possible sense." She told the audience that eugenics in its widest possible sense meant "nothing less than a super race." Through "racial hygiene," an early Progressive-era idea that had scientific and lay support in Britain and the United States, social reformers like Johnston predicted that "human stock" would improve by giving "the more suitable races or strains of blood a better chance of prevailing speedily over the less suitable."[40] Led in Britain by Charles Darwin's cousin, statistician Francis Galton, and Harry Laughlin, Charles Davenport and Paul Popenoe in the United States, eugenicists argued that civilization could be rapidly improved through "positive" eugenics— the encouragement of "better" peoples to reproduce in greater numbers—and "negative" eugenics, which included sterilization (both forced and "voluntary"), forced segregation, restrictions on immigration, the establishment of mental and physical "screens" (most notably the IQ and "character" tests), and the creation of social service agencies and programs, including school curricula, that sought to improve the quality of the race through "sex hygiene."[41] In the United States, Britain, and later Nazi Germany, eugenics—the making of a "super race"— gained favor as a legitimate means to improve on "natural selection."

Johnston's "super race" would come, she told her Pittsburgh audience, when the human race abandoned its "animal fecundity," her rather crass term for over-population. Her vision for the "super race" rejected a world of "... teeming millions, more crowded even than in China and India, packed together each one with no room for mind or soul to expand." Eugenicists wanted something better for humankind. Johnston said, "Their vision is the moral nature of man raised to the strength and stature of the angels." Johnston saw on the horizon a "sweetness and light" emanating from just beyond those "Delectable Mountains."

For many progressive, social reformers like Johnston, America's future as the land of "sweetness and light" required racial purification. Ridding society of the "unfit," the "mongrel," and the "socially inadequate" could be done through the compassionate application of the "science of hereditarianism." The starting point, at least for Johnston and her suffrage sisters, always came back to feminism and ultimately the suffrage question. "Never, never, never ..." she said to her Pittsburgh listeners, "will you get your super race until you get your super woman." Johnston's "inescapable fact" was that feminism and eugenics "are inseparable." She concluded her speech by telling those assembled, "Believe me there are many ways of serving the Future, but binding the mind and chaining the activities of the mother of the human species is not among them"[42]

Looking back, it may be difficult to comprehend how turn-of-the-century progressives could have been so misled by the pseudoscience of eugenics. Johnston mentioned in her Pittsburgh speech, and in many other eugenic talks, that the "super race" could be created through classroom instruction. In other words, teachers would make students aware of "race thinking," the early-century notion that "improper" sexual habits would foul the human race. We can now see that just behind the slogans of "betterment" and "progress" lay practices that were blatantly racist, violent and, ironically, misogynist. Most of the forced sterilization procedures that occurred in the United States were performed on women.[43] However, it is of little consequence to apply our present-mindedness to Johnston and her fellow social reformers turned eugenicists. Instead, it is more profitable to situate Mary Johnston and the eugenics movement in the larger concerns that motivated intellectuals and educators during the Progressive era before the Great Depression and the rise of German fascism.[44]

From the wellspring of the industrial revolution, with its unchecked growth in urban sprawl and its "teeming millions" came the fear of "race suicide," a term that gained favor among white, middle-class reformers during the first two decades of the 20th century. The millions of Southern European immigrants— the darker races—coupled with the decline in the birthrate for white, middle-class families, provoked deeply felt anxieties over the future of the "white race." Demographers told horror stories of declining births among the "best families," and the upper classes saw the "lesser" peoples rapidly increasing. The masses of poor, darker-skinned people, the "hunger-bitten hordes" according to sociologist Edward A. Ross, were reproducing at such an alarming rate around the world that "our more fecund rivals" would be able to "colonize the waste places," and our status as a superpower would be threatened. As it was in South Africa, Ross wrote at the turn of the century, that whites in America "stand aghast at the rabbit-like increase of the blacks."[45] At home, it was more of the same. Grounded in an oddly contradictory mix of conservatism and progressive reform, social Darwinists turned hereditary studies into the pseudoscience of eugenics and pushed for the sterilization of the "socially inadequate," a broad-stroke label defined as "schizophrenics, manic depressives, feebleminded, epileptics, sufferers of Huntington's Chorea, inebriates, drug addicts, tramps, the homeless, orphans, paupers, criminals, ne'er-do-wells, the blind and deaf, syphilitics, lepers and the tubercular."[46] Eugenics became a national campaign to make a better America through both selective breeding and the elimination of impure stock.

The eugenic crusade distrusted Darwinian natural selection as the way to "cleanse" society—natural selection simply took too long and the problems of urban America with its "teeming millions" precluded patience.[47] So Johnston's "super race" would come only when an "objective" social science—eugenics—was used to combat society's "animal fecundity." Well-known eugenicists such as psychologists G. Stanley Hall and Edward L. Thorndike (the leading promoter of the IQ test) wanted to "control society more efficiently and effectively through the scientific manipulation of mankind's instincts."[48] If the "objective" social sciences could sort out the "biologically inferior" and public policy could limit their reproduction, the "better classes" would be free to reproduce in larger numbers, resulting in a more "perfect" civilization.

At the core of the eugenics movement, indeed at the heart of progressivism at the turn of the century, were individuals like Mary Johnston, who projected their class prejudices and fears of "race suicide" as "objective" science. The "laws of nature" during the height of the Progressive era were seen as synonymous with the values of the privileged. To Mary Johnston and thousands of middle-class white women, ministering goodness to the nation was their "natural" duty as "mothers of the race." Hindsight tells us those ministrations were all too often subordinated by evil.[49] In Charlottesville, Virginia, such was the case of Carrie Buck and her daughter, Vivian.

RACE SUICIDE AND THE STERILIZATION OF CARRIE BUCK

In January 1924, Carrie Buck was committed to the State Colony for Epileptics and Feeble-Minded in Lynchburg, Virginia. She was 18, white and six-months pregnant. Born a few miles away in Charlottesville, Carrie was the daughter of Emma Buck, who had earlier been committed to the same Lynchburg hospital. Emma also had been born in Charlottesville, not long after the end of the Civil War. Carrie Buck was one of many supposedly illegitimate children born to Emma. As a baby, she had been given over to the care of a foster family, the Dobbs, who lived on Grove Street, literally on the wrong side of the tracks, in a poor section of Charlottesville. Less than three months after her commitment, Carrie Buck gave birth to a daughter of her own and named her Vivian.

The same year Carrie Buck was committed, the state of Virginia enacted a compulsory sterilization law, modeled on one advanced by Harry Laughlin. Laughlin was the superintendent of the Eugenics Record Office, the leading depository of eugenics data and considered the ideological epicenter of the eugenics movement in America. Laughlin was trained as a biologist and had taught at a Missouri normal school before he came to the Eugenics Records Office. His expertise was immigration policy and he based his study of the "lesser races" on the premise that "[white] women were the salvation of the social order, racially and morally ..."[50] Laughlin tried to prove the biological relationship between the immigration of darker-skinned people and cultural degeneration. He felt it was crucial that,

> American women keep the nation's blood pure by not marrying the colored races ... for if men with a small fraction of colored blood could find mates among white women ... the gates would be thrown open to a final radical race mixture of the whole population.[51]

Laughlin was a zealous racist and his model sterilization law, written in 1922, was draconian even by the standards of his era. He advocated the elimination of what he called the "worthless" by calling for the forced sterilization of the "blind, including those with seriously impaired vision; deaf, including those with seriously impaired hearing; dependent, including orphans, ne'er-do-wells, the homeless, tramps, and paupers."[52]

Charles Davenport, one of Laughlin's most trusted colleagues, wrote, "The life of the commonwealth takes precedence over the right of reproduction of the individual."[53] Radical eugenicists such as Davenport and Laughlin (and on the West Coast, Paul Popenoe and Ezra Gosney of Pasadena's Human Betterment Foundation) advocated that the technology of racial purification—eugenics—should advance its sinister form of goodness in the name of the survival of the commonwealth. The use of the new sciences would intercede and the "super race" Johnston saw just beyond the "Delectable Mountains" would begin in the mental hospitals with patients like Carrie Buck.

Virginia decided in 1924 to sterilize Carrie Buck because, according to the state, she was feeble-minded, the daughter of an incarcerated feeble-minded woman, and the mother of an "illegitimate, feeble-minded child." The state had an obligation to stop the spread of what eugenicists called defective "germ plasm." The superintendent of the hospital where Carrie Buck was held ordered her sterilization. Interestingly, it was conservative Christians who came to Carrie Buck's defense, arguing all the way to the U.S. Supreme Court that Buck's "natural rights" as an individual were being violated by excessive state intervention. Judge Oliver Wendell Holmes and seven of his colleagues on the bench would hear none of it. The majority opinion, written by Holmes, concludes with his now (in)famous final sentence: "Three generations of imbeciles are enough."[54]

The Supreme Court had determined, largely because of written testimony from Laughlin, that Carrie Buck had inherited her "imbecility" from her mother. Both women had been given the Stanford-Binet IQ test, and each had scored a mental age of less than 10 years. In his letter to the court, Laughlin told the justices that Carrie Buck's family "... belong[ed] to the shiftless, ignorant, and worthless class of anti-social whites of the South."[55] Laughlin, who never appeared before the court (nor did the court ask any clarifying questions regarding his written testimony), continued to make subjective, disparaging comments about Carrie Buck: "[she] has a rather badly formed face; of a sensual emotional reaction ... is incapable of self-support and restraint expect under close supervision." Laughlin's medical determinations were drawn from observations made by hospital staff and doctors. Laughlin never examined Buck, because he was not a trained physician.

Laughlin told the Court that feeble-mindedness is typically caused by the "inheritance of degenerate qualities ..." except in rare instances when "it is caused by environmental factors which are not heredity." Laughlin wrote "... the evidence points strongly toward the feeble-mindedness and moral delinquency of Carrie Buck being due, primarily, to inheritance and not the environment." Laughlin's damning testimony helped seal Carrie Buck's fate.

Carrie Buck was morally delinquent, claimed Laughlin, because she was now a young mother. Being supposedly "shiftless, ignorant, and worthless" made unnecessary any attempt to name her mate. The court and Laughlin assumed he was from that same class of poor whites. What Laughlin probably did not know was that a relative from the Dobbs family had raped Carrie Buck. But the superintendent who admitted Carrie knew, and her foster family knew. What was clear was that the Dobbs family had Carrie committed as a feeble-minded inmate to hide her pregnancy—and possibly her attacker—from the Charlottesville community.[56]

The case of Carrie Buck and the Supreme Court made headlines around the country. Laughlin's testimony was prominently featured. But according to Stephen Jay Gould and other contemporary scholars, it was not so much Laughlin's damning testimony as it was the testimony from a Charlottesville Red Cross social worker that Vivian Buck, Carrie's six-month-old daughter, was feeble-minded. The U.S. Supreme Court ruled that Carrie Buck should be sterilized because there was "evidence" that her daughter Vivian had "inherited" her supposed "imbecility." The court had admitted as evidence testimony that the Red Cross social worker had observed the baby and had determined that "there was a look about it that is not quite normal ..." Carrie Buck was sterilized against her will and based on that testimony and on what Justice Holmes later wrote were his feelings that "real reform" was close at hand.[57]

We now understand that Carrie Buck was committed and sterilized because she was poor and undereducated. In the early 1980s, Stephen Jay Gould reported in *Natural History* that a medical researcher had determined that the hospital where Carrie was committed had performed over 4,000 sterilizations, some as

Fig. 10. Carrie Buck and her mother, Emma Buck, in 1924. *(Photo courtesy of Arthur Estabrook Papers, M.E. Grenander Department of Special Collections and Archives, State University of New York at Albany)*

late as 1972. Gould wrote that the researcher had found Carrie Buck still living, not far from the Lynchburg hospital. She was no imbecile. She read daily, worked with a friend on the crossword puzzle in the local newspaper and, when examined by mental health professionals, was determined to be far from mentally retarded. Her only daughter, Vivian, had died at the age of eight.

In addition to Gould, other scholars have examined the Carrie Buck story. In his *Eugenic Sterilization in Virginia,* Paul Lombardo tells us that there was no imbecility in three Buck generations.[58] Ironically, her mother's foster family, the Dobbs, adopted Vivian. She attended Venable Elementary School in Charlottesville. According to her report card, she was an average student, receiving Bs and Cs, and, by every account available to us today, a very normal child. She died at the age of eight of *enteric colitis,* an inflammation of the intestine, a generic term used then by medical examiners to describe an assortment of diseases, mostly associated with poverty. Vivian Buck died because she was poor.

Maybe trying to fix the human condition is part of the human condition. In the U.S. Supreme Court chambers, a well-known Virginia trial lawyer, Aubrey Strode, argued the Buck case. A former high-school principal, newspaper publisher and at the time of the Buck trial, a two-term Virginia state senator, Strode was an "untiring progressive," who "instinctively" pressed for standards that he thought promoted equality and fairness for all under the law. In one statement, his biographer cuts to the heart of Strode's progressive social reform: "... he believed in the notion of progress, but not the kind of progress that would come by itself."[59] For Strode and many other progressives during the years before the world got turned upside down by the Great Depression and war, "progress had to be dragged out of the mire of ignorance and poverty and disease that plagued the world."[60] Noble words indeed that too often have been in advance of ignoble deeds.

For Mary Johnston, racial betterment through sterilization may have been necessary for the feeble-minded but her eugenic advocacy was not so severe. For Johnston, classroom instruction would change the nature of humankind. Through education, middle-class children would come to understand the necessity of racial purification. There was a debt each generation owed to each successive generation, a responsibility Johnston believed was of the highest order. She spoke of "an army" of "passionate" men and women who wished to see "inaugurated an era of proper instruction to children, to boys and girls, in the physiology of sex, the essential sacredness and high office of the sexual organs, the basal facts of life and reproduction."[61] Johnston's sex education had a moral purpose—she wanted white, middle-class children to understand "the necessity of self-control," and the "honorableness of practicing it" was their responsibility to the future, a "noblesse oblige of cleanliness of body, mind and soul."[62]

In a 1912 speech, which she titled "The Eugenical Point of View" and delivered at the Virginia State Conference on Charities and Corrections, Johnston previewed a new movement in schools: "sex hygiene" and, if practiced, it meant "efficient living," "fair temperance," and "service ... to the race." She wanted children (especially the charitable cases and misfits found in the state's wards and orphanages) to understand the rudiments of sexual reproduction because, she said, ignorance breeds "gutter talk, ancient obscenities, vulgar mystery ... a muddy and slimy cup of knowledge taken from whatever soiled hand is first outstretched." The child had a right to know, and know they would, except that the knowledge gained from the "wrong book, the wrong paper, the wrong person" would "stain the mind." And a stained mind, she told her audience of wardens and social workers, was "so hard to cleanse."[63]

Despite her flair for the melodramatic—she told the conference audience that conception, if done by the "right people," was "noble, pure and clean"— Johnston's eugenic message was intended to hit home. Ignorance, she said, "was an animal quality." To Johnston, ignorance was man's indiscriminate fouling of future generations through his reckless distribution of the "sacred and immortal" germ plasm. Without a "proper" education, the unfit would spread their "bad" seeds, possibly tainting the "better races" and future generations, just as "a piece of soiled and smutted and defiled paper" would be "sorrowfully of little account."[64] Most eugenicists were not so naive to think that the medical community could sterilize all those "of little account." It would be through education that middle-class whites, the better race, would learn how they could advance their kind. In the period between the world wars, in progressive places like Pasadena, eugenics, "the making of a better race," would morph into the "science of education."

NOTES

1. To see what Charlottesville read of the *Potemkin* mutiny, see "Sea Fight Has Commenced," 25 May, p. 1; "Fighting in Moscow," 7 June, p. 1; and "Fleet Starts in Pursuit," 6 July, 1905; all *Charlottesville Daily Progress.* Also see Robert Weinberg, *The Revolution of 1905 in Odessa* (Bloomington: Indiana University Press, 1993) p. 132–138, and Richard Hough, *The Potemkin Mutiny* (Englewood Cliffs: Prentice-Hall, Inc. 1960). The mutiny was made famous by Sergi Eisenstein's 1927 film, *Battleship Potemkin. The Richmond Times-Dispatch* was delivered to Charlottesville via train.

2. "Idealism Has Ruled America," *Charlottesville Daily Progress,* 6 July 1905, p. 1.

3. William A. Link, *A Hard Country and a Lonely Place* (Chapel Hill: University of North Carolina Press, 1983) p. 91.

4. Ibid., p. 91, 93.

5. Walter Hines Page, *Rebuilding Old Commonwealths* (New York: 1902) p. 150–151, cited in Link, p. 89.

6. Link., p. 93.

7. Link., p. 89.

8. Louis Harlan, *Separate and Unequal: Public School Campaigns and Racism in the Southern Seaboard States, 1901–1915* (Chapel Hill: University of North Carolina Press, 1958) p. 92–93.

9. Ibid., p. 80.

10. Link, p. 102.

11. Harlan, p. 42–43.

12. Harlan, p. 39, 43–44, 92–96; James McPherson, *The Abolitionist Legacy: From Reconstruction to the NAACP* (Princeton: Princeton University Press, 1975) p. 143–241. In *The Education of Blacks in the South, 1860–1935* (Chapel Hill: Univ. of North Carolina Press, 1988), historian James Anderson disagrees with both historians' assessment, p. 80–81.

13. Grace Elizabeth Hale, *Making Whiteness: The Culture of Segregation in the South, 1890–1940* (New York: Pantheon Books, 1998) p. 51–53.

14. Hale, p. 51–53, 59–61, 61–64; David Brion Davis, *New York Times, "This Week In Review,"* 21 August 2001; W. Fitzhugh Brundage, "White Women and the Politics of Historical Memory in the New South, 1880–1920," in *Jumpin' Jim Crow: Southern Politics from the Civil War to Civil Rights* (Princeton: Princeton University Press, 2000) p. 115–139.

15. Hale, p. 284–285.

16. Anderson, p. 79–80.

17. Ibid., p. 91.

18. M.F. Armstrong and Helen W. Ludlow, *Hampton and Its Students, with Fifty Cabin and Plantation Songs* (New York: G.P. Putnam's Sons, 1874) p. 22.

19. Ibid., p. 22–23.

20. Ibid., p. 33–34.

21. Ibid., p. 37–42.
22. Anderson, p. 82.
23. Ibid., p. 38–39.
24. Ibid., p. 118.
25. Link, p. 178; The Miller Manual Labor School of Albemarle County, Va., was established in 1877 from Samuel Miller's estate. Miller was a self-made man who donated the funds upon his death. See Helen Gray, "Educating Poor White Children," *Leslie's Weekly,* 24 April 1902, p. 394–395; and "The Miller School: Its History, Work, and Results," a speech by Charles E. Vawter, delivered at the Capon Springs Conference, 24 June 1900, in the *Miller School Papers,* Special Collections, University of Virginia, [9844–6], Box 1.
26. Edgar Gardner Murphy, *Problems of the Present South,* p. 80, as cited in Link, p. 178.
27. Lucy Randolph Mason, "Standards for Workers in Southern Industry," *National Consumers' League,* 1931; Jean Charlotte Shelton, "Woman Suffrage and Virginia Politics, 1909–1920" (Master's thesis, University of Virginia, 1969); Desha Breckinridge, "Women and the Schools," p. 10–18; "The Relation of the Public Schools to Kentucky's Commercial Development," p.19–31; *Kentucky Federation of Women's Clubs: School Betterment for Kentucky,* 1908; , F. Ray Marshall, *Labor in the South* (Cambridge: Harvard University Press, 1967).
28. Clayton McClure Brooks "Proper Voices, Radical Words: Mary Johnston, Lucy Randolph Mason, and the Process of Racial Liberalization," (Master's thesis, University of Virginia, 1999) p. 4, 38.
29. Ibid., p. 30.
30. John Salmond, *Miss Lucy of the CIO: The Life and Times of Lucy Randolph Mason, 1882–1959* (Athens: University of Georgia Press, 1988).
31. Lucy Randolph Mason, *To Win These Rights: A Personal Story of the CIO in the South* (New York: Harper and Bros., 1952) p. xii.
32. Ibid., p. 1.
33. Ibid., The Roosevelt quote is in the book's foreword.
34. Salmond, p. 77.
35. Brooks, p. 34.
36. "Autobiography," unpublished in *Mary Johnston Papers,* Special Collections, University of Virginia, [acc. No. 3588], Box 22.
37. Edna C. Green, *Southern Strategies* (Chapel Hill: University of North Carolina Press, 1997) p. 162–163.
38. She used that line in her many speeches, see " The Woman Movement in the South," 1910, *Mary Johnston Papers,* Box 27.
39. Trudy J. Hanover "A Divine Discontent: Mary Johnston and Woman Suffrage in Virginia," (Master's Thesis, University of Virginia, 1972) p. 13.
40. "Pittsburgh," 1911, not paginated, *Mary Johnston Papers,* Box 27.
41. Ibid.
42. Ibid.
43. Donald K. Pickens, *Eugenics and the Progressives* (Nashville: Vanderbilt University Press, 1968) p. 3–22.
44. Ibid., p. xi.
45. Linda Gordon, *Woman's Body, Woman's Right, Birth Control in America* (New York: Penguin Books, 1990) p. 136.
46. Harry H. Laughlin, "The Relation of Eugenics To Other Sciences," 11:2, *The Eugenics Review,* July 1919, p. 1.

47. Pickens, p. 3.
48. Ibid., p. 4.
49. Ibid., p. xi.
50. Ibid., p. 65.
51. Ibid., p. 67, quoted in Pickens, from Laughlin's *Conquest by Immigration,* p. 30–31.
52. Stephen Jay Gould, ed., *"Carrie Buck's Daughter." The Flamingo's Smile: Reflections in Natural History* (New York: W.W. Norton and Company, 1985) p. 311.
53. Pickens, p. 92.
54. Gould, p. 310.
55. Harry L. Laughlin "The Legal Status of Eugenical Sterilization," a supplement to the Annual Report of *The Municipal Court of Chicago,* 1929, p. 17.
56. Gould, p. 314.
57. Ibid., p. 315.
58. Paul Lombardo, "Eugenic Sterilization in Virginia: Aubrey Strode and the Case of Buck V. Bell" (Ph.D. dissertation, University of Virginia, 1982) as quoted in Gould, p. 318.
59. Ibid., p. 257.
60. Ibid., p. 258.
61. "The Eugenical Point of View," Johnston's speech at the Virginia State Conference of Charities and Corrections, 1912, not paginated, in *Mary Johnston Papers,* Special Collections, University of Virginia, Box 27.
62. Ibid.
63. Ibid.
64. Ibid.

CHAPTER 5

"WINNING THEM INTO GOODNESS"
Progressive Pasadena Between the Wars, 1920–1940

In 1905, Ezra S. Gosney decided he would retire to Southern California. A successful and wealthy attorney who had made his fortune working for the railroads and the livestock industry, Gosney settled in Pasadena because of the climate (he had wintered there) and the schools, specifically one private school, Polytechnic Elementary. "Poly," as it would come to be known, was the spin-off from the consolidation of Troop Polytechnic Institute into the California Institute of Technology—Caltech. Gosney had been one of the principal founders before his retirement and, for more than 25 years, he was president of the Polytechnic Board of Trustees. In addition to his schoolwork in Pasadena, Gosney kept busy with a lemon "ranch" and various business ventures, including serving as legal counsel for banks and financial corporations in the city. His lemon ranch grew into one of the largest concerns of its kind in the world.

Gosney's philanthropic efforts were not limited to the Polytechnic Elementary School. In the mid-1920s, he cast about for a man who could assist him in making the world a better place. Gosney had come to believe that the country was suffering from "race suicide." Eugenics was the answer and Gosney wanted to do something to further that "noble concept." He was interested in organizing like-minded men "in the education of citizens in such practical and important matters as will reduce dependency and the necessity for the usual forms of charity ..." Gosney's goal, driven by his need for "efficiency" and "race purity," was to better educate Americans in the "practical and important matters" of sterilization.[1] His brainchild would be Pasadena's Human Betterment Foundation.

Gosney found his man in Paul Popenoe. He was just what the foundation needed. Popenoe had had an eclectic career by the time he joined Gosney. He had been educated for two years at Occidental College and then spent one year at Stanford but had to leave to care for his ailing father before he could graduate. (Later, he would receive an honorary doctorate from Occidental College, which led him to refer to himself as "Dr. Popenoe.") His Kansas family had come to

Pasadena just before the turn of the century and, like many Midwesterners, they relished the climate and profited greatly in the wide open economy of the new West. By the time he helped create the Human Betterment Foundation (HBF) in 1926, Popenoe had worked as an editor of the *Pasadena Star News,* an "agricultural explorer" in the employee of his father, a retiree turned nurseryman, a date palm "rancher" in the Coachella Valley of Southern California and as editor of the Washington, D.C.–based *Journal of Heredity.* Paul Popenoe would later be described by his son as the consummate progressive; he believed that the "path of human betterment lay in the application of science to society."[2]

During World War I, Popenoe enlisted and, because of his connections in Washington, was put in charge of vice and liquor control around stateside military bases. It was, according to his son, a perfect assignment for a man who was a lifelong moralist and antidrink crusader. After the war, he served as the executive secretary of the American Social Hygiene Association, a group trying to achieve through public education what Popenoe tried to achieve while in charge of vice and liquor control. Social hygiene was Mary Johnston's cause—race cleansing through sex hygiene. When Popenoe joined Gosney in the mid-1920s, he was well respected within the eugenics movement. He had authored *Applied Eugenics* (1918), *Modern Marriage* (1925), *The Conservation of the Family* (1926) and *The Child's Heredity* (1929) along with numerous articles and other research publications. The HBF was located in a suite of offices in one of the major business buildings on Colorado Boulevard. Pasadena was about to become a world center for eugenics studies.

THE HUMAN BETTERMENT FOUNDATION

Upon his return from a trip to California's state hospitals, Popenoe suggested that the first major project of the HBF be a "thorough-going and impartial" analysis of the sterilizations that had been performed in the state since before the war. Popenoe had scouted around the state, looking at the sterilization records of the various state hospitals. In the last 15 years, California's mental hospitals had performed 4,000 to 5,000 sterilizations, and Popenoe suspected there was much to learn and teach as a result of those operations. He told Gosney the data was open to their investigation, and "it ought to be possible to frame a program for further action, which might be adopted in California and thence taken by other regions."[3]

Paul Popenoe wielded no axe like the antidrink Carrie Nation. He advised Gosney that the HBF should be the "compiler of the data" and remain "merely an impartial scientific body" away from the political fray, therefore able to "inspire the movement, rather than lead a lobby for it." Popenoe knew that any expansion of sterilization would be bitterly opposed by many groups, especially the Catholic Church and the Christian Scientists.[4] Success in the "practical and important matters" of enlarging the scope of human sterilization would depend upon how well the HBF could avoid the fallout from the political skirmishes to follow.

Popenoe and Gosney began to collect the data, and in the late 1920s, the HBF published a series of studies on eugenic sterilization in California, all reporting benefits to the patients and the larger community, including 28 "voluntary" sterilizations of poor and destitute Pasadena women. Between 1927 and 1930, Popenoe authored 16 reports in a half-dozen professional journals, variously titled "Sterilization and Criminality," "Fecundity of the Insane," "Parole After Sterilization," "Marriage After Sterilization" and the "Social and Economic Status of the Sterilized Feeble-Minded."[5] In less than five years, the HBF would rival Harry Laughlin's Eugenics Record Office at Cold Spring Harbor, New York, as the world's leading center of eugenic studies.

Knowing that the general population would never consume such technical material as "Fecundity of the Insane," Gosney and Popenoe summarized the studies and coauthored a laymen's eugenic reader, *Sterilization for Human Betterment,* which Macmillan published in 1929. In the introduction, they wrote that the book "gives all the information needed" about the positive side of sterilizations and the benefits received from "race cleansing."[6] In a subsequent publication the next year, Gosney said the dissemination of the "valuable results of the research" was not a "short-cut to any eugenic millennium."[7] Rather, sterilizations were but one among many "protective measures." The world was watching, and the two men sensed that just over those "delectable mountains" that Mary Johnston dreamed of, was a society without the problems of the "unfit" that plagued modern America.

Indeed, the world was watching. Paul Popenoe left the HBF in the early 1930s to join the Institute of Family Relations in Hollywood, a marriage-counseling business that spun eugenics into family values. The HBF continued to churn out hundreds of thousands of prosterilization pamphlets to thousands of high schools, colleges and universities. Knowing the future of the Western (white) world was in the genes of intelligent youth around the country, the HBF focused its outreach on classroom instruction. Hence, the most requested pamphlet the foundation sent to schools began, "Shall the fit or the unfit make up the next generation?"[8] Here in America's classrooms was where the race wars would be won or lost.

Although the HBF concentrated on American schools, it also distributed its propaganda worldwide. Throughout Latin America and Europe, the HBF countered the Catholic Church and other groups that opposed mass sterilization. Popenoe's books, especially *Sterilization for Human Betterment,* were printed in many languages, including Spanish, French and German. But it was in Germany that Gosney and Popenoe received their greatest attention.

The new government of Adolph Hitler had taken a keen interest in this American form of progressive "race cleansing." Gosney and the HBF were flattered and eager to assist the Nazi government in its efforts to make a better Germany. In March 1936, the German consul in Los Angeles wrote to express his "great pleasure" in announcing that his government had passed its National Hygiene Legislation, which ultimately led to the forced sterilization of 400,000 Germans. The German government was "thankful to all those American organizations and men who have worked in the line of Human Betterment," particularly, the consul went on to say, Paul Popenoe and Ezra Gosney, who had just that year spoken and written in support of Germany's hygiene legislation. According to the consul's letter, Gosney and Popenoe were "very well known in Germany" and had been valuable contributors to the sterilization legislation. Both men would later furiously backpedal away from their Nazi connection, but the damage was done. As the horrors of Hitler's regime became known and the scientific community exposed the flaws in hereditary "science," the HBF lost credibility. It closed when Gosney died in 1943.

Still, for long afterward, eugenic reconstruction remained fixed in the progressive consciousness as one form of cultural salvation, although sterilizations occurred with alarming frequency in mental institutions around the country for decades after the closing of the HBF. Long after the fall of popular forms of hereditary studies, schools blandly continued to disseminate information—often embedded in instructional texts and teaching "habits"—that eugenics was a "noble concept, which most people can agree on." That quote comes from a widely used college introductory biology text which asked its young readers to accept the concept of IQ as infallible: "How long would our society function, if by a wave of a magic wand we all suddenly became one type with an IQ of 125 or better? Who would dig the ditches, who would collect the garbage, and who would do many of the jobs that are necessary in society?" The authors argued that there still needed to be a "sane program" of eugenics based on "practical, scientific, and democratic methods." That college text was still in use as late as the mid-1960s.9

The question of "who would do those jobs" had perplexed progressive places like Pasadena for a generation before that biology text was in use. How would Pasadena create those "democratic methods" that would determine who was best suited to reap the rewards of the new century? The eugenics idea may have been progressivism taken to excess, but progressive educators around the country firmly believed they could "fix" culture through the schools. To do so, however, Americans—especially the millions of school-age children—needed to be sorted into their "natural" groupings. Progressives had such untrammeled faith in science that the "natural groupings," which before were difficult to manifest as "needs," became known through the "new science" of intelligence tests and rating scales that "determined" character, attitude, behavior and aptitude. It was not a coincidence that along with the arrival of the HBF in the mid-1920s, the city of Pasadena emerged as one of the leading school systems in the country in the use of "scientific" determinism. No city in America epitomized the progressive impulse as well as Pasadena. If the 1920s were the golden age of the New Education, then Pasadena was the jewel in the crown.

PROGRESSIVE EDUCATION DURING THE 1920S

In September of 1928, the newly appointed superintendent of schools for the city of Pasadena submitted his first annual report to the board of education.[10] John Amherst Sexson (who has the distinction of being the only superintendent in the history of the city to survive longer than 15 years—he lasted 20) inherited a school system that was considered among the most "modern" in the country. Sexson arrived when Pasadena was one of the fastest growing cities in the United States. At the end of the First World War, the student population had been less than 5,000. When Sexson submitted his initial report to the board in 1928, it exceeded 20,000. Two years later 24,000 students would be enrolled in Pasadena's 32 schools. Grouped in age-graded clusters called the 6-4-4 Plan, students first attended kindergarten before beginning six years of elementary school, then four years at a junior/senior high school, followed by four more at a senior high school/junior college, the last two years devoted to the first two years of college.[11] This was a "seamless," 14-year educational experiment that was considered so unique in scope and enterprise that only a community like Pasadena could pull it off. And it did, with panache. Keeping the 6-4-4 Plan intact during the Depression and the war years took political will and pedagogical know-how coupled with strong community support. It also took money—a lot of it. By the time Sexson was asked to retire in 1947, amid accolades from the city's business and political leadership (but grumblings from disgruntled and underpaid teachers), he was one of the most respected and influential school administrators in the country.[12]

John Sexson was a Midwestern farmer's son, educated by his schoolteacher mother in a one-room sod schoolhouse on the Nebraska prairie. Like many of his contemporaries, after earning his normal-school degree, Sexson combined teaching and administration in small Western communities, mainly in Colorado. Pasadena recruited Sexson out of Bisbee, Arizona, a small copper mining town, where, as superintendent, he had grown weary of budget fights with company engineers serving as school-board members. The Pasadena job must have looked heaven-sent. In this town that was sun drenched in winter and liberally pro-gressive—city leaders referred to themselves as "modern" and "forward thinking"—the superintendency was his next step. It also did not hurt that the city was the wealthiest in the country.

Sexson found Pasadena in the midst of an economic boom unparalleled since the turn of the century. During the 1920s, shaking off the effects of World War I, Pasadena began a major capital building campaign of which schools were a key part.[13] In less than a decade, the city erected a grand central library with branch satellites that made good on the promise that every citizen would have a library within walking distance. Pasadena then created an 18-hole municipal golf course and Olympic plunge and diving facility at Brookside Park adjacent to the 80,000 seat—later expanded to 100,000—world-class Rose Bowl stadium. Finally, as a fitting tribute to the finest city in the country, Pasadena built a stunning Italian Renaissance-style civic auditorium and city hall that dwarfed any municipal structure of any comparable-sized city in the country. Pasadena's elite knew they had no equal. During the 1920s, they created the material representation to match their civic ego.

By the time Sexson settled into his office near the city hall complex, he knew his new home was thoroughly "modern." The community's boosters—led by an increasingly powerful coterie of professional real estate agents—continued to market Pasadena (as they had since well before the century's turn) as the city of stable, upper middle-class families commingling with the very wealthy. In reality, the city continued to attract a mix of lower middle-income families while maintaining a sizable population of working-class laborers. When Sexson took over in 1928, Pasadena had emerged from its 40-year battle with organized labor over control of the city's economic and cultural resources. Sexson's schools would come to mirror a community that was segregated into particular neighborhoods defined by color and caste. From the early days of the 1880's boom, the all-encompassing task of "meeting the needs" of the city's children, especially the poor and working class had increasingly fallen to the schools. During the Sexson years, the schools responded to the needs of the children with the vigor and professional zeal that was characteristic of a progressive community fixed on what one earlier superintendent had called "winning them into goodness."[14]

Sexson's predecessor, John Franklin West, has to be credited with establishing the groundwork for Pasadena's progressive system of educational and social services. West was the consummate "administrative progressive," a school leader steeped in the new era of efficiency, order, function and a key term, *equity*. For him, as for most of his contemporaries, including Sexson, the definition of equity would prove to be his most contradictory legacy.

West and his progressive administrators saw nothing wrong with wanting schools to be factories, efficiently dispensing knowledge and goodness to children. He urged the 1919 board of education to increase the number and type of schools. He wanted all the buildings to be highly efficient, "standardized" two-story

Fig. 11. Pasadena's City Hall, designed by the noted architectural firm of Bakewell and Brown, cost the city $1.3 million when it was erected in 1927. To convey the sense of civic accomplishment, Bakewell and Brown turned to the style of 16th-century Italian architect Andrea Palladio, who had studied and admired the Roman architect Vitruvius. The photograph was taken from the entrance of the equally inspiring Pasadena Central Library just after the city hall was opened. *(Photo courtesy of the Pasadena Museum of History)*

"plants" with classrooms flanking a central hallway. Pasadena had older structures and many were considered unsafe firetraps. West wanted to consolidate, to bring the students together into large, well-ventilated, efficiently organized, fire-safe schools, where the town's children would receive a "modern" education.

The board met his every wish and then some. In what was becoming an expectation for a very wealthy *belle arts* Pasadena, the buildings would be anything *but* utilitarian, unimaginative "plants." West's board of education members were the same men and women supporting the creation of Pasadena's magnificent civic structures and sporting arenas. Apparently, they took Dewey at his word: "What the best and the wisest parent wants for his own child, that must the community want of all its children." West had used this Dewey quote in his 1925 annual report, two years after the city had overwhelmingly approved a $3 million school improvement bond. Why would they not create the same grand buildings for the children?

By the end of the decade, Pasadena had a network of highly stylized school buildings that captured the flavor of Southern California's sunny, outdoor lifestyle. Altadena Elementary School, opened in 1926, was typical. A sprawling complex of buildings with Mexican red tile roofs, open courtyards (some with fountains), arched passageways, and thick, white-washed walls, Altadena Elementary evoked the imagined past of California's Spanish dons. Pasadena's children attended schools with up-to-date kitchens, cafeterias, auditoriums, libraries and large, fully equipped playgrounds, staffed, of course, by progressively trained recreation leaders. In 1919, when West called for his new plants, the school system owned 64 acres. In 1927, the city schools were the largest landowner in the community, holding title to 148 acres.[15]

Under West's leadership, the system was structured to be all things for nearly all children. Pasadena had interpreted "modern" schooling to be a network of "scientific" responses to a student's academic, social and emotional needs. This included earlier attempts with "Special Study Rooms" that evolved into "Opportunity Rooms" for underachieving students. There were vocational and academically tracked junior high schools, a technical high school, a part-time high school for working youth, a 24-hour high school for predelinquent students, an adult school and, by the time of West's departure, one of the first "gifted" education experiments in the country. Pasadena's educators were beginning to believe that to educate the "whole child"—a euphemistic term used by progressives to mean education for *all* social and academic needs—the system must embody the very educational ideals of Dewey himself. Schooling was more than preparation for living, it was *life itself*.[16] This was no easy task, for what educators in Pasadena came to define as life itself meant, for many students, a life fraught with the ailments associated with living in an industrial economy. Although Pasadena was a community of small businesses and homes—indeed, many were grand mansions—poverty was no stranger. For many children in the immediate postwar years, "life itself" meant being stranded on the streets, hungry, without adequate clothing, housing and medical care. The city would begin to accommodate the needs of its youngest citizens by measuring, classifying and then categorizing them, so as one administrator said, "[we] do not employ the de-humanized method of importing goodness into children; but rather the common sense method of winning them into goodness."[17] The results were nothing short of spectacular.

Fig. 12. Two of the many schools that symbolized the creation of progressive Pasadena during the 1920s and 1930s' Altadena Elementary School and Eliot Junior High, were built a few blocks from each other in north central Altadena. Both remain part of the Pasadena Unified School District. *(Altadena photo courtesy of the Pasadena Unified School District. Eliot photo courtesy Pasadena Museum of History.)*

By the end of the 1920s, the social services provided by the city's schools were invasive. Just after World War I, West created the Department of Child Welfare and Guidance with three employees, a doctor and two nurses. When Sexson took over eight years later, there were 33 full-time workers in the office with an untold number of support staff and part-time employees. Child Welfare and Guidance coordinated the efforts of the other city welfare services. The various school PTAs, the Citizens' Milk and Hygiene Committee, the Welfare Bureau, the Police Department, the Mexican Settlement House, the YMCAs and YWCAs, the Red Cross, the Boy Scouts, the Pasadena Dispensary, Day Nursery, Boy's Preventorium, the Juvenile Court and the Council of Social Agencies were but the most visible. Serving the schools were three medical teams—doctors with full-time nurses, a dentist and a half-time volunteer dentist (assisted by six dentists who performed their services *pro bono*) and two oral hygienists. The dentists examined every child's mouth annually—that was 24,000 by 1930—but the medical and dental teams could not provide the needed services to cover the increasing "problems" flooding into the city with the ever-expanding population.[18]

Pasadena's goal of "meeting the needs" of its "less fortunate" citizens had far-reaching consequences. "Meeting the needs," the all too familiar refrain of progressive educators during this period, meant first defining the needs of a population that mystified, perplexed and frustrated school officials. In 1927, truant officer Earl Smith's workday had became increasingly complex. Whereas he once simply took out-of-schoolers back to school, Smith now reported that during the school year in 1927, he and his staff rounded up 312 children found on the streets (there had been 25 in 1920), made nearly 900 home visits (down from 1,120 in 1925), responded to 183 police calls (there were none in 1920), granted 743 work permits (up from 303 in 1924), visited schools 3,223 times (up from 710 in 1923), oversaw 4,460 transfers (up from 286 in 1920), and dealt with 170 "incorrigible" cases—mostly boys—(up from 26 in 1924). During the 1927–28 school year, Smith's staff had contact with Pasadena's children 14,003 times. In this small enclave tucked up against the foothills of the San Gabriel mountains, Smith drove his car nearly 10,000 miles in less than a year.[19]

These statistics filled page after page of both West's and Sexson's annual reports. Pasadena's progressive bureaucrats, like progressives around the country, were increasingly obsessed by the quantification of culture. Progressivism had come to mean social efficiency and Pasadena's turn toward the New Education meant its officials were consumed by an ideology of form, segmentation and hierarchy. They researched, planned and then made efforts to organize everything down to the last minute detail. In 1926, the principal of Longfellow Elementary School, the largest elementary school in the city with over 1,100 students, reported that he and his staff were most proud of how the school had "sanely and efficiently reorganized the school supply room in a most progressive fashion."

Superintendent West believed wholeheartedly that the city was meeting the needs of "every boy and girl who knocks on our doors." West and John Sexson wanted the city's schools, their schools, to be the full embodiment of Dewey's admonition about what the best and wisest parent wants for his own child. Both superintendents knew, as Dewey did, that "any other ideal for our schools is narrow and unlovely." In 1925, three years before he was fired, West boasted to his board, "It is very gratifying that in Pasadena this ideal approaches realization."[20]

"SHOULD STUDENTS BE SORTED?"

The irony of progressivism is that the more the school bureaucrats reached into the community to meet the needs of students, the more the schools became engaged in trying to "fix" or "cure" complex social behaviors exhibited by students who, in many ways, were responding to the very institutional arrangements created by progressivism. School attendance officers like Earl Smith were needed because progressives determined that keeping students in schools was paramount. Youngsters on the streets were considered, at best, predelinquents. Depending on their social station (most likely determined by social class and skin color), out-of-schoolers were labeled as "miscreants" and "social deviants" apt to engage in "anti-social behaviors."[21] The aim of administrators was to bring children off the streets and into the classrooms. In doing so, schools took on the enormous problems associated with industrial society.

Among Superintendent West's most important accomplishments was the creation, in 1922, of the Department of Research and Service. Under the direction of psychologist W. Hardin Hughes, the department was charged with managing the enormous data generated by a system that was fixated on creating and then tracking "individual differences." By 1927, just five years after West brought Hughes to Pasadena, the city had established one of the most far-reaching testing, counseling and guidance systems in the country. Schooling had begun to effectively echo the eugenics zeitgeist. The "better race" would use science to "fix" the lesser ones.

In his first annual report in 1919, West told the board that he had been "keenly interested in the psychological investigation and developments" that were being carried on by Lewis Terman, E.L. Thorndike, James Cattell and others. He was aware of how Terman had used army recruits during the war as test subjects and told the board that the intelligence tests "were both logical and scientific and give promise of providing us with a most useful means of improving instruction and teaching ..." He was confident that intelligence tests would lead to great things for education. If they could devise "a means by which we can secure in each classroom a thought-provoking lesson instead of a textbook recitation, education will have taken a big leap forward." The superintendent, like many during this time, believed IQ tests would transform instruction, providing schools with much-needed information that would compel teachers to change their approaches to student learning. He told the board that "this great work" has "pointed the way" and Pasadena should take the lead and "profit by it."[22]

Take the lead they did. Pasadena educators were caught up in the postwar zeal of measuring capabilities, categorizing students and predicting outcomes. Ultimately, they created schooling so those predictions would come true. Although Hughes reported more than once that he was in favor of a "conservative program of testing" that would not "accumulate a large number of test scores," the city schools nevertheless had begun an intensive measurement program that tended to reinforce what they believed everyone knew—those with material wealth were more "intelligent."

We must keep in mind that the city's efforts to measure and then track "intelligence" was not some back-room plot hatched to justify a very hierarchical social order. Hughes and his colleagues believed intelligence tests merely named "the distinctions."[23] The differences between the haves and the have-nots had always existed. Intelligence testing gave educators a huge advantage over their predecessors in that they could now *scientifically* sort children into different groups, thereby providing for more efficient, customized services that could meet their needs.

The IQ test was grounded in the notion that intelligence was predetermined, that once the results were in, the score was immutable. Once determined, an individual's intelligence was then used to determine what type of education he or she would receive. Rather than seeing the environment as the main determinant of intelligence, many within the mental measurement movement attempted to prove that differences were inborn and impermeable. Most important, the IQ test reinforced, through the sanctity of numbers, the long-established belief that society was naturally stratified by evolution. Each group occupied its rung on the social ladder. Progressivism tended to want to make those on the lower rungs of the ladder less violent and less hurtful, as well as make the positioning on the rungs less contentious and less competitive. Although some educators argued the ladder itself was a device to keep certain less favored groups marginalized, most educators and social scientists believed the positioning on nature's "order" was quite useful. Testing only tended to substantiate one's placement. In retrospect, sadly, it is clear that the tests were self-fulfilling prophecies and one of the most glaring examples of school-based scientific racism.[24]

Hughes, in his weekly newspaper column, told Pasadena how natural, "genetic" differences were observed everyday in the form of material wealth and social status—in the more wealthy neighbor who owns a Cadillac, wears better clothes, gets job promotions quicker, is in *Who's Who* and "generally has more fame and prosperity." All these "facts," wrote Hughes, constitute "aspects of life that one must adjust to." Schools, he went on, "therefore need to teach [the child] how to acquire such an attitude toward the inequalities of life ... [so] he may adjust himself to its conditions with the least possible friction."

One week, Hughes titled his article, "Should Students Be Sorted?"[25] For Hughes and his staff, the answer was an emphatic *yes*. Tests gave the Pasadena educator the means of instructional differentiation. Ultimately, some in Pasadena believed that IQ measurement had the potential to eliminate the need for ability groups, as instruction would be so precise it would meet the unique needs of each individual.

To be able to achieve that ultimate differentiation, Hughes sensed that he needed more than mental measurement. He was concerned that IQ tests alone could not provide as complete a picture of the student as was needed. Hughes had written that the natural order found in a meritocratic society such as Pasadena was reflected in its school intelligence tests. "In the ordinary affairs of life" he said, "we judge intelligence by attainment."[26] It was no different in schools. Hughes wrote, "We can never be certain that we have prepared a perfect situation in which the individual has a natural and complete incentive for doing all that he is capable of doing." High scores on tests were never doubted—"one cannot make a high score unless he has the ability to do so." But lower scores, especially from students who came from Pasadena's wealthy and middle-class families, could be confusing and misleading.[27]

Hughes and his colleagues believed that defining and then quantifying "character" was as important as measuring innate intelligence. They were puzzled by the lack of a positive correlation between intelligence scores as determined by the tests and academic success of the system's graduates when they went to college. There should be a logical connection between high intelligence as measured by the tests and excellent grades at Stanford, the University of California or the University of Southern California, where most of the system's college-bound graduates went. This was exactly the type of "educational problem" Hughes wanted his research department to tackle.[28]

In 1923–24, Hughes and a research team of 18 Pasadena educators set out to "determine in as scientific a fashion as possible the traits that should be included in a rating scale for students." Their "scientific" approach was to first determine the "psychology of each trait" and then how that trait was "expressed in behavior." Once this was accomplished, the team would then "ascertain the methods and school procedure essential for developing the trait." They called their measurement device the Graphic Rating Scale (GRS), and in various iterations, the scale was used extensively throughout the system for the next two decades.[29]

Teachers and counselors would observe students and then determine where on the scale a set of defined behaviors fell. As an example, the characteristics of the "industrious" student "... are that he works regularly and on time; habitually completes his work; and makes judicious use of time." If the opposite were observed, then teachers and counselors would rate a student accordingly, answering questions such as "did he work sporadically; seldom complete his work; use time injudiciously." Thus, in Pasadena, preselected "attitudes, habits and interests" were evaluated through observation without taking into account the myriad variables in each observed context. Hughes thought he had escaped this weakness by having each student's GRS averaged over time, because, he wrote, "[We are] aiming at greater justice." Yet, too often "adjustment" decisions, in other words vocational or academic course selections and grade placements, were made after only one or two years of GRS observations, with only a handful of teachers reporting. What Hughes meant by "justice" was his attempt to soften the impact, if he could, of the all-powerful—and in his mind exceedingly unscientific—

teacher letter grade. He surmised that if students believed that the characteristics found on the GRS were important to adults, then students would feel that the "attitudes, habits and interests" were as important as "those [teacher grades] on which they are regularly rated." Thus, he concluded, "Students of mediocre ability could feel accomplished even if they did not achieve much success in book work" because such a student "... knows that the school is observing and making record of the fact that he is acquiring habits and attitudes most conducive to successful living."[30]

Hughes and the team initially came up with 12 character traits, then, two years later eliminated certain traits that proved too unscientific for definition: "Trustworthiness," "Respect for Authority" "Confidence in Own Ability" and "Force of Personality."[31] Apparently, junior—and senior-high schoolteachers complained that certain traits did not correlate well to their particular subjects— "Respect for Authority" to mathematics instruction and "Trustworthiness" to English classes. The scale was narrowed to reflect only what was believed to be most important.[32] Given the love affair the system had with IQ tests, the traits deemed most important were those that correlated most highly with IQ tests. Ranked in descending order of perceived importance were:

1. "Industry"
2. "Accuracy"
3. "Initiative"
4. "Quickness of Thought"
5. "Control of Attention"
6. "Retentiveness of Memory"

Two additional traits that remained from the original scale of twelve, "Co-operation" and "Leadership," were relegated to classroom situations where group work was prominent. In the junior/senior high school and junior college, that meant classrooms least likely to be valued as solidly academic.

Under the guise of "scientific infallibility," the GRS reinforced the dominant white, middle-class Protestant perception that subjectively defined behaviors like "industry," "persistency," "aggressiveness," "cooperativeness," "trustworthiness" and "respect for authority" as the essential characteristics of a successful student. Those students whose demeanor did not fit within the acceptable range of definitions were determined to be lacking. Even when the later versions eliminated the more idiosyncratic traits, the scale remained fixed on evaluating students' "character" according to a set of traits that were defined as much by who did the observations as by those who originally determined the definitions of "interests, abilities, and habits." The GRS simply reinforced that "otherness" was a legitimate multidimensional standard by which the dominant white, middle-class culture could be defined as "superior."[33]

The GRS was made legitimate when it was introduced at Muir Junior High School during 1923–24. Muir, which began as an "opportunity school," was increasingly geared toward vocational work. Although initially skeptical of the scale, the head counselor reported that teachers had become "sympathetic" to the rating scheme. Teachers wanted to develop a "well-defined plan" so the positive side of "character," absent in certain students, could be improved upon. According to the counselor's report to the superintendent, teachers identified classroom situations where "difficulties could be most easily observed." They did this because a "list of causes" was necessary for "accurate diagnosis." With plan in hand, the teachers began "ascertaining and stating concretely the things to do to remove the causes which hinder the development of good traits."[34] What might have been those "causes which hinder development" of good character? Using the GRS along with the IQ tests, teachers determined that particular courses of study were incompatible with certain students' observed "interests, abilities, and habits." In Pasadena, teachers and counselors were reminded that the aim of scientific measurements was to "adjust children to the system."[35]

The Muir teachers and counselors made home visits to those they had identified as most in need. By the end of the year, the plan had been modified to include "definite vocational guidance." The counselors and teachers gave "the boys" (for there is no mention of girls in the initial study) a list of vocations. Then groups of boys were brought to the auditorium for individual interviews. During those interviews, teachers and counselors guided the students as they created the next year's schedule of classes. This guidance resulted in a boy "choosing his course [academic or vocational] and selecting his electives." The "guidance" in making these decisions was given "in light of ... grades, intelligence quotients, the teacher trait ratings, the students' and parents' interests" and something the counselor called "economic considerations."[36] In Pasadena, the largest number of occupations open to the greatest number of white, working-class boys at Muir would have been the trades—carpentry, plumbing or masonry. "Economic considerations" meant white boys were guided into courses of study that "met their needs." Mexican, African American and Japanese boys were "adjusted" into their respective career tracks in domestic services like gardening, driving or cooking.[37]

Pasadena's 6-4-4 Plan and testing practices helped institutionalize divisions within the city. The poorer, white working-class students and the city's increasing population of color attended particular elementary schools—all, with the exception of one segregated Mexican school in the unincorporated northeast, were on the west side of the city. Under the 6-4-4 Plan, those students, or at least those who chose to stay in school, moved on to a four-year junior high school, usually George Washington, located in the northwest corner of Pasadena. For those planning on a full high school or vocational education after Washington, the system provided Muir Technical High School, also located in west Pasadena. A demographic snapshot of Pasadena in 1930 shows large, white, working-class neighborhoods in the west and central sections. With the exception of a small Mexican *colonia* located in the unincorporated northeast, Pasadena's neighborhoods of color were restricted to the western portions of the city. Pasadena's white middle-class and wealthier neighborhoods and schools were in the eastern sections and along the city's Southern boundary with San Marino and South Pasadena, both small, white-only bedroom communities.

In a general way, teachers used the "scientific measurements" of the GRS and the IQ to determine students' overall attitudes toward school; in other words, their "fit." When a student did not "seem to respond favorably to the instruction given them," Hughes and his staff wanted teachers to recommend further testing. By the end of the 1923–24 school year, the "Adjustment Division," a newly created branch of the research department, had administered nearly 400 individual IQ tests and an unknown number of group tests, nearly all requested by principals and teachers. I. Grace Ball, the division head, was pleased with her work, especially the increasing number of requests for group IQ tests "so teachers [might] measure scientifically the abilities of their group for purposes of analysis, classification, and promotion." When Ball administered the intelligence tests, she found that a majority of the 400 recommended students were classified as "mentally retarded" and "dull normal," labels that had been created by the testmakers. In addition, Ball classified 15 students as "predelinquent" and two as "mentally superior." She focused on meeting the needs of all of the students, except the two "superior" ones.[38]

Most of her work appears to have been focused on trying to convince the parents to agree to place their children in the vocational school or in one of the many "special study rooms" scattered around the system. Many refused, testimony to the reluctance of parents to trust tests, teachers and institutional power that attempted to classify their children as less than able. Still, the number of students who were "adjusted" to the system, meaning removed from their classrooms, was large enough to warrant Ball's urging that additional space be found. What she wanted were classrooms devoted to "industrial work" because "adjustment" for the "slower" children meant a modified curriculum, including "shop-work, cooking, sewing, gardening"—much of which necessitated transfer to the vocational school. She recommended additional shop, cooking and sewing space at Garfield, Lincoln, Madison and Longfellow and asked that Fremont School be given "laundry, cobbling, cooking, sewing, and shop equipment to meet their needs for concrete instruction." The students at each of these schools were predominately working class, and, at Lincoln, Garfield and Fremont, many were of the "darker races." She also recommended a 24-hour school for predelinquents and classes for "children of superior intelligence." Nearly all of her recommendations became realities within the next few years.

At one level, the system's progressive practices worked. By the middle of the 1920s, Attendance Officer Earl Smith noticed marked decreases in out-of-school children, court appearances, institutional placements and warning notices sent to parents. These decreases were matched by dramatic increases in his home and school visits and in his granting of work permits. The changing nature of Smith's work reflected changes brought about by the city's progressive programs.[39] By the end of the decade, the city had devised a network of educational and social services that "met the needs" of all of Pasadena's citizens, including the wealthy, the middle class, and the burgeoning population of poor immigrants from Mexico. By 1930, Mexican immigrants had been sorted into a settlement house, at least five churches—three of them Protestant—a privately (white) owned, for-profit "Mexican Housing Association," and two (de jure) segregated Mexican schools.[40]

Early in the 1920s, there had been hundreds of Mexican children out of school. Pasadena had never made any substantial effort to bring them into schools, and when the initial efforts were made, just before World War I, the Mexicans resisted. In 1909, there were more than 500 children out of school and many of those were Mexican.[41] In 1923–24, Pasadena further reinforced its mandatory attendance laws, and nearly 300 Mexican children, once left to their own devices, were sitting behind desks in two segregated, all-Mexican schools. The James C. Fremont School was located in an unincorporated northeast *colonia,* devoted mainly to citrus orchards. Junipero Serra, the other all-Mexican school, was tucked between two railroad spurs along South Raymond Street—the traditional industrial section of the city, where the Chinese laundrymen had been banished in the 1880s.[42] Because of the "special needs" of the Mexican population, the city did not initially include the two schools in the 6-4-4 Plan. Instead, both Fremont and Serra were K-8 schools, the only such arrangement in the city. In the 1920s, other than the two Mexican schools, Garfield and Lincoln were the only predominately multiethnic K-6 schools in the system, with growing populations of African Americans, Japanese and Southern Europeans.[43] All of the other schools in the city were nearly all white. Fremont and Serra ended at the eighth grade because it was the conventional wisdom that Mexican children did not attend school after that.

One reason that many children did not attend school before the 1920s was because the community had refused to accommodate increases for *any* schools. During 1923 and 1924, at the urging of superintendent West and with the backing of the community's influentials, the city approved more than $3 million in school construction bonds that included funds for the expansion of Fremont and the building of an entirely new school for the Mexicans living in the city's densely populated industrial area. Junipero Serra was built, as one board member said, "for the industrial needs of the community."

The building program reflected the increasingly strict interpretation of the unwritten rule that in Pasadena certain cultural groups lived within certain neighborhoods. The intended focus of the school building program was to alleviate the overcrowding of the white schools, which would reduce the threat of Pasadena's white children having to sit next to "other" children.[44] The new school construction tended to further segment an already highly stratified community. Although anecdotal, when asked about contact with and perceptions of the "others," older white Pasadena residents who have been interviewed cannot recall any association with Mexicans. Older residents acknowledge that Mexicans existed in the city, but they have no memory of any Mexican schools, Mexican *barrios* (neighborhoods) or of Mexicans actually living in the city. Moreover, the social distance that resulted from this segmentation was somewhat color blind; older African American residents, too, seldom recall the location of the Mexican schools or having much contact with Mexican residents.[45]

MEETING THE NEEDS OF MEXICAN PASADENA

We know little about early Mexican Pasadena. By the time of incorporation in 1884, the few remaining *Californio* families had all but disappeared. The *Chronicle* in 1883 noted that four families sold their homesteads and returned to Mexico.[46] In the early 1890s, Eulogio Carrillo, the second son of John J. Carrillo, president of the Santa Monica Board of Trade, married Pasadena's Grace B. Westover, but the young couple lived in Santa Monica. Arturo Bandini, a sheep rancher and accountant (and former landowner of vast properties in the San Gabriel Valley) married into one of the founding families, the Elliotts. After the marriage, the new Californio/Indiana Colony alliance had some influence on the community's affairs, as the couple was mentioned prominently in the newspaper.[47] Grace Westover Bandini was one of the founders of the Shakespeare Club, and Arturo Bandini was active in a number of political and social organizations. In the late 1890s and just after the turn of the century, there were scattered references to a Mexican Union Club, organized to celebrate Mexican independence from Spain, and the Club Mexicanos de Pasadena, but both of these organizations might very well have been whites pretending to be dons from old California.[48]

With the economic boom at the turn of the century, immigrants flooded into Southern California by rail. In Pasadena, two railroad companies, the Santa Fe and the Southern Pacific, ran spurs into the center of the city along what was then called Broadway Street (now Arroyo Seco Boulevard) and South Raymond Street. At about this same time, Henry Huntington's Pacific Electric interurban rail system was reaching Pasadena, and hundreds of workers, many Mexican but also

Filipino and Japanese, entered the city to work laying the new line. Within the corridor between the two lines, the rail companies built section houses just north of Glenarm Street, at the base of Raymond Hill. Huntington's company erected sheds along Glenarm Street. This "industrial section" of the city was where Mexican immigrant laborers made their homes, along with smaller numbers of Chinese, African American, Greek and Japanese.[49] By the turn of the century, hundreds of Mexican workers and their families were living within the South Raymond corridor. The population was dense enough that by 1910 city officials began to take notice.

The Raymond Street *barrio* was not the only area that Mexican immigrants called home. A second neighborhood, referred to as a colonia because of its rural location, was northeast of the city center in an unincorporated area of Los Angeles county. This was home to a number of Mexican families, numerous enough so that St. Andrew established another small mission. White Pasadenans referred to this area as "Titleyville," but to Mexicans it was "Chihuahuita" or "little Chihuahua," after the northern Mexican state. One longtime Mexican resident of Chihuahuita remembered using "Titley" as slang, but to be referred to as from "Titley" was an insult to a Mexican from Chihuahuita.[50] A third, smaller Mexican *barrio* lay just to the north of the city center in the neighborhood around Waverly Street. By the 1960s, Waverly Street was home to some 4,000 *Mexicanos*. The neighborhood, removed when the 210 Freeway was built, was one of the city's most populous working-class neighborhoods. For the most part, its history has been lost.[51]

The 1910 census counted 258 Mexicans living along South Raymond, but those numbers are not an accurate representation of the population. Itinerant laborers are typically evasive, seldom trusting a prying, inquisitive outsider asking questions about where one lives and works. Further confusing the census count were the housing conditions, which were deplorable even by turn-of-the-century standards. In fact, there was little decent housing anywhere in the *barrio*. What we know of the neighborhood indicates that mixed with standard wood-framed houses and barns were tents, shacks, lean-tos and wood and tin sheds—almost anything that might offer a minimum of protection from the elements. The few standard houses supported far too many people. One report in the early 1920s indicated that some houses had as many as six to a room. The *barrio* had almost no plumbing or electricity. As late as the 1930s, infectious disease was a constant concern. Cooking was often outside over primitive brick ovens or open fires. Then the 1910 census count was only as accurate as the census taker was able to locate and count a population that did not wish to be counted. The "fact" that there were 258 Mexicans along South Raymond is wrong. There were more.

Mexican immigrants had no other place to live in the city center except in the Raymond Street *barrio*. Unemployment and vagrancy worried city leaders.

These immigrants were not like the Chinese who came to Pasadena as single males. Mexicans came north in family units, or, as was often the case, the women came sola and then later had their extended families join them.[52] Mexican women counted in the 1910 census were often caring for young children. To the Pasadena matrons concerned about health and education, women and children only tended to increase the complexity of the *cholo* community. The census indicates that in 1910 Mexican women did not work for wages but, again, just how completely Mexican women answered a stranger's rather intrusive questions—in English no doubt—is open to interpretation. The women may have said they did not work for wages, but one suspects they were employed as domestics and laundry workers and as day laborers for a large, seasonal fruit processing plant near the section house. We know that these women did perform wage work, because a group of white Pasadena matrons established a small nursery so the Mexican mothers could leave their children while they went off to work. A nursery, to these reforming matrons of Pasadena, went a long way toward solving the "problem" of the children, especially those of school age. Before this, Pasadena had not paid much attention to Mexican youth. It was not until the immigrant community became so large and scores of Mexican children began attending Garfield School that this progressive city decided to act.

SEGREGATION AS AMERICANIZATION

Located just to the west of the railroad tracks on the corner of California Street and Pasadena Avenue, the James A. Garfield School was the *barrio's* "neighborhood school." Further west, less than a mile from the school, was Orange Grove Boulevard. Here, along "Millionaire's Row" and its slightly less fashionable, more upper middle-class tributaries like Grand Avenue and Bellfontaine Street, lived families that also sent their children to Garfield School. As the Orange Grove neighborhood increased in size and the Mexican *barrio* increased in numbers, Garfield School became contested territory.

Garfield's first principal in 1888 was Arthur L. Hamilton. In 1907, after a long career as teacher and principal, Hamilton became Pasadena's Superintendent of Schools. In his first "State of the Schools" speech, Hamilton, who also had been a member of the Throop Polytechnic faculty, proposed the most massive reorganization of schooling in the city's brief history.

Hamilton knew Pasadena well. He also knew the issues confronting education. Recognizing that the schools were not meeting the needs of many of the students, he was the first superintendent to call for special study rooms, where children who were classified as "about to be behind,"[53] or had been out of school, would have a more individualized education. His first two special study rooms were at Garfield and Wilson Grammar, which in a few years would become the city's "Opportunity School," where young boys who had not succeeded in their prior classrooms might have another chance. The programs at Wilson Grammar would later migrate to Muir.

Hamilton saw public education as a legitimate extension of the social network of the modern, progressive city. He believed the public schools might serve the needs of the working-class family. He called for a "Mother's School" for "infant hygiene, general care of babies, in sick-room diet, home ventilation, and sanitation."[54] In addition, Hamilton asked the board of education for funds to bring in a medical team of doctors and nurses to begin health examinations for all boys classified as "confirmed truants, or otherwise undesirable school citizens."[55] He was convinced that through science—in other words, proper medical evaluation—problems could be diagnosed, and these "incorrigible boys" could be made into desirable school citizens.[56] Although he recognized truancy as a continuing problem, he turned his attention to what was, in his view,, a major crisis—the 510 children not in school at all. What Pasadena needed, Hamilton told the board, was to "extend [its] services" and, as a result, the board voted unanimously to hire its first attendance officer, a man, Hamilton surmised, who would not only locate and bring in the out-of-school child but would then "look after the irregular student and save him from a worthless life of a criminal."[57] This was the staff position Earl Smith occupied in the 1920s. Many of the children that Hamilton proposed adding to the attendance rolls (as well as keeping there) had not been part of the traditional school culture. These were the children of labor, especially, it appears, the *Mexicanos* residing along South Raymond.

By 1908 there was growing tension over Garfield's multiethnic classrooms. In that year, the board called for a bond issue to raise money, some of which would be used "to remodel and reconstruct the old Garfield school building so that it can be used for classes in manual training and domestic science and for any other purpose."[58] The "old Garfield school building" was the original (1888) grammar school, now located next to the newly opened (1907) Garfield School. It was a "ramshackle," poorly lit, poorly ventilated, two-story frame building that some on the board feared might "fall down." Immediately after the announcement, a group of parents from Garfield strenuously objected to the board's decision to use the building for manual training and domestic science.[59] These were parents from the west side of the Garfield attendance area, along the Orange Grove/Bellefontaine axis. Although there is no conclusive evidence that Hamilton's special study rooms at Garfield were intended for the exclusive use of Mexican children, it is logical to assume that a population that so befuddled and frustrated school administrators would be segregated, given the prevailing attitude toward those "who wait at her doors."[60]

Enter Clara Morgan Odell, patron parent of Garfield. Odell and her family—husband Samuel and two young children—had moved to Pasadena in 1909

Fig. 13. A gathering of Mexican children on the steps of Garfield School in 1914. The photo, taken by a member of Pasadena's Meza family, is one of the few surviving images of the Mexican community in the early 20th century. *(Photo courtesy of the Pasadena Museum of History)*

from Santa Monica. She and Samuel had followed their temperance-minded Methodist minister, Reverend F.G.H. Stevens who, like the Odells, had disliked "wet" Santa Monica. Relations were strained between Clara and Samuel, so the move may have been as much intended to save the marriage as to avoid alcohol. Before long, Mr. Odell was spending his time in Santa Monica, and Mrs. Odell, having hired a housekeeper, was throwing herself into school and city politics, becoming active with the Garfield Parent-Teacher Association (PTA). Clara Odell was a fierce social reformer, active in the Women's Christian Temperance Union (WCTU) and the Methodist church. For the Mexicans, as well as the city leadership, Clara Odell was impossible to ignore.[61]

Odell was intent on fixing what she saw wrong in her new city. Aware of the rapidly increasing Mexican population at Garfield—by 1913 there were 150 Mexican students at the school, nearly half of the total attendance—Odell was concerned that more Mexican mothers were not attending the school's PTA. She began home visits to encourage immigrant mothers to come to Garfield School meetings. What she found along South Raymond deeply disturbed her. She was sympathetic to the plight of the Mexicans. "They should not be blamed," she said, because it was more the fault of "the conditions."[62] Nor did she blame Henry Huntington, who owned some of the "conditions," that cluster of sheds and shacks along South Raymond and Glenarm streets where so many destitute Mexican laborers and their families lived. Instead, Odell and her Garfield School PTA sisters began a municipal campaign to clean up the "conditions," which included fixing the Mexicans themselves. Attempting to better understand their new students, the Garfield teachers enrolled in Spanish language courses.[63]

Odell recognized that the housing was so frightful, "you might be able to keep chickens ... if they weren't very fancy chickens."[64] A high fence surrounded Huntington's Pacific Electric camp. Inside, more than 100 men, women and children lived in abject poverty, sharing 12 small rooms built in the form of long, low sheds. Scattered among the sheds were tents for single male *traqueros*. Accompanied by a reporter from the *Pasadena Daily News,* one of Odell's PTA sisters walked through the camp in January 1913.

> We entered the hovel of the sick woman slowly dying of tuberculosis and met Miss L.M. Sewell, visiting nurse for the Associated Charities. The home consisted of a narrow entry, in one corner of which was the stove fashioned out of bricks and smoking badly. The stench of cooking and washing pervaded the next room, which opened into the kitchen. In here was a single bed on which the sick woman was resting. A stack of clothes and bedding was on the floor ... dozens of rats run from house to house coming up through the cracks [in the floors and walls] ... The furniture was for the most part made of soap boxes.[65]

The *Daily News* reporter, clearly repulsed by the camp, made repeated references to the "degenerate" inhabitants, including the "Spanish, negroes [sic], Japanese and Chinese." "Immorality," said the writer, "may well be imagined," because entire families were forced to sleep in one room "... rolled in blankets on the floor [or] on the beds." Most of the sheds accommodated more than eight persons to a room. Because the Mexicans were "thrown together" as they were, the the *Daily News* reporter assumed there was "no morality" among them.[66]

But the "problem" was not just the "immoral" and unsanitary conditions bred by substandard housing, but the people themselves. It was "not enough to furnish them with better houses, it is needful to teach them how to live in those houses ... Their moral nature was scarcely developed." To Odell and her WCTU allies, the temperance crusade had provided ample proof that changing an aberrant culture required drastic measures. The Americanization program in Pasadena would concentrate on the children. Odell understood that to Americanize the Mexicans they needed "to raise the standard of mentality in the children," because older Mexicans "do not like to change."[67] Odell and her Americanizing sisters were zealous Christian crusaders. Less than six months after the *Daily News* article appeared, the city ordered Huntington to demolish the camp at his expense and then rebuild.[68]

In addition to the railroad camps, Odell's crusaders went after the *barrio*'s slum landlords. Mexican *traqueros* were paid on average $1 a day for 12 to 14 hours of backbreaking labor with pick, sledgehammer, wagon and wheelbarrow. Housing in the *barrio* was substandard and overpriced. Rents in some of the larger structures were by floors, and gouging landlords charged as much as $11 a floor, forcing Mexican families to take in as many boarders as possible. When beds were full, people slept where they could. Many of the structures had packed earth for floors. Odell described one house where the "floor"—a mosaic of wood scraps—"oozed" as she walked because it had been laid directly on wet earth. Odell and the Garfield matrons "agitated the matter," as she said, until the land-lord lowered the rent. They also forced other owners to repair poor housing, pro-viding better ventilation, light and sewage.[69]

Odell and the Garfield matrons also pressured the city to begin to enforce its school attendance laws. The result was that ever-larger numbers of Mexican chil-dren began coming to school. Yet all was not well at Garfield. There were far too many Mexicans. Superintendent Hamilton's special study rooms were overflow-ing. In a lengthy newspaper interview, Odell explained that many children came to Garfield overage and "they feel the difference between themselves very keenly—and the American children aren't slow to remind them of it." Clearly Odell was compassionate, but she was alarmed at the consequences of so many Mexicans. "When they find themselves so much older and bigger and cannot do their best work," she wrote, "the whole class has to be held back if the races are mixed."[70] The only reasonable solution was to segregate the Mexicans because, Odell said, the "[Mexican children] work better when they are by themselves."

Trapped by a narrow, ethnocentric view of "us" and "them," Pasadena's edu-cators did not know what to do with these "strangers." There were simply too many "differences" and not enough special study rooms to accommodate them. Conventional wisdom determined that what was needed was a special school, just for Mexicans. A special school would "meet the needs" of the Mexicans, while not holding back the white children. Pasadena was about to put its own progressive spin on the recent U.S. Supreme Court *Plessy* decision. "Meeting the needs" meant separation.

In the fall of 1911, the population of the city's more affluent southwest neigh-borhood and the South Raymond *barrio* could no longer coexist. In October the board of education announced that they were considering opening a "school for Mexicans." According to the Pasadena newspaper, the school system needed to respond to a population of immigrants who were "breaking the law" by "not sending their children to school." More likely, the population along Raymond Street posed too many special problems for the Garfield School patrons. Jeremiah M. Rhodes, who had replaced Hamilton as superintendent, told the newspaper that the Mexicans were keeping their children close to home rather than having them "mingle with their white-skinned scholars." He also told the press that Mexicans at Garfield were so ill kept that "it was necessary last year to introduce a number of the brown skinned pupils to the bathtub before they were allowed to enter the classroom."[71]

The impression that Mexicans were best served in a separate environment had become the consensus. Although no existing documents have survived, the system's annual report for 1914 says that the Mexicans were polled by school officials and asked if they wanted "segregation." The annual report says the Mexicans "chose segregation."[72] The survey results may or may not have been exactly as reported, but if presented with a "plan" to create "their own school" within "their neighborhood," and knowing that at Garfield School their children were being scorned by white students and were being segregated into separate rooms, the Mexicans may well have voiced support for a separate school.

In the fall of 1912, the board ordered the purchase of the less expensive of two tracts of land along South Raymond Street for the "industrial needs" of the Mexican children living in the *barrio*.[73] In the spring of 1913, the board's intention to segregate the Mexicans into a special school was a matter of public record. Yet some of the school patrons wanted more. The district PTA, "petitioning on behalf of the patrons of Garfield school," asked that the new South Raymond school be "a residential school rather than an ordinary school, believing that "the Mexican children would receive more benefit in a school of that character."[74] The South Raymond Street School, renamed Junipero Serra in a few years, was for the exclusive needs of the *Mexicanos*. The white patrons of Garfield wanted assurances from the board that the Mexican population would be further restricted to their neighborhood by a residential school. Efforts at Americanization would be more efficient, or so they said, if the children occupied a segregated residential setting. In fact, that school never was residential, but the idea of a Mexican boarding school in Pasadena was realized on a lesser scale when, in 1914, the Wallace Home for "orphaned or near orphaned" children was opened in the Chihuahuita area. Pasadenans continued to be intrigued with the idea of boarding Mexican children. In 1915, a group from the city visited the newly opened Spanish-American Institute in Gardena, a home for boys that was operated by the Methodist Church and modeled on the Hampton Institute in Virginia. In a few years, the Gardena school would be known as the Hampton Institute for Mexicans.[75]

The South Raymond Street School, known officially as the Raymond-Ritzman Industrial School, opened on Monday, September 14, 1914. For Clara Odell, it was her crowning achievement. Recently elected to the board of education, Odell chose all the supplies for the school, including "everything from a tiny desk for the kindergarten to gas stoves for domestic science." The white community was not exactly sure what to teach the Mexicans, except "practical things" that will "instruct them in the better manner of living." Garfield, for years "overcrowded with children from the Mexican district," would now be able to devote more time to white children, just as the new "industrial school" would "offer more opportunity for individual instruction" to the Mexicans.[76]

Fig. 14. In stark contrast to Pasadena's commitment to progressive school build-
ings such as Altadena and Eliot were the two *de jure* segregated Mexican schools.
The top photo is of South Raymond Street School, just after it opened in 1914.
The bottom photo is of Chihuahuita School, c. 1915. *(Photos courtesy of the
Pasadena Unified School District)*

The board did not invest much in the children of Spanish-speaking laborers.
The Raymond-Ritzman Industrial School would not be a residential school but
just an assortment of bungalows and other portable buildings until a permanent
structure was built after the school bond was passed in 1923. Instead, the board
relied on the municipal budget, charitable organizations, church and civic groups,

parents, children and even students in the city's manual training classes to provide the school with a playground and support facilities built with volunteer help
and donated equipment, on rent-free land adjacent to the school.[77] When a
group of parents asked "for a bungalow to serve free lunches to the children of
South Raymond School," the board agreed, and moved a building from Garfield
School with one stipulation. The moving costs would be charged to the city
rather than coming from the school system. Church and civic groups lent a hand
and the school was furnished with desks and other equipment, all without much
direct cost to the school district.

Even with the relocation of most of the *Mexicanos,* Garfield School
remained a multiethnic and multiclass mix of affluent and working-class whites,
Mexicans, African Americans and Southern European students. In the spring of
1916, a group of more affluent white parents petitioned the board to create a
school further southwest and deeper into the wealth of the Orange Grove neighborhood. The petitioners were willing to provide rent-free land and would tolerate "temporary circumstances" if the board would only install portable buildings. The board voted unanimously in favor of the petitioners and within a
month had moved a bungalow onto Grand Avenue near Belfontaine Street,
approximately a mile from Garfield School. The board paid the full cost of the
move.[78] By 1924, that bungalow expanded into the Arroyo Seco Elementary
School. In that year, a taxpayer group recommended its closure as the 6-4-4 Plan
was instituted, but the affluent neighborhood refused and the school remained
open. Over the next 30 years, as white parents from the Garfield attendance area
refused to have their children in classrooms with so many darker-skinned students, Arroyo Seco became the system's "transfer school." Pasadena came to call
the area around Garfield and Arroyo Seco the "neutral zone." In the early 1950s,
the National Association for the Advancement of Colored People (NAACP) filed
suit against the city arguing that this "neutral zone" was nothing more than an
escape hatch that allowed white families to leapfrog Garfield School for "better"
all-white schools. That lawsuit was the opening salvo in Pasadena's bitter school
desegregation case that would eventually find its way to the U.S. Supreme Court.

AMERICANIZING THE MEXICAN

The progressive impulse to segregate Mexicans into "their own school" was a
complex social and political undertaking. What was this need to segregate and,
once separate, to create a specialized environment and curriculum? Simply label-
ing the process as racist limits our understanding of the complex interplay
between the political economy of the nation and the immigrant groups coming
to Southern California during the first quarter of the 20th century. Segregating
Mexicans into the Raymond Street School gave Pasadena reformers a way to

avoid "strangers" and provided an opportunity to reconstruct a preindustrial, "foreign" culture into one more compatible with the needs of industrial America. To be sure, the effort to remake Mexicans was not without direct benefit to the Mexican community. The Americanization program brought much-needed medical assistance and education. At the same time, the many Americanization programs further pushed these "strangers" to the edge of society. Pasadena's educators were no different from other progressives in the Southwest who saw Mexicans as a social and educational "problem." To the white, middle-class reformer, Mexicans were "foreign" and *very* different. The differences began with language but did not end there.

With the opening of Raymond Street School in 1914, the majority of Mexican children were removed from Garfield. In his annual report, F.J. Becker, Raymond Street's supervising principal wrote that "class recitation is an important part" of the day. Phonics instruction, according to Becker, "[was] completely removed ..." because it was that "old time drudgery, [that] lack of personal interest, which causes him [the Mexican] to become inactive." Teaching English was a matter of keeping the child's interests alive. To Pasadena's educators, Mexicans were "child like" and more interested in "actions and emotions." If given a comparable academic program—comparable that is, to what was expected of white children—it was thought that Mexicans would grow listless under the "purely mental effort."[79] Mexicans were musical and artistic, apparently born to dance because they "naturally [could] keep step, showing a stronger sense of rhythm" than the "American" children. They were more engaging to white observers when involved with color and music. Their "penmanship, drawing, and handiwork ... are on the whole superior to the work done by other children." Anglo educators thought Mexican boys were prone to reject the more mental aspects of learning and did better when involved with activities around the shop or the garden. Mexican boys were "naturally inclined" to menial labor, just as Mexican girls had a "natural" inclination to handicrafts and sewing.[80]

To the Anglo Pasadenan involved in the "Mexican problem," differences had become synonymous with "otherness." Therefore, the expectation was that Mexicans would respond differently to "typical" (white) schoolrooms. These perceptions of difference required a specialized curriculum so Mexicans could be successfully "adapted," and a major focus of the adaptation was the industrial economy.

White educators created the data to fulfill their expectations that Mexicans were a lesser people. By the early 1920s, educators had begun using IQ tests to "compare the intelligence of children of different races ..." with "American" children. Mexican children were given individual and group IQ tests, and the results were plotted alongside results from similar tests administered to white children. The testers were unaware of the impact that language dominance had on the test takers. They were apparently unaware that different environmental variables would skew the scores. In any case, they were convinced that the results would assist them in finding the appropriate classifications and adjustments for the Mexican children. The results only tended to reinforce the existing relations of power. One educator in Roswell, New Mexico, went so far as to rank nationalities by "average IQ." The first two steps on his comparative ladder were occupied by "American" and "English," followed by "Hebrew," then the "Chinese," "Mexican," "Indian," "Slavish," "Italians" and, at the bottom, the "Negroes."[81]

Throughout the southwest states of the former Mexican Empire, Americanization reformers struggled to convince immigrants to abandon their ways, including their native Catholicism. Reformers pushed Mexicans to convert to the more familiar Protestantism, to see that their children drank more milk and ate more vegetables and beef instead of beans and tortillas. Believing cleanliness was next to godliness, Protestant reformers wanted Mexicans to bathe more often, to wear shoes (with socks) and brush their teeth. In Pasadena, teachers at the South Raymond Street School gave children toothbrushes after their "penny lunches"—simple meals of hot soup, bread, fruit and milk, the cost supplemented by the charities. Mexican mothers were instructed in the "better ways," how to make wheat bread instead of traditional tortillas, how to use sewing machines instead of needle and thread and to use "proper" methods for bathing their babies.[82]

To the middle-class Pasadena reformers like Clara Odell, remaking the preindustrial Mexican laborer meant "efficiency." In the South Raymond street School, recitation may have been intended to keep the Mexican child engaged but it also was an efficient method used to ensure that English was the only language spoken. Principal Becker's initial report in 1915 told the majority of white Pasadenans what they wanted to hear, "More attention is given to hand work in [South Raymond Street School] than in the other schools of the city. The basketry work accomplished by Miss Fobs' room has been especially commended this year."[83]

SEGREGATION AND RESISTANCE

A central question for historians is how to interpret social change and what occurs when less powerful groups come into contact with a more dominant culture. Conventional wisdom in Pasadena suggests that after a period of "adjustment" (conflict), the Mexican immigrant "blended" (assimilated) into the "American" culture. Indeed, the public transcript suggests there was little if any resistance to Americanization. Resistance, however, has a history in many forms.[84]

For centuries, subordinate groups have resisted the strong arm of those who wield privilege and power. From passive noncompliance, or what one might call "cultural lethargy"—Mexican laborers moving just fast enough so as not to draw retribution from the boss (Anglos might call this the "manana" syndrome)—to open rebellion in the face of overwhelming odds, those with little privilege have bartered for what ideological safe space they could. Written by the powerful, the "public transcript" most often gives legitimacy to the dominant worldview, and, in fact, is "a self-portrait of how they would have themselves seen."[85] Recent scholarship reveals that there is a different reality behind "our history." Those at the bottom of the ladder take on the appearance of being deferential. As political anthropologist James Scott has written, "They bow and scrape, they seem amiable, they appear to know their place and to stay in it, thereby indicating that they also know and recognize the place of their superiors."[86] Scott points out that this "conformity" to ruling standards is, in reality, tactical. Subordinates engage in "an art form in which one can take some pride at having successfully misrepresented oneself."[87] From the Untouchables in India to African slaves working the plantations of the American South and generations of *campesinos* working the haciendas in Mexico, those with little status in the eyes of the ruling class have "tactfully disguised [their] true aims and intentions from [their] social adversaries." Behind the public transcript lies a world of resistance to oppression that is the terrain of undeclared ideological warfare. To understand it "requires [us to] enter the world of rumor, gossip, disguises, linguistic tricks, metaphors, euphemisms, folktales, ritual gestures, [and] anonymity."[88]

We can infer that Mexicans in Pasadena resisted the intrusions of the industrial Anglo culture because Mexicans rejected the politics of Americanization. They resisted the New Education by refusing to participate on terms other than their own. They smiled; they deferred; they said *"gracias,"* they apologized—and then they went on with their lives.

Despite all that the board of education and charitable organizations (including a very intrusive Methodist church) tried to accomplish with *Mexicano* families, officials realized that their Americanization programs were futile because they could not get the Mexican community to be more efficient. Odell and the others believed that the path to successfully changing the Mexican home was through the children and especially their sense of time. "We can teach the children better things, and we can hope in this way to make improvements," said a city social worker, but not until the Mexicans came to school—and on time.[89]

Punctuality was critical to the progressive Pasadena educator, but the Mexican community did not respond to the structures inherent in school bureaucracy. The "American" notion of time, with bells, class schedules and specific allotments of time rigidly designated for specific tasks, was in direct contradiction to the Mexicans' long-standing cultural norms that had been established over centuries of pastoral life.

Emory Bogardus, a leading sociologist from the University of Southern California, believed Mexicans "live so largely in the present, that time has no particular meaning to them. With them time is not commercialized as with us. Their wants are not aroused as are ours and as is natural they consequently do not drive themselves as we drive ourselves."[90] After all, school absenteeism in Mexican Pasadena was chronic. Reports made repeated references to children in the railroad camps not attending school, being chased by the truant officers, and generally flouting directives regarding school attendance. To compound the problem, few houses in the *barrio* had clocks. Changing the "conditions" meant cleaning up the slum, but, just as important, it meant correcting the Mexican's lethargic ways. So Clara Odell decided to do something.

In July of 1917, Odell, in her capacity as a member of the board of education, asked that the city power station, just a few blocks south of the Raymond Street School, blow its steam whistle precisely at 8:45 a.m. on school days. Odell and the school administration had become convinced that the Mexican community needed an intrusive reminder that school started precisely at a predesignated time. If this community would not self-regulate, then the rhythms of an entire community would be dictated by the blast of a horn, much like the mill towns in the East. As it turned out, the city engineer refused Odell's request, citing that the disruption to the larger community was more of a problem than tardy Mexican students and their families. The board, instead, installed a steam-powered horn on the school grounds. As it turned out, the horn was defective. By the end of the year Odell and the board settled for a large, manually operated bell they called "an early warning bell."[91]

To Odell and the board, "Mexican time" and *manana* was a worldview incompatible with the efficient, modern city. Stereotypic characterizations of the Mexican laborer are, in fact, not so much symptoms of cultural lethargy as coded forms of resistance that have allowed groups working in oppressive situations to settle and then survive on foreign, hostile turf. Odell and other reformers may have had a Christian Utopia in mind as they struggled to educate "the Mexican," but the reality of their ideology required those who were culturally different to situate themselves on the lower rungs of a social order that offered little upward mobility.

When the board opened South Raymond in September 1914, principal Becker commented on how the *Mexicano* community reacted to segregation:

> A great change has come over the pupils and parents of this school in regard to the segregation of this class of pupils. At their removal from the Garfield School, there were many exclamations in Spanish of *"regretas"* [sic] *"Que* Lastima," "What a shame," but when those who have finished the fourth grade this year were told that they would have to continue their work at another school this coming year, they expressed a desire of wishing to continue in "their own school."[92]

Indeed, what a shame. There could very well have been another, hidden meaning in the Mexican lament, *"que lastima."* As thinly veiled threats often are, *que lastima* might have been ripe with sarcasm. The public transcript in Pasadena shows that Mexicans consciously and actively "chose segregation," but it is unlikely that they actively pursued a school setting where they would be further marginalized.[93] *"Que Lastima"* was a code of resistance that in one form or another complained, ever so gently, about being shunted about by the ruling class. To openly complain and reject a segregated environment invited retaliation. To mutter or grumble "what a shame," nuanced the complaint without making Mexicans vulnerable to counterattack.

THE SETTLEMENT HOUSE ASSOCIATION AND THE "MEXICAN QUESTION"

Pasadena educators and reformers intended for the Raymond Street School to be a community center for the Mexicans. The epicenter, though, of the "Mexican quarter" was the settlement house administered by the charitable women of the Edna Alter Mexican Settlement Association. Named after a head of the Pasadena Charities, who had died in a train wreck, the settlement house and the school were the most intrusive of the city's many intersections between the dominant white culture and the Mexican immigrant. The Mexican Settlement Association was part of a network of institutions and programs—including the school, the settlement house, a day nursery, and a cooperative laundry—where Odell and other Protestant reformers could carry on their needed work. Pasadena's social services and progressive charities attempted to deculturalize Mexican children in the two segregated schools—South Raymond and, in a few years, Fremont School in the unincorporated northeast. The teaching of the middle-class, Anglo "better ways" would follow the children when they came to the after school and vacation programs at the settlement house. Here, reformers could extend their work through the children directly into Mexican homes.[94]

The charity women, all Protestants, saw rescuing Mexican women and children as Christian fellowship. Work with Mexican families was also an extension of their idealized "separate sphere," that turn-of-the-century feminist effort to "maintain the family unit," as historian Eileen Boris writes, "and protect motherhood, domesticity, and [above all else] children." Clara Odell and the Garfield PTA women played a key role in attempting to reconstruct "public life in accordance with their own ideal of womanhood." The charity women accomplished much, including improved life conditions for the immigrant families and, no less important, new professional roles for themselves. Odell would become the first woman president of the Pasadena Board of Education. Other women, such as Ester Mack, would emerge as leaders within the increasingly complex network of Pasadena social services. Still, historian Boris points out, women reformers ended up using a definition of feminism that relied on ideals—nurturance, altruism and domesticity—that were difficult for working-class immigrant women to aspire to.

The requirements of Americanization made cultural redefinition nearly impossible for Mexican women, which is one reason immigrant women are often cast as passive players. Yet, for all that, in Pasadena and elsewhere in the Southwest, Mexican women were active agents in Americanization programs and religious charitable outreach, taking from both what they needed to protect and nourish their families.[95]

The Mexican settlement house began in 1913 as a "neighborhood house ... no better than many of the houses" they lived in, Odell claimed, but "clean and pleasant" and always "open to the mothers." Not long after Odell's 1913 description, the association moved its fledgling enterprise to a building on South Marengo Street, just east of the *barrio*.[96] The new settlement house opened to a howl of protest from the more affluent white neighbors who "resented" the "location of the settlement house in their midst." The association packed up and moved to a rented house on California Street. Then, in 1915, after the construction of the Colorado Street Bridge that spans the Arroyo Seco, a larger house was saved from the wrecker's ball and relocated at 699 South Raymond Street, where the association settled in for the next 20 years. Intending to provide a "haven of refuge," the matrons focused on improving the lives of women and children. Furnished with "some simple things," the house initially was a place where Mexican women could come with their children to rest, talk or just sit and "rock their babes." They could also "join in the sewing classes [and] get advice from the woman in charge."[97]

The first outreach effort of the settlement association was the Mexican Woman's Day Nursery.[98] It was originally located in that small house on South Marengo Street, but soon the association purchased a bungalow (they had it painted red) and moved the nursery to the settlement grounds on South Raymond. With the goal of using children to "[win] its way into the Mexican homes," the women of the association established the nursery to care for young children who had either been left to their own devices while their mothers worked or had been left with older, school-age siblings. Teachers at Garfield reported that girls were coming to school with babies and toddlers in tow. More distressing to the Garfield teachers was that some of the young girls were staying at home two and three days a week to care for their younger siblings.

The nursery was the nucleus of a network of programs that aided the immigrant in Americanization but also increased the subservient status of Mexican women. The stated goal of the matrons was to help relieve the mothers of childcare and also to furnish the women with the means to become self-sufficient. It was believed that if Mexican mothers could go off to their jobs free from the constraints of caring for their children, they would more easily merge into the class of wage laborers, thereby easing the burden on relief organizations. Progressive Pasadena considered handouts too easy for the immigrants. They thought that the Mexicans would take advantage of the city's relief programs wherever possible, and will "make no effort to be self-supporting so long as outside aid can be secured."[99] Charity, to these Protestant women, meant giving of their time and skills, but they expected a return on their investment.

White Pasadena reassured itself that its "better ways" were valued by some of the Mexicans. As the nursery opened, the newspaper quoted a Mexican mother—in perfect Standard English—saying self-support was also *her* goal. "The day nursery opens next week," she was quoted as saying, "... just as soon as I can leave the babies there, I can get a job and pay my own rent." The mother had earlier been offered a rent-free house but had refused the handout, proving, said the newspaper, the "inestimable benefit of self-support."

The newspaper reporter's use of Standard English reinforced the idea that "good" Mexicans were learning the "better ways." In much the same way Southern whites altered the language of freedmen to reinforce a perception of the inarticulate "darkie," white Pasadenans created accounts of inarticulate Mexicans stumbling through dialog in non-Standard English. "I been terrible sick," one older Mexican woman supposedly said in 1913. "The doctors almost starve me. Pretty soon they don't give me bread. Then I starve altogether."[100] It is highly unlikely the woman would use the phrase, "Then I starve altogether." More likely, the conversation was an invention of the reporter. Its intended effect, though, was clear—this Mexican had not learned the "better ways."

Americanization and its programs of reculturalization were not restricted to the work of the charity associations and its middle-class white matrons. The Protestant churches, specifically the Methodist-Episcopal church, also waded into the *barrio* with the full intention of altering "the Mexican." The Pasadena First Methodist and the Lake Avenue Methodist, in the center of the city, opened a "little chapel" on Ritzman Avenue that furthered the separation between Anglo Protestants and Mexicans. The first pastor of the Ritzman Avenue chapel was Francisco Olazabal.

In the spring of 1915, Olazabal and the two white Methodist churches began a cooperative laundry specifically to employ Mexican women. Apparently only the converted Methodists could work at the laundry. The churches rented a four-room house on Ritzman, across the street from the Mexican chapel. The house was remodeled and "thoroughly cleaned." They erected a seven-foot fence around the rear of the property to "prevent intrusion and provide safety." The church leaders were careful to dispel any concern that the laundry would compete directly with larger laundries in the area. This was a nonprofit charity operation intended to improve the human condition. It was named the Bonita Cooperative Laundry. The local newspaper pointed out that laundry work—washing and ironing—was the only kind of "labor that can be performed by Mexican women." It explained that the women were in need of work because they had been barred from working in any of the larger laundries in the city. Apparently the "American girls" refused to work with them.[101]

Much like the other settlement association programs, the Bonita Cooperative functioned as a site of cultural reconstruction. Here, unemployed "deserving" families—"many widows with children ... or with husbands who have deserted [them]"—might live without being dependent on Pasadena charities. Rather than have the families leave the *barrio* to look for work, the churches wished to "establish a central place where they [the women] can come and work and where there is work." Laundry workers would pick up and deliver Pasadena's dirty clothes, thereby keeping white Pasadenans from having to come into the *barrio*. The profits were divided among those who did the work. The goal of the laundry, as part of the network of reform institutions in the city, was to wean Mexicans away from their "natural" inclination to rely on others for assistance. The Bonita Cooperative motto—"There is no help that helps people like the help that helps them to help themselves"—was stamped on each laundry list.[102]

Reverend Olazabal left Pasadena in 1916 to become the first Mexican Methodist pastor in Northern California. His replacement was Ambrosio C. Gonzales from Santa Ana in Orange County. The newspaper said that he had "made 243 converts" in three years. Gonzales, who had opened four Methodist churches in New Mexico, had been educated at the "Hampton Institute for Mexicans" in Gardena.[103] Like Olazabal, however, Gonzales did not succeed in converting Mexicans to Methodism. The immigrants used the laundry for employment, and no doubt, they used the little chapel on Ritzman Street to meet other needs. As to a return on the Protestant investment, Mexicans remained firmly Catholic. By the mid-1920s, Gonzales's congregation was made up of a mere 12 Mexican families.[104]

The charity association's vision of a multifunctional community center was fast becoming a reality. Behind the South Raymond house was a small garage, no more than a shed, but roomy enough so that Odell and the women had it repaired and painted white. This was the Mexican "maternity hospital."[105] Initially it was set up with two beds. In 1922, through a gift from an anonymous donor, the maternity hospital was rebuilt in a nearby spot as a "thoroughly modern" ward with four beds. The move was needed because the Los Angeles Gas and Electric Company (LAG&E), the largest landowner other than the railroads in that part of the city, erected a natural gas holding tank within 15 feet of the little maternity ward, and the county health inspector declared the hospital closed. Out of necessity, the donor gave the settlement association $8,000 because, where else would the expectant Mexican women deliver their babies? A member of the board of directors gushed that the little Woman's Hospital, as it would later be called, would "meet the needs of all those requiring its services, recognizing no color or creed except that of the Golden Rule and the need of the women applying for admission." The maternity hospital recognized the "Golden Rule," because the nearby Pasadena Hospital—soon renamed the Huntington Memorial Hospital after the railroad magnate bequeathed it $2 million—refused to admit any patients not defined as "American."[106]

The Mexican Day Nursery, the settlement house, the Bonita Cooperative laundry, the Maternity Hospital and the school were among the many "strand[s] in the weaving of the web named by us the Mexican Question," as one of the charity women said in 1916.[107] The Pasadena charities that operated the settlement association saw in the "Mexican Question" their greatest fear. This perfect place, this most Christian City on the Hill, was being threatened by "otherness," just as the city had been nearly 30 years before when "that class of men" occupied Beebe's saloon. But the "Mexican Question" was different and would require a different response. Anglo Pasadena feared Mexicans would spread their violence, crime, disease and social unrest. Radicalism from the Mexican Revolution was already creeping north. In 1907, anarchists of the *Partido Liberal Mexicano* (PLM) had settled in nearby Los Angeles. According to the press, no Mexican men living in Pasadena wished to return to the fighting in Mexico, but white Pasadenans feared more what might occur if radicalism found fertile ground.[108] This dread of Mexican radicalism may have been amplified because it came at the height of Pasadena's socialist experiment. Helen Firmin, the Socialist candidate for the school board in 1909, had been one of the first visitors allowed to see the Mexican PLM revolutionaries, led by Ricardo Flores Magon, while they were imprisoned in Los Angeles.[109] The Socialists had made a point of linking their party goals to the plight of workers. Pasadena's industrial and commercial base required cheap labor to expand and maintain the regional transportation systems, to work the fields, dig the ditches, clean the houses, pull and carry the heavy loads, and repair, clean and perform all the required backbreaking labor many whites had begun to reject. As long as the labor of "the others" could be bought cheaply, then the monied class would find ways to rationalize "the conditions."

Progressive Pasadena seldom appeared uncomfortable with the disparity between Orange Grove wealth and Raymond Street shacks. It was believed that the deplorable conditions were the result of unfortunate circumstances that were beyond any Pasadenan's control, because Mexicans, blacks and the Chinese were responsible for their own state of affairs. The descriptions of the slum by white Pasadenans were embedded in a class-bound, ethnocentric worldview that defined the camps through a self-affirming question: "How could anyone live like that?"[110] Clearly, the charities felt it was their obligation to help the women and children, especially the children. So Odell and the Garfield PTA mothers pushed and "agitated" for benefits to the Mexicans living along the railroad tracks. Attention was focused on the conditions, but not much was accomplished. Henry Huntington tore down the railroad sheds. South Raymond Street was paved. The sewers were installed, albeit slowly, but the city leaders paid scant attention to the quality of life within the "embryonic slum." That leadership, including Mayor William Thum, was roundly criticized by charity and civic bodies after Thum said, in 1915, that he "thoroughly understood the problem but could not see his way clear for action." A member of one of the civic reform organizations then told the press, "If we cannot get the city officials to act peacefully, a little coercion would be a good thing."[111]

What coercion the civic organizations had in mind was unclear. The municipal government still did not see its way to address the problem until Charles Cheney, the secretary of the California Conference on City Planning, criticized Pasadena in June of 1915 for having the "worst housing conditions in the state." The Women's Civic League, one of the charity societies that pressured city government, sponsored his talk. Cheney blasted city leaders, admonishing them to "soften the sharp line that breaks South Orange Grove Avenue, the garden of the wealthy, and plunges one into the depths of the embryo slums in the Mexican district."[112] He told the charity women that the state planning commission had no "worst record for housing in the entire state, barring none of the large cities," than what was present in Pasadena's Mexican *barrio*. Cheney scolded Pasadena, saying "There must be something radically wrong in a city noted for its beautiful homes and gardens ... and also having the worst housing conditions in California." But he was sympathetic to Pasadena's dilemma, and admitted "the great problem" was what to do next. What turned out to be next was Cheney's recommendation that a "systematic, impartial collection of significant facts" be gathered, so that the "city government could save waste."[113]

The California Commission on Immigration and Housing, one of the most influential state-level Americanization efforts in the country, conducted a survey of Pasadena housing the next year. The study told Pasadena what it did not want to hear. Its slum was no longer "embryonic." When it was released in the fall of 1916, the city commissioners refused to make it immediately public, needing, they said, additional time to decide how to respond. The survey covered the four most depressed areas in the city: the Vernon District, where 40 percent of the neighborhood was African American; a semirural area along Lincoln Boulevard in the northwest; the downtown rooming houses; and the industrial area along Raymond Street. As was expected, the report on the "Mexican problem" received the most attention. Pasadena had too many immigrants, too little decent housing and too many unemployed and underemployed, who earned wages averaging less than $1 a day.

The housing survey, written by the labor camp inspector for the state Immigration and Housing Commission and two Pasadena women familiar with the city's housing, had few recommendations. The inspectors implied, though, that there might be a way out of the dilemma. "We can never expect Mexicans to be clean," the survey stated, "while we place insurmountable difficulties in their way and do not demand very much of them." The inspectors believed there was ample evidence that Mexicans might be reconstructed given correct conditions. There were "numerous gardens [in the *barrio*] ... immaculately clean front yards ... [that] suggested a pride which the Mexican might take in a better home." The report focused on the dilemma of trying to "fix" the immigrants, who showed signs of understanding the "American ways" but lived in an environment unfit for further cultural development. Compounding the "problem" was the fear that the *barrio* could no longer contain the population. Given the rapid birthrate, the increasing number of new arrivals, the wretched conditions and the lack of jobs, the "problem" might spill over into the rest of progressive Pasadena. The fear of Mexicans pushing at the edges of the *barrio* was palpable.

The reform imperative meant keeping Mexicans within well-defined limits— not only geographic, but also clear cultural boundaries that would mark the lines that separated progressive Pasadena from those dark-skinned "strangers." Within the language of progressive Pasadena, "outreach" presupposed the Mexican to be somewhere else, away from the center of civic life. As Pasadena sought to help the destitute immigrant, the settlement outreach programs attempted to contain the immigrant laborers along the edges of white society. The settlement house, the school and other charitable programs defined the Mexican *barrio* as "their neigh-borhood." The threat of these "others" would only intensify as whites in Pasadena learned more about the "conditions" that defined the "differences."

White Pasadena came to loathe Mexican "filth" and "degeneracy." News-papers and the housing reports criticized the unkept, "primitive" and "barbaric" Mexicans. Their children were most often in need of baths, haircuts and clean clothes. Observers pointed to glaring differences: Mexicans cooked their food over open fires, slept in groups, were idle, wore tattered and dirty clothes and were intemperate. White Pasadena reformers were preoccupied with the state of order and cleanliness. Everything and everyone was described by the press as appearing "dirty," "slovenly" and living "in huts." Newspaper writers made the labor camps into repulsive places. One writer described passing by a "row of houses, swarming with rats and filth, and with an odor so nauseous that it per-vaded the district for blocks ..."[114]

The observations of the slum, which was a multiethnic community made up of Mexicans, Chinese, Japanese, Greek and African-American workers, many with extended families, were apparently written by women. There are no obser-vations, interviews or declarations made about the habits of males living within the *barrio*. One observer said she was not allowed into a camp because the men were just coming off the night shift and were sleeping. Few newspaper reports directly mention males. For a slum supposedly occupied by unemployed and idle males, the women's observations do not confirm the official reports.

It may have been that the women writers purposely focused on the lives of women and children to kindle sympathy. Their observations further fueled concerns over the conditions, yet contradictions abound. The camps were filled with "idle" yet "affectionate" children engaged in no orderly play or function. One observer walking through the *barrio* described disorder everywhere. She also noted that, "Tuesday seems to be washing day in the Mexican quarter" as "all the mothers" had lines filled with clean clothes. During the summer of 1916, in an effort to "clean up" the *barrio*'s refuse "problem," the city wanted the Mexicans along Raymond Street to buy garbage cans and pay 25 cents a month to have them emptied, "as do the other citizens of Pasadena." But when the department of public safety surveyed the area, they found the conditions "remarkably clean." Most of the backyards in the *barrio* were found to have flourishing flower and vegetable gardens. Some landlords had left large garbage cans, and they had been filled with stones, ashes, tin cans and garbage. But the city collectors refused to pick them up because they "declined to risk their backs." Progressive, urban Pasadena wanted everything in its place. Rocks and ashes were meant to be disposed of in one container, garbage in another. Progressive Pasadena understood this distinction; "primitive" Mexicans did not.[115]

While "primitive" Mexicans repulsed the reformers, it was the perceived violence of the *barrio* that most frightened white Pasadena. There were newspaper reports of gunfights and brawls in dark, back allies "down in Sonora town" and of knife-wielding drunks in bloody fights over women. The newspaper said that these "foreigners" were "murderous" and "savage" and white Pasadena had no reason to believe otherwise. The police did what they could to contain the violence, recommending an extra officer to patrol the *barrio,* suggesting the police did not visit "little Mexico" on a regular basis. The problem, as the police saw it, was that they could not get the inhabitants of the *barrio* to cooperate. Witnesses had a habit of disappearing or failing to swear out complaints. The "Mexican problem" was made worse by the presence of Greeks, Chinese, Japanese, Southern Europeans and African Americans.[116] Within the boundaries of the slum existed a Pasadena few whites knew or understood. Reformers like Odell wanted the *barrio* fixed before something tragic happened.

The tragedy came late on the night of April 23, 1918, when the rented barn and storehouse of the Chinese-American Cooperative Vegetable Company was set ablaze. Three adjoining buildings, home to dozens of Mexicans and Chinese, were lost. Fourteen horses were burned to death and nearly 50 Chinese and Mexicans were made homeless. The Chinese fruit and vegetable peddlers owned the horses, 17 in all, as well as carts, wagons and a truck. The three horses that survived were badly burned, and the newspaper reported that they would probably be shot. The Chinese lost everything, including all of their savings, totaling thousands of dollars. With no insurance, the prospects of a quick recovery appeared dim.[117]

These were wooden buildings and, since the fire began in the largest barn, the blaze exploded through the dry hay and feed and quickly enveloped the four adjoining buildings. This was a raging inferno. With a hard wind blowing north toward the city center, burning embers were carried for blocks. For a time, "the whole district was threatened." The fire moved so quickly that the Chinese and Mexicans barely had time to get out with their nightclothes. Just south of the Chinese Cooperative barn was the Union Feed and Fuel Company, with its wood-filled storehouse. If the wind had shifted, the flames would have consumed the stored fuel. Beyond the storehouse was the power plant and, up the hill, the Raymond Hotel. The Raymond had once before burned to the ground back in April 1896. This was the "new" Raymond, just as spectacular. Now it had been threatened. Only one Chinese male was seriously injured, his face and hands badly burned as he went back into the barn in an attempt to save the truck. Although the fire department said the cause was unknown, the authorities were suspicious of "incendiarism." The speculation the next day was that boys—presumably white boys—had been harassing the Chinese peddlers and had set the fire. The Chinese told the reporter that on the night of the fire, they had difficulty "driving away" a group of boys who were "bothering them."[118]

The city was lucky. The alarm had been sounded because a dog began to bark, alerting the night watchman, who called the fire department. But the *barrio* nearly went up in flames and, since more affluent neighborhoods bordered the slum, Anglo Pasadena felt threatened from within. The homeless were a more immediate consequence of the fire. The city charities were not equipped to house 50 men, women and children. Two months later, in June 1918, a hundred citizens, concerned with the volatile situation within the *barrio,* appeared before the city commissioners and demanded that Pasadena "erect and maintain municipal quarters for the Mexican population." The citizens, mostly civic-minded women, wanted, at city expense and "within the industrial district," a bungalow court to be erected and then rented "for our Mexican population." Their petition called for the city to "employ a person to oversee and instruct the tenants to be cleanly [sic] and keep their homes in a sanitary condition."[119]

Long before municipal, state and federal governments went into the business of low-cost housing for the poor, Pasadena's civic minded wanted the city to marshal its resources and rebuild the neighborhood. It was an efficient idea. The city would erect a court of bungalows, small houses closely grouped with common walkways, for the exclusive use of the immigrants. It would not be charity, because Mexicans would rent the houses from the city. The city reformers would then have a more direct influence over the lives of the laborers, thereby enabling them to be more efficient in learning the "better ways."

If the civic-minded women could not get the city government to remember to install sewers, then building housing for the Spanish-speaking laborer at taxpayer expense was out of the question. The commissioners did not act on the petition. Then, early in 1921, another disaster struck the *barrio*. This time it was the LAG&E, the same business that erected the natural gas tanks that closed the first woman's hospital. The LAG&E, extending its ownership further into the *barrio*, tore down a number of houses occupied by Mexican workers and their families. Once again, the city had a homeless problem.[120]

Sensing the city's image was at stake, the Chamber of Commerce stepped in with its special housing committee, chaired by William Grassie, a former member of the board of education. It was made up of a mix of socially active women—including the head of the settlement house, Francis Boniface, and Ester Mack of the Garfield PTA—and some of the city's most influential and wealthy businessmen, including psychiatrist McBride from the California Commission on Immigration and Housing. The chamber soon commissioned yet another study of slum housing.

The survey that the Chamber ordered turned out to be one of the few surviving documents that described the Mexican *barrio* in any detail. The study was Christine Lofstedt's master's thesis, completed under the direction of Emory Bogardus at the University of Southern California. "A Study of the Mexicans Living in Pasadena" is as thorough as Lofstedt's worldview would allow. She gathered data on the numbers of Mexicans living in the city (1,736), their places of origin (mostly the northern states of Chihuahua and Durango, but some were from Zacatecas), and why they came to Pasadena (for work and to escape the Mexican Revolution).[121]

Lofstedt's data confirmed what the chamber already knew—these were poor people, with little education, working as day laborers in cement work, gardening, ditch digging and fruit picking. Mexican employment was as unsteady as it was seasonal. Old timers who remember these days say that the *barrio* would empty during picking season, as families headed south to pick berries in Buena Park or over to Walnut, in Orange County, to pick grapes.[122] Interestingly, the Lofstedt study pointed out that Mexicans were buying homes, mainly within the Chihuahuita *colonia* but also along South Raymond. Lofstedt's survey told the chamber that Mexicans were living in overcrowded, unsafe and unsanitary houses in both areas. There were less than 200 toilets to serve 1,700 people, fewer than 100 sinks and only 50 bathtubs. Compounding the conditions, there was little running water, electricity or city services.[123]

The Lofstedt study also told the chamber what its members did not know—that the neighborhoods made a vibrant, multidimensional community. There were *mutualistas* (mutual assistance leagues), communal gardens, political organizations and a strong sense of cultural pride—or *raza*. They danced, sang and

partied. There were real *fiestas,* not those put on for the benefit of Anglos roman-
ticizing an imagined *Californio* past.

The chamber learned that the *barrio* was, indeed, growing despite the new
restrictive immigration laws placed on *Mexicanos.* In 1919, one census report put
the *barrio*'s population at 1,200, but Lofstedt's count indicated that there were
nearly 600 more Mexicans living in the city. The Immigration Act of 1917 was
intended to slow down circular migration by requiring a head tax and literacy test
when the border was crossed, but apparently it did not impact Pasadena. One
reason might have been that the immigration officials, mindful of the needs of
growers, allowed Mexicans to enter the United States if they said they were agricultural workers.[124]

We can use Lofstedt's data and the few oral histories to create a very different picture of the *barrio* than what was depicted in the Pasadena press. This was
a defensive, protective community. Mexicans resented the racist attitudes in
Pasadena, and Lofstedt recognized that their "passivity" was, in reality, a community in protest. Mexicans, "in mute protestations" of the "derogatory" and "sen-
sationalist" newspaper articles, "became distrustfully"[sic]. She was suggesting
that there was more to see than the Anglo (mis)perception of the untrustworthy
Mexican. She wrote that during the winter of 1921–22, a Mexican man living in
the *barrio* had been arrested in connection with the drowning death of his son.
The papers sensationalized the event, but then went silent when the police later
determined that the boy had died accidentally.[125] Lofstedt thought this was
reprehensible.

Both the *colonia* of Chihuahuita and the Raymond Street *barrio,* although
strapped for resources, managed to remain informed. Lofstedt found just 37
homes with books in all three Mexican communities—South Raymond, Chihuahuita and the Waverly area—but men and women read the newspapers, and not
just Pasadena papers, but Spanish and English language papers from Los Angeles.
Nearly 100 households subscribed to papers, and knowing the patterns of recy-
cling, newspapers were handed from *Mexicano* to *Mexicano* throughout the community. Lofstedt found no evidence of *The Los Angeles Times,* but she did find
The L.A. Examiner and the Spanish language papers, *La Prensa* and the more conservative *El Herald de Mexico.*[126]

For Mexicans and other poor, Pasadena was a dangerous place, and as in
many laboring communities, residents did what they could to escape the drudgery of seemingly endless days of risky and backbreaking work on the lower rungs
of the capitalist ladder. They listened to music on dozens of gramophones and
Victrolas. More than one newspaper writer commented on the "singing and
laughing" of the women and children as they crowded around the phonograph.
The South Raymond community formed a boys' band—with dented and banged
instruments—under the direction of a recently arrived music director, who had

trained in Mexico City. Lofstedt describes Mexican men listening and singing to recordings of "La Boheme," "Carmen" and "Rigoletto."[127]

There was a kind of defiance within the *barrio,* a sense of *raza* and communal pride in being Mexican that Anglo Pasadena never understood. It was not arrogance—the unequal relations of power made outright defiance dangerous. Although, certainly, individual members of the community would occasionally crack heads with the police. More often, demonstrations of *raza* were careful, pick-your-spot expressions of resistance. In the public rituals of domination, it is not far-fetched to think that the elite, as anthropologist Scott maintains, would submit to a kind of self-hypnosis—a "buck up their courage, improve their cohesion." These displays of power convinced the dominant of their "high moral purpose." Embedded in those public rituals are hidden jewels of defiance.[128]

In 1922, Francis Boniface, the settlement house director, was asked by the city's Shakespeare Club to "provide entertainment" for the guests of the Maryland Hotel, now the most prestigious hotel in the city. The Maryland was winter home to some of the most wealthy and powerful people in the world. The settlement house sent dancers and musicians, mainly youngsters, to the Maryland for an evening performance. They were "dressed in the typical Mexican gaily colored clothes, glowing with natural vivacity and spontaneity and portraying an atmosphere of formality, dignity, and innate curiosity," said Lofstedt. The presentation so impressed the audience that a guest stopped one of the dancers and asked, "Where do you come from?" The girl looked at the woman and said, "Lower Raymond Avenue." This was evidence to Lofstedt of Anglo-Pasadena's ignorance about what went on within the *barrio.* It was also evidence of the *barrio's raza.*[129]

THE MEXICAN HOUSING ASSOCIATION

The chamber and the city government needed to send a message that homelessness was under control. Even before Lofstedt completed her study, members of the chamber's special housing committee signed incorporation papers creating the Mexican Homes Association.[130] Its aim was to build low-cost housing ("cheap but comfortable and sanitary homes") that would keep Mexicans within the *barrio.* It sold bonds, drawing 7 percent interest. For investors, the association advertised the possibility of a secure investment and a profit. The Chamber's response to the "conditions" was to build "homes for the Mexicans" which they intended to rent for $20 to $25 a month. In this way, the Chamber of Commerce hoped to "do away with the slum" and still make a profit. As a chamber member said, "Purchase of the stock is a practical way of taking part in a very constructive social welfare program ..." Together with the "City Beautiful" association and the recent successful bonding of the new civic center and city hall, Pasadena was sending a message that "[t]here was no place for squalor and unsanitary conditions for Pasadena."[131]

The first step was to purchase the requisite land in the *barrio*. The association did so in 1923 when it took ownership of a large lot on South Broadway, just north of Glenarm Street. The land would accommodate 24, four-room stucco houses. Each home was to have natural gas, electricity, a kitchen and a bathroom, complete with a bathtub. The chamber advertised that its plan was to build 50 homes grouped in "a community arrangement," rather than single homes on individual lots. The Pasadena Realty Board met and supported the chamber plan to rent the homes but, ever mindful of the business of home ownership, called for the houses to be "bought outright" by the Mexicans. Throughout the bond campaign, the chamber members hammered home the idea that the "Broadway Court," as it was called, would keep the "Mexican population together" instead of "being allowed to spread in the city." The secretary of the realty board told his fellow businessmen that the intention of the home association was not to segregate, because, after all, "there is no need to worry." He continued, "These people do not want our choice residence section. They would sooner remain where they are with their splendid $200,000 up-to-date school, their modern churches and the settlement hospital and home to serve their needs."[132]

THE "UP-TO-DATE" JUNIPERO SERRA SCHOOL

The Mexican Homes Association opened in September 1923 with the first eight houses of what eventually would be a court of 24. To celebrate the opening of a new Junipero Serra School, the settlement association, the school board and the chamber held an "open house" day in May 1924. The Mexican consul from Los Angeles, Gaiza Leal, was the featured guest as hundreds toured the school, the settlement house and the Broadway Court homes. The "up-to-date" school was an object of pride in the city. Pasadena officials referred to Serra School as one of the most modern of its kind in the country and surely "better than any school in the Republic of Mexico."[133]

The city had every reason to be proud. The new Junipero Serra School was a fitting addition to Pasadena's efficient network of Americanization efforts. Noted architect Cyril Bennett designed it on the same site as the old one but now facing Fair Oaks Avenue rather than South Raymond. The school was intended to be a "community center," with an auditorium that would accommodate 300, manual arts and domestic science workshops, a swimming pool, showers, a kindergarten room with a fireplace and large classrooms with sinks and hot and cold water. When it tore down the hodgepodge of frame buildings that was the old school, the school board ordered one small building to remain as the caretaker's residence. In one of the few surviving photographs, one can see two gigan-

Fig. 15. Erected on the same lot as South Raymond Street School, the newly opened Junipero Serra School is shown here in an undated Pasadena School District photograph. The looming natural gas tanks just behind the school gave it its unofficial name, the Gas Tank School. *(Photos courtesy of the Pasadena Unified School District)*

Fig. 16. Discovered tucked away in a long forgotten file in the Pasadena school district archives, this photograph is of children from Junipero Serra, excited and ready for a performance. To the right, we can only guess what has caught the little girl's attention. *(Photos courtesy of the Pasadena Unified School District)*

tic "L.A. Gas Co." natural gas storage tanks looming behind the school. The school took on a new name in the community, the "Gas Tank School."

In 1929, Christine Lofstedt was appointed principal. She was the last administrator for Junipero Serra. In 1932, after only eight years of operation, the school was closed. Ironically, the student body, which had just 17 years before been removed from Garfield School, was now transferred back to that west side school.

Superintendent Sexson and the city's leadership said they had decided to close Junipero Serra School to save money. Although justified as a fiscal necessity of the Depression, the closing remains somewhat of a mystery. Sexson reported that the Mexican school-age population was declining at both schools, yet the 1930 school census is inconclusive.[134] Serra was a new school; Garfield an old one. As early as 1925, a board-appointed survey had recommended closing Garfield and moving the students to Junipero Serra. The California Taxpayers' Association, in its 1931 cost analysis of the city schools, recommended the same thing. Yet Sexson and the board did the opposite. The school remained vacant until it was torn down after the 1933 earthquake.

In 1932, the *barrio* was firmly established around the settlement house and Serra school. By moving the students, all 267 of them, to Garfield, the boundaries of "Mexican town" were expanded. Later, during the mid-1930s, an additional component of that expansion was contested when the settlement association attempted to move its house to a location across the street from Garfield, on the south side of California Street. The homeowners in the immediate area, all white, were up in arms. One resident complained that moving the settlement house to California Street "would let down the bars," because the "Negro and Mexican population is north of California Street."[135] The boundary lines that marked the white/colored neighborhoods were rigidly enforced and the Planning and Zoning Commission rejected the association proposal. The settlement house remained on South Raymond Street.

THE CRISIS BEGINS

The richest city in the country had spent millions on civic improvements, programs and personnel. But in 1931, two years into the economic downturn known as the Great Depression, Pasadena was on the edge of a serious financial crisis. Although it appeared to be working, the grand social experiment of the 1920s was just too expensive to maintain. Revenue was off, unemployment was rising, and the city, always edgy about its image, needed to appear stable, prudent and prepared. For a decade, Pasadena's school administrators and the board of education got almost everything they asked for. They called it "pay as you go," but, together with the $3 million in construction bonds, the building of Pasadena's *belle artes* schools ended up costing over $8 million.[136] The result was a national reputation as one of America's finest cities.

Then in 1929–30 it all began to unravel. Pasadena was forced to retrench, and its schools, the "jewel in the crown" of this perfect place, were subjected to demands for massive cuts in personnel and programs. A taxpayer group demanded the closing of six elementary schools, of which Junipero Serra was one. In 1931–32, Superintendent Sexson maneuvered through a minefield of potential calamities as he negotiated with conservative, business-oriented taxpayer organizations that looked at the bottom line in municipal expenditures. In flush times these organizations and associations were Sexson's allies. He had a gift for currying the favor of the Downtown Businessmen's Group, The Twentieth Century Club and the Metropolitan Businessmen's Association. Now the business and taxpayer associations, in an effort to "keep taxes down," set out to dismantle Pasadena's progressive school infrastructure by cutting salaries, eliminating "surplus" teachers and closing schools. Beneath the cost-cutting rhetoric was a fervent, antiprogressive tone that equated anything beyond the "basics" with "frills." It would be Sexson's successor, Willard Goslin, who would suffer the whirlwind of the antiprogressive forces in the city.

At least Sexson's shrewd gamesmanship prevented the taxpayer groups—most notably the Property Owners' Division of the Pasadena Realty Board—from taking the schools apart program-by-program. As demands for cuts crested before budget hearings, there always seemed to be a proschool group ready in defense. It was the superintendent's behind-the-scenes maneuvers that put those proschool groups at the podium. He manufactured alliances between his schools, the board, and the various parent and civic groups. His inner circle of central office associates—especially the board secretary, Courtney Monsen, and the assistant superintendent, George Meredith—were his loyal shock troops.

The full credit for saving the schools from the worse proposals of the conservative antitax hounds must go to Sexson. The superintendent saved most of the schools from closing and many of the progressive programs remained in place. Despite his alliance building, he lost the teachers. The superintendent ran *his* schools with an iron fist. Courtney Monsen, the board secretary, called Sexson "ruthless."[137] Democracy was merely a word to Sexson. Each member of his inner staff believed "the boss" was "a great guy," but none of them believed he understood what democracy meant. He demanded loyalty and would display a volatile temper when a subordinate disagreed. He reportedly threatened to put a disgruntled teacher "in [the] little Mexican school on the outskirts of town."[138] His assistant superintendent, Meredith, was apparently Sexson's hit man. He was described by many as "crude," mean spirited, "tactless," and "sarcastic" as he negotiated with individuals or groups that had dealings with the superintendent. Mostly, it appears, those negotiations were with teachers. When Sexson was advised that Meredith's bulldog behavior was doing more harm than good, the superintendent smiled and said, "But some of those people need to be told ... they are not doing a good job."[139]

The Depression and the war kept opposition to Sexson at a minimum. Then, in 1948, Sexson's 20 years of autocratic rule finally got the best of him. Believing that the superintendent had ignored repeated pleas by teachers for salary relief, the Pasadena Education Association backed two anti-Sexson board candidates— one a former teacher—and their election ended any hope of a compliant board of education.[140] Harriet Sterling, the retired teacher elected to the board, said the teachers were "fed up" with the superintendent's administration. The "boss" talked "a lot about democracy," said Sterling, but "he [was] an absolute dictator." The new board decided Sexson had reached retirement age. Amid praise reserved for a prince, John Amherst Sexson—in private, bitter and frustrated over his removal—left the office he had ruled since 1927. Pasadena's schools have never been the same since.[141]

NOTES

1. David A. Valone, "Eugenic Science in California: The Papers of E. S. Gosney/Human Betterment Foundation," a biographical sketch located in the Ezra S. Gosney/Human Betterment Foundation Papers, California Institute of Technology Archives. Hereafter cited as "Gosney Papers"; the "noble concept" quote is from *College Biology*, below.
2. David Popenoe, "Remembering My Father: An Intellectual Portrait of 'The Man Who Saved Marriages'" (New York: Institute for American Values), working paper for the Symposium on Fatherhood in America, November 1991, p. 4, 56.
3. Paul Popenoe to Ezra Gosney, letter dated 10 January 1926, in the "Gosney Papers," California Institute of Technology Archives, Pasadena, California.
4. Ibid.
5. E.S. Gosney, *Collected Papers on Eugenic Sterilization in California: A Critical Study of Results of 6000 Cases* (Pasadena, CA: The Human Betterment Foundation, 1930); "Pasadena Cases," folder 12.7, box 12, "Gosney Papers," California Institute of Technology Archives, Pasadena, California.
6. E.S. Gosney, and Paul Popenoe, *Sterilization for Human Betterment* (New York: Macmillan Company, 1929).
7. *Collected Papers on Eugenic Sterilization in California,* introduction, not paginated.
8. *"Human Sterilization Today,"* A Publication of the Human Betterment Foundation, 325 Security Building, Pasadena, California, a pamphlet in the "Gosney Papers," folder 4.7.1–2, Box 4, California Institute of Technology Archives, Pasadena, California, p. 3. The pamphlet said that "births among families habitually living on public charity are often 50 percent higher than births among self-supporting families ... the generally admitted trend of the population toward degeneracy is real and vital."
9. Wilbur H. Johnson, *General Biology* (New York: Henry Holt and Company, 1957), p. 525.

10. "Annual Report of the Superintendent," John Sexson, 1926–1917, City of Pasadena. Also see Vincent Booth Claypool, "John Amherst Sexson, Educator" (Ph.D. diss., University of California, Los Angeles, 1948).

11. William Martin Proctor, ed., *The Six-Four-Four Plan of School Organization in Pasadena, California, A Report to the Board of Education, the Patrons and the Staff.* Pasadena: Pasadena Board of Education, 1933. Pasadena was one of the pioneers in the new organization plan.

12. See Claypool for Sexson's retirement. The "seamless" comment is from an author interview with Sid Gally, 8 January 2002.

13. West's 1924–1925 "Annual Report of the Superintendent," shows that the city school building expenditures had declined from 1913 until 1919. Yet in 1923, the city schools had the highest "holding power" or retention of any city with a population of more than 100,000 in the country. That same year, the city passed a $3 million school construction bond. See West's report, p. 16–17.

14. See Jeremiah Rhodes, "Pasadena Kindergartens, 1901–1919," p. 6. This was one of many special publications printed by the city schools. Rhodes was superintendent from 1912 to 1918.

15. "Annual Report of the Superintendent," John Franklin West, 1923–1924, City of Pasadena, p. 12.

16. Claypool, p. 62. Sexson quoted Kilpatrick and Dewey often in his annual reports. See his 1931–32 report, p. 33.

17. Jeremiah Rhodes, "Pasadena Kindergartens, 1901–1919," p. 6.

18. See Earl Smith's report in the "Annual Report of the Superintendent," John Franklin West, 1926–1927, City of Pasadena, p. 13–20.

19. Ibid., p. 17.

20. John Franklin West, "Annual Report of the Superintendent," 1925–1926, City of Pasadena, p. 11–12.

21. I. Grace Ball, "Typical Work of the Adjustment Division," *Educational Research Bulletin* 3:3 (November 1924), p. 6–8.

22. John Franklin West, "Annual Report of the Superintendent," 1926–1927, City of Pasadena, p. 7.

23. W. H. Hughes, "What About Intelligence Tests?" *Pasadena Star-News,* 9 January 1926, p. 8.

24. The literature on testing is substantial. An excellent starting point is Raymond E. Fancher, *The Intelligence Men: Makers of the IQ Controversy* (New York: W.W. Norton and Co., 1985).

25. Hughes, "Should Students Be Sorted?" *Pasadena Star-News,* 20 March 1926, p. 8.

26. Hughes, "What About Intelligence Tests?" *Pasadena Star-News,* 9 January 1926, p. 9.

27. Ibid.

28. Hughes established his "Research Department" under West. He then created the *Educational Research Bulletin* to disseminate what they had learned. The first volume appeared 26 September 1922.

29. John Franklin West, "Annual Report of the Superintendent," 1923–1924, City of Pasadena, p. 20–22.

30. Hughes, "Studying the Individual Child," *Pasadena Star-News,* 2 January 1926, p. 11.

31. John Franklin West, "Annual Report of the Superintendent," 1923–1924, City of Pasadena, p. 36–38.

32. W. Hardin Hughes, ed., "Reliability of Traits," *Educational Research Bulletin* 3:4 (December 1924), Pasadena City Schools, p. 23–25.

33. W. H. Hughes, ed., "A Guidance Program in the Junior High School," *Educational Research Bulletin* 4:6 (February 1926), Pasadena City Schools, p. 17–25.

34. John Franklin West, "Annual Report of the Superintendent," 1924–1925, City of Pasadena, p. 25–27.
35. Ibid., p. 23.
36. Ibid., p. 27.
37. "Fitting the Commerce Course of the High School and Junior College to the Needs of the Community," *Educational Research Bulletin* 4:9 (May 1926), p. 3–48. The occupations data is drawn from the U.S. Census, 1930, found in William Proctor's 1933 report on the 6-4-4 Plan, "Vocational Opportunities in Pasadena," p. 93, discussed below.
38. Ibid., p. 23–25.
39. See John Franklin West, "Annual Reports of the Superintendent," 1923–1927, especially Earl Smith's "Attendance Department" reports.
40. The exact number of churches remains difficult to pinpoint. In the industrial section, there was the Methodist chapel, a Nazarene chapel, and the Catholic mission. In the northern section there was a Methodist church and probably the Catholic mission.
41. See Arthur L. Hamilton, "Annual Report of the Superintendent," 1909, City of Pasadena, p. 18–20.
42. As late as the early 1930s, Manny Contreras reported that there were only a few "oakies" at Fremont.
43. John Franklin West, "Annual Report of the Superintendent," 1926–1927, City of Pasadena, p. 110–120. There were smaller populations of Mexican children at Cleveland School and at Thomas Jefferson School, but by early 1930 those populations had been absorbed by Garfield and Lincoln. Until Fremont opened, there were Mexican children at Emerson Elementary School. Also see the "Hart-Peterson Survey," published by the Pasadena Board of Education, 1926.
44. See West's "Annual Report" on lack of school funds, 1923–24, and the school bonding election. Also see the history of the system written by the board secretary, Cortney Monsen, in the 1936 Pasadena Junior College Homecoming program, located in the Pasadena Unified School District (PUSD) archives.
45. Sid Gally, interview with author, Pasadena, Calif., 10 March 2002; Jessie and Mary Moses, interview with author, Pasadena, Calif., 21 July 1994; Edna Griffin, interview with author, Pasadena, Calif., 16 July 1993; Ruby McKnight Williams, interview with author, Pasadena, Calif., 16 March 1994; Sara and Walter Shatford, with author, Pasadena, Calif., 10 March 2002; Katie Nack, interview with author, Pasadena, Calif., 13 March 2002, and Elbie Hickambottom, interview by author, Pasadena, Calif., 22 March 2002. Also see Marguerite Duncan-Abrams, "Pasadena's Forgotten Neighborhoods: Residential and Cultural Aspects of Pasadena's Commercial Sector in the Early Twentieth Century" (graduate paper, University of California, Irvine, June, 1990) and Carson Anderson, "Ethnic History Research Project," City of Pasadena, March 1995.
46. *Chronicle,* 20 September 1883, p. 1.
47. Roberta Martinez, community activist, interview by author, Pasadena, Calif., 13 January 2001.
48. For the reference to the "Mexican Union Club," *Pasadena Daily Evening Star,* 13 August 1896, p. 5, col. 1; the reference to the *Club Mexicano* is in the *Pasadena Star,* January 25, 1903, p. 1, col. 6.
49. "Gangs of Men Working Hard; Mexicans, Japanese and Greeks Transform the Streets into Bee Hives of Activity," *Pasadena Daily News,* 17 July 1903, p. 1. The newspaper put the labor gangs at "350 cholos, 100 Japs, and the remainder Greeks" working in crews of 100.
50. Manny Contreras, interview by author, Pasadena, Calif., 21 March 2001.

51. Roberta Martinez, interview by author.

52. Vicky Ruiz, *Out of the Shadows: Mexican Women in Twentieth-Century America* (New York: Oxford University Press, 1998), p. 3–50.

53. Arthur L. Hamilton, "Annual Report of the Superintendent," City of Pasadena, 1908, p. 20.

54. Ibid., p. 20–21.

55. Ibid., p. 21.

56. Ibid., p. 21.

57. Ibid., p. 21.

58. See, "Garfield School Bond," *Pasadena News,* 6 March 1908, and *Minutes,* Pasadena Board of Education, 6 March 1908.

59. *Minutes,* Pasadena Board of Education, 6 March 1908.

60. The comment, "wait at her doors" was a common saying among the nation's social workers that dealt with immigrant groups. In this case, it refers to Mexicans "coming to California," a place for centuries that was Mexico. The term "waiting" carries a double meaning, as Mexicans would, indeed, need to wait to be admitted. But "waiting" also meant needing to wait for social acceptance. See "Friends Visit Mexican Day Nursery," *Pasadena Star,* 15 January 1916.

61. Karen Odell Wilkes, "Clara Morgan Odell," (undergraduate research paper prepared by Odell's great granddaughter, March 1991), not paginated, in author's possession.

62. "Mexicans are Problem for Workers," *Pasadena Star,* 20 December 1914, col. 1, p. 13.

63. Ibid.

64. Ibid.

65. "Further Facts on Mexican Huts," *Pasadena Daily News,* 14 February 1913, col. 2, p. 7.

66. Ibid.

67. Ibid.

68. "Will Demolish Unsanitary Shacks," *Pasadena Star,* 14 August 1914, p. 1.

69. "Mexicans are Problem for Workers," *Pasadena Star,* 20 December 1914, col. 1, p. 13; Wilkes, not paginated.

70. "Mexicans are Problem for Workers," *Pasadena Star,* 20 December 1914, col. 1, p. 13.

71. *Pasadena News,* 9 October 1911, p. 1; Odell commented in her interview that a bathtub had been installed the previous spring.

72. Jeremiah Rhodes, "Annual Report of the Superintendent," City of Pasadena, 1915, p. 53.

73. *Minutes,* Pasadena Board of Education, 9 September 1912. The tract was purchased for $1,600 on 14 October 1912.

74. *Minutes,* Pasadena Board of Education, 14 March 1913.

75. See "The Wallace Home," *Pasadena Star-News,* 8 January 1927, col. 2, p. 23 and "Mexican School is Big Success," *Pasadena Star,* 11 February 1915, col. 2, p. 1. Interestingly, the founder of the Gardena school was Frank S. Wallace, but there is no known documentation that would connect the two institutions. The author of the newspaper article on the Wallace Home referred to its director as "Mother Wallace."

76. Ibid., *Pasadena Star,* 11 February 1915.

77. *Minutes,* Pasadena Board of Education, 13 August 1914; 28 September 1914; 16 February 1915; 26 September 1916.

78. *Minutes,* Pasadena Board of Education, 27 June 1916, *Minutes,* Pasadena Board of Education, 7 August 1916.

79. Grace Stanley, "Separate Schools for Mexicans," *The Survey* (15 September 1920), p. 714–715.

80. Ibid.

81. "The Intelligence of Mexican Children," *The Survey* (2 February 1924), p. 139–142.

82. See the many articles in the Pasadena newspapers, e.g., "Mexican Women of City are Taught Ways of Americans," *Pasadena Evening Post,* 27 May 1920, p. 1; "Teach Care of Households as Part Work," *Pasadena Star-News,* 17 May 1921, col. 5, p. 20; "Feed Eighty Mexican Pupils," *Pasadena News,* 16 November 1921; "Teach English to Mexican Children," *Pasadena Star-News,* 7 November 1916, col. 6, p. 6; "Mexican Parents Will be Given Instruction in New Local School," *Pasadena Star-News,* 24 September 1914, col. 5, p. 1; "Teaching Them to Care for Babies," *Pasadena Star,* 7 July 1915, col. 5, p. 6.

83. Ibid., p. 54.

84. James C. Scott, *Domination and the Arts of Resistance: Hidden Transcripts* (New Haven: Yale University Press, 1990). For the following discussion, I draw heavily from Scott's seminal work.

85. Ibid., p. 18.

86. Ibid., p. 33.

87. Ibid., p. 33.

88. Ibid., p. 137.

89. "Mexicans are Problem for Workers," *Pasadena Star,* 20 December 1914, col. 1, p. 13.

90. Emory Bogardus, "The Mexican Immigrant," *Sociology and Social Research*" vol. 11 (1926–27), p. 478, 487, cited in Mario Garcia, "The Americanization of the Mexican Immigrant, 1880–1930" *The Journal of Ethnic Studies* 6:2 (Summer 1978), p. 27.

91. *Minutes,* Pasadena Board of Education, 10 July 1917 and 26 December 1917.

92. Jeremiah Rhodes, "Annual Report of the Superintendent," City of Pasadena, 1915, p. 55.

93. Ibid., p. 56.

94. See "Praise Edna Alter," *Pasadena News,* 21 July 1913, on her death; as early as October 1911, the "Titleyville" area had a one-room "school" for the "benefit of the Mexicans"; see "School for Mexicans" *Pasadena Daily News,* 11 October 1911.

95. Eileen Boris, "Reconstructing the 'Family': Women, Progressive Reform, and the Problem of Social Control," in Noralee Frankel and Nancy Dye, eds., *Gender, Class, Race, and Reform in the Progressive Era* (Lexington: University of Kentucky Press, 1991), p. 73–74 and Ruiz, p. 45.

96. "Edna Alter Society Moves," *Pasadena News,* 11 November 1915, p. 10.

97. See "Edna Alter Society Moves for Protest," *Pasadena News,* 11 November 1915; on the house moving, see Manuel Pineda, *Pasadena Area History* (Los Angeles: James Anderson Publishers, 1972), p. 41–42; see Odell interview in "Mexicans are Problem for Workers" for comments on "simple things"; and "Aid is Needed for Mexican Children," *Pasadena Star-News,* 21 March 1916 for comment on "rocking babes" and "advice."

98. "Friends Visit Mexican Day Nursery," *Pasadena Star,* 15 January 1916. Odell mentions work with mothers as early as 1913 in the first settlement house, which, incidentally, Odell does not give us an exact location.

99. "Mexicans Here Will Not Go to War," *Pasadena Star,* 5 May 1914, col. 6, p. 6.

100. "Clean Up Slums is Slogan of United Civic Bodies," *Pasadena Daily News,* 13 February 1913, col. 2, p. 1.

101. "Mexican Women Will Be Hired," *Pasadena Star,* 15 March 1915, col. 1, p. 1.

102. Ibid.; and also "Novel Laundry Now Ready to Open," *Pasadena Star,* 3 April 1915, col. 3, p. 16.

103. See "Rev. Gonzales Has Plans for Church," *Pasadena Star-News,* 12 October 1916, announcing his arrival and Olazabal's departure, for comments on the Latin American Institute, see "Will Tell of Work among Mexicans," *Pasadena Star-News,* 8 July 1920, col. 1, p. 6.

104.   See Christine Lofstedt, "A Study of the Mexicans Living in Pasadena" (Master's thesis, University of Southern California, 1922), p. 21, which is discussed at the conclusion of this chapter.

105.   "Health Service Enlarging Scope of Its Activities," *Pasadena Daily News,* 8 March 1919.

106.   "Single Gift Brings New Building," *Pasadena Star-News,* 5 December 1922, p. 1.

107.   "Aid is Needed for Mexican Children," *Pasadena Daily News,* 21 March 1916.

108.   Douglas Monroy, *Rebirth: Mexican Los Angeles from the Great Migration to the Great Depression* (Berkeley: University of California Press, 1999), p. 127; "Mexicans Here Will Not Go to War" *Pasadena Star,* 1 May 1914, col. 6, p. 6.

109.   Ricardo Romo, *East Los Angeles: A History of a Barrio* (Austin: University of Texas Press, 1983), p. 92; "Pasadena Department," *The Citizen,* 15 March 1908, p. 3.

110.   See the two-part expose, published by the *Pasadena Daily News* during the winter of 1913: "Clean Up Slums is Slogan of United Civic Bodies," *Pasadena Daily News,* 13 February 1913, col. 2, p. 1, and "Further Facts on Mexican Huts," *Pasadena Daily News,* 14 February 1913, col. 2, p. 1. The same woman reporter who identified herself only as a "staff representative" presumably wrote both. She concluded her first article with the following, "It is almost impossible that people could live in such places, regardless of nationality." She concluded her second article with, "Mere descriptions fail to convey an adequate idea of the degradation in which these people live."

111.   Under the headline, "Clean Up Slums is Slogan of United Civic Bodies," the newspaper ran a separate article, subtitled "Menace to Entire City," in which W. Z. Taber of the New Century Club called for a "little coercion."

112.   "Takes Whack at Slums of City," *Pasadena Daily News,* 7 June 1915, p. 1.

113.   Ibid.

114.   "Clean Up Slums is Slogan of United Civic Bodies" *Pasadena Daily News,* 13 February 1913, col. 2, p. 1.

115.   "Refuse Disposal Must Be Solved," *Pasadena Star-News,* 29 August 1916.

116.   "Mexicans in Fierce Fight," *Pasadena Daily News,* 16 July 1907, col. 3, p. 5; "Murderous Mexicans Use Pistols Freely," *Pasadena Daily News,* 2 February 1906; for comment on increased police patrols, see "Mexican Shot in Fight," *Pasadena Daily News,* 18 March 1914, p. 5.

117.   "Fire Loss Felt By Many," *Pasadena Star-News,* 24 April 1918, col. 1, p. 1.

118.   Ibid.

119.   "Ask Municipal Quarters for Mexicans," *Pasadena Star-News,* 21 June 1918, p. 1.

120.   The bulldozing of Mexican homes is mentioned in "Housing of Mexicans is Aim," *Pasadena Star-News,* 22 September 1921.

121.   Lofstedt, p. 4–5.

122.   Manny Contreras, interview by author, Pasadena, Calif., 21 March, 2001; Manny Contreras and John Contreras, interviewed by N.H.C. [Chris] Sellers, Chapel Hill, N.C., 3 June 1999, p. 7.

123.   Lofstedt, p. 1, 5, 7, 11–13.

124.   Ruiz, p. 12; Mario T. Garcia, *Desert Immigrants: The Mexicans of El Paso, 1880–1920* (New Haven: Yale University Press, 1980), p. 46–48. "Mexicans to Have Good Homes," *Pasadena Star-News,* 23 March 1923, p. 1.

125.   Lofstedt, p. 24–25.

126.   Ibid., p. 26.

127.   Ibid., p. 27.

128.   Scott, p. 67.

129. Lofstedt, p. 35.

130. "Housing of Mexicans is Aim," *Pasadena Star-News,* 22 September 1921, p. 1.

131. "Better Homes for Mexicans," *Pasadena Star-News,* 3 January 1923, p. 16; "Fifty Houses in Plan for Mexicans," *Pasadena Star-News,* 16 March 1923, p. 1.

132. See "Mexicans to Have Good Homes," *Pasadena Star-News,* 16 March 1923, p.15 for comment on land purchase; see "Fifty Houses is Plan for Mexicans," *Pasadena Star-News,* 24 November 1922; for comments on group plan, see "Better Homes for Mexicans Aided," *Pasadena Star-News,* 1 June 1923; also see, Lofstedt's thesis, Appendix D: "A Double Opportunity," a typewritten version of the chamber advertisement for stock purchases. The reference to "Double Opportunity" meant social good as well as profit.

133. "Open House in Mexican Section," *Pasadena Star-News,* 23 March 1924, p. 11.

134. "School to Close," *Pasadena Evening Post,* 12 August 1932, col. 1, p. 1; Hart-Peterson Survey, *Pasadena City Schools,* February 1926, p. 73. The city's largest newspaper, the *Pasadena Star-News,* did not cover the story.

135. "Zoners Deny Permit for Aid Group," *Pasadena Star-News,* 11 March 1938, col. 3, p. 1.

136. "Survey of the Pasadena City Schools," *California Taxpayers' Association,* Association Report No. 119, Los Angeles, California (1931), p. 96–97.

137. Courtney Monsen, interview by John Claypool, in "John Amherst Sexson," 2 January 1948, not paginated, in appendix.

138. Harriet Sterling, interview by John Claypool, 14 January 1948, in "John Amherst Sexson," not paginated, in appendix.

139. Harriet Sterling, interview by John Claypool, 14 January 1948; Courtney Monsen, interview by John Claypool, 2 January 1948; Gladys C. Rinehart, interview by John Claypool, 13 January 1948; Drummond McCunn, interview by John Claypool, 4 March 1948; Milton Wopschall, interview by John Claypool, 5 March 1948. The "Mexican school" quote is from Sterling interview. The "they are not doing a good job" quote is from Rinehart interview.

140. Claypool, p. 185.

141. Harriet Sterling, interview by John Claypool, 14 January 1948, p. 267; John Claypool believed Sexson was despondent, angry and frustrated with his removal.

CHAPTER 6

SOUTHERN PROGRESSIVISM
DURING THE GREAT DEPRESSION
Creating the "New South" in Virginia's Schools 1900–1940

For many, the Great Depression of the 1930s is captured in the photographs of Dorothea Lange—images of squalor and despair; the dirty, scuff-grays and somber moods of poor whites and destitute blacks; innocent faces that seemed to tolerate the present as they looked to some distant future with little hope. In the large cities, breadlines and "Hoovervilles," violent strikes and payless paydays mocked a nation that to millions had been God's Promised Land. But it was the hopelessness of rural, backwoods poverty that was so poignantly conveyed in the images Lange made as she wandered the depressed countryside. In the South, to white and black sharecroppers, to laborers, section hands and, generally, the poor and working class, the 1930s brought havoc to an already impoverished land-scape. Like the "Great War" it followed, this holocaust was to be forever cursed by its victims as the "Great Depression," a cuttingly ironic description of a decade of revolution that changed the world.[1]

If the Great Depression was hard on poor whites, it was harder still on Southern blacks. Caught in a culture of seemingly inescapable poverty that grew out of a rigidly segregated social system, Southern blacks during the Depression apparently had few choices. They could live within a biracial society or leave. All over the South, Afro Southerners voted with their feet, as migration became one form of social protest.[2] Thousands abandoned the land and headed north and west to places like Harlem in New York and Watts in Los Angeles. In Virginia, the rural black population continued to fall throughout the first three decades of the 20th century, while the numbers of urban black dwellers remained fairly con-stant.[3] Pasadena's well-established black community would complain about these "country bumpkins" causing "trouble." Some blamed the new arrivals for the city's changing racial climate.

To the African American, the much-heralded New South of the 20th century was merely another version of the old. Poverty for most was constant, as everyone endured a society that socialized whites and blacks into believing their world was preordained to be divided by color and class. This biracial state was no more apparent than in Southern schooling, where, starting with the end of Reconstruction, children attended schools according to the color of their skin. In Virginia, by the turn of the century, black children were educated almost universally by African-American teachers. In nearly every black school in the state, black men (seldom women) served as principals and administrators. Always though, whites controlled educational policy for Negro schools, as in every Southern state.[4]

Throughout the South, the Supreme Court's *Plessy* ("Separate But Equal") ruling was seldom if ever equal. Black children attended schools that were woefully underfunded and understaffed, with equipment and supplies that were often nonexistent, and a school year that was nearly always shorter than that of its white counterparts. Education for Southern black children was, as historian Carter Woodson wrote early in the 1930s, "mis-education."[5] With the coming of the Depression, even that was severely curtailed. School terms were further reduced and teachers' salaries cut to a point where many in rural schools earned much less than half of what their white colleagues earned in the cities. All over the region, white and black schools alike—but more often the latter—hit bottom and closed their doors. In Red Hill, a small farming community not far from Charlottesville, the white school board closed two black schools, transferring the funds and one teacher to another black school in an effort to save money.[6] Politicians talked of sacrifice, and in communities all over the country, teachers responded. In Richmond, Virginia, the state superintendent told a backslapping, self-congratulatory assembly in May of 1933 that the success in keeping an eight-month term (for white schools) was due more to teachers staying on even when the money ran out rather than to the solvency of the state treasury.[7] Teachers could not, though, in Virginia and elsewhere, continue to carry the schools. As despair deepened, the mood of many turned to a mix of rage and hope. For blacks and whites, working class, middle class, teachers and tenant farmers, there was a sense that something was about to change.

PROGRESSIVE EDUCATION AND THE GREAT DEPRESSION

By the winter of 1932, millions were out of work and there apparently was little President Hoover would, or could, do about it. Paydays came and went without paychecks. For those who had jobs, salaries were cut 10 to 30 percent or more. Chicago's teachers went weeks without pay, many taking in fellow teachers who were broke and homeless. In Pasadena, half the kindergarten teachers lost their jobs, and at least 20 percent of the workforce was out of work. All over the country, people lost their homes. Banks seized farms, or farmers simply walked away, abandoning family lands that had been worked for generations. Hard money seemingly vanished overnight as banks and savings institutions were forced to lock their doors. Children left school by the thousands in the futile attempt to find work somewhere, anywhere. Three years after the "Panic of '29," it appeared to many that the country was dangerously close to economic Armageddon. The hard-and-fast rule of capital and cheap labor producing wealth—and jobs—had turned to myth. How could this land of plenty, with its rich and abundant natural and human resources, suffer such misery? From progressives and the socially elite to those in breadlines and on the family farm, there was a growing resentment toward what Sinclair Lewis called the "monied aristocracy" and a laissez-faire economic system that promoted selfish individualism, conspicuous consumption and extravagant wealth for the few.

As the Depression worsened, well-known, mainly northern educators, who for a generation had relied on a child-centered, progressive pedagogy to frame their cultural agenda, joined with the political and social Left to embrace a newly broadening philosophy. They proposed a series of far-reaching, radical proposals for ameliorating the tensions that existed between the American liberal tradition and the lure of Marxian economic systems that seemed to offer some release from the vicissitudes of capitalist declines, booms and busts. Calling themselves Social Reconstructionists, educators, philosophers and social critics, including Sidney Hook, John Dewey, William Heard Kilpatrick, Theodore Brameld and George Counts (who had just returned from an automobile trip across the Soviet Union to see for himself if the proletarian revolution was real), advanced the notion that teachers and the work they perform should aid in easing the crisis.[8] The reconstructionists believed the crisis had been exacerbated because schools—child-centered and traditional, public and private alike—reflected the moribund values of a class-bound society bent on self-protection at all costs. In 1932, George Counts, in his now famous *Dare the Schools Build a New Social Order?* wrote a biting condemnation of the middle class:

> They ... possess no deep and abiding loyalties, possess no convictions for which they would sacrifice over-much, would find it hard to live without their customary material comforts, are rather insensitive to the accepted forms of social injustice ... and in the day of severe trial will follow the lead of the most powerful and respectable forces in society and at the same time find good reason for doing so.[9]

For the reconstructionists, the principal aim of schools and teachers should be to prepare individuals, as Kilpatrick wrote in 1933, to "take part intelligently in the management of their lives, to bring them an understanding of the forces which are moving, and to provide them with the practical tools with which they themselves can enter into the direction of these forces."[10] Kilpatrick, a longtime member of Columbia's Teacher's College faculty and the most famous of John Dewey's students, called for an educational system that functioned at the cutting edge of social change, rather than reacting in knee-jerk fashion to successive crises, oblivious to the larger cultural voices of status quo and reaction. The educational reconstructionists and a wide array of socially progressive intellectuals wanted schools to take the lead in reshaping culture away from the hierarchical notions imbedded in 20th-century industrial capitalism. Schools and teachers would then participate equally in a cultural redefinition of America—a collective society dependent less on the wealth of the few and more on the planning of the many. The social reconstructionist agenda cut at the very nature of how America thinks about culture and order and threatened the very definition of power and who governs. Later, during the postwar era of anticommunism, Kilpatrick would come face to face with a vitriolic, conservative backlash that branded him and his followers as traitorous "REDucators." In 1949, his mere presence in Pasadena would aid in the downfall of the city's new progressive superintendent.

For those bent on reclaiming what they believed was a more democratic culture, these early 1930s were heady times. Radical forces were at work; revolutionary ideas were capturing the imagination of workers, farmers, blacks, young and old. In the South, the early years of the decade invited, as historian George Tindal wrote, "radical agitation."[11] Communists and trade unionists in the cities organized industrial and textile workers, and, in the countryside, the Share Croppers' Union was formed chiefly among poor whites and blacks. All over the region there was "desperate but nebulous talk of revolution."[12] Even the self-proclaimed patriarch of a reactionary and racist South, Governor Theodore Bilbo of Mississippi, told reporters in 1931 that "folks are restless ... communism is gaining a foothold ... I'm even getting a little pink myself."[13] Bilbo's assessments of communist gains—and his self-proclaimed political coloration—are far fetched. Yet the economic base of a progressive New South was seriously threatened by the Depression. By 1933, one third of the region's railroads were in receivership. Farm profits had all but disappeared, and financial institutions, both at the state and local levels, were ill equipped to deal with the crisis.[14] State revenues continued to dry up, and, in Virginia as throughout the South, that meant fewer dollars for schools.

It is somewhat paradoxical that in the midst of this great economic and social catastrophe, when both white and black schools were subject to gross underfunding and the very fabric of Southern society was unraveling, black educators in Virginia made significant gains in the struggle against inequality and segregation.[15] By seizing the ideology and language of the social reconstructionists, African-American educators in Virginia were able to carve out a tenuous foothold in state educational policy making. What makes the study of Virginia education—both black and white—during the 1930s especially ironic, is that social reconstruction, with its themes of radical community change being initiated by a vanguard of teachers liberating the masses and creating a "new kind of society," was never intended for African Americans. At least in Virginia, the very idea of social reconstruction may have been merely a transitory illusion, for the ideals of progressive community rebuilding turned out to be more a conservator of the status quo than the hoped for mechanism of radical democratic change.[16]

In Charlottesville, as in many of Virginia's New South communities, the culturally transformative themes of a reconstructed "new kind of society" were subsumed by color and caste. The result was further alienation and social stratification, the exact opposite of what progressive theorists like Hollis Caswell and William Heard Kilpatrick were advocating. As it turned out, reconstructing society in Charlottesville would prove to be as complex and contradictory as it was in Pasadena.

RECONSTRUCTING VIRGINIA

Progressive pedagogy and the idea of a socially reconstructive educational system came to Virginia when Sidney Hall was appointed state superintendent of public instruction in 1931.[17] A native Virginian and former director of secondary education at the Virginia State Department of Public Instruction, Hall was on the faculty of George Peabody College in Nashville at the time of his appointment. Hall had progressive views on educational change. Given the reticence of Virginia's political establishment to invest much—either funds or liberal ideas—in schooling, Hall's appointment appears to be contradictory at first glance.[18] In the private correspondence between Senator Harry Byrd and his lieutenants, it is clear that Hall's appointment came with strings attached. The Democratic party in Virginia ("the Organization") controlled state politics and Harry Byrd controlled the party. Hall was a dark-horse candidate, and only when the leading candidate withdrew at the 11th hour, did Byrd agree to him.[19] The reason came out during the early years of the decade, when Hall repeatedly told Byrd and his lieutenants that he could deliver the state's teachers to the "Organization," though at a cost of supporting some of Hall's ideas. For the next decade, Hall and Senator Byrd would struggle over who was to control the state's schools. In the end, it was to be Byrd.[20]

Sidney Hall was an astute politician who saw himself becoming president of a major university. There was speculation throughout his tenure as state superintendent that he was about to jump ship for William and Mary, Peabody or the University of Virginia.[21] A persuasive public speaker, Hall was enigmatic and handsome (some said he had the look of Cary Grant), energetic, and, from the very first days of his appointment, clearly the one in charge, as much as one could be with Byrd's organization looking over his shoulder. He believed the ideals of a progressive New South—science, efficiency, industry and democracy—would free Virginia from the old ways of waste, ignorance, political cronyism and paternalism.[22] His was an educational enterprise that would equalize school funding, systematize bureaucracy, improve teacher pay and retirement and, most important, redesign the very experience of school. In the spirit of true progressivism, education would bring Virginia into the 20th century. He understood, though, that any fundamental change in school experience would necessitate changes in educational governance. Reforming schools in Virginia would require the building of coalitions, and it would begin with the most powerful professional organization in the state, the High School Principals Association. By 1932, Hall's Virginia Curriculum Revision Project, with the enthusiastic blessing of most administrators in the state, was under way.[23]

Logistically, the project was spread over eight curriculum centers including the University of Virginia, the State Teachers College and Virginia State College for Negroes at Petersburg, the center set aside for curriculum design for the state's entire black school population.[24] The State Department of Public Instruction in Richmond asked each of the institutions to recommend a committee of local talent to monitor the creation of new curricula, ostensibly to be designed through the input of some 12,000 to 15,000 classroom teachers, as they worked in study groups all over the state from 1931 to 1932. In reality, the structural components of revision were in place long before the "workers" (teachers), who have been characterized as the real force behind this movement, ever got to their study groups. What has been characterized as a prodemocracy, grass roots, teacher-led statewide reform effort, was in reality the creation of a small group of men, most notably Hollis Caswell from Teachers College, who served as Hall's curriculum consultant, and Frederick Alexander, principal of Newport News High School and chair of the Aims Committee.[25] It was Caswell and Alexander who probably wrote the project's guiding "aims" during the summer of 1932.[26]

As the revision program unfolded, it was clear that the language of school reform in Virginia was to be democratic, participatory, liberating, cooperative and reconstructive.[27] Caswell, whom we have to believe was the real architect of the program, idealized a "Democratic Man," his vision of the activist-citizen whose education had prepared him to be responsive to society's ills. Caswell had come to believe that social ills were the result of what he called "disordered social functions." Schools can aid in the correction of social functions by introducing early in a child's education a set of key ideas, "woven," as one curriculum historian would later write, "right into the child's performance."[28] Formal education, then, could take the lead in the reconstruction of culture. Experience, in the truest sense of progressive pedagogy, would liberate society from the old ways.

However, this educational and culturally reconstructive process needed "guideposts." In other words, there had to be central, functional ideas classroom teachers could employ as they wrote units of study. These organizational structures were the "aims, understandings, and generalizations" that Alexander and

Caswell wrote during the summer of 1932. Ironically, what was created for this very conservative Southern state, bound by the traditions of white aristocracy and slavery, were some of the most far-reaching, radical educational ideas to come out of any statewide revision program. Alexander admitted that he had tried to answer George Counts' call for a reconstructive America. The guidelines he created gave the revision program, at least on paper, a decidedly anticapitalist flavor. Alexander suggested teachers design curriculum around generalizations. "Individuals and powerful minorities have always sought to control and to subjugate," and, as a result, "many of the significant movements of history have been caused by man's effort to throw off the yoke of oppression and slavery."

"Democracy," then, should be seen as "... a new thing in the world, as an experiment in the effort to establish human rights for all men." Since the theoretical base of educational progressivism had broken with absolutism, Alexander wanted teachers to instill in their students the idea that "the present social order is not fixed and permanent. Man continues to modify it in search for justice and freedom." To some, especially those in the black community, these were ideals to be taken seriously. Later the notion of a reconstructed social order would come back to haunt both Hall and Alexander.[29]

As far as "Big Business" and laissez-faire capitalism were concerned, Alexander offered as aids for curricular innovation a collection of provocative themes. Educators and their students should understand that "the material prosperity of the modern world has been attained under the capitalistic system," but "capitalism is based on the principle of profit to the owner rather than to service to the masses of the people." As a result, "the distribution of goods in a capitalistic society tends to direct social products into the hands of the few." If teachers were aware that "production is based on the amount of goods purchasers can be induced to consume, rather than upon their needs," then they would understand that "the capitalistic system is not planned and lacks direction, thus waste and economic cycles result." Alexander concluded by telling teachers "the dependence of the laborer upon capital tends to reduce him to a servile status."[30] These were, indeed, revolutionary ideas. One wonders, years later, if Alexander really believed Virginia was ready for a revolution in its schools.

In an article he wrote in 1934 for the *Clearing House* magazine, Alexander said that high school students involved in the revision program could be "discussing ways in which the church, the school and the press restrict thinking and conduct to bring out the ways in which you are denied the intellectual and social freedom that you should have." They might be "arranging bulletin board[s], showing how the press tends to interfere with the realization of the democratic ideal." Students could be "visiting courts and industrial plants and interviewing laborers, lawyers, and people who have been convicted of crimes to learn in what ways the poor and nonconformists are deprived of justice." Classroom materials, said Alexander reassuringly, were carefully selected so they "present a well-balanced discussion ..." Alexander concluded that subject matter was used to broaden the pupil's "experiences through engaging in socially useful activities that will enable him to realize attitudes and understandings that he can use in managing and re-creating a new kind of society."

It is quite possible that Frederick Alexander was caught up in the heady spirit of radical social change. But he was no radical; he was well connected to the Newport News business community and never established himself as being left of center in his political or educational views. Before his work on the project's aims and after he left the revision program, Alexander did not speak the language of social reconstruction. His daughter believed he was a political independent but tended to vote Democratic.[31] As principal of Newport News High School he was known by students and faculty alike as authoritarian, a "no nonsense administrator." When faculty members saw him walking down the hall with a stack of books tucked under his arm they wondered aloud if they were about to experience a 30-minute or three-hour meeting. In 1936, when he was appointed Director of Negro Education, he quickly established himself as a conservator of the biracial status quo rather than a moderate looking toward change. His authoring of aims that were decidedly anticapitalist, antichurch, and near Marxist in language (if not intent), perhaps indicate that he had been swept up by the drama of Counts's culturally transformative ideology. In the early days of the decade, when talk of revolution and reform were laced throughout the popular as well as educational press, Alexander might have believed what he wrote. His *Clearing House* essay was carefully crafted to emphasize the most revolutionary, antistatist aspects of the revision program. If he did not believe in the ideals of social revolution, then why did he single out those activities that had students "interviewing school officials, ministers, and newspaper editors to determine their part in building a new social order?"[32] On the other hand, he might have known that the teachers of Virginia, bound as they were by Southern conventions of hierarchy and order, would never take seriously the more radical aims of the revision program. In that case, his contribution to the revolutionary literature of the old Left would take on a cynical, hollow ring as a ploy to further his career rather than as inspiration for social change.[33]

Hall, Caswell and Alexander expected that, at least, the less controversial parts of their plan's content would be put into practice around the state. To an extent, those expectations were correct. Subject integration—what progressive educators at the time called "core work"—was experimented with in schools all over the state. Caswell's belief that schools would become *the* major site for community reform turned out to be an illusion, thanks to an entrenched system that was embedded in hierarchal definitions of caste and color. Although the architects of the program—namely Alexander—appeared to center the themes of the project squarely within the conflicts generated by class divisions, the overarching intent of the Virginia Curriculum Revision Project was never to trifle with social class conventions. In other words, Alexander's Aims Committee tackled class conflict but never challenged the ways in which social class is constructed.

As with any new school curriculum, how it gets translated at the local level is the measure of its "usefulness," a term we have seen with multiple interpretations. Sidney Hall told James Johnson, school superintendent at Charlottesville, that Waynesboro, Radford, Matthew Whaley High School in Williamsburg and Creadock High School in Norfolk were "some of the more sanely progressive schools" engaged in core work.[34] What Hall meant by "sanely progressive" is unclear. Was he suggesting other Virginia schools were dabbling in reconstructive experiments that are more radical? Probably not, as there is little evidence to suggest Alexander's aims of revolution were operating anywhere in white schools in Virginia's New South experiment.

THE NEW SOUTH AND CHARLOTTESVILLE'S PATRIARCH

The New South had begun to take shape in the cities during the first decades of the 20th century. Although rural schools were rapidly being consolidated, it was in the cities that ideas of change spread most rapidly and where schooling was, by necessity, being bent to the needs of a new urban age. Since World War I, and for blacks well before that, the rural Southern population had begun to spill into the cities, creating for educators the perplexing problems of managing accommodation while simultaneously adjusting the educational enterprise to a changing technological culture. For a rapidly expanding city like Charlottesville, the symbol of the New South in all its complexity and paradox would be its schools. At the center (and not by coincidence exactly at the geographical, civic center), was to be the new white-only high school, Lane High School.

The story of how Lane became a reality reflects a central theme in understanding how progressive ideals of community building got twisted into social fragmentation. The board of education mediated a complex set of contradictory impulses to establish a school thought to be so modern in its construction and curriculum that every student would come to know his or her purpose in life—and more important, come to fulfill that purpose. A building that served as a symbol of white civic pride, Lane High School was offered up to all as an icon of Southern progress in this New Age. Lane epitomized not only the "coming of age" of white Southern youth but the community of Charlottesville itself.[35]

Charlottesville's schools and its superintendent James Johnson were, to many in the community, one in the same. Appointed in 1909, Johnson ruled the schools, both white and black, as if they were his own. The superintendent personally supervised everything, from the daily accounts and attendance to the

Fig. 17. James Johnson, Charlottesville's superintendent
of schools, in a 1940 photograph for the *Frontiersman
Magazine.* Johnson was appointed teaching superintendent in July of 1909. He retired in 1945. *(Photo courtesy of
the Albemarle County Historical Society)*

installation of toilets at a new elementary school. He was always the center of
attention. At a special board meeting, called because six plumbers complained
Johnson was meddling in their work at the new Clark Elementary School site,
Johnson said that he had appointed himself "plumbing inspector." Although the
plumbers and the board objected, Johnson remained the "inspector." Nothing
escaped his watchful eye, including the political dynamics of the board of education. Nominally his employers, the Charlottesville board was, in reality, subservient to Johnson. He was captain of the ship and everyone knew it.[36]

By 1932, after more than 20 years of service to the community, Johnson's
dominance began to be challenged. Early that year, longtime president of the
board, Thomas Michie, one of the venerable old men of Albemarle County,
resigned due to ill health. Albert Balz, professor of philosophy at the University,
replaced Michie. A few years later Balz would be joined by one of his colleagues
from the engineering department, A.L. Hench. Together the two would begin to
wrest control of the city's schools from Johnson.[37]

Michie's departure marked the end of an era for Charlottesville. By way of
comparison, the industrial cities of the Northeast during much of the 19th
century had administered schools through the advice and consent of a board of

education made up of local businessmen, ward politicians and civic leaders, many of whom were either owned outright by political machines or compromised to near paralysis by indebted tradeoffs. Superintendents were continually subject to the maneuverings of a board that reflected the contestation between and within boroughs and their constituencies. As the 19th century drew to a close, progressive educators had campaigned for a more "professional" school administration that would be immune to the vicissitudes of local politics. A professionally trained superintendent and his assistants who would oversee the day-to-day operation of the schools would administer public education. Boards of education, instead of seating political hacks, would be made up—or so the progressives hoped—of enlightened, "successful businessmen" who in effect would refrain from micromanaging schools. These "administrative progressives," to use historian David Tyack's term, would be free to remake the educational enterprise to benefit the entire community.[38]

By contrast, the evolution of Southern school systems after the Civil War took a decidedly different turn, due to the lack of any publicly supported universal education. Mostly rural and divided by color and class, the governance of public education was ignored in the mainstream until the turn of the century. In 1900, small cities like Charlottesville, with one or two white schools and (maybe) a black primary school, had developed political structures that were negotiated through compromise and personal fiat. With the coming of the New Age, the South was buffeted by dramatic shifts in demographics as former slaves abandoned the old plantation system in favor of cities. Progressive social and political ideologies challenged brittle Old South alliances and exposed shopworn ways.[39]

By the early 1920s, cities like Charlottesville, whose population had absorbed some 4,000 new faces since the 1910 census, were confronted with the contradictory impulses of urbanization. Yes, the community profited greatly by the accumulation of capital and its concomitant technological advances, but at what cost? Throughout the country, the New Age of industrial capitalism and urbanization brought community dismemberment and individual alienation. Small industrial centers, fed by the growth in railroads, expanded rapidly and generated tremendous wealth. Yet an intuitive sense of communal loss plagued the new middle class; something was terribly wrong. Soon civic leaders, business and philanthropic interests, social critics and educators began to ask if schools, as physical centers of neighborhoods, might not serve as the vehicle for communal revitalization.

By the end of the 1920s, Charlottesville was no longer isolated from urban tension. Residents were sensing that something was, indeed, amiss in their little corner of Eden. Repeatedly, the *Charlottesville Daily Progress* editorialized for "modernity." No longer was small-town parochialism good enough for such "a thriving and rapidly growing city." What was needed was a chamber of commerce, a retail merchants association, new buildings, sidewalks, paved streets (with curbs) and traffic lights—in other words, all the trappings of urbanity. Auto traffic needed to be orderly. Shops needed to open—and close—consistently. Merchants needed to advertise because the New Age of capital was preaching that wives needed to be convinced that their lives could be made easier if only they would convince their husbands to purchase something new. The city also needed to be cleaner. Tourists from the metropolitan areas of Washington and New York were coming to the Blue Ridge mountains, and Charlottesville should reap the benefit. In April of 1925 the paper's editor wrote, "Why should we stand back and see ... enterprising people go forward along modern, progressive lines while we stagnate and dawdle our time away?" He concluded, "Money is in a city, not in the country or a small town."[40]

In the public mind, Johnson and the board represented stability in a rapidly changing, unstable world. During the 1920s, the superintendent and his board continued with what they knew best. Johnson ran his schools his way and would continue to do so with a nearly free hand. The lean war years, coupled with the increasing numbers of both white and black students and the perplexing and often confusing changes in educational thinking associated with progressivism, led the board to depend on Johnson. Johnson was seen as a master at making what was impenetrable seem simple, as if it were common sense. The coming of the Great Depression—and Albert Balz—changed it all. By 1932, the world was no longer simple and common sense was no longer enough. To Balz and Hench, the city had outgrown not only its schools but also Johnson's single-minded capabilities.

"HE'S BEEN ASLEEP AT THE SWITCH."

As the Depression wore away Charlottesville's meager resources, the rift between what Johnson could do and what New South advocates like Balz and Hench thought needed to be done became all too apparent. The superintendent was not what historian Tyack would call an administrative progressive. Johnson was the anti-New Age, small town patriarch of Charlottesville's schools, and his actions made it clear that he despised the University of Virginia's inroads. Years before Balz took his seat on the board, Johnson, though himself a University of Virginia graduate, had been at war with the university's education department. The disagreement involved a less than cooperative venture that allowed secondary education students to practice their craft in Charlottesville's old Midway High School. Johnson repeatedly sabotaged the collaboration to such an extent that the university field supervisors resigned in disgust. Johnson either altered, refused or simply ignored whatever the university attempted to implement. The superintendent wanted nothing to do with the university and its new ideas. The battle was a classic "town and gown" struggle.[41]

The cooperative venture, funded mostly by Rockefeller's general education board and the university—little if any money had come from the city—placed University of Virginia (UVA) students and their faculty mentors in the dilapidated Midway school. By the middle of the decade, it was no longer able to accommodate the increasing numbers of students moving into Charlottesville and was ready to fall down. The building was referred to as a firetrap on more than one occasion. The board finally authorized a new high school to be built for white students. Using very little local money (there was none), the board instead relied on federal and state dollars. Balz and the board hoped that the new school would serve as a "physical plant" to make Charlottesville proud. But they also hoped that the new school would address an increasing concern associated with urbanization: how does public education meet the needs of a modern, technological culture? How would Charlottesville, having outgrown the notion of the country common school, create an educational enterprise that reproduced the social and economic strata found in 20th-century capitalism?

Balz and the board saw social stratification as cultural sophistication. Students at the high school came from homes that reflected the growing economic diversity in and around Charlottesville. Some students would go on to the university or other colleges, but Balz realized that not everyone would—or should—attend college. Increasing numbers of children came to the high school from the emerging commercial classes, replacing to an extent the dwindling numbers from the rural communities who were being educated (if they chose to continue their education past the eighth grade) by county schools like Red Hill, located not far from Charlottesville. By far the largest increase in Charlottesville's student body came from children of the working class.

Since its founding before the turn of the century, Midway School, like Pasadena High School, had one curriculum, academic. Students either succeeded or failed in Greek, Latin, algebra, geometry, ancient history and English. The large number—nearly half—that did not succeed disturbed Balz and his colleagues. They either repeatedly failed courses or, worse yet, dropped out at an early age. Progressives all over the country, including Charlottesville's board of education, shuddered at the thought of out-of-school children wandering the streets without much, if any, formal education.

By 1935, there were nearly 900 students at Midway, a school built for far fewer. Yet at June's graduation, only 95 received diplomas and of those only 35 made plans to go on to college. What particularly upset Balz was the city's ranking within the state's 75 white accredited high schools. The school was 15th from the bottom. Balz was determined that the new high school—and for that matter the entire (white) system—should address the problem. This was Charlottesville, home of Mr. Jefferson's university, and the city's schools should reflect that status.[42]

For philosopher Balz and engineer Hench, the answer to the "problem" was science, specifically, the New Science of psychological testing. This "New Science" told them that intelligence, as defined by Lewis Terman, Alfred Binet and others, was the only real objective factor in making educational choices. IQ testing in Charlottesville's schools—along with its rational and practical bedfellow, guidance counseling—told Balz and his board colleagues that the college preparatory curriculum, for years the staple of academic offerings at the school, had abandoned the overwhelming majority of Charlottesville's white children. What was needed was a curriculum that reflected the growing diversification of culture, a differentiated curriculum that would guide children into careers that were meaningful and productive. Not everyone was suited for life at the university. A majority of children would remain in Charlottesville, and the new school needed to adjust, as Balz said, "literally to the conditions of life and work in this community." The new curriculum needed to provide "for each pupil in the degree of his educatabilty ..." In other words, as Balz would clarify later, the students needed "some specialized training in anticipation of vocational and allied activities."[43]

The linchpin of his proposed curriculum was how he and others defined "in anticipation." If the curriculum was differentiated, how would educators determine which children got which curriculum? Apparently, there were no epistemological arguments, no "chicken and egg" philosophical debates. The curriculum came first. Children were then fitted, through intelligence (and other kinds of tests), and then "counseled" or "guided" into certain "tracks." Like schools in Pasadena and elsewhere, Charlottesville's new high school was going to be a model of efficiency and modernity. Balz summed up his intentions when he told the community that the new Lane High School would "house the programs, rather than adjust the programs to the building." The school would, in Balz's mind, reflect the differentiation of Charlottesville. What mattered too was the elimination of waste, and the old ways certainly had been wasteful. The New South, like much of the rest of the country idolized efficiency. The urban schools of this modern age, which were drafted from the ideological blueprint of industrial capitalism, were created to be synonymous with efficiency and modernization.[44]

The formal structure of Balz's new high school proposal would require a complete overhauling of the city's traditional approach to public education. He recommended adding a year, thus creating a seven-year elementary (kindergarten and then grades one through six) and a five-year high school (grades seven through 11) system. Although Pasadena and many Northern and Western communities had established separate junior high schools 20 years before, there was no junior high school building in Charlottesville. The eighth year was, as Balz termed it, a "transition year." The eighth-grade students would be housed in the high school. To Balz, the eighth year was preparation for high school. Most important, that crucial year "would provide," as he argued, a "program of instruction for those pupils not educable beyond the limits of a junior high school."[45]

The tension that existed between Johnson and Balz had not lessened. In fact, it spilled over to the remaining members of the board. During the two-year period devoted to planning the new high school, Johnson stonewalled, ignored or belittled suggestions, proposals and recommendations made by the board's curriculum committee, now chaired by a new member, attorney George Starnes. A frustrated Starnes wrote Balz during the summer of 1940 and complained that Johnson was spending entirely too much time "with the books" and not enough with administering the system. Balz had made similar observations, once claiming that the superintendent was "wed to his books," referring to the compulsion Johnson exhibited in managing the system's ledgers. Starnes, Balz and Hench believed it was no longer an efficient use of time to have the superintendent sit at his desk and check the attendance list, count the number of requests for supplies or balance his "books." When it came to reforming the curriculum, Starnes told Balz, "You know as well as I do what ... Johnson has in mind. He has been asleep at the switch and he hates to admit it. How can we ever make progress under such conditions?" To Johnson, the conflict between the board and its superintendent revolved around how definitions of "progress" determine hierarchy and control.[46]

"THINGS ARE IN UNUSUALLY SATISFACTORY SHAPE"

When Lane High School opened in the fall of 1940, amid brass bands and parades, speakers, led by university president John Newcomb, praised the city for its contributions to a modern age. On that beautiful fall day, the all-white crowd could look a quarter mile away up toward Vinegar Hill, the black business and residential district in Charlottesville, and see Jefferson High School, built on the foundation laid by Anna Gardner during Reconstruction nearly 75 years before. The present red brick building had been erected in the mid-1920s paid for partly by donations collected by the black community. Next to the high school on the same piece of land was the Jefferson Elementary School. Education at Jefferson had little if any resemblance to what occurred down the road at Lane. Charlottesville, like cities all over the South, had all but refused to underwrite the development of black education.[47] Public taxes, even though drawn equally from both white and black, were spent unequally. When Lane opened its doors in 1940, Jefferson High was a plain, unassuming building with a single-track academic curriculum supplemented with only a few manual education courses. Jefferson was only one of a dozen accredited black high schools in the state, and its classrooms were overcrowded and its teachers overworked and underpaid.

Fig. 18. Lane High School, in August 1941, a month before opening its doors to Charlottesville's white students. Albert Balz, the president of the board of education, planned for the school to be a model of progressive efficiency by "housing the programs rather than adjusting the programs to the building." *(Photo courtesy of the Albert and Shirley Small Special Collections Library, University of Virginia)*

For the most part, whites in Charlottesville went about their daily tasks as if the black community was another world. The vast majority of whites would have never found themselves along South 6th Street, in a neighborhood known as Scottsville Road, unless they were landlords collecting rent. Scottsville Road, at the bottom of the "Hill," was in a gulch, its houses without indoor plumbing and lit only by kerosene lamps. Its occupants lived off the use of a single outside water hydrant. Not far from Scottsville Road, down in the hollow away from Main Street and Vinegar Hill, was the Gas House District, where a small rivulet carried away waste and other refuse. Houses were shacks, and many were without glass for windows, heat or plumbing. Then there was Happy Hollow, with a reputation only a little less "unsavory" than Scottsville Road. Happy Hollow, according to the white UVA observer who recorded the "unsavory" comment, received its name from the "care-free attitude" of those that use to live there. Happiness aside, crime and violence were common. So were children, many of whom dropped out of school. These dropouts spent time on the streets, scorned by whites that saw them as shiftless, "up to no good" and, in the words of the UVA observer, "degenerate."[48] Other black neighborhoods were less grief stricken than Scottsville Road and Happy Hollow. That same UVA observer described some as areas of "high respectability and high morality."[49] Charlottesville's African-American community was not a single, uniform black mass but a community marked by divisions in social class. All of Charlottesville's African Americans had one thing in common, though—their children passed through Jefferson Elementary School. Education was common ground for the black community, and it was here that much of the tension between whites and blacks was to be played out.

As far as the board and Johnson were concerned—at least publicly— Jefferson, during the Depression, was "in unusually satisfactory shape."[50] Beneath that public transcript, however, the black community was seething, continually pushing and prodding the board to improve the quality of education at both the high school and the elementary school. During the 1930s, a group of school patrons, referred to as the "Charlottesville 400," the city's black elite, brought petition after petition to the board. The petitioners at first pleaded, and then politely requested that improvements be made. Later in the decade, they made outright (but nevertheless "polite") demands that white leadership address the inequalities at the schools. While the white schools continued to expand, the two black schools were directed by principals who were required by overcrowded conditions to teach classes. By the early 1940s, there were four white elementary schools and the new high school, each administered by (nonteaching) personnel. In 1933, Miss Maude Gamble, teaching administrator at the primary school, buckled under the pressure of doing two jobs in the most trying of environments. She resigned and returned to the classroom. The board appointed Cora Duke as teaching principal, giving her the same meager administrative stipend of $100 that it had given Gamble.[51]

In black communities throughout Virginia, the reoccurring theme of inequality, overwork and too little money provoked educators to take seriously what Richmond's State Department of Education was proposing during the Depression decade. Although Sidney Hall, Hollis Caswell and Frederick Alexander never intended the Virginia Curriculum Revision Project for the black community, progressive black educators seized upon the project's reconstructive ideals in an effort to carve out increased ideological elbowroom for themselves and the community. There is no evidence that the "Charlottesville 400" ever endorsed any politically left, radical measures to address inequality.[52] But Charlottesville's Jefferson High School did have its "vanguard of social reconstructionists" working "for a new kind of society."

BLACK RECONSTRUCTION

Hall's revision project, regardless of its language of reform, never intended to democratically reconstruct the inequities in Southern society. When D.W. Peters, director of instruction at the state department of public instruction, asked President John Gandy of Virginia State College to recommend a committee to oversee the design of school-based materials, it was evident that white leadership envisioned something very different for black children. The college was to serve "as a center for all work in the state which involves any special adaptations that may be proposed for Negro Children."[53] Gandy and his faculty were furious. "Special adaptations" could mean only one thing—a curriculum designed to further segregate, by substantiating, through school practice, the fallacy that intelligence was color-bound. For the previous 15 years, black educators and social scientists had argued long and well that educational performance could not be predicted by intelligence testing.[54] Gandy's faculty saw "special adaptations" as further proof that their arguments had fallen on deaf white ears.

John Gandy, who had been the patriarch of black education in Virginia for 30 years, asked Edna Colson, a young professor of elementary education at the college, to recommend an advisory committee to answer the state department of public instruction.[55] Colson, working on her doctorate at Teachers College, Columbia, under George Counts and Mabel Carney (two of the more radical social reconstructionists), assembled the brightest and most progressive educators in Virginia. Among her selections was a young colleague, Doxey Wilkerson, director of the high school program at the college since 1927. It was immediately evident that Wilkerson was a brilliant and politically passionate young man, who understood the nexus between race and social class. His early writing was often about choice and the power that comes from community organizing.[56] Later in the decade, he would leave Virginia for Howard University. He served on President Franklin D. Roosevelt's Advisory Committee on Education and, then, in the early 1940s, as vice president of the American Federation of Teachers. Wilkerson joined the Communist party after the war, edited the Harlem weekly *The People's Voice*, and taught at the Communist party–sponsored Jefferson School for Social Science in New York and at Yeshiva University. Throughout his career, whites attacked him for his turn to communism, but black Virginians never lost their admiration for Wilkerson and his lifetime of work to equalize educational opportunity.[57]

Colson and Wilkerson were to become the catalyst for much of the reconstructive material to come out of Virginia during the Depression. Wilkerson believed one of the greatest impediments to black education was a system of social relations that created dissolution, despair and futility. He often used the parable of a dog that, bound for years by a fenced yard, was unable to see the open gate.[58] It was through schools that Wilkerson and other black progressives saw the open gate. Young children should be taught that they had the power to reconstruct the world. They should know that their world is not limited. Through struggle and planning, Wilkerson believed that children could make this "new kind of society," that Alexander had alluded to.

It was evident from the outset that Wilkerson, Colson and the advisory committee intended to use the progressive rhetoric of the Virginia Curriculum

Revision Project for purposes different than those Richmond had intended. In Colson's words, the committee "launched itself into a course of study" that, within a year, would result in a brilliant rebuttal to the state department's request for "special adaptations."[59] Leadership in Richmond, symptomatic of a separate and unequal social system, paid little attention to what black educators wanted or needed to accomplish their task. Throughout the revision process, Colson complained frequently and at times bitingly that Peters and his staff were slow, vague, noncommittal, and, above all else, unresponsive to "the needs of the Negro."[60] Frustrating as this was, the Virginia State College group was left to its own devices, and they responded accordingly.

Some nine months after the initial call for revised materials, Peters requested his first meeting at Virginia State College to "discuss the things Negro teachers can do in the State Curriculum Project." Gandy, the committee, teachers and principals all met to hear Peters, who showed up late for the meeting. He could only make a brief comment or two about the need for "understanding ... the nature and function of the curriculum by the average classroom teacher ..." and "... the proper organization of materials considered especially important in the education of the Negro."[61] In a June 1933 letter, Wilkerson cautioned curriculum makers throughout the state to follow the procedures prescribed by the state department. He knew the state department would respond to an attack on Jim Crow. It was no use having their efforts thrown out by a technicality.[62] In mid-August, after Peters paid a second visit to the college, the committee sent its work to Richmond. In December, the committee published its recommendations in the college magazine, the *Gazette*.

The advisory committee rejected any notion that curricular adaptations were necessary because of "inherent racial differences in intellectual ability or special aptitudes." Then Wilkerson and the advisory committee departed significantly from prior arguments:

> Curricular adaptations because of race can justifiably be proposed, then, only in the light of social problems which result from racial factors. If there be such problems, it seems to follow that they represent social needs which make demands upon education, needs to which special curricular adaptations should be made.[63]

Any social problems came as a result of the nature of a biracial state not as a result of some misguided idea that intelligence was color-bound. Accordingly, "the approach of education in meeting these needs, therefore, must also be biracial." And if social problems that result from segregation were to be solved by education, then the committee reasoned, schools of both races should be involved in the solution.

Wilkerson and the others had effectively turned the revision program on its head. Along with the "Basic Philosophy" that rejected differences in racial intelligence, the committee laid out 15 social problems that called for "special adaptation in the curriculum of all children," including political problems, racial stereotypes, problems of health, economics, crime and delinquency. The committee sent Richmond a set of "guiding aims," calling for a common course of study, inclusion of reconstructive materials in teacher education, model units and a comprehensive bibliography. It also included a program of study for the secondary schools on black education that was remarkably similar to what today might be called an Afro-centric curriculum.[64] Above all else, Colson stressed that "the materials lose their significance when the philosophy of education which justifies their use is not understood."[65]

The advisory committee understood the significance of what it had done. After Colson gave Peters the committee's statement and the materials, she told Gandy it was "a momentous occasion."[66] She was optimistic that Richmond would incorporate the committee's views when the *Tentative Course of Study for Elementary Schools* was published in September of 1933, no doubt because Peters had assured her that the state department would include the committee's materials. The state department had no such intentions. The course of study carried the following comment about black education, which Colson termed unfortunate: "The Committee for Negro schools suggests units of work in connection with the aspects of the several centers of interest that will be especially valuable in Negro schools." The state then listed the themes that the committee intended for all children, as if they were to be used exclusively by black schools.[67]

For the next three years, black educators, especially Colson and her colleagues at Virginia State, worked to have their viewpoint included in official state department bulletins. Despite Peters' assurances that what they produced would be published, the state department continually altered or omitted the committee's position on how best to achieve the New South in Virginia.[68]

What Wilkerson, Colson and the advisory committee had written was more than an answer to Richmond. It was a call for black social reconstruction through education. The advisory committee and the scores of black teachers who participated in the revision program used the language of progressive reform to attempt to remake their communities. Black history and culture, African colonization and slavery were all more than just topics proposed by higher education faculty members for use in black schools. Many were incorporated in teacher-designed units for use in classrooms throughout the state, intended to be used by both white and black students. Yet, the reconstructive materials never made it into white schools. Colson and her colleagues at Virginia State, the Hampton Institute and Virginia Union were in public schools on a regular basis working with teachers interested in designing and implementing progressive and reconstructive curricula. From the middle of the decade on, faculty members and students participated in a series of community surveys, gathering data on demographics, health, housing, and economics and voting patterns. The surveys were apparently utilized by Luther Jackson, a professor of history at Virginia State when he formed the Virginia Negro Voters League in the early 1940s.[69]

One of Colson's graduate students was Carrie Michie, a history teacher at Jefferson High School in Charlottesville. Michie was a longtime resident of the city and, under Colson's direction, she began a comprehensive survey of "withdrawals" (today's dropouts) at Jefferson High. Michie's study is the only indepth analysis of Depression-era black schooling in Charlottesville and, like Christine Lofstedt's thesis on Mexican Pasadena, is revealing in what it tells us about the state of the community.[70]

Michie began her thesis with a resounding call for social reconstruction through education. "The ideal[s] ... of democracy cannot be realized unless all of the children are provided with public school training and cultural resources in keeping with their capacities." What separates Michie's social reconstruction from other tamer approaches to progressive education is that the data she and Colson collected had an activist purpose. Colson, her colleagues and students like Michie used their data to "... examine present practices in an attempt to determine those elements which are most likely to affect the happiness, efficiency, and capacity for social service." Michie's study was intended to alter her community. [71]

Like many, if not most, high schools in the country, Jefferson had the contradictory problem of too many students and too many dropouts. Unlike the dropouts in many white high schools during the Depression, Michie's data indicated that the staggering number of withdrawals from Jefferson signaled more than a declining economy. Michie interviewed 60 of the nearly 300 dropouts who had left school since 1926. The data illustrated what black Charlottesvillians already knew about the community. The parents of these students that had jobs worked in low-paying positions as cooks, janitors, butchers, laundresses, maids and orderlies at the university hospital. Of the 60 dropouts she interviewed, 70 percent were "over aged," meaning they had failed at least one year and more likely three or four years of school. Fifteen year olds were still in elementary school. Twelve year olds were still in the primary grades. These students (and the schools) simply ran out of options and quit.

Michie discovered that many of the dropouts were rural children, who had come to live in Charlottesville because their parents realized backwoods schools were not on the same level as more urban schools. Only in Charlottesville, would Albemarle's rural blacks have any chance at an education. At great personal expense, families sent their children off to relatives in the city to attend school, but the impact of years of poor, rural education left its mark. The country kids were behind when they arrived, and without resources, they remained behind. In this segregated community, there were no resources for black education beyond the simplest, barest necessities. Charlottesville's black primary and secondary school was ill equipped to deal with the hometown students let alone poor émi-grés from the countryside.

Michie did not leave it at that. She was biting in her condemnation. Charlottesville's schools were "undemocratic in that [they] caused pupils of small means to feel unable to cope with classmates." Her study pointed out the great disparity between city children from stable families and children from backwoods impoverished families. She called for the school system "to adjust its programs to better meet the needs of the community," and offer additional courses, better guidance and vocational education programs. Michie, perhaps because of Edna Colson and Doxie Wilkerson's influence, understood that the negatives of segre-gation were greatly magnified by social-class differences within the black com-munity. Like her mentors, Colson and Wilkerson, she called for an end to segre-gation by color and caste:

> Any acceptance of a caste system is so far removed from the aims of democracy that it is distasteful to true Americans; but if those eliminated from our schools are destined to the less desirable positions, it may tend to affect the family for several generations, and result in deprivations and non-participation in the material comforts and cultural resources of society. 72

If the white school board knew of Michie's recommendations, they ignored them. But they would not be able to ignore Carrie Michie for long.

By the end of the decade, the state department had become aware that the reform process instituted by Hall and guided by Alexander's aims was contribut-ing to a reconstructed definition of black civil rights. Teacher study groups had formed to examine and evaluate the status of black education within the context of an overall, statewide assessment of the revision process. There were more than 200 black study groups in 42 counties. Study conferences were planned at three regional centers, including Virginia State College. The groups discussed, among a wide-ranging set of problems and issues, "civic participation," an idea antithet-ical within a segregated society. The discussion groups were apparently so offen-sive to certain local (white) officials that the state department ordered the con-ferences and study groups cancelled.

Even so, one observer noted that the groups and conferences had "... made the Negro more conscious and dissatisfied with his educational plight," some-thing not intended by the original revision process nor the late decade evalua-tion.73 Virginia's African-American community continued to push, pressure, chide and confront Jim Crow over issues that were vital to the quality of life in the black community. The advisory committee, through its work and the work of countless black teachers, did more to turn progressive theory into practice than did progressive, white educators anywhere in the South. The number, scope and especially the reconstructive content of articles published in the *Bulletin* far exceeded what appeared in *The Virginia Journal of Education,* the white teachers' association magazine. Moreover, the work of the advisory committee marked the beginning of a new era in black political power in Virginia.

SIDNEY HALL AND BLACK POWER

Sidney Hall appears to have had little direct contact with the revision process other than by educating audiences about the general virtues of curriculum reform as he traveled the state. What consumed Hall far more throughout the decade was keeping schools open full term and diluting the effects of the Depression on budgets, especially his own. This meant feuding with Harry Byrd as Hall tried to prod an unmoving assembly to fund his "Three Point Plan," an average minimum salary, improved retirement and free school textbooks.[74] Extremely active in the national arena, Hall was an editor of the *New Frontier,* the radical journal inspired by Teachers College that did much to promote the ideals of social reconstruction. He also served as chairman of the National Education Association (NEA) legislative committee. By the end of the 1930s, the superintendent was one of the most politically powerful educators in the country. Perhaps realizing the futility of pushing for increased funding from the Virginia Assembly, as well as sensing the changing mood of the Congress during Roosevelt's second administration, Hall threw his energies into securing federal aid for schools.

By the winter of 1936–37, there appeared to be enough support on Capitol Hill to pass legislation granting large sums of money—$300 million within a few years—to assist them in equalizing "educational opportunity" to the states. This was not intended to equalize white and black schools, instead, "equalizing educational opportunity" was NEA-sponsored legislation (known as the Harrison-Black-Fletcher bill) to bring poor and wealthy states into some balance with each other. The NEA lined up support for the campaign, including what it thought was tacit approval from the White House.[75]

In the spring of 1937 as the hearings were being held, a new coalition led by the American Federation of Teachers (AFT), NEA's rival union, together with the NAACP, was demanding significant changes in the bill. This was in addition to the expected conservative political and religious antipathy to federal aid to schools. As drafted, the bill made no provisions to guarantee that federal money would not be used disproportionately by Southerners to perpetuate the inequality between white and black schooling. The AFT/NAACP opposition to the un-amended Harrison-Black-Fletcher bill was problematic. Both organizations knew Southerners would never support federal aid with strings attached, especially if those strings dictated to states where federal dollars were to be spent. Yet the NAACP and AFT were not opposed to federal aid. On the contrary, both organizations recognized the need. So the AFT sponsored a rival bill that not only included safeguards sought by the NAACP but allocated more money. The sponsors of the Harrison-Black-Fletcher bill realized it would succeed only if it received support from the AFT and NAACP as well as other black and labor organizations.[76] The art of political compromise seemed necessary. Instead, Sidney Hall chose to gamble.

As chair of the NEA's legislative committee, Hall had worked closely with Willard Givens, NEA's executive secretary, and John Studebaker, F.D.R.'s Commissioner of Education. He had met personally with the president, stretching a five-minute interview into 15. He was optimistic that there was a growing resolve on both sides of the aisle for federal aid. He knew the fragile nature of coalition building and knew better still how quickly this opportunity might evaporate. F.D.R. was not about to support any legislation that might damage his Southern alliance, and any bill requiring that federal funds be color blind might alienate Southerners from future New Deal legislation.[77] The president's inherent distrust of "school people," as he called public educators, further clouded the issue and made the timing of the bill crucial.[78]

Indicative of his political power and ambition (but also because of NEA concern that its efforts might go awry), Hall chaired the week-long congressional hearings, calling before the Committee on Education a series of speakers to buttress not only the NEA position but to blunt AFT/NAACP opposition.[79] The NEA and Hall could not control the testimony of black leadership, such as Charles Thompson of Howard University or Charles Houston of the NAACP, but Hall could show the committee that not all black educators were against the bill as it was written. Hall placed two black Virginians on the calendar. One was T.C. Walker, a conservative Richmond attorney, who for years had influenced the Negro Organization Society, a community-based school support group that later merged with the state's PTA. Walker countenanced no controversy nor opposition to the white-controlled school system in Virginia. "Discriminations," said Walker, "have always existed, but there is no need of advertising them; we think the best way of getting rid of them is by taking no notice of them." He told the committee "... this bill, it appears to me, is a God-send to the school system of Virginia and to the school systems of the whole country so far as the Negro people are concerned." Walker concluded by assuring Hall and the committee that "there are some things we have to be mighty careful about in this matter; we do not want to excite in any of your activities anything that would bring about race friction."[80]

Following Walker came Archie Richardson, the first African American to be appointed to Virginia's State Department of Public Instruction. Richardson's praise for the Harrison bill was gushing; he repeatedly called for passage of the bill without amendments:

We should like very much to see this bill passed. We feel that to earmark the bill in its present stage of development may defeat the purpose of the bill ... we feel that [to do so] is challenging the honesty and integrity of the white people in Virginia.[81]

Richardson's accomodationist testimony led him to argue that in Virginia "if you want honey, you do not kick over the beehive." He went on to tell Hugo Black, Senator from Alabama,

I believe that the future success of the Negro lies in his intelligent cooperation with the most intelligent leaders of the white group, and that by resorting to any drastic action, we are simply raising red flags that give the other group an opportunity to strike back and possibly wound more seriously.[82]

To the committee, Richardson's Virginia was one of compromise, cooperation, fairness and opportunity. Because of his tenuous position as Assistant Director of Negro Education, to keep his job, Richardson would have been hard pressed to advocate anything other than the Hall party line. No doubt his comment about "intelligent cooperation with the most intelligent leaders of the white group," was in reference to his boss, who was sitting directly in front of him. Richardson also did not have to tell Senator Black from Alabama about the inequalities in Richmond. The segregated state department building was so illequipped to deal with a black male, Richardson had to relieve himself in the basement, bring his own lunch to eat alone in his office or leave the building to lunch at a local black diner. A few years later when Hall appointed his second black administrator, Sam Madden, WPA Director of Vocational Education for Negroes, the state department denied him an office in Richmond and sent him packing to Hampton.[83] As far as the aid legislation was concerned, the four-year NEA-sponsored campaign went for naught. F.D.R. refused to support funding if it would jeopardize his Southern alliance, which apparently it did as a result of the AFT/NAACP effort to amend the Harrison bill.

The bill was dead—for the meantime—but out of the campaign, the NAACP and AFT had significantly enhanced its ability to serve as power brokers within national politics.[84] In Virginia, black educators were able to broker a new political reality for themselves because they publicly confronted Hall and his choice of witnesses.

Hall's political gamesmanship on the Hill had backfired. When it was reported that Richardson, and to a lesser extent Walker, had spoken for the entire black community—their repeated use of "we" was perhaps intentional—the outcry from the black press, not only in Virginia but nationally, embarrassed and angered Hall.[85] It is highly unlikely the superintendent was so naive that he failed to understand that Walker and Richardson were speaking for themselves rather than the majority of black educators. Hall's anger and embarrassment more likely came because the black community contradicted his position. Hall's efforts to represent Virginia, and by implication the entire South, as a united, cooperative, biracial front had collapsed. Opposition to the bill within the black community was solid, and the NEA and Hall were forced to back down at substantial political cost. Not only had Hall's witnesses become suspect but, closer to home, representatives from the black Virginia State Teachers Association (VSTA) publicly refused to back the Harrison bill.

Hall was furious, but according to William Cooper of the VSTA legislative committee, the superintendent was "now interested in the Association in a new way."[86] Once back in Richmond, Hall ordered Frederick Alexander, now Director of Negro Education, to set up a meeting between himself and the VSTA. Alexander told the association's leadership, which was made up of many of the same individuals who had served with Wilkerson and Colson on the revision project, that Hall wanted to "get together with our group."[87] Cooper, from the Hampton Institute, was selected to meet with the superintendent. According to Cooper's notes, an aloof Sidney Hall reaffirmed, "without any personal feeling," that his position on the Harrison bill should have been accepted. No doubt sensing his changing political fortunes and too smart to let this opportunity pass, Hall asked the leadership of the black teachers' association to form a committee to "act with the Virginia Education Association." He also asked the VSTA to select "someone to whom he [Hall] might turn to find out the attitude of the Negro teachers in such matters."[88] Candidly, Cooper told Hall that "they too had been embarrassed." From this newly won position of strength, he went on to tell Hall that if they had only been consulted from the beginning, they would not have had "to go against him."[89] Cooper does not tell us how the meeting ended, only that the Superintendent sent him down the corridor to the Virginia Education Association office, where he was given ballots to send "thru-out the state," probably to secure black opinion on federal aid. For the first time, black teachers in Virginia had secured a toehold in white school politics. Cooper referred to the meeting as a first "cooperative effort" between white teachers and the black educational community. That community's newly won political power would quickly lead to tangible gains; Hall and the Virginia Education Association would drop from the Three Point Plan the term "average" when referring to a minimum salary. By 1939, the Three Point Plan referred simply to a "minimum salary of $720."[90]

Cooper's notes were made while he was in executive session at the November 1937 Richmond meeting of the VSTA. In that same meeting was Thurgood Marshall from the national office of the NAACP. Marshall told the committee, and then later the entire Virginia State Teachers Association, that he and the association appreciated VSTA's stand on the Harrison-Black-Fletcher bill. Marshall told them that the "[House] Committee learned exactly the position of the

Southern Negro on this bill."[91] Marshall was there not only to applaud the association for its stand on federal aid but also to report on the court battle in Maryland over salary equalization. By the early 1940s, the association's efforts to equalize salaries between white and black educators would succeed as the U.S. Supreme Court decided that the Norfolk board of education could not pay equally qualified black teachers less than whites.[92]

SALARY EQUALIZATION: "THE UNSOUND AND VICIOUS ECONOMIC POLICY..."

Both black and white Virginians had been watching for the announcement. When it came, it shocked both communities, though for different reasons. The U.S. Supreme Court refused to hear the Norfolk salary case, agreeing with the lower court that white teachers could not be paid a higher salary than equally qualified black teachers. The black educational community was elated by the court's decision. The salary struggle had been long and painful. The first litigant, Arlene Black, lost her job bucking Jim Crow. Six more teachers in Richmond, active in the salary case, would lose their jobs even though the suit had already been settled. Black teachers were on average paid less than half what white teachers were paid, and there were numerous instances in which the discrepancy was much higher. When the board appointed Cora Duke as teaching principal, she was paid $900. That was less than half what an equally qualified white classroom teacher without any administrative responsibilities would have made at Lane High School.[93]

Although Balz had warned his colleagues well before the court decision that they should be prepared for the worse, he and the board were stunned by the announcement.[94] At first, they refused to admit that they had a separate schedule for black teachers. Balz wrote a memo in February 1941, just after Lane had opened, saying that it might be appropriate for other cities to state that they no longer had separate schedules, but as far as he was concerned:

> It does not seem advisable for our own system. I have therefore omitted ... any reference to race, color, or sex. We have taken the position that such differences have not defined our salary policy in the past, and I do not see why we should say that we shall follow such a policy in the future.[95]

What Balz wanted was a minimum/maximum salary schedule with the board free to operate within the publicly stated parameters. By confining the schedule to a minimum, the city was free to establish what he called "flexibility." To justify his proposal, he gave as an example what he surely knew to be a cultural absurdity:

> An elementary teacher, because of exceptional value, might receive the highest salary [paid any teacher]. And indeed, so far as the system's definitions go, such a teacher might

be a negress. The point is that, however improbable the case might be, nothing in our system would prevent its occurrence.[96]

Nothing except past practice. The criteria Balz set for salaries would, in addition to information concerning length of service and training, contain an escape clause that Hench later complained was "vague." Balz concluded his list of five salary criteria with "the concrete needs of the system ... and the practical conditions under which the system must operate." His vague "practical conditions under which the system must operate" was all too clear to the African-American community. Historically in a school system divided by color, "practical conditions" meant a biracial system where blacks would receive far less than whites.

Balz's initial five-step salary proposal collapsed under the weight of its own illegality and inefficiency. Another board member, Homan Walsh, had admitted privately that they had been discriminating on the basis of color, and it was time to redress the grievance. Still, Balz and the board refused to admit that there was any necessity for salary equalization, even as they designed a public schedule that began to balance salaries. Instead of referring to the new schedule as "salary equalization," which might imply some prior wrongdoing, on a draft of the schedule Hench crossed out the word "equalization" and wrote "adjustment."[97]

Fig. 19. The Charlottesville Board of Education, on the steps of the George Rogers Clark Elementary School. *Back row from left to right:* George T. Starnes, W.H. Snyder, B. Lee Hawkins, W.T. Dettor, A.L. Hench and Edwin L. Turner. *Front row from left to right:* John F. Harlan, H.W. Walsh, Harry H. Robinson, James G. Johnson, A.G.A. Balz, Randolph H. Perry and Hope W. Gleason. *(Photo courtesy of the Albemarle County Historical Society)*

On the eve of the war, Charlottesville, in Balz's estimation, was providing a "well rounded, modern education" for their children. Gone was the single-track old high school, replaced by a thoroughly modern school that was a tribute to the rise of the New South. Gone too were thoughts that the city could continue to function with a dual salary schedule for its black and white teachers. What remained, much to the chagrin of Balz, Hench and George Starnes, was that venerable old Charlottesville patriarch, Superintendent James Johnson. He turned out to be more than the progressives bargained for and remained until 1945 when, on his terms, he retired amid accolades, ironically provided by the very board he warred with for years.

THE END OF PROGRESSIVISM AND SIDNEY HALL

Salary litigation would be the final chapter in Sidney Hall's professional career in Virginia. His recurring run-ins with Byrd's Democratic Organization over issues of money and power repeatedly placed him outside the machine. Apparently his ongoing feud with Byrd also placed him outside the organization's protective cover. Amid rumors of a possible scandal involving an extramarital affair, he resigned during the summer of 1941 to become director of continuing education at George Washington University in Washington, D.C. When he announced his resignation, which had been leaked to the press while he was in Florida, he told the educational community that his work in Virginia was done, and he wanted to return to a more tranquil life in higher education. The Richmond press, though, smelled a story and reported that the capitol was "uncharacteristically closemouthed."[98] When *The Richmond Times-Dispatch* asked the governor to comment, James Price refused. Yet when Hall returned to the capitol, he contradicted Price and told reporters he had "acted with the Governor." The superintendent's "retirement," as he referred to his departure, remained shrouded even as Hall was packing his bags. Days later, Price still refused to comment. This lack of closure by the Governor, either words of praise or damnation for a state leader with a national reputation, only tended to mystify an already confusing affair. The last words *The Richmond News Leader* wrote about Hall came a few days later when the paper concluded, "He has already transferred his interests in property on Seminary Road to his wife, Mrs. Stella R. Hall. The deed of bargain and sale was filed in Henrico County on August 8."[99]

It remains unclear why one of the most respected educational leaders in the country would voluntarily leave his seat of power at the height of his influence to assume an obscure position in continuing education. Hall may have tried to strike some kind of deal with Byrd's liberal Democratic party opponents in Price's administration. Or he may have become expendable to Price just because he would not cooperate with Virginia's new democratic liberalism. There is the pos-

sibility that gossip about his private affairs was his undoing. He may have alienated the organization to such a degree, it refused to protect him. The fact
remains, however, that no matter where Hall stood in relation to Price and his
group, good friends of the organization do not suddenly walk away, left professionally penniless. Almost from the day of his resignation, Hall became *persona
non grata*. Educators around the country knew his name, but he no longer was a
force in national educational debate. His work at NEA dried up during the war
years, probably due to the nature of his position at George Washington. He no
longer had any political base. It was as if he had been banished from the
kingdom.

Hall's departure did not hamper the movement within the black community
to remake Virginia. By the end of the 1940s, it was clear that the attack on Jim
Crow was quickening. The all-white graduate and professional schools had been
forced to accommodate black students. The University of Virginia was now
accepting both black graduate students and women as undergraduates, and
salaries between white and black teachers were quickly being equalized. The
pedagogical promise long associated with progressive education—child-centered
instruction, less reliance on textbooks and more on exploration and discovery—
may have been less important to progressive, black educators than teaching young
children the history and culture of the African and African American. It was that
legacy—self-knowledge and the power of education—that is the essence of social
reconstruction in any community, white or black. The efforts by black educators
like Edna Colson, Doxey Wilkerson, John Gandy and Carrie Michie to reconstruct black Virginia helped create a foundation that served to buttress what we
have come to call the civil rights movement.

Carrie Michie and her colleagues at Jefferson High School would bring their
grievances to the white school board during and after the war but to little avail.
Then, in May of 1954, came the U.S. Supreme Court's *Brown vs. Board of
Education* decision. The world Charlottesville and Pasadena had come to know
would be forever changed.

NOTES

1. Under the guidance of no one and drawing funds from F.D.R.'s Farm Security Adminis-
    tration, photographers such as Lange, Marion Post Wolcott, Ben Shahn, Russell Lee and
    Jack Delano drove the highways and backroads of the country documenting the ravages of
    the Depression. Lange hoped her work would alleviate some of the suffering. Apparently
    it did, as she and the sociologist Paul Taylor's documentation of migrant workers led to
    government-sponsored camps. See David P. Peeler, *Hope Among Us Yet: Social Criticism and
    Social Science* (Athens, Georgia: University of Georgia Press, 1988), p. 57–48; *Dorothea*

Lange, with introductory essay by George Elliott (New York: Museum of Modern Art), distributed by Doubleday, 1966.

2. See *The Great Migration in Historical Perspective: New Dimensions of Race, Class, and Gender,* ed. J. W. Trotter, Jr. (Bloomington: Indiana University Press, 1991), especially his "Introductory Essay," p. 1–21; and Earl Lewis, "Expectations, Economic Opportunities, and Life in the Industrial Age: Black Migration to Norfolk, Virginia, 1910–1945," p. 22–45; see also Nicholas Lemann, *The Promised Land: The Great Black Migration and How it Changed America* (New York: Alfred Knopf, 1991).

3. From 1910–1920, in Albemarle County, in which Charlottesville was the only incorporated city, the overall county population (white and black) declined by 3,866. Yet the city of Charlottesville grew by nearly the same number due in part to annexation as well as rural out-migration. Nearly 2,100 African Americans left the county during the same period and increased the city population by 423. See Marjorie Felice Irwin, *The Negro in Charlottesville and Albemarle County: an Exploratory Study* (M.A. Thesis, University of Virginia, 1929), published by the Phelps-Stokes Fellowship Papers 9 (1929), p. 24–25.

4. James Anderson. *The Education of Blacks in the South, 1860–1935* (Chapel Hill: University of North Carolina Press, 1988). Regarding black administrators and teachers in Virginia, see J. Rupert Picott, *The History of the Virginia Teachers Association* (Washington, DC: National Education Association, 1975), p. 72. For a discussion on white teachers in black schools in the late nineteenth century, see *Bulletin of the Virginia State Teachers Association* 10:3 (May 1933), p. 4, on the Richmond board of education finally giving in to VSTA pressure to allow blacks to secure administrative positions in the city's black schools, a practice long-urged by VSTA and apparently practiced throughout most of the state. The statement on school administrators being black men needs no additional commentary. Typically women did not administer schools in Virginia.

5. Carter Woodson, *The Mis-Education of the Negro* (Washington, DC: Associated Publishers, 1933).

6. See David Tyack, Robert Lowe and Elisabeth Hansot, *Public Schools in Hard Times* (Cambridge, Mass.: Harvard University Press, 1984), p. 32, for comments on school closings around the country. See William Leap, "Red Hill" (Master's Thesis, University of Virginia, 1929) and Tyack, Lowe and Hansot p. 188, 201–203, for discussion of consolidation.

7. *The Richmond News Leader,* 25 May 1933, p. 13.

8. C.A. Bowers, *The Progressive Educator and the Depression* (New York: Random House, 1969).

9. George S. Counts, "Dare Progressive Education Be Progressive?" *Progressive Education* 9 (April 1932), p. 258.

10. William H. Kilpatrick, *The Educational Frontier* (New York: Appleton-Century-Crafts, 1933), p. 71.

11. George Tindal, *The Emergence of the New South, 1913–1945* (Baton Rouge: Louisiana State University Press, 1967), p. 385.

12. Ibid., p. 385.

13. Ibid., p. 385–386, cited in Hilton Butler, "Bilbo-The Two-Edged Sword," *North American Review* CCXXXII (1931), p. 496.

14. Tindall, p. 365–367.

15. William Link, *The Paradox of Southern Progressivism, 1880–1930* (Chapel Hill: University of North Carolina Press, 1992).

16. Ronald Goodenow, "Paradox in Progressive Educational Reform: The South and the Education of Blacks in The Depression Years," *Phylon* (March 1978), p. 49–65.

17. Hall's appointment was announced just before the new year, 1931. See the *Charlottesville Daily Progress,* 30 December 1930, and the *Virginia Journal of Education,* 16 January 1931. There were progressive ideas being discussed during the late twenties by William Smithey's UVA-based secondary school administrators organization, but it was not until Hall, a long-time friend of Smithey, came to the superintendency that any real effort was made to reorganize practice around the state. For information on the secondary education movement in Virginia, see *The Virginia Teacher,* conference proceedings of the High School Conference held annually at UVA beginning in 1921.

18. For comments regarding Hall's appointment, see Herbert Kliebard, *The Struggle for the American Curriculum, 1893–1958* (New York: Routledge and Kegan Paul, 1987), p. 223–227; Barry Franklin, *Building the American Community: The School Curriculum and the Search for Social Control* (London: Falmer Press, 1986), p. 127–131; Mary Louise Sequel, *The Curriculum Field: Its Formative Years* (New York: Teachers College Press, 1966), p. 173; Michael James, "Schools and Cultural Change-Retrospect and Prospect: The Virginia Curriculum Revision Project, 1931–1941," *The National Social Science Journal* 1:5 (Spring 1990), p. 13–24; Lynn Burlbaw, "Hollis Caswell: An Intellectual Biography" (Ph.D. diss., University of Texas, 1989).

19. *The Charlottesville Daily Progress,* expressing a sentiment that typified newspaper sentiment around the state, commented "The appointment of Dr. Hall to become the state's educational leader came as a distinct surprise to educational circles as well as the general public." 30 January 1930, p. 1.

20. See the correspondence between Byrd, Hall and E.R. Combs, one of Hall's closest advisors, in the Harry Flood Byrd Papers, Alderman Library, University of Virginia, 1911–1965 (Acc 9700), Box 116, Box 140, Folders: "Sidney B. Hall," 1930–1933, 1933–1936, and Box 93; Folder: "E.R. Combs," 1930. Hall was clearly one of the organization's staunchest supporters, but he was adamant that Byrd support the schools during the crisis. More than once he let Byrd know that the teachers were solidly behind the organization, but if the Minimum Education Program, which was Hall's plan for revitalizing public education, was not passed, then he was in no position to guarantee anything. He pleaded with Byrd to support the schools, and if he would, "your name would not only be remembered for your great achievements as Governor, but that you would more than ever be remembered as the individual who helped save the schools ... for the State in the most serious crisis which we have ever experienced." Hall to Byrd, 9 January 1933.

21. In a letter William Smithey wrote to Hall while Hall was teaching at Peabody, he encouraged Hall to try for the presidency at Fredericksburg. Hall later told Smithey he did not feel the time was right "to enter the scramble for Fredericksburg." Not long after Hall took over as state superintendent, *The Richmond News Leader* reported that he was in line for the position of superintendent of Richmond's schools. Later in the decade, his name was repeatedly mentioned as a candidate for president of William and Mary, Peabody and once, UVA. See Hall to Smithey in the William Royall Smithey Papers, Alderman Library, University of Virginia, [acc RG-21/54.801;861], folder: "Correspondence: 1928–1929"; see *The Richmond News Leader,* 20 and 24 May 1933, for commentary on the city superintendency. For speculation on Hall leaving for a college presidency, see *The Richmond News Leader,* 21 August 1935, and the *Richmond Times-Dispatch,* 17 July 1936. Regarding Hall leaving for William and Mary, historian Richard Sherman of William and Mary believes Hall was passed over for the presidency in 1934 just because he was "a school man." There was concern that the institution, which had a rocky financial and intellectual base, would be perceived as a teacher education college if Hall was appointed. The trustees instead turned to

the aging John Stuart Bryan. See Douglas Southall Freeman, *John Stuart Bryan,* unpublished biography, *Virginia State Historical Society,* Chapter 16, for comments on Bryan's presidency. Sherman's comments came in a telephone conversation with the author, 14 July 1992.

22. For an excellent analysis of the social policies of the New South see William Link, *The Paradox of Southern Progressivism, 1880–1930* as well as Edward Ayer, *The Promise of the New South: Life After Reconstruction* (New York: Oxford University Press, 1992).

23. See the many articles and editorials in the *Virginia Journal of Education,* the white teachers' association magazine. Hall's first speech was before the high school administrators. Hugh Sulfridge, principal of Lane High School in Charlottesville and president of the Virginia Education Association, believed Hall's plan was brilliant. Regarding the lofty goal of reconstructing Virginia schools, Sulfridge wrote, "No greater importance could claim our attention." see *Virginia Journal of Education* 25:3 (November 1931), for coverage of the Annual Convention in Richmond. The theme of the convention was "Curriculum Revision." In Hall's meeting with the high school principals, he discussed his 14-point plan for reconstructing education in Virginia.

24. In addition to UVA, the centers included Fredericksburg, Radford, Harrisonburg, Farmville and William and Mary. Virginia Polytechnic Institute served the entire state for agriculture.

25. See Hall's introduction to the State Department of Education *Bulletin* of 1932, in which he comments on Alexander et al., "Procedures for the Virginia State Curriculum Program" (Richmond: State Board of Education, 1932).

26. See Lynn Burlbaw, "More Than Ten Thousand Teachers: Hollis Caswell and the Virginia Curriculum Revision Program," *Journal of Curriculum and Supervision* 6:3 (Spring 1990), p. 233–254 for an analysis of the process. Alexander and Caswell worked during the summer on the aims. The others on the committee turned the work over to Alexander, but no reason was given. It may have had to do with limited funds.

27. Hollis Caswell, interview by Tom Hogan, tape recording transcription, July 1969, *Columbia University Oral History Project* 107. In the interview, Caswell called the aims "radical" and "controversial." He had essentially the same comments regarding the controversial nature of the aims when O.L. Davis of the University of Texas interviewed him eight years later. In the Davis interview, though, Caswell disavows any connection between the Virginia program and Counts's ideas on reconstruction. See Hollis L. Caswell interview by O.L. Davis, Jr., 17 October 1977. Tape Recording, Oral History Collection, Center for the History of Education, The University of Texas at Austin.

28. See Mary Louise Sequel, *The Curriculum Field: Its Formative Years* (New York: Teachers College Press, 1966), p. 173.

29. *Bulletin* (Richmond, Virginia: Virginia State Department of Education, 1932), p. 16–17, 24–26.

30. Ibid., p. 24–26.

31. Margaret Lee (Mrs. James A. Craig) Alexander, telephone interview with author, 21 January 1989.

32. Alexander, p. 81.

33. See the James biography of Alexander for citations and source notes. *The Virginia Journal of Education* had numerous articles with titles suggesting reconstructive content, such as "The Schools and the New Social Order," but overwhelmingly these essays prove to be commonplace. For comments on Alexander's role as director of negro education, see the William Mason Cooper Papers located at Hampton University, Hampton, Va. Cooper was an officer of the VSTA and later president of Virginia Union University.

34. Sidney Hall to James Johnson, 12 April 1940, in the Charlottesville School Board Papers, The Papers of Albert G. A. Balz (mss 3795), Box 1, Folder "1940 Curriculum Committee: Lane High School (new white High School)." Balz was president of the board in the late 1930s and a member of the philosophy department at UVA.

35. See for the migration patterns, *The Great Migration in Historical Perspective*, ed. J. W. Trotter, Jr., especially his introductory essay (Bloomington: Indiana University Press, 1991). For Leap's comments on Red Hill High School, see "Red Hill," p. 88–96.

36. For one illustration of Johnson's compulsion with "the books" and his relations with the board, see the 21 August 1930 entry in the *Minutes of the Board of Education,* Charlottesville, Va.; also see the 16 April 1931 entry detailing the plumbing at the new Clark Elementary School.

37. *Minutes,* Charlottesville Board of Education, 21 January 1932.

38. See David Tyack's *The One Best System* (Cambridge: Harvard University Press, 1974) for a comprehensive discussion on the bureaucracy associated with urban schooling. Tyack makes no mention, though, of the South.

39. See William Link, *The Paradox of Southern Progressivism, 1880–1930* (Chapel Hill: University of North Carolina Press, 1992).

40. See the many editorials in the *Charlottesville Daily Progress* during 1925–1926, especially "Urge Need of a Chamber of Commerce Stressed," 4 April 1925, p. 4; "Curing Our Small Town Ways," 20 April 1925, p. 4; "Organizing for Local Development," 15 April 1925, p. 4, and "Advancing Our Home Town," 18 November 1925, p. 4. On improved streets, see "Streets and Sewers," 1 June 1926, p. 4.

41. See the correspondence between Albert Balz and A.L. Hench found in The Charlottesville School Board Papers, The Papers of Albert G.A. Balz, mss. 3795, Box 1 and the correspondence of William Smithey, UVA professor of secondary education in William Royall Smithey Papers, Acc RG-21/54.801;861, Box 5: Cooperative Relations between UVA and Charlottesville 1927–1929, 1933–1934.

42. Balz correspondence with Hench, 1 July 1935.

43. Balz papers, 14 October 1937.

44. Balz papers, 28 September 1938; 10 January 1940.

45. Ibid.

46. Starnes to Balz, Balz papers, no date, marked "confidential" and signed "George," probably written sometime in the fall of 1940.

47. See Anderson for an analysis of the meager support given black education, especially chapters 4–5. Also see Louis Harlan, *Separate and Unequal* (Chapel Hill: University of North Carolina Press, 1958). In Red Hill, one of the four black elementary schools petitioned the county board to extend the school year from seven months to nine. The board told the school patrons that if they wanted the year to be longer, they would have to pay for it. They compromised and closed one school at the mid-year and sent the teachers to another school. See Leap, p. 92.

48. See Marjorie Felice Irwin, *The Negro in Charlottesville and Albemarle County* (Phelps-Stokes Fellowship Papers Number 9, University of Virginia, 1929), p. 19–22; also see Helen Camp de Corse, *Charlottesville—A Study of Negro Life and Personality* (Phelps-Stokes Fellowship Papers Number 11, University of Virginia, 1933), p. 7–10. Irwin made the "degenerate" comment.

49. Irwin, p. 21.

50. "Minutes," Charlottesville Board of Education, comment made by the board vice president, Virginia Mann, 16 October 1933.

51. "Minutes," 25 May 1933.

52. In the O.L. Davis interview, Caswell comments that blacks were not interested in the revision program.

53. See the correspondence between Gandy and Colson in "The Colson-Hill Family Papers, 1834–1984," (Acc. 1965–13) Virginia State University Archives. Petersburg, VA Box 65, Folders: "V.S.U. correspondence with John Gandy, 1930–1931," #463 and #464, "1932" 25 January 1932; 24 October 1932; 1 November 1932.

54. See the many articles in the *Journal of Negro Education, The Virginia State Bulletin* and *The Southern Workman,* all relating to the inequality of intelligence testing, viz. black intelligence and children.

55. "Colson to Gandy, November 1, 1932." Colson and Gandy had already organized a committee to study curriculum development long before the state department request. In a letter dated 7 January 1931, she recommended to Gandy a list of names for a revision study group. The staff from the college agreed that the revision process would be difficult, at best. "What there is of value not included in the bibliography is so likely to be of equal difficulty, that we recommend such organization of study groups as will provide the most able leadership available and extension of time for those who are slow of comprehension." She recommended William Cooper from Hampton; Winston Douglass from Richmond; Eva Mitchell from Hampton; L.F. Palmer, principal from what would later in the decade be the most progressive black high school in the state, Huntington High School in Newport News; and Archie Richardson, who in 1936 would be appointed by Hall to the state department as Assistant Director of Negro Education. Cooper, Douglass and Palmer would serve as VSTA presidents and later college presidents. Mitchell would serve as director of research at VSTA during most of the 1930s.

56. See his many articles in the VSTA *Bulletin* and the *Journal of Negro Education,* especially his analysis of the black tobacco workers' strike, which won the right to organize and higher wages, January 1938 in the *Journal of Negro Education.* In that study, he compared the tobacco workers' wage increases to the wage of a black Virginia teacher. See the VSTA *Bulletin,* 30 November 1930, April 1931, 19 January, November 1932, March 1933, January 1934 and March 1935 as examples.

57. Wilson Record criticized Wilkerson in his polemic on communism and blacks, *The Negro and the Communist Party* (Chapel Hill: University of North Carolina Press, 1951). Closer to home, Blair Buck, who came to the state department in the late 1920s from Hampton and later would be appointed director of instruction, wrote in his unpublished autobiography that Wilkerson, no matter how Buck tried to talk him back into the fold, had "thrown it all away" by joining the Communist Party. He, like Record, referred to Wilkerson's years with the Communist Party as "a waste." See Michael James, "Blair Buck," *Virginia Dictionary of Biography* (Richmond: Virginia State Library Volume 2, in press). A copy of the autobiography is in the author's possession. Wilkerson died in June 1993 in Norwalk, Conn. See his obituaries in the *New York Times,* 18 June 1993 and in the Norfolk, Conn., *The Hour,* 18 June 1993.

58. Sam Madden, interview by author, Petersburg, Virginia, 29 July 1992.

59. Colson to Gandy, 24 October 1932.

60. Colson to Gandy, 15 September 1934, 4 March 1935; Colson to Ruth Henderson, 22 November 1935, 5 April 1935, 5 February 1936. Colson also criticized the state department in the Virginia State College *Gazette,* December 1933, 1–5 and in a letter to Charles Thompson, editor of the *Journal of Negro Education* 31 January 1934, 2–3. Wilkerson was struck by Colson's ability to attack, without apparent fear of reprisal. In a letter to Colson,

he wrote that he "wish[ed] he had the gift for saying bitingly pertinent things diplomatically, inoffensively, though none the less forcefully." See Wilkerson to Colson, from Ann Arbor, 2 December 1933. Wilkerson was in Ann Arbor working on his doctorate.

61. *Virginia State College Gazette* 38:4 (December 1933), p. 5.

62. Ibid., p. 4.

63. Ibid., p. 6.

64. Ibid., p. 17.

65. Colson to Charles Thompson, 31 January 1934.

66. Colson to Gandy, 19 July 1934.

67. Colson to Gandy, 20 July 1934. She advised Gandy that they had met with Peters and "the meeting was a momentous occasion ... we hope our offerings will be properly incorporated in the forthcoming bulletin of the State Department."

68. Colson to Thompson, 31 January 1934, and Colson to Henderson, 22 November 1935 and 5 February 1936.

69. Colson to Gandy, 11 October 1935 and 14 November 1935 for her annual reports on how the department was aiding the development of the "new curriculum." Also see Ronald Goodenow, "Paradox in Progressive Educational Reform: The South and the Education of Blacks in The Depression Years," *Phylon* (March 1978), p. 49–65.

70. Michie, Carrie Welbrock, "An Investigation of the Causes of Withdrawals from Jefferson High School Charlottesville, Virginia" (Master's thesis, Virginia State College, 1939).

71. Ibid., p. 2.

72. Ibid., p. 4.

73. Archie Richardson, *The Development of Negro Education in Virginia, 1831–1970* (Richmond: Phi Delta Kappa, 1976), p. 52.

74. See the correspondence between Hall and Byrd in the *Harry Flood Byrd Papers* at UVA, especially Hall to Byrd, 14 January 1932, 30 January 1932, 16 June 1932, 13 December 1932, 15 December 1932 and Byrd to Hall, 12 and 14 December 1932 and 18 June 1932. In a letter Hall wrote in January of 1933, he told Byrd that he was having difficulty keeping the teachers "in line." The fiscal crisis and Byrd's reluctance to support the teachers' needs apparently were causing Hall to openly criticize the organization (Hall to Byrd, 26 January 1933). He told Byrd that he did not want the next general session to be like the last, where "only after serious difficulties that I was able to keep the school organization in line."

75. Anne Gibson Buis, "An Historical Study of the Role of the Federal Government in the Financial Support of Education" (Ph.D. diss., Ohio State University, 1953), p. 213–283; Marjorie Murphy, *Blackboard Unions: The AFT and the NEA, 1900–1980* (Ithaca, New York: Cornell University Press, 1990), p. 131–149. Murphy mistakenly has Hall coming from West Virginia.

76. Buis, p. 146–149; Gilbert E. Smith, *The Limits of Reform: Politics and Federal Aid to Education, 1937–1950* (NY: Garland Publishers, 1982), p. 56–60.

77. Smith, p. 56–57; Murphy, p. 141–149; Andre R. O'Coin, "Vocational Education During the Great Depression and World War II: Challenge, Innovation, and Continuity" (Ph.D. diss., University of Maryland, 1988), p. 265–296. He mistakenly lists Hall as NEA president, see p. 283, fn. 79; see Martha Swain, *Pat Harrison: The New Deal Years* (Jackson: University Press of Mississippi, 1978), p. 210–218 for an excellent analysis of Harrison's role in federal school aid legislation.

78. David Tyack, Robert Lowe and Elisabeth Hansot, *Public Schools in Hard Times* (Cambridge, Mass: Harvard University Press, 1984), p. 107.

79. *Hearings Before the Committee on Education House of Representatives,* 75th Cong., 1st Sess., HR 5962, "To promote the general welfare through the appropriation of funds to assist the states and territories in providing more effective programs of public education, 30 and 31 March, 1, 2, 6, 8 and 13 April 1937." Hall presided over the House hearings and arranged the calendar for both the Senate and House.

80. *Hearings Before the Committee on Education and Labor United States Senate,* 75th Cong., 1st Sess., 9–11 and 15 February 1937, on S. 419, p. 216–219. See Elizabeth Cobb Jordan, "The Impact of the Negro Organization Society on Public Support for Education in Virginia, 1912–1950," (Ph.D. diss., University of Virginia, 1978), for a discussion on Walker's views of schooling.

81. Senate Hearings. p. 222–227. Although it does not mention his appearance before the Senate, see Richardson's historical sketch.

82. Senate Hearings, p. 226.

83. Richardson, p. 50; also see the author's interview with Sam Madden.

84. Murphy, p. 149.

85. See Charles Thompson's editorial in the *Journal of Negro Education* (April 1937), p. 131–132. He cited numerous editorials in national weekly newspapers that were critical of Hall and his "...'hand-picked' Negroes from Virginia," as one editorial commented. Thompson quotes a letter from Gandy, written the day after Richardson's appearance in which he criticized supporters of the bill. In a pointed reference to Richardson's "intelligent Negroes" comment, Gandy wrote: "I think I know the sentiment of the intelligent Negroes of Virginia very well, and I would unhesitatingly bear witness to the fact that in my opinion they do not approve of the Harrison-Black-Fletcher Bill as drawn ..." He concluded, "We do not know anything about the appearance of the two Virginia witnesses before the Committee in the interest of the Harrison-Black Bill."

86. See Cooper's comments in the Virginia Teachers Association Papers, Executive Secretary Record Books, Acc. # 0069-14, Box 1, 13 November 1937, n.p.

87. Ibid.

88. Ibid.

89. Ibid.

90. Ibid. See the *Virginia Journal of Education* 33:1 (October 1939), p. 4 which makes no mention of average. Gandy first mentioned the issue of salary equalization in 1919, and then throughout the 1930s, VSTA actively worked to have "average" removed from the Three-Point Plan.

91. Cooper.

92. Ibid.; Mark Tushnet, *The NAACP's Legal Strategy Against Segregated Education, 1925–1950* (Chapel Hill: The University of North Carolina Press, 1986), p. 78–80, 102–103. Cooper claimed that Marshall was not there to recruit salary litigants.

93. See the correspondence between Hench and Balz in the Papers of the Charlottesville School Board, 1939–1948, "The A.L. Hench Papers," mss 927-A, -B. Box 1 (eight folders: 1939–1940), "Hench-his stuff as member of the Charlottesville School Board"; (2); 1943–1945; Committee for the Office of the Superintendent; (1) Curriculum Committee (2); Curriculum Committee for new white high school (2); 1940–1941 Committee on Educational Facilities for Negroes and the Personnel Committee: Black teacher's equalization of pay (1). For commentary on the firing of Arlene Black and the "Richmond Six" see the *Bulletin* of the VSTA.

94. Balz to board, 2 May 1940.

95. Balz to board, 3 February 1941.

96. Ibid.
97. Balz to Hench, 3 April 1941. Hench had crossed out the typewritten word "equalization" and penciled in "adjustment," the term Balz had used since early in the year.
98. *The Richmond News Leader* and *The Richmond Times-Dispatch,* 12 August 1941, p. 1.
99. *The Richmond News Leader* and the *Times-Dispatch,* 14 August 1941, p. 1. The *Virginia Journal of Education* 35:1, September 1941, p. 3 quoted Hall as saying he had accomplished much and therefore, "felt free to return to university teaching."

CHAPTER 7

PROGRESSIVE EDUCATION IS REDUCATION!
Civil Rights in Pasadena, 1930–1975

On the first day of May 1937, 22-year-old Myrtle Ward and her four-year-old daughter, Jeannette Louise, took a walk along Pasadena's Colorado Street Bridge. Myrtle, married to an out-of-work accordion player named Clarence Ward, was terribly depressed. She had recently given up her job, and the family's financial situation was crushing her. There apparently was little to encourage her—or anyone else in depressed America—that things would improve quickly. As talented as Clarence was with the accordion, he could only find work as a musician with the Works Progress Administration, a federal assistance program created during the Depression to support everything from building new schools to helping down-on-their-luck artists like Clarence.

Myrtle had driven the family car to the east end of the world-famous bridge, a concrete and iron Beaux Arts creation erected in 1913. The Colorado Street Bridge was the tallest structure in Pasadena, standing more than 150 feet above the boulder-strewn floor of Arroyo Seco Canyon, and it connected Pasadena to the northeastern edge of Los Angeles. Myrtle Ward's mother later told the press that her daughter was bitter, that for unknown reasons she had "given up" her job so Clarence could work. After parking the car, Jeannette and Myrtle walked hand in hand to a small alcove near the middle of the bridge where there was a granite bench. Myrtle pinned a note to Jeannette's coat. It read, "I am Myrtle Ward, 4329 Van Horne Avenue." She picked up her daughter and threw her off the bridge. Myrtle then climbed the guardrail and jumped to her death.[1]

Myrtle Ward was the 95th suicide from Pasadena's bridge. Four-year-old Jeannette Louise, though, was not the 94th. She survived, her fall broken first by the branches of a pepper tree and then, as luck would have it, by a spot of soft sand in the dry streambed. The tragedy of an overwrought mother who threw her four-year-old daughter from the span "touched the hearts" of Pasadena, as the *Star News* reported, but the suicide also refocused attention on the bridge itself, symbolic as it was of the condition of the world in 1937. Over the years since the stock market crash of 1929, the Colorado Street Bridge had taken a new name that rankled Pasadenans who cared about such things. The bridge was now called "Suicide Bridge," and that was not good for the city's image. No matter that the majority of suicides were Los Angeles residents who used the bridge to end their misery, Pasadenans felt, as the *Star News* reported the day of Myrtle Ward's death, the need to "safe-guard the bridge." It was as if the structure—and the city's image—was somehow threatened by the suicides. Three months after Myrtle Ward died, and after the city held a competition of Pasadena architects to design an aesthetically pleasing barricade to stop would-be jumpers, the city manager decided to save money and put up a chain link and barbed wire fence. The "hog run" as it was then called was immediately decried as an eyesore. The number of suicides from the bridge declined, although that may have had as much to do with the coming end of the Depression as with the barricade. But the span over the Arroyo Seco could not shake off its Depression-era name so easily. For decades after Myrtle Ward jumped to her death, it remained Pasadena's "Suicide Bridge."[2]

Most of the suicides at the bridge were attributed to the collapse of the world's economy. Pasadena was a city of extreme wealth, but by the end of the decade of Depression, no longer the country's richest city. It had fallen to third behind Montclair, New Jersey, and Brookline, Massachusetts. Initially, it appeared to withstand the social and political turmoil that accompanied the Depression. The tourist season during the winter of 1931–32 began as any other season. In December and then increasingly throughout January, trainloads of wealthy visitors, mostly from the East Coast, spilled into the city. They took up residence at their mansions along Orange Grove Boulevard and its tributaries or in one of the city's ultra-plush hotels, the Maryland or the exclusive Castle Green Apartments.[3] But this tourist season turned out to be very different. The world Pasadena had come to know and trust had turned upside down. There were transient labor camps on the outskirts of the city, and folks were hearing crazy, scary stories that a newborn baby had starved to death at one of them. Maybe even more alarming were reports in the press that longtime employees of city government—not merely laborers but engineers, surveyors and stenographers—were being terminated as the city cut its payroll in an effort to lower expenditures so taxes could be reduced. Although there was no apparent panic, Pasadena's staid and reserved veneer was showing signs of stress.[4]

During the winter of 1931–32, as the city was immersed in the usual rush of fame and grandeur, Pasadenans were witnessing the debris of the Depression. On a daily basis, hundreds of out-of-work men were wandering the streets, looking for work or a meal. Many had taken up temporary residence at Memorial Park, only a few blocks from the recently erected Central Library. Now, as Christmas approached, increasing numbers of out-of-work women appeared at Memorial Park. There were so many, that by early spring the city was forced to close the park bathrooms temporarily so they could be expanded. By the summer of 1932, Memorial Park was the daily rendezvous point for hundreds of indigent men and women searching for work—any work. Many sensed it was work that would not come.[5]

By the early spring of 1932, nearly 20 percent of the city's workforce—in excess of 8,000 Pasadenans out of a total working-age population of just over 40,000—had registered as unemployed.[6] The perception in the community was that there were even more. These were staggering numbers for a city that just a few years before had been riding the crest of an economic boom that saw the construction of the Rose Bowl and the palatial City Hall and the building or rebuilding of 32 schools, including the scientific epicenter of the modern world, the California Institute of Technology. In a book published that year, Morrow Mayo, the venerable wit of Southern California journalism during the interwar years, said, "Pasadena is ten miles from Los Angeles as the Rolls Royces fly. It is one of the prettiest towns in America, and probably the richest."[7] Mayo was pointing to the 400 millionaires in residence and "perhaps twice that many if you count (as Pasadena did not) those who had homes in the city but spent most of their time elsewhere." Mayo thought the fashionable winter season brought a thousand new millionaires.[8]

Also at the end of the 1930s, psychologist Edward L. Thorndike, one of the scions of the movement to quantify differences (he wrote dozens of books on ranking everything from children's intelligence to workplace habits), published his Carnegie-funded study of 310 American cities. In *Your City,* Thorndike wrote of the outcomes of "nearly a million items [measured] by modern quantitative methods." He boasted that the results were "for all intelligent citizens." When one examines the questions Thorndike posed, it was clear that wealth spoke volumes. The chances of a baby dying within the first year of life, the number of girls aged 10 to 14 working for wages, and the amount of public funds spent per person for recreation were, for Thorndike, not class bound but reflective of a city's "goodness." Thorndike's "modern quantitative methods" determined that Pasadena was "America's Finest City."[9] The realtors drooled—at least those with jobs.

We will never know the secrets of Myrtle Ward's relationship with Clarence, but her mother believed her suicide was due in no small part to her having given up her job so her husband could work. Did Myrtle have to stay at home to care for Jeannette because Clarence went off to work? Or did Clarence merely succumb to chauvinism and force Myrtle to give up her job because he could not tolerate his wife as the primary breadwinner? Clarence disappeared after Myrtle's death, so the story remains incomplete. Whatever his motivations or the circumstances of Myrtle's work, the Depression was clearly forcing many to rethink cultural norms. The monetary crisis was fast becoming a social crisis. The city was changing so quickly, that what many perceived as rock solid cultural realities were very quickly being exposed as little more than manufactured illusions. Certainly, the Depression was forcing a redefinition of "women's work."

During its 60-year existence, Pasadena had developed a public face that was crafted by the circumstances of migration, wealth, housing patterns, religion and a rather bizarre social conservatism. Morrow Mayo was amused that no movie star had ever lived in Pasadena. He was convinced they were made to feel unwelcome. Mayo laughed that Pasadena's conservatism could embrace eccentricities ("quacks, fortunetellers, swamis and purveyors of 'electronic vibrators'") but never the perceived instability associated with the *nouveau riche* of the movie industry. For Mayo, the epitomes of Pasadena were the wealthy, middle-aged matrons on "whose diamond-studded hands, time, alas, hung heavy." With protégées of young matrons and debutantes, these middle-aged women went in mainly for "Junior League high-jinks [and] homes for Mexican orphans and genteel whoopee." Mayo, perhaps too unkind, was nevertheless perceptive. He recognized the tensions that existed in a city that welcomed wealth with its "quirkishness" yet recoiled at the perception that the city catered only to the wealthy. Millionaires, mused Mayo, would join the Chamber of Commerce for the unique purpose of keeping commerce out of the city. Although he confessed he never knew exactly what was going on, he was sure that Pasadena's businessmen, like businessmen everywhere, were nothing more than "natural vandals." So, in the garden called Pasadena, greedy younger businessmen would "chop down every unprogressive, obstructing tree" if not for the "moss-backed, retired millionaires" who served on the city-planning commission.[10]

Pasadena may have embodied Morrow Mayo's paradox, but the city's founders had all been the paragons of clear-headed, Victorian stability. They were middle-class, Protestant Midwesterners who envisioned a Utopian Christian City on the Hill. Until the Depression, their city's public face suggested that the women who mattered were white, middle-class (more likely wealthier), conservative, Protestant and committed to a moral community anchored by the ideal of the home. In other words, women who mattered worked—but never for wages. Clara Odell, Ester Mack, Charlotte Perkins Gilman and Mrs. Calvin Hartwell anchored the city's early feminist legacy. This image of Pasadena's women as selfless, moral mothers was not unusual for the progressive period.[11] What makes Pasadena's women of status noteworthy is how persistent and deepseated their image became. The public transcript reflected the idea that women who mattered tended unpaid to the needs of their families and the charitable needs of the poor. These women saw their emancipation not in the boardroom or the courthouse but in protecting their homes. The city's public sense of self valued these "social mothers" in places like the Mexican camps or as temperance "workers" and "City

Beautiful" crusaders. Obviously, thousands of women labored for wages in Pasadena, but those were women who mattered less—white, working class and poor women of color. What would be different about the year 1932 was that the chaos of the Depression was starting to alter the long-standing assumption that social class and color were the only determinants of women's wage work. The economic crisis would eventually expose a new reality in Pasadena. Middle-class white women were not relying solely on charitable mothering as a means to community status. Increasing numbers of women were working for wages.

As the middle of 1932 approached, the Depression drained every relief organization in the city. Stunned at first by the sheer numbers, relief workers also began to detect a shift in who was registering for assistance. Initially, it had been "building tradesmen, truck drivers, mechanics, gardeners, and domestics," logically those first hit by a collapsing economy. Now there was a "decided shift in classifications ... more being from clerical, sub-professional and executive fields."[12] And increasingly, these newly unemployed were women. In September of 1932, 35 percent of the registered out of work were women. One city agency forecast the number of unemployed women filing for relief would increase by as much as 40 percent.[13] The appearance of large numbers of wage-earning *middle-class* women peeled away the all-too-thin veneer of social custom and exposed for the first time the fact that wage labor, *not* social mothering, was the chosen route to women's emancipation in Pasadena.

The Depression and the war that followed forever changed Pasadena's gendered sense of self. No longer was the home the single locus of control. No longer did a narrow band of the populace debate the public definition of what constituted the "public good." Increasingly, working women—married, single, black, white and Latina, working in business, in education and in agencies devoted to the public welfare—were negotiating their status through their paid labor. Elite women continued to do what they had always done, but now—and especially during and after the war—women reimagined women's work. After World War II, Pasadena's workingwomen increasingly commanded positions within the social hierarchy. No longer was women's status in the community defined merely by wealth. The 1950 census reported that there were 7,000 professionals living in the city, 3,000 of whom were women. Among the women were accountants, auditors, clergy, chiropractors, editors and engineers. There were six pharmacists, 31 physicians and surgeons, two surveyors, two dentists, six chemical engineers, one veterinarian, a radio operator, three embalmers and 25 actresses, 21 of whom were employed. The census does not tell us if they were movie stars.[14]

HAZEL BARKER, DOLLY BRADY AND THE GIFTED

Some of the professional women who filed for unemployment relief in 1932 were Pasadena's teachers. The tax hounds had called for the closing of six schools, cutting teacher and administrative salaries, and, if necessary, eliminating scores of jobs. Superintendent John A. Sexson, his administrative staff and the Pasadena teachers' and parents' associations worked to prevent the wholesale undoing of the city's progressive school system, but attrition was unavoidable. A number of teachers were laid off as the board began the unpleasant task of trimming budgets and increasing class size. During the summer and fall of 1932, the debate turned to what programs and which schools would be eliminated. The Taxpayers' Association called for closing six elementary schools (the junior and senior high schools were spared). They were Garfield and Grant; Roosevelt, which was a special education facility; Arroyo Seco, the small school located in the affluent area south of the Rose Bowl; and Emerson and Columbia, both located on the west side. The board and Sexson quickly agreed to close Grant (it was a worn-out brick building that had been declared unsafe) but instead of Garfield, they closed Junipero Serra. The fate of the remaining four schools, as well as the rest of the difficult budget decisions, were under discussion when, in the spring of 1933, a natural disaster struck Pasadena, the likes of which had never been experienced. The argument to close schools to save money was suddenly moot.[15]

The Long Beach earthquake rumbled through Southern California late in the day of March 10. Left in its wake were hundreds of crumbled buildings (many were schools) and nearly 200 dead. Hundreds more were injured. Fortunately, the quake, which measured 6.3 on the newly developed Richter Scale created by Caltech seismologist Charles F. Richter, arrived after the children had left school. No one died in Pasadena, but many school buildings were little more than rubble. For the remaining weeks of the school term, children attended makeshift classes in whatever structures were deemed safe. By the summer of 1933, engineers had determined that nine buildings would need to come down (including Junipero Serra) and an additional 13 would require extensive structural reinforcement (including Garfield). The cost would be enormous. Given the depleted education budgets both locally and at the state level, the school board turned to Pasadena's voters for help. On the second try, the city was able to secure from its voters, along with grants-in-aid from the Federal Emergency Administration of Public Works, $3.5 million in school reconstruction bonds.[16] For the next two years, while Pasadena rebuilt its schools, 5,000 students were in double session, attending classes in everything from partitioned auditoriums and expanded janitor's closets to a tent city erected on the grounds of Pasadena Junior College. By 1937, Sexson reported that the system "had stabilized," but school people knew it would only be a matter of time before new funds would be required to accommodate the ever-expanding population.[17]

Before the earthquake, one of the schools the Taxpayers' Association and the board had readily agreed to close was Grant.[18] Built in 1908 as a "modern" two-story brick building, Grant was located a few blocks from the Caltech campus.

In the late 1920s, during Superintendent John West's tenure, the school was selected as the site for the system's first "gifted" education experiment, probably because of its available space (there were wooden outbuildings located just south of the main building) and its close proximity to Caltech. Apparently, too, a number of professors whose children attended Grant School pressured the board of education to create something special. I. Grace Ball, the administrator in charge of intelligence testing for the system, was put in charge of creating a program, finding the students and hiring the teaching staff. The Director of Research, Hardin Hughes, and his staff made the decision to skim the "highly intelligent" students—those with IQ scores exceeding 140—from the other schools and bring them together at Grant. Hughes had determined that the "very intelligent" were not meeting expectations, and an enriched curriculum was necessary. Three classrooms were established for combined grades one-two, three-four, and five-six. One of Grace Ball's first staff decisions was to appoint Hazel Barker as the teacher for the "5-6" group. Barker was apparently the perfect fit, highly creative and even-tempered yet not so idiosyncratic she might challenge the order of things.

The Grant plan was to use the three gifted classes as a field experiment for Dewey's more radical versions of child-centered progressive practice. Most public school adaptations of progressive education had remained fairly tame throughout the post–World War I decade. The majority of elementary aged students in the nation remained engaged in classroom practice rooted in the traditional notions of the teacher as the single arbiter of curricular decisions. Regardless of the hyperbole that swirled around the changing nature of American education in the 1920s, progressivism—in other words, a more child-friendly, psychology-based (mostly Freud, seldom Jung), activity-oriented classroom structure responding to children's readiness and interests—had not replaced the typical desks-bolted-to-the-floor elementary classroom. By 1930, in most schools around the country, classrooms still revolved around teacher decisions. Textbooks remained the major sources of information, and schools were focused on the traditional definitions of what was important, the "3 Rs."[19] West and others—presumably those Caltech families—wanted to challenge that traditional definition, and what better place than a classroom filled with the best and brightest?

As different as Grant's classrooms became, Pasadena's "enriched education program," as it was called, never intended to alter the social order. Giftedness was not to be risky business in Pasadena. This was not "social reconstruction" either in intent or content. Those who attended Grant came from Pasadena's growing number of professional families and were white and middle class.[20] Once the IQ tests determined qualification, students came from all over the city. Initially, the board told parents that transportation was not part of the deal, but, within a year, children were riding yellow school buses to Grant.[21]

Two of those students were Sara Brady (she was "Dolly" to her young friends) and Blanche Murphy. When the two second graders stepped off the bus at Grant, they walked into a very different world than most other children experienced in Pasadena. To a degree, it was a world the students could make for themselves.

With the California sunshine, all instruction need not be indoors. Hazel Barker and her colleagues—Ruth Campbell and Naomi Chambers—took the students outside, and it was there that much of what came to define Pasadena's early gifted education experiment took place. Children learned to read, write and compute but not from textbooks and certainly not by sitting at desks. Skills were acquired and practiced through "projects." Sara, Blanche and their classmates built a playhouse and then went about stocking it with furniture they con-structed, including rugs they wove and chairs they made. They planted and tended a garden complete with its own "irrigation system," a series of earthen "dams" and trenches that channeled water from a faucet to the garden. They raised barnyard animals, including rabbits and chickens (which they could describe in husbandry terms) and performed "scientific experiments" which tested their novel hypotheses. They wrote plays and performed them for the entire school. The older children produced a complete "symphony," conducted by one of their own—and constructed many of the musical instruments out of common materials. The students were not graded in the traditional sense. Instead, at the end of the year, each student would respond to questions the teachers posed. This "self assessment" constituted their report card. Seventy-five years later, Sara Brady and the others who attended these early, child-centered classes at Grant remembered two essential qualities that John Dewey and his pro-gressive colleagues believed were central to the mission of schools. As Sara Brady put it, "We could make anything we needed or solve any problem." She now admits she could not quite solve *any* problem, but during those gifted days at Grant, nothing seemed out of reach.[22]

Not everyone agreed with Dewey's more child-centered philosophy. "Making things" and "solving problems" apparently made Hardin Hughes increasingly uncomfortable. Given his faith in scales, graphs and numbers, the lack of precise pedagogical definitions in a child-centered classroom (or more likely the question of what role children should play in determining classroom hierarchy) concerned him. So, when the board and Sexson decided to follow up on the Taxpayers' Association 1931 report with their own data collection to support the 6-4-4 Plan, Hughes chaired the elementary education segment of the study team.

In July 1931, the board, at Sexson's recommendation, hired Stanford University professor William Proctor to outline a program of research studies to determine if Pasadena's schools were successful under the 6-4-4 Plan. The public rhetoric made the Proctor study appear as if it had gathered value-free data. In fact, Proctor's study was anything but value-free. The report, titled

Fig. 20. Sara "Dolly" Brady, (far left) lunches outdoors with some of her 1st and 2nd grade class-mates—and a few farmyard friends. *(Photo courtesy Sara Brady Shatford)*

"Kindergarten Six-Four-Four Plan of School Organization," was Sexson's counter to the Taxpayers' Association report. Scores of educators and laypersons looked into every aspect of the system and its organization and then reported to the city that the schools were on solid philosophical, programmatic and fiscal ground. "The Six-Year Elementary School" study team, chaired by Hughes, was made up of an eclectic group of mainly sympathetic progressives, including L. Thomas Hopkins, professor of education from Teachers College, Columbia, a nationally known figure who was in charge of curriculum work at one of the nation's most progressive schools, Lincoln School in New York. Hopkins, a friend of Sexson, had been employed on a parttime basis as a consultant since 1929. Joining Hopkins was Barbara Burks, a psychologist assigned to Grant school, Grace Ball and two education professors, James Sinclair from Occidental College and Junius Meriam from the University of California at Los Angeles, one of the nation's leading authorities in elementary school curriculum development.[23]

SCHOOLING AS "LIFE-ACTIVITY"

What came from the Proctor studies was a public, systemwide affirmation of progressive, child-centered practice. But the Proctor studies, published by the board in 1933, shied away from endorsing more radical Deweyian approaches. In fact, the system was focused on progressive appearances but was not engaged in authentic, child-centered education. Hughes and his team were not concerned much with academic achievement. Hughes' research department had gathered abundant data to indicate that, in the elementary grades, progress in the "fundamental subjects had been normal or better." Instead, the team was intent on investigating how far the system had moved toward "life-activity," a progressive education term meant to reflect the ways in which classrooms integrated the study of "real-life" projects (gardens, boats, airplanes) through an "activity" curriculum (making things, solving problems) rather than traditional subjects taught by textbooks and recitation.24

The team relied on Hopkins' definition of "life-activity" and, therefore, divided the investigation into three distinct levels.

1. The teacher remains in control of the environment, tying the projects to traditional subjects.

2. The teacher remains central to the learning but the activities are now more independent of the traditional curriculum.

3. The most child-centered approach, where the teacher is "practically free" from curricular requirements and the students select their projects based on their interests.

Hughes reported that every elementary school had activity work in progress, and fully 90 percent of all classrooms were engaged at level one, noting that the majority of classrooms were not equipped for full-blown child centeredness because teachers were either not trained sufficiently, or the room itself was ill-equipped.

More to the point, Hughes' report clearly states that Pasadena's school leadership was not ready for authentic child centeredness. The report clarified the extent to which teachers only tried to create the *illusion* of "free choice." In other words, teachers consciously set out to trick students into thinking they were sharing power. In many instances, Hughes reported that teachers succeeded in introducing the activity "in such a way that it seemed to the pupils that they had suggested and initiated the activity themselves." The report went on to state that "no classrooms were free from general curricular requirements," but that the gifted rooms at Grant (and the fifth- and sixth-grade classrooms at Linda Vista School, which were not part of the gifted program) were engaged in "modified" child centeredness, which was a blending of levels two and three. Grant's teachers, however, were not operating independently of the expectations of the system. As in the rest of the schools, real authority remained with the teacher. Hughes tried to calm any fears that Pasadena was slipping into more radical progressivism or schooling for social reconstruction when he reported that teacher leadership "had more to do with the selection of the activities around which the curriculum would be built than the exercise of free choice by the children."[25] This was risk-free progressive education or, as historians Daniel and Laurel Tanner mockingly called it in a history of educational philosophy written in 1970, "educational Machiavellianism."[26]

But was this pretense of child centeredness, as the Tanners claim, little more than "teachers map[ing] out their classroom strategies with Machiavellian cunning"? The Tanners were writing about the national progressive education movement, yet one wonders if there might not be more complexity to the intentions of teachers in any community—including Pasadena—than merely attempting to fool children into thinking they had made particular decisions. During the 1920s and 1930s, progressive educators were struggling with ways to correlate new notions of child development with traditional ideas of subject matter knowledge and competence. The belief that a child's highly idiosyncratic interests should rule the classroom was generally discredited by the 1930s, especially by John Dewey. The Tanners correctly point out that it was Dewey who cautioned teachers in the early 1930s to be aware that, too often, "interests had come to mean choices expressed orally by the child." The Tanners paraphrase Dewey when they say that it was up to the teachers "to identify and cultivate those interests that are prized by the community and lead in the direction that the demands of society would take."[27] Pasadena's teachers were following an evolving form of progressive pedagogy and also an established set of rules for professional conduct in their community. This meant that traditional subjects—and teacher authority—would continue to take center stage in classrooms. After all, community leadership was fixed on the preservation of the social order. It was only after World War II, when new school leadership began to challenge Pasadena's ruling class on other educational issues, that the city's elite reacted with a vengeance to progressivism and "life-activity."

GRANT SCHOOL AND L. THOMAS HOPKINS

Hughes' lack of enthusiasm for radical progressive practice may have come because L. Thomas Hopkins (whom Hughes and the committee relied on as a "national authority" in activity learning) was highly critical of Grant's self-contained gifted program. Though normally sympathetic to more experimental forms of progressive practice, Hughes criticized the school for its "social snobbishness ..." and especially for its antisocial pupil behavior. "Never before," he wrote, "have I ever visited such a chaotic institution." Years later, in his unpublished memoirs, Hopkins said:

If the purpose of education was to help pupils understand and develop themselves by their normal process of learning, it was an outstanding failure. If it was to teach them subject matter by the usual traditional psychology, it was also a failure ...

From Hopkins' viewpoint, "this school offered a high type of miseducation." He recommended closing Grant's gifted program and admitting the students to other schools with a "more normal classification of pupils." Sexson apparently rejected Hopkins' recommendation, because the program was transferred to Madison School after the 1933 earthquake and then, in 1934, moved back to Grant where it remained in bungalows until it was closed permanently in 1943.[28]

There was possibly more to Hopkins' criticism of the gifted program than mere concern about antisocial behavior or classroom chaos. In a world of super-egos—his included—Hopkins chose to tangle with two of the biggest. First, the Grant gifted program was heavily influenced by none other than Lewis M. Terman, one of the legends of the IQ test. It was Terman, a professor from Stanford University, who, in 1916, rewrote the Binet version of the intelligence test into the "Stanford Binet," the standard for virtually all IQ tests that followed.[29] Terman was interested in a longitudinal study of gifted children, and, in the mid-1920s, he and his colleagues tested more than 250,000 California school children in order to find a sample of 150 boys and girls with IQs above 140. Some of that sample came from Pasadena. Terman was in Pasadena when Hopkins made his recommendation to close the school. Outraged, Terman let everyone within earshot know of his displeasure. Hopkins' memoirs also indicate he took some pleasure in tangling not only with Terman but also with the Caltech professors whose children were in the program. When the school eventually closed, Hopkins, who had earlier criticized the professors for assuming proprietorship of the school and assuming that all "their offspring were gifted," approvingly said the Caltech parents "felt a deep loss of prestige for themselves and their children." Hopkins wrote, "I never chatted with Terman thereafter. He was not interested."[30]

At about the same time that the Grant school discussions were being conducted, Hopkins, who was never shy about speaking his mind, squared off with a second ego, the president of Caltech, Robert Millikan, during a Taxpayers' Association budget hearing at the school board. Millikan spoke for the association, and, according to Hopkins, he ridiculed the Nobel Prize–winning Caltech president for assuming he could be an authority on public education as well as physics. When, at the conclusion of the hearing, Hopkins extended his hand to greet the president, Millikan turned his back and walked out. In less than two years, L. Thomas Hopkins, Sexson's friend and consultant, had alienated two of the most powerful academics in the world.

Regardless of Hopkins' criticisms, the teachers and administrators—including Hazel Barker and Grace Ball—believed that they had created an environment where students practiced the use of power without any of the associated risks. This was a safe progressivism and given the politics of such a conservative place, one suspects the Grant teachers may have gotten as close to real power sharing with children as the system would tolerate. Criticisms such as the Tanners' regarding "teacher manipulation" seem out of place. Teachers were attempting to incorporate their incipient knowledge of Deweyian "motivation" (interest plus effort leads to meaningful purpose) while remaining within the circumscribed boundaries imposed by their leadership. Seventy-five years later, former Grant students report that they understood they were not making all the decisions. They played along with the system, and out of that they negotiated something special for themselves and, possibly, even for the teachers. The adults pretended to let the students in on decision making. In turn, the students pretended they were making independent decisions. In the end, it was the students who fooled the teachers, for they understood that by not openly challenging authority they gained more than the system intended. Sara Brady and Blanche Murphy, as well as others interviewed more than seven decades later, believe that the measure of freedom and responsibility they achieved sustained them ever since.

After completing her sixth-grade year with Hazel Barker, "Dolly" Brady went on to Pasadena's Eliot Junior High School, which she detested for its rigidity and boredom. Sara describes herself as "maladjusted" at Eliot, which seems more of an indictment of the school than an honest appraisal of her social skills. After graduation from Pasadena Junior College, she attended UCLA, where she blossomed into a Phi Beta Kappa. There she ran into a friend of her older brother, who now was a dashing, soon-to-be lawyer. His name was Walter Shatford. They were married during the war. Sara admits she never became a good speller but refuses to blame her early progressive education. She also says she was never taught cursive but she never missed spending time on such an "unnecessary skill" because the neat and highly stylistic manuscript she learned at Grant was perfect for every task. Spelling and cursive aside, Sara Brady Shatford believes her progressive education at Grant School gave her and her classmates something very special:

> I still know some of the people who went to Grant. I don't know that we, as a group, were major contributors to the world but those I have stayed in touch with are fine citizens, have professional careers, are funny, great friends, and to my mind are sound thinkers, liberals, who do what they can to help in big and little things, and are willing to stand up publicly for what they believe in. Grant encouraged us to think.

L. Thomas Hopkins may have been critical of what Grant School defined as "thinking," but Sara and Walter Shatford made a career out of standing up for what they believed in. After the war, they moved into Sara's family home on Washington Boulevard, on the west side of the city. With the coming of the civil rights movement in the early 1950s, these two young liberals would find themselves in the eye of the storm.[31]

THE COMING OF WILLARD GOSLIN

During the fall of 1947, just after John Sexson had publicly announced his "retirement," the school board met to decide the best way to go about hiring a new superintendent. In November, board president and attorney Vernon Brydolf wrote Willard Goslin, the superintendent of schools in Minneapolis, asking if he would suggest three administrators he thought were qualified to become superintendent of Pasadena's schools.[32] Brydolf and the board wanted Goslin's suggestions, because the Minneapolis superintendent had just been elected to the most influential school leadership position in the country. In February of 1948, Willard Goslin would become president of the American Association of School Administrators (AASA). During Goslin's era, the AASA was a branch of the National Education Association and was the most powerful professional education organization in the country.[33] Little wonder that Brydolf and the board wanted Goslin's opinion. Goslin wrote Brydolf on the last day of the year and suggested three names. We do not know who they were, but we do know he did not nominate himself. That would not have been his style. On January 6, Goslin received a return letter from the board secretary, Courtney Monsen, asking if he would consider meeting the board to discuss his candidacy as superintendent. Monsen suggested the board could come to the February AASA meeting in Atlantic City. Goslin agreed.[34] Given what happened in Pasadena over the next two years, it was a decision he would come to regret.

Hiring a superintendent 50 years ago was much less transparent than today. There was no formal search committee, no public input into the process, no formal interview. Instead, the board met Goslin in his Atlantic City hotel room. They chatted and then invited him to come to Pasadena to "look us over." After an early springtime visit of a few days, in which Goslin toured the community and met with individual board members and other community leaders, he sat down with the board and agreed on a contract. Considering Goslin's stature in the world of public education, why would the most prominent administrator in the country, a well-respected superintendent of a large urban system, decide to move his career to Pasadena? The answer was simple: his tenure as the head of Minneapolis schools was over, at least as far as Goslin was concerned. For months, the Minneapolis teachers and board had been at odds over a new contract, and he was caught in the middle. In the winter of 1948, as the Minneapolis teachers went on strike, Goslin had reached his limit. With the Pasadena offer on the table—they had met his every wish, including relative freedom to continue as AASA president—Goslin decided it was time to move.

Goslin's appointment created little publicity outside the city. His contract was not unusual. His salary was competitive but not out of the ordinary. He made sure the board understood his commitment to the presidency of AASA, although his out-of-town work would turn out to be a sore point for some in the community. He also made sure the board understood his commitment to "modern" education, in other words progressive practice. No one on the board gave him any indication that his views were controversial. In fact, the board had actively recruited Goslin specifically because of his progressive ideas.

Willard Goslin, no matter the inflammatory publicity that would explode around him in less than a year, was no radical reconstructionist. He never proposed a socially reconstructive theme at any time in his career. He never saw schools—and classroom practice—as anything more than the nexus of individual freedom and community building. He was well versed in establishing administrative policies and procedures that would make schools efficient, community centered and accessible to all. Yet, it was his ideas of efficiency, community and, above all else, accessibility that got him into hot water.

Goslin's definitions of what constituted the community school ended up running counter to social custom in Pasadena. Civic leadership had been comfortable with progressive education and its Deweyian themes of child centeredness until those approaches challenged the time-honored assumptions about power, order and race in the city. It was then that progressive education became what opponents described as a "cancer" that needed to be cut from the body politic. In November 1950, two-and-a-half years after his arrival, Willard Goslin would be forced to resign amid an atmosphere of near-hysterical, McCarthy-like charges that "Progressive Education is REDucation!" When one examines the allegations leveled against Goslin and his administration—the supposed abandonment of letter grades, elimination of competition, rejection of traditional subject matter, and, most important, usurping parental authority—it becomes very clear that there was little relationship between actual classroom practice, progressive or otherwise, and the campaign to oust the superintendent. There is no conclusive evidence that Goslin radically altered the content of Pasadena's schools, nor is there any evidence to suggest that Pasadena teachers were teaching anything other than traditional subject matter. Goslin was removed, not because he was an aloof administrator who ignored parental concerns or so radical that he was a "fellow traveler," but because he was progressive enough to actualize the nexus between social class and what he and other progressives called the "good life." When the dust finally settled, many in the city understood that Goslin's downfall in the end came because he challenged the prevailing construction of race.

A year after he arrived, due to the necessity of changing school boundaries because of the long overdue construction of two new school buildings, Goslin announced that his administration was going to do away with the "neutral zones" around the Arroyo Seco neighborhood. For 30 years the city's race-based transfer policies had allowed affluent white families in those zones "school choice," so they could flee the multiracial Garfield School attendance area. Within a month after Goslin's announcement, the "anti-progressive education" campaign had begun. But as we shall see, at the center of the Goslin controversy was race and power, not progressive education as the anti-Goslin forces claimed.

Civic leadership in Pasadena would not admit it, but Willard Goslin had inherited a divided city. African Americans and Mexicans on one side, whites on the other. In 1948, it was an arrangement that was becoming increasingly precarious. After the war, Pasadena's black community had gained more than a measure of political power through the rising effectiveness of the National Association for the Advancement of Colored People (NAACP) and its national, antiracist school campaign. In addition, Pasadena's vigorous civil rights campaign of the 1950s was precipitated by a dramatic increase in the black population, from 3,000 just before the war to more than 9,000 in 1950. At the time of Goslin's tenure, Pasadena's African-American community was the second largest demographic group in the city, having surged ahead of Mexican Americans and Japanese.[35] Within a year of Goslin's dismissal, the Pasadena branch of the NAACP filed suit in the superior court to end the use of transfers and the Arroyo Seco neutral zone. For the next two decades, the black community would challenge the city's prevailing notions of race and power. Then, late in the 1960s, the federal government brought the first federal school desegregation case west of the Rocky Mountains, making Pasadena a national symbol of non-Southern racism.

THE MYTH OF A GOLDEN AGE OF RACIAL HARMONY

The rising political power of the black community in postwar Pasadena was long in coming. With the arrival of the first African-American settlers in the 1880s— 75 years before the NAACP neutral zone suit—a nascent struggle against racism and oppression began. One of the most enduring myths of early Pasadena, nurtured by similar forces to those that perpetuated the idea that "ladies" do not work for wages, is that there was a "Golden Age of race relations." Supposedly, from just after the city's founding in the 1870s until the turn of the century, whites and blacks lived in "harmony" and "mutual respect." The Golden Age only ended when the homogeneity of the early white population—mainly the Midwesterners and New Englanders of Republican stock who had opposed slavery before and during the Civil War—was tainted by the arrival of increasing numbers of working-class whites, who did not share the city's abolitionist fervor. However, when the historical record is carefully analyzed, any idea of a Golden Age appears far-fetched, if not contradictory. As we have seen, there has always been racial and class tension in a city founded on the principals of exclusion, speculation and profit. The evidence is overwhelming. The working class was further marginalized as a means to incorporating the city in 1884. The Chinese community was burned out and then thrown out of the civic center in the late 1880s. During the 1890s, the city had an energetic nativist organization that was racist and anti-immigrant. Mexicans were segregated into particular residential and school zones. Regarding race, there has never been a Golden Age in Pasadena.

One convenient source for the assertion of a Pasadena devoid of racial and class conflicts appears to be a few comments made by one of the earliest black settlers, Frank Prince, in an interview conducted by a graduate student in 1947. Prince told the student that sometime before the turn of the century, he and his father were having a meal at Charlie Grimes' café on south Fair Oaks Avenue, and a white customer, newly arrived in the city, objected to their presence. Grimes told the man, "in a voice that could be heard by all present," that the Princes were "good people who paid their bills and kept out of trouble." The graduate student then suggested that Grimes' attitude was typical of Pasadena's majority white population before 1900. Prince did not make that claim. It was an assertion by his interviewer. The Prince story and the student's analysis have been spun into all sorts of grand pronouncements about 19th-century "equality," "access" and "respect." The myth of the Golden Age arose from a need to keep Pasadena's founding Utopian myth of Paradise from being tainted by Pasadena's dismal record of race relations.[36] Instead of relying on a single interview to describe a quarter of a century, a more realistic approach to the early history of race, racism and social class divisions in Pasadena would be an analysis of the founding of the first black civic institutions, the churches.

As former slaves and their extended families fled the South after the Civil War, religion in the black community took on new and varied representations. African Americans after the Civil War began to expand their religious institutions, but they always linked belief in divine law with their pursuit of freedom. The white community has been particularly unable to fully understand how African Americans and their churches have refused to accept the Anglo-European virtue of "rugged individualism" and its notions of segmentation, separateness and hierarchy. Further, early religious demonstrations have led black-church scholars to call the church the first authentic theater in the African-American community, a marked contrast to evangelical Christianity's hostility to theater (if hardly to theatricality).[37] Little wonder then that many within the white, European-American community saw the multiple forms of religious expression by African Americans as comical or dangerous—usually both.

It is impossible to determine exactly how many African Americans lived in Pasadena in the late 19th century, but certainly the population was large enough to support more than a single church. Among the earliest settlers in Pasadena's Indiana Colony of the 1870s had been a handful of ex-slaves, but the number of

African Americans living in the area around the time of incorporation in the mid-1880s was small. The first black church in Pasadena, the First African Methodist Episcopal, was organized in 1888 in the home of Silas Carnahan, a blacksmith who had migrated with his family from Texas. The small congregation rented various rooms and halls until, by 1910, it was prosperous enough to purchase a building lot on the corner of Kensington Avenue and North Vernon Street, a neighborhood that by the turn of the century had become the center of the black community. Frank Prince and his son William, together with the other men from the community, had to stand armed to defend the church from repeated attempts to burn it down.[38]

The arson attempts on the African Methodist Episcopal church were only a few of many incidents as blacks attempted to put down roots in the community. By the turn of the century, a general rule had been established: when the black community expanded, it met with white resistance. In 1903, a small group of black Methodists broke from the African Methodist Episcopal church and established the Scott Methodist Chapel (known later as the Scott United Methodist Church). The small congregation purchased an old Presbyterian church building in South Pasadena and attempted to move it to a location outside the boundaries that had been prescribed as "colored." Just as whites attempted to locate the Mexican settlement house outside of white neighborhoods, white Pasadenans prevented the black community from establishing its institutions wherever it thought best. The church building sat on the South Pasadena street until the church secured a lot in a more "acceptable" area, on Fair Oaks Avenue south of California Street, not far from the Mexican barrio.[39]

The Scott Methodists were not the first group to splinter from an established church. In 1893, the black population was large enough to support the founding of a Baptist church. Beginning as a Sunday School in the home of Mrs. Maria Hill (who had come with her son Archie and two daughters from Atlanta), the congregation eventually built the Friendship Baptist Church in 1897 on South Vernon Avenue, in a neighborhood both blacks and whites had come to consider "colored." By the turn of the century, the city was supporting its second African-American Baptist congregation, the Metropolitan Baptist Church. A decade later, as the Metropolitan congregation attempted to erect a new church building within the now well-defined black neighborhood, the white community reacted.

In June of 1909, two black-occupied homes on Cypress Avenue in a working-class enclave, were burned. Two weeks after these "mysterious" arsons, dozens of flyers were found tacked to gateposts and fences at 128 Waverly Drive, which is adjacent to Vernon Avenue. The signs said, "WARNING If you niggers build upon this property Remember—Cypress Avenue." This property, owned by the Metropolitan Baptist Church, was to be the home of its new church building. The church elders at first decided to keep quiet about the threat but later went to the police. There were no arrests and the church was eventually built on the Waverly site. The elders, expressing concern about the future of African Americans in the community, said the building would be fireproof.[40] The message from the white community was clear—black expansion, even within a circumscribed neighborhood called "colored town," would be countered with white violence.

REVEREND BUSHNELL

The black community in Pasadena has always been a rich tapestry of differences, a multiclass, multi-ideological community, despite the persistent belief by whites to the contrary. One sign of its inner diversity is that older African Americans advanced the myth of racial harmony. Longtime black residents, at least many of those interviewed by historian Robin D.G. Kelley for the city's centennial celebration in 1984, also came to believe that the pre–World War I era was a period when whites and blacks lived in harmony but the black community was homogenous and "close knit." Trouble came to the black community around World War I, according to Kelley's interviews, because of the increasing flow of "uneducated bumpkins"; in other words, poor, rural Southern blacks, who were migrating west to find their fortunes.[41] The assumption was that the racial violence that struck Paradise Pasadena was class bound. The white community had not rejected the "black pioneers," because those first arrivals were somehow more compatible, less different than their white neighbors. Even with the home and church burnings, many blacks came to believe, as one older black resident said of the period, that "many White friends of the Negroes came to their defense."[42]

The conservative black community's reluctance to see a grittier reality was epitomized in the reception of the first pastor at Metropolitan Baptist, Reverend J.D. Bushnell. Just after the church was established in 1903, Bushnell left to take over the pulpit at Friendship Baptist Church. He may have left Metropolitan because the Friendship Baptist congregation was larger, fairly prosperous (given the limited access to better-paying jobs) and active in the community. Around the time Bushnell arrived, the congregation began to fracture over what the press said was the "holiness doctrine" or sanctification. Clearly, Bushnell was attempting to alter the direction of the congregation, but was the split merely over church doctrine?

Reverend Bushnell's problems over a possible shift in church doctrine arose as early as December 1903, when a threat of possible violence was reported in the *Pasadena Daily News*. Friendship Baptist had held a revival meeting, and a group led by James Griffin, the editor and publisher of the Los Angeles African-American newspaper, *The Enterprise*, clashed with others in the congregation over whether the church should follow a "holiness doctrine." Whites have come to call those who practice sanctification "holy rollers." There were threats of "razors and knifes[sic]" and "cutting," and the police dispatched officer Reynolds to keep order in the congregation. The controversy was posing a serious threat to church and community stability.[43]

But J.D. Bushnell was not a holiness preacher. He was a Socialist. Apparently, the church elders decided he had gone too far, and, possibly using sanctification as a diversion, they dismissed him. By the summer of the following year, Ethel Whitehead, president of the Pasadena branch of the Woman's Socialist Union (WSU), wrote that Bushnell had left the Friendship Baptist Church rather than be "gagged." He was now conducting services on Sunday night at a local public hall, "convincing his congregation that his race here in America, when freed from chattel slavery 40 years ago, merely changed for a worse form of servitude known as industrial slavery." Bushnell's socialism was what had driven a wedge into the Friendship Baptist congregation. Later, in the fall of 1906, Bushnell appeared once more in Whitehead's column, having attended her "Sock Social" fundraiser, which she held in her home. He sang, accompanied by Whitehead on the piano, but Whitehead does not tell us if he spoke about his views on socialism and the black community to those in attendance. There is no indication that the all-white WSU or the all-male Socialist party saw Bushnell and his congregation as potential allies, and there is no indication any attempts were made to forge a multiracial Socialist front in Pasadena. After the 1906 newspaper articles, Reverend J.D. Bushnell disappeared from Pasadena. He reappeared in 1908 in East Nashville, Tennessee, as the pastor of the First Baptist Church, a religiously conservative church with no ties to the holiness movement. In 1913 Bushnell left for New York City, where he authored and arranged a number of Baptist hymns still in use today.[44]

Why did the perception of racial harmony linger so stubbornly? Both the Anglo-European and African-American communities in Pasadena have seized on it to put distance between themselves and the contradiction of racism in Paradise. The rejection of Bushnell and the controversy over the holiness doctrine may have had as much to do with black attitudes about religious differences as with class politics. But the ouster of a prominent Baptist pastor is only one of many of the surviving stories that indicate Pasadena's African-American community was never free from ideological and class differences.

ARCHIE HILL

If nothing else, the murder of a white streetcar conductor in 1903 by the son of the founder of Friendship Baptist should forever lay to rest the perception that uneducated country bumpkins were responsible for the demise of Paradise. Archie Hill, the son of Maria Hill, one of the founders of Friendship Baptist, was an educated and successful African-American tailor residing in turn-of-the-century Pasadena. Maria Hill had migrated to California in the early 1890s from Atlanta, Georgia, with her son and two daughters, Rowena and Myrtis. With them came Rowena's two children, Myrtis and Porter Hill Ballard. The extended Hill family lived first in Los Angeles and then moved to the North Vernon Avenue neighborhood in Pasadena. Mrs. Hill was a "trained nurse," who, according to newspaper accounts, was prosperous enough when she reached Southern California so as not to need employment. Archie Hill's father had been a wealthy white man in Atlanta. It was probably his death in the early 1890s that led to the family's migration west. The press indicated that Maria had been in Hill's employ before the Civil War and remained with him afterwards, bearing her three children. These were "quality niggers," as *The Los Angeles Times* called them, who "scarcely show their African blood." The Hills were well connected in Pasadena's growing black community and a close-knit family. The *Pasadena Daily News* also reported that Archie had a reputation as a "quarrelsome customer."[45]

In January 1903, 25-year-old Will Carleton, who was white, arrived in Pasadena from La Junta, Colorado, with his young, pregnant wife. They moved into a second-floor flat above T.F. Twinting's grocery store, close to the power station on South Fair Oaks Avenue. Carleton took a job as a railway conductor with the Pacific Electric Rail Road (PERR). His wife, who remained nameless in the media throughout her husband's ordeal, gave birth to their only child, Virginia Sayre Carleton, in early May 1903, just a few weeks before her husband's unfortunate demise. Not long after he took his job, Carleton joined the carmen's union. He also joined the Odd Fellows, a fraternal order whose membership was mainly working-class tradesmen.[46]

At eight in the evening on May 31, Hill had jumped on board Carleton's No. 88 railcar at the corner of Colorado Street and Fair Oaks Avenue. Hill said he gave Carleton a $5 gold piece and waited for his $4.95 change. Carlton insisted Hill had done nothing of the sort, suggesting Hill had given him the exact fare. The two men argued briefly, then Hill jumped off the car at the next stop and walked to the butcher shop to pay his account. He told Mr. Flourney, the butcher, that he had just enough money to cover his bill because the conductor had made a mistake and owed him change from a $5 gold piece. Hill then jumped back on car No. 88 as it returned from the loop around Marengo Street. He told Carleton, "Just give me $4.90 and call it even." Carlton again told Hill he was mistaken. By Carleton's account, he opened his pockets to show Hill he did not have the $5 piece. Unsatisfied, "the dark shifty-eyed little tailor" pulled out his .38 revolver and shot Carleton at point-blank range. The bullet passed through the conductor's stomach and colon, piercing the peritoneal gland and finally lodging between his eighth and ninth ribs. After the shot, Hill either jumped or was pushed off the car and was immediately apprehended by a nearby police officer, J.O. Reynolds. When officer Reynolds asked Hill what he had

Fig. 21. The "quarrelsome customer," Archie Hill,
from an undated portrait located in the Black History
Collection of the Pasadena Museum of History. *(Photo
courtesy of the Pasadena Museum of History)*

done, Hill's stunned reply was "I shot a man." He turned over his revolver to
Reynolds without a struggle and went quietly to jail.[47]

Word of the shooting spread like wildfire. Later that night, although Carlton
was still alive, his union brothers "and others" sought to take matters into their
own hands. The threat of lynching on their lips, a mob of well over 100 men surrounded the city jail, and they frightened Chief of Police Freeman enough for
him and his armed deputies to take Hill by wagon to the Los Angeles county jail.
Freeman told the *Daily News* that he was not concerned so much about losing his
prisoner to a mob as about injuries to someone trying to protect Hill. The crowd
dispersed, but not the talk. Freeman kept Hill in Los Angeles until the trial nearly
five months later.[48]

The next day, the press reported that "the boys had gotten up a petition"
demanding that Charlie Grimes refuse service in his cafe to "negroes who may
wish to patronize his establishment." The motormen and conductors from the
PERR, who the *Daily News* said were "stirring up" trouble against the black community, were incensed over the shooting. Grimes played coy, telling the *News*
reporter that he knew there was talk of a petition but refused to comment until
he read "the boys' demands." Whether the petition ever got to Grimes or what he
did once it did arrive is unknown. However, black citizens who were interviewed

by the *Daily News* distanced themselves from Archie Hill. The general sentiment in the press reports was that the African-American community was trying to ignore the incident. "We are in no way responsible for the shooting of Carleton," said an unidentified black citizen, "and it strikes me as foolish to attempt to cast such a reflection upon us either as individuals or as Negroes." No doubt the community was not ignoring the Carleton shooting as much as it was trying to put some distance between itself and any complicity with Hill's actions. Its members understood the racial tension in the city. Even with Carleton still alive, the potential for violence by the white community was too real to suggest any measures in support of Hill. So they let him alone.[49]

Four days after he was shot, Carleton died of complications from lead poisoning. He was buried on Saturday, June 5. His funeral "was one of the largest ever held in Pasadena." His "comrades in the railway service" came out in force, dressed in full uniform and wearing black crepe armbands. Special railcars were used to bring PERR men from Los Angeles. Hundreds marched behind a five-foot, flower-adorned model of a railcar carrying Carleton's badge, No. 128. At the head of the procession were the PERR superintendents bearing three immense links of white and pink carnations. The "Filharmonic Quartette of Los Angeles" furnished music, "their melodious voices blending tenderly and sweetly ..." Among the flower arrangements sent by the Odd Fellows and Rebekahs was, according to the *Daily News,* "a cross of white carnations and ferns from the colored people ... who by this simple but thoughtful expression spoke eloquently of their grief at the action of one of their number who caused the death of this young man." Other than Hill's mother, sister, and her two children, the only support Archie Hill received was from Reverend Bushnell, who sat directly behind the accused when he went to his arraignment. There is no mention of Bushnell during the trial in Los Angeles.[50]

Archie Hill was tried for first-degree murder in Los Angeles by a jury—all white—drawn from cities scattered around the county. Only one juror was from Pasadena. It is doubtful Hill would have received a fair trial in Pasadena, given the near-hysterical atmosphere in the city. Hill's attorney, a Pasadena lawyer by the name of John "Judge" Rossiter, argued self-defense. Rossiter was a "strenuous Republican" and for years Pasadena's city recorder, hence the title of "Judge." Archie Hill claimed that Carleton had struck him repeatedly while they were arguing and that he had warned the conductor that he would shoot him if he did not stop. Hill admitted he drew his .38 but said the gun accidentally discharged during the quarrel. Rossiter claimed that a stunned and beaten Archie Hill had fallen backwards off the car. Police officer Reynolds and the examining physician both acknowledged that Hill was badly bruised from blows other than those received by the fall from the car. Witnesses testified that Hill had in his possession that Sunday a $5 gold piece. The butcher told the jury that Hill had told him the conductor had mistakenly kept his change from the gold piece, and more than one witness claimed Hill and the conductor struggled on the steps of the car. The trial got under way in October, and within a week, the jury found Hill guilty. The district attorney's office, with assisting attorneys provided by Pacific Electric, demanded Hill be hanged but the jury (after convincing two who were holding out for manslaughter) unanimously chose instead to sentence Archie Hill to life in the state prison.[51]

A member of a prominent black family was found guilty of murder in the first degree. In a highly publicized affair, no white "friend" showed any support for Hill or his family and only Reverend Bushnell came from the black clergy to support him. The press made note that there were no blacks in the courtroom the first day and only a few African Americans in the courtroom during the following days. Granted the observations were from a white press that had found Hill guilty before all the facts were in. However, given the description of his "quarrelsome" nature, it is possible the black community distanced itself from Hill because its members suspected he was guilty. One person was reported to have said, "It is a little far fetched ... to think that we as a class sympathize with Archie Hill, when as a matter of fact, we do not." Of course, the quote may reflect antipathy toward Hill's social position within the black community. More likely, however, it was the sentiment of a community predicated on surviving within a world that was hostile, no matter what the folklore of harmonious race relations attributed to the period.[52]

ORGANIZING THE COMMUNITY

Surviving meant organizing political structures that would enable Pasadena's African Americans to combat the racism and prejudice around them. In March 1898, black Pasadena, "in a mass meeting," organized its first political association to "act and vote as a unit in the upcoming city, county, and state elections." That summer, the city hosted a statewide meeting of the Afro-American League (AAL), the first of what would be many such AAL conventions held in Pasadena.[53] The league had been founded in Chicago in 1887 to support the Republican party, to work toward better employment opportunities for blacks, and support the emerging African-American community. The 1898 Pasadena meeting was such a success that the city's black leadership decided to unite all political organizations in town under its banner. In 1903, after Booker T. Washington had come to Pasadena in January to speak to thousands at the white Methodist Episcopal Church, the league met again in Pasadena.[54] Nearly 100 men and women from around the state met at Woodman Hall for four days of debate, organizing and social gatherings. The congress had serious business on its agenda. Washington's visit—he was greeted by the widow of President James Garfield and introduced to John Brown's daughter, both Pasadena residents—may have been a public relations delight to those comforted by a racially harmonious Pasadena, but it did little to assuage the increasing ill will toward African Americans, both in the city and elsewhere. Before the convention opened in August, the state Afro-American League asked rhetorically, "Is the mob to rule in this country?" The question was significant, coming so close to the Archie Hill murder trial. The league scattered hundreds of circulars around town urging the city's residents to attend the upcoming congress to discuss "The Race Question."[55] The delegates were concerned with the "disastrous increase" in lynching around the country and the consequences of recent laws in Southern states like Virginia that disenfranchised the black voter. But it was Booker T. Washington's call for the Negro to "quit politics" that most stirred the delegates.

Washington's Atlanta Compromise speech of 1895, in which he called for blacks to abandon any political challenge to white rule and instead devote all their energy toward economic self-sufficiency, divided African-American communities around the country. On the evening of August 19, an audience of 300 crowded into Pasadena's Woodman Hall to listen to speeches on that subject and others. Half of the audience was white and, according to the press, were there "partly out of curiosity, partly out of genuine sympathy and interest in the cause." The following day, beneath a large portrait of President Theodore Roosevelt flanked by smaller pictures of Frederick Douglass and Booker T. Washington, the delegates overwhelmingly rejected Washington's plea to abandon politics. The vote was not even close—33 voted against the resolution, with only six in favor. The *Daily News* reported that support for the resolution rested mainly with the older delegates and clergy but did not identify which, if any, clergy voted with the majority. Reverend J.D. Bushnell, the state chaplain to the AAL, was in attendance. Two of Pasadena's delegates, including William Prince, the state president of the league, and Seaborn B. Carr, who would later write the Pasadena column for *The California Eagle,* the Los Angeles–based black newspaper, led the floor fight against the resolution.[56] Clearly, Pasadena's early black leadership were committed to decisive political solutions to social and economic problems. Further, it is equally clear that the black community at the turn of the century believed Pasadena had sufficient race problems to warrant such political action.

Regardless of the critical perspective on white society black delegates expressed throughout the convention, the *Daily News* put its own spin on the four-day congress. Reflecting on the consciousness of its parent majority community, the *Daily News* reassured white Pasadena that the African-American segment of the population had remained within acceptable limits. The newspaper reported that "white visitors" were "genuinely surprised" that "the Negroes showed surprising progress in self-control ... and logical argument ..." The addresses were the result of "painstaking investigation and care," and even with the highly charged issue of mob violence, the *Daily News* reported that stress was laid on the black man "being a quiet, law abiding citizen" rather than focusing on the violence against the black community. The newspaper reporter went on to say that black women, especially black mothers, were subscribing to the progressive ideal of the home as the locus of the community; indeed, "well trained children," the *Daily News* reported, "laid the foundation for future progress." The *Daily News* was redefining the AAL meetings to suggest that the problems within the black community were attributable to the black community. The *Daily News* did not mention the stinging rejection of Booker T. Washington's recommendation to stay clear of the white man's political machinery. Instead, the reporter summed up the conference with Washingtonian themes of accommodation, cooperation and conciliation:

> Indeed, today, educational, moral and industrial progress is the tricolor flag under which the race is marching to victory—victory of themselves and of adverse conditions and circumstances.[57]

By the end of the year, however, any thoughts of racial "harmony" were apparently rapidly evaporating. The world-famous Fisk Jubilee Singers, who had "won distinction before the crowned heads of Europe," could not get a hotel room in Pasadena for reasons that the press openly acknowledged had to do with their race.[58]

The Negro Taxpayers' and Voters Association

Amidst near-constant pressure to conform to white notions of community, Pasadena's African Americans—in 1910 less than 800 out of a total population of 30,000—continued to build their institutional base. The AAL, increasingly racked by internal divisions over its nearly unquestioned support of the Republican party, came to the city for the last time during the summer of 1910. The sense of urgency over the "race question" in the city had intensified since the meeting in 1903. The previous spring, the local branch of the AAL had unanimously supported the hiring of the city's first black policeman. William Reynolds, a former U.S. Army cavalry officer and a tailor, hatter and dyer by trade, had applied to the city commissioners but nothing had come of it. A year later, the AAL convention agenda was focused on local as well as national issues. The delegates heard from "Mrs. Palmer, a preacher," the same evangelist who had helped spark the sanctification fight at Friendship Baptist seven years before. This time Sister Palmer had more on her mind than church doctrine. In an impassioned speech before the delegates, she urged the state league to demand an investigation into the house and church burnings on Cypress Avenue and Waverly Street. She also called on the AAL to pressure the city to hire at least one black teacher, something the city would refuse to do for the next 40 years. It would not be until well after World War II that Pasadena would finally relinquish its "no colored need apply" hiring policy for police as well as teachers.[59]

With the eventual breakup of the AAL, the black community in Pasadena formed its most strident political organization to date, the Negro Taxpayers' and Voters Association (NTVA). In the fall of 1914, with the purpose of "defending, prosecuting, ascertaining and perpetuating the rights and privileges of the members ..." the association installed its officers in a ceremony at Forester Hall. Foreshadowing alliances to come, attorney E. Burton Ceruti, secretary of the Los Angeles chapter of the NAACP, was master of ceremonies and the guest speaker was Dr. J. Alexander Somerville, the first black man to graduate from the University of Southern California. Somerville, who was a Jamaican by birth, told the audience of the political and philosophical alliances between the NAACP and the NTVA.[60] After that, the NTVA would meet twice a month in the evenings at Garfield School to discuss "various civic affairs." When Matt Solomon, the association secretary asked the school board for permission to use the auditorium at Garfield, the board agreed but cautioned Solomon, and through him the black community, that discussion of "civic affairs" must not "... conflict with school work," and the use of the building after hours "was subject to the same restrictions as in all cases." The board made no such provisions known to any of the many other groups using the schools after hours.[61]

The next spring, as the board of education was preparing for the June election, the NTVA gave the city an indication of what it had meant by "civic affairs." The association asked the board to select "three or four clerks or judges ... from the colored people for services at several voting places ... during the election for members of the board of education on June 4, 1915." The black community was apparently backing a candidate for office and wanted to assure itself that the election was fair and above reproach. The association also requested, "that four colored people be given [positions as janitors] in the public schools of Pasadena."[62] The board never publicly responded to the request. There were to be no colored poll watchers in Pasadena, and certainly there were to be no colored employees, a long-standing practice that was only overturned after World War II. The board did, however, react to the efforts of the NTVA and the black community, in making its grievances known. A few months later, when the association asked to renew its regular, twice-monthly meeting place at Garfield, the board agreed but then charged $2 for every meeting, the only such fee requirement the board made for after-school use.[63]

SCHOOL SEGREGATION

The creation of the NTVA reflected deep ideological and social class divisions within the African-American community. The NTVA agenda was decidedly political and that rankled conservative black Pasadenans. In December 1915, secretary Matt Solomon rose to defend the NTVA in *The California Eagle,* saying that the black community needed to understand that discrimination and racism had to be "met with stubborn resistance in a legitimate way by all Negroes of this municipality ... and [we] are not of one mind." Solomon said the association was designed to "bridge this chasm." He pointed out that racism and discrimination in the city impacts every black citizen. He was especially critical of those members of the community who believed that by having friends in higher places they were somehow immune to racism: "If you are a friend of these law makers ... [and so long] as your skin is black you are ill-concerned."[64] Political and class divisions within the black community were not restricted to Pasadena. *The California Eagle,* the principal black newspaper in Los Angeles for the first 50 years of the century, more than once editorialized about the harmful effects of "not getting together."[65]

By 1919, the NTVA was apparently unable to meet the political needs of Pasadena's black population. In February, William Reynolds, the same man who the city commissioners had rejected earlier for a position on the police force, took over *The California Eagle* column from S.B. Carr. Reynolds reported that a number of progressive African Americans in Pasadena had come together to discuss "live and pertinent questions concerning the race here in Pasadena ..." In a few months, those progressives under the leadership of John Wright and Reverend A.E. Shattuck would organize the Pasadena branch of the NAACP. Reynolds claimed in his February column that there was a great need in Pasadena to "circulate propaganda for the guidance of the race" in this, the "greatest crisis of the nation's progress and reconstruction." There was little in the way of a united black political front in Pasadena. Reynolds once again urged "the fast growing Negro population to come together and agitate for the things necessary for their betterment."[66]

One issue that was apparently without discord, at least in Pasadena, was school segregation. In 1915, the California legislature proposed funds to establish a segregated school for the all-black town of Allensworth, in the San Joaquin Valley of central California.[67] Carr, writing in *The California Eagle,* said, "Fully 90 percent of the 1,900 colored [Carr's estimate of the black population in Pasadena] are opposed to the ... bill." Carr may have been exaggerating slightly about the size of the population and its unanimity of opinion, but certainly no one can doubt that the community was opposed to school segregation. This may have been due to the prevalent belief that schools in Pasadena were the only remaining public institutions in Pasadena where the black community had equal footing with whites. When four local African-American students graduated from Pasadena High School in 1916, Carr exclaimed: "We have no segregation in this city and are satisfied with conditions as far as schools are concerned."[68] But by the early 1920s the threat of separate schools—even with California law prohibiting *de jure* segregation—was on Pasadena's political landscape.

The white community in Southern California had historically been opposed to black enterprise. Whites had seen the effort by Henderson Boone and others to establish a Tuskegee-plan black industrial school as dangerous. Any African-American institution outside white control was a means to increase black political power. Yet without irony, whites early in the century also saw separate schools for the children of African Americans and Mexicans—as long as the schools were under the dominion of whites—as necessary and "good." The contradiction did not elude the black community. Mayor Early's thinly veiled criticism of the black community's lack of support for the polytechnic school was apparently provoked by African Americans suspicious of white institutional expansion, especially when the stated purpose of the school was "for their own good."

During the period just after World War I, the black population expanded in the U.S. West as undereducated, rural Southern blacks came to Southern California searching for the good life.[69] Their mixing with Pasadena's established African Americans was not without conflict, as revealed by the repeated references by older black residents to newly arrived "bumpkins." During the war, blacks had access to better-paying jobs, but the end of the war brought pressure to return to domestic labor. Yet with competition from the new Pasadenans, including the Japanese who were moving into service labor, even domestic jobs became scarce for blacks. The city's racial profile was increasingly problematic for white leadership as pressure to accommodate the new arrivals—blacks, Mexicans, Japanese and poorer whites—competed with the market-driven image of a placid Shangri La. If the school system was to continue to expand its reach as it also perfected its "modern" approaches to progressivism, then maybe it was time for an all-black school.

In April 1922, the local chapter of the NAACP met at the Scott Chapel on south Fair Oaks Avenue. This was a special Sunday meeting, and the featured speaker was Dr. Frederick Bull, the president of the Pasadena Board of Education. Dr. Bull, known around town as "Fred," had been elected to the board in 1921 during John Franklin West's term as superintendent. The city was in the full flush of scientific progressivism. Discussions were under way for what would soon result in vocational and academically tracked junior high schools, a technical high school at Muir, a part-time high school for working youth, a 24-hour high school for predelinquent students, and an adult school. Mexicans were efficiently cordoned off into "their schools" in the industrial area and in the northeast. Pasadena's "modern" schools were being reshaped to meet the needs of all children, so why not a special school for the colored? Board of education president Bull was there to advocate just that. Sharnette Boyce, who had taken over *The California Eagle*'s Pasadena column, dismissed Bull as a "minor official," but his message was worrisome. Boyce advised her readers to reject the board's argument. "There's no use taking sides with an issue of this kind," she wrote, "in order to give a few persons work as teachers or janitors." She was alluding to Bull's proposal that segregated black schools would offer employment to the black community, thereby giving jobs to black teachers who were otherwise prevented from working in Pasadena's schools. But she also may have been reminding the community that, given the bleak employment opportunities afforded African Americans in the city, the majority of graduates would be working as janitors.[70]

Boyce's anti-Bull column hit home. Dr. Bull was trying to get a "few colored people together to put something over," so later, whites would say "they wanted it." Although school segregation was illegal in the state constitution, if the black community "wanted it," then what would prevent the city from creating a "colored industrial school"? Ironically, 40 years later during the civil rights struggles of the late 1960s, Muir High School was to many white liberals fast becoming just that, a segregated "industrial school."[71]

By 1930, the school system reflected the rigid social and economic segregation that defined progressive Pasadena. Elementary schools such as Garfield, Lincoln and Cleveland—all on the west side—saw ever larger numbers of black students in attendance. A 1930 graph used by the city showed that of the 17 schools, only two—Emerson and Washington—had a white population as low as 92 percent. The other 15 were above 95 percent and many were all white. The three westside schools mentioned—Garfield, Lincoln and Cleveland—had significant or majority populations of color. The two *de jure* segregated schools, Junipero Serra and Fremont, were obviously all *Mexicano*. By 1939, the segregation had intensified. Cleveland Elementary School was now 88 percent minority. Lincoln was 53 percent. Garfield had jumped to 94 percent.[72] The race- and class-based scientific model of progressivism had reassured Pasadena's whites that segregation was not only a good idea, it was the only logical idea. The same 1930 graph showing school rankings by race, indicating that every majority white or all-white elementary school was superior to colored schools in every criteria that mattered to the white community: promotion, progress, achievement and IQ. Who could argue with that? The prevailing (white) assumption was that the system merely reflected the natural order of society.[73] For minority communities of color, progress, achievement, promotion and test scores have always mattered. But in an illogical race-based system that was constructed to minimize potential, Pasadena's schools ended up being counterproductive for nearly everyone.

SEGREGATION AND BROOKSIDE PARK

Other than jobs and schools during the first decades of the 20th century, the most problematic issue in the black community was Brookside Park and the city's decision to segregate the public swimming pool when it opened in 1914. The segregation of the pool served as a catalyst to organize the black community, spurring the creation of the NTVA.[74] From the first order to exclude blacks (as well as the Chinese, Japanese and Mexicans), the African-American community became galvanized. The chairman of the city commission, R.L. Metcalf, told the black community that they could use the pool Wednesday afternoons and evenings. The city's argument, provided by the city attorney John Munger, was based on an 1880 school segregation decision (*Ward v. Flood*, 48 Cal. 36). Munger told the commissioners that, in his opinion, the city's management of the plunge was "not to be questioned for legal reasons, and certainly not for ethical or social reasons." Munger's interpretation of *Ward v. Flood* was flawed, for the state had already overturned the school segregation clauses, but the interpretation was nonetheless anchored in Booker T. Washington's Atlanta Compromise speech of 1895. After the NTVA corrected Munger's interpretation of the law, he flatly told the black community that its argument that the city was violating the 14th Amendment was erroneous, "The 14th Amendment guarantees equal *political* rights not equal *social* rights [Munger's italics]." Swimming was, by the city's definition, a social right. Munger then threw Washington's Atlanta speech back into the community, "In all things that are purely social we can be as separate as the fingers, yet one as the hand in all things essential to mutual progress."[75] The community fumed.

It was little wonder that there was a need for a political response to the city's ruling. Chairman Metcalf had told the press that some within the black community were in favor of a separate day, but they were scarce. Mr. M.H. Davis, who resided on South Vernon, derided the segregation of the pool for his own particular reasons. His daughters, "the better class of Negro girls," would have "no protection from the rougher element" if there was only one day for blacks to use the pool. Most of the African-American community was outraged for different reasons. In its first public statement, the newly formed NTVA considered the order an "affront to our self respect and a direct infringement of our civil rights." Ever cautious in an increasingly hostile world, the NTVA, through its Los Angeles attorneys Tyler and Macbeth, did not demand specific redress but instead stated that it was "the sense of the Colored people ... that we be accorded equal privileges with all the other citizens of the city in the use and enjoyment of all the utilities ... on the same days and under and upon the same terms that every other citizen is accorded them."[76] They did, though, demand a formal public hearing. The commissioners filed the demand without comment.

How often Pasadena's citizens of color used the pool on Wednesday afternoons is unknown. There was mention in the press that the community would boycott the separate day, but there is no proof that it was ever attempted. In 1916, the coalition of black churches requested use of the pool and park for the Union Sunday School Picnic, the grand, all-church summer get-together, when thousands of African Americans would celebrate God and summertime. The city agreed, but the churches then voted to go instead to Eastlake Park in Los Angeles.77 The churches returned to use the park on a special day during the summer of 1920 when, as the *Star News* reported, they celebrated "Racial Progress." In actuality, the community was raising funds for an "Old Age" home in Los Angeles and celebrating the poetry of Paul Lawrence Dunbar. Over 1,000 children plunged into the pool that day, and the park superintendent said it was one of the most orderly crowds ever.78

Black protest never ceased, but it paled in comparison to a masterful public relations move only Pasadena's white elite could fully appreciate. In 1930, the city renamed the separate swimming day, calling it "International Day." The city also moved the segregated day from Wednesday to Tuesday, because according to Ruby McKnight Williams, a longtime black activist, "Tuesday was the traditional day off for black servants." McKnight Williams was suggesting the change came as a way to lessen black pressure and to head off any potential black protest. To heap insult onto injury, the city began to advertise that after each "International Day" it would drain the Olympic-sized pool, clean it, and then refill it so whites could use it the next day—an engineering feat extraordinaire, if it was ever completed, never mind the enormous cost in labor and materials. One suspects that many within the black community knew the city did not drain the pool, but having to tell the world that the use of a swimming pool by children and adults of color was so offensive that it necessitated pool cleaning was outrageous. In small ways, Pasadena's African Americans expressed their rejection of the white pool rule.

Children would jump the fence at night, including Jackie Robinson's Pepper Street Gang, which made a habit of evening dips in the forbidden waters. The Pepper Street Gang was a mixed race group of boys from Robinson's westside neighborhood. They had scrapes with the law, but none were terribly serious. Woody Strode, later one of Robinson's UCLA athletic teammates, said Robinson's anger, greater than many of the other black athletes at the university, was the result of his living in Pasadena. Other stories told of boys who climbed the fence, swam and left without a trace—except for the urine marks on the edge of the pool.79

In 1939, with support from the national office of the NAACP as a "friend of the court," the local branch, now presided over by Dr. Edna Griffin, brought suit against the city for its segregated plunge at Brookside Park. Thurgood Marshall and Los Angeles attorney Thomas Griffith sued the city board of directors (formerly the commissioners) and the park superintendent. The local branch of the NAACP, on behalf of Charles Stone and five other African Americans, charged that the city had willfully discriminated against its citizens of color by denying them equal access guaranteed under the 14th Amendment. In 1939, city attorney Harold Huls, a small, bespectacled man originally from Indiana, continued to argue that the 14th Amendment did not have jurisdiction over "social" rights, and there was no precedent for the NAACP suit. Huls and the city argued that if blacks had equal access, then the pool, which was supposedly self-sufficient, would go broke because whites would never share the water. In private, the white elite were outraged that the black community had enlisted the national office of the NAACP. These outsiders were the real "instigators" and not the local colored, who, everyone understood, were happy living in Pasadena. Early in 1940, the court rejected the NAACP suit but on a technicality. Griffith and Marshall, in consultation with Dr. Griffin and the local branch, agreed to appeal. On January 13, 1942, the Supreme Court of the State of California ruled that the city had violated the constitutional rights guaranteed by the 14th Amendment. The black community was overjoyed but the celebrations were short lived. The city immediately closed the pool to everyone. If whites could not swim alone, then no one would swim.[80]

After repeated suits during the war years brought on-again, off-again pool use, the city allocated $10,000 for repairs and reopened the pool during the summer of 1947, a year before Willard Goslin was to take over the school system. City officials had always insisted that whites would not use an integrated pool and that there was not enough money to keep it open for only a few colored children. When the pool reopened, under the watchful eye of Bob Snow, the new pool supervisor (whom city leaders had ordered not to promote "colored patronage"), many whites predicted that only children of color would use the pool. Blacks may have won the legal right to use the pool, they said, "but they will be given only what the law insists upon."[81] On the day the plunge reopened only a few black, Asian and Mexican children swam. It was proof, said the "influential [white] Pasadenans" from the Merchants Association, that whites would not swim in integrated waters.[82] But by week's end Snow began to report increasing numbers of white children, and by the end of summer, he told his bosses the pool was a happy mix of many children. The white elite fumed.

When Superintendent Goslin moved to Pasadena in 1948, his new city was thoroughly segregated. Not in the same sense as Webster Grove, Missouri, where he had once served as superintendent or any Southern town like Charlottesville, Virginia, with its de jure separate school system. Nonetheless, Pasadena's African American, Mexican and, to a lesser extent, Japanese citizens had limited access to theaters, restaurants and cafés, to neighborhoods and parks of their choice, and to good jobs. For much of the 20th century, the black community had been restricted to narrowly defined pockets of land that whites deemed less valuable. Two principal residential areas comprised the majority of black housing—the industrial area around Vernon Street west of Fair Oaks Avenue and the northwest region of the city, on rocky, dry land that Pasadena's founders from Indiana considered useless. The Mexican population, now considerably smaller than the African-American community, occupied the industrial section and the northeast *colonia* of Chihuahuita. The northwest had become the primary residential area for Pasadena's black community. During the Depression, as the African-American community increased in numbers, there were repeated rumors that blacks were attempting to "infiltrate" white neighborhoods. So in 1939, a group of prominent "business and professional men" formed the Pasadena Improvement Association to keep the northwest "black-only."

The Pasadena Improvement Association's strategy for keeping the northwest for blacks only was to restrict the remaining residential property in the city to whites. Led by A.B. Smith, one of the city directors, the association worked for at least two years to create or renew restrictive covenants on homes and vacant building lots outside the northwest area. Smith was the "greatest enemy to the Negroes in Pasadena," according to one report, and was to have said that as long as he had "anything to do with Pasadena government, the Negroes will not be accepted." He was known to have bought uncovenanted property for the sole reason of preventing African Americans from owning it.[83] But the association (made up of Smith, nine bankers, six real estate men, three attorneys and others) was generally subtler in its actions. The association employed a group of men who, on a commission basis somewhat like door-to-door salesmen, worked the residential neighborhoods, selling homeowners (for $5 apiece) the following covenant:

> That no portion or part of said lots or parcels of land shall be used or occupied by, or be permitted to be used or occupied by, any person not of the white or Caucasian race. That no person shall live upon said property at any time whose blood is not entirely that of the Caucasian race, but if persons not of the Caucasian race are kept thereon by such Caucasian occupant strictly in the capacity of servants or employees of such occupant, such circumstances shall not constitute a violation of this covenant.[84]

The $5 fee, which some complained was too high, covered the costs of recording and filing the document and the salesman's share. The association was formally endorsed by the city's power structure: the Chamber of Commerce, Pasadena Junior Chamber of Commerce, Pasadena Merchants' Association, Pasadena Civitan Club and the Pasadena Realty Board and its Property Owners' Division.[85]

The property on all sides of the northwest as well as the central (industrial) district became restricted. When one commissioned salesman was asked if he had found any objections to the campaign other than the fees, he replied, "Briefly, there are too many nigger-lovers in Pasadena." In spite of their objections, one account claimed that fully 60 percent of all the property in the city was restricted in 1941, maybe more.[86]

That account was written by James Crimi, a Pasadena resident and graduate student working with Emory Bogardus at the University of Southern California. Crimi's master's thesis, "The Social Status of the Negro in Pasadena, California," is a comprehensive and hard-hitting indictment of his city's dismal record on race relations. Crimi's data and analysis questioned city structures that marginalized black youth as he criticized government and social service agencies for their paltry efforts at reform. His survey ended up telling his readers that many within the African-American community believed Pasadena was no better than many cities in the South.[87]

The Pasadena Improvement Association mirrored other segregation policies and practices in the city. Theaters, including the Pasadena Playhouse, routinely practiced total exclusion or, if black Pasadenans were admitted, it was to "special" seating. The playhouse kept an empty seat between white and black theatergoers. The Pacific Theater restricted black patrons to the far left side seats or the balcony. Weekend dances at the Civic Auditorium, which during the war drew audiences in the thousands to some of the best jazz and swing bands in the country, did not allow African Americans.[88] Only a few restaurants and cafés openly welcomed multiracial dining. Edna Griffin, the first black woman physician in the city and its longtime NAACP president, told of a Chinese restaurant that had two menus, one with prices for whites, the other with higher prices for blacks. Whites could bowl, play miniature golf and roller skate but Pasadena's African Americans had to leave the city to find those forms of recreation. At the Pasadena Winter Gardens, the city's only ice rink, there were no signs proclaiming "Whites Only." That was unnecessary because management told any aspiring black skater that it might be dangerous for them to go onto the ice. "They (the white management) say that if a white person should object to them, he might push or shove them to cause them to fall. The Negro is then reminded how sharp and dangerous the skates are."[89] Mostly the confrontations were less aggressive. The owner of the miniature golf range, Everett Paine, said that he would occasionally see a "colored boy come in and play" during the day but that he made sure that they knew they were not welcomed. If groups of blacks came in during the evening, he would do what many proprietors of public places in Pasadena did: ignore them, treating them "coolly" until they gave up and left. Paine told an interviewer, "The ones for you to see are the realty people. They've spent lots of time and money on trying to control the Negroes."[90]

Trying to control "the Negroes" had become a central preoccupation for Pasadena's civic and business leadership. Crimi's study reveals a deep fear on the part of white Pasadena that the "colored were infiltrating" white neighborhoods to the east.[91] The majority of whites who responded to his questionnaire—a sample of 244 churchgoers, students, residents of working-class and middle-class neighborhoods, professionals, merchants and teachers—were intolerant, fearful and ignorant of black Pasadenans. Nearly 80 percent believed property values would go down if blacks moved into "their" neighborhood. "No one" would be "pleased," wrote Crimi, if a black family moved onto their street and nearly 70 percent would either move out or "agitate" to get the newcomer out. In fact, support for segregation by law ("impossible under the Constitution," wrote Crimi) received the greatest unanimity of opinion in his survey. Fully 90 percent wanted the city to enact laws to restrict the movement of black citizens or to create separate schools, separate parks and pools, separate transportation and recreation. More than one respondent wrote, "send them back to Africa." Many more admired the segregation policies of the surrounding all-white towns of Glendale, San Marino and Sierra Madre.[92]

When Crimi gathered his counterpoint data from the black community—interviews, essays from high school and junior college students, editorials from *The California Eagle*—the resentment toward white Pasadena was more than palpable. Black Pasadenans were outraged at the Pasadena Improvement Association and the role city government was taking in restrictive covenants. There were feelings of despair, futility and rage. And, Crimi pointed out, there were threats of impending violence unless the pervasive racism in the city was addressed in some fundamental, meaningful way. Crimi, a former student at Pasadena Junior College, was especially concerned with how black students were enduring the chasm between aspiration and reality. When Crimi compared future occupational goals of white and black junior college students, he found "remarkably" little difference.[93] The differences were, however, pronounced in parents' occupations. The majority of white parents were professionals or in skilled trades. The black parents were in domestic work or unskilled labor. Crimi lamented how black students "misunderstood well-intentioned" school counselors, who attempted to "guide them" into nonprofessional work.[94] Crimi's condescension, though, must be understood as situational. This was Pasadena, and, historically, the city had made it very clear it was not a future home for aspiring black professionals. Mack Robinson, Jackie Robinson's brother, fresh off the 1936 U.S. Olympic track team, came home with two medals, one gold and one silver. A college-educated, international sports hero, Robinson had beaten Hitler's Arian best and he expected more from Pasadena than what he got. Robinson was ignored by city officials and dismissed, as a friend recalled later, as one more "uppity colored boy looking for work."[95]

THE ZOOT SUIT RIOTS

Crimi's 1941 study foreshadowed the racial violence that was to come to Southern California. During the summer of 1943, festering wartime tensions turned to rage as white servicemen and cops rioted in Los Angeles and beat young Latino and black males called "zoot suiters." The racial violence spilled over into Pasadena. The "zooters" were mostly young Mexican-American and African-American males, who identified themselves through highly stylized clothing—baggy pants, fitted tightly at the ankles; long coats with watch chains; large, floppy, "pancake" hats; and long hair. There had been scrapes with local authorities—including servicemen—but nothing as serious as the blowup that occurred in early June 1943. For 10 days mobs of out-of-control servicemen, mostly sailors and marines, along with civilians roamed the streets in many Southern California cities—including Pasadena—hunting for the hated "zooters." A "crowd" of nearly 400 sailors formed at the Pike amusement zone in Long Beach "in search of Mexican and Negro youths sporting the reat pleats." Before police and navy shore patrols could disperse them, the sailors had chased one zoot suiter onto the stage of a theater and ripped off his baggy pants, "while spectators roared their approval."[96] It was only when the military ordered the servicemen out of downtown Los Angeles, where most of the violence transpired, did the riots cease. Hundreds were hurt, but there were no deaths and surprisingly few convictions despite hundreds of arrests. The authorities, both civil and military, criticized the soldiers and sailors for their uncivil behavior, but no one in government circles suggested the "zoot suit wars" were anything but the fault of the "gangster thugs" with their garish "costumes." Young males wearing "the zoot suit" were beaten, stripped of their pants and generally humiliated. One unidentified Pasadena zooter was beaten, stripped and then thrown into a garbage truck.[97]

During the height of the rioting in Los Angeles, paranoia was rampant in Pasadena and rumors flew around town that hordes of "zooters" were about to "attack." One night the police got a report that "two carloads filled with zoot suiters were headed for Pasadena," and a police "reception committee was organized to meet them."[98] Another night, two Pasadena boys (the press did not identify them by ethnicity) were chased by a mob of 150 servicemen until they were rescued when they ran into the police station. When asked why they were wearing the hated pants, the boys told the police, "Mister, that's all we got." Somehow the police and press came to the conclusion that the boys were not "zooters," possibly because the authorities were reluctant to admit that "gangsterism" could be homegrown. Chief of Police Anderson sent them home in a police car.[99]

The "zooters" represented much of what white America (and Pasadena) feared. Local press and wire reports described these young men (and women) as different, rebellious, contradictory and, as was often the case, prone to "vicious-

Fig. 22. In this 1942 photo, a group of "zooters" awaits arraignment in a L.A. jail. They had been arrested because they had allegedly crashed a wedding party. *(Photo courtesy of the Herald Examiner Collection, Los Angeles Public Library)*

ness." This was wartime America, and within the midst of patriotic, "law biding real Americans" were "gangs" of "thugs" that needed to be "taught a lesson." These "pachuco thugs" frequented "dark alleys" and "pool halls and beer joints," and when found, "they scurried into hiding." During the riots, they were reported in "carloads" and "truckloads" and in "gangs," but seldom as individuals. They were "hoodlums in raking [sic] clothing" or "gaudily-garbed youths who frequent dark streets and amusement areas."[100] The subordination into "otherness" was not limited to males. "Black-skirted" women were gangland "pachucas," razor-wielding girls who "ran with the pachucos." Officials in Los Angeles likened the riots to a "civil war"; the district attorney said it was "near anarchy."[101] To make matters worse, the wartime enemy was using the uprising for its own propaganda. The newspapers reported that Radio Tokyo broadcast that "American doughboys and sailors" were beating up civilians in Los Angeles.[102]

What was not lost, and in fact what was emphasized, was that the "zooters" were "colored." Yet, even though race was central to the altercations—these were in fact race riots—the recurring theme in public pronouncements from those in charge was that the disturbances were not racially motivated. Race, said government officials and the press, had nothing to do with the eradication of "hoodlumism." This was "gangsterism," editorialized the *Pasadena Star-News,* and it was a mistake to "catalogue them merely by costume or racial origin." Its origin, rather, was a resurgence of Chicago-style mobsters. These were the reborn "Lime-house toughs of London's gas-lit era":

> What makes this late crop of hoodlums especially dangerous is not where they come from or what they wear but their gangsterism. Individual toughs are bad enough but bands of them are intolerable. A mob is a very dangerous thing; more cruel than its component parts.

Though Pasadena was threatened, the point of origin was not Pasadena, but "out there" over the border, in Los Angeles or some other, lesser place frequented by "cholos," "niggers" and "coloreds." If there was blame to be leveled (other than the "zooters," the Los Angeles Police Department got most of it) then the *Star-News* wrote that it was because the city of Los Angeles, where the hoodlums "originated," had not been diligent in finding "where they lived, what their habits were, where they got their cars ..." Like the eradication of a deadly disease, the implication was that if the authorities had gotten to the root of the problem sooner, then they might have "scotched some of this hoodlumism at the source."[103]

However, other less shrill voices were heard during the riots. Carey McWilliams, a Pasadena resident and attorney, who would later move to New York to take over the reins of the *Nation* magazine, deplored the racial violence exploding around him. McWilliams and 150 other Pasadena-area citizens met at the McKinley Junior High School auditorium and drafted a resolution to the board of directors urging them to use its good offices to "eliminate any racial discrimination which may exist here." McWilliams said there was a "tendency to exaggerate [any rise in] delinquency ..." but pointed out that since the start of the war, "statistics show that [any increase in delinquency] has been lower among Mexican youth."[104] Stephen Reyes, the director of the Mexican Settlement House, was on the stage with McWilliams, but there is no record of what he said. A local writer and a member of the Congress of Industrial Organizations (CIO) helped organize the meeting. Although the multiracial rally was focused on racial violence in Pasadena, the *Star-News* minimized the criticisms of the speakers and instead emphasized a theme of "friendly relations with Latin America." Facts, whomever presented them, were of little consequence in a near-hysterical atmosphere. The *Star-News* asked if the "zoot suit psychology" would spread? Due process of law was important, wrote the *Star-News* the following week, but the solution to eliminating these "gangsters" was finding the "causes" of the "zoot-suit psychology" and then "making these boys right-minded again."[105] Many believed that education would be the key to "right mindedness."

Carey McWilliams was not the only voice on the left. George Sanchez, professor of Latin-American education at the University of Texas, was an outspoken critic of society's usual responses to the so-called "Mexican problem." As early as 1932, Sanchez wrote of the "frequent prostitution of democratic ideals to the

cause of expediency, politics, vested interests, ignorance, class and 'race' prejudice." Sanchez always brought his readers' attention to the term "race," because
legally, Mexicans and other Latinos were considered, at least by the census takers,
as "white." His voluminous writing documented the instances in which Mexicans
were excluded in schools, the marketplace, the military, housing and jobs. The
"zoot suits" and the "pachuco question" were, for Sanchez, questions of "race" and
class—and neglect. He saw the "maladjustment" of a generation of young men
and women as an American problem of "oppressive self-righteousness." He
wrote, "The so called 'Mexican Problem' is not in fact a Mexican problem. It is a
problem foisted by American mercenary interests upon the American people. It
is an American problem made in the USA."[106]

By the war's end, Pasadena suffered from a near-siege mentality. For many
in America, the tensions generated by the decade of Depression, with its rise of
Fascism and Communism followed by a world war that ended with the atomic
bomb, tended to exacerbate already prevalent feelings of vulnerability. A special
postwar census had been conducted in 1946 and it verified what many in Pasadena suspected—the "others" had significantly increased their numbers.

THE GOSLIN BEGINNING

This was the Pasadena Goslin found when he arrived from Minneapolis to start
the school year in the fall of 1948. That first year passed without any noticeable
rancor. The only blip on the horizon had been the formation of a conservative
group—ostensibly a parents' organization—that called itself the School
Development Council. Goslin spent the 1948–49 school year doing what school
administrators typically do to get to know a new system. He visited with every
conceivable club and organization in his community, except the School
Development Council, which few knew existed. He considered his role as the
educational leader a community responsibility, and what better way to get to
know the community than to meet the interested (and not so interested) groups
in the city. As part of his effort, he set out on what he called the "knife and fork
circuit," meeting (and dining) with the Chamber of Commerce, and most of the
civic and businessmen's organizations.[107]

Goslin also met with every school PTA that first year. He considered those
meetings vital to his educational program, because at the intersection of school
and community, he could be reasonably assured that his message about progressive, modern education would be heard. That fall he met LuVerne LaMotte, the
PTA president at Burbank School, a small elementary school located near the
border of Altadena and east Pasadena in a well-to-do, all-white neighborhood.
LaMotte was the wife of Donald LaMotte, the manager of the Pasadena Sears and
Roebuck store. Both were moderate Republicans interested in civic affairs. Mrs.

LaMotte noted that Goslin was a "dynamic speaker" and that his talk about a mountain camp for Pasadena youth was well received by the Burbank elementary school mothers. Later, after the explosion over Goslin's supposed Communist-inspired "REDucation," LaMotte became increasingly active on the moderate side of school district affairs, honing her political skills through various offices until she was elected to the board of education in the late 1950s.[108]

Later that year, Goslin visited with the PTA at San Rafael School, a button-sized elementary school just across the Arroyo Seco on the far southwestern edge of Pasadena. A few of the mothers put on a luncheon for the new superintendent at the swank Allendale Country Club. San Rafael School once had served the children of a nearby orphanage, but now its children came from one of the toniest neighborhoods in the city. Goslin told his San Rafael audience that he was excited about the upcoming summer workshop. He had invited his good friend, none other than John Dewey's most famous student, William Heard Kilpatrick, to open the five-week summer session. The theme of the workshop would be "We Learn What We Live," a quintessentially progressive theme, one that defined Kilpatrick's lifetime of educational work.[109] In the audience that day were Louise Hawkes Padelford and her friend Cay Halberg. Padelford was the daughter of Albert Hawkes, past president of the U.S. Chamber of Commerce and former archconservative U.S. senator from New Jersey, and she shared her father's sympathies. The senator's daughter was married to Morgan Padelford, a technical advisor at Hollywood's Technicolor Studio. Louise and her friend did not like what they heard that day. Padelford remembered lying awake at night thinking about the new superintendent and his "progressive" ideas. The School Development Council was about to get two new members.[110]

Goslin's summer workshop plan was not a new idea in school circles but was new to Pasadena. Goslin drew its inspiration from the recommendations of the Eight Year Study, a national research project that during the 1930s matched college success rates from progressive secondary school students with a control group from traditional schools. What interested Goslin and many of his fellow school superintendents was the recommendation that a period during the summer be set aside for teachers to meet with experts, hold formal and informal discussion groups, and generally come together in ways that were impossible during the hectic school year. Goslin, according to the journalist David Hulburd, had not become enamored of Pasadena's teachers. "Frictions," said Hulburd, "were at an all-time high ..." Cliques had formed under Sexson and various department heads were not speaking to subordinates. A number of older administrators were planning on retiring and a third of the teachers were new and in need of evaluation. Later, Goslin's assistant, Mary Beauchamp, added that for a system with a reputation for excellence, Pasadena's classrooms were exceptionally average. The Summer Workshop would be a new start, and with William Heard Kilpatrick

Fig. 23. Willard Goslin, at his desk, in this undated school district photograph. His schools were accused of many transgressions including teaching sex education, which one anti-Goslin foe said "would lead to free love and free love leads to communism." *(Photo courtesy Pasadena Unified School District)*

as its leader, Goslin and Beauchamp were confident it would mark an auspicious beginning for postwar Pasadena. [111] Less than a year later, Goslin would sacrifice Beauchamp in an attempt to keep his administration from collapsing under the School Development Council's assault, led by Louise Padelford and her friends.[112]

Goslin had brought Beauchamp from Minneapolis because he believed she was perfectly suited to the task of helping reconstruct Pasadena's schools. The system was in dire need of an overhaul. The buildings were in poor repair, and the elementary schools were severely overcrowded. Many were on half-day schedules. The enrollment projections were for the elementary school population to double by 1955, a mind-boggling proposition since the city had not constructed a new elementary school since the 1933 earthquake. During his first year, Goslin oversaw the completion of two new junior high schools that were in progress when he arrived, but those buildings would barely ease the overcrowding at the upper end of the 6-4-4 grouping. The Pasadena school system had, over the years, come to serve many of the students from surrounding Temple City and La Canada, two all-white towns with contiguous borders to Pasadena.[113] The two new junior high schools were in Temple City and La Canada. Before the La Canada school was built, in what we now call "reverse busing," eastside children were bused to Eliot Junior High School in Altadena along a route that took them past the increasingly minority Washington Junior High School.[114] Goslin put Beauchamp in charge of coming up with a plan, including new bus routes that would maximize the use of all the junior high schools once the new buildings were ready. Beauchamp began to examine where Pasadena's students lived and where they went to school. Goslin then turned his attention to more pressing needs, namely finding the money to build new elementary schools.

When Goslin arrived, he and the board did not haggle much over the political costs associated with raising bond money to build new schools. During the summer of 1948, the superintendent and the board decided that at least three new elementary schools were needed and to pay for them they authorized a $5 million bond election for that October. The bonds passed in a four-to-one landslide. The voters—at least 80 percent of them—understood the system's needs, as did the chamber, the Pasadena Realty Board, and the Shakespeare Club, all of which endorsed the election.[115]

All a successful bond election authorizes is an increase in general indebtedness, not an increase in property taxes. Goslin and the board agreed they could not keep going back to the voters every time the budget ran short. The costs of public education in Pasadena and its surrounding towns had risen a staggering 111 percent since 1940, and the meager income from the local tax base was simply insufficient to meet the needs of a growing system. The solution would be to raise local property taxes. Each municipality in California set its own rate of taxation, called the tax levy, and in Pasadena the levy had been last set in 1937 during the Depression. Then came the war years in which public education everywhere took a back seat when it came to public funds. As Goslin and the board prepared the 1950–51 budget, the superintendent proposed that the next time the schools went to the electorate, it would be to change the property tax levy from the prewar level of 90 cents per $100 of assessed value to $1.35, a 50-percent increase. He told the community that there "isn't any way for this town to talk its way out of the situation or to dodge it. We either raise the limit of the tax rate or we educate the children less well." Over the years, some have questioned the wisdom of such a large increase, coming as it did on the heels of the war, but Goslin and the board knew the system would be in dire straits without sufficient funds. If there was a debate over the amount of the tax request, it was behind closed doors. Publicly, the superintendent and his board were one. In April 1950, the board authorized a tax election for June 2, two months hence.[116] Goslin would be dismissed by November.

THE SCHOOL DEVELOPMENT COUNCIL AND "REDUCATION!"

Initially, the School Development Council (SDC) was neither a council nor much involved with school development. It was a politically naive, unorganized grassroots group of dissatisfied customers—parents who came together to complain about the schools for all sorts of reasons. Membership waxed and waned throughout 1948 and 1949. There was little cohesion and not much in the way of a proactive agenda. Interestingly, its first two presidents were both men without school-aged children. What the SDC tapped during the 1949–50 school year was a highly organized ideological leadership and Pasadena's long-festering fears about "the other."

The SDC agenda changed significantly when Louise Padelford, Cay Halberg and other conservative women joined the organization sometime in 1949. Padelford was the inspirational force behind the newly energized council but never assumed the public reigns of elected leadership. That was left to Frank Wells, a local businessman with two children in the school system. Wells's greatest strength appears to have been his ability as a public speaker. On the other hand, Padelford was a dynamo, a relentless, nonstop workaholic with ties to conservative political organizations around the country. She had worked on her father's senatorial campaign, traveled with him on his numerous speaking engagements as president of the national Chamber, and made friends (and a few enemies) as she rubbed elbows with reactionary and political conservatives from Wendell Wilkie to the populist anti-Semites; the Reverend Gerald L.K. Smith, the Glendale preacher of hate; and Father Charles E. Coughlin, the "radio priest." Both men were vehement anti-Communists, who used their influence to bash "minority-ism" in the United States. She was the immediate past president of ProAmerica, the national, Republican woman's organization, and the founder of its Pasadena chapter. This was no vain, self-effacing political maverick. Padelford (her friends and family called her Lou Lou) was a graduate of Vassar with a master's degree in sociology and a Ph.D. in romance languages from Columbia. She had traveled the world many times, studied at the Sorbonne and had been a member of the founding faculty at Scripps College for Women in Claremont, California. She thrived in her causes, and, in rare moments when there were none, she languished without focus.[117]

Like mythic Atlas, Louise Padelford carried the weight of the world on her shoulders. She would rise at 3 a.m., unable to sleep, to compose letters (with carbons) to "Daddy and Mum," then wake the children, take them to school, go to various club and committee meetings, back home to meet the children, then off to meetings in the evening or the theater and a dinner party. Her calendar was never empty. She had her fingers in everything, forever it seems, complaining that she could not keep it all under control but unable to let go. Her politics, like her beloved "Daddy," were reactionary. In the early 1950s at the height of Senator McCarthy's witch-hunts, she was the darling of conservative causes, having either correspondence with or membership in dozens of reactionary organizations in the country, including a number of openly anti-Semitic and racist groups. Later, during an interview sometime in the early 1950s, while she was still a resident of Pasadena, she refused to concede that race had anything to do with Goslin's ouster. Goslin and his friends were simply the embodiment of everything she despised. Her friend Cay Halberg agreed, "We were such a small, loose group of parents" upset with the schools. "Desegregation was no part of our argument, nor any part of our interest, our dispute or our purpose." Halberg thought they were Goldwater Republicans before Barry Goldwater. When the national press had a field day criticizing Goslin's forced resignation, Padelford and Halberg were shocked, confused and angry. Neither could understand all the fuss. The enemy was in Pasadena but it was not Louise Padelford and her friends, it was progressive education, Willard Goslin and his friends.[118]

Fifty years later, just who was "The Enemy," to use a Carey McWilliams' line, still remains clouded by innuendo, half-truths and gossip. Conservatives saw the coming "school fight," as Padelford called it, a test of resolve. Could they defend American democracy from an enemy out to undermine its values of liberty, individuality and the pursuit of free enterprise? In 1950, a conservative's definition of democracy was radically different from how a progressive like Goslin or Kilpatrick would define the idea. Padelford's democracy was the outgrowth of a competitive system of free enterprise. Individual success would come "according to a man's own ability and self-reliance." Padelford and her friends were convinced postwar America was under attack by those who wanted to "collectivize" the country.[119]

Goslin and his friends would have agreed that the country was threatened but not by the same enemy. Goslin was no radical social reconstructionist. Rather, he was a liberal progressive whose school philosophy had never been openly challenged, at least not to the extent that Padelford and her friends were about to challenge it. Although race was seldom explicit in his public discourse, Goslin's progressivism was firmly rooted in equity. For Kilpatrick and Beauchamp, however, race was far more explicit. All three were active in "Human Relations" workshops, a term used in the 1940s and 1950s to describe a progressive educator's understanding of how to achieve "better racial relations." But for Kilpatrick and Beauchamp, the workshops were a significant public aspect of their educational beliefs. Goslin saw improved race (and social class) relations as one more reason progressive education was democratic education. Goslin and Kilpatrick were Deweyan pragmatists—they meant for public education to encourage children, individually and in groups, to explore their world and take risks, although for most progressives, the risks were seldom risky. Nonetheless, in

1950, Goslin's progressivism prevented him from ignoring racial exclusion in Pasadena. Although he never put integration (or desegregation) at the cutting edge of his school politics, equity was embedded in how he understood his role as the community's educational leader.

For Padelford and her friends, the progressive's love affair with educating "the whole child" was little more than a precursor to collectivizing and little more than an attempt by the school "to subvert the social order by taking possession of the child." To Goslin and the others, educating the "whole child" through group work that explored intercultural values and human relations was a core worth fighting for. With conservative ideologues like Padelford on one side and committed progressives like Goslin, Beauchamp and Kilpatrick on the other, the stage was set for an epic battle over how community in Pasadena would be defined. Although the language is different, that battle remains as central to today's definition of democracy in Pasadena—and elsewhere—as it was during Goslin's era.[120]

With Frank Wells as its president and Padelford and friends increasingly active, early in 1950, the SDC leadership decided to invite board president Milton Wopschall and newly elected board member Lawrence Lamb, a local mortician, to lunch in an effort, said Wells, to "reach out a hand in friendship."[121] This was well before Goslin and the board had confirmed the necessity of the tax election, and well before the SDC had any significant local press. Goslin was now aware of the SDC, as he had attended its December 1949 meeting—the first and only meeting he would attend—and had subsequently squared off with Padelford over federal aid to schools, an idea that horrified Padelford but intrigued Goslin. Then, just after the lunch meeting, at the regularly scheduled February board meeting Goslin dropped the rezoning bombshell—there would be no more neutral zones and no more transfers.[122]

During the board meeting, Wopschall peppered Goslin with questions he had received from, as he put it, "parents and patrons of the schools." The board president demanded answers about grading, competition, patriotism and core curriculum as well as rezoning. The questions paralleled Kilpatrick's themes that were discussed during the summer workshop, except that Kilpatrick never specifically mentioned rezoning, though the professor from Colombia did emphasize "human relations." Wopschall's queries were the first early hints that the SDC had sufficiently mobilized its opposition to have caught the ear of the board president. Moreover, Wopschall's interest in rezoning was a clear indication that Goslin's views on race and segregation would be opposed.

Goslin answered all of Wopschall's questions. The superintendent said "yes" about grading, "Grades were being recorded at the junior high school." Concerning competition, Goslin told Wopschall that too much competition was unhealthy. Although the teachers encouraged student competition, it was "competition with themselves" rather than with each other that was emphasized.

When the last question came, Goslin told Wopschall that rezoning was necessary because the permit system and neutral zones were burdensome and unfair. "New schools," Goslin told the board in reference to the new junior highs, "necessitate new boundaries." It was his intention "to move steadily toward the elimination of neutral zones." He said the transfer situation had "gotten out of control." It had become "a hot potato, and if you don't think so, just try holding it." In the year before Goslin arrived, there were nearly 300 transfer applications, but his staff had managed to whittle that number down to less than 200. He went on to tell the sparsely attended meeting that it was his intention to thoroughly investigate the demographics of transfers. His staff had already begun to plot where children lived and where they attended school. He concluded by telling his audience that he would have "a new set of boundaries" for the board within two months.[123]

The last speaker that evening was Louise Padelford, speaking on behalf of ProAmerica. Padelford asked Goslin who was responsible for bringing Theodore Brameld, another noted progressive educator from Ohio State University, to Pasadena to speak about "better human relations." Goslin told her that the district PTA had invited Brameld to Pasadena, and the Los Angeles County Office of Education was covering the costs. Goslin then surprised Padelford when he asked her if she saw no reason to improve human relations in Pasadena. The question made her uneasy and she responded angrily. Later, she said Goslin twisted her question, but, she said, his gamesmanship "was such a typical technique of left-wingers." She said she did feel that human relations should improve, but not "through the efforts of someone who does not believe in what our community stands for ..." not someone like Brameld who was an "avowed believer in collectivizing our society." There must be, she said, "good Christians who are able to meet with our parents and our teachers and give them some suggestions ..." Her use of "good Christians" may have been in reference to Brameld being Jewish. She then returned Goslin's question with her own and asked, "When you say human relations, you really mean racial relations in this community, don't you?" Goslin told her his definition was "far greater than racial relations."[124]

That was the only mention of race Goslin made that night. He did not mention race, or for that matter, parental concern when he spoke to the board about rezoning. Furthermore, he made no mention of maintaining Pasadena's traditional definition of community schools. Goslin's answers to Wopschall's questions about classrooms—core curriculum, grading, patriotism and competition—cannot be considered significant enough to cause the fight that was about to occur. The bombshell that ignited Pasadena was his statements on the redistribution of children regardless of "tradition." In effect, Goslin's new boundaries would begin to desegregate the system. Before that moment in February 1950, Goslin's opposition had been weak, unorganized and seemingly disinterested in mounting any kind of campaign to discredit the superintendent and progressive education.

Almost overnight, the SDC and other groups intensified their efforts. Later, Padelford would say the February board meeting was the beginning "of my interest and activity in the school fight." But rather than concentrate on rezoning and segregation, Padelford and the rest of the SDC leadership focused on the soon-to-be-announced special June tax election. As it turned out, they seized upon the perfect tool, for embedded deep within the community's collective pockets was the fear that with more money Goslin's schools would alter the traditions of Paradise.[125]

SMOKESCREENS AND RAT PACKS

During the late winter and early spring of 1950, the SDC became the progenitor of an inflammatory broadside against the tax increase and public education, accusing schools of using tax dollars to practice treasonable activities, from doing away with the "3 Rs" to usurping parental authority and teaching sex education, an activity, remarked Dr. Ernest Brower, an SDC member, "that leads to free love and free love leads to communism."[126] Goslin's opposition used the board of education meetings, their own public council meetings, pamphlets, telegrams, the radio and, most importantly, the two city newspapers, the *Star-News* and especially *The Independent*, to launch and carry the attack.

The anti-Goslin/antiprogressive education coalition, with the SDC at the ideological controls, exploited the postwar insecurities of Pasadena. Through its judicious and well-funded use of media—they sent 10,000 telegrams the day before the election, but especially its use of the newspapers and radio—the SDC furthered an already paranoid atmosphere. Goslin's opposition in a little more than three months galvanized the city and the surrounding towns in a way that was unheard of before or since. The campaign, in an effort to rid the community of the subversive educationists, made it so difficult to discern what the real issues were, most Pasadenans were convinced there was some truth to the charges that the schools were going to hell in a handbasket. Goslin and his administration, the teachers and many of the parents were blindsided by the barrage of near-slanderous material spewed by the SDC and its affiliates. Lost in the strident "Progressive Education is REDucation!" witch-hunt was any hope for rational community dialogue over schools and desegregation.

During the spring of 1950, the city was subjected to an intense campaign of rumor, innuendo and fear. Not coincidentally, at the same time the SDC was attacking Goslin at meetings throughout the city, *The Independent* began a series on Pasadena's schools.[127] The antiprogressive education rhetoric heated up noticeably as *The Independent*, ostensibly neutral, according to the former publisher, began a series of "eye-witness" reports on Pasadena schools under the banner "What Are Our Schools Teaching?"[128] Publisher Fred Runyon had taken his cue from *The Los Angeles Herald Express,* which had run a similar series in January under the banner, "What's Wrong with Our Schools?" Carey McWilliams would later belittle Runyon's paper as a "former shopping guide." From early March until just before the election, *The Independent* featured articles with bold titles such as "College Professor Says Schools Deplorable," "Films Help Second Graders at Allendale; Wandering Permitted, Forced Learning Out."[129] In an attempt to rebut *The Independent* (and, no doubt, to sell its newspapers), Goslin was asked by the rival *Star-News* to write a short series on "Modern Education, Explained." Robert Gilchrist, Goslin's assistant superintendent, and his staff wrote the articles. They wrote, "Modern education sees a wider role than drilling the three Rs for themselves alone ... isolated exercises in memory work will not teach the Pasadena child to think for himself." It was a familiar child-centered theme from the 1930s.[130] Whether "Progressive Education" or "Modern Education," the labels did not matter to conservative parents fearful that these "new" methods were little more than "fads" and would ultimately leave their children behind. Now, *The Independent* was telling parents that the schools were relying on movies and play and the administration had all but rejected drill and memorization.[131]

The day before the election, when the campaign had reached an emotional crescendo, *The Independent* had as its front-page headline: "Forecast Record School Vote on Tax Hike Today." Directly below the headline, filling nearly a third of the page, was a photograph of a young man behind bars, sitting on a stool, doing what appears to be schoolwork. The caption read: "Progressive Education?" It turns out that the photograph was of an ex-GI, who was in jail because he had four parking tickets at overcrowded Pasadena Junior College.[132] One suspects the scene was staged. At an SDC rally at Madison School, the week before, Frank Wells charged that Goslin's progressive education led to juvenile delinquency. The SDC text was drawn nearly verbatim from Allen Zoll's infamous red-baiting National Council for American Education (NCAE) tract, "Progressive Education Increases Delinquency."[133] Zoll was a hate-monger who, like Father Coughlin and others, sprinkled anti-Semitic references throughout his pamphlets. Zoll's tracts, which he always opened with the attribution, "By Allen A. Zoll, Ph.D. Internationally Known Sales Consultant," were little more than character assassinations, carefully constructed to look like "objective" analyses.[134] Although the SDC disavowed any formal relationship with Zoll's organization, Wells more than once read from NCAE literature. At the Madison School rally, Zoll's pamphlets were distributed to the audience.[135]

Goslin smelled a smokescreen. He told the community at the board meeting before the tax election that there were always a few people opposed to public education. There were, he said, "a few in Pasadena" but, in his opinion, not too many. However—and here his voice rose—when an attack on the tax levy drifts off so that "attempts are made to split, weaken, and divide the board of education," when efforts are made to discredit and destroy the confidence of his staff and "come dangerously close to accusing the teachers of this community of being subversive," then the opposition has gone too far. These attacks, he said, "are nothing more than a smokescreen." He told the standing-room-only audience that the assault on the school programs under the guise of "socialism," and "collectivism," was an attack on a philosophy of education that "this community has supported for a long period of time."[136] Supporters of the superintendent were puzzled and angry. Pasadena's classrooms had not changed much since Goslin arrived, so why were the schools now being singled out for attack?

Behind the "Progressive Education is REDucation!" smokescreen was a deep fear of social change, and the harsh attacks on the schools and Goslin tended to frighten and confuse many in the community. Rumors—many bizarre with no connection to any evidence—took on a life of their own. A proposed new health and guidance curriculum was a devious plan to indoctrinate the children to be mindless "commies." Goslin's talks about camping got turned into stories about "stealing children," a progressive education version of Nazi Germany's Youth Corps. There was a persistent rumor that an elementary school arithmetic text compared doctor's fees under free and nationalized medicine even though no such text existed. Wopschall had to intervene in a argument that had broken out at a board meeting between two speakers, one perplexed by the hysteria, the other ridiculing the schools for "communistic connections."[137] And through it all the SDC pushed at the system. Once the tax election was announced, the council wanted the schools to provide information on all educational expenditures. Goslin and Wopschall had no choice; begrudgingly they diverted staff time to gather the requested data.[138]

The tensions only increased when in mid-April, as promised, Goslin came to the board meeting with his rezoning plans. For the first time, the board had to move the meeting across the street to the junior high school auditorium because 500 people showed up, many angry that the administration was going to end their "freedom of choice," as one parent put it. Ironically, it was "Public Schools Week," and Lawrence Lamb read a proclamation urging the public to support its schools, "because they are worth the costs." Speaker after speaker filed to the microphone to express opposition to the rezoning plan. Most said their property would be devalued, implying that it would be caused by African-American and Mexican-American children attending school at Linda Vista or Arroyo Seco Elementary or by white children attending nearby multiracial Washington Junior High instead of being bused to all-white McKinley Junior High, which was farther away. When Dr. A.R. Traylor, president of the Pasadena NAACP, asked for someone to please clarify how property values would decline because of the presence of black children, no one rose to answer. John Holmes, president of the

East Arroyo Homeowners' Association, argued that their children should be included in the Linda Vista attendance area, thereby ensuring that they would continue to go to school with all white classmates. Later, Holmes admitted that the opposition to rezoning was about race and entitlement. A few years after Goslin's departure, Holmes' group would reappear before a different Pasadena board of education, arguing that the East Arroyo neighborhood should be allowed to leave the system and join La Canada's newly formed—and all-white—school district.[139]

When it was finally Goslin's turn to speak, he was hardly less than straight-forward. After reviewing the criteria for setting new boundaries, he said, "The Administration has no interest in who lives on which side of the boundaries ... but we are interested in putting the right number of children into the proper facilities, and that [we] proceed on that basis alone." Supporting the administration's rezoning plans was a long list of progressive groups including the Human Relations Workshop, the Pasadena Area Council of Churches, the NAACP and Arthur Hutchins of the Central Labor Council. According to a *Los Angeles Times* reporter (who was not sympathetic with the Goslin side), many in the audience supported the rezoning plan, and they greeted the East Arroyo opposition with catcalls and boos. *The Los Angeles Times* reporter said the number of prepared and memorized speeches supporting the plan "stunned" the opposition. The SDC saw this as one more example of a left-wing plot to "distort everything to cause confusion and unhappiness." Supposedly, Beauchamp had organized the redistricting "demonstration." Board secretary Courtney Monsen told the *Times* reporter that the liberals had created a tempest in a teapot. Only a few junior high school children would be affected. Nevertheless, the East Arroyo faction openly fought the proposed boundary changes because, as one resident said, "the elementary schools are next."[140]

The board set the start date for the new boundaries on July 1, 1950, but allowed those already enrolled in out-of-area junior high schools to remain until graduation. The board minutes read, "Under no circumstances was the new territory created by the new boundaries to be considered a neutral zone." *The Daily People's World,* the Los Angeles-based communist newspaper, applauded the decision with the headline, "Pasadena Schools Give Jim-Crow the Heave Ho." Thirteen years after Goslin's dismissal, the California Supreme Court, in *Jackson v. Pasadena City School District,* would find that the city, over many years before and after the vote, had gerrymandered school boundaries to keep black students isolated from white students. The court ruled that the school board was "not innocent" but rather had consciously created boundaries that "were [not] fixed on a nonracial basis.[141]

Race fears in Pasadena were not confined to Goslin's rezoning plans. *The Independent* ran a series of articles during the spring on the dreaded "Rat Pack."

In April and May, the newspaper began to report unrelated crimes that occurred in different parts of greater Los Angeles as the work of "gangs of thugs," and "hoodlum gangs [that] have swept over Southern California lately." The "gangs," which more often than not consisted of no more than two young men, were reported as "swarthy, Mexican gangs," and their acts described as "terrorism."[142] A week and a half before the June tax election, now considered by all to have developed into a referendum on progressive education, subversion, and Willard Goslin's future, *The Independent* ran an article on the front page under the title "Rat Pack Beatings Reds' Work." The article quoted Los Angeles city councilman Ed Davenport, who said that the Los Angeles Police Department was engaged in "neighborhood sweeps and curfew arrests," in the black and Latino areas of the city. Davenport's comments came during a council meeting where hundreds had protested the police sweeps and the curfews. *The Independent* referred to the mainly black and Latino protesters as "Red sympathizers."[143]

On the heels of the "zoot suit" paranoia, uncontrollable forces outside their neighborhoods seemingly were threatening Pasadenans, forces described by *The Independent* as evil and violent. Just days before the tax election, the reported assaults were not random but were under the direction of the feared "Reds" and coming out of neighborhoods similar to those Goslin was planning to open. This not-so-subtle threat, juxtaposed with the oft-repeated rumors that the schools were now openly teaching socialism and communism, was more than enough.[144] The proposed tax increase was crushed nearly two to one. More voters turned out in this school election than at any time in the history of the system. Of the 71 precincts, 70 voted no. The only precinct in the system voting in favor of the increase represented the northwest. The African-American and Mexican-American voters turned out in huge numbers and resoundingly approved of the increase, apparently not taken with a campaign of misspent tax dollars, rat packs, mountain camps or "REDucation!"[145]

THE END OF GOSLIN

One precinct does not make an election. Goslin and the board were confronted with a budget that would need slashing and a conservative coalition that was growing bolder by the day. A month after the election, the SDC pressed its agenda, demanding that all Pasadena teachers, administrators and "outside consultants" be subjected to a loyalty oath written by the council that included a teacher oath never to deviate "from the textbook." The SDC also called for "an ideological investigation of curriculum, methods, and personnel ..." The council wanted the investigation to be conducted by "patriotic organizations such as the American Legion or the Sons of the American Revolution."[146]

The SDC's call for an ideological investigation and loyalty oath was contained in a five-page, single-spaced "petition" signed by the nine-member executive committee. Much of the petition was devoted to what Wopschall called "vague generalities" about the content of the curriculum and teaching practices. Padelford probably wrote the letter. There are repeated references to her favorite themes: "The Columbian Cult," meaning John Dewey and Kilpatrick from Teachers College, and attacks on the "politico-social aims of the present school administration," including suggestions that certain books be censored because of the fear of "insinuation." The SDC wanted its "ideological investigators" to determine what it meant when a senior high school social studies teachers' guide stated that one of the lesson objectives was "understanding why democracy often failed in the past." Padelford and the others were apprehensive that somehow this book contained "insinuations" which were part of a larger subversive plot "to 'sell' the children on the collapse of our way of life and the substitution of collectivism." Padelford and the executive committee saw conspiracy everywhere. There were plots to overthrow the "American way," and they were being fomented in places like New York and Columbia's Teachers College by professors like Kilpatrick and school administrators like Goslin.[147]

Wopschall and the board answered Padelford and the SDC, but it was too late. There was little reason to believe that the community would be able to engage in a rational dialogue about schooling. Wopschall defended the schools and the administration and challenged the SDC to bring specific charges rather than "vague generalities." Padelford and the SDC then charged that the schools were using communist propaganda because an "Intercultural Relations" pamphlet had recommended Langston Hughes as outside reading. Padelford then cited a Hughes' poem, "Goodbye Christ" with the lines:

> Goodbye
> Christ jesus, Lord God Jehova,
> Beat it on away from here.
> Make Way for a new guy with no religion at all—
> A real guy named
>   Marx Communist Lenin Peasant Stalin
> Worker Ye

Wopschall said he would look into the matter.[148]

Race, after all, ended Mary Beauchamp's stay in Pasadena. Earlier in the spring, as the SDC attacks intensified, Goslin asked Beauchamp to come to his office. He was sympathetic, he said, but her presence had become too controversial. She reluctantly agreed. Beauchamp, who Goslin respected and admired, was never one to back down from a fight but was depressed and exhausted. The superintendent then announced that she was resigning and heading off to New York University to complete her doctorate. Many had criticized her open advocacy of a more multiracial community, especially her work on the rezoning controversy. Others, including some of Goslin's friends, criticized her blunt tone and agreed she should leave because she had become a lightning rod around which Goslin's opponents could concentrate the attack.[149]

Padelford blamed Beauchamp for the "new emphasis" on race in Pasadena. She later said, "None of us were very much aware of a racial problem until Mr. Goslin arrived bringing with him a very charming lady ..." She "speeded up the human relations program" because, according to Padelford, she openly shared a room with a woman who was "half Negro but did not look it." The woman, Diane Gray, later married "a Negro communist organizer." That organizer turned out to be Don Wheeldon, a reporter for the *Daily People's World (DPW)*, the communist newspaper. Wheeldon, from Hartford, Connecticut, covered the Pasadena school fight for the *DPW*. Later, in the early 1960s, Wheeldon, his good friend Elbie Hickambottom and their wives would be the first African Americans to "bust" the segregated Civic Auditorium dances.[150]

What bothered Padelford was that Mary Beauchamp and Diane Gray were having "mixed parties." Beauchamp's friendship with Gray and Gray's subsequent marriage to Wheeldon convinced Padelford that Beauchamp "had more than a personal eagerness to speed up this whole thing than what was really good for our community ..." Padelford, though, appreciated Beauchamp's openness because "if she hadn't pushed so hard perhaps we wouldn't have realized ... what Goslin was tied in with, what he was trying to accomplish." Padelford's friend, conservative author and Pasadena resident Mary Allen, accused Goslin and Beauchamp of "racial agitation," "over emphasizing inequalities" and promoting "class divisions" that were nonexistent before the two arrived from Minneapolis. Beauchamp was Goslin's agent. She began "propagandizing in the Human Relations Workshop" for an end to the neutral zones. It was Beauchamp, said Allen, who "organized and led the forces which agitated a small rezoning problem into a racial demonstration." Allen also said "there was wealth in Pasadena but no poverty," and those who supported the neutral zones did so not because of any racial discrimination but because "they were protecting the interests of their own children."[151]

Padelford may have denied that race was at the center of the school fight, but her comments about rezoning tell us quite differently. At about this time, she told an interviewer, "We have a very good Negro population [here in Pasadena]. They have very good schools, two good schools in their—what used to be their—zoned district." The fight, she said, came because "they wished to rezone so that a group of white children who had always been permitted to go across the Arroyo to the school on the other side would be sent into this Lincoln School where it was 95 percent colored ..." She revealed what many white middle-class and wealthier

East Arroyo residents feared—the removal of their most-favored status in the community. The privilege and entitlement that had been purchased through decades of political bartering had brought to the Arroyo—and all of prestigious Pasadena—institutionalized access to the material and social capital of the community. Padelford and her friends were not going to give up that entitlement without a fight. Progressive education was the enemy because, to Padelford and the others, it challenged long-established assumptions about power and privilege in Pasadena.152

Although Goslin tried to carry on with business as usual, in November, while he was in New York, the board sent him a telegram asking for his resignation, and, feeling he no longer had the necessary support, he agreed.153 By November and probably sooner, most of the board had given up on the superintendent. Only the former teacher, Gladys Rinehart, remained a loyal supporter. With Goslin's resignation, the city was in a state of shock. What *had* happened in Pasadena? After less than a few months, one of the country's most respected and admired school systems was in shambles. The city was now being described around the country as either a seedbed of communist conspiracy or the home of postwar fascism. The final straw came when the California Senate Committee on Un-American Activities arrived in October to "investigate." They had come at the request of Assemblyman Bruce Reagan who was one of Padelford's neighbors. The committee, on which the House Committee on Un-American Activities (HUAC) was modeled, put on a McCarthy-like show in the city hall. Media, including newspapers from around the country and television cameras from Los Angeles, covered the affair. The SDC leadership was prominently on display, but Padelford, in keeping with past practice, did not appear. Witnesses, including Goslin, were called. The superintendent told the senators, "Pasadena is on the threshold of one of the healthiest periods in the history of its educational system." Other testimony was taken, and the half-truths and innuendo continued unabated. This was national publicity the city fathers would not tolerate. Wopschall, Lawrence Lamb and the others—except Gladys Rinehart—voted to ask for the superintendent's resignation in the name of "harmony."154

Goslin departed for George Peabody College in Nashville, the same school Sidney Hall had come from when he came to Virginia's Department of Education in 1930. Goslin served on the faculty of the Department of School Administration until his retirement in 1965. He died in 1969. He was brought to Peabody by president Harry Hill, specifically because of his views on race. Hill knew that a Supreme Court decision on racial segregation eventually would change the South and he wanted a Southern man with liberal views about schooling and desegregation. After Goslin left Pasadena, he did not speak or write much about the school situation, although he did speak about the growing attacks on public schools. His professional papers are kept at Vanderbilt University and con-

Fig. 24. The Pasadena Board of Education in 1950. Gladys Rinehart, the lone Goslin holdout, is at the left, next to Vernon Brydolf. Carl Wopschall, the board president is center, with Lawrence Lamb to the right. At far right, wearing the stunning chapeaux, is Harriet Sterling. Standing behind the group is their secretary, Courtney Monsen. *(Photo courtesy Pasadena Unified School District)*

tain much of what he wrote before he came to Pasadena and much of what he wrote after he left, but nothing remains about Pasadena.[155]

Not long after Goslin left for Peabody, Louise Padelford moved to Claremont, California, where she and Morgan had first met in the 1930s. Her letters and diary indicate her relationship with her father was always tense. Albert Hawkes was generous but an extremely controlling man. One Christmas morning in her Claremont home, there was a tremendous fight between them and their relationship was strained to the breaking point. Louise could never seem to live up to her father's expectations. Hawkes had once told her that only two people in his life had never disappointed him, his mother and Louise. She and Morgan divorced not too long after her father died. Louise, who traveled around the world 15 times, became, in her later years, a devotee of Buddhism and transcendental meditation. She was a frequent visitor to Japan. For someone so rigid in her views of the world as a younger woman, she came to the end of her life believing in reincarnation, mysticism and Eastern religion. She died in 1974.[156]

Looking back, the Pasadena school controversy was the first of what would be many postwar assaults on public education around the country. The attacks on Pasadena's schools by a small, strident and well-organized group was an ideological assault that no one saw coming, least of all Willard Goslin. The superintendent was not politically naive—he was blindsided. Goslin understood there was opposition to his philosophy of education, but no one was prepared for the anger that exploded in 1950. What he and his friends learned, to their own sorrow, was that in the future there would be more small groups with shrill voices using language that touched on deep fears and unresolved dilemmas. The Pasadena controversy stirred a national debate. School people urged the country to begin preparation for another war, a different conflict where public schools would be the prize. Liberals cautioned that "The Enemy" was going to come after unsuspecting communities. In Scarsdale, New York, the school board deflected criticism from a small, SDC-like group, when they refused to allow the board meetings to erupt into attacks on books and teachers. They may have learned how to counterpunch from what happened in Pasadena.[157]

Yet the center of American society remained convinced something was terribly wrong with the country. Conservative scholars, bolstered by persistent questions about the ability of schools to combat the threat of world communism, said "modern education" had become infected by an "anti-intellectualism" that was undermining America's preeminent position in the world. What was needed was a return to the "common values" of the past. America should once again put stock in the subjects most easily recognized as "Western civilization." But Western civilization had always been at the core of Pasadena's school curriculum long before Goslin arrived, and there is little evidence that Pasadena schools changed its pedagogy much after he left. His immediate successor, Frank Walkup, a longtime Pasadena school administrator, reinitiated summer workshops, because he thought them a good idea. Only this time there were no Kilpatrick or Brameld to stir the waters.[158]

The attacks on Pasadena's schools also reflect an anxious nation, suspicious of how the world was changing. It was not coincidental that along with unchecked rumors about summer camps and math texts, Pasadenans—and the rest of the country—were fearful of "invasions" from outer space, mysterious "disappearances" of children and the Armageddon of atomic holocaust. Was no one safe? Even art was under attack. *Life Magazine* claimed Jackson Pollack's wild, crazy splatters of paint were "art." But to many, Pollack and the others were little more than barbarians at the gate and their art only tended to reinforce fears that Doomsday was just over the horizon.[159]

THE BEGINNING OF THE END

The Goslin affair shattered Pasadena's collective confidence in its schools. In an effort to restore order and find out, as the SDC charged, if the system was teaching un-American values and was hiding "The Enemy," the city endorsed a school survey, the first since the Taxpayers' Association Survey of 1931. Padelford was a survey member, but one suspects the work was too dull, and she resigned, charging that the committee was "stacked" with proadministration appointments. Two highly respected professors, Clyde Hill of Yale and Lloyd Morrisett of UCLA, chaired the survey. The 939-page report, published in 1952, found nothing to support the SDC claims. There were hundreds of participants scattered across 16 committees, including a Professional Advisory Committee and a Citizens' Survey Committee that Padelford had served on until her resignation in February 1951. The survey was comprehensive—the table of contents alone was 36 pages in length—but Goslin is not mentioned by name.[160]

The city had been forever changed. The prewar days when Sexson and powerful businessmen dominated all school decisions were over. Sexson's administration had remained in power for two decades partly because important decisions were passed through a network of business connections before being submitted to the board for final approval. Sexson's door was always open to those dominant interests. When Goslin closed those doors, word spread that he was "aloof" and "unresponsive to parental concerns." More to the point, the new superintendent would not use his office to continue to broker privilege and entitlement to a minority of residents at the expense of many. After the rezoning controversy, there was no going back. Maybe Milton Wopschall put it best when he said, "The colored question was with us and will always be with us."[161]

Ironically, the beginning of the end came when the adjoining towns of Temple City and La Canada, perhaps seeing the increasingly darker shades of Pasadena's school children, voted to leave the school system. Temple City left first, right after the Goslin fight, amid bitter debate over the quality of education in the Pasadena system. Temple City was all white and its departure led to increasing segregation within Pasadena's schools. The school board was left with a smaller system, fewer dollars and insufficient incentive to retain a very expensive 6-4-4 plan. The next year the board went back to the conventional 6-3-3 alignment. Then, in 1960, La Canada pulled the plug and voted to leave the Pasadena system taking with it a junior high school and 900 white children. The board of education, with newcomers LuVerne LaMotte and Walter Shatford, was confronted with an East Arroyo faction demanding continuation of its most-favored-status and an African-American community growing more restive by the day.[162]

LuVerne LaMotte and Walter Shatford

In June of 1957, Pasadena's superintendent, Dr. Stuart McComb, the successor to the short-lived superintendency of Frank Walkup, resigned. He was fed up with a board of education that repeatedly sabotaged his attempts to create new programs and reestablish the status of Pasadena's schools. The great fear of Pasadena's conservatives had been the threat of the schools being "captured" by the communists. The boards of education that followed Goslin's administration, led by conservatives Lawrence Lamb, Edgar Barratt, and attorney Robert Mardian, exhausted the system's reputation by looking for the "communist conspiracy" in every classroom, book and teacher dossier. McComb came to loathe the board, especially Lamb and Barratt, and refused to stay on after his contract expired in 1957. The board majority had stonewalled salary increases, censored books and speakers, and had become positive the "Reds" had infiltrated the schools. They opposed the United Nations and any association with it or programs like UNESCO. When a disenchanted Lawrence Lamb decided not to run for reelection in 1957, his supporters blamed "Jewish connections" and "minority groups" that were seeking "to control the board."[163]

LuVerne LaMotte had seen enough. She had recently chaired a successful tax election committee and worked closely with superintendent McComb. On April 1, 1957, she filed her candidacy for the upcoming election in June. She said, "It seemed like the time to do something *for* the teachers rather than *to* them." The three incumbent communist hunters charged that "there [was] a shocking attempt to capture the Pasadena schools" and that "minority groups are seeking control of the schools." As the date of the election came closer, Lamb, Barratt and Mardian began a "secret investigation" of "conspirators," including McComb and Roland Walker, the former acting superintendent who had assumed the assistant superintendency when McComb was appointed.[164]

Running with LaMotte was Walter Shatford, a young attorney who lived with his wife, the former Sara Brady from Grant School, and their children on Washington Boulevard on the west side of Pasadena. Like LaMotte, Shatford was disturbed by the direction the system was taking. Shatford believed Lamb and Barratt were not focusing on schools while they hunted for imagined infiltrators. So he teamed up with LaMotte and Steve Salisian, a local automobile tire salesman, and the three ran as an opposition ticket. In private, Shatford referred to the three as "the good guys."[165]

The three were swept into office by a huge plurality. Many believed the system had turned the corner. Maybe the communist witch-hunt was over. Although Barratt and Robert Mardian remained, they no longer constituted the majority. Then, in July, Mardian suddenly resigned, leaving Barratt the lone conspiracy theorist. Later, Mardian would be tapped by Richard Nixon to manage his "Committee to Re-elect the President" in 1972. One year later, Robert Mardian was convicted during the Watergate scandal as a co-conspirator.[166]

The LaMotte/Shatford/Salisian board was immediately confronted with trying to get the system back on track. They appointed Robert Jenkins from New

Jersey as the new superintendent. In 1958, they put in place a revised transfer policy with what turned out to be two contradictory clauses. First, the board stated that "it shall do nothing that promotes racial or other types of segregation," nor would it allow parents to alter the "faithful representation of the geographical area served by each school." But past practice continued, and transfers, mainly from west to east, were routinely granted "to avert cases of proved hardship." Later, during the federal trial that ended Pasadena's segregated schooling, the federal court ruled that the permits still had been freely granted to avert cases of whites attending "minority schools."[167]

In the fall of 1960, two years after the three were elected, came La Canada's vote to "unify" its schools. Heard often during the campaign was the refrain "we want to educate our children at home." Many in Pasadena heard it as a thinly veiled rationale for the idea that La Canada, a community with no African-American residents, wanted to avoid having to continue to send its children to Muir High School, with its growing population of black students.[168] With the unification vote, the critical issue facing Pasadena was how to compensate for the loss of La Canada's 900 white students. The La Canada Junior High School, built when Willard Goslin was superintendent, was now no longer part of the Pasadena system and, more importantly, no longer open to the all-white East Arroyo residents. There were choices to be made. Immediately, the East Arroyo parents began to pressure the board to allow their children to attend nearly all-white McKinley Junior High School instead of the geographically closer, but increasingly minority, Washington Junior High School. The board was fully aware that its decision also would impact the student composition of Muir. If the East Arroyo students were sent to Washington, they would fall within the Muir High School attendance area, thus lessening the impact of the La Canada withdrawal. If, on the other hand, the board sent them to McKinley, they would end up attending Pasadena High School on the east side of town, leaving Muir to become even more a school for black and brown students. Shatford, as president of the board, took Silesian's suggestion and held the next regularly scheduled board meeting at Linda Vista Elementary School, perched along the western rim of the Arroyo. The intention was to hear directly from "all those affected."[169]

McKinley or Washington?

Throughout the history of Pasadena, civic and business leadership has had opportunities to address racial and class isolation. Nearly always, policies were enacted that ended up reinforcing *de jure* and *de facto* racial and class segregation. In May of 1954, when the city heard about the *Brown v. Board of Education* Supreme Court decision, Pasadena had been sufficiently divided by color and caste so that five elementary schools were either significantly or entirely populated by children of color. By 1960, the number had grown to eight. Washington Junior High was more than half black. Muir High School was the only one of the two high schools with any significant population of color. The black community was hemmed in along a narrow residential corridor, prevented from expanding because of restrictive covenants still being enforced by the city's realtors, even though the Supreme Court had declared the covenants illegal. The race and class divisions in the city had only worsened. The median black income in the city was less than $5,000, one third the median income of the Linda Vista neighborhood. The median level of education for African Americans and Mexican Americans over 25 years of age was less than 12 years, whereas the Linda Vista adults were mainly college educated. Many whites apparently believed the *Brown* decision did not apply to their city. Pasadena was not segregated but, rather, Negroes and whites just "chose to stay with their kind."[170]

But the *Brown* decision did pertain to Pasadena. Well before the Supreme Court ruling, Thurgood Marshall and the national office of the NAACP, looking for a far western case to join with its Southern and Mid-Western lawsuits, considered Pasadena's 1953 neutral zone suit a likely addition. During the summer of 1953, the board of education was confronted with serious overcrowding at Arroyo Seco Elementary, one of three nearly all-white elementary schools serving the hillside canyon neighborhood. Instead of transferring children to the nearby, less crowded and multiracial Garfield, the board decided to spend $15,000 to build "portable" classrooms at Arroyo Seco. The NAACP protested, accusing the board of using taxpayer money to "support segregation." The association attorney, Charles Johnson, argued that Garfield was underutilized because at least 65 white children from the school's attendance area (the "neutral zone") were allowed "easy" transfers for "the slightest reason" to the now overcrowded Arroyo Seco Elementary. Johnson and the association president, Dr. I.B. English, told the board that unless the plan to build the additional classrooms was abandoned, the NAACP would file suit, contending that the constitutionality of the board's action was "open to serious question."[171]

Board president Ray Untereiner, a Caltech professor elected just after Goslin was fired, asked the association not to take legal action because the board was "voluntarily" going to arrive at a "good decision." Johnson and Dr. English urged the board not to cave in to "pressure and coercion" from those "not in sympathy with a racially integrated school system." But Untereiner and his colleagues went ahead and ordered the portable classrooms. It was not the first time (nor would it be the last time) that Arroyo wealth would exert undue pressure on the board. Nor would it be the last time a Pasadena board of education would utilize "voluntary" as a racialized strategy. Johnson and English tried one last time. With shades of what would be the association's national strategy during the *Brown* litigation, Johnson told the board he was prepared to bring "a psychiatrist and sociologist to testify on the effects of segregation." Untereiner said no. On the same day the press announced that Earl Warren had been appointed Chief Justice of the Supreme Court, the association sued the city.[172]

The neutral zone case in Los Angeles County Superior Court never got past the depositions. The court ruled in favor of the NAACP and ordered the city to "cease and desist" its race-based transfer and neutral zone practices. The school board then announced it would not appeal. If the board had appealed, Johnson believed Thurgood Marshall would have added the suit as one of the companion cases in the *Brown* decision. What the local NAACP did not know at the time was that the school system would continue to allow white families around the Arroyo "facing hardships" to transfer to all-white schools.[173]

Four years after *Brown,* the city faced another litmus test. In 1958, Pasadena passed bonds to create a new high school to replace the older building that had been shared with the junior college during the 6-4-4 arrangement. The new school was built at the farthest eastern edge of the city, in an area that was rapidly being developed as white-only housing. When Pasadena High School opened in 1960, Muir and the new school were literally and figuratively at opposite ends of the system. The new school on the eastern edge was white and surrounded by white elementary and junior high schools. Muir, at the farthest western edge of the system, had a student body that was 50 percent black and Mexican American. No one could argue that the city needed a new high school to fulfill the needs of its newest neighborhoods but Muir's activist parents would later contend that the school's resources were rapidly bled off to support the continued expansion of the new eastside high school.[174]

The continuation of illegal transfers and the siting of the eastside high school are but two illustrations of the city rejecting opportunities to redraw attendance boundaries and adjust the student population to make its schools less segregated. Instead, city leaders, including civic and business leaders, continued to refuse to recognize their legal and ethical responsibilities. With the withdrawal of La Canada, the ethnic balance at the west side high school would become progressively more disproportionate unless the board acted. Amidst a growing national civil rights movement and pressure from an increasingly well-organized and focused black community with its supportive white liberals, the LaMotte/Shatford/Salisian board had its first major civil rights test of the 1960s. It failed.

It was clear from the outset of the November board meeting that the heavily white East Arroyo community, including the Linda Vista neighborhood, was vexed over the "interracial problem" at Washington Junior High School and wanted to know how the board planned to "fix it." Shatford, the parent of two children who attended Washington, told the audience of nearly 300 that "there was a misapprehension concerning Washington." There was "no problem." The teachers at Washington were carefully chosen because of their ability to understand and "cope" with the interracial environment. Furthermore, there was no guarantee that La Canada Junior High School was a better environment. He told the parents that the integration of the Washington, D.C., schools had proven to be quite successful for both black and white students. Then, in an attempt to mollify the crowd, he reminded the all-white assembly that the junior high schools were academically "tracked," meaning "their children would be with others of like ability."[175]

That did not placate Mrs. Raymond Davis, a Linda Vista parent, who told Shatford and the board that the objections they were hearing that evening were not to "integrated classes, but were concerns about the great concentration of the colored students ..." "These children," said Mrs. Davis, "were not as well educated morally as [our] children." Shatford disagreed. He said that all children profited by an integrated education, and there were "no incidences of thievery at Washington." This was, apparently, in reference to Davis's comment about morals. Still others took up Davis's questions about race. One parent told Shatford that he did not want his children attending a school where the teachers had to "cope." Another claimed the "problem" was not about "integration," but "merely the parents wanted to have their feelings taken into consideration when the boundary lines were drawn." Mr. Byron Guyer, a resident of Linda Vista Avenue, then pushed the discussion to a new level. "Is it possible for this group of parents," he asked, "to consider asking permission to withdraw from the Pasadena's school district and associate itself with another?" Although the meeting was ostensibly to discuss options relative to time spent on buses and distances from Linda Vista to one of the junior high schools, race was on everyone's mind. Now there was the threat that the East Arroyo community would withdraw if the board did not acquiesce to its demands. Immediately James Stivers (a conservative incumbent), LaMotte, Salisian, Shatford and Dr. Robert Freeman (who had been appointed to the board when Mardian resigned), appealed to the crowd not to consider withdrawal. Although no decision was made that night, the threat by the Arroyo wealth to pull out of the system hung over the city as the board prepared to make its most difficult decision to date.[176]

To assist the board in making that decision, Jenkins recommended the appointment of a multiracial "Citizens' Advisory Committee on Redistricting." Although the committee recommended that the city pursue the widest possible distribution of ethnicity within its schools, after three months of deliberations, it nevertheless recommended that Linda Vista students go to McKinley. Jenkins touted the committee's multiracial membership, even having the final recommendations presented at a news conference by one of the African-American members. Shatford counterproposed a plan to send Linda Vista students to Washington, and then shift students from that school to partially integrate McKinley. But, in March 1960, the board caved in to the East Arroyo community and took the citizen's committee recommendations. By a 3-2 vote, it redrew the boundary so Linda Vista students would attend McKinley Junior High School.

Voting no along with Shatford was Dr. Robert Freeman. The original three "good guys" were now down to one. Although Steve Salisian had gained office with the "liberals," he made his position clear at the Linda Vista meeting. He supported "neighborhood schools." Shatford was equally clear on the other side. Washington *was* the Linda Vista neighborhood school. LaMotte was the swing vote. She told the press that both junior high schools were "integrated" (McKinley had less than a 10 percent African-American student population), so she supported a redistricting policy that she found was minimal and "color-blind." Shatford then asked the rhetorical question: what if the black population was the majority at McKinley, and Washington was predominately white? Would his fellow board members make the same decision? No one answered.177

JACKSON V. PASADENA CITY SCHOOLS

The black community's response was immediate. In the summer of 1961, the father of Jay Jackson Jr., an incoming black eighth grader at Washington, applied for an intradistrict transfer to Eliot Junior High School in Altadena. Eliot was all-white and as near to the Jackson home as Washington. Jay Jackson Sr., a banker, asked for the transfer because he was "convinced that at Washington [his son was] not getting the best education available ..." His transfer application concluded with, "I am convinced that the recent deliberate acts of the Pasadena school board, permitting Linda Vista area school children to attend McKinley Junior High rather than Washington Junior High, were designed to and in fact did intensify and continue Washington's racially segregated character, thereby making an inferior school which I do not desire my son to attend and continue to be damaged."178

The transfer request was a strategic response to the board's McKinley decision, although the school board never saw it coming. The administration denied Jackson's request, giving as its reason the following, "the conditions stated in your application do not qualify under existing policies." Sam Sheats, the legal redress chairman of the Pasadena NAACP, was Jackson's attorney, and he immediately brought a writ of mandate before the County Superior Court. The speed by which Sheats filed his petition indicates that the suit was prepared well before the transfer was denied. Just as the *Brown* decision came as a result of precedent-setting cases over decades of NAACP struggle, the Jackson case would lay the foundation for the federal suit that ultimately forced the city to desegregate its schools in 1970. Sheats charged in the petition that the board "deliberately, arbitrarily, unreasonably and illegally manipulated, altered and gerrymandered the McKinley Junior High School zone ... for the purpose of instituting, maintaining, and intensifying racial segregation at Washington Junior High School." According to the *Brown* ruling, school segregation was "inherently unequal," hence the allegation that Jay Jackson Jr. would be "damaged." The Superior Court judge upheld the school decision denying the transfer, stating the administration was well within its legal right to determine where students went to school.[179]

Sheats was not working alone. Loren Miller, the NAACP attorney who had handled the association's restrictive covenant case before the federal appeals court, told the press that the national office of the NAACP would now take charge of the *Jackson* proceedings. Joining in the appeal would be A.L. Wirin of the American Civil Liberties Union, who had worked with Miller on the restrictive covenant suit. Miller added, "The case will be taken to the highest court if circumstances warrant." A few months later, after the *Jackson* suit was sent to the California Supreme Court on appeal, Roy Wilkins, of the national NAACP, announced in Washington, D.C., that the association was beginning a concerted campaign to end school segregation in both the North and the South. Twenty-three communities outside the South were targeted. Pasadena was on the list, the only city west of Illinois.[180]

Sam Sheats would remain connected to the case; it was, in many ways, his. He would be one of the team of attorneys to argue its merits before the Supreme Court. In June of 1963, the state Supreme Court overturned the lower court, adopting the notion of "affirmative integration." The justices ruled that Pasadena had gerrymandered the McKinley boundaries, in effect creating *de jure* (intentional) segregation as well as perpetuating *de facto* residential segregation.[181] The state Supreme Court had for the first time applied the *Brown* ruling to California. In the opinion of the court, Pasadena and other segregated communities were obligated to do more than just "refrain from affirmative discriminatory conduct." The consequences of segregation require that school boards take steps insofar as reasonably feasible, to alleviate racial imbalance in schools regardless of its cause ..." In this landmark case, the California Supreme Court ordered the city to "take steps insofar as reasonably feasible" to repair the damage.[182] Instead, the board majority for the next seven years "engaged in a verbal minuet," said Shatford, "mincing back and forth and sideways," avoiding the real work of finding common ground in a rapidly deteriorating situation.[183]

PLANS GONE AWRY

For the next few years, Shatford and Freeman would be the odd men out in a tug of war between the liberal minority and a conservative board majority. Just before the *Jackson* decision, the board and the school administration created "The Geographic and Controlled Open District Plan," modeled on similar open enrollment plans operating in places like Charlottesville, Virginia, and other Southern communities. Open enrollment was supposed to reduce the high concentration of black children in westside schools by allowing them the "opportunity" to leave for less segregated schools—on a space-available basis. Instead, the opposite occurred—the only students who left were the stranded white students who fled for whiter schools further to the east. The administration had once again put the onus for change squarely within the black community. The predominately white schools along the Arroyo or those further east were not part of the board's plans. Only those schools within what was called the "Negro community" were allowed to participate. Muir's student body remained nearly 50 percent minority; Pasadena High School nearly all white. If the intent of Pasadena's open enrollment was to voluntarily desegregate its schools, it was not working. Many suspected the plans were nothing but a ruse to defer concerns over an increasingly segregated community. Plans such as the one in Pasadena relied on the assumption that black students should leave "their" schools to attend white schools. In the many open enrollment plans and modifications of those plans, "voluntary" movement like that of Pasadena's white children from east to west was never proposed. Eight years later, when the city found itself in court over its segregated schools, the federal judge found the supposed "voluntary plans" in a direct violation of the 14th Amendment.[184]

Shatford was defeated during the next election. He, LaMotte and Salisian, ran for reelection, but the two former "good guys" decided to team up with a more conservative newcomer. Their campaign slogan was "preserving neighborhood schools," and Walter Shatford went down in defeat.

In 1965, Pasadena's integrationists—both white and black—were still in the minority, at least among those who voted. The city was a racial battleground. The specter of violence that had shadowed Pasadena since before the zoot suit riots now threatened to explode. It had already exploded during the hot, humid August when Watts, in Los Angeles, went up in flames. During four nights of open rebellion, there had been sporadic gunfire in Pasadena, but no one was killed or seriously injured. There had been a few Molotov cocktails (the police said most were "poorly constructed"), and 40 buildings were damaged. But as the Star-News put it, the city only got the "overflow," as if somehow the grievances expressed in the northwest corridor during those four nights were not homegrown. By the second night, the police had arrested 70 black youths (all below the age of 25) they considered the "core" of the city's African-American "troublemakers." There was a cross-burning on Kinneloa Avenue on the eastside of town, and a number of black-owned businesses along North Fair Oaks Avenue put up signs telling the discontented on the street, "I'm a brother." By the end of the violence a few days later, everyone was jittery, afraid the rioting had become a portent of things to come.[185]

Watts illustrated that the use of race for political gain is an enduring theme in America. In November 1965, Pasadena and Los Angeles area hardliners, calling themselves The Greater Los Angeles Citizens Council, brought Jim Clark, the notorious white-supremacist sheriff from Selma, Alabama, to speak at Pasadena's eastside Wilson Junior High School auditorium. Clarke had been responsible for the infamous attacks on civil rights marchers as they attempted to cross the bridge into Selma. In protest of Clark's presence, hundreds circled the Wilson auditorium, chanting civil rights slogans, singing "We Shall Overcome" and carrying pickets denouncing Clark's racism. Some were there in support of the Selma sheriff. Clark's presence galvanized the liberals. Many carried picket signs for the first time, including Skipper and Pat Rostker and Walter and Sara Shatford. Inside, amidst waving Confederate flags, were 175 uniformed Los Angeles county deputy sheriffs. Clark—who wore a gold medallion on his coat with "NEVER" engraved on it to symbolize his defiance of the civil rights slogan, "We Shall Overcome"—was eventually heckled off the stage by hundreds of antiracist partisans. More than a few wondered if the city's political soul had been won over by the segregationists.[186]

Over the next few years, the new board continued to tinker with open enrollment plans. But the only open enrollment plans working were for whites moving east. The board tinkered some more with the voluntary concept, permitting transfers from designated (black) schools, only if the transfer "improved ethnic balance," meaning no longer could white students leave predominately black, westside schools. Whites, steeped in years of entitlement, vigorously objected to this less liberal, narrower definition of "voluntary," arguing it was "reverse discrimination" and once again suggesting that "color blind," like "community," were subjective determinations.[187]

Jenkins resigned in 1967 to take the superintendency at San Francisco. Dr. Paul Salmon, who came to Pasadena because, he said, he liked being "challenged by a difficult situation," was his replacement. Salmon faced a daunting task. Bond elections to raise funds were rejected by an electorate fearful of any further erosion of white rule. Conservative groups worked to defeat integrationist school policies and prointegration candidates. One such group was "SAM" ("Silent Aroused Majority") a spin-off from a 1960's slogan (The Silent Majority) used by conservative whites to bolster the prevailing arrangements of power in the country. Another group, "Taxation," was blunt in its attacks on poor blacks. Preying on the mushrooming fear in Pasadena's white neighborhoods, "Taxation" handed out a flyer that said,

> The vote of a prostitute living on welfare payments (your tax money) for her illegitimate children and paying no taxes whatsoever has a vote equal to yours on a proposal to increase taxes, which are a first lien against your house.

The same group told voters that the bond issue in question was the work of "left-wing extremists who use children as pawns in the game of 'remaking the USA.'"[188]

Muir High School parents and area homeowners began to press the board because they believed there was ample evidence that the school was rapidly becoming a physical wreck. Further, the community was disturbed because they believed the conservative board had all but abandoned the campus in favor of the more affluent eastside. Two essential buildings containing classrooms and laboratories had to be closed due to mandated earthquake repairs that the board refused to authorize because, it said, there were insufficient funds. Some in the community believed the money was available; still others, such as the president of the Muir PTA, believed the board majority purposefully kept the buildings closed to keep capacity down and thereby prevent any transfers of white eastside students to Muir.[189]

Fig. 25. In happier times, Muir High School, c. 1955. *(Photo courtesy Pasadena Museum of History)*

Salmon, like Goslin and McComb before him, repeatedly clashed with his board. The enrollments at many of the schools—and especially at the high schools—continued to reflect a growing racial "imbalance" that frightened the majority whites. As long as the "minority" population had remained minor—and contained within strictly enforced racial zones—the white community remained content. But now, the city's white population was decreasing faster than the city's black population was increasing. Realtors told the board that whites were leaving because of the "quality of education," and few failed to understand the meaning of "quality." Seeing no way out but the transfer from east to west, Salmon drafted what he called Plan A, which would send 500 students from Pasadena High School to Muir over the next three years. Other than Salisian, who continued to hold out for his racialized definition of "neighborhood schools," Salmon was able to gain the necessary board support. LaMotte, her views slowly changing, and the three others may have seen this as a "last chance." Certainly that was the - prevalent view within the liberal, white community. The distribution of Muir's student body reflected continued "white flight." In 1964, 63.3 percent of the student body was white. Three years later, it had fallen to 55 percent. Salmon believed Plan A would address that decline and it was the least "intrusive" proposal in light of the continual failure of open enrollment plans. Plan A was the system's first stab at compliance to *Brown* and *Jackson* without relying on the use of volunteers.190

"Busing" did not, in 1967, evoke the same knee-jerk reaction it gets today. Still, the word "bus" was heavy with meaning in 1967. (Salisian had said that he saw nothing wrong with "bus transportation," but he would not support "transportation for integration.") The majority of the white community refused to support Salmon's Plan A and showed its collective displeasure with the superintendent and the board majority by electing two candidates, Brad Houser and John Welsh. Both were adamantly opposed to "gerrymandering" and "social engineering," terms they failed to recognize had historically aided in the creation of a hierarchical Pasadena they both wanted to preserve.191 The two had run on a campaign theme of "Rescind Plan A," and they both stated that their first official act would be to throw out the integration plan. They did just that at a special board meeting on July 10, 1967. The board voted three-to-two to rescind Plan A. LuVerne LaMotte and Joseph Engholm voted no. Two years before it was Engholm who had defeated Walter Shatford, campaigning on a "neighborhood schools" platform. Sam Sheats of the NAACP and others said the city was at a "crossroads." There were threats of a lawsuit and the board dug in its collective heels.192

SPANGLER V. PASADENA CITY SCHOOLS

Board politics had turned nasty. Given the openly racialized position taken by Welsh and Houser, along with Salisian's continued swing to the political right, LuVerne LaMotte, once a moderate conservative, was now recast as a moderate liberal. The rescission of Plan A turned out to be what the liberal community feared; it was the final straw. On July 18, three families, James and Bobbie Spangler, Skipper and Pat Rostker (both white) and Wilton and Dorothy Clarke, African Americans, filed an injunction in the County Superior Court on behalf of their high school children. The three knew each other through school politics, but were not close before the lawsuit. Skipper and Pat Rostker, who had campaigned for Steve Salisian and the "good guys" back in 1957 and carried their first picket sign in protest of Sheriff Jim Clark, lived on the eastside. The other two families lived within the Muir area. It was known as the Spangler suit, because James and Bobbie Spangler were the instigators, and as the Rostker's tell it, the "driving force behind the case."

The initial Spangler suit was limited to high school rezoning. The three families wanted the board to restore Plan A, thereby stopping, or at least slowing, they believed, the decline that had characterized the Muir community's most recent past. But the crisis that was looming over the conditions at Muir was more than a clash over crumbling buildings and resource allocation. What was at the heart of the Muir controversy was privilege, social class and race. For years, especially after World War II, wealth in the city had been shifting east leaving behind pockets of established professional-class neighborhoods like those around the Arroyo Seco. At the same time, increasing numbers of poor and working-class black families had moved into Pasadena, and since the traditional black enclaves in the northwest were contiguous with the Arroyo neighborhoods, the fear was that Muir would become what it was 50 years ago—a trade school for the "others."

In August, Judge Ralph Nutter of the Superior Court refused to issue the Spangler injunction, citing that the court needed to let the new board make its first move. "Judicial action," said Nutter, "should be the last resort." But, he warned, if the new board did nothing over the next year to adequately address the concerns of the plaintiffs, then "another judge might be asked to look at it in a different light." At the next board meeting, the attorney representing the three families told the board they would "wait and see" but, like Judge Nutter, they would return if nothing were accomplished.[193]

Somewhat analogous to rearranging deck chairs on a sinking ship, the board continued to offer only half-hearted, voluntary open enrollment plans, even one without school district transportation. They did, however, authorize a new track for Muir's athletic field at $168,000, which was 80 percent of the cost needed to repair the school's two closed classroom buildings. The board majority told the Muir parents that the track would be "the finest in the country." For many within the community, the board's decision to build a track at the expense of academic classrooms was openly racist; the message being sent was that African Americans were athletes, not scholars.[194]

But a new athletic track was not what Judge Nutter and the others wanted to see from the board. The board's opposition began to snowball. In April 1968, 13 white and African-American plaintiffs filed charges in Pasadena against the school district citing intentional segregation. Known initially as *Williams v. Pasadena,* the suit was later transferred to the County Superior Court and, over time, has come to be known as the "NAACP suit" because Sam Sheats and the association represented the 13 plaintiffs. In June 1968, when the board refused to authorize work on the classrooms at Muir, the principal and two vice principals resigned, citing "harassment by adult pressure groups and ... deteriorating administrative conditions." Later that summer, the new attorney for the Spangler's, Edgar Boyko, addressed the board, advising them that unless they moved to fix the situation at Muir, the three families would be compelled to resubmit the lawsuit, only this time at the state and federal level. Boyko also told the board that he would ask the Department of Justice to intercede. The board did nothing. In August, Boyko filed the "Spangler" complaint at the federal level.[195]

Then in October, superintendent Salmon resigned, citing his disgust with an obstructionist board of education. LaMotte, now the spokesperson for the moderate side of the board, wrote an "Open Letter to the Community," in which she cited the numerous wasted opportunities to repair the community. She apologized for the board's behavior and regretted Salmon's resignation. In April of 1969, she was reelected along with Houser and Welsh. But Steve Salisian, citing "exhaustion," stepped down. Later he would open a conservative Christian bookstore in the city. Taking his seat was Albert Lowe, a liberal and a Chinese American, the first "minority" ever elected to the board of education. Lowe had first appeared in school politics as a member of the Citizens' Advisory Committee on Redistricting. Some have speculated that Lowe's presence had more to do with Salisian's decision to not seek reelection than his "exhaustion." Now Houser and Welsh were the odd men out as the balance of power swung to the other side. But it was too little, too late. The board had lost any chance to remain the appointed arbiter of school policies. The federal government was about to step in.[196]

The Justice Department had been waiting in the wings. In May 1969, an "advanced team" of "civil rights surveyors" from the Department of Health, Education and Welfare (HEW) "suddenly" appeared at the administrative offices to conduct what they said was a "routine survey" of the school district and its federally funded programs. At least the board and administration were surprised. One of the HEW attorneys explained that Pasadena was merely one of five cities in the state slated for review, and the city's "card just happened to fall out of the computer first." In June, the Office of Civil Rights (OCR) (which at the time was contained within HEW) showed up, and for 10 days a "first string" team of attorneys canvassed the westside, talking to officials, school administrators and community members. The city and the board were told by the OCR attorneys that when the report was completed the superintendent and the board would receive a copy. [197]

Maybe for the board and the media, the arrival of the HEW surveyors was "sudden" and "surprising," but many believed they had come to the city by invitation. The federal government was fully aware of what was happening because quiet discussions with the Justice Department had begun months before the HEW team arrived. James and Bobbie Spangler had found their first attorney through a family friend and the initial lawsuit had been prepared *pro bono*. After Superior Court Judge Nutter rejected the suit and the board continued to drag its feet, the three families realized the original law office, with its single *pro bono* attorney, was insufficient. That is when Lynne Vernon, an active, westside mother of three, stepped into the fray. Vernon, who was white, was one of those quiet, behind-the-scenes activists who accomplish much but few come to know. She had been involved in her local PTA and then, during the rezoning controversy, had begun to collect data relative to the shifting demographics in the city. Her data collection was wide-ranging and meticulous. For a single individual without a professional staff—or any professional training as a demographer—Vernon's work gave the Spangler team more than enough ammunition to counter the board. Some believe it was Vernon who recommended attorney Boyko to the Spanglers. Regardless of who made the recommendation, when the Spangler team met Boyko they were immediately impressed with his quick grasp of the situation. It was Boyko who then suggested the suit be submitted at the federal level and it was Boyko who began the behind-the-scenes discussions with the Justice Department attorneys. If there was a mole, then it surely was Lynne Vernon. Without her active participation, the Justice Department might not have been as successful in its intervention.

In November, when the board's attorneys appeared in court to file a routine motion to dismiss parts of the *Spangler* suit, they were shocked to find a team of Justice Department lawyers petitioning federal Judge Manual L. Real. The federal petition asked Real to allow the Justice Department to intervene as a plaintiff in the suit known as *Nancy Anne Spangler et al v. the Pasadena City Board of Education*. The board's attorneys cried foul, complaining that the federal government had "broken its promise" to deliver a copy of the HEW findings. In a statement heavy with irony, acting superintendent Ralph Hornbeck said, "I must admit, I am concerned when we receive broken promises, contradictory statements and evasive answers from agencies of our federal government with whom we have been honest and open." For decades, individuals within Pasadena's communities of color had been saying the same thing about the city's government.[198]

In its 10-day swing through the city, the "first team" of OCR attorneys had found what they had been looking for. In September, instead of sending the report to the board and superintendent Salmon (who had yet to resign), they sent it to the Justice Department. Salmon later told the press that he knew the report was ready in August and "kept waiting for the other shoe to drop." It did, only it dropped into the offices of the Justice Department in Washington, D.C. When LaMotte and the others found the federal government was petitioning to intervene, she said, "The next six months will tell whether Pasadena lives or dies." Judge Real not only rejected the board's petition to dismiss parts of the *Spangler* suit but also allowed the federal government to join the suit as a plaintiff. The *Spangler* suit would be the first federal desegregation case west of the Rocky Mountains and, true to LaMotte's prediction, the trial would be a life or death determination.[199]

It only got worse for the board and the administration. In November 1969, over Judge Real's objections, the federal government was allowed to expand the suit to include the entire system (not just the high schools as originally filed) when it joined the *Williams v. Pasadena* petition with the *Spangler* grievance. Sam Sheats' NAACP suit was a class-action complaint filed on behalf of all the children attending Pasadena schools. It called for the board to end its "unreasonable and arbitrary" practice of "rigidly maintaining" segregated schools. Of the 13 families named in Sheats' complaint, six were black and seven were white. The *Williams'* suit, named after Chris Williams, an African-American student at Washington Junior High School, was far-reaching in scope and intent but called for no monetary damages as the *Spangler* suit would. It is unclear why Judge Real objected to the Justice Department request to expand the initial suit and it remains unclear why Real (or the Justice Department) did not fold the *Spangler* suit into the *Williams'* complaint. If that had happened, then Real would have heard a NAACP-sponsored case.

The newly constituted *Spangler* suit caused the board's attorney, deputy county counsel Raymond Schneider, to complain that the Justice Department was asking for something "entirely outside the scope of the law—a program of busing students ... to end racial imbalance." Although a *Spangler* attorney (but not a Justice Department lawyer) said busing was not pertinent to the case, everyone was aware of the implications. If the federal government had its way, yellow school buses would move back and forth across town and redefine Pasadena's neighborhood schools.[200] LaMotte and her colleagues thought it prudent to appeal the ruling but then waited because new lawyers were coming to their assistance. The *Spangler* case had now taken on proportions larger than anyone could have imagined just a few months before. The Los Angeles County counsel's office declared it would be unable to provide for the board's defense. Immediately, LaMotte, Engholm and the others hired private attorneys and began negotiations with the government lawyers in an attempt to settle out of court.[201]

There would be no out-of-court settlement. The government attorney, Charles Quaintance, made it clear that to settle, the board would have to agree to fully desegregate the high schools by the fall of 1970 and all the elementary schools by the start of the 1971 school year. When LaMotte and the board said they needed more time, Quaintance and the Justice Department attorneys said no. Comparing the progress of negotiations to the Vietnam War peace talks underway in Paris, one attorney said the litigants were still far apart and added, "You might say we haven't even decided on the shape of the table yet." Meanwhile, Real set the trial date for November. In a last-ditch effort to give the litigants more time to settle out of court, he postponed the start date until early January 1970.202

On New Year's Day 1970, as flower-adorned floats glided east down Colorado Boulevard, *The Los Angeles Times* reported that white families were leaving Pasadena in record numbers. Nearly 1,200 white students had pulled out since the end of the last school year, and the year before the district had lost more than 1,000 Anglo students. That was more than 2,000 white students in less than two years. A distressed board president LuVerne LaMotte said, "We must do something to reverse the trend." LaMotte also knew that nearly a third of the city's school-age children, just over 13,000, were attending private and parochial schools in and around the city. The system, so long revered as the jewel in the Crown of the Valley, was breaking apart. Engholm remained upbeat, even though he believed the federal government had singled out Pasadena because of its "reputation." He had "high hopes that one of these days we are going to get back to the status we once enjoyed of having one of the finest school systems in the nation." He further hoped "fine responsible people of all races will join hands to see that this happens in the future." White folks with means continued to flee.203

On January 6, 1970, in Judge Manuel L. Real's court in the federal building in downtown Los Angeles, the *Spangler v. Pasadena City Schools* trial opened. *The Los Angeles Times,* perhaps acknowledging the national publicity the city was receiving, referred to the trial by the headline "United States vs. School Board." Engholm said the city was not fighting the suit to oppose integration but because the community needed more time to "understand why we are integrating ..." The board attorney, John Pollock, was more direct, "The school district doesn't need the intervention of the government to solve the problem." Pollock's "problem" had only "worsened." In seven years, from May of 1962 to October of 1969, the African-American enrollment had nearly doubled, from 5,252 to 9,173, while the number of white students had decreased from 22,453 to 17,859. With 250,000 pages of documents and between 85 and 100 witnesses, the *Spangler* trial was expected to last through March. Two weeks after it began, however, the judge surprised everyone when he handed down his ruling. LaMotte was correct. Her Shangri La had come to an end.204

Real ordered the city to fully desegregate its schools by the start of the next term. When school opened in September 1970, the judge required that the more than 30 Pasadena-area schools would have "no majority of minority" children in attendance. Given that the city was "rigidly segregated," as Sam Sheats, the NAACP attorney alleged (and Real had concurred), the task for LaMotte and the other board members appeared enormous. In less than a month from announcing his decision, Real wanted a plan on his desk for how the board intended to address his "no majority of minority" decree. By September, 14,000 children would be bused around the city in an effort to meet the judge's order.[205]

As expected, the conservatives on the board were irate. If the court had its way, then the city's elite would lose its first-ever school war. Board members Welsh and Houser were not about to let that happen. They demanded that the board's politically moderate majority, made up of LaMotte, Lowe and Englehorn, appeal the court's decision. The majority decided they would not, since attorney Pollard advised them that they would be unable to dispute any of the court's 54 findings against the system. The majority thought it prudent to put the unrest behind them and move in a direction that would fulfill the court's order and benefit the city's schoolchildren.

In late January, at the first board meeting after the judge's decision, Welsh walked out in a very dramatic display of barely contained anger. He wished them all "God speed" but refused to participate in carrying out a decision he believed grossly unfair and "unconstitutional." He called Real's judgment "an insult and an injustice to the citizens of the district." Welsh and Houser thought that by not appealing, the board was admitting guilt. In his resignation speech, Welsh told a crowded boardroom,

> We are in effect saying, 'You are right judge. For the last eight years our efforts have been a sham, our policies tokenism, our long-range plan has been a stall, our master plan is only for effect [and] our superintendents have been insincere.'[206]

Sam Sheats and others in the audience probably agreed with his assessment. Immediately after Welsh's resignation, Houser began a public petition drive to appeal the court order. The appeal campaign quickly got spun into a recall campaign against the hated three.

The board majority had made its critical decision not to appeal because the court had made it clear the city was in violation of the 14th Amendment and, as LaMotte pointed out, all the members of the board, even Welsh and Houser, had testified in court that they were committed to integration. To appeal now, LaMotte inferred, would be hypocritical. Lowe told the press that to him, Real "had told us to do that which we ought to be doing—with or without a court order." Superintendent Hornbeck thought the chance of a successful appeal was less than 50 percent. A group of Muir students offered the board their help in selling the idea of integration to the community.[207]

Others, however, were less gracious. One parent said, "nobody is going to bus my child out of the area no matter the ethnic balance." He said he did not believe in "destroying a child's psychology for a socialist belief." Furthermore, he threatened to lie down in front of the bus and it "could [roll] over my dead body." Others said the ruling put the city "under martial law." One resident asked the city directors to intervene on behalf of the appeal committee. They refused, saying the board of education was an autonomous body. The resident, Paul Leonard, then suggested that the directors "prohibit [the] use of city streets for busing students." The directors did not comment.208

THE "FUNDAMENTALIST BOARD"

By mid-February 1970, the judge had the city's first authentic desegregation plan. Real had required that no school have a student population greater than 50-percent minority but the board majority decided each school would reflect the ethnic composition of the entire school district. Ironically, the two schools that had been the focus during the 1960s—Muir and Pasadena High School—would, under Real's order, be considered sufficiently integrated. LaMotte, Lowe and Englehorn, however, wanted every school to be "balanced." It was, as LaMotte said, the "only fair thing to do." She and her more moderate colleagues were also concerned that they would have hell to pay if their plan did not impact every neighborhood equally.

In an effort to meet the goal of "balance," the board's plan, called "The Pasadena Plan," divided the district into four east/west attendance zones. The traditional K-6 elementary grades were reconfigured into K-3 and 4-6 schools. The plan called for every child at the elementary level to attend his or her "neighborhood school" for half the elementary years, and then be bused to a "paired" school somewhere else in the attendance zone. As an example, a child living in the posh San Rafael School area might go to that school, which under the plan was now fully integrated, for grades K-3, and then get bused to Washington Elementary School, in the northwest, for grades 4-6. Under the board's arrangement, which Real approved in March, the elementary grades got the lion's share of disruption simply because racial segregation was endemic at the elementary level. Sixty percent of the elementary students were bused as opposed to half of the junior high students and only 20 percent of the high school students. In September, when school opened, 14,000 students moved around the city in hundreds of yellow buses.209

When Welsh resigned, the board appointed its first African-American member, Henry Clark. There had been speculation that the majority might appoint Sam Sheats, but the NAACP attorney was too outspoken. Meanwhile throughout the spring, Houser's appeal effort was gathering strength. Twenty-three white individuals, all parents in the school district, asked that the U.S. District Court of Appeals to overrule Real's desegregation order. When the court refused, the committee, known as the Pasadena Appeal Committee, took its petition to the U.S. Supreme Court. Finally, in early May, the effort to block the court-ordered integration appeared finished as the court refused, without comment, to hear the petition. One of the organizers said, "This would seem to be the end of the case." He was wrong. It was only the beginning of the struggle to return Pasadena to "neighborhood schools."210

Next came a recall attempt. Thousands of signatures were gathered and in October 1970, Pasadena went to the polls. The question before them was whether LaMotte, Lowe and Engholm should remain, in effect keeping the Pasadena Plan in place. The issue was "neighborhood schools" and of the 14 recall candidates, 13 were opposed to "forced busing." The campaign was bitter. Led by Henry Marcheschi, a white resident who lived on the eastside, the antibusing faction promised what could not be delivered—a return to the past. The recall was barely defeated. The voting patterns reflected a divided city. On the predominately white eastside, the three incumbents were badly beaten. However, fewer than half the precincts—35 of 75—voted for the recall. In the heavily black sections of the westside and the northwest, the recall was defeated by a resounding 10 to 1 margin. The black and Latino vote saved the incumbents, but the prointegration community knew it was only a matter of time before the opposition would come at them again.211

Marcheschi was elected the next year to replace Houser, who decided not to seek reelection. Then, in the summer of 1971, Clark moved out of the area and the board majority appointed Sam Sheats to serve out Clark's term. It was now LaMotte, Lowe, Sheats and Engholm's replacement, Ann Hight, whom the moderates had appointed in 1971 when he resigned. Marcheschi stood alone against the majority, now more liberal because of Sheats and Hight. By the spring of 1973, though, the stage was set. Three seats were up for grabs and LaMotte had announced her retirement.212

Opposing the board majority were Henry Myers, Lyman Newton and Richard Vetterli. Myers and Vetterli, along with Marcheschi, lived in a middle-class, eastside housing tract known as Hastings Ranch, a post–World War II development with a virulent reputation of "white-only." Newton was from the west Arroyo. Their campaign was not merely "dirty" in the conventional sense of politicians throwing "mud" at each other. The ugly name-calling, flagrant lies and misinformation generated against the incumbents served to drive a wedge even deeper into the city's collective soul. Myers, Newton and Vetterli concentrated on the white precincts, flooding neighborhoods with campaign flyers stating schools were, as a result of busing, places of "intimidation, assault and violence." The opposition camp more than hinted that "race mixing" was destructive to the white community because of the "lower morals" of black families. Myers campaigned on a "get tough" policy. "Discipline, respect and common courtesy," he said, "must be restored to the classroom" and "violence must be dealt with firmly." The message was clear. End busing, restore "neighborhood schools," and "order" and "discipline" will return.213

Thirty years before, in 1950, during the Goslin administration, and 40 years before that, in 1909 during the socialist school board campaign, the voters of Pasadena were convinced their world was collapsing because of threats from within. Now, in 1973, it happened again. Pasadena had listened to its deepest fears about the loss of status and power. This time, the rallying cry was "Neighborhood schools," a late-century reincarnation of "Treason in our schools!" and "Communists in our schools!" Myers, Vetterli and Newton used race and the city's historical preoccupation with entitlements and prestige in an effort to restore the old order. All three moderate incumbents were defeated. The three newcomers would join Marcheschi, and together they would direct considerable energy at destroying the Pasadena Plan. Sheats was the lone holdover from the moderate side, and he said it was like swimming in a tank of sharks. For the next six years, the city would be a battleground, as the new "fundamentalist" board would attack the desegregation plan—and "progressive education"—in an effort to reconstruct their America.214

FUNDAMENTAL EDUCATION

At the core of what emerged from the conservative board was a plan to "restore" Pasadena and its schools. The new board would simultaneously contest the desegregation order ("stop forced busing!") and rid the schools of what they believed to be wrong with America. Their plan was called "Fundamental Education" and its leading proponent—Vetterli went as far as to say its founding father—was board member Henry Myers. Fundamentalism, as the name implies, rejects progressivism, stressing, instead, a "back-to-basics" approach that emphasizes "standards," "patriotism," "respect" and "competition." Slogans do not do justice to the conservative restoration the board majority intended. It was not merely the rejection of progressive ideals like "cooperative learning," "subject integration" or "multiculturalism." Myers, Marcheschi, Vetterli and Newton wanted to purge the city's schools of all things they considered "un-American," including "offensive" books, "radical" teachers and administrators, and "forced busing," which Myers and the others blamed for the destruction of "the finest educational system in the country."215

Within a month of taking office, the board majority—with Sheats in dissent—created its first fundamental school, transforming John Marshall Junior High School into John Marshall Fundamental School, grades K-8. The board's decision looked capricious, as there was no prior study, no fact finding, and no pilot program. Myers announced that there was a "growing demand" for "fundamental education" and that the school district would now provide for those wishing such an experience. He would write a few years later that "Fundamental schools have been studied and proven on this continent alone for well over two hundred years. Only when educators strayed from basic fundamental precepts did they get into trouble." Some complained that Marshall's purely voluntary attendance suggested an attempt at resegregation but the board was careful to balance the student body. More blatant attempts at resegregtion would come later.216

Marshall's curriculum and organization reflected Myers' fundamentalist philosophy. No federally funded programs were allowed because the board felt federal influence was academically (and ideologically) suspect and strings were always attached. The following list of "Fundamental School Requirements" comes from Myers' book, *Fundamentally Speaking*, which was published in 1977.

1. Emphasis will be on fundamentals: reading, writing, arithmetic, discipline, and respect. Reading will be taught by the phonics method. Traditional, basic mathematics, not "new math," will be utilized.

2. Homework will be assigned in each subject, at every grade level, on a regular basis.

3. No child will be passed on to a higher grade until he has mastered the minimum requirements set for his grade level.

4. Achievement and IQ testing will be performed upon admission and periodically thereafter.

5. Classes will be ability grouped.

6. Strict discipline will be maintained. The teacher is authorized and expected to maintain order in the classroom. Paddling and detention are permitted at the discretion of the teacher.

7. Parents and guardians must meet with the teacher periodically to discuss the progress of the child.

8. Letter grades will be given periodically in each of the basic subjects.

9. After school help will be provided where required.

10. Dress, for the students and the teachers, must comply with minimum standards. Neatness and cleanliness are mandatory.

11. High moral standards, respect, courtesy, and patriotism will be emphasized at all grade levels.217

Marshall's older male students wore white shirts and ties; females wore dresses. Male teachers wore coats and ties and the women on the faculty wore dresses and heels—the dress code prohibited women from wearing pants. In the classroom, when students were recognized (only after raising their hands), they stood before they spoke. All school flag-raising ceremonies were conducted every day, patriotic songs were sung and "American heritage" was emphasized. Many in the city applauded a return to normalcy after the turbulent 1960s. Others were less sanguine.

When the board announced the creation of the fundamental school, Myers said there were 3,500 applications, with 130 arriving from private school parents. Little wonder the outpouring of interest. Fundamentalism promised an easy cure for a troubled city and nation. After all, the problems associated with school integration were not Pasadena's alone. Since the beginning of the most active period of the civil rights movement in the early 1960s, communities around the country experienced massive—and sometimes violent—disruptions to public education. Coupled with the national angst over Vietnam and the racial unrest exploding in the largest cities, the country was in a state of turmoil not experienced since the Civil War and its aftermath. During unsettled times, simple solutions are appealing. In Pasadena, during the early 1970s, the lure of "fundamentalism" and its promises of a safe return to the stability of "neighborhood schools" were too much for many to pass by. Myers and his colleagues were "ecstatic" over the number of applicants, and that only encouraged more attempts to "fundamentalize" Pasadena.[218]

Myers and the others were increasingly vexed that American society had become infected by "progressivism" and "permissiveness" and the bedrock values that made America "strong" were being corroded by "liberals," "communists," and meddling "do-gooders." As it was during Cary McWilliams' time, identifying "The Enemy" in Pasadena depended upon one's ideological colorations. But that remains too narrow a definition to fully understand Myers and the fundamentalist movement. At one level, they believed the enemy was John Dewey's progressive education and its tenets of "cooperation" and "caring about the whole child." They saw "permissiveness" as a communist conspiracy designed to undermine America's historical reliance on the strengths of the individual. Myers, like the crusaders of the city's Americanization programs that came 50 years before him, was focused on "fixing" the miscreants, the riffraff that belonged to a disheveled social order he called "slobism." Whereas the Americanization zealots saw immigrants and their aberrant cultures as the threat, Myers saw "slobism" everywhere, even in kindergarten classrooms where "Litter and trash are everywhere. Soda straws. Candy wrappers. Milk cartons. Lunch sacks. All strewn thoughtlessly about." This was "proof" that the "advanced stages of the disease" was "spreading like wildfire ..."

Looking back, Myers' ranting about milk cartons and lunch sacks seems a bit eccentric, if not hysterical. Even during the early 1970s, many thought Myers and his fellow board members were paranoid actors in a Faustian drama of national proportions. Yet, it is crucial to understand that within this atmosphere of extremism, he and his followers recognized an essential truth. The old order was breaking apart. Many who opposed the fundamentalists were quick to accuse them of racism and much of the fundamentalists' actions would support such a contention. But Myers and his moral crusaders were about more than race and the integration of schools. Of course he and his friends objected to integration, but Myers' hostility to black and Latino children sitting next to white children represented less about race (and racism) than it did the potential loss of long-standing entitlements that historically have come because of race and racism. Integrated classrooms at San Rafael Elementary School, that toney neighborhood close to the Arroyo where 30 years before Louise Padelford and her friends first heard Willard Goslin spin his stories about progressive education, meant that San Rafael no longer represented exclusivity, prestige, status and wealth. The same thing could be said about Myers' "neighborhood school," Don Benito Elementary, located in the Hastings Ranch subdivision. As it was in Charlottesville, the impact of court-ordered desegregation would be begrudgingly tolerated by Pasadena's white conservatives—but only if policies were in place to control the extent of integration.[219]

The fundamentalists in Pasadena yearned for a return to trusted values of order, hierarchy and discipline. "Patriotism" was to Myers and his cohort merely an expression of how the community should worship the old order. Communal introspection—the willingness to rectify racial and class grievances—was not part of their agenda. Beneath their patriotic "America First" rhetoric, was a reliance on Spencerian ideals of "fitness" and "survival." To Myers, parental "choice" meant creating a structured approach to public schooling, where the marketplace would dictate who survived and who failed. If parents had school choice, then the schools would have to respond or, like unhealthy fruit on the vine, the less favored would wither and die. Myers knew that his children—and the children of his allies—would succeed. The class structure in America would assure that. The "others" would just have to work harder to catch up. It was a simple solution to a complex problem—and we have heard it before, as far back as the turn of the century when the city made one of its initial stabs at "fixing" the poor, at the Mexican School on South Raymond Street. Then, "choice" meant shipping poor Mexican immigrants to a "special school" so white, middle- and upper-class students could enjoy the fruits of their "neighborhood school."[220]

There was immediate resentment toward the new board. Increasingly, the politically left and moderate opposition saw the fundamentalist movement less as libertarian, than ironically, as a dangerous movement toward another kind of totalitarian state. Myers wrote that his definition of a "good" education was "simply a school where basics of education are stressed with little or no experimentation; where discipline reigns and patriotism flourishes." It was, he said, "the new conservative alternative." That scared many who believed the movement was a direct attack on communities who believed differently; who viewed progressive social change as necessary and good—and long overdue. To Myers' opponents, "discipline," "order" and "patriotism" were slogans that meant more than pedagogical techniques and curricula. Those terms signaled that "The Enemy" was organizing to purge the community of all things determined to be "progressive."221

The new conservative board so unnerved many in the community that board meetings, those typically bland monthly affairs, became Pasadena's own version of a circus under the tent. It was great theater. The more Myers and the others pushed their agenda, the more the opposition became galvanized. In raucous meetings, the Pasadena Federation of Teachers demanded an end to book censorship. Liberal and leftist groups ridiculed threats against so-called liberal and leftist teachers. Myers and Vetterli, the most outspoken of the fundamentalist board, became increasingly suspicious. They saw the disruptions as a communist conspiracy and repeatedly ordered board meetings into executive session. That left Sam Sheats to carry on alone, telling standing-room-only crowds of 500 to 600 his views of a world turned upside down.222

Restoring the old order meant six years of fighting with the courts, trying to reestablish some semblance of "freedom of choice"—which Judge Real refused to permit. The fundamental schools grew in number—the waiting list of students approached 1,400—and, in a blatant effort to circumvent the desegregation order, the board allowed out-of-district transfers to bypass the waiting list. Myers and the others knew that the transfers were white families, living in Pasadena, who had fled the court order. They saw the transfer policy as a legitimate means of "attracting more white students back to the public schools." Myers repeatedly stated that fundamentalism would "return stability" to the system, promising a "basic education" that he said was common before the progressive's seized power. If the promise was "stability"—which returning white families may have perceived as controlling the number of minorities in any one school—then the transfer policy was necessary. Those who were in line, waiting for their share of "stability," howled at the blatant unfairness shown by the board.223

It was Myers' contention that if parents could choose fundamental education with all its promises of constancy and order—then, yes, whites that had left the system would come back for an integrated education. To Myers, fundamentalism went beyond race, and, as proof, he told Real that 30 percent of the applications for fundamental schools came from black families. Perhaps the court saw Myers and his movement as disingenuous. The common perception—buttressed by Real's many legal opinions—was that race was at the core of "white flight." It was, but Pasadena's struggle for community was about more than a knee-jerk reaction to "race mixing." Like in Charlottesville and other Southern communities, the conservative white board majority in Pasadena was trying to control the extent of school integration and, to do so, it needed more white families back in the schools. Real was unimpressed and refused to back down.224

At the deepest level, the conservative board was less about "communists" and "race mixing" than about the struggle for power. Pasadena has always been about who controls the resources. The city, founded on the principals of speculation and profit and the design of its public institutions, especially its schools, has historically underscored who wins and who loses. Schools are important arenas in the contestation for power. The city came to understand that fact during one of its first culture wars, when the Socialists campaigned for the school board. A "good" education—meaning access to advantage and social status—has always been costly. The wealthy have understood that. Just ask them about the costs associated with sending their children to boarding schools. Just ask parents today about the cost of sending their children to Caltech or its 100-year-old spin-off, the very private Polytechnic School. Wealth and race buys "choice" and choice buys advantages. Myers understood that and he still does.

The conservative, antibusing school board collapsed in the late 1970s. The city, one suspects, grew tired of the constant battles. Or maybe it was because the white majority school-age population was reduced to a minority as those with enough capital left for "safer" places. Judge Real released the city from his oversight when the moderates regained control of the board in 1979.225 Myers remained until the mid-1980s and then left for one of those "safer" neighborhoods, in the white-flight bastion of Orange County. In 2000, on the 30th anniversary of the court decision, he said that the Pasadena Plan was "unproductive and costly," which to many in the city rings true. He also said that white families who have left the city's schools have done so for good reasons.

> If you were a white parent ... and only 16 percent of the kids are white and all of his friends are other races, do you think you would keep your child there if you had a reasonable opportunity to go to a place that's 50-50? What's your child's opportunities for dating, finding friends or choosing a life partner?226

Were his comments racially motivated? Probably, given that he went on to say that dating and "choosing a life partner" in Pasadena in the year 2000 might lead to mixed-race couples—and mixed-race grandchildren—which, given a choice, were not his preferences. Perhaps the fear of race mixing was at the core of Myers' fundamentalism. Yet the struggle for power reflected more the fear that Myers and his community were about to be cut off from the advantages associated with Pasadena's time-honored pathways to privilege. Today, more than 30 years after the end of the court order, the old definition of "neighborhood schools" no longer works. The emerging redefinition might confuse the likes of Henry Myers. It certainly confuses many who remain in the "Crown of the Valley."

NOTES

1. "Tosses Child Off Bridge, Then Dies," *Pasadena Star-News,* 1 May 1937, p. 1; "Victim Whom 'Suicide Bridge' Spared," *The Los Angeles Times,* 23 November 1984, San Gabriel Valley edition, p. 1, col. 1.

2. "In Pasadena, a fence helped," *Pasadena Weekly,* 11 July 1984, p. 8; "Bridge is Born Again," *Pasadena Star-News,* 12 December 1993, p. A-1, col. 1; Richard Joseph Schmidt, "Weathered Crossing," *Westways Magazine,* December 1978, p. 56–59.

3. "Great Human Wave West Started," *Pasadena Star-News,* 17 January 1931, p. 1, col. 1. The writer called it the "annual hegira of excursionists from the East and North ..." The Pasadena Chamber of Commerce had already sent flowers and greenery to decorate various train stations in Eastern states, an inducement to travel to the warm West during the winter deep freeze. Los Angeles expected nearly 4,000 excursionists from four special trains in one day in January.

4. On the labor camps, see "Relief Camp Opening is Arranged," *Pasadena Star-News,* 27 May 1932, part 2, p. 1, col. 4; "County Work Plan at Flats," *Pasadena Star-News,* 25 May 1932, part 2, p. 1, col. 5; on the death of the baby, see "Block Drive Volunteer Writes," *Pasadena Star-News,* 26 May 1932, part 2, p. 1, col. 2; on the city employee reductions, see "City to Drop Many from Payrolls," *Pasadena Star-News,* 19 June 1931, part 2, p. 1, col. 1.

5. "Frank Views on Jobless Are Told," *Pasadena Star-News,* 21 May 1932, p. 1; "Park's Rest Room To Be Opened," *Pasadena Star-News,* 27 May 1932, p. 4; "Social Center at Park Begun," *Pasadena Star-News,* 27 June 1932, p. 1; "Programs Fill Need in Lives of Jobless Women at Park Here," *Pasadena Star-News,* 13 December 1932, p. 6.

6. "Block-Aid Work Given to Many," *Pasadena Star-News,* 22 June 1932, p. 1; 1930 Fifteenth Census, 1930, vol. III, *U.S. Government Printing Office,* p. 247.

7. Morrow Mayo, *Los Angeles* (New York: Alfred Knopf, 1932), p. 211.

8. Ibid., p. 212.

9. Edward L. Thorndike, *Your City* (New York: Harcourt Brace and Company, 1939) preface, p. 8–9. Also see Manual Pineda, *Pasadena Area History* (Los Angeles: John Anderson Publishers, 1972), p. 24.

10. Mayo, p. 216.

11. Noralee Frankel and Nancy Dye, *Gender, Class, Race and Reform in the Progressive Era* (Lincoln: University of Kansas Press 1990), p. 3.

12. See the "Block-Aid" collection in the *Myron Hunt Papers,* Huntington Memorial Library, San Marino, California. Hereafter cited as *Hunt Papers.* When the Depression struck, Hunt and his wife, Virginia Pease, former principal of Polytechnic School and a close confidant of E.S. Gosney, organized "Block-Aid," a community-based charitable effort designed from the New York City model to help white-collar male workers and middle-class women. Residential neighborhoods, or blocks, were canvassed and funds were solicited to help out-of-work Pasadenans. Apparently the districts were in the east and south sides of town. There is little indication that black or Mexican neighborhoods were canvassed. Certainly out-of-work

African Americans did not have the same access to institutional assistance as whites. "Block-Aid," however, did provide "colored" help to the swank Zonita Club during one of its posh dinners. "A Negro woman performed the 'southern cooking' in her own home and sent down the delectable viands. Five Negro musicians entertained right royally." See "Block-Aid Group is Providing Dinners in Various languages," *Pasadena Star-News*, 5 August 1932, p. 12.

13. "Pasadena Employment Commission," 21 September 1932, in *Hunt Papers*.

14. *Census of the Population: 1950*, Seventeenth Decennial Census of the United States, Characteristics of the Population, Vol. II, Part 5: California, p. 5–119.

15. See Sexson's 1933 *Annual Report*, "The Public Schools Face the Depression," Pasadena Board of Education, for his thorough discussion of how the system went about its defense given the numerous attacks on its policies, practices and budget. See especially p. 15–22, citing the impact of the Depression on the system and p. 27 that graphs the downsizing of personnel. Between 1931–32 and 1932–33, the number of kindergarten teachers were reduced by more than half and all supervisory positions were eliminated. Most of the remaining personnel, some 95 percent, were retained.

16. "81 Years of Public Education in Pasadena," ed. by A. Roland Walker (Pasadena: Superintendent's Annual Report, 1955), p. 36.

17. The "had stabilized" quote is attributed to Sexson, cited in ibid., p. 37.

18. "Survey of the Pasadena City Schools" *California Taxpayers' Association Report No. 119* (1931), p. 322–324.

19. See Larry Cuban, *How Teachers Taught* (Cambridge: Harvard University Press, 1992) and Herbert Kliebard, *The Struggle for the American Curriculum, 1983–1958* (New York: Routledge and Kegan Paul, 1987) for an analysis of what constituted curriculum and pedagogy in American schools in the 20th century.

20. Sara Shatford mentions one African-American girl attending Grant School for a short while but she left. Sid Gally mentions the possibility of a Mexican-American boy but is not sure. Sara Shatford, interview by author, Pasadena, Calif., 10 March 2002; Sid Gally, interview by author, Pasadena, Calif., March 10, 2002.

21. *Minutes,* Pasadena Board of Education, 21 June 1928; Sara Shatford, interview by author; Blanche Murphy Jaggi, telephone interview by author, 16 June 2002; author correspondence with Shatford and Murphy Jaggi, in author's possession.

22. Murphy Jaggi, interview by author; correspondence with Shatford and Murphy Jaggi.

23. William Martin Proctor, "The Kindergarten-Six-Four-Four Plan of School Organization in Pasadena," *City of Pasadena* (1933), p. 25. Meriam's *The Traditional and the Modern Curriculum: An Emerging Philosophy*, published just after Meriam's death in 1960, remains a classic study of the elementary school.

24. Proctor, p. 27.

25. Proctor, p. 29.

26. Daniel Tanner and Laurel N. Tanner, *Curriculum Development: Theory into Practice*, 2nd ed., (New York: Macmillan Publishing Company, 1980), p. 297.

27. Ibid., p. 297; Dewey's paraphrase from "Comments and Criticisms by Some Educational Leaders in Our Universities," Chapter 5, in *The Activity Movement*, Thirty-Third Yearbook of the National Society for the Study of Education, Part II (Bloomington, Ill: Public School Publishing Co., 1934), p. 85.

28. Walker, p. 59, 77–78.

29. Stephen Jay Gould, *The Mismeasure of Man* (New York: W.W. Norton, 1980), p. 175; Raymond E. Fancher, *The Intelligence Men: Makers of the IQ Controversy* (New York: W.W. Norton and Co., 1985), p. 132–149.

30. L. Thomas Hopkins, *My Pasadena Experience*, 1929–1941, p. 3–5. The memoir was never published and is found at the University of Texas, Austin, Center for Oral History, O.L. Davis, director.

31. Sara Shatford, interview by author and Shatford correspondence.

32. David Hulburd, *This Happened in Pasadena* (New York: Macmillan Co., 1951), p. 3.

33. Edgar B. Wesley, *NEA: The First Hundred Years* (New York: Harper and Brothers Publishers, 1957), p. 282–286.

34. Hulburd, p. 4–7. This is the only monograph published on the Goslin affair. As a result of Goslin's firing, there were scores of newspaper and news magazine articles, numerous scholarly journals and book chapters devoted to Goslin's superintendency. Many were supportive, but many were critical of Goslin and schooling in general. Hulburd was a journalist for *Time* and was dispatched to Pasadena by his boss, Robert Larson, the magazine's publisher. None of Hulburd's Pasadena notes were found in the *Time-Warner* corporate archives.

35. *Census of the Population: 1950*, Seventeenth Decennial Census of the United States, Characteristics of the Population, Vol. II, Part 5: California, p. 5–101. In 1950, Mexican Americans were counted in the census report as "white." Therefore, the exact population of Mexican Americans cannot be determined. The total population in 1930 was 76,086, with a black population of just over 3,000. In 1940, the total population had grown to 81,864 and the black population was 3,929. See *Census of the Population, 1940*, Volume II, Part 5, "Characteristics of the Population," p. 608–609. The Japanese population had declined slightly to just fewer than 800 in 1940, down from 850 in 1930. In 1950, there were 1,500 Japanese living in Pasadena. See *Sixteenth Census* for data on Japanese in 1940 and 1930, p. 568; and the *Seventeenth Census* for the population in 1950, p. 602.

36. Earl F. Cartland, "A Study of Negroes Living in Pasadena" (Master's thesis, Whittier College, 1948), p. 12. See Ann Schield, *Pasadena: The Crown of the Valley* (Pasadena: Pasadena Historical Society, 1995), p. 97–98, for her analysis of black/white relations based on the Cartland story. There was a general sense of frustration by historian Robin D.G. Kelley when, as a graduate student at UCLA, he conducted interviews with older black residents who were fixated on "firsts" at the expense of more recent history. He was also equally frustrated with the prevailing notion that the black and white community at the turn of the century was forever altered because of the sentiments of incoming white migrants. Kelley believed that the changes came as a result of competition over jobs and ever increasing numbers of black workers. See Kelley's notes in the *Black History Collection*, Pasadena Museum of History, hereafter cited as PMH.

37. See Eric C. Lincoln, and Lawrence H. Mamiya, *The Black Church in the African American Experience* (Durham: Duke University Press, 1990), for an excellent analysis of the changes in the black church in the 19th century.

38. See Kelley's notes, *Black History Collection*, PMH.

39. See pamphlet, "Scott United Methodist Church Seventy-Fifth Anniversary, 1903–1978," p. 7, *Black History Collection*, "Churches," Box 11/2, BH-D-18-32, PMH.

40. "Threats to Burn Church," *Pasadena Daily News*, 30 June 1909, p. 1, col. 1.

41. See "Introduction" in Kelley's notes, *Black History Collection*, PMH, p. 2.

42. See James Crimi, "The Social Status of the Negro in Pasadena, California" (Master's thesis, University of Southern California, 1941), p. 49.

43. "Threatened to Use Razors and Revolvers in Church," *Pasadena Daily News*, 1 December 1903, p. 1, col. 1.

44. Dr. Floyd Lacey, telephone interview by author, East Nashville, Tennessee, 11 May 2002. Dr. Lacey is the pastor of the First Baptist Church of East Nashville. Dr. Lacey read from a church history documenting Bushnell's musical contributions to Baptist hymnals.

45. "Conductor Carleton Hovers Between Life and Death," *Pasadena Daily News,* 3 June 1903, col. 1, p. 1.

46. See "Conductor Carlton Has But Small Chance of Recovery. Warrant Served on Hill," *Pasadena Daily News,* 1 June 1903, p. 1 for description of Carlton. For references to Carlton's labor affiliation and Odd-Fellows membership, see "Wounded Conductor is Very Much Improved Today," *Pasadena Daily News,* 2 June 1903, p. 1.

47. "Preliminary Examination of Archie Hill for Murder," *Pasadena Daily News,* 17 June 1903, p. 1. For the "shifty eyed" comment, see "The Slayer of Carlton Object of Much Interest," *Pasadena Daily News,* 10 June 1903, p. 1. See "Conductor Carlton Hovers between Life and Death," *Pasadena Daily News,* 3 June 1903, p. 1 for officer Reynolds' description of Hill's arrest.

48. "Conductor Carlton Has But Small Chance of Recovery. Warrant Served on Hill," *Pasadena Daily News,* 1 June 1903, p. 1; "Archie Hill's Trial begins Today Before Judge Smith," *Pasadena Daily News,* 12 October 1903, p. 1.

49. "Railway Employes [sic] Object to Eating With Negroes," *Pasadena Daily News,* 2 June 1903, p. 1.

50. "Conductor Will Carlton Dies," *Pasadena Daily News,* 4 June 1903, p. 1. For references to the funeral, see "Funeral of Conductor Carlton This Afternoon," 6 June 1903, *Pasadena Daily News,* 6 June 1903, p. 1. Also see "Preliminary Examination of Archie Hill For Murder," *Pasadena Daily News,* 17 June 1903, p. 1 for reference to Bushnell. The *Pasadena Daily News* reported that a "motley crew" of observers came to the police court for Hill's arraignment but there was no mention of any visitors of color. Apparently, other than Hill, the only African Americans in the courtroom that day were Hill's two sisters and Bushnell.

51. See "Archie Hill's Trial Begins Today before Judge Smith," for comments on jury selection. Rossiter is mentioned in John S. McGroarty, *Los Angeles Mountains to Sea,* Vol. II, p. 322. For details on the trial, see "Fights For His Life," *Pasadena Daily News,* 13 October 1903, p. 1; "'Justifiable Action,'" *Pasadena Daily News,* 14 October 1903, p. 1; "Evidence Before Jury," *Pasadena Daily News,* 15 October 1903, p. 1; "Case Near Close," *Pasadena Daily News,* 16 October 1903, p. 1; "Hill is Found Guilty," *Pasadena Daily News,* 17 October 1903, p. 1.

52. "Railway Employes [sic] Object to Eating With Negroes," *Pasadena Daily News,* 2 June 1903, p. 1.

53. Pasadena hosted Afro-American League (AAL) conventions in 1898, 1903 and 1910. In 1896, William and Charles Prince of Pasadena played significant roles in organizing the Los Angeles branch of the AAL. By 1910, the league had declined significantly because of its blind obedience to the national Republican Party, which was, by the turn of the century, beginning to alienate blacks throughout the country. See *A Brief History of the Afro-American league with Some references to Its Objects and What It Has Accomplished* (San Francisco, 1895), cited in Kelley's notes, "Politics and Organization," *Black History Collection,* PMH.

54. "Booker T. Washington Speaks to Thousands," *Pasadena Daily News,* 5 January 1903, p. 1, col. 1.

55. "Local Negroes Alarmed At The Frequency of Lynching," *Pasadena Daily News,* 28 July 1903, p. 1, col. 3.

56. For comments on the resolution, see "Afro-American Council Decides to Keep in Politics," *Pasadena Daily News,* 20 August 1903, p. 1, col. 1. For comments on the mixed-race audience, see "Negroes Disagree Over a Resolution to Quit Politics," *Pasadena Daily News,* 19 August 1903, p. 1, col. 4.

57. "Close of Ninth Congress of Afro-American Council," *Pasadena Daily News,* 21 August 1903, p. 6, col. 2.

58. "Turned Down in Pasadena," *Pasadena Evening Star,* 19 December 1903, p. 1.

59. See "Colored Man Wants Position," *Pasadena Daily News,* 26 April 1909, p. 8, for comments on application. Reynolds went on to write a Pasadena column for the *California Eagle,* succeeding Seaborn B. Carr in 1919. See "Afro-Americans Will Adjourn Tonight," 28 July 1910, p. 2, col. 2, for comments by Sister Palmer. See "Afro-Americans of State in Council," *Pasadena Daily News,* 26 July 1910, p. 6, col. 1, for Early's comments on education and the AAL infighting over Republican politics.

60. "Negroes Install Their Officers," *Pasadena Star,* 12 December 1914, p. 7, col. 2; J. Alexander Somerville, *Man of Color: An Autobiography by Dr. J. Alexander Somerville* (Los Angeles: Lorrin J. Morrison, Printing and Publishing, 1946).

61. *Minutes,* Pasadena Board of Education, 12 October 1914.

62. *Minutes,* Pasadena Board of Education, 14 May 1915

63. *Minutes,* Pasadena Board of Education, 11 October 1915.

64. "The Secretary Speaks," *California Eagle,* 4 December 1915.

65. "Editorial," *California Eagle,* 12 December 1917.

66. See "Crown City News," *California Eagle,* 12 April 1919, for notes on NAACP founding. Also see "Crown City News," 8 February 1919, for Reynolds' comments.

67. *California Eagle,* 6 February 1915.

68. "Pasadena Department," *California Eagle,* 24 June 1916.

69. The black population numbered 1,094 in 1920, which constituted two-and-one-half percent of the total population of 45,354. See Kelley's notes on "Immigration," PMH.

70. "Pasadena Department," Sharnette Boyce, editor, *California Eagle,* 29 April 1922.

71. See Fred Bull's obituary, *Star-News,* 30 August 1940, located in A.L. Hamilton's scrapbook, Box 2, vol. 4, page 102, PMH.

72. Edwin A. Cottrell, *Pasadena Social Agencies Survey* (Pasadena: Pasadena Council of Social Agencies, 1940), p. 320–321. Cottrell was a professor of political science at Stanford.

73. California Taxpayers' Association, *Survey of the Pasadena City Schools, Association Report No. 119* (Los Angeles, California, 1931), p. 166–167.

74. "Negroes Meet To Discuss Plunge," *Daily News,* 15 July 1914, p. 1:4; "Negro Taxpayers Form Association," *Pasadena Star,* July 17, 1914, p. 7.

75. See James Crimi, "The Social Status of the Negro in Pasadena, California" (Master's thesis, University of Southern California, 1941), p. 77. Crimi's study is discussed below.

76. Correspondence, Tyler and Metcalf to R.L. Metcalf, 29 July 1914, "Brookside Pool Controversy" folder, Pasadena Central Library.

77. "Negroes Given Use of Park For Day," *Pasadena Daily News,* 8 July 1916, p. 5, col. 1, and "Negro Residents Alter Picnic Plan," *Pasadena Daily News,* 11 July 1916, p. 5:5.

78. "Negro Pageant of Nations Next Week," *Pasadena Star-News,* 7 August 1920, p. 13:1; "Thousands of Negroes at Outing," *Pasadena Star-News,* 12 August 1920, p. 13:1.

79. Jackie Robinson *I Never Had It Made* (New York: G.P. Putnam's Sons, 1972), p. 18; Don Wheeldon, interview by author, Pasadena, Calif., 1 August 1991 and 15 January 1992.

80. See the correspondence between the national office of the NAACP and Thomas L. Griffith Jr., the Los Angeles NAACP attorney in charge of the suit, in The Papers of the National Association for the Advancement of Colored People, Branch Files, Series D, The West; and the Pasadena Central Library clipping file on "Brookside Plunge"; Harold P. Huls, *Pasadena Community Book* (1943), p. 248–249, PMH.

81. Cartland, p. 61.

82. Ibid., p. 61.
83. Cartland, "A Study of Negroes Living in Pasadena," p. 17.
84. Crimi, "Social Status of Negroes in Pasadena," p. 73.
85. Ibid., p. 72.
86. Ibid., p. 74.
87. Ibid., p. 117–118.
88. See Ronald Cohen's essay, "Music Goes to War: California, 1940–45," in *The Way We Really Were,* ed. Roger W. Lotchin (Urbana: University of Illinois Press, 2000), p. 47–67.
89. Cartland, p. 66.
90. Ibid., p. 64.
91. Crimi, p. 20.
92. See Crimi, ibid, for sample size and composition, p. 50–51, on property values and "agitation," p. 54, 58, on segregation, p. 59–61.
93. Ibid., p. 41.
94. Ibid., p. 46–47.
95. Wheeldon interviews, 15 July 1991, 10 August 1992.
96. "'Zoot Suit' Riots Hit Suburbs; Car Injures Policeman," *Pasadena Star-News,* 9 June 1943, p. 1, col. 2.
97. Historians of the West have tended to not pay much attention to the "Zoot Suit" riots. For a blame-the-victim depiction, see Gerald R. Nash, *The American West Transformed: The Impact of the Second World War* (Bloomington: University of Indiana Press, 1985), p. 115–118. For a different view of the riots, see Mauricio Mazon's *The Zoot-Suit Riots: The Psychology of Symbolic Annihilation* (Austin: University of Texas Press, 1984); "Act To Curb 'Zoot Suit' Violence," *Pasadena Star-News,* June 8, 1943, p. 1, col. 1.
98. "Act to Curb 'Zoot Suit' Violence," *Pasadena Star-News,* 8 June 1943, p. 1, col. 1.
99. "Two 'Zooters' Chased By 150 Soldiers Into Police Station," *Pasadena Post,* 11 June 1943, p. 1.
100. See the many articles in *The Los Angeles Times* and the Pasadena newspapers for the inflammatory language of the riots, especially "'Zoot Suit' Riots Hit Suburb; Car Injures Policeman," *Pasadena Star-News,* 9 June 1943, p. 1, col. 2; "Grand Jury Probe of 'Zoot' Rioting Due; Girl Knifed," *Pasadena Star-News,* 10 June 1943, p. 1, col. 1; "Youth Probe Opened By Governor," *Pasadena Star-News,* 12 June 1943, p. 1, col. 1.
101. "Grand Jury Probe of 'Zoot' Rioting Due; Girl Knifed," *Pasadena Star-News,* 10 June 1943, p. 1, col. 2.
102. "Jap Radio Seizes On 'Zoot Suit' Riots to Spread Propaganda," *Pasadena Star-News,* 11 June 1943, p. 1, col. 2.
103. "Zoot Suit War Is Not Costume Piece Nor International Incident But Gangsterism," *Pasadena Star-News,* 13 June 1943, p. 4, col. 1.
104. "Pasadenans Urge Race Tolerance," *Pasadena Star-News,* 18 June 1943, p. 1, col. 3.
105. "Elimination Of The Zoot Suit Psychology Is The True Task At Hand, *Pasadena Star-News,* 16 June 1943, p. 4, col. 1.
106. See George Sanchez, "Pachucos in the Making," *Common Ground,* December (1943), p. 13–20.
107. Hulburd, p. 24.
108. The term REDucation comes from Kitty Jones and Robert L. Olivier, *Progressive Education is REDucation* (Boston: Meador Publishing Company, 1956); LuVerne LaMotte's "My Board Years," in author's possession, was part of the original LaMotte collection, but when donated to the Pasadena Museum of History, the autobiography was for some unknown reason not among the papers.

109. "We Learn What We Live: The William Heard Kilpatrick Conference," Pasadena: Pasadena
      City Schools, 1949. Author's copy was given to him by Mary Beauchamp Lane and has a
      small photo of Beauchamp Lane with W.H. Kilpatrick at the Pasadena train station.
110. Cay Halberg, telephone interview by author, 12 August 1995; Louise Padelford to "Dearest
      Mum and Dad," 19 January 1949, Box 5, Louise Hawkes Padelford Papers, Special
      Collections, Vassar College. The Padelford papers have not been catalogued by Vassar
      College.
111. See Hulburd, p. 23, for Goslin's views on the teaching staff.
112. Mary Beauchamp Lane, interview by author, San Francisco, 13 January 1992; John Beineke,
      And There Were Giants in the Land: The Life of William Heard Kilpatrick (New York: Peter
      Lang Publishing, 1998), p. 323–338; Hulburd, p. 53–54.
113. In 1950, the population of Pasadena was 104,000; Altadena 35,753; Sierra Madre 7,228; La
      Canada 9,750; and Temple City 28,751. The total population served by the system was
      approximately 200,000.
114. James and Bobbie Spangler, telephone interview by author, 13 August 2002. Jim Spangler
      lived in the Linda Vista area and was bused to Eliot. He moved away in 1946, then returned
      to the Pasadena-Altadena area with his wife Bobbie in 1962. They sued the city schools in
      1968 for its discriminatory practices. Their name was attached to the federal lawsuit that
      ended segregated schools in Pasadena.
115. *Minutes,* (Elementary) Pasadena Board of Education, 28 September 1948, p. 5426–5427.
116. *Minutes,* (Elementary) Pasadena Board of Education, 24 May 1950, p. 5820; Hulburd,
      p. 62–66.
117. In the Louise Hawkes Padelford Papers held in Special Collections at Vassar College, Box
      12, are numerous folders with literature and correspondence—including membership cor-
      respondence—with conservative and far right organizations including the National
      Conservative Public Affairs Council; "Yardstick Project" a joint project from the American
      Heritage Education Corporation and Grinnell College, a conservative mid-1950's organiza-
      tion that educated against socialism; the Committee for Constitutional Government; Pro-
      America; National Society Daughters of the American Revolution; National Council for
      American Education; The Freedom Club; The Foundation for Economic Education;
      National Industrial Conference board; John Birch Society; and the National Association of
      Manufacturers. There are also file folders labeled "Anti-Catholic publications" and "anti-
      Negro publications" which contained the "Republic of Negrael, (for our eyes only)" a pro-
      posal to set up two (Mississippi and Alabama) state republics for African Americans, sup-
      ported by contributions from Harlem African-Americans. The "Anti-Jewish and Zionist
      propaganda" folder is a mix of pamphlets and broadsides attacking Zionism and Jews in gen-
      eral, including the anti-Semitic *Defender* magazine; and George Robinett's The America
      Nationalist and his Christian Nationalist Crusade.
118. Cay Halberg, telephone interview by author; correspondence with author, 6 November
      1995.
119. See Carey McWilliams, "The Enemy in Pasadena," *Christian Century* 68, 25 January 1951;
      "Open Letter to Milton Wopschall from The Executive Committee of the SDC," 11 July
      1950, located in the "School Development" folder, Pasadena Board of Education Archives,
      Pasadena Unified School District, hereafter cited as PUSD archives. Although the entire
      executive committee signed the letter, there is strong reason to attribute its authorship to
      Louise Padelford.
120. Fred M. Hechinger, education editor for the *New York Herald Tribune,* wrote three articles
      on Goslin and the Pasadena schools titled "Aftermath in Pasadena," *New York Herald*

Tribune, 6–8 August 1951 and subsequently reprinted by the American Jewish Committee, New York.

121. Hulburd, p. 68.

122. Lee Hines, past president of the Pasadena League of Women Voters, interviewed by author, Pasadena, Calif., 2 August 1992. There are no records of any deliberations regarding the establishment of the neutral zones, nor any opposition until the Pasadena branch of the NAACP threatened to sue the city in 1953. See "NAACP Hits School Board for 'Waste of Tax Fund,'" *The Independent,* 28 September 1953, p. 2; "NAACP Hits Plan to Erect Classrooms," *Pasadena Star-News,* 28 September 1953, p. 8; "Board Nixes Plea of Negroes for Schools Hearing," *The Independent,* 30 September, 1953, p. 3; Hulburd, p. 69–70.

123. *Minutes,* (Elementary) Pasadena Board of Education, 15 February 1950, p. 5750–5752.

124. Transcription of a Louise Padelford interview, Padelford Papers, Box 5, p. 21–22, no date. The interviewer is also unknown, with the initials "PLF." Also, see the *Minutes,* (Elementary) Pasadena Board of Education, 15 February 1950, p. 5750.

125. Padelford interview, p. 22.

126. *Education in Pasadena,* Senate Investigating Committee on Education, Eighth Report, Nelson Dilworth, Chairman, Senate of the State of California, 1951, p. 11–12.

127. "What Are Our Schools Teaching?" *The Independent,* 1 March 1950, p. 1.

128. Fred Runyon, former publisher of *The Independent,* interview by author, Arcadia, Calif., 8 July 1991.

129. "College Professor Says Schools Deplorable," *The Independent,* 5 March 1950, p. 10; "Films Help Second Graders at Allendale; Wandering Permitted, Forced Learning Out," *The Independent,* 9 March 1950, p. 3.

130. Robert Gilchrist, former assistant superintendent of Pasadena, telephone interview by author, 14 October 1991.

131. See the series, "Modern Education Explained" *Pasadena Star-News,* 3, 7–12 March 1950, and "Pasadena Schools Defend Modern Use of Three Rs," *Christian Science Monitor,* 9 March 1950.

132. "Forecast Record School Vote," *The Independent,* 2 June 1950, p. 1.

133. See the pamphlet, *Progressive Education Increases Delinquency,* National Council for American Education, no date.

134. "Zoll, Hate-Monger, Promotes New Racket," *New York World-Telegram,* 25 August 1948, p. 6.

135. McWilliams, p. 10–15.

136. *Minutes,* (Elementary) Pasadena Board of Education, 24 May 1950, p. 5820.

137. *Minutes,* (Elementary) Pasadena Board of Education, 8 August 1950, p. 5920.

138. Willard Goslin to Frank Wells, 25 May 1950, folder, "School Development Council," PUSD archives. Goslin's reply to Wells was blunt: "We will make any and all such information ... available to your representative ... We will do so in spite of the element of disrespect of the Board of Education ands its Administrative Staff, which is implied in your continuing to send outside persons into the board offices ..."

139. *Minutes,* (Elementary) Pasadena Board of Education, 19 April 1950, p. 5795; John Holmes, interview by author, Pasadena, California, 29 July 1991.

140. "School Zones Stir Debate in Pasadena," 26 May 1950, *The Los Angeles Times,* sec. II, p. 1; "Stirred Furor in Pasadena," *The Los Angeles Times,* 26 May 1950, 20 June 1951.

141. *Minutes,* (Elementary) Pasadena Board of Education, 19 April and 3 May 1950, p. 5795, 5803–5804; *Daily People's World,* 5 May 1950, p. 1; *Jackson v. Pasadena City School District,* 382 P. 2d 878,882, 31 (1963), cited in Meyer Weinberg, *Race and Place: A Legal History of*

the Neighborhood School (Washington, DC: U.S. Government Printing Office, 1965), p. 68–69.

142. "'Rat Packers' Stab Man With Ice Pick," *The Independent,* 17 May 1950, p. 1; "Rat Pack Beats Up Man Defending Wife," *The Independent,* 19 May 1950, p. 1; "Rat Pack Terror," *The Independent,* 20 May 1950, p. 1.

143. "Rat Pack Beatings Reds' Work," *The Independent,* 22 May 1950, p. 1. See the "Civil Rights Congress Papers" at the Southern California Library for Social Studies and Research, "Rat Packs" folder.

144. LaMotte, "School Activities and Board Years." Hulburd, p. 96, 129.

145. *Minutes,* (Elementary) Pasadena Board of Education, 7 June 1950, p. 6743–6744. The total vote was 22,210 against, 10,032 for. The one precinct voting in favor of the increase was 170 for, 137 against.

146. "Open Letter to Milton Wopschall," 11 July 1950, folder, School Development Council, PUSD archives.

147. Ibid.

148. Dr. Ernest Brower to Milton Wopschall, 5 September 1950; Milton Wopschall to Dr. Ernest Brower, 15 August 1950, both in folder, School Development Council, PUSD archives.

149. Mary Beauchamp Lane, interview by author; Robert Gilchrist, telephone interview by author.

150. Padelford interview, p. 31; Don Wheeldon, interview by author; Elbie Hickambottom, former member of the Pasadena Board of Education, interview by author, Pasadena, Calif., 6 January 2001.

151. Mary L. Allen, *Education or Indoctrination* (Caldwell, Idaho: Caxton Printers, Inc., 1955), p. 152–153. Allen's book was intended as a rebuttal to Hulburd's *This Happened in Pasadena* and the NEA report, *The Pasadena Story.* Also see Charles Wollenberg, *All Deliberate Speed: Segregation and Exclusion in California Schools, 1855–1975* (Berkeley: University of California Press, 1976), p. 139–141.

152. Padelford interview, p. 30–31.

153. Hulburd, p. 133–153; Allen, p. 198–206.

154. *Education in Pasadena,* Senate Investigating Committee on Education, Eighth Report, Nelson Dilworth, chairman, Senate of the State of California, 1951.

155. "Harry Hill," transcription of the interview of Felix Robb by Weldon T. Ellis, Special Collections, Jean and Alexander Heard Library, Vanderbilt University, no date, p. 28–32; The NEA report, *The Pasadena Story,* was published under the auspices of the "National Commission for the Defense of Democracy Through Education," an NEA organization established years before the Goslin affair in an attempt to defend public education from political attacks.

156. Charlie Padelford, telephone interview by author, 12 March 1999. See the many folders on Zen Buddhism and meditation, Box 6, Padelford Papers, Vassar College.

157. Robert Shaplen, "Scarsdale's Battle of the Books," *Commentary,* January 1951, p. 530–540.

158. The most vitriolic of attacks was Albert Lynd's *Quackery in the Public Schools* (New York: Grosset and Dunlap, 1953). Then there was Arthur Bestor's *Educational Wastelands: The Retreat from Learning in Our Public Schools* (Urbana: University of Illinois Press, 1952), in which Bestor blamed progressive education for too many national evils, including poor teacher education programs. See John Beineke's *And There Were Giants in the Land,* for a perceptive analysis of the antiprogressive attacks during the 1950s, p. 389–409. Later, during the 1960s, there were others, such as Richard Hofstadter's *Anti-intellectualism in American Life* (New York: Alfred A. Knopf, 1963), especially Part V: "Education in a Democracy,"

p. 299–392, in which he attacks progressive education's infatuation with "The Child and the World."

159. "Jackson Pollack," *Life Magazine,* vol. 29:6, 8 August 1949, p. 42–45.

160. *Report of the Pasadena School Survey,* 1951 (Pasadena: Pasadena City Board of Education, 1952); "Louise Padelford to Dearest Dad," 12 February 1951, Padelford Papers, Box 8.

161. "Aftermath in Pasadena," *New York Herald Tribune,* 6–8 August 1951; Hulburd, p. 41–42. For Wopschall quote, see "Stirred Furor in Pasadena," *The Los Angeles Times,* 20 June 1951, p. 5.

162. Walker, p. 41.

163. "Are Our School Boards Being Captured?" FACTS Vol. V:3 (May–June 1957), p. 1; "Crisis in the Summertime," *News COPE,* Vol. 8:1 (24 October 1957); LaMotte, "School Activities and Board Years."

164. "Crisis in the Summertime," *News COPE* Vol. 8:1 (24 October 1957); LaMotte, "School Activities and Board Years."

165. Walter Shatford, former member of the Pasadena Board of Education, telephone interview with author, Pasadena, Calif., 22 July 2002.

166. Skipper and Pat Rostker, telephone interview with author, Monrovia, California, 31 July 2002; see Carl Bernstein and Bob Woodward, *All The President's Men,* 2nd ed. (New York: Touchstone Books, 1994), p. 59–63, 82–83, 90, for Mardian's post-Pasadena story. Bernstein and Woodward refer to Mardian as "the housecleaner."

167. "Transfer Permits and Releases—Policies and Regulations," *Superintendent's Bulletin* Number 8, 22 July 1958, vertical files, PUSD archives; Donald McAlpin, "Analysis of the Efforts to Promote Racial Desegregation within the Pasadena Unified School District as Directed by the Court Order of Judge Manuel L. Real in January of 1970" (Ph.D. diss., Walden University, 1972), p. 105. Donald McAlpin, a longtime school counselor in the Pasadena system, used files, documents and interviews to assemble his data. The dissertation is an excellent and useful contribution to the literature on Pasadena's schools.

168. "La Canada Votes School Unification," *Pasadena Star-News,* 19 October 1960, p. 19. The *Star-News* reporter quoted James Reynolds, chairman of the Committee for a La Canada Unified School District, who said the vote was "an expression of political maturity ..." Also see "Future of Linda Vista Area Students Poses New Problem," *Pasadena Star-News,* 20 October 1960, p. 19.

169. See William Cohen's case study, "Pasadena," in *Law and Society Review* Vol. 11:1 (November 1967), p. 44–45. The November issue was devoted to eight case studies based upon reports prepared for the U.S. Office of Education. On the complaints the board had been unduly influenced by the East Arroyo parents, see the correspondence between Franklin H. Williams, Assistant Attorney General, State of California to Dr. Robert Jenkins, Superintendent of Pasadena Schools, 20, 28 December 1960, 17, 20 January 1961. Also see the transcript of audio tape, "Minutes of the Regular Meeting," Pasadena City Board of Education, November 29, 1960, held at Linda Vista Elementary School, p. 12, 500–516, all at PUSD archives.

170. For income data, see Cohen, p. 42; for data on schools, see McAlpin, p. 77.

171. "N.A.A.C.P. Hits Plan To Erect Classrooms," *Pasadena Star-News,* 28 September 1953, p. A-1, "NAACP Hits School Board for 'Waste of Tax Fund,'" *The Independent,* 28 September 1953, p. 2.

172. "Board Nixes Plea of Negroes for Schools Hearing," *The Independent,* 30 September 1953, p. 3. See "Warren to Be Chief Justice," *The Independent,* 30 September 1953, p. 3.

173. Charles Johnson, attorney for the NAACP, interview by author, Pasadena, Calif., 21 January 1992; see "Reporter's Transcript of Depositions," 5 December 1953, Superior Court, State of California, County of Los Angeles, no. 621, 618, PUSD archives.

174. McAlpin, p. 66; Lynn Vernon "A Review of the Pasadena Unified School District's Pasadena Plan for Desegregating Pasadena's Schools," p. 1–2, photocopy, in author's possession. The report was authorized by the PUSD in 1993 and released, with editorial changes unknown to Ms. Vernon, under the same title.

175. *Minutes,* Pasadena Board of Education, p. 12, 504–505; Cohen, p. 44–45; Walter Shatford, interview by author.

176. *Minutes,* Pasadena Board of Education, p. 12, 505–506, 510–511.

177. Cohen, p. 45; for Salisian's "neighborhood schools" comment, see *Minutes,* Pasadena Board of Education, p. 12, 515; also see the "Confidential Correspondence, Superintendent Jenkins to County counsel, James Briggs," 26 September 1961, in La Canada Withdrawal folder, PUSD archives.

178. See Jackson's "Application for Intra-District Transfer" in *Jackson v. Pasadena* folder, PUSD archives.

179. *Jackson v. Pasadena* folder, PUSD archives; Cohen, p. 48–50; McAlpin, p. 79; Wollenberg, p. 141–142; James Coleman et al., *Equality of Educational Opportunity* (Washington, DC: Government Printing Office, 1966), p. 480.

180. "New Action Looms in Racial Case," *Pasadena Star-News,* 29 September 1961; "NAACP Starts Drive on Schools in North, South," *The Los Angles Times,* 13 February 1962; "Pasadena Target of NAACP School Integration Drive," *The Independent,* 13 February 1962.

181. Charles Wollenberg, *All Deliberate Speed: Segregation and Exclusion in California Schools, 1855–1975* (Berkeley: University of California Press, 1976), p. 141–142.

182. *Jackson v. Pasadena School District,* 59 Cal. 2d 978,82 (1963).

183. Cohen, p. 50.

184. Vernon, p. 2–3; McAlpin, p. 80–83. In June 1965 the editors of *Know Your Schools,* which was published in Pasadena by a group of volunteers, reported that of the 13 percent who transferred to eastside schools, over a third were white. The editors also pointed out that the transfers came from wealthier families. See *Know Your Schools,* Vol. 7:6 (June 1965) as cited in Julie Salley Gray, "To Fight the Good Fight: The Battle Over Control of the Pasadena City Schools, 1969–1979," *Essays in History* 37 (1995), http://etext.lib.virginia.edu/journals/EH/EH40/steinh40.html, p. 3.

185. "Vandals Strike In Pasadena," *Pasadena Star-News,* 14 August 1965, p. 1; "Riot," *Pasadena Star-News,* 16 August 1965, p. 1–3.

186. Stanley Siegel, "Incident in Pasadena," *Frontier* 17 (December 1965), p. 11–12; author interviews with Walter Shatford, Don Wheeldon, Skipper and Pat Rostker.

187. Lee Austin, "Pasadena School Board Vows to Push Anti-Segregation Plan," *The Los Angeles Times,* 8 May 1966, p. 1, 3, sec. 2; Vernon, p. 3–4, McAlpin, p. 82–84.

188. Roy Reed, "Schools In Pasadena Confronted by Classic Segregation Crisis," *The New York Times,* 7 April 1968, p. 24.

189. Vernon, p. 7.

190. Vernon, p. 4–5, McAlpin, p. 87–88; author interviews with Spangler, Rostker and Walter Shatford.

191. The gerrymandering quote is from "Schools Dispute Nears Eruption," *The Independent,* 1 December 1968; also see "Dispute Arises Over Courses on Minorities," *The Los Angeles Times,* 4 April 1968. Houser and Welsh objected to "singling out the Negro and Mexican-

American for special [curriculum] study; they wanted a "broader course ... on all minorities to how they assimilated into American society."

192. Lee Austin, "Pasadena Nears Crossroads on Integration of Schools," *The Los Angeles Times,* 18 June 1967, p. 1, 10, sec. 2; Vernon, p. 5–6, McAlpin, p. 87–88; Walter Shatford, interview, by author.

193. Spangler and Rostker, interviews by author; also see Vernon, p. 6, McAlpin, p. 90, and "Court Denies Injunction In Shifting of Students," *The Independent,* 16 August 1967.

194. Vernon, p. 8, McAlpin, p. 92; Spangler, interview by author.

195. Spangler and Rostker, interviews by author; *Chris Williams et al. v. Pasadena City Board of Education,* in *Williams v. Pasadena* folder, PUSD archives; McAlpin, p. 90–91; Vernon, p. 8; Austin and Snyder, p. 1. Vernon cites a Muir meeting on 2 July 1968 when 1,200 people filled the auditorium "with speaker after speaker" imploring the board to act. Boyko told the board that if they "did not sit down with my clients for a prompt and frank face-to-face discussion ..." he would resubmit the suit. Only LaMotte and Engholm expressed interest in such a meeting.

196. Vernon, p. 9–10; Walter Shatford, interview by author; Spangler and Rostker, interviews by author.

197. Lee Austin, "U.S. Probes Pasadena's Schools on Civil Rights," *The Los Angeles Times,* 6 June 1968, p. 1, 2.

198. For Hornbeck quote, see "Schools Dispute Nears Eruption," *The Independent,* 1 December 1968, p. 1.

199. LaMotte, author interview; for LaMotte quote see, "Schools Dispute Nears Eruption," *The Independent,* 1 December 196, p. 1. Also see Wollenberg, p. 149–153.

200. "U.S. Permitted to Join Pasadena School Suit," *The Los Angeles Times,* 5 December 1968.

201. "School Trustees Hire Attorneys To Fight Lawsuit," *Pasadena Star-News,* 10 January 1969, and "Race Suit Study Due For Board," *Pasadena Star-News,* 4 November 1969; "Integration: Laws, Guidelines and Plans, Ethnic Distribution in Pasadena's Schools," *League of Women Voters of Pasadena* (December 1968), p. 2.

202. "De Facto Bias—Is City Guilty?" *Pasadena Star-News,* 2 November 1969, p. 1.

203. "White Students Leaving Pasadena School System in Record Number," *The Los Angeles Times,* 1 January 1970, p. 1.

204. "United States v. School Board: Pasadena Racial Test Case Starts Tuesday," *The Los Angeles Times,* 4 January 1970; "U.S. Court School Suit Due Today," *Pasadena Star-News,* 4 January 1970.

205. Lucie Lowery, "Judge Orders Schools to Integrate," *Pasadena Star-News,* 19 January 1970, p. 1; Vernon, p. 11.

206. Lucie Lowery, "School Board Rejects Appeal; Welsh Resigns," *Pasadena Star-News,* 28 January 1970, p. 1.

207. Ibid.; Vernon, p. 14.

208. Ibid. For the comments on the city streets and busing, see "Directors Refuse City Intervention in School Case," *Pasadena Star-News,* 28 January 1970, p. 3.

209. Vernon, p. 13.

210. Vernon, p. 14; Lucie Lowery, "New Suit Looming for City Schools," *Pasadena Star-News,* 1 January 1970, p. 1; Lucie Lowery, "23 Parents Ask School Suit Entry," *Pasadena Star-News,* 3 March 1970, p. 1; Lucie Lowery, "Intervention Plea On School Denied," *Pasadena Star-News,* 4 March 1970, p. 1; Lucie Lowery, "School Appeal Studied," *Pasadena Star-News,* 13 April 1970, p. 1; "Pasadena Appeal Rejected," *Pasadena Star-News,* 10 May 1970, p. 1, 3.

211. "Recall Election Divides Pasadena," *The New York Times,* 11 October 1970, p. 64; "Pasadena Voters Support School Board Members Who Back Integration," *The New York Times,* 15

October 1970, p. 28; Tom Wicker, op-ed, "Some News for the Court," *The New York Times*, 18 October 1970, sec. IV: p. 15; Vernon, p. 15. The Mexican-American community organized against the recall, one of the few recognized public displays of political power by the Latino community in some time. It would not be the last. "Mexican-Americans Against the Recall," a flyer located in LuVerne LaMotte's papers at the Pasadena Museum of History, was signed by the president of the Mutualista Club of Pasadena, founded early in the century and the president of MECHa, the Movimiento Estudiantil Chicano de Aztlan (Chicano student movement), a more radical student organization in the 1960s that continues to stir the waters around the country.

212. Vernon, p. 15–16. Just after he was elected, Marcheschi, in a rather transparent move to undo the court order, presented his "New Pasadena Plan," in which he outlined a "recommended new approach to achieve voluntary integration and equality of educational opportunity." In effect, his "plan" divided the district in two, one white, the other not. See "The New Pasadena Plan," 25 October 1971, in Samuel Sheats Papers, PMH.

213. Vernon, p. 16–17.

214. Julie Salley Gray, "To Fight the Good Fight: The Battle Over Control of the Pasadena City Schools, 1969–1979," *Essays in History* 37 (1995), http://etext.lib.virginia.edu/journals/EH/EH40/steinh40.html, p. 1–18. Salley Gray, the daughter of Robert Salley, longtime head of the Pasadena Federation of Teachers, offers a perceptive analysis of the fundamentalist board. She argues that the fight is better understood as a local example of the national restoration of the political far right. She does not, though, situate the fundamentalists in any historical context. She errs when she refers to the board as a "Mormon board," meaning, she says, that the majority belonged to the Church of Latter Day Saints. In fact, as former board president George Van Alstine pointed out in correspondence with the author, the board did not have more than two members from the Mormon Church at any time during the 1970s.

215. Salley Gray, p. 8; Henry S. Myers, *Fundamentally Speaking* (San Francisco: Strawberry Hill Press, 1977), p. 51; Vernon, p. 16–17.

216. Myers, p. 53; Vernon, p. 19; Salley Gray, p. 6–8.

217. Myers, p. 53, 123; for his comments on federal "interference," see p. 40–42.

218. Ibid., p. 54.

219. Myers, p. 11.

220. Ibid., p. 18–19.

221. Ibid., p. 56.

222. Richard Vetterli, *Storming the Citadel: The Fundamental Revolution Against Progressive Education* (Costa Mesa: Educational Media Press, 1976), p. 3. Vetterli wrote, "Often meetings are characterized by hissing and booing, catcalls, etc., sometimes even during the prayer and Pledge of Allegiance that open each meeting." Vetterli said that Myers would adjourn the meetings, fearing that "the disruptions might place spectators in some jeopardy." For comments on the board meetings, see Salley Gray, p. 10–11. For comments on Sheats, see Noel Greenwood, "Pasadena Schools: How Much Turmoil Can They Take?" *The Los Angeles Times*, 7 July 1974, sec. III, p. 1.

223. Myers, p. 57; Vernon, p. 23; Salley Gray, p. 12.

224. Myers, p. 57; Vernon, p. 18.

225. Becky Bartindale, "Schools freed of court control," *Pasadena Star-News*, 7 June 1979, p. A1, col. 5.

226. David Zahniser, "Busing: 30 years After Landmark Decision," *Pasadena Star-News*, 23 January 2000, p. A-6.

CHAPTER 8

MASSIVE RESISTANCE
"Freedom of Choice"

In one of his last official acts as superintendent of Charlottesville's schools, Dr. James Johnson, about to retire after 40 years of service to the community, submitted to the board of education his end-of-year report. Written early in May 1945, the report reflected Johnson's typical compulsive detail. For the last few years, the city had been "adjusting" to the federal court order equalizing salaries between black and white teachers, so Johnson's report listed every teacher in the system, both black and white, with his or her current salary and the proposed increase for the following year. What set Johnson's end-of-year report apart from prior teacher "re-elections," was his recommendation that five teachers be "let go."

In a growing city the size of Charlottesville, releasing a handful of teachers might not have caused much of a stir except that all five were from the same school. The teachers were experienced educators, without any apparent blemish on their personnel records. Most important, all were from Jefferson High School, the only black secondary school in the city. In the preceding few years, seven teachers at Jefferson had quit or been fired. Now, in one end-of-year recommendation, the superintendent wanted to replace nearly a third of the teaching staff. In notes penned along the margin of his copy of Johnson's memo, A.L. Hench, a longtime member of the board, made it clear that something serious was unfolding at the school. "It is said," Hench wrote, "that these [five teachers] have been attempting to incite insubordination to [principal] Duncan. Hence we dropped consideration of the re-election of any teacher in the Jefferson High School."[1] Until Hench and his colleagues on the board got to the bottom of the supposed insubordination, no black teachers (including the librarian and school clerks) were to be reappointed for the following year.

Owen Duncan, the target of the alleged insubordination, was principal of the city's only black high school. The building contained both the "grammar grades" (what would be called a junior high school if in a separate building) and the secondary school. It appears that his main administrative duties were at the high school. Duncan had taken over the school before the war, and the break with some of his faculty is the first indication that the white community had of any significant discord at Jefferson. That is not to say that the white school board did not have knowledge of the substandard conditions at the two schools. Throughout the Depression decade, black educators and school patrons had been feuding with the board over the quality of education at Jefferson. Until the spring of 1945, however, there had never been any indication that there was concern within the black community over the quality of school leadership.

Insubordination is serious business and grounds for immediate dismissal, so the board moved quickly but cautiously. Johnson's recommendation to terminate the Jefferson teachers had come at Duncan's request, but the board suspected there might have been more to the situation than the principal's side of the story. Along with the reelection memo, Johnson sent board members a copy of a letter he had received from a "citizen's committee" of concerned parents and patrons. A few weeks before, at a community meeting in late April, the entire Jefferson High School faculty—all 18 teachers as well as the librarian and school clerk—had risen in protest against Duncan. Before a "large group of citizens," the Jefferson teachers aired their many grievances. They accused Duncan of all sorts of antiprogressive school practices, including managing the school as if it were his personal fiefdom. As a result of his "autocratic" and "dictatorial" leadership, there were no longer "harmonious relations" between the teachers and the principal. Furthermore, many teachers were afraid of the man: he was "threatening," "sarcastic," "belittling," "coarse" and "offensive" to nearly everyone but especially toward the five he wanted removed. As the board would soon find out, these were some of the most experienced and respected teachers at the school.

At the community meeting the teachers said they had no idea how Duncan evaluated their teaching. There were no known criteria or standards of classroom performance. One of the teachers on Johnson's dismissal list had been at the school five years but never had an evaluation that questioned his ability. The teachers said Duncan "disrespected [their] intelligence," and if a teacher challenged his authority, he would retaliate by announcing that Jefferson was "overstaffed," implying their positions were "temporary." Maud Gamble, who once was the head teacher at the elementary school, said the sixth- and seventh-grade teachers (the grammar grades) kept quiet because they "feared for their jobs." As far as she was concerned, this controversy was between Duncan and the high school teachers. What most disturbed the black community was that the teachers said student discipline was "deplorable." According to one of the teachers, the students so disrespected Duncan that when he rose to speak at an assembly, they "booed and hissed."[2]

Ten influential black leaders—including a minister, the head of the parent-teacher association, and a prominent businessman and former newspaper pub-

Fig. 26. Jefferson Colored High School, c. 1939. *(Photo courtesy of the Albert and Shirley Small Special Collections Library, University of Virginia.)*

lisher (who also happened to be the husband of a Duncan adversary)—sent the protest letter to Johnson and the board.[3] It was clear that some in the African-American community had a serious problem with the school's leadership. Duncan and a majority of the high-school teachers had developed a profound dislike for one another. The white board of education needed to investigate—but from their perspective, this was not about "race relations." Duncan was black and so were all the teachers. The blowup at Jefferson was apparently caused by bad blood between the teachers and the principal. Board Chairman Albert Balz put together a "Special Committee to Investigate Conditions at Jefferson High School," including himself, Hench and Superintendent Johnson. Another board member, George Starnes, an attorney in Charlottesville, would chair the proceedings. The next week Starnes began to call in the teachers, one by one.

The board, reflecting the marginal status of the black community, decided that the interviews would be held at Lane High, the new white high school, rather than at Jefferson. The board wanted to know if the controversy was confined to interpersonal relationships—was Duncan a poor administrator causing the teachers to react to the lack of "harmonious relations?" Or was the principal being challenged by a group of "hot heads," or worse yet, "radicals?" As the testimony began to unfold, the answer turned out to be both. The interviews went on for two weeks and included meetings with members of the "Charlottesville 400," the core of the city's African-American elite. But Starnes, Balz, Hench and their fellow board members could not see that the Jefferson School controversy was about more than "bad blood." This was, after all, about race and caste.[4]

"Morale Cards" and the Balance of Power

As the interviews began—even though Starnes told each teacher that his or her testimony was to be "given freely, was entirely confidential, and questions need not be answered if the teacher did not wish to do so"—one suspects that the teachers and clerks thought twice before being entirely candid. This was the board that hired Duncan. They paid his salary (and theirs) and had complete oversight of the educational affairs at the school. The black teachers were meeting alone with their white employers at the white high school, so deference to the powerful was in order. Even so, each was polite and cordial, the teachers were clear—the school was in "poor shape," and Duncan was mainly at fault. The principal was "uncouth," "dogmatic," "insecure" and "spasmodic." One teacher said, "He can be as nice as you please; sometimes he can turn around and be otherwise." Most feared the man—yet few stood up to him. These were the teachers most invested in the school, from coaching after-school team sports to directing the drama club, student government and debate. Duncan called them the "troublemakers." They and other teachers and clerks reported "screaming" confrontations in the hallways between some teachers and Duncan. During faculty meetings, which one teacher referred to as "torture chambers," there were repeated clashes.

One of the teacher leaders was Carrie Michie, though she was not on Johnson's termination list. Her 1939 master's thesis, written under the direction of Edna Colson at Virginia State College, stressed "cooperation in a democratic society" as the means by which democratic schools can solve problems. Duncan thought Michie "weak" and later said that "all the weak ones" gather about the "troublemakers." Duncan portrayed the crisis as a plot to challenge his leadership. He told the school board investigative committee that he "had been fighting subversive ... means," and the teachers' charges had been "taken entirely out of their circumstances." It was the "troublemakers" who were behind the "ruckus," and they were out to destroy his authority.[5]

According to the teacher testimony, Owen Duncan was no progressive. His leadership, indeed, was flawed. Again and again, the committee heard how the principal would publicly reprimand the teachers while students stood and watched. He would challenge teachers' authority and belittle their lesson plans, often displaying his displeasure by tearing up those plans in front of the shocked and embarrassed teacher. One teacher told the committee that Duncan curried favor with the students by abandoning long-established school rules and regulations. He was "uneven" in his student discipline, often having different punishments for the same offense. His "Morale Cards," a pseudonym for his teacher disciplinary cards ("You can contribute to the morale of the school by observing the regulations concerning the subject indicated below ..."), were particularly irksome. He would have a student messenger deliver the bright blue "Morale Card" to a classroom teacher, and the students would know Duncan had struck. Teachers were convinced he was purposely undermining their authority.[6]

Morale at Jefferson was dreadful, and his hated blue cards only made it worse. Once Duncan made the teachers write lengthy "Philosophy of Education" statements. After more than a week of laboring during after-school meetings, he told the teachers he was "disappointed" because all of the philosophies were "weak" and "unscholarly." He told them he had "thrown them in the trashcan." When they protested, he had them write new philosophies. The teachers never heard what happened to those, although Duncan told Starnes and the committee that he had included them in his state Department of Education report.[7]

Duncan's testimony before the committee was, as Hench said in his notes, "startlingly inconsistent." According to Duncan, there was no disciplinary problem with the students. He suggested the teachers had not told the committee the truth. He "always took recommendations and suggestions from the faculty." And although the school had its problems, he said Jefferson was far from "deplorable." When pressed by Starnes, Duncan said the problem was the five "troublemakers" he had recommended for dismissal. Specifically, it was two veteran teachers, both women. He told the committee that one of these teachers had "been on the spot" regarding her professional "fitness" just as he took over as principal. She had been "rescued," he said, by the other teacher, and, ever since, the two of them had formed "an alliance ... to weaken his influence among the teachers." He finished his testimony by telling the committee he did not "tend to dominate," and he relied on the faculty in a "very democratic procedure."[8]

A half century later, reading from the committee transcripts and the notes from Balz and Hench, one can sense the enormous gulf between Duncan and the teachers. Starnes had asked a teacher (one of the two women Duncan most disliked) if she had any idea why Duncan might not "get along" with the teachers. She told the committee that Duncan was "insecure" and that he "didn't have tact" in making friends, and, as a result, he was "hostile to everyone." He had "an inferiority complex," and she thought his "attitude was really a defense mechanism." None of the teachers came out and said Duncan was miscast in the role of principal—that would have been too risky—but the implication was clear: before Jefferson High could be fixed, Duncan had to go. Many—but only those *not* on Duncan's dismissal list—said the teachers should shoulder some of the blame. When Starnes asked one of the "troublemakers" if the fault lay entirely with Duncan, she said, "If everyone said nothing, there would be no trouble, but would that be best for the system?"[9]

What was "best for the system" was the long-festering question that divided white Charlottesville from the black community. Everything in this small Southern city was about race. As a result, the board's options were limited. The testimony pointed to a poorly equipped administrator who practiced a kind of school leadership rooted in an authoritarian tradition. The situation was so dreadful that the five targeted teachers (three were women) had become confrontational, argumentative, disrespectful and insubordinate toward a male authority. From the teachers' perspective, the situation had become unmanageable. Yet, outside the school, an element of black leadership in the community praised Duncan. After the committee had taken the teachers' testimony, its members interviewed eight influential citizens, including Thomas Inge, a merchant, two doctors and a minister. Duncan had lived in the Inge household when he first arrived, and the grocer vouched for his dedication and work ethic. Whether the committee had solicited these interviews is unclear. One citizen told the committee that "he and the group had come down merely to see what they could do to help ..." None of the eight were critical of Duncan. Many praised his leadership, which may have been more an act of deference to white power than outright support for the principal since to openly criticize a black leader appointed by a white board called into question white rule.

Perhaps the controversy was more a reflection of the class-based conflicts Michie described in her master's thesis. Michie had criticized the school for not effectively meeting the needs of rural children who had come to Charlottesville to attend school. According to Michie, Jefferson was "undemocratic," because country kids were made to feel inadequate compared to their more cosmopolitan classmates. There was friction between those who were succeeding at Jefferson and those who were not. The community leaders who came before the board's investigative committee, perhaps reflecting their middle-class accomodationist sensibilities, felt that morale suffered because some students were not getting the needed "discipline."[10]

"DOWN WITH DUNCAN!"

The need for increased "discipline" seemed particularly salient because the city was also abuzz with talk of a student strike. The white community heard about a possible strike the same day it read about the rift between Duncan and the teachers. On May 7, the *Charlottesville Daily Progress,* the largest white newspaper in the city, reported that the school board was not investigating a "lack of harmonious relations" between Duncan and the teachers, but rather was looking into efforts by "certain teachers" to organize a student walkout. According to the newspaper, the black Parent-Teacher Association (PTA) was solidly behind Duncan. A spokesperson named Helen Smith from the PTA's "publicity committee" told

Fig. 27. The photo is an edited composite taken from the Crimson and Black, the 1943 Jefferson High School yearbook. *Top row left to right:* Owen J. Duncan, Jr., Carrie W. Michie, Eleanora B. Sellers. *Bottom row left to right:* Elsie C. Heiskell, Booker T. Reaves, Leon W. Armistead. *(Photo courtesy of the Albert and Shirley Small Special Collections Library, University of Virginia)*

the newspaper that there was a "small group" of discontented citizens against Duncan but they did not represent the majority of the PTA. Smith implicated "certain faculty," telling the press that the board's investigation had nothing to do with the principal's fitness. As far as Charlottesville's white community was concerned, the Jefferson blowup was about a few "radical" teachers and their disruptive students.[11]

The *Daily Progress* failed to check the Helen Smith story. The next day, Douglass Edwards, the PTA president, told the newspaper that no one on the PTA knew a Helen Smith. She apparently was a fraud, as was her "publicity committee," something Edwards said did not exist. Further, her charges that the PTA was solidly behind Duncan were, according to Edwards, "a vicious ... hoax." Edwards told the newspaper that, although the PTA had yet to take an official position, the issue before the board's investigative committee was about Duncan's fitness as principal, not a student strike. Edwards saw the threatened student walkout as symptomatic of Duncan's failure to lead.[12]

The board knew that there had been strike plans, and, further, they knew some of the teachers were involved. But the investigative committee did not know which teachers and to what extent the strike plans had progressed. One teacher told Starnes that the students in his class thought the walkout was "all in fun." Another said he had seen a sign in a classroom window that said "Down With Duncan," but it had been quickly removed. Some of the teachers denied any knowledge of the strike, while others said the newspaper report was the first they had heard of it. When asked about the threatened strike, Duncan told the committee that the "troublemakers," specifically the two women he most disliked, were behind it. To Duncan, the potential walkout was "the culmination of the group's subversive activities." He told the committee that getting rid of the two women was "for the good of the school."[13]

One of the women Duncan wanted out was Eleanora Sellers, wife of T.J. Sellers, the former publisher of the city's first black newspaper, *The Reflector*. The newspaper had had a short history—it was in business for only a few years during the 1930s—but T.J. and Eleanor Sellers had made their mark. The Sellers were pillars of the community, actively engaged in the political and social affairs of Charlottesville. Eleanora Sellers helped organize some of the first black women's organizations in the city. She and her husband were two of the most visible and respected members of Charlottesville's black elite. T.J. Sellers was one of the 10 members of the community who first brought the complaints about Duncan to the board. He was an outspoken critic of white rule, and his editorial writing often took the city's white leadership to task for its unequal distribution of funds in the name of public education. After the war, he had become the Charlottesville editor of *The Roanoke Tribune,* an influential black weekly newspaper.[14]

The Sellers did not go unnoticed by some in the white community. A few years after the war ended, Sarah Patton Boyle, a white liberal from Charlottesville, sought T.J. Sellers' aid in helping her understand why her offer of "assistance" to Gregory Swanson, the first African American admitted to the University of Virginia law school, was rebuffed. Swanson had angrily walked out on Boyle when she read him a draft of a newspaper article she had written. Although she had never met him, Boyle knew Sellers' reputation in the community and contacted him in the hope that he could shed light on why Swanson had become so angry at her offer of "help." When Sellers read Boyle's proposed newspaper article, he accused her of "gross paternalism" that arose out of what he called "the 'Master class' turned liberal" syndrome. Over the ensuing months, the two continued to meet and talk. Boyle ended up referring to those meetings as "The T.J. Sellers Course for Backward Southern Whites." The lessons she learned from

Sellers about paternalism and race became her best-selling book, *The Desegregated Heart*. Later in the decade, she would be one of the most outspoken white critics of Virginia's "Massive Resistance" to school desegregation. Boyle learned that being quiet was not in the Sellers' family tradition. During the Duncan controversy, it was Eleanora Sellers who told the investigating committee that being quiet about Duncan was not "best for the system."15

WHITE POWER AND BLACK AGENCY

As the board's investigative committee gathered for its final deliberations in late May of 1945, what was "best for the system" turned on two crucial questions. Would students carrying signs and chanting "Down With Duncan!" have walked out, organized (maybe) by two "radical" teachers? Or was this "ruckus," to use Duncan's term, the result of a very personal, long-simmering grievance between the principal and the two women? The second question may have become a significant concern to the board's investigation, because during the teacher testimony the committee was stunned when Eleanora Sellers' colleague—the other woman Duncan disliked—accused him of sexual misconduct. This was the teacher who earlier had told the committee that Duncan was "tactless" and "spasmodic" due to his "inferiority complex."

During the testimony, the woman told Starnes and the committee that at the end of Duncan's first year as principal, he had filed a complaint against her with the superintendent, and, as a result, Dr. Johnson had withheld her salary increase. Duncan never told her of his complaint. When she found out, she confronted Duncan, but he denied having any knowledge of why her pay raise had been turned down by Johnson. She later met with the superintendent, and, as she said to Starnes, "the matter was cleared up." The exact nature of Duncan's initial complaint against her remains a mystery, but just as Starnes and the committee were getting ready to make their final recommendations, Hench wrote, "... If [she] charges D ... then we will have to have a real trial. Or she must drop the matter since it is an old matter and she did not bring the matter up at the time." He concluded with, "Can we make a decision without having D. face [the teacher]?"16

Was the struggle between Duncan and the Jefferson teachers provoked by the personal conflict between the woman and Duncan? If that was the case, what would the board tell the public? Balz and his colleagues concluded they needed to discipline Owen Duncan, but they also needed to discipline the teachers. In Charlottesville's biracial system, however, any decision the white board made could not be construed as sanctioning any increase in black political power. Therefore, the board would not dismiss Duncan. To do so would embolden the teachers and the larger black community that had first aired the grievances. Equally important, the board could not fire the five teachers. To do so would only encourage a near-tyrannical principal. Central to the board's public position was its belief that it must remain above the internal bickering in the black community. To Balz, Hench, Starnes and the others, this dispute was none of their doing.

On May 23, at a special board of education meeting, Balz and the board scolded everyone in the black community, including the parents, teachers and Duncan. They did not fire Duncan nor dismiss any of the teachers Duncan wanted out of the school. The board told the black community that the principal "has strangely failed to stimulate eager cooperation ... [and] by autocratic manner and contemptuous treatment he has repressed constructive criticism and suggestions by the teachers ..." The board accepted the explanation "that these features of the administration are not due to disrespect for the ability of the teachers but rather to certain unfortunate mannerisms."[17]

On the other hand, the board criticized "some of the teachers" for their failure to cooperate with Duncan and their "unwillingness to accept the advice of the principal in matters properly within his jurisdiction." The board reported considering dismissing certain teachers (probably the five originally listed, though the committee did not make the names public) but instead said it had decided to "recommend no change so drastic." The board then told the superintendent to "observe carefully" the dynamics between Duncan and the teachers during the upcoming year.[18]

As to the alleged student strike and the general "laxity of discipline" at the school, the board blamed Charlottesville's changing culture. The initial draft of the committee's report blamed the students because they "come from a backward race," but either Hench or Balz crossed that out and replaced it with "many pupils come from homes where there is no family unity or home training." The final report went on to say that the lack of "family unity" and "home training" was equally true of the white students at the end of the war. The report blamed the unsettled conditions caused by World War II, especially the anticipated early induction of some of the boys into the military. (When the *Charlotteville Daily Progress* reported the board's findings, the newspaper left out the board's criticism of white households.) The committee went on to warn black parents against "carping" about Duncan in front of their children. To do so was just one more reason the school did not have "respect for authority [which was] fundamental in an ordered and orderly society."[19]

By doing nothing, the board did everything the biracial state required. The board solidified power within the white community by keeping an ineffective administrator in control, which further served to undermine black agency. In a complex and rapidly changing social order, the rules of segregation required the board to pit oppositional forces against one another rather than to search for common ground. For the white board, solutions arising from common ground in the black community were a non sequitur. As far as the school board was concerned, the "problem" was *within* the black community and had nothing to do with the white community. Unless black Charlottesville's "problems" threatened white social and economic stability, it was the duty of the board to remain disconnected.

Yet, the board was never disconnected. The norms of language in this unequal, hierarchal social arrangement made exclusion legitimate in the eyes of the white world. During the teacher testimony, the woman who alleged Duncan's improprieties said something in reference to the principal. We do not know what, but it may have been the assertion about his personal misconduct. One can imagine the stunned silence that followed. George Starnes responded with derision and ridicule when he said, "Not that we are particularly interested in that." Despite his dismissive remark, he and the others were indeed very interested "in that." Hench complimented Starnes's rebuke by writing, "Nice understatement ... George."[20]

The Charlottesville Board of Education might have believed it had resolved the "problem," but the problem did not go away. Less than a year later, the school board received a petition signed by nearly 250 people demanding the removal of Owen Duncan. In a letter cosigned by Douglass Edwards, president of the PTA, and L.B. Burns, president of the City Federation of Women's Clubs, the petitioners charged that Duncan was "dictatorial and intolerant of the views of others." He had "lost control" of the school, because he was "emotionally unstable" and "this unfortunate weakness" had caused numerous "unnecessary brawls with students, teachers and patrons." The community was concerned that students were getting the wrong message. There were too many students off-grounds during the school day, hanging about Vinegar Hill's pool halls and shoeshine parlors, unsavory places to Charlottesville's black elite. This time the petitioners held Duncan wholly responsible for the school's "laxity of discipline." The petitioners recommended ("respectfully" they said) that the board remove Duncan because it was "necessary" and in "the best interests of the students and community in general." The petitioners said Duncan's removal was "necessary" so they could "cooperate with the school administrator and authorities in building a more progressive community."[21] Once again, those on the margin defined "progressive" in ways most majority whites did not appreciate.

The board of education responded by appointing another committee, only this time the new superintendent, G. Tyler Miller, possibly intending to blunt any criticism from the black community, asked the state's Assistant Supervisor of Negro Education, Archie Richardson, to come to Charlottesville and "thoroughly investigate the situation." Richardson, as we will recall, had been the first African American appointed to the Virginia State Department of Education by State Superintendent Sidney Hall. When Richardson appeared before the congres-

322   The Conspiracy of the Good

sional committee on federal aid to education before the war, it was clear that he spoke the language of accommodation.

In April of 1946, Archie Richardson interviewed patrons, teachers, students and Duncan, though he was not vested with any power or authority. His role was to "investigate" and "report," but the final decision was left to the board. Superintendent Miller, writing to the City Federation of Women's Clubs and the PTA, concluded that the board, once again, "does not consider removal of the Principal justified."22

Language will often reinforce arrangements of power. In his response to the black community, Superintendent Miller, who in a few months would depart for Richmond to become state superintendent of public instruction, said the Charlottesville board had "carefully checked" all signatures on the petition. Miller told the community that 52 signatures were from patrons from the high school and 14 were from the primary school. There were 138 "other signers." Miller went so far as to "disqualify" 19 names, because he said the signatures were "uncertain." More important, the board knew who had not signed the petition, and that turned out to be most of the high school faculty. Only seven teachers and a departing visiting nurse took the risk of signing the petition. Could fear of retaliation have kept the others away? Miller's report told the board that improvements were at hand because "further changes in [Jefferson] personnel will take place in the coming year."23 And changes did take place. By the start of the 1946–47 school year, nearly all the "troublemakers," including Eleanora Sellers, had left the school, presumably discouraged by the futility of their efforts.

By taking an instrument of community solidarity—the petition—and dividing it into "classifications," the white community effectively used the petition against the black community. By "classifying" most of the petitioners as "others" and showing that the majority of teachers at the high school had not signed the petition, the board made its inaction legitimate. Miller told the black community that Duncan, although flawed, was not principally "at fault." Once again, the "conditions" at the school were the result of a "breakdown of discipline" within the black community. Miller wrote "After careful consideration of the petitions, the communications from the City Federation of Women's Clubs and the PTA, the report by Mr. A.G. Richardson, and the report of the Special Investigative Committee ..." the has board decided "unanimously" to do nothing except blame the black community for its "lack of support of the principal and the teaching staff."24 If the parents and teachers worked together, there would be no more attempts at a disruptive student "strike" and no more complaints of students leaving school to frequent Vinegar Hill's gas stations, pool halls and shoeshine parlors.25

Five years later in 1951, Burley High School was opened not far from Jefferson. It was a joint project of Albemarle County and the city of Charlottesville, a segregated black high school that served "all the needs" of the African-American children living in the city and county. The board of education then converted Jefferson into an elementary school. They hoped that the larger facility would contain the rapidly expanding black population in Charlottesville. Owen Duncan, however, was not the principal at either school. For reasons that remain unclear, he left that year to teach in rural Rustburg, Virginia.

In cities all over the South, segregation was deemed necessary to the white community, because they believed that black society was "different" and required separateness. In her 1929 University of Virginia master's thesis, "The Negro in Charlottesville and Albemarle County," Marjorie Felice Irwin, who was white, wrote that segregation was both "voluntary and compulsory." She concluded that the "differences" seen by white society quickly became "aversions," and blacks then sought the "advantages" associated with segregation. The legal and extralegal mechanisms by which whites tied status to color and caste were reinforced in a thousand direct and subtle ways every day in Charlottesville. Irwin described how blacks would sit at the rear of the bus and streetcar, come to the back door of a white-occupied house, sit in the "colored only" balcony of local movie houses and attend separate, "colored" schools. Irwin concluded, "This segregation has resulted in the formation of Negro organizations, and has compelled them to depend on themselves."[26]

That communal dependence would eventually undo *de jure* segregation. Most of the public awareness of civil rights history has focused on the epic battles and larger-than-life men and women—the Montgomery Bus Boycott, the Poor People's March on Washington, Dr. King, Thurgood Marshall and Rosa Parks. Yet, in small towns and large cities, the everyday opposition to racist practice was conducted by men and women most of us will never know. That certainly was the case in Charlottesville.

MASSIVE RESISTANCE

When the *Brown* decision was announced on May 17, 1954, many of Virginia's white politicians were cautiously (maybe naively) optimistic that some compromise—"some rational adjustment"—as the State Attorney General J. Lindsay Almond wrote, might be forthcoming. Governor Thomas Stanley said, "I contemplate no precipitate action ... [but] to work toward a plan which will be acceptable to our citizens and in keeping with the edict of the court." Others were less optimistic. Senator Harry Byrd, the powerful leader of the state's Democratic party machine, called the ruling "the most serious blow that has been struck against the rights of the states" stressing that Virginia "faced a crisis of the first magnitude." Byrd gave no hint of compromise.[27]

The black community was ecstatic. The Charlottesville branch of the National Association for the Advancement of Colored People (long dormant but recently reborn under the leadership of three ex-GIs) said the decision was "a great victory not only for the American Negro, but for all true Americans." They called for "all Americans to join our crusade for freedom." But not everyone in Charlottesville was as pleased—or ready for a crusade. Homer G. Richey, who soon would organize the region's most effective prosegregation organization, The Defenders of State Sovereignty and Individual Liberties, told Charlottesville's *Daily Progress* that if the schools admitted a single black child, "it would mark the beginning of the end for Virginia." The editor of the *Daily Progress,* Chester R. Babcock, was less pugnacious when he wrote that although segregation was "gradually" ending through "voluntary" means, the court order would have an adverse effect on public schooling. The only "encouraging" thing Babcock could report was that "extreme haste will probably not be necessary." He predicted that there would be no integration for "some time." He was correct.[28]

For the next few years, Charlottesville (and nearly all of white Virginia) argued that access to public schools was the state's prerogative and the federal government had no jurisdiction. There were calls for "interposition," "nullification" and "secession," although the latter idea had already been tried once, ending with Lee's surrender at Appomattox. Interposition, however illusionary (and ultimately illegal), had nonetheless come to the segregationists as a promising option. Retrieved from long-abandoned, 18th-century constitutional doctrine (Virginia historian Benjamin Muse thought the idea had been "disinterred"), interposition argued that a state had a right to "interpose its sovereignty" between the federal government and "its people." Resisters everywhere in the South now had a weapon to oppose the reviled Washingtonians. "States' Rights!" became the regional rallying cry, and, more often than not, the loudest calls against the federals and the integration order came from Virginia newspaperman James "Jack" Kilpatrick, the fiery 31-year-old editor of *The Richmond News Leader.* Initially the newspaper had called for compliance to *Brown* but not now. In the summer of 1956, "Massive Resistance," a term used by Byrd the previous spring, was an idea ready to be tested.[29]

By the spring of 1956, Southern moderates (white liberals calling for limited, "controlled" integration) had been shouted down. With mounting pressure from the NAACP and the threat that the judicial appeals process was about to run dry, Senator Byrd and 100 other Southern legislators drafted the "Southern Manifesto," calling for open defiance of the court's ruling. They also feared that a solid segregationist front was breaking down when some communities with smaller black populations went ahead and drafted integration plans. No longer advocating "local control," which only months before had been the mainstream white response to the federal order, Virginia legislators moved quickly during August to put into place a package of laws that would defy the court order by making school integration illegal. If the federal courts ruled that a Virginia community must desegregate its schools, then the state was prepared to close those schools.[30]

There were repeated delays as the appeal process ran its due course but by the summer of 1958, it appeared that Virginia was about to test its "right of interposition." The NAACP had focused its resources on four communities: Norfolk, Warren County, Prince Edward and Charlottesville. As early as October of 1955, the Charlottesville branch of the NAACP, represented by Oliver Hill, Spottswood Robinson and a team of attorneys from the Richmond office, petitioned the school board on behalf of 44 children, asking that the board open the city's white schools to integration. The board took the petition "under review." In the spring, Hill and the others came back, asking the board for its decision. The board reported no progress and the NAACP filed suit in federal court on May 6, 1956. Meanwhile, the city council retained the services of a local attorney, the former governor of the state, John Stewart Battle, Sr.[31]

Battle went to court in July, arguing before Federal District Judge John Paul—who historian Muse pointed out was a native Virginian and son of a Confederate soldier—that the federal government had no jurisdiction over the state's schools. Battle asked that the suit be dismissed. Judge Paul rejected that argument and told the city—and by implication, all of Virginia—that "I am not willing that this court be a knowing and willing accessory to a policy which has as its purpose delay and evasion ..." He ordered Charlottesville to desegregate in September.[32]

In Judge Paul's decision, though, were the makings of a school integration plan that city leaders apparently did not recognize or more likely refused to acknowledge. Paul told the city,

> If the complainants receive a favorable decree, it doesn't necessarily mean that all schools are open and everybody can rush in.
>
> When the school board is presented with an application, it will have to evaluate it on whether the particular school being applied for is overcrowded. And it will have to consider the qualifications of the applicant to attend the school he is applying for.
>
> There are many valid reasons why a Negro may be turned down, but he may not be turned down because he is a Negro.
>
> The decree wouldn't say: you can go to any school you want to.
>
> There is the question of residence. Many cities designate areas for particular schools and all pupils within that area go to the same school.[33]

Paul was suggesting that if the city could accept minor changes in the racial makeup of its schools, then the court would look favorably upon quotas, admissions' screens, and, if not outright gerrymandering, then certainly neighborhood "zones." Yet, by the summer of 1956, deliberations over school desegregation had devolved to such a state that rational debate in Charlottesville was rare. No longer were moderates heard above the din of segregationist rhetoric. Choosing to ignore

Paul's order, the city went back to court requesting a stay of execution, arguing that the September start would "most certainly be disruptive from an administrative point of view."[34]

For many Charlottesvillians, the summer of 1956 was like no other. The city began to attract national attention, and, as in Pasadena, it was the kind of attention city fathers could do without. F. John Kasper, head of the Seaboard White Citizens' Council located in Washington, D.C., came into town. The first White Citizens' Council was formed in Mississippi just after the *Brown* decree, and its purpose was to "protect" Southern "heritage," namely to ensure that segregation remain the law of the land. Kasper was pushing a villainous harangue that worried town officials so much, they seriously considered banning "inflammatory" public meetings. Kasper had announced that his group planned to use "every means available, preferably legal," to stop school desegregation, and, although he had no intention of instigating violence, his group "would meet violence firmly." Kasper left the city and was later arrested in Tennessee on charges of bombing an integrated school. Also in town that summer was Asa Carter, who spoke at a pro-segregation rally held at McIntyre Park. Carter's race-baiting career would eventually take him to Alabama, where he would hook up with George Wallace and write the governor's infamous "segregation now, segregation forever" speech. Petitions were circulated that summer, and nearly 9,000 Charlottesvillians—over a third of the total white population—demanded that schools remain segregated. Then, in late August, during one of Kasper's vitriolic rallies, Sarah Patton Boyle, the head of the local Human Relations Council, had a burning cross planted on her front lawn.[35]

Boyle, who had been befriended earlier by newspaperman T.J. Sellers, was the most outspoken white integrationist in Virginia, and was scorned by most for her support of the movement. By the summer of 1956, she had grown somewhat accustomed to the minor harassments that came with a white Southerner taking a public stand against segregation. There were threatening telephone calls, nasty letters and even an occasional photograph of the burned, mangled body of some poor lynched man with a "you're next" message scribbled at the bottom. Boyle took all these in stride, even gaining some measure of strength from the encounters. She refused to give the segregationists any quarter, believing that if her knees buckled in public, her adversaries would take it as a sign they were succeeding. The way she handled her run-in with the burning cross was a perfect example.

Late in August, after what she described as a particularly trying day, she retired early. But a flickering light outside her window made her rise, and there, just "a slipper's throw from the house" was a six-foot-tall burning cross with "flames stretching eastward in the light like banners of evil." No matter, thought Boyle. She "felt tall and strong ... I lifted up my being to the cross's wild beauty—like skyrockets and Roman candles—and suddenly I laughed aloud." This deeply religious woman found humor in the idea that a cross, a symbol of "eternal love," could be used in "an attempt to torment me." She ran to her 13-year-old son's room and, wanting him "to share the best of the experience," shouted, "Look! They're burning a cross for mother. Isn't it beautiful?" Reckless as it now may appear, Boyle and her son ran to the yard and took photographs of the cross. Boyle was sure the cross setters were watching and she wanted to give them a show of defiance. She and her son doused the flames with a bucket of water and took the smoldering thing inside the house. Indicative of the stubbornness of this very remarkable woman, Boyle and a few of her "liberal friends" immortalized the event by having a framed inscription from World War II hero "Vinegar Joe" Stillwell hung about the charred wood. The inscription read, "Illegitimus Non Carborundum," which according to Boyle, translates to "Don't let the S.O.B.'s grind you down."[36]

Tensions were at a breaking point as Judge Paul heard the arguments for a stay of his desegregation order. Less than a week before Boyle's burning cross, he agreed with the school board that to implement the desegregation decree in September would, according to the newspaper, "cause an unusual degree of confusion, and, perhaps in some instances, chaos." A week after Boyle's cross, another was burned, this time on the lawn of a Human Relations Council officer, Mrs. Morris Brown. She told the press that this one was "a dud," as it never fully ignited and "fell over" of its own weight.[37]

In December, the city and school board took the next step in the judicial process and argued the case (*Allen v. School Board of the City of Charlottesville*) before the U.S. Fourth District Court of Appeals. In January 1957, that court ruled in favor of the plaintiffs and ordered the city to desegregate its schools. The Court of Appeals, however, did not stipulate when the city had to comply, and the school board, following its now familiar course of action, appealed again, but this time the only remaining judicial avenue available was the Supreme Court. The Fourth District Court of Appeals then ruled, at the city's request, that its order to desegregate be delayed pending the higher court's ruling.[38]

In March 1957, the Supreme Court refused to hear *Allen v. Charlottesville*, thereby ending any further appeals by the city. Charlottesville was now firmly "behind the eight ball," as a member of the school board told the press. If the city refused to comply with the court order, it would be cited for contempt. If, however, the city decided to comply and desegregate its schools, the state government had legislation in place to seize the schools and close them. There was one last option. The city now put its faith in the state's Pupil Placement Board, part of Byrd's Massive Resistance legislation.[39]

The Pupil Placement Act authorized the establishment of a state "placement board" that would oversee "admissions tests" that "determined" the "suitability" of African-American students petitioning to attend white schools. Though academic "tests" were administered, neighborhoods were "examined," and interviews held for each applicant—everyone knew that no black child would be admitted to a white school. The NAACP went back to court, arguing that the Pupil Placement Act was unconstitutional. Pending the result of the NAACP suit, the city asked for another delay, and the court agreed.[40]

The daily routine for Charlottesville had not changed much since the *Brown* decision. The schools opened in September of 1957, much as they had for years. Most students, black and white, gathered on street corners and walked or rode buses to the five elementary schools and two high schools in town. Black children went off to Jefferson Elementary School, which occupied the former high school building near Vinegar Hill in the center of town. Older African-American students attended Burley High School, jointly opened by the city and the county in 1951. Albemarle county and Charlottesville had approved a $1 million bond in the late 1940s for the construction of a segregated high school.

Fig. 28. Venable Elementary School, c. 1936. *(Photo courtesy Albemarle County Historical Society)*

White working-class mothers living in the Belmont section of town (close to where Carrie Buck had lived before she was shipped off to the state hospital to be sterilized) sent their children out the door to walk to the recently opened Johnson Elementary School, named after the former superintendent, James Johnson, who had died the previous year. The more affluent moms living in the upscale neighborhoods close to the university dropped their kids off at Venable Elementary School, which had opened in 1925. Venable was a two-story, red brick building dominated by a sweeping set of steps that disappeared under four huge white columns. This was the neighborhood of the university's professors, and city professionals and it was, of course, all white. Venable and Lane High School were the symbolic racial and educational epicenters of Charlottesville, and that fact was not lost on the NAACP. The petitions for student transfers were for Venable and Lane, and the NAACP lawsuit marked those two schools for desegregation. By the spring of 1958, white families, now more than ever aware that the appeal process had run its course, began to prepare for the worst.[41]

But in a city as divided as Charlottesville, what was the worst? On one hand, there was the inevitability of a dreaded court order that would put black students in white schools. How would the white community respond to African-American children sitting next to their kids? To many, even more alarming was J. Lindsay Almond, the newly elected prosegregationist governor, rattling the swords of Massive Resistance, threatening to close schools if the courts won. The prospects were anything but optimistic. The city faced either integrated schools or no schools, and that was just not acceptable to Charlottesville's white professional class. So, 10 Venable School mothers began to organize.

THE BASEMENT MOTHERS

There were two competing interests regarding education that emerged in Charlottesville during the spring and summer of 1958. The Charlottesville Educational Foundation (CEF), a group committed to keeping the city's schools segregated, was in effect another name for the area chapter of the Defenders of State Sovereignty and Individual Liberties. The Defenders, a statewide organization formed in response to the *Brown* decision, organized the CEF to run segregated private schools if the governor intervened and closed the city's schools. The Massive Resistance legislation called for the creation of public tax–supported tuition grants (vouchers) to enable white families to escape integrated public schools and attend segregated private schools. If the federal courts ultimately succeeded—which most believed would happen—then the CEF hardliners intended the private schools to become permanent, in effect abandoning the public schools to the black community and the few white integrationists.[42]

Others with less strident beliefs, fearful that public schooling would be denied their children, began to organize an alternative to the CEF plan. Most whites in Charlottesville wanted the schools—and the larger community—to remain segregated, but as the crisis deepened during the summer, a group of 10 Venable School mothers planned an alternative if the state intervened and closed the schools. The women, all wives of either university professors or well-heeled professionals, formed the Parent's Committee for Emergency Schooling (PCES). They jokingly referred to themselves as the "basement mothers" because during the summer, the women quietly went about organizing temporary classrooms—many in donated basements around the city. Regardless of the outcome—even if the schools reopened with integrated classrooms—the mothers insisted they would fold their operation and return to being supportive public school parents. They had no intention of turning any of the basements into permanent classrooms, and, further, they required that any family enrolling a child in the PCES program sign a pledge to return to the public schools when they reopened, integrated or not.[43]

On September 13, 1958, Judge Paul signed the order to admit 10 black children to Venable and two black students to Lane High School. Three days later, the Court of Appeals refused to hear the city's appeal. Three days after that, Governor Almond did what many feared—he invoked the Massive Resistance laws, seized the schools and closed Venable and Lane. Contemporary observers said the city was "powerless" to do anything about the ruling, arguing that the governor and the legislature had ended the city's jurisdiction over its schools. The school board passed a resolution stating, "Because of circumstances beyond the control of the City Council and the School Board ..." parents should seek the "best private arrangements." Interestingly, this was the same city government that was powerful enough since 1954 to defy the Supreme Court. There were no "appeals" from the city government, no suits filed in any court against the state's ruling, and no defiance of the Massive Resistance "laws." Further, there was no expressed outrage at the loss of "local control." Instead, 4,000 white Charlottesvillians signed a petition supporting Almond's school closings. It would take a group of white Norfolk parents to file suit against Almond and the state (*James v. Almond*), alleging that the school closings were unconstitutional. Meanwhile, the CEF and the Venable mothers went to work, each pursuing an opposite goal.[44]

The segregationist organization, the Charlottesville Educational Foundation, opened an "elementary school" in a large house it had leased for the year. They named the school after the icon of Southern resistance, Robert E. Lee, and 182 Venable students filed through its doors the day it opened. The remaining 340 Venable students—minus the 10 African-American children the court had admitted—attended the PCES basement schools. Teachers from Venable taught for both organizations, although the PCES mothers had convinced not only the majority of the students' families but also the majority of the teachers that the temporary—they called them "emergency basement schools"—were best.[45]

The high school was another matter. When it became public knowledge that both the CEF and PCES were competing for students, the Lane High School faculty decided that they "would rather work as a group" to educate "all the children." Refusing to be split by the two organizations, the faculty appointed itself as mediator, and, in early September, the PCES and CEF leadership struck a "deal." The two organizations partnered a "cooperative" high school program for the city's white students, meeting classes in basements, rooms and halls around the city. The CEF plans for a segregated high school, using the Lane faculty as its instructional core, ended when the cooperative plan was created. The CEF then sought a permanent home for a private high school. The next June, with three local contractors pouring the foundation *gratis,* Rocky Hill Academy was begun. In a few years, it would house hundreds of white children, their tuition paid by state vouchers.

No other schools in the city were impacted by the closures. Jefferson and Burley remained open as did Johnson and the other white elementary schools. Meanwhile, the 12 African-American students who the court ordered into Venable and Lane refused to return to Jefferson and Burley and were tutored, mainly in private homes but also at the board of education offices. Judge Paul had ruled that the teachers, being paid by state and local school funds, were working in publicly constituted schools; therefore, the black students could not be denied admission to either of the organization's programs. The NAACP decided against trying to enroll the students in either of the two emergency "schools," taking a "wait-and-see" position. Besides, Randolph White, the editor of *The Charlottesville-Albemarle Tribune,* the local black newspaper, said the idea of "emergency schools" was a "silly mess ... foisted on white parents by their so-called leaders."[46] However, some in the white community appealed directly to the NAACP leadership to challenge the legality of the emergency schools—for reasons other than integration and the community good.

Throughout the fall and early winter, the emergency school plan appeared to be working. The PCES basement classrooms scattered around the city operated on a shortened day. Some parents at Venable thought so much of a kindergarten teacher, Miss Trevillian, they privately contracted her services, and she held class in her basement, separate from the PCES program. Forty-five children showed up the first day. The high school students attended classes at the Elks Club, Buddy's Restaurant and a local business that offered what passed for science labs. To get around the logistical difficulties associated with classrooms scattered about the city, the high school teachers devised a six-day-a-week plan, with each day devoted to a single subject. The Lane principal reported great enthusiasm for the daylong, single-subject instruction, and morale "was just as high as it could be." In the middle of November, Lane classrooms were "consolidated" into two larger spaces at two Christian churches, and mechanical drawing was moved from Buddy's Restaurant to the Greek Orthodox Church. The girls attended physical education classes at the country club. For some, it would be the only time they would be allowed on the plush grounds. More than one parent commended the emergency schools, suggesting that these "no frills" schools could be a model for the future. Enrollment, though, was troublesome, as 200 high school students were "missing." Many later turning up at nearby schools. The two organizations did not report daily attendance, although one suspects it was erratic. "For Sale" signs, ominous signals of community dissatisfaction, began to appear around the Venable neighborhood.[47]

The split system of private schools had, indeed, divided the community. A Venable mother, Mrs. Peter Manson, remembered 30 years later that it was the only time in her life when people turned and "walked across the street from me so they wouldn't have to speak." But Mrs. Manson admitted she was "no diplomat," and the Parents' Committee stayed together because there were "a lot calmer heads" than hers during the meetings. Friendships ended, families were torn over divided loyalties, and violence seemed just under the surface, despite the temptation to think that Charlottesville was "too cultured" to resort to tactics already displayed in lesser places in the South.[48]

Given the frequent references in the press to racial violence in other Southern communities—on November 10, the *Daily Progress* reported that a "mysterious" bomb had blown apart an integrated high school in West Virginia—there were no violent acts against blacks or whites in Charlottesville. Some considered the absence of violence the result of the community's good fortune to be blessed with "intelligence"... and a university. Others thought it was the city's good fortune in having Thomas Michie as mayor. Michie, the son of the former school board president, was levelheaded, firm and very much in command. Violence, he told the police, was not to be tolerated. The only incidents directed at the schools were a bomb threat at Burley and vandalism at Lane. The Lane vandalism was apparently the doing of two young black boys, ages seven and 10, who along with a few other boys (including a white boy), raided the school's art room and then went off to trash a local florist and another downtown business. Inflammatory letters continued in the *Daily Progress,* attempting to influence whites that "Negro domination" was at hand but to Charlottesville's credit—whatever the reason—no bloodshed marred the city.[49]

The PCES mothers, as well as another newly constituted moderate group, the Committee for Public Education, were not content to let the basements and the scattered high school classes suffice as legal or effectual alternatives to the public schools. There was too much at stake, and the "For Sale" signs were just the tip of the iceberg. When, in early January, it appeared that the Massive Resistance laws were going to be struck down, representatives from the PCES and CPE urged the Charlottesville board to reopen the schools as soon as possible once the court had spoken. The board, at its mid-January meeting, told the audience that the schools' reopening was "complicated" by the appeals under way, and they would "play it by ear" if the courts ruled that Massive Resistance was unconstitutional.[50]

On January 19, 1959, the Virginia State Supreme Court of Appeals ruled that the school closings were unconstitutional. It was, ironically, the anniversary of Robert E. Lee's birth. Almond capitulated a week later, telling the state that he would not order the General Assembly to consider any further legislation to prevent desegregation. Many whites around the state cried betrayal, but the *Daily Progress* editorialized that the governor had little choice. Editor Babcock advised his readers that there were options available to circumvent "enforced integration." He saw the end of the Massive Resistance laws as fortunate. "Wipe away the slate clean," he said. The Supreme Court's decision, he emphasized, "does not *require* integration." All it did was "*forbid* racial discrimination" in public schools. The task before Virginia was to prevent nondiscrimination from producing "forced integration." His solution was state-supported tuition vouchers, and, he said, "there is nothing complicated about it." The "problem" had a solution—it was "freedom of choice" between private and public schools. On the same day that Almond told the state there were no legal means left to enforce segregated public schools, he ordered the assembly to repeal the school compulsory attendance laws and enact a tuition-grant program, in effect signaling that his administration would continue to thwart any plans for full integration.[51]

The Charlottesville board met immediately after hearing the court's decision, but did not immediately reopen the two schools. Instead, the board appeared to waffle, suggesting the competing pressures to keep the schools closed and reopen them. City attorney John S. Battle Jr., the son of the former school board attorney (who had left the city to join President Eisenhower's Civil Rights Commission), told the school board it had no alternative but to reopen the schools on an "integrated basis within a reasonable amount of time." Members of the city council told the press that they favored a referendum to gauge public sentiment about reopening, but Mayor Michie thought holding a referendum was a waste. "I don't see what the question could be," said Michie, other than to ask "Should the School Board obey the law?" Most politicians, though, were uneasy about pushing ahead, fearing public backlash about integrated schools. The majority of the city officials expressed "complete confidence" in the school board to make the "right decision," creating, perhaps, some safe distance between themselves and the potential fallout over the board's upcoming decision.[52]

The board had failed to move quickly, because it was not sure exactly what to do. On one hand, there was a split system of private, white schools that appeared to be succeeding—with many public expressions of satisfaction with the "new" status quo. On the other hand, the court's order needed to be implemented—and the city attorney had made it clear that the board would be held in contempt if it refused to desegregate schools. Complicating matters, various groups now began to pressure the board. The CEF and the Defenders, of course, wanted the schools to remain closed, because without state funds to pay the teachers, the organization had no ready means to keep going. Contrary pressure came from the League of Women Voters, the basement mothers of the Parents' Committee for Emergency Schooling, the Committee for Public Education, and, for the first time, an as yet unnamed downtown business organization. All wanted the schools reopened. The board met January 26 and passed a resolution that reopened the two schools on January 31.[53]

The businessmen's organization—an "alliance" of politicians, university administrators and professionals—had surfaced just as the crisis was ending, telling the board that the school closings were bad for Charlottesville's image as a "modern" city. Although it has been argued that business support for Massive Resistance around the state was never strong, the CEF leadership was, in fact, a cross section of the city's business leadership. Business support for closing the schools—enthusiastic or not—began to disappear as a University of Virginia (UVA) report appeared in the fall, pointing out that private schooling was going to cost money—lots of it. The report, "Some Aspects of Virginia's Current Educational Crisis" authored by a university economist, warned that to retain employees, business would need to raise salaries and wages to offset the increased costs of private schooling, necessary even if the state provided tuition grants. A handful of commercial and political leaders quietly began to press for an end to the crisis. They maneuvered behind the scenes, avoiding any public notice, concerned about appearing pro-integration.[54]

As historian Andrew Lewis points out, business support to end private schooling came after it was clear public sentiment had swung toward reopening the schools. Once the court determined the schools must reopen, business began to demonstrate how capital had done its part to save the community's schools. Knox Turnbull, an investment broker and spokesman for the downtown business group, said, "Let's get back to as near normal operations of our schools as smoothly as we can ... and in the process let's seek together to recapture our community solidarity and strength which always has been a great asset to Charlottesville and Albemarle." Maybe the businessmen had something to worry about: nearly 30 years later, Homer Richey, one of the leaders of the local Defenders, still blamed the "merchant class" for knuckling under for fear of losing the "Negro dollar."[55]

Once the board made public its decision to reopen, there was an outpouring of support for public education. Petition after petition arrived congratulating the board. The heads of three Charlottesville banks endorsed the board's decision—careful, though, to keep their names separate from their banks. Twelve hundred signatures congratulating the board appeared in the newspaper under the title "a non-political statement by a group of independent citizens," indicative of fears on

Main Street that the business community might be held responsible. White moderates, fearful for months that the schools would be taken away from them, breathed a sigh of relief. Over 150 UVA professors offered their congratulations. Many were confident, as the university president Colgate Darden said, that "limited desegregation was an experiment well worth the effort." If money could be found to continue to pay for private school tuition, then those families that feared an integrated school environment could continue at the CEF schools—at public expense. To ensure that the necessary funds could be secured, Governor Almond brought the recently retired state controller back to Richmond to assist the legislature in finding the money. Darden advised local boards to make plans for a "dual system of public education," in which most whites would attend segregated tuition-grant schools and the African-American community would be left with the public schools.[56]

CONTROLLING INTEGRATION

Perhaps the greatest contribution the Venable mothers made to the civil rights struggle in Charlottesville was, in the words of historian Lewis, that they "uncoupled support for public education" from the longstanding Southern allegiance to segregation, thereby allowing the majority of white citizens to argue that the school closings were an "educational crisis," not a "race relations crisis." Lewis aptly points out that the mothers never saw their responsibility as anything other than returning the white children to the schools. Discussions never ensued over the logistics—or the ethical considerations—of an integrated school setting, and, as Lewis argues, this "narrowness" exposed the mothers' definition of public education as more self-serving than community building.

Repeatedly in Charlottesville and other Southern communities, whites responded to desegregation orders only when the vested interests of the white community were seriously threatened. White entitlement, built through decades of Jim Crow laws and unwritten edicts, created an educational environment that whites came to see as their exclusive privilege. An empowered black community was viewed as a threat to that entitlement. As in Pasadena, when the more affluent white community sensed its long-standing privileges were endangered, legal (and illegal) resistance followed. The greatest failure of the Southern white community during the immediate post-Brown period was that its hysterical preoccupation with "race-mixing" prevented any mutually beneficial solution from being hammered out. The Charlottesville school board met representatives from the black community only once, just after the court's decree and that was in an attempt to get the NAACP leadership to quit the case because it might be "disruptive" to the community.[57]

Looking back at Charlottesville's reaction to race, one would expect that any angst over the emergency schools would fix blame on African Americans and the imminent threat posed by "race-mixing." But in fact, apprehension in the white community, at least in the neighborhoods of the middle and professional classes, was less about integration and more about how desegregation could lessen the advantages that came from racial preferences. The university newspaper, *The Cavalier Daily*, interviewed teachers, parents and students at the makeshift high school in mid-November. As "smoothly operating" as it was, the emergency schools were criticized because parents and students were beginning to fret that the "situation" was undermining their entitlements. One parent, after complaining about the "conditions," said the state should have had a "program ready (for this problem)" because her child's chance "to get into a college" was now jeopardized. A junior said that the private schools were "hurting the educational system" and she would rather go to school with "a few Negroes," because with the private school her "social life has come to a stop." At the extreme, a mathematics teacher (the former Lane High School principal) believed the "no frills" private schools could be useful in the future to weed out "undesirables." He said that the private schools encouraged the more independent student and the only students "suffering" were "the unambitious" [sic]. He implied that the private school experience might revise "our whole system of education" once the schools reopen. The mathematics teacher said, "I don't think we should clutter up our schools with those that don't want to be here." But a very perturbed city detective (the only anonymous interviewee) may have best captured the mood of the more affluent white community when he asked rather incredulously, "how can two little niggers hurt Lane High School?"[58]

To what ends would the white community go to protect the needs of its children? According to one black activist, at least once during the crisis white leadership met the black community over the school closings. George Ferguson, one of the three ex-GIs who helped revitalize the NAACP, said that during the fall of 1958, unnamed members of the emergency school coalition approached him with a "plan" that, to Ferguson and other black parents, was all too transparent. Ferguson, who had been elected NAACP president in 1958, was asked to enroll black children in what he called the "little [white] private schools," but the request had nothing to do with integration. Quite the opposite, Ferguson was convinced that these whites were acting more out of self-interest than concern for the larger community. According to Ferguson, some in the emergency school coalition had become apprehensive that "discipline" at the emergency schools had deteriorated to such an extent that the schools needed to be closed. Members of the emergency school organization—it may have been Charlottesville's teachers, maybe the teachers at Lane—tried to convince him to enroll black students in the makeshift schools. If Ferguson and the parents had agreed, the court would have ordered the emergency schools to desegregate. The Massive Resistance laws would then have kicked in, and the "little private schools" would have been closed, thereby ending the "discipline" problem. Were these emissaries from the white schools pleading for a better Charlottesville? Or was their inspiration mainly self-interest? Ferguson answered that question when he refused to play along, saying "they wanted to use us like goats."[59]

Venable and Lane remained segregated when they reopened on January 31, because, once again, the Federal Court granted the city a delay in its school desegregation case. City attorney Battle presented the school board's first-ever desegregation plan to the Appeals Court. With assurances that the few black children involved would be tutored at city expense, Judge Simon Sobeloff stayed the order until the following September. The city argued that the 12 African-American children were "way behind" their white counterparts, because they had not attended school during the crisis. In a gush of civic munificence, Battle and the board implied they would "lose out" if they had to "compete" with more qualified white students. The NAACP leadership suspected what lay behind the board's "concern" was a ploy to get the kids to return to Burley and Jefferson. The black parents refused and the students did not return to Jefferson and Burley. Instead, they were tutored at the board of education office at city expense.[60]

The white community repeatedly failed to comprehend what was occurring on the other side of town. Battle and the white leadership mistakenly assumed that the students had not received any instruction during the crisis. However, during the crisis, retired teachers had coached the 12 students by day and Burley and Jefferson teachers had continued with the lessons at night. Although these 12 children were from the families of Charlottesville's black elite, whites never understood that the "coloreds" were capable of "competing." So tutoring was in order, more as it turned out to satisfy the white community than to "catch up" so-called backward children. Judge Sobeloff agreed with the board, and commended the city by expressing "full confidence in Mr. Battle" and Charlottesville's desegregation plan. For the remainder of an uneventful spring, Lane and Venable remained white-only.[61]

In September 1959, Charlottesville and the rest of the country watched a handful of black children desegregate Venable and Lane. There were nine black students at the elementary school and three at the high school. It was said that there were more cameramen and reporters than parents at the two schools that first day. But there were no hostile demonstrations as there had been at Little Rock, Arkansas, or at Front Royal, Virginia, another of the state's Massive Resistance hot spots. But then again, in Charlottesville there were hundreds of white students attending private, segregated schools operated by the CEF. Fully 30 percent of the student population from Venable and Lane opened the year at Robert E. Lee Elementary School and at the newly constructed Rock Hill Academy. The state had enacted a tax-supported tuition-grant system that paid all but $15 of the educational costs at the private schools. Over the years that the vouchers were made available to parents, the CEF would wait until the state established its grant formula and then add the $15 "surcharge," presumably to avoid any implication that the CEF schools were "public."[62]

The two segregated CEF schools were often referred to as a "safety valve" for the city, meaning those families that found desegregation repugnant had an alternative. The tuition grants were called "freedom of choice," and proponents marketed the vouchers as a "human rights" issue not as an escape from "race-mixing." Yet "freedom of choice" was not free. It cost the city taxpayers, both black and white, thousands of dollars every year. The city spent so much, in fact, that one UVA researcher said that the funds spent to send kids to private, segregated schools could pay for a substantial raise for the city's public school teachers, kindergarten classes for 200 students, or five new counselors at the high school.[63]

The desegregation of Charlottesville's schools over the next decade moved at a snail's pace because the city's desegregation plan was to block, delay and appeal every new court order. Judge Paul had accepted the city's "school assignment plan," which was little more than a bogus arrangement to contain African Americans in "their" neighborhoods. Under the city's court-approved plan, Charlottesville was divided into six zones or districts. In a transfer policy that was remarkably similar to what was used in Pasadena a few years later, black, elementary school children who lived within a predominately white district were routinely "transferred" or assigned to Jefferson. To attend any other school, black families would need to apply to the school board for a "transfer," which came only after interviews and tests—and then only begrudgingly. On the other hand, whites living within the Jefferson district were routinely assigned to the nearest white school. Those transfers required no interview or test. The majority of blacks in the city lived within the Jefferson district, and there were no transfers to any white school. Only after repeated court tests did the school assignment plan get struck down. Only when the 1964 Civil Rights Act threatened to withdraw federal funds, did the numbers of black students in all the city's public schools begin to approach the proportion of the overall African-American population. Until the late 1960s, hundreds of families received state vouchers to attend the Robert E. Lee Elementary School and Rocky Hill Academy. When the state grants finally ended, the schools dried up and disappeared.[64]

Yet, even with the end of the vouchers and the segregated private schools, the two communities remained bitterly divided. During the 1970s, Charlottesville followed a national trend as middle-class whites moved out to the newer housing developments in the suburbs and blacks, often underemployed and undereducated, moved into the city. Tensions again became high, only this time the issues were about unemployment, police overreaction and crack cocaine, not civil rights lawsuits and school closings. In April of 1975, and then two months later in July, the racial violence that was absent during the school closings exploded when angry rioters roamed the streets in a predominately black neighborhood known as Westhaven. Stores were firebombed, one police officer was wounded and the air was filled with rioters' gunshots. Dozens were arrested. Contemporaries said the gulf between the two communities was wider than at any time in memory. the *Charlottesville Daily Progress* reported that "Black Problems Were Priority Items," suggesting white Charlottesville was unaware of the "conditions" in the black community.[65]

Westhaven, where the riot took place, had been the city's answer to "urban renewal." During the same year that the *Brown* decree was handed down, Charlottesville had (barely) passed a referendum authorizing a "Housing Authority." In 1960—after much wrangling, diversion and disagreement—the city passed its first redevelopment referendum, authorizing the demolition of much of Vinegar Hill's housing and business. The center of Charlottesville's historic black neighborhood would be removed—housing, shops, social halls and businesses were plowed under in an effort to "salvage" or "reclaim" the city center. As "compensation," Charlottesville built Westhaven Housing Project in a white, working-class section of town. The poor, substandard housing on the Hill, some without running water or indoor plumbing, had been replaced by white-owned businesses, including a large hotel and a federal courthouse. But 20 years after the Hill had been "redeveloped," large tracts of land still were undeveloped. Gone was the center of black social and commercial life in Charlottesville, with its numerous black-owned businesses—including the shoeshine parlors, gas stations and barbershops the city's black elite did not want their children frequenting. Gone, too, was the Blue Diamond Night Club with its racy Saturday night jazz. The old Jefferson school remained, used in the 1990s as a city "annex," housing a preschool and other city services. Some white civic leaders have suggested that Jefferson should be looked at for its potential redevelopment dollars. Others, namely older black teachers and those interested in historic preservation, have argued that the old school should be preserved as a symbol of community hope and struggle. Westhaven ended up becoming what urban housing projects have come to symbolize in America—a monument to hopelessness and isolation.[66]

NOTES

1. Dr. James Johnson to Dr. A.G.A. Balz, Chairman of the School Board of the City of Charlottesville, 3 May 1945, in Albert G.A. Balz papers (mss 3795), Box 3, Folder: "Special Committee to Investigate Conditions at Jefferson High School." Other than the central players in the Jefferson school controversy, all teachers have remained anonymous.

2. All quotes are from notes taken by Balz and A.L. Hench and the typed transcripts of interviews conducted during the board's investigation, located in Balz's "Special Committee to Investigate Conditions at Jefferson High School," hereafter cited as Special Committee folder.

3. City School Board, Charlottesville, Va., from The Committee, 3 May 1945, in Special Committee folder.

4. Based on the charges brought against Duncan, Starnes prepared for the investigative committee eight questions that he believed would uncover whether Duncan or the teachers were at fault. Following the teacher testimony, Starnes then prepared another seven questions for Duncan.

5. See the interview transcripts in the Special Committee folder; for teacher interviews, p. 1–13; Duncan interview, p. 14–18; community leaders, p. 19–20.

6. Duncan interview, p. 14–18, including Balz's notes on Duncan's use of the Morale Cards. See teacher interviews on teacher plans, p. 8; on abandoning school rules, p. 9.

7. See the many references to the philosophy of education papers in teacher interviews, p. 3–5, 7–8. See Duncan's response to the teacher accusations, p. 16. He told the committee that "... he had given the teachers no reason whatsoever to say that their papers were unscholarly and disappointing."

8. Interview with Duncan, p. 14–18.

9. Interviews with teachers, p. 5.

10. Interview with community leaders, p. 19–20.

11. "Jefferson P.T.A. Defends Duncan," *Charlottesville Daily Progress,* 7 May 1945, p. 7.

12. "Hoax Claimed By P-T.A President" *Charlottesville Daily Progress,* 8 May 1945, p. 8.

13. Interview with Duncan, p. 17.

14. See the few surviving issues of *The Reflector,* the black newspaper founded by T.J. Sellers, on-line at the University of Virginia Library, http://www.vcdh.virginia.edu/afam/raceandplace/news_main.html.

15. Sarah Patton Boyle, *The Desegregated Heart: A Virginian's Stand in Time of Transition,* with an introduction by Jennifer Ritterhouse (New York: William Morrow and Company, 1962; reprint, Charlottesville: University of Virginia Press, 2001), p. xii–xiii. Also see, Bradley Charles Mittendorf, "From Discussion to Confrontation" (Master's thesis, University of Virginia, 1993), p. 35–43. T.J. Sellers was one of the 10 who brought the charge of incompetence before the board of education.

16. Hench's notes, 23 May 1945, in Special Committee folder.

17. See the final report of the "Committee to Investigate Certain Complaints of Conditions at Jefferson High School," 14 June 1945, Special Committee folder.

18. Ibid.

19. Ibid. See "School Head and Staff Criticized: But Board Retains Jefferson Faculty," *The Daily Progress,* 29 May 1945, p. 1.

20. See Hench's notes, 23 May 1945, Special Committee folder.

21. L.B. Burns and Douglass Edwards to the Charlottesville Board of Education, no date but carries date stamp, 15 April 1946, Special Committee folder.

22. G. Tyler Miller to The President of the City Federation of Women's Clubs and to the President of the Parent Teachers Association, 27 May 1946, Special Committee folder.

23. Ibid.

24. Ibid.

25. Ibid. *The Daily Progress* did not cover the second Jefferson school controversy.

26. See Marjorie Felice Irwin, *The Negro in Charlottesville and Albemarle County* (Phelps-Stokes Fellowship Papers Number 9, University of Virginia, 1929), p. 42.

27. Benjamin Muse, *Virginia's Massive Resistance* (Bloomington: Indiana University Press, 1961), p. 4–5.

28. For the NAACP quotes and Homer Richie's response, see "U.S. Supreme Court Rules Against Segregation," *The Daily Progress,* 18 May 1954, p. 1, col. 6; for Babcock's editorial, p. 4, col. 1. For the Defenders' organizational response, see "Citizens' Group Formed Here to Combat Integration," *The Daily Progress,* 8 March 1955, p. 8. Also see Dallas R. Crowe, "Desegregation of Charlottesville Virginia Public Schools, 1954–1969: A Case Study" (Ph.D. diss., University of Virginia, 1971), p. 27–28; Andrew B. Lewis, "Emergency Mothers: Basement Schools and the Preservation of Public Education in Virginia," p. 76, in Matthew Lassiter and Andrew Lewis, eds., *The Moderates' Dilemma: Massive Resistance to School Desegregation in Virginia* (Charlottesville: University Press of Virginia, 1998). I have used the terms desegregation and integration somewhat interchangeably, as was the case during the period.

29. Muse, p. 20–24.

30. Ibid., p. 27.

31. See Crowe, p. 46, on the NAACP and the hiring of Battle. Also see Lewis, p. 76.

32. For comments on Battle and the court, see Crowe, p. 47; for the comment on Judge Paul, see Muse, p. 54.

33. *The Daily Progress,* 12 July 1956, p. 1, col. 8, cited in Crowe, p. 50–51.

34. Crowe, p. 53.

35. Crowe, p. 55–58; Lewis, p. 83; Muse, p. 64; Boyle, p. 253–254.

36. Boyle, p. 253–254.

37. Crowe, p. 62, cited in *The Daily Progress,* 7 September 1956, p. 3, col. 3.

38. Crowe, p. 64; "Charlottesville Granted Desegregation Delay," *The Richmond Times-Dispatch,* 27 July 1957, p. 1, col. 1.

39. Crowe, p. 66.

40. Crowe, p. 66–70.

41. "Fond Memories and Hick'ry in Venable's Golden Year," *The Daily Progress,* 7 May 1976, p. 1, col. 1. Also see James Robert Saunders and Renae Nadine Shackelford, *Urban Renewal and the End of Black Culture in Charlottesville, Virginia* (Jefferson: McFarland and Company, Inc., 1998), p. 48–49.

42. Lewis, p. 72–73, 79–80; Robert Becker, "Massive Resistance: When City Schools Closed, Education Continued," *The Daily Progress,* 26 April 1987, p. 1–2, sec. E; Muse, p. 78; "Citizens' Group Formed Here to Combat School Integration," *The Daily Progress,* 8 March 1955, p. 8.

43. Lewis, p. 86.

44. For the "powerless" observation, see Paul M. Gaston and Thomas T. Hammond, "Public School Desegregation: Charlottesville, Virginia, 1955–62," A report presented to the Nashville Conference on "The South: The Ethical Demands of Integration," a consultation sponsored by the Southern Regional Council and the Fellowship of Southern Churchmen, 28 December 1962, (mimeograph), p. 4; on the school board resolution, see *Minutes,* Charlottesville School Board, 19 September 1958, p. 1; on the petition supporting the closing of schools, see Crowe, p. 109; on the Norfolk suit, see Crowe, p. 113 and Lewis, p. 95.

45. Lewis, p. 89–90; Becker, p. 2; Crowe, p. 92–110; Gaston and Hammond, p. 3–7.

46. For comments on the high school "cooperative plan," see Lewis, p. 87–88; Crowe, p. 108, for comments on tutoring. See Lewis, p. 89, and Crowe, p. 111, for Randolph White's "silly mess" quote.

47. For the Miss Trevillian story, see "Fond Memories and Hick'ry in Venable's Golden Year," *The Daily Progress*, 7 May 1976, p. 12, sec. A. For the "high morale" comment and the status of the high school program, see "Lane Program Said Progressing Well," *The Daily Progress*, 7 November 1958, p. 13; for comments on the consolidation and the missing 200 students, see "Joint Committee to Centralize Classes," *The Daily Progress*, 11 November 1958. The editorial on "Schools Without Frills," is in *The Daily Progress*, 10 November 1958, p. 4. On the declining enrollment, see "Sixteen Percent of Lane Students in Other Schools," *The Daily Progress*, 23 December 1958, p. 13. The "For Sale signs" observation is found in "Board Asked to Oppose Policy," *The Daily Progress*, 7 November 1958, p. 1.

48. Becker, p. 2.

49. See "Thunderous Explosion Rips Integrated School," *The Daily Progress*, 10 November 1958, p. 3 and "Boys Who Ransacked Lane High School Art Room are Charged in Two Other Vandalism Cases," *The Daily Progress*, 21 November 1958, p. 5. See the many letters to the editor found in "Your Right to Say It," *The Daily Progress*, p. 1, 7, 9, 11, 14, 21 November 1958, all p. 4. Lewis, p. 89, 95.

50. "School Board Says Action 'Premature,'" *The Daily Progress*, 9 January 1959, p. 15, and Crowe, p. 119.

51. "Court Voids Massive Resistance Laws," *The Daily Progress*, 19 January 1959, p. 1; "The Road We Must Take," *The Daily Progress*, 20 January 1959, p. 4. See Crowe, p. 121, on Norfolk closings and p. 126 on Almond's order.

52. For Battle's and Michie's quotes, see "City School Decision May Be Made Monday," *The Daily Progress*, 24 January 1959, p. 1. Also see Crowe, p. 121, on board meeting.

53. See Crowe, p. 123, on the CEF wanting schools to remain closed. Also see "City Council Backs Board's Decision to Reopen Schools," *The Daily Progress*, 27 January 1959, p. 1.

54. Lewis, p. 80, 93–95.

55. Ibid. For the Richie quote, see Becker, p. 2.

56. On the bank president's support, see "Bank Heads Endorse School Board Action," *The Daily Progress*, 28 January 1959, p. 15. See "1,200 Signers Back School Board Action," *The Daily Progress*, 27 January 1959, p. 11. For the UVA professor's comments see, "Faculty Statement Supports Schools," *The Daily Progress*, 30 January 1959, p. 19. On Darden's plan, see "Darden Asks Areas to Adopt Dual Education System," *The Daily Progress*, 28 January 1959, p. 15. For a larger discussion of desegregation and Southern business interests, see Elizabeth Jacoway and David R. Colburn, eds., *Southern Businessmen and Desegregation* (Baton Rouge: Louisiana State University Press, 1982).

57. Lewis, p. 72–73, 101–103, and Crowe, p. 38.

58. "Dissatisfaction Expressed Over Private Schools," *The Cavalier Daily*," 19 November 1958, p. 2.

59. Saunders and Shackelford, p. 50.

60. Ibid., p. 50–51.

61. Ibid., p. 49–51; "Lane and Venable Open Wednesday," *The Daily Progress*, 30 January 1959, p. 1, and Crowe, p. 127–128. For the "full confidence" quote, see Gaston and Hammond, p. 6.

62. For comments on the opening of school, see Becker, p. 1, and Gaston and Hammond, p. 7. On the white resistance at Warren County schools, see "White Students Boycott Warren County School," *The Daily Progress*, 8 February 1959, p. 1; "White Students Again Boycott Warren School," *The Daily Progress*, 9 February 1959, p. 1, and "Two Students Withdraw at Front Royal," *The Daily Progress*, 20 February 1959, p. 1. At the start of school in Front Royal, there were 22 students, all black, at a school built for 1,000. Also see Lewis, p. 96–101, and Crowe, p. 134–138.

63.   Gaston and Hammond p. 10–14, for comments on the private schools as a "safety valve." The local newspaper editor strongly supported a "freedom of choice" plan advanced by Leon Dure, a retired newspaper man. It was not free. See Gaston and Hammond, p. 10, 14, for data on the cost to the city to support the tuition grant (voucher) plan. Also see Lewis, p. 100–101. For additional comments on the tuition grants, see Crowe, p. 149–150, and Lewis, p. 98.

64.   Gaston and Hammond, p. 10–14. Also see Crowe, p. 130–198 and Lewis, p. 100–101.

65.   See Charles Giametta, "City's Black Population Increases; Whites Move Out, Census Shows," *The Daily Progress,* 24 February 1981. On the city riots in 1975, see "Youths Pelt City Police With Rocks," *The Daily Progress,* 2 April 1976, p. 1; "Police on Full Alert After 2nd Night of Incidents," *The Daily Progress,* 3 April 1975, p. 1; "Black Problems Priority Items," *The Daily Progress,* 3 April 1975, p. D1; "City Tension Cools; Police Still on Alert," *The Daily Progress,* 4 April 1975, p. 1; "Police Officer Shot in City Disturbance," *The Daily Progress,* 22 July 1975, p. 1; "Confrontation Spurs Reaction," *The Daily Progress,* 22 July 1975, p. 1, sec. C.

66.   During the school closings, *The Daily Progress* carried reports on the redevelopment of Charlottesville's Vinegar Hill. See "Housing Authority Makes New Vinegar Hill Survey," *The Daily Progress,* 10 November 1958, p. 13, and "Federal Loan Approved for Vinegar Hill," *The Daily Progress,* 6 November 1958, p. 25. On the relocation of Vinegar Hill residents, see Saunders and Shackleford, p. 61–85. For comments on the potential redevelopment of Jefferson High School, see David Cho, "Charlottesville Split Over What To Do With Former Black High School," *The Washington Post,* 13 February 2002 [Internet copy, n.p.].

EPILOGUE

LOOKING BACK
Perceptions of Renaissance

Not far from Pasadena's civic center is Martin Luther King Village. Located at the intersection of Washington Boulevard and Fair Oaks Avenue, it is a cluster of angular, off-white, stucco buildings that look as nondescript as too many other Southern California condominium sprawls. Like Charlottesville's Westhaven Housing Project, "King's Village" is Pasadena's answer to urban renewal. Late in the 1960s, fearing the continual decline of housing in the north central section of the city—a neighborhood that had become increasingly African American during the 20th century but had always been working class—Pasadena began a project not dissimilar to the "renewal" of Vinegar Hill. Using federal dollars to finance the project, the city, amid pronouncements of "decent" housing for the "working poor," declared eminent domain. Properties were purchased, bulldozers came in and (mainly) black families were moved out. In 1971, the first phase of King's Manor, its original name, was completed. The waiting list far outdistanced the available "units."[1]

On the corner across from the entrance to the village, was a large supermarket that had served the neighborhood for years. Not long after the projects opened, the market closed. The owners, a heavily diversified corporation, said the store was no longer profitable. When pressed by activists in the black community, corporate spokespersons said the supermarket was subject to too many thefts, was unsafe and, in a highly competitive retail environment, was ultimately a drain on the corporation's already thin profit margin. Once the store closed, the only alternative open to the poor in the "units" across the street was either to patronize the nearby mini-markets, with their small selection and high prices, or to travel miles away to the closest large market. Many in the complex did not own cars, so public transportation—in Southern California that means buses—was necessary. Twenty years after the market closed, the neighborhood still had not managed to convince corporate America and the city that "the conditions" in the projects deserved services.

Almost immediately after they opened, the projects went into a downward spiral. The poor who occupied the buildings organized as best they could in an effort to bring some relief to "the conditions," but there was more futility in the air than hope. In 1984, the president of the tenants' association said, "It's promises after promises after promises and not one of them kept." He made those comments as the city was once again trying to sell off the projects to a private developer, who, in turn, was promising another renewal of the original renewal. Mayor Jo Hickman, who is white, said at the time, "I'm delighted we're finally going to make a better way of living for those people ..."[2]

King's Village, like Westhaven, had become a physical and social wreck. Just seven years after its opening, public housing in Pasadena "had been allowed to deteriorate" to the point that 104 of the 313 units were so badly in need of repairs they were closed and an additional 39 units were demolished. There was enough blame for fingers to be pointed in all directions. Services at the Village were sparse, but kids were plentiful, and drug violence seemed everywhere. At least that was the perception of many in white Pasadena. As with public housing elsewhere, what Pasadena's municipal leaders got with King's Village was the opposite of their stated good intentions. Instead of decent housing, the city had created a residential sinkhole. If the unstated goal, however, was to mark a particular place for "those people," then the Village was a success. Years later, the city and corporate wealth finally have created a shopping area not far from the projects. It is a grand affair, complete with a grand title—"Renaissance Plaza"—and it was built with no small amount of municipal funds. But I suspect "those people" still remain leery of the city's "good intentions."

Charlottesville's public housing, too (the city has three government-sponsored projects, Westhaven, Garret Square and Prospect) has been a constant concern to some city leaders. Others, however, appear not to see the city's projects as their problem. In January 2003, for the first time ever, the board of education met with the city's Redevelopment and Housing Authority "to try to begin closing the education achievement gap in students living in public housing." This initial meeting came more than 30 years after the opening of the projects. Dave Norris, the director of the housing authority, told the board that the number of children in the projects who drop out of school was exceptionally high, greater than any other student cohort in the city. If those children lived in any other neighborhood, he said, "Community leaders would consider it a crisis." Instead, he said that when dropouts occur in public housing, "people just expect it." Years before, when Vinegar Hill was a racially segregated enclave, the perception was that the most important factor defining the community—perhaps the only factor that mattered—was color. But there had always been poor whites living on the Hill. After the collapse of state segregation and the advent of Westhaven, the poor—black *and* white—were moved into public housing. In places like Westhaven—as before, on Vinegar Hill—the common denominator was and is poverty, not race, despite the perception that the latter is all that matters. Norris, who arrived from Richmond in 1997, described Westhaven as a "walled-off enclave," and, he said, it was "symbolic of what we do to poor people in this community." His observation could just as easily have been about King's Village.[3]

Yet the perception marketed by both communities is very different from what Norris and the president of the King's Village tenants' association reported. In places like Pasadena and Charlottesville, the public transcript gets an unhealthy dose of altered reality. In April 1997, *Reader's Digest* conducted its annual "best city" poll and Charlottesville—though not Pasadena—ended up in the top 10 for cities that the magazine rated "as the best places to raise a family." The *Digest* used the Roper Center for Public Opinion Research, and out of 1,000 parent interviews, the center culled 13 factors that were then used to rank hundreds of cities and towns across America. The magazine reported on what it called the "50 winners."[4]

The 1,000 parents told the magazine that a low crime rate, together with a low drug/alcohol problem, "good" public schools and quality health care were the most important factors in choosing a neighborhood. Right behind those factors, the parents said that "many private schools" and "access to colleges" were critically important, as was a thriving economy, affordable housing and a clean environment. Charlottesville was ranked seventh in the *Digest* poll. The magazine quoted one parent who said Charlottesville was a "very wholesome town with a very low crime rate." The parent who made that statement clearly had nothing to do with Westhaven or any of the other public housing projects in the city. I imagine that a majority of the parents used by the pollsters were somewhat affluent because who else would emphasize "many private schools" as an important criterion for selecting a neighborhood? Certainly not the poor and working class.

As the authors of *Urban Renewal and the End of Black Culture in Charlottesville, Virginia* point out, the *Digest* did not disclose the racial breakdown of the parents that were tapped to create the "winners." Without knowing who these people are—where they live, their income, ethnicity and politics—we are unable to gauge the authenticity of the rankings. But the magazine is in the business of selling copies, and the April 1997 issue pronounced that the 50 "winners" were "family-friendly places" where people "work with each other, trust each other, count on each other."

The third-ranked city in the 1997 poll, behind the two small, very homogeneous white Wisconsin towns of Sheboygan and Kenosha, was Loveland, Colorado. Loveland is a suburban community 60 miles north of Denver. Loveland is not dissimilar to another Denver suburb with a similar sounding name, Littleton. In fact, Littleton and Loveland have about the same number of people, are predominately white (more than 90 percent) and prosperous. Both have

thriving local economies, a clean environment and excellent schools. So what separates Loveland from Littleton except perceptions? The magazine said that
Loveland was "a wonderful place to bring up children," and was rated first in
available youth services. Littleton had always prided itself on its public schools,
but what affluent, suburban community has not? Pasadena created a national reputation for itself due, in no small measure, to the "success" of its schools. But we
know that success is a sliding signifier, changing as definitions of quality, community and standards change. Littleton could very well have been Loveland, that
is, until April 1999, when perceptions of Littleton were changed forever. Two
years after the *Digest* announced its 1997 winners, on April 20, 1999, Eric Harris
and Dylan Klebold, two teenage students wearing their trademark black trench
coats, entered Columbine High School and killed 12 classmates and a teacher
before they turned their weapons on themselves. Columbine is in Littleton. The
tragedy that was Columbine could very well have happened in Loveland or any
number of other affluent suburban communities. So much for perceptions of
family-friendly places where people trust each other.

My point here is that "stability" and "success" are artificial constructions, created to sell everything from houses, cars and clothes to status and privilege. To
Charlottesville's boosters, Westhaven and the rest of public housing are simply
nonexistent, invisible places. But there are people who live in those "units"—
black and white—who deserve better. "Best city" rankings (like "failing" school
rankings) are wrongheaded because they separate communities rather than create
them. I suspect that the poor who live in Westhaven and King's Village could care
less about the *Reader's Digest* poll. I doubt they are aware of its existence. What
they do care about, however, is the misguided perception that "the conditions"
that characterize public housing are self-inflicted. Ironically, after April 1999, the
affluent neighborhoods that make up the Columbine community feel the same
way about the perceptions being spread about their community.

For decades, the well-respected public opinion Gallup poll has reported on
the state of America's schools. When parents have been asked about their community's schools, respondents have generally seen the public schools in a favor-
able light. No matter where the Gallup pollsters visited—urban, suburban or
rural—parents reported satisfaction with their neighborhood schools.
Interestingly, however, when the pollsters asked about schools around the country, parents gave a negative view. Poor and working-class parents of color living
in large cities said their neighborhood schools were okay, but it was the "other"
schools that had problems. Wealthy, white parents who lived in the suburbs said
their community schools were satisfactory but the "other" schools had issues.
These perceptions varied little with race, region and class.[5]

Since the end of the 1960s, America has heard a steady drumbeat about failing schools, declining standards, rampant school violence and incompetent

teachers. It has been a miserable assessment of the nation's classrooms, but, apparently, if we can trust the Gallup poll, the decline in America's public education has been located in "other people's schools" not "our own." The perception of "otherness"—no matter where we live or the income we earn—gets reinvented again and again. The great divide in the country is marked by how little we know about who lives on the other side of the proverbial bridge. That certainly appears to be the case in Pasadena and Charlottesville.

Walter and Sara (Dolly) Shatford live a short distance from King's Village. The Shatfords—Walter, the former board of education member and Dolly of the gifted program at Grant School—remain active; both have seen the other side of their 80th birthdays. Walter still goes daily to his law practice. Their children, all graduates of the city's schools, live nearby. Today, more students of color attend Pasadena Unified School District than white children. The schools are ethnically mixed, but not evenly. A few schools are mainly black and Latino, while others are nearly half white. Many of the schools, though, are severely overcrowded. Schools in the center of the city and in the northwest corridor are so densely packed that double sessions have been used more than once since Judge Real's desegregation order. To many in the city, board president LuVerne LaMotte's declaration that Real's January 1970 order would destroy the schools has become a reality. Now that court-ordered desegregation has come, there are still those—not only whites but also blacks and Latinos—who want it to go away. Each community has its own reasons. Recently, a white resident living in the more affluent southwest neighborhood told an audience of interested citizens that it was time to "end this social engineering," meaning a return to "neighborhood schools." The current superintendent, Percy Clark, an African American who is the city's third black superintendent, came to Pasadena in 2001 after a long career as a school administrator, most recently managing a cluster of charter schools with the Edison Project in Michigan. To some observers, Clark's enthusiasm was reminiscent of a revival meeting. His public affirmation that his goal was to change the perception of Pasadena's schools ("Are you with me?" he would shout) was met with qualified support. He said what some in the city wanted to hear. His "Quality Schools" initiative, which included a plan to reduce busing, jolted the city. Did he want a return to "neighborhood schools?" On that assumption, praise came from many, including city officials and the president of the board of education, who was black, but uncomplimentary language was directed at Clark, much of it from the African-American community. He was reportedly sent a cotton plant, more than hinting that his political aspirations were somewhere else than in the black community.[6]

Since he arrived in August 2001, Clark's superintendency has been marked with controversy. But in many ways, he continues in a line of administrators—John Sexson, Willard Goslin and Paul Salmon to name only a few—that have struggled to lead a system burdened by political infighting, neighborhood enti-tlements, diminishing expectations and now, declining resources. The crisis over who rules Pasadena and its schools continues unabated. When Judge Real handed down his decision more than 30 years ago, many thought the city had finally turned the corner. Looking back over the last three decades, the city is as divided today as it was when Real ordered the schools integrated.

THE NEW MILLENNIUM

In the year 2000, Pasadena had more in common with its past than one might imagine. Although the public schools are predominantly Latino and black, many of the city's neighborhoods, as well as the school district's participating suburbs of Altadena and Sierra Madre, remain majority white. If busing ended today, as some wish, then Sierra Madre's schools would be 90 percent white. Smaller neighborhoods in the northeast and southwest would be nearly the same, but the northwest Pasadena schools—the few that are there—would be 90 percent Latino. That is what got Percy Clark in such hot water. His redefinition of Pasadena's educational enterprise promised a return to "neighborhood schools." I suspect he had not done his homework. He had no idea the bombshell such a proposal would create.

The shifting definitions of "community" and "neighborhood" in Pasadena today continue to defy easy analysis. In neighborhoods around the city, there are after-school programs, soccer matches and pick-up street games where race takes a back seat. I stood on a corner close to the Shatford home recently and watched a friendly game of basketball with equal parts black, Latino and white. But in classrooms at the local "neighborhood school," the perception is that race is in the driver's seat.

Faith in the enterprise called public education has diminished since the 1960s. Even before Real's desegregation order, whites (the more affluent kind) were on the move—not just out of Pasadena but out of all of the metropolitan area—to new suburbs carved out of the former citrus groves of Orange County and the bean fields of the San Fernando Valley. Perceptions of private school success and public school failure have accelerated to such an extent that in Pasadena, the middle class and wealthier clientele, many white but also Latino and black, has signed on with private schools. There are now over 10,000 students in nearly 50 private schools in Pasadena and its surrounding suburbs, and many of those schools are nearly all-white establishments. But others have carved out special niches, like one school that promises an Afro-Islamic education, and its tuition is not cheap, by any definition. In 2000, two members of the school board sent their children to private schools and so did the executive director of the Pasadena Education Foundation, the nonprofit that raises money for the system's schools.

When these community leaders were interviewed, they consistently argued that private schools promised the advantages of stability and access, which is something that public schools have failed to deliver, or at least that is the observation in the new millennium.7

In many ways, Pasadena mirrors much of America. The city remains divided, or more accurately, chopped up into small enclaves with particular wants and needs. In some neighborhoods, wants and needs are hotly debated and the divisiveness remains largely unresolved. In the more affluent southwest section of the city, the issues are smog, traffic and taxes. There is little debate about public schools because so many parents have their children in the privates. In the northwest, that historically poor and dark-skinned section of the city, there are still fewer schools per student than any other section of the city. The northwest corridor also has more children than any neighborhood in the system. Of the 2,500 students who are bused daily, all but 200 come from the northwest. Most are Latino. They get sent out to places like Sierra Madre and Linda Vista near the Arroyo, areas with higher percentages of white students—and empty seats because so many students have gone off to private schools.8

What we find in 2000 is that LaMotte's "sacred concept" of neighborhood schools is undergoing redefinition. One northwest parent said she did not "give a rodent's rear end what color the students are." She passionately argued that it did not matter if a new northwest neighborhood school was "segregated" with black or Latino children. What mattered was that the school, if it ever comes, "reflects the surrounding community" and delivers on the promise of "quality educational opportunities." Others were less impressed with her argument. A local executive, who is white, and was running for the school board in 2000, said that if the city has to "revisit 1970 (the desegregation order) in 2010 because we still have segregated schools, we will have wasted 40 years for nothing." Apparently, at least in the northwest neighborhoods, there is a new debate over what constitutes "segregation."9

LOOKING BACK

I began *The Conspiracy of the Good* with two "snapshots" from Pasadena. One told the story of the 1993 Halloween killings, when three young African-American boys were gunned down in a senseless act of cold-blooded murder. The other was about the reopening of the city's famous bridge, with its moonlight revelers from the city's toney neighborhoods, dancing away the night as if the murders had occurred a million miles away. Too often, in my opinion, the city's powerful have ignored what is on the other side of that bridge. The image of a tranquil, stable community, with parades and progressive thinkers living in magnificent old homes, continues to remain firmly a part of what the city's boosters market to the outside world.

We now know that more than a century ago, Pasadena's elite began to craft a vision of a privileged class of residents and guests who lived in grand homes and even grander hotels—built by labor that no one was supposed to see. Whenever that vision was threatened, the city's business and social elite used whatever resources were available, including the press and the machinery of government, to create new "ordinances" to promote a worldview they believed was best for everyone, including those that were excluded.

Now, more than 100 years later, after whiskey wars and labor wars, segregated Mexican schools, church burnings and "whites only" swimming pools, much of Pasadena's past has been forgotten. In this aristocratic town, stories of radical socialists, trade union organizers and vibrant Labor Day parades have been buried under layers of bluestocking history. Today, when New Year's Day crowds walk past a downtown Pasadena movie theater, they see poster-sized photographs from turn-of-the-century Rose Parades. Except for one of the photos, which depicts a trade union plasterer and some children. It is not from the Rose Parade. It is from a long forgotten Labor Day parade. How do we know? Because the early parade organizers, the chic Valley Hunt Club, never recognized the legitimacy of trade unions. As a result, the early parades rarely had labor union participation. Certainly, the Rose Parade organizers would have never sanctioned a working-class laborer to walk alongside its swank flower-adorned carriages. So how did the photo get misappropriated? Most likely because Pasadena's conventional wisdom has so marginalized the city's working-class history that an old photograph of a plasterer in his Sunday best, carrying a banner celebrating his union, just *had* to be from the Rose Parade—even though the working class was not part of the early parades. It is Pasadena double-think. From a new millennium-marketing stand-point, the photograph appealed to the theater owner (or the building's architect) because it lent sophistication to an otherwise new but nondescript stucco building. Those old photos give the building an aura of age, despite the misappropriation of the trade union image, and selling an image has always meant something in Pasadena.[10]

As historian Herbert Gutman tells us, the struggle to reconceptualize the present (what Percy Clark has in mind) has rich connections with the past. Apparently, Superintendent Clark has failed to understand this or he would have been more sensitive to the city's history of neighborhood schools. Gutman was a labor and working-class historian, who spent his long and fruitful career writing about collective responses to the inequalities associated with capitalism. He railed at the narrow definition of a "national history" that glamorizes "possessive individualism" as the only sure cure to social ills. Gutman was despondent—and I must agree—that the past is too often pillaged to celebrate what in fact were deep

Fig. 29. An unknown representative from the Plasterers Union
No. 134, on display in his Sunday best. Caught in the Sid Gally
photograph is a reflection of Colorado Boulevard, now marketed
as "Old Pasadena." *(Photograph courtesy of Sid Gally)*

inequalities of race, class and gender. The theater photo is but another example.
An American history that ignores the collective struggle for community becomes
a consumers' history, to be used as justification for anticommunal commitments
to the greed of what Gutman called "entrepreneurial economics," and what I have
come to call the politics of selfishness cloaked as "communal goodness." Gutman
reminds us that historians should be around to explain that the struggle between
individual and collective responses to social change is not new. He further
reminds us that the core value of the American experience is conflict, not consensus, regardless of what our national history tells us.[11]

Today, in buildings once occupied by Socialists engaged in passionate debate
over working-class politics, trendy teenage clerks sell GAP, Benetton and other
clothing to upscale shoppers. Developers have reclaimed Pasadena's turn-of-the-

century commercial district on the west end of Colorado Boulevard. This new shopping district is now called "Old Pasadena," a clever marketing device that effectively uses the past to sell the present. Narrow alleys that jut off from Colorado are packed with shoppers looking at everything from $5 café lattes to $500 cotton shirts. Scattered throughout "Old Pasadena," to give the flavor of stability to things new, are brass plaques commemorating bits and pieces of the city's history—"This building was once ..." or "On this spot once stood ..." Pasadena Heritage, the city's upscale version of historic preservation and the same folks that organized the Colorado Street Bridge reopening, put the plaques there. Across the street from J. Crew and Starbucks, where the Carpenter's Local 769 and the Women's Union Label League met at century's turn (and not far from the theater with the trade union photograph), is the main entrance to a shoppers' lane called Mills Alley. The alley has a plaque that reads "Once known as Wards Alley ... a fire at this site destroyed a laundry establishment owned by Chinese settlers."

Not quite. We know that the Chinese laundry did not merely go up in flames in some blameless accident. It happened in one of the city's first fits of violence against "outsiders," when a mob drove out more than 100 Chinese workers, looting their rooms, destroying their property and stealing their money. The day after, the "Chinaman" was hanged in effigy from a street pole to symbolize the death of the "other." In a highly nuanced act of class and racial distancing, the city's elite wished the land cleared of the "Celestials" for expansion of the commercial district—the same district that now entertains all those shoppers looking for their lattes. The myth of tranquility persists because it sells better than conflict.

Let me conclude with two additional "snapshots" from Pasadena and Charlottesville today, 10 years after the snapshots with which I began. I believe each informs us about how the struggle for our American community continues.

Pasadena:

> On the evening of June 16, 2003, the Pasadena Board of Directors passed an ordinance prohibiting employers from recruiting day laborers, a twist on the restrictions cities pass against panhandlers soliciting money on the street. This time, the restriction is intended to prevent employers in cars from hustling five-dollar-an-hour immigrant workers, almost always Mexicans or Central Americans. The directors claimed certain street corners where the day laborers congregate—which, not coincidently, are in the city's prime business district—are "traffic hazards." Because the immigrants rush onto the pavement when a car slows, the city attorney said the situation was "dangerous for the workers." Since soliciting work is not a crime in California, the city could not prevent the day laborers from looking for work. City leaders say what is behind the new ordinance is an effort to lure the immigrants away from their designated street corners to a "safer" city-run employment center a mile and a half from the business district. But for laborers

dependent on drive-up employers at the local paint store or lumberyard, the employment center might as well be in Tijuana.[12]

Charlottesville:

During January and February of 2002, the University of Virginia campus and the city of Charlottesville, which has always prided itself on its safe streets, were stunned by a series of assaults on university students. The victims, 10 in all, were white, East Asian and East Indian. When their attackers were caught, the city was shocked. Those responsible for the beatings were 10 Charlottesville High School students—and they were all black. Motives were hard to come by. Wallets were left in pockets and the attackers said little to their victims. Just a string of beatings, sometimes with clubs, that caused cracked heads and broken bones. There were allegations that the beatings were racially motivated. David Duke, the former KKK leader, brought his European-American Unity and Rights Organization (EURO) to town, demanding that the 10 be charged with hate crimes. In a soul-searching community meeting, which was attended by some of the victims, one citizen said, "We don't have a problem here ... somebody just blew this out of proportion. I believe the kids were just being kids ... they never intended to hurt anyone." Concerned Charlottesville residents organized a bake sale to help victims pay their medical bills—and to help the assailants pay for their legal defense. No hate crime charges were filed.[13]

NOTES

1. Jim Tranquada, "King's Manor: City hopes for rejuvenation of housing project," *Pasadena Star-News*, 30 January 1984, p. A32.
2. Ibid.
3. Reed Williams, "Building Up; Public Housing, Playground Improvements Among Goals of New City Development Leader," *The Daily Progress*, 12 August 2002 (Lexus/Nexus, online edition, n.p.) and Braxton Williams, "Groups Join Forces to Discuss Public Housing, Education" *The Daily Progress*, 14 January 2003 (Lexus/Nexus, online edition, n.p.). James Robert Saunders and Renae Nadine Shackelford, *Urban Renewal and the End of Black Culture in Charlottesville, Virginia* (Jefferson: McFarland and Company, Inc., 1998), p. 112. Also see Nancy B. Nyman, "The Politics of Public Housing: The Case of Charlottesville, Virginia," (Master's thesis, University of Virginia, 1968), and Christopher McLean, "The City of Charlottesville's Proposed Development of Vinegar Hill," (Master's thesis, University of Virginia, 1984).
4. "The Best Places to Raise a Family," *Reader's Digest*, April 1997, p. 74–81.
5. Stanley M. Elam, ed., *A Decade of Gallop Polls of Attitudes toward Education, 1969–1978* (Bloomington: Phi Delta Kappa, 1978) and Stanley M. Elam, ed., *The Gallup/Phi Delta Kappa Polls of Attitudes toward Public Schools, 1969–1988: A Twenty-Year Compilation and Educational History* (Bloomington: Phi Delta Kappa, Educational Foundation, 1989).
6. David Zahniser, "Busing: 30 Years After Landmark Decision," *Pasadena Star-News*, 23 January 2000, p. A1, for statistics on school population. For "social engineering" comment, see Andy Samuelson, "Quality Schools plan stirs debate," *Pasadena Star-News*, 27 February

2002, p. A1. Clark opened school in September 2001 with a stirring speech entitled, "Why Not the Best?" He stood on the Pasadena Civic Auditorium stage in front of the system's employees, and, with arms raised above his head, shouted, "Are you with me?" According to Tommy McManus, the black school board president, the focus was on attracting "middle-class students back to the system," but many read that as a thinly veiled call for more white students. See Andy Samuelson, "'Are You With Me?' Superintendent Clark vows to take PUSD to the top of the mountain," *Pasadena Star-News*, 5 September 2001, p. A3, col. 2. The black and Latino community, however, grew apprehensive. Some, including former board member Elbie Hickambottom, were outraged. He said Clark's initiative would destroy the schools. He said he had no confidence in Clark and, further, said whites had not returned because "they don't want to go to school with blacks." Joe Hopkins, the editor of the black *Pasadena Journal*, slammed Clark more than once in his column, calling him a sell-out. See "Black Power at a Crossroads, Again," *Pasadena Journal*, 31 January 2002, p. 2, col. 1. Larry Wilson, the editor of the *Pasadena Star-News*, who is white, then waded into the fray by criticizing Hopkins, calling into question his intelligence when he faulted Hopkins' writing style, saying it was "artless" and "odious." See Larry Wilson, "Venomous ink has gone too far," *Pasadena Star-News*, 23 March 2002, p. A16, col. 1. For comments on the cotton plant, see Erika Hayasaki, "Task Tough for Ambitious Schools Chief," *The Los Angeles Times*, 11 August 2003 (Lexus/Nexus online edition, n.p.).

7.   See David Zahniser, "Public, private school chasm grows wider," *Pasadena Star-News*, 23 January 2000, p. A1, col. 2, for comments on private schools and the perception of public school failure.

8.   Ibid. Community activist Porfirio Frausto, who attended the southwest community meeting, made the observation that southwest residents were concerned more with smog and traffic than the schools.

9.   David Zahniser, "Northwest neighborhood finds schools scattered," *Pasadena Star-News*, 11 October 1999, p. A1, col. 2.

10.   I am indebted to Mary Borgerding, longtime Pasadena resident and historical museum volunteer, for informing me about the selection process for the theater photos. Borgerding, however, was unaware of the origin of the electrician's photo, believing it an image from the Rose Parade.

11.   Ira Berlin, ed., *Power and Culture: Essays on the American Working Class* (New York: Pantheon Books, 1987), p. 5.

12.   Bob Edwards and Mandalit del Barco, "Pasadena enacts regulation to curb hiring of day laborers from the street," *National Public Radio*, morning edition, 17 January 2003 (Lexus/Nexus online edition, n.p.).

13.   Adam Hochberg, "Reaction within Charlottesville, Virginia, community to string of assaults my black teens," *National Public Radio*, morning edition, 22 March 2002 (Lexus/Nexus online edition, n.p.); Carlos Santos, "Hate-Crime charges will not be filed; Charlottesville attacks at issue," *Richmond Times-Dispatch*, 29 March 2002 (Lexus/Nexus online edition, n.p.).

BIBLIOGRAPHY

MANUSCRIPT COLLECTIONS

California Institute of Technology Archives
  Amos Gager Throop Collection
  E.S. Gosney Papers
Hampton University
  William Mason Cooper Papers
Huntington Memorial Library
  Amy T. Bridges Journal
  Jeanne Caroline Carr Papers, 1842–1903
  Myron Hunt Papers
Jean and Alexander Heard Library Vanderbilt University, Special Collections
  Willard Goslin Papers
The Papers of the National Association for the Advancement of Colored People
  Branch Files, Series D, The West
Pasadena Museum of History
  Black History Collection
  Lynn Vernon Papers
  Samuel Sheats Papers
  Tournament of Roses Collection
Southern California Library for Social Studies and Research
  Civil Rights Congress Papers
University of Texas, Austin, Center for Oral History
  L. Thomas Hopkins Papers
University of Virginia, Alderman Library Special Collections
  The A. L. Hench Papers
  Harry Flood Byrd Papers
  Mary Johnston Papers
  Miller School Papers
  The Papers of Albert G. A. Balz
  William Royall Smithey Papers
Vassar College, Special Collections
  Louise Hawkes Padelford Papers
Virginia State University Archives
  The Colson-Hill Family Papers, 1834-1984
  Virginia State Teachers Association Papers

Books

Allegor, Catherine. *Parlor Politics: In Which the Ladies of Washington Help Build a City and a Government.* Charlottesville: University of Virginia Press, 2000.

Allen, Mary L. *Education or Indoctrination.* Caldwell, Idaho: Caxton Printers, Inc., 1955.

Anderson, James. *The Education of Blacks in the South, 1860–1935.* Chapel Hill: University of North Carolina Press, 1988.

Armstrong, M. F. and Helen W. Ludlow. *Hampton and Its Students, with Fifty Cabin and Plantation Songs.* New York: G.P. Putnam's Sons, 1874.

Ayer, Edward. *The Promise of the New South: Life After Reconstruction.* New York: Oxford University Press, 1992.

Beineke, John. *And There Were Giants in the Land: The Life of William Heard Kilpatrick.* New York: Peter Lang Publishing, 1998.

Berlin, Ira, ed. *Power and Culture: Essays on the American Working Class.* New York: Pantheon Books, 1987.

Bernstein, Carl and Bob Woodward. *All The President's Men,* 2nd ed. New York: Touchstone Books, 1994.

Bestor, Arthur. *Educational Wastelands: The Retreat from Learning in Our Public Schools.* Urbana: University of Illinois Press, 1952.

Blocker, John. *American Temperance Movements: Cycles of Reform.* New York: Twayne Publishers, 1989.

Blocker, John S. *"Give to the Winds Thy Fears:" The Women's Temperance Crusade, 1873–1874.* Westport: Greenwood Press, 1985.

Bloom, Jack. *Class, Race, and the Civil Rights Movement.* Bloomington: Indiana University Press, 1987.

Bond, Horace Mann. *The Education of the Negro in the American Social Order.* New York: Prentice Hall, Inc., 1934.

Bordin, Ruth. *Women and Temperance.* Philadelphia: Temple University Press, 1981.

Bowers, C.A. *The Progressive Educator and the Depression.* New York: Random House, 1969.

Boyer, Paul. *Urban Masses and Moral Order in America.* Cambridge: Harvard University Press, 1978.

Boyle, Sarah Patton. *The Desegregated Heart: A Virginian's Stand in Time of Transition,* with an introduction by Jennifer Ritterhouse. New York: William Morrow and Company, 1962; reprint, Charlottesville: University of Virginia Press, 2001.

Brundage, W. F., ed. *Under Sentence of Death; Lynching in the South.* Chapel Hill: University of North Carolina Press, 1997.

Buhle, Mary Jo. *Women and American Socialism, 1870–1920.* Champaign: University of Illinois Press, 1981.

Butchart, Ronald. *Northern Schools, Southern Blacks and Reconstruction.* Westport, Conn.: Greenwood Press, 1980.

Carew, Harold D. *The History of Pasadena and the San Gabriel Valley.* Los Angeles: S.J. Clarke Publishing Co., 1930.

Carpenter, Thomas D. *Pasadena: Resort Hotels and Paradise.* Pasadena: Castle Green Times, 1984.

Cash, Wilbur. *The Mind of the South.* New York: Knopf, 1941.

Caton, Bruce. *A Stillness at Appomattox.* New York: Doubleday and Company, 1953.

Ceplair, Larry, ed. *Charlotte Perkins Gilman: A Nonfiction Reader.* New York: Columbia University Press, 1991.

Cherrington, E. H., ed. *The Anti-Saloon League Yearbook of 1913.* Westervale, Ohio: Anti-Saloon League Association, 1913.

Cherrington, Ernest Hurst. *The Evolution of Prohibition in the United States of America.* New Jersey: Patterson Smith Publishing Company, 1920.

Coleman, James, et al. *Equality of Educational Opportunity.* Washington, DC: Government Printing Office, 1966.

Cronon, William, George Miles and Jay Gitlin, eds. *Under an Open Sky: Rethinking America's Western Past.* New York: W.W. Norton, 1999.

Cuban, Larry. *How Teachers Taught.* Cambridge: Harvard University Press, 1992.

Davis, Mike. *City of Quartz.* New York: Verso Press, 1990.

Deutsch, Sarah. *No Separate Refuge: Culture, Class, and Conflict on an Anglo-Hispanic Frontier in the American Southwest, 1880–1940.* New York: Oxford University Press, 1987.

Dumke, Glen. *The Boom of Southern California.* San Marino: The Henry Huntington Library, 1944.

Elam, Stanley M., ed. *The Gallup/Phi Delta Kappa Polls of Attitudes toward Public Schools, 1969–1988: A Twenty-Year Compilation and Educational History.* Bloomington: Phi Delta Kappa, Educational Foundation, 1989.

Elam, Stanley M., ed. *A Decade of Gallop Polls of Attitudes toward Education, 1969–1978.* Bloomington: Phi Delta Kappa, 1978.

Epstein, Barbara Leslie. *The Politics of Domesticity: Women, Evangelism, and Temperance in 19th Century America.* Middletown: Wesleyan University Press, 1981.

Fancher, Raymond E. *The Intelligence Men: Makers of the IQ Controversy.* New York: W.W. Norton and Co., 1985.

Fass, Paula S. *Outside In: Minorities and the Transformation of American Education.* New York: Oxford, 1989.

Foner, Phillip S. *American Socialism and Black Americans.* Westport: Greenwood Press, 1977.

Frankel, Noralee and Nancy Dye. *Gender, Class, Race and Reform in the Progressive Era.* Lincoln: University of Kansas Press, 1990.

Franklin, Barry. *Building the American Community: The School Curriculum and the Search for Social Control.* London: Falmer Press, 1986.

Garcia, Mario T. *Desert Immigrants: The Mexicans of El Paso, 1880–1920.* New Haven: Yale University Press, 1980.

Gardner, Anna. *Harvest Gleanings in Prose and Verse.* New York: Fowler and Wells, 1881.

Gilman, Charlotte Perkins. *The Living of Charlotte Perkins Gilman.* New York: D. Appleton-Century Company, 1935.

Gordon, Linda. *Woman's Body, Woman's Right, Birth Control in America.* New York: Penguin Books, 1990.

Gosney, E.S. *Collected Papers on Eugenic Sterilization in California: A Critical Study of Results of 6000 Cases.* Pasadena, CA: The Human Betterment Foundation, 1930.

Gosney, E.S. and Paul Popenoe. *Sterilization for Human Betterment.* New York: Macmillan Company, 1929.

Gould, Stephen Jay. *The Mismeasure of Man.* New York: W.W. Norton, 1980.

Green, Edna C. *Southern Strategies.* Chapel Hill: University of North Carolina Press, 1997.

Greenstein, Paul. *Bread and Hyacinths: The Rise and Fall of Utopian Los Angeles.* Los Angeles: California Classic Books, 1992.

Gullett, Gayle. *Becoming Citizens: The Emergence and Development of the California Women's Movement, 1880–1911.* Champaign: University of Illinois Press, 2000.

Hacker, Andrew. *Two Nations: Black and White, Separate, Hostile, Unequal.* New York: Charles Scribner's Sons, 1992.

Hale, Grace Elizabeth. *Making Whiteness: The Culture of Segregation in the South, 1890–1940*. New York: Pantheon Books, 1998.

Harlan, Louis. *Separate and Unequal: Public School Campaigns and Racism in the Southern Seaboard States, 1901–1915*. Chapel Hill: University of North Carolina Press, 1958.

Hill, Mary. *Charlotte Perkins Gilman: The Making of a Radical Feminist, 1860–1896*. Philadelphia: Temple University Press, 1980.

Hofstadter, Richard. *Anti-intellectualism in American Life*. New York: Alfred A. Knopf, 1963.

Holder, Charles Frederick. *All about Pasadena and its vicinity: The climate, missions, trails and canons, fruits, flowers and game*. Boston: Lee and Shepard/ Charles T. Dillingham, 1889.

Holder, Charles Frederick. *Southern California: Its Climate, Trails, Mountains, Canyons, Watering Places, Fruits, Flowers and Game. A Guide Book*. Los Angeles: Los Angeles Times-Mirror Company, 1888.

Hough, Richard. *The Potemkin Mutiny*. Englewood Cliffs: Prentice-Hall, Inc., 1960.

Hourihan, James. *The History of St. Andrew's Parish, 1886–1986*. New York: Custombook, Inc., 1986.

Hulburd, David. *This Happened in Pasadena*. New York: Macmillan Co., 1951.

Jacoway, Elizabeth and David R. Colburn, eds. *Southern Businessmen and Desegregation*. Baton Rouge: Louisiana State University Press, 1982.

Johnson, Wilbur H. *General Biology*. New York: Henry Holt and Company, 1957.

Jones, Kitty and Robert L. Olivier. *Progressive Education is REDucation*. Boston: Meador Publishing Company, 1956.

Kilpatrick, William H. *The Educational Frontier*. New York: Appleton-Century-Crafts, 1933.

Kliebard, Herbert. *The Struggle for the American Curriculum, 1983–1958*. New York: Routledge and Kegan Paul, 1987.

Knight, Edgar W. *Public Education in the South*. New York: Ginn and Co., 1922.

Lane, Ann J. *Her Land and Beyond: The Life and Work of Charlotte Perkins Gilman*. New York: Pantheon Press, 1990.

Lazerson, Marvin. *Origins of the Urban School*. Cambridge: Harvard University Press, 1971.

Lemann, Nicholas. *The Promised Land: The Great Black Migration and How it Changed America*. New York: Alfred Knopf, 1991.

Lincoln, Eric C. and Lawrence H. Mamiya. *The Black Church in the African American Experience*. Durham: Duke University Press, 1990.

Link, William. *The Paradox of Southern Progressivism, 1880–1930*. Chapel Hill: University of North Carolina Press, 1992.

Link, William A. *A Hard Country and a Lonely Place*. Chapel Hill: University of North Carolina Press, 1983.

Lukas, J. Anthony. *Big Trouble*. New York: Simon and Schuster, 1997.

Lukas, J. Anthony. *Common Ground*. New York: Alfred A. Knopf, Inc., 1986.

Lynd, Albert. *Quackery in the Public Schools*. New York: Grosset and Dunlap, 1953.

Marshall, F. Ray. *Labor in the South*. Cambridge: Harvard University Press, 1967.

Mason, Lucy Randolph. *To Win These Rights: A Personal Story of the CIO in the South*. New York: Harper and Bros., 1952.

Mayo, Morrow. *Los Angeles*. New York: Alfred Knopf, 1932.

Mazon, Mauricio. *The Zoot-Suit Riots: The Psychology of Symbolic Annihilation*. Austin: University of Texas Press, 1984.

McPherson, James. *Ordeal By Fire: The Civil War and Reconstruction*. New York: Alfred Knopf, 1982.

McPherson, James. *The Abolitionist Legacy: From Reconstruction to the NAACP.* Princeton: Princeton University Press, 1975.

McWilliams, Carey. *Southern California Country.* New York: Meredith Press, 1946.

Members of Writers' Program of the Work Projects Administration, ed. *The Negro in Virginia.* Richmond: Hastings House, 1940.

Monroy, Douglas. *Rebirth: Mexican Los Angeles from the Great Migration to the Great Depression.* Berkeley: University of California Press, 1999.

Monroy, Douglas. *Thrown Among Strangers: The Making of Mexican Culture in Frontier California.* Berkeley: University of California Press, 1990.

Moore, John Hammond. *Albemarle County: Jefferson's County, 1727–1976.* Charlottesville: University of Virginia Press, 1976.

Mowry, George. *The California Progressives.* Berkeley: The University of California Press, 1951.

Murphy, Marjorie. *Blackboard Unions: The AFT and the NEA, 1900–1980.* Ithaca, New York: Cornell University Press, 1990.

Muse, Benjamin. *Virginia's Massive Resistance.* Bloomington: Indiana University Press, 1961.

Museum of Modern Art. *Dorothea Lange, with introductory essay by George Elliott.* New York: Doubleday, 1966.

Myers, Henry S. *Fundamentally Speaking.* San Francisco: Strawberry Hill Press, 1977.

Nash, Gerald R. *The American West Transformed: The Impact of the Second World War.* Bloomington: University of Indiana Press, 1985.

Newmark, Harris. *Sixty Years in Southern California, 1853–1916,* 3rd ed. New York: Houghton Mifflin Company, 1930.

Nordoff, Charles. *California for Health, Wealth and Residence.* New York: Harper and Bros., 1873.

Olsen, Laurie. *Made in America: Immigrant Students in Our Public Schools.* New York: Norton, 1997.

Page, Henry Markham. *Pasadena, Its Early Years.* Los Angeles: Lorrin L. Morrison, 1964.

Peeler, David P. *Hope Among Us Yet: Social Criticism and Social Science.* Athens, Georgia: University of Georgia Press, 1988.

Pickens, Donald K. *Eugenics and the Progressives.* Nashville: Vanderbilt University Press, 1968.

Picott, J. Rupert. *The History of the Virginia Teachers Association.* Washington, DC: National Education Association, 1975.

Pineda, Manual. *Pasadena Area History.* Los Angeles: John Anderson Publishers, 1972.

Pitt, Leonard. *The Decline of the Californios: A Social History of the Spanish-Speaking Californians, 1846–1890.* Berkeley: University of California Press, 1966.

Pittenger, Mark. *American Socialists and Evolutionary Thought, 1870–1920.* Madison: University of Wisconsin Press, 1993.

Pomeroy, Earl S. *In Search of the Golden West: The Tourist in Western America.* Lincoln: University of Nebraska Press, 1957.

Record, Wilson. *The Negro and the Communist Party.* Chapel Hill: University of North Carolina Press, 1951.

Reid, Hiram. *The History of Pasadena.* Pasadena: The Pasadena History Company, 1895.

Richardson, Archie. *The Development of Negro Education in Virginia, 1831–1970.* Richmond: Phi Delta Kappa, 1976.

Robinson, Jackie. *I Never Had It Made.* New York: G.P. Putnam's Sons, 1972.

Roland, Charles P. *Albert Sidney Johnston, Soldier of Three Republics.* Austin: University of Texas Press, 1964.

Romo, Ricardo. *East Los Angeles: A History of a Barrio.* Austin: University of Texas Press, 1983.

Ruiz, Vicky. *Out of the Shadows: Mexican Women in Twentieth-Century America*. New York: Oxford University Press, 1998.

Rumbarger, John J. *Profits, Power, and Prohibition*. Albany: SUNY Press, 1989.

Salmond, John. *Miss Lucy of the CIO: The Life and Times of Lucy Randolph Mason, 1882–1959*. Athens: University of Georgia Press, 1988.

Saunders, James Robert and Renae Nadine Shackelford. *Urban Renewal and the End of Black Culture in Charlottesville, Virginia*. Jefferson: McFarland and Company, Inc., 1998.

Schield, Ann. *Pasadena: The Crown of the Valley*. Pasadena: Pasadena Historical Society, 1995.

Scott, James C. *Domination and the Arts of Resistance: Hidden Transcripts*. New Haven: Yale University Press, 1990.

Sequel, Mary Louise. *The Curriculum Field: Its Formative Years*. New York: Teachers College Press, 1966.

Sinclair, Upton. *The Autobiography of Upton Sinclair*. New York: Harcourt, Brace, and World, Inc., 1962.

Smith, Gilbert E. *The Limits of Reform: Politics and Federal Aid to Education, 1937–1950*. NY: Garland Publishers, 1982.

Somerville, J. Alexander. *Man of Color: An Autobiography by Dr. J. Alexander Somerville*. Los Angeles: Lorrin J. Morrison, Printing and Publishing, 1946.

Stadtman, Verne. *The University of California, 1868–1968*. New York: McGraw-Hill Book Company, 1970.

Starr, Kevin. *Inventing the Dream: California Through the Progressive Era*. New York: Oxford University Press, 1985.

Stimson, Grace. *Rise of the Labor Movement in Los Angeles*. Berkeley: University of California Press, 1955.

Swain, Martha. *Pat Harrison: The New Deal Years*. Jackson, Mississippi: University Press of Mississippi, 1978.

Tanner, Daniel and Laurel N. Tanner. *Curriculum Development: Theory into Practice*, 2nd ed. New York: Macmillan Publishing Company, 1980.

Teitlebaum, Kenneth. *Schooling for "Good Rebels" Socialism, American Education, and the Search for Radical Curriculum*. New York: Teachers College Press, 1995.

Thorndike, Edward L. *Your City*. New York: Harcourt Brace and Company, 1939.

Thurston's Directory of Pasadena. Pasadena: The Thurston Company, 1906–07; 1908–09; 1911.

Tindal, George. *The Emergence of the New South, 1913–1945*. Baton Rouge: Louisiana State University Press, 1967.

Trotter, J.W., Jr., ed. *The Great Migration in Historical Perspective: New Dimensions of Race, Class, and Gender*. Bloomington: Indiana University Press, 1991.

Tsai Shi-Shin, Henry. *The Chinese Experience in America*. Bloomington: Indiana University Press, 1986.

Tushnet, Mark. *The NAACP's Legal Strategy Against Segregated Education, 1925–1950*. Chapel Hill: The University of North Carolina Press, 1986.

Tyack, David. *The One Best System*. Cambridge: Harvard University Press, 1974.

Tyack, David and Larry Cuban. *Tinkering Toward Utopia*. Cambridge: Harvard University Press, 1995.

Tyack, David, Robert Lowe and Elisabeth Hansot. *Public Schools in Hard Times*. Cambridge, Mass: Harvard University Press, 1984.

Van Orman, Richard A. *A Room for the Night: Hotels of the Old West*. Bloomington: Indiana University Press, 1966.

Vaughn, William Preston. *Schools for All: The Blacks and Public Education in the South, 1865–1877.* Lexington: University of Kentucky Press, 1974.

Vetterli, Richard. *Storming the Citadel: The Fundamental Revolution Against Progressive Education.* Costa Mesa: Educational Media Press, 1976.

Violas, Paul. *The Training of the Urban Working Class.* Champaign: University of Illinois Press, 1978.

Weinberg, Robert. *The Revolution of 1905 in Odessa.* Bloomington: Indiana University Press, 1993.

Wesley, Edgar B. *NEA: The First Hundred Years.* New York: Harper and Brothers Publishers, 1957.

West, Elliott. *The Saloon on the Rocky Mountain Mining Frontier.* Lincoln: University of Nebraska Press, 1979.

White, Richard. *"It's Your Misfortune and None of My Own": A New History of the American West.* Norman: University of Oklahoma Press, 1991.

Wollenberg, Charles. *All Deliberate Speed: Segregation and Exclusion in California Schools, 1855–1975.* Berkeley: University of California Press, 1976.

Wood, J.W. *The Concise History of Pasadena.* Los Angeles: 1923.

Wood, J.W. *Pasadena, California, Historical and Personal.* Pasadena?: printed by author, 1917.

Woodson, Carter. *The Mis-Education of the Negro.* Washington, DC: Associated Publishers, 1933.

Woodward, C. Vann. *Origins of the New South, 1877–1913.* Baton Rouge: University of Louisiana Press, 1951.

Zangrando, Robert. *The NAACP Crusade Against Lynching, 1909–1950.* Philadelphia: Temple University Press, 1980.

CHAPTERS AND ARTICLES

Anderson, John. "Fitting the Commerce Course of the High School and Junior College to the Needs of the Community." *Educational Research Bulletin* 4:9, Pasadena City Schools, W. Hardin Hughes, ed. (May 1926): 3–48.

"Are Our School Boards Being Captured?" *FACTS* Vol. V:3 (May-June 1957): 1.

Ball, I. Grace. "Typical Work of the Adjustment Division." *Educational Research Bulletin* 3:3, Pasadena City Schools, W. Hardin Hughes, ed. (November 1924): 6–8.

Banner, Lois. "Religious Benevolence as Social Control: A Critique of an Interpretation." *Journal of American History* 60:1 (June 1973): 23–41.

Bogardus, Emory. "The Mexican Immigrant." *Sociology and Social Research* 11 (1926–27): 470–488.

Boris, Eileen. "Reconstructing the 'Family': Women, Progressive Reform, and the Problem of Social Control." In *Gender, Class, Race, and Reform in the Progressive Era,* edited by Noralee Frankel and Nancy Dye, 73–86. Lexington: University of Kentucky Press, 1991.

Brundage, W. Fitzhugh. "White Women and the Politics of Historical Memory in the New South, 1880–1920." In *Jumpin' Jim Crow: Southern Politics from the Civil War to Civil Rights,* edited by Jane Dailey, Glenda Elizabeth Gilmore, and Bryant Simon, 115–139. Princeton: Princeton University Press, 2000.

Burlbaw, Lynn. "More Than Ten Thousand Teachers: Hollis Caswell and the Virginia Curriculum Revision Program" *Journal of Curriculum and Supervision* 6:3 (Spring 1991) 233–254.

Butler, Hilton. "Bilbo-The Two-Edged Sword." *North American Review* CCXXXII (1931): 496–504.

Carr, Jeannie. "Pasadena: The Crown of the Valley." *Historical Society of Southern California* 3 (1893): 80–87.

Cohen, Ronald. "Music Goes to War: California, 1940–45." In *The Way We Really Were,* edited by Roger W. Lotchin, 47–67. Urbana: University of Illinois Press, 2000.

Cohen, William. "Pasadena." *Law and Society Review* 11:1 (November 1967): 42–53.

Counts, George S. "Dare Progressive Education Be Progressive?" *Progressive Education* 9 (April 1932): 257–263.

"Crisis in the Summertime." News COPE Vol. 8:1 (24 October 1957). Daniel, Harrison W. "Virginia Baptists and the Negro, 1865–1902." *Virginia Magazine of History and Biography* 76 (1968): 340–386.

Cronin, William, Miles, George and Gitlin, Jay, "Becoming the West." *Under an Open Sky: Rethinking America's Western Past,* edited by W. Cronin, G. Miles and J. Gitlin, 3–21. New York: W.W. Norton, 1992.

Deutsch, Sarah. "Landscape of Enclaves: Race Relations in the West, 1865–1990." In *Under an Open Sky: Rethinking America's Western Past,* edited by W. Cronin, G. Miles, and J. Gitlin, 110–131. New York: W.W. Norton, 1992.

Fields, Barbara Jean. "Origins of the New South and the Negro Question." *The Journal of Southern History* 67:4 (November 2001): 811–827.

Freudenberg, A. and J. Casteen, eds. "John B. Minor's Civil War Diary." *Magazine of Albemarle County History* 22 (1964): 45–55.

Garcia, Mario. "The Americanization of the Mexican Immigrant 1880–1930." *The Journal of Ethnic Studies* 6:2 (Summer 1978): 19–34.

Gemmill, Chalmers L. "The Charlottesville General Hospital, 1861–1865." *Magazine of Albemarle County History* 22 (1964): 91–160.

Gonzalez, Gilbert. "Segregation of Mexican Children in a Southern California City: The Legacy of Expansionism and the American Southwest." *Western Historical Quarterly* 16:1 (January 1985): 55–76.

Goodenow, Ronald. "Paradox in Progressive Educational Reform: The South and the Education of Blacks in The Depression Years." *Phylon* (March 1978): 49–65.

Gould, Stephen Jay. *"Carrie Buck's Daughter." The Flamingo's Smile: Reflections in Natural History,* edited by Stephen J. Gould, 306–318. New York: W.W. Norton and Company, 1985.

Gray, Julie Salley. "To Fight the Good Fight: The Battle Over Control of the Pasadena City Schools, 1969–1979." *Essays in History* 37 (1995). http://etext.lib.virginia.edu/journals/EH/EH40/steinh40.html.

Greenberg, Ivan. "The Half-Day Mill School Movement of the 1870s." In *Education in Massachusetts: Selected Essays,* edited by M. Konig and M. Kauffman, 65–77. Westfield: Institute for Massachusetts Studies, 1992.

Gullett, Gayle. "Women Progressives and the Politics of Americanization in California, 1915–1920." *Pacific Historical Review* LXIV:1 (February 1996): 71–94.

Gutman, Herbert. "Work, Culture, and Society in Industrializing America, 1815–1919." *Journal of American History* 63 (Fall 1973): 531–587.

Hughes, W. Hardin, ed. "Reliability of Traits." *Educational Research Bulletin* 3:4, Pasadena City Schools (December 1924): 23–25.

"Jackson Pollack." *Life Magazine* vol. 29:6 (8 August 1949): 42–45.

James, Michael. "Schools and Cultural Change-Retrospect and Prospect: The Virginia Curriculum Revision Project, 1931–1941." *The National Social Science Journal* 1:5 (Spring 1990): 13–24.

Johnson, James. "The Participation of Negroes in the Government of Virginia From 1877 to 1888." *Journal of Negro History* 14:3 (July 1929): 251–271.

Johnston Denis, Alberta. "Mrs. Albert Sidney Johnston." *Texas Magazine* 11:13 (May 1897): 429–431.

Katz, Sherry. "Socialist Women and Progressive Reform." *California Progressivism Revisited,* edited by William Deverell and Tom Sitton, 117–143. Berkeley: University of California Press, 1994.

Kazin, Michael and Steven Ross. "America's Labor Day: The Dilemma of a Workers' Celebration." *Journal of American History* 78:4 (March 1992): 1294–1323.

Kelley, Robin D.G. "'We Are Not What We Seem': Rethinking Black Working-Class Opposition in the Jim Crow South." *Journal of American History* 80:1 (June 1993): 78–112.

Kingsdale, Jon M. "The 'Poor Man's Club:' Social Functions of the Urban Working-Class Saloon." *American Quarterly* XXV: 4 (October 1973): 472–489.

Laughlin, Harry H. "The Relation of Eugenics To Other Sciences" *The Eugenics Review,* 11:2 (July 1919): 53–64

Lewis, Andrew B. "Emergency Mothers: Basement Schools and the Preservation of Public Education in Virginia." In *The Moderates' Dilemma: Massive Resistance to School Desegregation in Virginia,* ed. by Matthew Lassiter and Andrew Lewis, 72–106. Charlottesville: University Press of Virginia, 1998.

Madison, James. "Taking the Country Barefooted: The Indiana Colony in Southern California History." *California History* LXIX:3 (February 1990): 236–249.

Mason, Lucy Randolph. "Standards for Workers in Southern Industry" printed by the *Consumers' League,* 1931.

McDaniel, Ralph Clipman. "The Virginia Constitutional Convention of 1901–1902." In *Johns Hopkins University Studies in Historical and Political Science* 46, 243–408. Baltimore: The Johns Hopkins University Press, 1928.

McWilliams, Carey. "The Enemy in Pasadena." *Christian Century* 68 (25 January 1951): 10–15.

Mink, Gwendolyn. "The Lady and the Tramp: Gender, Race, and the Origins of the American Welfare State." *Women, the State, and Welfare,* edited by L. Gordon, 92–122. Madison: University of Wisconsin Press, 1990.

Morton, Richard. "Life in Virginia by a 'Yankee Teacher', Margaret Newbold Thorpe." *Virginia Magazine of History and Biography* 64 (1956): 180–207.

Muraskin, William A. "The Social-Control Theory in American History: A Critique." *Journal of Social History* 9:4 (Summer 1976): 559–569.

Newby, Mary I. "A Guidance Program in the Junior High School." *Educational Research Bulletin* 4:6, Pasadena City Schools, W. Hardin Hughes, ed. (February 1926): 17–25.

Ong, Paul. "An Ethnic Trade: The Chinese Laundries in Early California." *Journal of Ethnic Studies* 8 (Winter 1981): 95–112.

Popenoe, David. "Remembering My Father: An Intellectual Portrait of 'The Man Who Saved Marriages'" (New York: Institute for American Values), working paper for the Symposium on Fatherhood in America (November 1991): 1–56.

"The Raymond Hotel, Pasadena, California: A Place for Particular People," pamphlet. San Francisco: Norman Pierce Company, 1904.

Robbins, William. "The 'Plundered Province' Thesis and the Recent Historiography of the American West." *Pacific Historical Review* (winter 1986): 577–597.

Siegel, Stanley. "Incident in Pasadena." *Frontier* 17 (December 1965): 11–12.

Small, Sandra. "The Yankee Schoolmarm in Freedmen Schools: An Analysis of Attitudes." *Journal of Southern History* XLV (August 1979): 381–402.

Smith, R.C. "Prince Edward County: Revisited and Revitalized." *Virginia Quarterly Review* 73:1 (Winter 1997): 1–27.

Sulfridge, Hugh L. "President Sulfridge Calls Attention to Important Convention Items of Business" *Virginia Journal of Education.* XXV, no. 3 (November 1931), pg. 103.

Zall, Alan. *Progressive Education Increases Delinquency,* pamphlet. National Council for American Education, 1949.

GOVERNMENT DOCUMENTS

Anderson, Carson. *Ethnic History Research Project.* Pasadena: City of Pasadena, March 1995.

California Taxpayers' Association. *Survey of the Pasadena City Schools, Association Report No. 119.* Los Angeles, California: California Taxpayers' Association, 1931.

Clark, Victor. U.S. Department of Labor. *Bulletin of the Bureau of Labor* XVII–1908. Washington: Government Printing Office, 1909.

Commission of Immigration and Housing of California. *Americanization: The California Answer.* Sacramento, California: California Printing Office, June 1920.

Cottrell, Edwin A. *Pasadena Social Agencies Survey.* Pasadena: Pasadena Council of Social Agencies, 1940.

Dilworth, Nelson, Chairman. Senate Investigating Committee on Education. *Education in Pasadena, Eighth Report.* Senate of the State of California, 1951.

Laughlin, Harry L. "The Legal Status of Eugenical Sterilization," *a supplement to the Annual Report of The Municipal Court of Chicago,* 1929.

League of Women Voters of Pasadena. Integration: *Laws, Guidelines and Plans, Ethnic Distribution in Pasadena's Schools.* Pasadena: League of Women Voters of Pasadena, December 1968.

Pasadena City Board of Education. *Report of the Pasadena School Survey, 1951.* Pasadena: Pasadena City Board of Education, 1952.

Proctor, William Martin, ed. *The Six-Four-Four Plan of School Organization in Pasadena, California, A Report to the Board of Education, the Patrons and the Staff.* Pasadena: Pasadena Board of Education, 1933.

Proctor, William Martin. *The Kindergarten-Six-Four-Four Plan of School Organization in Pasadena.* City of Pasadena, 1933.

Report of the Commissioner of Education, 1904, Volume 2. Washington, DC: U.S. Government Printing Office, 1906.

State of California, Department of Parks and Recreation. *The Chinese Laundry on Second Street: Papers on Archeology at the Woodland Opera House Site, California Archeology Reports,* No. 24. California: Department of Parks and Recreation, September 1984.

Superintendent's Annual Report of the Pasadena City Schools.

U.S. House of Representatives. *Hearings Before the Committee on Education House of Representatives,* 75th Cong., 1st. Sess., HR 5962.

U.S. Bureau of the Census: Census of the Population: 1950, Seventeenth Decennial Census of the United States, Characteristics of the Population, Vol. II, Part 5: California. Washington, DC: U.S. Government Printing Office.

U.S. Bureau of the Census: Census of the Population, 1940, Volume II, Part 5, Characteristics of the Population. Washington, DC: U.S. Government Printing Office.

U.S. Bureau of the Census: Fifteenth Census of the United States, 1930, vol. III. Washington, DC: U.S. Government Printing Office.

U.S. Bureau of the Census: Thirteenth Census of the United States, 1910 and the Fourteenth Census of the United States, 1920, Abstract with Supplement for California. Microform.

U.S. Bureau of the Census: Thirteenth Census and Fourteenth Census, Population, 1910,1920, Vol. II, General Report and Analytical Tables. Washington, DC: U.S. Government Printing Office.

U.S. Bureau of the Census: Twelfth Census of the United States, 1900, Township of Pasadena. Microform.

U.S. Bureau of the Census, 1880: Population Schedules, California—City and County of Los Angeles, "Pasadena Village." Washington, DC: U.S. Government Printing Office.

Virginia State Department of Education. *Bulletin.* Richmond, Virginia: Virginia State Department of Education, 1932.

Walker, A. Roland, ed. *81 Years of Public Education in Pasadena.* Pasadena: Superintendent's Annual Report, 1955.

Weinberg, Meyer. *Jackson v. Pasadena City School District,* 382 P. 2d. Cited in *Race and Place: A Legal History of the Neighborhood School.* Washington DC: U.S. Government Printing Office, 1965.

NEWSPAPERS

Charlottesville Chronicle
Charlottesville Daily Progress
Christian Science Monitor
Commentary
Common Ground
Common Sense
Common Speech
Daily People's World
Farmville Herald
International Socialist Review
Leslie's Weekly
Los Angeles Socialist
New York Herald Tribune
New York Times
New York World-Telegram
Pasadena Daily Evening Star
Pasadena Daily News
Pasadena Evening Post
Pasadena Evening Star
Pasadena Journal
Pasadena News
Pasadena Post
Pasadena Star
Pasadena Star News
Pasadena Weekly
Reader's Digest
Richmond Times Dispatch
Richmond Times-Dispatch
The California Eagle
The Cavalier Daily
The Charleston Gazette
The Citizen
The Daily News
The Hour
The Independent
The Los Angeles Daily Times
The Los Angeles Examiner

The Los Angeles Times
The Pasadena Guardian
The Pasadena Star
The Reflector
The Richmond News Leader
The Richmond Times-Dispatch
The Survey
The Valley Union
Tuscaloosa Observer
Union Labor News
Virginia Journal of Education
Virginia State College Gazette
Washington Post

UNPUBLISHED THESIS AND DISSERTATIONS

Abrams-Duncan, Marguerite. "Pasadena's Forgotten Neighborhoods: Residential and Cultural Aspects of Pasadena's Commercial Sector in the Early Twentieth-Century." Graduate paper, U.C. Riverside, 1990.

Allen, Ralph Kenneth Jr. "Substandard Housing: Glendale and Pasadena, California." Masters thesis, California State University, Northridge, 1968.

Brooks, Clayton McClure. "Proper Voices, Radical Words: Mary Johnston, Lucy Randolph Mason, and the Process of Racial Liberalization." Master's thesis, University of Virginia, 1999.

Buis, Anne Gibson. "An Historical Study of the Role of the Federal Government in the Financial Support of Education." Ph.D. diss., Ohio State University, 1953.

Burlbaw, Lynn. "Hollis Caswell: An Intellectual Biography." Ph.D. diss., University of Texas, 1989.

Camp de Corse, Helen. "Charlottesville—A Study of Negro Life and Personality." Master's Thesis, University of Virginia, 1933.

Cartland, Earl F. "A Study of Negroes Living in Pasadena." Master's thesis, Whittier College, 1948.

Claypool, Vincent Booth. "John Amherst Sexson, Educator." Ph.D. diss., University of California, Los Angeles, 1948.

Cotkin, George. "Working-Class Intellectuals and Evolutionary Thought in America, 1870–1915." Ph.D. diss., Ohio State University, 1978.

Crimi, James. "The Social Status of the Negro in Pasadena, California." Master's thesis, University of Southern California, 1941.

Crowe, Dallas R. "Desegregation of Charlottesville Virginia Public Schools, 1954–1969: A Case Study." Ph.D. diss., University of Virginia, 1971.

Duncan-Abrams, Marguerite. "Pasadena's Forgotten Neighborhoods: Residential and Cultural Aspects of Pasadena's Commercial Sector in the Early Twentieth Century." Graduate paper, University of California, Irvine, 1990.

Garcilazo, Jeffrey Marcos. "Traqueros: Mexican Railroad Workers in the United States, 1870–1930." Ph.D. diss., University of California, Santa Barbara, 1995.

Hanover, Trudy J. "A Divine Discontent: Mary Johnston and Woman Suffrage in Virginia." Master's Thesis, University of Virginia, 1972.

Herman, David George. "Neighbors on the Golden Mountain: The Americanization of Immigrants in California—Public Instruction as an Agency of Ethnic Assimilation, 1850–1933." Ph.D. diss., University of California, Berkeley, 1981.

Irwin, Marjorie Felice. *The Negro in Charlottesville and Albemarle County: an Exploratory Study.* M.A. Thesis, University of Virginia, 1929.

Jordan, Elizabeth Cobb. "The Impact of the Negro Organization Society on Public Support for Education in Virginia, 1912–1950." Ph.D. diss., University of Virginia, 1978.

Katz, Sherry. "Dual Commitments: Feminism, Socialism and Women's Political Activism in California, 1890–1920." Ph.D. diss., University of California, Los Angeles, 1991.

Leap, William. "Red Hill." Master's Thesis, University of Virginia, 1929.

Lofstedt, Christine. "A Study of the Mexicans Living in Pasadena." Master's Thesis, University of Southern California, 1922.

Lombardo, Paul. "Eugenic Sterilization in Virginia: Aubrey Strode and the Case of Buck V. Bell." Ph.D. dissertation, University of Virginia, 1982.

McAlpin, Donald. "Analysis of the Efforts to Promote Racial Desegregation within the Pasadena Unified School District as Directed by the Court Order of Judge Manuel L. Real in January of 1970." Ph.D. diss., Walden University, 1972.

McLean, Christopher. "The City of Charlottesville's Proposed Development of Vinegar Hill." Master's thesis, University of Virginia, 1984.

Michie, Carrie Welbrock. "An Investigation of the Causes of Withdrawals from Jefferson High School Charlottesville, Virginia." Master's thesis, Virginia State College, 1939.

Mittendorf, Bradley Charles. "From Discussion to Confrontation." Master's thesis, University of Virginia, 1993.

Morton, Richard L. "The Negro in Virginia Politics, 1865–1902." Phelps-Stokes Fellowship papers No. 4, University of Virginia, 1918.

Nyman, Nancy B. "The Politics of Public Housing: The Case of Charlottesville, Virginia." Master's thesis, University of Virginia, 1968.

O'Coin, Andre R. "Vocational Education During the Great Depression and World War II: Challenge, Innovation, and Continuity." Ph.D. diss., University of Maryland, 1988.

Shelton, Jean Charlotte. "Woman Suffrage and Virginia Politics, 1909–1920." Master's thesis, University of Virginia, 1969.

Sui, Paul. "The Chinese Laundryman; A Study of Social Isolation." Ph.D. Diss., University of Chicago, 1953.

Vance, Joseph Carroll "The Negro in the Reconstruction of Albemarle County, Virginia." Master's thesis, *University of Virginia,* 1953.

Webb, William Edward. "Charlottesville and Albemarle County, 1865–1900." Ph.D. dissertation, *University of Virginia,* 1965.

Wilkes, Karen Odell. "Clara Morgan Odell." Undergraduate research paper prepared by Odell's great granddaughter, March 1991, in author's possession.

INDEX

THIS SERIES EXPLORES THE HISTORY OF SCHOOLS AND SCHOOLING in the United States and other countries. Books in this series examine the historical development of schools and educational processes, with special emphasis on issues of educational policy, curriculum and pedagogy, as well as issues relating to race, class, gender, and ethnicity. Special emphasis will be placed on the lessons to be learned from the past for contemporary educational reform and policy. Although the series will publish books related to education in the broadest societal and cultural context, it especially seeks books on the history of specific schools and on the lives of educational leaders and school founders.

For additional information about this series or for the submission of manuscripts, please contact the general editors:

Alan R. Sadovnik   Susan F. Semel
Rutgers University-Newark   The City College of New York, CUNY
Education Dept.   138th Street and Convent Avenue
155 Conklin Hall   NAC 5/208
175 University Avenue   New York, NY 10031
Newark, NJ 07102

To order other books in this series, please contact our Customer Service Department:

800-770-LANG (within the U.S.)
212-647-7706 (outside the U.S.)
212-647-7707 FAX

Or browse online by series at:

www.peterlangusa.com